SOUTHERN LITERARY STUDIES

SOUTHERN LITERARY STUDIES
Louis D. Rubin, Jr., Editor

Gentleman in a Dustcoat

THOMAS DANIEL YOUNG

A Biography of

LOUISIANA STATE UNIVERSITY PRESS/BATON ROUGE

Gentleman in a Dustcoat

John Crowe Ransom

Designer: Dwight Agner
Type face: VIP Baskerville
Typesetter: The Composing Room of Michigan, Inc., Grand Rapids
Printer and Binder: Kingsport Press, Inc., Kingsport, Tennessee

1978 printing

LIBRARY OF CONGRESS CATALOGING IN PUBLICATION DATA

Young, Thomas Daniel, 1919–
    Gentleman in a Dustcoat.

    (Southern literary studies)
    Includes bibliographical references and index.
    1. Ransom, John Crowe, 1888–1974-Biography. 2. Authors, American-
20th century-Biography. I. Title. II. Series.
PS3535.A635Z9185   811'.5'2[B]   75–27667
ISBN 0–8071–0190–7
ISBN 0–8071–0255–5 pbk.

Winner of the
JULES F. LANDRY AWARD
for 1976

For Arlease

Contents

Illustrations

Preface

JOHN CROWE RANSOM was a modest man who was never convinced that anyone could possibly be interested in the details of his personal life. This deeply imbedded humility, which was enforced by his critical conviction that a proliferation of biographical and historical data can divert a reader's attention from the literary work at hand, led him to insist often that he wanted no biography and that he would prefer to let his published work speak for him. When the idea of writing Ransom's biography first occurred to me, I was thus hesitant to express my interest to him. When I did, he responded, as one would expect, with a statement that evaded the question: "Oh, a biography; that's a mighty fine thing, but I doubt if there's enough there." This was in the fall of 1961 while he was a visiting professor at Vanderbilt University. Although the matter never left my mind during the next several months when I was seeing Ransom almost daily, I did not broach the subject again for some years.

I did express my interest in writing the biography to Donald Davidson and Allen Tate, and in the next five or six years I began to collect letters and other sources of information and to talk to Ransom's former students and colleagues, as well as to his many friends, in Nashville and elsewhere. At different times in the mid-1960s I heard of two other would-be biographers who were discouraged by Ransom's lack of enthusiasm for their proposals. In the spring of 1968, at a meeting of some of the Agrarians at the University of

Dallas, Allen Tate was commenting on some of the activities scheduled to celebrate Ransom's eightieth birthday when he turned to his
old friend and remarked that since someone would surely write Ransom's biography, he should get the biographer started. "At least,"
Tate concluded, "you can help him keep his facts straight." Since
Ransom raised no objections, I gathered my courage, and the next
day at lunch I reminded him of my continuing interest in that project. His only response was, "I'm game, if you are."

Once we were under way, he cooperated completely. He gave
liberally of his time and on two separate occasions talked with me for
three or four hours a day almost everyday for a month. If these long
sessions were bothersome or if he ever fretted under my tedious
questioning, he successfully concealed his feelings. In fact he seemed
to enjoy reminiscing, talking about episodes from his boyhood and
telling anecdotes about his family, particularly those that concerned
his father and mother. After these two extended sessions, I saw him
every few months, and corresponded with him between visits, until
August, 1973, when I went to England for a year. In these later years
Ransom did not retain facts very well and his memory was most unreliable about dates; nevertheless he tried to provide what I requested.
He replied to my letters promptly and a few times wrote a second
letter to supply information he had omitted in an earlier one, to
amend an ambiguous or contradictory statement, or to correct a date
erroneously reported.

Ransom saved few of the letters he received from a large group of
correspondents, even fewer of the manuscripts of his poems and essays, and almost none of the materials relating to his literary career.
Donald Davidson told me of his going one Sunday afternoon in late
August, 1937, to Calhoun Hall on the Vanderbilt campus, where the
English faculty had offices. As he entered the building, he smelled
something burning, and a little later he saw smoke coming from one
of the offices. When he got to the open door, he saw Ransom dump-
ing the contents of his desk and filing cabinet into two burning trash
cans. "I am getting ready," he told Davidson, "to move to Ohio."
Fortunately, almost everyone saved Ransom's letters, beginning with
those he wrote his family from Oxford while he was a Rhodes Scholar.
For a half-century he and Allen Tate exchanged letters, and appar-

ently Tate kept nearly all of the letters he received. This rich collection, now at the Firestone Library of Princeton University, and the Jesse E. Wills Collection in the Joint University Libraries of Nashville—containing Ransom's letters to Davidson, Wills, Andrew Lytle, Robert Graves, Brainard Cheney, and others—have been invaluable to me.

Although biographers can rarely portray the lives of their subjects as they were actually lived, surely all biographers strive to come as close to presenting the real man as they can. With the abundance of available material, it seemed to me that the best manner in which I could present John Crowe Ransom was to let the evidence speak for itself. Wherever possible, I should resist the ever-present temptation to intrude to the point of informing the reader how I think he should interpret the material; how I believe he should react to Ransom's attitude toward a colleague, fellow poet, or a work of art; what I think is the real significance of Ransom's deciding to follow one course of action rather than another, especially when one would appear more reasonable or rewarding than the other. The biographer's attitude toward his subject will invariably be known: in the selection of the material, in the amount of space devoted to the development of some episodes, in the summary and editorial comment he will inevitably make.

One can never incorporate into a book of this kind nearly all of the material he collects, but I hope the narrative that follows will encompass enough facts representative of the qualities of a very complex human being for a reasonably accurate likeness to emerge. Ransom always insisted upon the importance of reason and common sense. Logic was the ultimate standard in judging a work of art: it was the most reliable means for defining the unique nature of poetic discourse, the final arbiter in determining the significance of literary form or social codes, even religious rituals. Yet many of the decisions that most affected his personal life seem to have been the result of developments over which he exercised little control. After his graduation from Vanderbilt, he thought he had settled on a career as teacher and administrator in the private secondary schools of Tennessee, but the receipt of a Rhodes Scholarship and his three years in England turned his attention toward journalism or college teaching. Even after

reading the Greats at Oxford and spending a year on the faculty of
the Hotchkiss School, no college position was available; consequently
he made plans to enter Harvard to study for the Ph.D. degree, to earn
the credentials he thought essential for a successful career in university teaching. During a visit home, however, he called on some of his
friends and former professors at Vanderbilt and was offered a position that had just become vacant in the English department. He accepted and remained there until he went into service in World War I.
While he was overseas he decided he would settle near New York City,
the literary center of the country, for he thought that location would
provide better opportunities than Nashville for pursuing his interest
in free-lance writing and journalism. With the help of Christopher
Morley, he acquired a position he thought might develop into the
kind of situation he wanted. He returned home for a brief visit, but
again chance intervened. Because his mother and father, then living
in Nashville, were so obviously disappointed that he planned to leave
again so soon after his two years in France, he decided to delay his
return to New York, but only for a year. He took another temporary
appointment in Vanderbilt's English department and remained almost twenty years.

The priorities Ransom established for his literary career displeased some of his friends and admirers. He was, Allen Tate once
said, "one of the great elegiac poets of the English language," who
produced ten or twelve almost perfect lyrics, poems which will be read
as long as poetry is regarded as a serious art. Yet almost all of these
poems were written in a period of two or three years. During the
remainder of his long and active literary career, much of his thought
and most of his creative energies were devoted to other activities: to
speculations on the nature and function of poetic discourse, on the
significance of religious myth and the need for an inscrutable God; to
discussions of the proper relations that should exist between man,
God, and nature; or, particularly during his later years, to the compulsive revisions of poems written many years before. The biographer
whose primary goal is to increase the general knowledge of Ransom,
the man as well as the artist, will likely appear to devote too much
space to the social and literary criticism and too little to the poetry. My
hope is that the pages which follow will make some contribution to the

assessment of Ransom's literary achievements as poet, critic, and editor, and that they will provide the means for a better understanding of and a deeper appreciation for a man who could both "fathom" and "perform" his nature.

Many persons have assisted me in the preparation of this biography, and I am happy to acknowledge my gratitude to as many of them as time, space, and memory permit.

In addition to John Crowe Ransom, to whom, of course, my debt is greatest, I owe much to Robb Reavill Ransom and Helen Ransom Forman, who allowed me to examine family papers, including a diary Helen Ransom Forman kept during her childhood. Several of the photographs in this book were provided by Robb Reavill Ransom and are used with her permission.

Many of Ransom's friends have shared with me their knowledge of him, allowed me to examine personal papers, and answered my inquiries. Among those to whom I owe most—a truer indication of the extent of my indebtedness is the number of times their names appear in the notes—are Cleanth Brooks, the late Donald Davidson, Andrew Lytle, Jesse E. Wills, the late Alec B. Stevenson, Robert Penn Warren, Peter Taylor, and Allen Tate. Many others have provided information essential to this book: Frances Cheney, Jane Sullivan, Herschel Gower, Dorrence Eaton, Corrine Eaton Watts, William A. Stuart, J. W. Phillips, Jordon Stokes, Ivar Lou Duncan, M. E. Bradford, Louise Cowan, Ada Young, and Frances McHaney.

Others who have assisted me in important ways are Jerry E. Brown, Thomas Richardson, William Reid, Kyle David Young, Susan Haddock, Paul Schwartz, Gary Cohen, Thomas B. Greenslade, and Owen T. McCloskey.

I owe a special debt of gratitude to Beverly Jarrett, Managing Editor of the Louisiana State University Press, whose expert and careful editing has improved almost every page of this manuscript.

Earlier drafts of parts of the manuscript were read by Jerry E. Brown, M. Thomas Inge, Joseph K. Davis, and Thomas D. Young, Jr. At a later stage it was read by Louis D. Rubin, Jr., Floyd C. Watkins, and George Core. I am immeasurably indebted to these scholars and critics because this manuscript was much improved by their suggestions. I owe special thanks to Marty Marina and Mary Floyd for their expert typing of the several versions this manuscript went through in its composition.

I gratefully acknowledge the many courtesies extended to me by several institutions and libraries, including permission to use letters, manuscripts, and other materials specifically designated in the notes: the Firestone Library of Princeton University, the Library of Congress, the Yale University Library, the Tennessee State Library and Archives, the Lily Library of Indiana University, the Chalmers Library of Kenyon College, the Haverford College Library, the Mona Van Duyn Collection and the William Jay Smith Collection of the Washington University Libraries, and the Jesse E. Wills Collection of the Joint University Libraries of Nashville.

I am grateful to Vanderbilt University for a leave of absence to complete the manuscript and to the Research Council of Vanderbilt University for grants that aided me at every stage in the preparation of the manuscript.

Most of all I am grateful to my wife, Arlease Lewis Young, without whose help and encouragement this project would probably have been abandoned long ago.

Thomas Daniel Young

Acknowledgments

THE AUTHOR wishes to express his grateful acknowledgment to the following periodicals in whose pages portions of this book first appeared: *Southern Review, Georgia Review, Sewanee Review,* and *Mississippi Quarterly.*

Author and publisher are grateful for permission to quote from the following:

John Crowe Ransom, *Selected Poems,* 3rd edition, revised and enlarged; copyright 1924, 1927, 1934, 1939, 1945, © 1962, 1963, 1969, by Alfred A. Knopf, Inc.; copyright renewed 1952, 1954, by John Crowe Ransom. Reprinted by permission of Alfred A. Knopf, Inc.

John Crowe Ransom, *The World's Body* (New York: Charles Scribner's Sons, 1938).

John Crowe Ransom, *The New Criticism;* copyright 1941 by New Directions Publishing Corporation, © 1968 by John Crowe Ransom. Reprinted by permission of New Directions Publishing Corporation.

John Crowe Ransom, *Beating the Bushes;* copyright © 1972 by New Directions Publishing Corporation. Reprinted by permission of New Directions Publishing Corporation.

Photographs used herein are reprinted by permission and with grateful acknowledgment of the author and publisher to: Robb Reavill Ransom; Kenyon College Archives; Ellene Ransom Papers, Tennessee State Library and Archives; and Jesse E. Wills Collection, Joint University Libraries of Nashville, Tennessee.

Abbreviations

Gentleman in a Dustcoat

I Loomings 1888-1905

R ICHARD POLIS RANSOM'S conversion, as one present that night at Winrow's campground observed, was "as clear and bright as you ever saw and I don't suppose he ever had a doubt of its genuineness." Shortly after this experience, he enrolled in La Grange College in Florence, Alabama; and, as soon as he had completed the ministerial course there, he migrated to Texas, where in March, 1847, just after his twenty-first birthday, he was admitted on trial into the Eastern Texas Conference of the Methodist Church. Although his health had always been excellent, within a few months after his ordination he began to have attacks of chills and fever which gradually grew worse, and by the end of his first year in the ministry he was almost completely incapacitated. "I think," he wrote his son John James thirty years later, "anxieties of mind in reference to my usefulness and success in my work had much to do in keeping up and aggravating my diseases."[1] He was received into the clergy of his church and given a charge, he was convinced, before he was prepared to accept the responsibilities of the appointment. During these months his feeling of incompetence was so great that he spent much of his time in "the woods and fields, reading, writing, and praying." Soon he "became speckled with sores and bumps from the bites of tick and other vermin." Convinced that he was doing no good, that he was "utterly worthless," he became so gloomy and despondent that he gave up his church and returned to Rutherford County, Tennessee, where he had been born in 1825 and where his family still lived.

This debilitating illness was not the only time R. P. Ransom's life was affected by physical ailment. Soon after he started to school his teacher sent a most disturbing report to his parents: "Dickie can not or will not learn." At first his father threatened punishment, but soon it was discovered that the lad simply could not see well enough to learn to read. From the age of twelve until his death, therefore, he was forced to wear glasses, the lenses of which became stronger and his vision poorer as the years passed. Late in life and very near the end of his ministry, he was convinced that the weakness of his eyes had seriously impaired his effectiveness in his chosen vocation:

I have lost much through life because of this infirmity. From my school days I have had to be cautious in the use of my sight and to give my eyes much rest from steady reading, both by day and by night. I have had to turn away from many a book altogether because of the fineness of the print. This weakness of sight has tended to reconcile me, more perhaps than anything else, to the appointments I have received, requiring much expenditure of time in travel and absence from my books. A station, with its superior opportunities for regular and systematic study, would be greatly my preference, were my eyes strong and capable of bearing the protracted strain of everyday study.[2]

One of his contemporaries in the Tennessee Conference, to which he was admitted in 1855, observed that R. P. Ransom would certainly have been "much more widely famous, but his defective eyesight did not allow him to catch inspiration from his audience."[3]

One who had known R. P. Ransom since his birth observed at the time of his death that he "had a different disposition from the rest of the children" in his family, that he was "very quiet and slow in his actions," "very sturdy in his habits," and that all his life he was a peacemaker; at home and at school he "settled all disputes."[4] The cast of character that allowed him to accept without complaint a series of appointments in the rural and village churches of Middle Tennessee is revealed in a letter to his son John James, who had just arrived in South America to take up his missionary post in Brazil. "It is right to desire success and to labor for it," he wrote on July 11, 1876, "but it is not right to harass our souls with brooding anxieties for results which it is unreasonable to expect nor even for results which we deem should be the legitimate fruit and outcome of our labors. There is a faith in God that will place us on higher ground than this—a faith which while it stimulates us to labor commits results entirely to the Lord and rests the issues in his hands. It is this faith alone, it seems to me, can keep the earnest servant of the Lord from ... cares and chafing anxieties of the soul." R. P. Ransom exemplified in his life the principles he preached. He never requested his presiding elder to place him in a particular church and even in his later years, when his assignments were to some of the most insignificant stations and charges in the conference, he never complained, but gave these small, and usually rural, churches "the same earnest care he gave his largest work."[5]

Shortly after chronic ill health brought him back to his native Middle Tennessee, R. P. Ransom married, on November 18, 1851, Frances Bass, also of Rutherford County. Before she died in 1865, she had borne him three sons: John James, the father of the poet, Richard B., and Robert P. Until they were almost grown, R. P. Ransom was both father and mother to his three sons. During this time, and until his death on September 12, 1897, when his grandson, John Crowe, was only nine years old, he was a minister in the Tennessee Conference of the Methodist Church. A scholarly man, thoroughly familiar with the dogma and principles of his church, he was also an able administrator and served for seventeen years, and in five different districts, as a presiding elder in his conference. A respected preacher, he was often called upon to address the annual conference, and on one such occasion it was reported that "the solemnity and grandeur of his message carried his hearers out of self and surroundings." "No man in the Conference," it was said, "can equal Dick Ransom in the purity of his English."[6]

The first son of Richard Polis and Frances Bass Ransom was born near Salem in Rutherford County, Tennessee, on July 8, 1853. Educated at home and in the schools of the small towns and villages his father served as pastor, John James entered Emory and Henry College in the fall of 1870. Dedicated since his fourteenth year to following his father into the Methodist ministry, he was immensely pleased to be able to report, shortly after his arrival on campus, that there had been a "gracious revival among the students of the college."[7] Evidently convinced that he and his son had done well in the selection of his college, R. P. Ransom responded that he hoped this resurgence of "faith in God and interest in his work" would "greatly improve the morale of the institution and give a religious tone to the place."[8] If John James's resolution to enter the clergy wavered during these early college years, it was strengthened by the even more obvious expression of faith and dedication which occurred during the winter of his junior year. "We are having a powerful revival here," he wrote his father on March 12, 1873, "far exceeding anything of the sort I ever knew at this place before. The very worst are seeking religion, and from Sunday night to this morning, 15 professions reported. More than twenty young men at the altar and additions expected to the number tonight."

At Emory and Henry, John James—called Johnny or John by his family and J. J. by his fellow ministers—was active in debate, liked his courses in elocution "almost better than anything I've had," and was one of the editors of the *Banner,* the student newspaper. In this last capacity he solicited contributions from his father. "Will you not assist us," he wrote on November 5, 1872, "by at least an occasional article? We wish to make the *Banner* as interesting as possible, and I know you could help us very much along that line. Write us something, a talk, an essay, a sermon, anything." After receiving two letters from his father and no reference to this request, John James wrote again: "If you have an aversion to writing, it would be ungrateful [of] me to worry you with entreaties to do so. You, however, know my desires, and should you feel inclined to avail yourself of the privilege—while I am editor—be sure that our colums [*sic*] are at your disposal."[9]

Apparently R. P. Ransom did not respond to his son's invitation, and there were no more requests. The next year John James decided the demands of his academic program were so heavy that he could not spare the time required by the office of editor-in-chief, to which he had been appointed; consequently he resigned and his letters home reflect some of his other interests and concerns. Once he wrote that there were seven cases of smallpox in Bristol, only twenty-four miles away, and that "something of a panic" prevailed among the students at the college. If the disease should reach Abingdon, ten miles from Emory, he concluded, "it is probable that the college would be left alone in its glory."[10] On another occasion he informed his father of his inclination to go into teaching rather than into the ministry. "You expect me to enter the Tennessee Conference next fall," he wrote on April 2, 1873; "as I have never said anything implying a different expectation, you will the more readily believe me that, until of late, I had no other idea than that of attaching myself to the regular itinerancy somewhere as soon as [I was] out of college." But within the past few weeks, he wrote, he had given serious consideration to another plan. Although he was not in a position to make a public declaration of his intentions, he expected to marry within the year.[11] Since he had no money of his own, he knew it "would seem imprudent to enter so solemn a compact without the means of support." This new intention had caused him to investigate carefully an opportunity of employment that he had learned of only within the past few weeks:

[I] am offered in N[orth] C[arolina] a situation as follows—the school catalogued 176 students last year, and the daily attendance was 116; if I consent to take the position of prof. there, I get one third of all the profits. In addition to this, I have "the refusal" of the school buildings, dormitories, etc. at $2200 if, at the close of the year, I choose to buy them or any proportional part of the same. The gentleman who makes the offer thinks I may count on at least $1250 for my year's work.[12]

If his father did not approve of the plan, he promised that he would "break off any further correspondence," give up "all ideas of marriage for years," and enter the ministry immediately, but likely not in the Tennessee Conference. Since he knew his father would be as "careful of my interest as I would," he concluded, he was perfectly willing to let him make the decision. But one thing he wanted to make absolutely clear: he was not "giving up the idea of preaching"; he merely wanted to delay his entry into the ministry for a few years.

The advice from his father, which must have come by return mail, was clear and to the point. John James should not leave college before graduation either to teach or to enter the ministry. If he had assumed that his father would have to go deeply into debt in order to keep him in college and his younger brothers in boarding school, he was assured that such was not the case. "I do not intend to embarrass myself with debt," R. P. Ransom wrote on April 23, 1873: "[I] will teach or farm myself before I will submit to such embarrassment." Since he was interested "above all else" in his son's graduating with his class in June, 1874, he urged him to come home as soon as his examinations were completed so that together they could make arrangements for the next year. Somehow he would raise the money, even if he had to open a school in Franklin, where he was serving his second year as presiding elder of the churches in that district.

John James Ransom returned to Emory and Henry in the fall of 1873 and was graduated with his class the following spring. That he was much aware of the cost of his education is demonstrated by the fact that during his senior year he boarded himself and decreased the $13.50 charged monthly by the college nearly by half.[13] On June 3, 1874, he wrote his father that having completed mathematics, the only course he was really concerned about, he was assured of graduation. As pleased as his father must have been with this information, he was even more delighted by the next item included in the letter. He had "received and accepted a call," John James reported, to a "preacherless circuit." Although he had been reluctant to accept the appointment without consulting his father, he was confident he would approve and feared that if he delayed the assignment would be given to someone else. "I do not know its name or anything about it," he continued, "except the Presiding Elder wrote that he had no preacher on it and asked if I would take it." Since he did not relish the thought of "floating around" until the meeting of the annual conference in October, he had accepted, a decision he thought especially prudent since it made him officially a member of the Tennessee Conference. But his real interest, he had decided, was in foreign missions, and only a lack of knowledge of Spanish had kept him from volunteering for service in Mexico.

The following year he was appointed "Preacher-in-charge of the Sawrie Chapel" in Nashville. At the general conference, which met in Louisville, Kentucky, a request came from the Reverend Mr. Junius E. Newman—who had gone to Brazil in 1867 and set up there a unionist church composed of Baptists, Methodists, and Presbyterians—asking that the Board of Missions organize an official mission of the Methodist Episcopal Church, South, in that country.[14] Sometime later that fall, when John James Ransom visited the office of the Reverend Dr. D. C. Kelley, the presiding elder of the Nashville

District and assistant missionary secretary, he was asked if he would do something for the board. Since he had written at Kelley's request occasional articles for one of the church papers, Ransom thought he was being asked to undertake a similar assignment and readily accepted. But Kelley had in mind an endeavor of a much different kind. Fifty years later Ransom reported their conversation:

"Brother Ransom, I want you to go somewhere for the Board. . . . The trip I want you to take is a long one." I replied that whether the destination be far or near I was at the service of the Church. Dr. Kelley then said that he wanted me to go as a missionary to Brazil. I replied that I would be glad to undertake the work.

'But," said Dr. Kelley, "we have no money to support you or even to pay your travel expenses." I replied that I would be glad to make my own way.

"No," said Dr. Kelley, "I cannot ask you to do that. I will raise enough money in the Nashville District to send you to Brazil, but we will have no funds to support you after you arrive, and you will have to provide for your own support, although the board will send you such money as it may be able to obtain from time to time." [15]

In the fall of 1875, at the annual conference which met at Fayetteville, Tennessee, John James Ransom was ordained deacon and elder and appointed missionary to Brazil, the first such appointment ever made by the Methodist Episcopal Church, South. The Reverend Dr. Kelley having been able, as he had promised, to raise boat fare and an extra hundred dollars for other expenses, Ransom left Baltimore, a few months after his twenty-second birthday, the only passenger on the sailing vessel *Keplar,* which with a full cargo of lard was bound for Rio de Janeiro.[16] After a voyage of fifty-two days the ship arrived at its destination on February 2, 1876. Ransom had "$100 and a little odd change" in his pocket and no knowledge of Portuguese at all, and he was faced with the immediate prospect of having to earn a living. He went from Rio de Janeiro to Campinas, where he was offered a position teaching Greek and mathematics in a small college operated by the Presbyterian church. As soon as he was settled, he arranged to teach English to Dr. Manuel de Marals Barras, member of a distinguished Brazilian family, in exchange for instruction in Portuguese. Soon he was able to speak and understand the language well enough to get by in the marketplace, and, of even more importance at the moment, with the help of Dr. Barras he prepared in Portuguese a Greek grammar for use in his classes at the college.

John James Ransom remained at the college for almost two years before accepting a position with the American Bible Society so that he could visit other sections of his adopted country. In the fall of 1878 he received a letter from the Board of Missions instructing him to set up headquarters in Rio, enclosing a check for several months' salary and promising a minimum support of $800 a year—a pledge that was not always honored. Since his knowledge of the language was good enough to allow him to preach in Portuguese, which the Reverend Mr. Newman could never do, Ransom undertook the very difficult task of trying to convert some of the natives to Methodism. He became, therefore, the first real missionary to Brazil because Newman had confined his activities almost entirely to the former residents of the southern part of the United States who had migrated to Brazil at the end of the Civil War. Beginning immediately to preach to congregations wherever he could find them—in private homes, on street corners, in vacant lots and rented halls—he founded at Cattete in September, 1878, the first permanent Methodist church in Brazil.[17]

As soon as John James Ransom was settled in Brazil, he naturally sought out Junius E. Newman, the man responsible for his being there. During the following years this association became much closer; Ransom visited as often as he could in the Newman home, where he became acquainted with the two daughters Mary and Annie, who had opened a boarding school for girls at Piracicaba. In 1878 he and Annie Newman were married, but she died in childbirth the next year. Upon her death the school was closed, and in the summer of 1881 John James toured Europe and returned to the United States for the annual conference, at which time he persuaded the Board of Missions to send Miss Mattie Watts to reopen and operate the Piracicaba Girls' College.

Shortly after his return to Brazil in the winter of 1881, he took up again a correspondence, which he had initiated the year before, with a young lady named Ella Crowe, a distant cousin of his stepmother, the second Mrs. Richard P. Ransom. Miss Crowe had expressed some interest in becoming a missionary and he had answered her request for information about Brazil with extended comment on the country, its people, history, climate, and customs. In an early letter he had described the carnival season—"when Rio goes mad for diversion's sake," the streets "are full of fantastic maskers," and thousands of flags of all descriptions, some "quite rich and costly flutter in all the principal streets." There are also, he continued, processions in which "fantastically beautiful carriages adorned with the utmost richness beauty and taste" and filled with "maskers of all kinds and descriptions" are drawn through the streets. If one looks at all of this pageantry in a superficial way, he wrote on February 21, 1881, "the fun, the jollity, might seem an adequate apology for the vast expense," but he could not overlook "the crime and immorality" which accompanied these festivities, not to mention the "thoughtless, incontinent spirit they encourage." He just could not forget that these spectacular exhibitions were genuine hindrances to his accomplishing what he was there to do.

In other letters he commented on the beauties of the Brazilian summers. "The flowers," he wrote on March 18, 1881, "are just now in their glory. We have in my garden at least six varieties of lily, all of which, except the Lily of the Valley, would perhaps be strangers to you." In his yard he had, too, chocolate plants, cinnamon trees, several varieties of peaches and plums, the celebrated "manja fruit," custard apples, and alligator pears. Altogether his garden contained "more than thirty kinds of fruit." In almost every letter he insisted on the need for missionaries and commented at length on the special pleasures one could get from such work. Once, soon after his return from the States, he chastised her for her apparent loss of interest in the field. "But what about your missionary schemes? Have they all evaporated on the ambient air?"[18] She must not forget, he insisted, that everywhere in South America "brave hearts and pure souls" are needed for the "great task of bringing a nation to God." If you are sure, however, that God has given you a work where you are, "far be it from me to say a word to the contrary. The ordinary chain of Providence for women and for men too for that matter, leads to a home and love and—." The paragraph ends abruptly and a postscript added the next morning indicates that he no longer has any idea how he would have completed the sentence, that he had not been able to complete it the previous evening because of a "sudden attack of billiousness," the aftermath of a serious and prolonged siege of yellow fever suffered the year before.

From this time the tone of the letters changed. Although they began "My dearest cousin" or "Dear Cousin Ella," they became more personal, and he always assured her how much her letters meant to him, for he was in great need just then of "assurance of affectionate regard." His lingering illness was a constant reminder of his weaknesses, of his incompleteness, of his need for friendship and affection. Soon, in order to convince her of his "cousinly affection," he began to enclose some of his own verse, which he said he had been composing for "a year or more."[19] Although the letter of December 30, 1883, opened in the customary manner, "My dear Cousin Ella," it immediately presented a question which made this salutation, he realized, "somewhat inappropriate." On three previous occasions he had tried to express what was on his heart, but he could not bring himself to mail those letters. Now he could only say simply and directly: "Will you be my wife?" Although he knew she loved him as a cousin, he also hoped she had a "grain of tender emotion" for him, the kind of "affection she would give to the man whom she would marry." He concluded with a statement of his feelings: "You are daily, almost hourly, in my thoughts, and I think I can promise to give you all the honor, the sympathy, the tender affection that before the world and between ourselves you would have a right to expect as my wife."

Even this fourth letter of proposal he could not mail. He held it for almost ten days before including it in a longer letter written on January 8. Her answer of February 18 was predictably cautious. Although she did have more than a mere "spark of affection" for him, she could not give him a "decided answer" because her father was opposed to her marrying anyone at present. But even this most guarded response was enough to convince John James that he should return to Tennessee to woo the young lady in person. Immediately after arriving in New York on May 17, 1884, he went directly to Nashville to attend a meeting of the Board of Missions, from which he had requested and received permission to remain in the United States for the remainder of the year to attempt to raise $50,000 for the Piracicaba Girls' College. After a few days in Nashville, he went down to Pulaski to see the young lady who had tentatively consented to be his wife, her acceptance on the condition that he could persuade her father to give his permission.

The young lady whom John James Ransom pursued so ardently was a member of a well-established Middle Tennessee family. Born in Marion, Alabama, on December 5, 1859, she had moved with her parents, Nannie P. and Robert Bruce Crowe, to Pulaski, Tennessee, in 1867. As a child, according to an account she wrote many years later, she "took part in the planning and making of the regalia of the original KKK."[20] The ladies who "patterned and constructed the costumes" of the Klan often came to her grandmother's, and young Ella tended the fire and did other chores so that she could listen to the conversation and watch the strange and bizarre costumes take shape. Her grandmother, Mrs. Andrew Lewis Crowe, her uncle, Captain James R. Crowe, and her uncle-in-law, Richard Reed, were three of the six organizers of the Klan.[21] Her memories of these early experiences were sharp and clear nearly seventy years later:

I very vividly recall witnessing two parades and weird maneuvers of the Klan at night on the streets of Pulaski. And I understand now, as I did not then, the reason for a visit and demonstration by the Klan at my father's home near Aspen Hill, Giles County, one Saturday night when my father, who was then a farmer, was weighing up cotton and paying the pickers for the week's work. I did not understand why my father always took my mother, who was a frail, delicate woman, and his family of small, helpless children with him on these occasions. And I was as much frightened and awed as was the crowd of grumbling and contentious darkies by the wonderful feats of the "Klu Klerke," as the darkies called them, swallowing a whole ham, drinking a whole bucketful of fresh spring water, etc.[22]

Her mother who died in 1882 at the age of forty-six, apparently of tuberculosis, left seven children, the youngest of whom was seven. With Ella Crowe's father's health already beginning to fail—he was feeling the first serious effects of tuberculosis, the disease from which he would die six years later—the care of the family fell increasingly on Ella and her sister Irene. Educated in the local schools and at Martin College from which she was graduated at the head of her class, Ella had taught school for five or six years before her engagement to John James Ransom. At the time her betrothal was announced, she was listed as a member of the faculty in the "Literary Department" and as

"Principal of the School of Art" by Howard Female College in Lebanon, Tennessee. She taught English, French, and music, and had
twenty-five students under her supervision.

After several delays, which John James found almost unbearable,
the young couple was married at 3 P.M. on Tuesday, September 2,
1884, in the Methodist Church of Pulaski, R. P. Ransom having come
from his station at Rock Hill to assist with the ceremony. After a brief
honeymoon trip to Mammouth Cave, Kentucky, and a longer visit
with the Ransom family in Rutherford County, Ella returned to
Pulaski and John James resumed his travels trying to raise funds for
the Piracicaba Girls' College.[23] When the young couple sailed from
New York, shortly after the first of the next year, he had traveled
more than twelve thousand miles in a little more than seven months,
had visited fifteen states and received cash and pledges exceeding fifty
thousand dollars.

Back in Brazil with his new wife, John James resumed the demanding and time-consuming work in which he had been engaged
for nearly ten years. Almost as soon as they reached Rio, he had to
leave Ella in order to visit the scattered churches and missions for
which he was responsible. A homesick young woman in a strange
country, whose language she was never able to speak very well, Ella
found these first few months very trying indeed. "Can you realize how
lonesome I am," she wrote her husband on March 29, 1885, "and how
much I miss you. . . . I've roamed all over the place; went to the study,
but it looked so lonesome and cheerless. I left it immediately."[24] But
she was determined to be a good wife and often during his frequent
absences she "prayed earnestly," she wrote, "that I might be of help to
you in your life's work." Soon they found a "beautiful, two-story
house" at a rent they could afford, and Ella threw herself completely
into the task of making it into their first home. After their first child,
Richard Bruce, was born, on September 2, 1885, she found her time
"well occupied."[25]

John James Ransom's work was more successful than it had ever
been. His letters to his father, those to his clerical friends at home, and
the official reports to the Board of Missions include accounts of accomplishments of which he was justifiably proud. But some differences of opinion developed between him and some of the other mis-

sionaries in Brazil, and after three unsuccessful attempts to resign he
was finally allowed to return to the United States. On August 4, 1886,
John James, Ella, Dick and his twenty-year-old Brazilian nurse, who
came along to assure that he learned Portuguese, sailed for New
York, arriving twenty-three days later after the "most miserable voyage" John James had ever experienced.[26] Soon after they left land
Dick developed croup, and they were convinced, despite the doctor's
lack of concern, that he also had whooping cough; this malady was
followed by a heat rash so intense that upon doctor's orders he was
kept below deck for almost the entire voyage. The third day at sea the
ship went through a tropical storm and Ella became seasick and was
confined to her bed for nearly three weeks. Only the presence of the
nurse made the voyage "barely tolerable," and when they arrived in
New York Ella had eaten nothing for almost a week and was so weak
she had to be helped from the ship.[27] They stayed in New York for a
few days to allow her to regain her strength, arriving in Pulaski near
the end of the second week in September. They remained there until
John James had to leave to attend the meeting of the annual conference, which began on October 12 in Clarksville. There he learned that
he had been transferred to the Pacific Conference and assigned to the
station at Mojave, California. He left Tennessee, immediately after
the conference was adjourned, to assume his new duties, stopping en
route to preach in Bay St. Louis, Mississippi, and El Paso, Texas,
before arriving in Mojave on the afternoon of the eighteenth.[28] Ella
and Dick joined him a month later, and their second child, Annie
Phillips, was born in San Francisco on February 11, 1887.

After one year in California, John James was received back into
the Tennessee Conference and assigned to the Richland circuit. Since
they knew this appointment was temporary, Ella, pregnant again,
spent most of her time in Pulaski, helping Irene nurse their father in
his terminal illness. He died on January 3, 1888, in the family home
on East Hill, and here, on April 30, 1888, John James' and Ella's third
child was born. In honor of his father and in memory of his
grandfather, he was christened John Crowe, the official ceremony
being performed by his other grandfather, the Reverend Mr. Richard
Polis Ransom, when the infant was barely three weeks old. On October 18, before John was six months old, his father was appointed

Missionary to Cuba. Since there were now three children and the oldest was barely three, Ella and John James agreed that she should remain in Pulaski so that Irene could help her with the children.[29] As soon as he found a suitable place, and surely within the year, he would come for them. He landed in Havana on December 19 and spent Christmas in the Hotel Telegrafo, from which he wrote on December 26 how much he missed the "innocent prattle of the dear children." The political situation was so unsettled, he saw immediately, that he was extremely pleased he had left the family in Tennessee. Eight months later, although he sorely missed his "dear wife and precious children," he had decided that he could not risk their "presence in this city for a single day."[30] Shortly thereafter, when revolution seemed inevitable, he and the other missionaries were called home. In the fall of 1889 John James was assigned to the West Nashville Mission for the remainder of the year. At the next conference, in October, 1890, he was appointed presiding elder of the Lebanon District, which included fifteen churches and over six hundred members, and Ella was delighted to return to the community in which she had been teaching when they were married six years before.

Between 1891 and 1899, from the time John Crowe Ransom was three until he was eleven, his father served four churches in Middle Tennessee: Spring Hill—where Ella Irene (she later changed her name to Ellene), the fourth child, was born on July 26, 1894—Franklin, Springfield, and North High Street, Nashville. While John James and his family were living in Springfield, his father was serving as pastor of the church in Elkmont. There on Sunday, September 5, Richard P. Ransom preached on "Heavenly Recognition." Some members of his congregation who heard him thought he had never been more eloquent, but immediately after the service he went to bed and never arose. He died exactly one week later.[31] John James and other members of the family thought the fatigue had been brought on by nursing in his last illness his youngest son Richard B., who had been practicing medicine in Texas for some time before he contracted tuberculosis and had to return to Tennessee. The shock of his son's death, on August 30, was too much for the old man's weakened heart. John James Ransom agreed completely, he told Ella, with the sentiment expressed by his old friend D. C. Kelley, in the obituary for the

Christian Advocate: "His was an ideal Christian home-going. The hindrances of age were at the door, the boys were mature, the saint was ready either for life here or in heaven."

Because the annual conference came in October each year and the Methodist minister never knew when he would be moved to a new station, the education of his children was often difficult. Many years later John Crowe Ransom recalled how his father would say to him each fall when school opened: "John, there's no need to enter school because we might move. We'll teach you."[32] So Dick, John, Annie, and, later, Ellene were taught at home, Ella paying particular attention to Annie's music. John never attended public school until he was ten years old. Because books were scarce almost everywhere in the South during the latter part of the nineteenth century, and almost unavailable in some of the rural churches John James Ransom served, early in his ministry he collected what must have been regarded in that time as a considerable library. These books were not only for his use and that of his family but for the benefit of his parishioners, particularly the children. Although a large number of the books were related to the church—sermons, biblical commentary, and discussions of Sunday school materials—most of the standard British and American writers, especially Shakespeare, the Victorians, and the American poets of New England, were well represented. From these poets John James chose quotations to illustrate points in his sermons and often after dinner he would read from Shakespeare, a Dickens novel, or "The Visions of Sir Launfal." As a child John spent many hours among these books, complementing the excellent instruction he received from his parents. He spent so much time there, in fact, that he knew better than anyone else in the family the order in which the books were shelved; consequently he soon acquired the assignment of packing and unpacking the books during their frequent moves.[33]

Although his father's salary during John Crow Ransom's youth was meager indeed and cash was exceedingly hard to come by, life for him and his family was usually pleasant.[34] Attached to the parsonage or available nearby was always enough land to keep a cow or two as well as a sufficient number of hogs and chickens to supply the family's need. If the minister's cow "went dry" during the year, someone in the neighborhood always lent him another until his "freshened." John

James always had a vegetable garden large enough to provide bounti-
fully for his family, to share with his neighbors, and to allow Ella to
can enough peas, beans, corn, and tomatoes for the family to have
during the winter. When a new preacher arrived, as well as at Christmas and on other special occasions, he was "pounded," the members
of his congregation bringing him food and other supplies for the
parsonage. At Springfield, John James was "pounded sixteen times"
during his three years, and before each meeting of the annual conference he was given a new suit.[35]

A lover of nature, John James Ransom always planted a tree as
soon as he arrived at a new parsonage—so that future preachers and
their families could enjoy it, he often told the children—and as soon
as they were settled he, Ella, and the children took long walks, searching out points of particular interest and beauty. Although he was far
more learned than most of the parishioners he served, he was an
effective speaker and worked hard on his sermons, trying to provide
something for all levels of people in the congregation. One of his
favorite subjects for sermons was the natural beauties of God's world.
Once after such a sermon in which his father had concentrated particularly on the beauties of the Great Lakes, Ransom asked him while
they were eating dinner if God would want such beauty disturbed for
the benefit of man. Although his father answered in the affirmative,
Ransom was not convinced and brought up the subject on several
other occasions. Finally his father said, "Ella, this boy will surely be a
lawyer. He would argue with a mile board."[36]

John James Ransom was a firm believer that boys with idle time
were likely to get into mischief; consequently John and Dick were
assigned regular jobs around the place. In summer they fed the cows
and chickens, helped gather and clean the vegetables, and assisted
their father in the garden. Each morning John James arose very early,
often before the sun was up, and worked in the garden for an hour or
two while the rest of the family slept. Then he would come by the well,
draw a tub full of fresh water, and bathe before going to the house to
awaken the children. After breakfast, which Ella would have ready by
the time the children got to the table, he would go about his pastoral
duties, leaving instructions for the specific tasks John and Dick were
to do in his absence. On one occasion they were to weed two rows of

corn. Since it was late June and unseasonably warm, Dick got his mother's umbrella from the house and held it over John while he hoed. After a few minutes, their father, who they thought had long since gone, loudly cleared his throat, and Dick quickly exchanged the umbrella for a hoe.[37]

Always inquisitive, John James Ransom read widely and liked to discuss what he read with his friends; thus there were often visitors, usually clerical, in the house. One of these, a fellow Methodist minister whom John James addressed fondly as Rabbi, would sometimes spend the night; and John Crowe would often lie awake, long after the other children were asleep, listening to the old friends discuss and argue until midnight and after.[38] John James would travel, sometimes to considerable distances, to hear a fellow minister preach, particularly if he had been recommended by a friend whose opinion he respected or if he thought the minister's message was likely to be provocative or enlightening. Once after going into Nashville to hear a minister whose published work he especially liked, John James returned home disappointed because the man had read a published sermon with which he was thoroughly familiar. On another occasion John James invited the minister of one of the most affluent congregations in the conference to hold a meeting in his church. Before one of the services the minister came for dinner at the parsonage. Since the children thought he was "somewhat haughty," they were delighted when he excused himself to go to the study to look over his sermon, walked into a coat closet, and closed the door behind him.[39] Although his father frowned when John Crowe laughed aloud, the boy was not too concerned because he could see his mother smiling, and he thought his father also found the episode amusing.

On October 25, 1898, John James Ransom was appointed pastor of the North High Street Methodist Church in Nashville. A church with more than five hundred members, it was not only the largest congregation he had ever served, it was also the only station, since his return from Brazil, in which he had an assistant. As soon as the family was settled into the bright new parsonage, built only three years before, their father made arrangements for John, Dick, and Annie to enter the public schools. Since John had never been formally enrolled in school before, he was shifted around from grade to grade and submitted to a series of examinations before, at the end of November, he was assigned to the eighth grade. Ransom was only ten and the school officials were reluctant to place him in classes with students four or five years older than he, but they were soon convinced that he could do the work.

At the end of the year the principal and some of the teachers encouraged Mr. Ransom to send John to one of the excellent college preparatory schools that had opened in the area because of the demanding entrance examinations required by Vanderbilt, a new university that had opened in Nashville not long after the end of the Civil War. After some investigation his father decided to enroll him in the school operated by Angus Gordon Bowen at the corner of 15th Avenue and Broadway.[40] Established only two years before, when its owner and headmaster had received his degree from Vanderbilt, the Bowen School had already assembled an able faculty and enrolled boys from some of the most distinguished families in Nashville. With the intention of preparing these young men for admission to Vanderbilt and other similar universities, Mr. Bowen and his faculty had developed a rigorous course of study. Four years of Latin and at least two of Greek were required of all students, and this instruction in the classical languages and literatures, the foundations of the entire curriculum, remained under the direct control of the headmaster himself. He was assisted by his younger brother Albert, when he was home from his missionary assignments in China, and, in his absence, by one or more Vanderbilt seniors on a part-time basis. English and German were taught by Dr. E. E. Severy, and Ransom's instruction in German must have been especially good. Not only did he decide to continue his study of German at Vanderbilt, but years later he surprised his fellow Rhodes Scholars with his ability to speak the language fluently enough to get them through that country during some of their summer vacations, a skill none of the others had. Instruction in mathematics was given by James McClure and Ransom's foundation in this subject was so sound that he submitted a perfect paper on the entrance examination given by Vanderbilt at the end of his junior year.

Ransom's memory of Angus Gordon Bowen was still vivid fifty years after his graduation. "Certainly he did more for my own educa-

tion," he wrote in 1957, "than any other man."[41] Although at the time
he appeared to be a "stern and tireless" teacher, Ransom later remembered him as a "warm and true friend." Not only was he determined to "teach the boys who came" to him, he was equally intent on
making them "do their part to receive it." Housed in a single building
on a small lot, the school provided so little playground space that the
boys had to stay indoors and work most of the day. When weather
permitted, however, Ransom, who liked to participate in competitive
athletics, was usually one of the boys involved in a game of stickball,
baseball, or football on one of the vacant lots.

A demanding teacher, Mr. Bowen gave long homework assignments, and the boys who did not complete them on time were required to come in on Saturday. After these sessions, which usually
ended just before noon, the headmaster sometimes rewarded those
students who had done outstanding work during the week by allowing
them to accompany him downtown for lunch in a German delicates-
sen and a visit to Goodpasture's Bookstore. By 1900 Goodpasture's,
located on the north side of Church between Cherry and Summer
streets (now Fourth and Fifth avenues), was already a favorite meeting place for a group of Nashville intellectuals who dropped in most
Saturday afternoons to discuss politics, literature (when Mr. Bowen
was present the topic of conversation was often Plato), and, sometimes, religion. Ransom was invited to participate in some of "Mr.
Bowen's Saturdays downtown," and they were occasions he never forgot. Mr. Bowen was also a strict disciplinarian, and often he punished
before the whole school the student who "had not come up with his
lesson" or whose "big animal spirits" had caused him to "get into
mischief." Although Ransom apparently was never made to "stand before" the entire student body or to have his hand paddled in public,
some of his friends were subjected to these unpleasant experiences,
one of which was usually enough to encourage the student thereafter
to do what was expected of him. The effect of his fellow students
upon Ransom was almost as strong as that of the headmaster and his
faculty. "There could not easily have been found," he recalled much
later, "assembled at that time in one place another hundred boys of
the general sort who were better entitled to education in a college
preparatory school."[42]

On Thursday, Friday, and Saturday, May 14–16, 1903, all members of the senior class from the Bowen School met those from similar schools in the area to take the examinations required for admission to Vanderbilt.[43] On Thursday, from nine until twelve, Ransom took the examination in English; on Friday, he had United States history; and on Saturday, Latin. Each year at the conclusion of these examinations Vanderbilt awarded two prizes: one went to the student who scored highest in Latin and Greek and the other to the one with the best marks in English, history, and mathematics. In 1903, the prize in Latin and Greek went to Arthur Jones of the Dresden (Tennessee) Training School and that in English, history, and mathematics to John Crowe Ransom.[44] Since his performance on this examination was ample proof of his intellectual ability and because Mr. Bowen attested to his emotional maturity, the officials at Vanderbilt allowed Ransom to enter the university at fifteen, a year younger than the minimum age specified in the bulletin. Although his father had been assigned to the New Providence Church near Clarksville, Tennessee, Ransom was able to live with a family friend in Nashville and avoid the expense of staying in the dormitory; therefore his father felt he could afford to allow his brilliant son to attend the university for at least a year, particularly since his prize money would pay half of the $100 required for tuition and fees.[45]

Although in September, 1903, when Ransom first enrolled, Vanderbilt was less than thirty years old, the bulletin of the institution could have commented not only upon its beautiful campus with "more than 150 varieties of trees" but also upon the quality of its faculty, which was particularly strong for a southern university of that time. Established in the period immediately following the Civil War, the university had the funds and the academic policies to attract well-qualified teachers and scholars from all sections of the country and especially from the South. "We demand first of all," Chancellor James H. Kirkland had proclaimed in his inaugural address, "that our professors shall be Christian men and competent scholars, but further than that we have no questions to ask and no instructions to give."[46] The attitude of the faculty was not particularly southern, because many of its members had been educated outside the region and some outside the country. Kirkland, who was also professor of Latin, held a

Ph.D. degree from Leipzig. Among Ransom's freshman teachers were Herbert Cushing Tolman, professor of Greek and later dean of the college, who had a Ph.D. degree from Yale, and Richard Jones, professor of English, whose doctorate was from Heidelburg.

Most of the students had been prepared, as Ransom had, in one of the many excellent private secondary schools that had sprung up in that section of the upper South in the last two decades of the nineteenth century. The best known of these was the Webb School of Bell Buckle, Tennessee, established by William R. "Old Sawney" Webb, who with Kirkland had been very active in the formation of the Southern Association of Colleges and Secondary Schools, an agency created to assist in setting standards for curriculum, accreditation, and other academic matters. The courses of study at these schools, though certainly restricted by modern standards, concentrated upon basic subjects in the traditional arts and sciences curriculum, providing their graduates with the preparation necessary to complete the requirements of institutions like Vanderbilt. Ransom's schedule, it would seem, was fairly standard for students of his day: in Latin he studied Basil Gildersleeve's grammar and read selections from Cicero, Livy, and Pliny. In Greek he read selections from Lysias, Demosthenes, and Plato. At almost every meeting of both classes each student had to translate from material he had been assigned to read before class, sometimes he was asked to translate material with which he was not familiar, and once each week he wrote extensive essays in prose composition. His English course consisted of a formal study of rhetoric and an introduction to English and American literature. Before closing with lectures on and readings from such contemporary southern authors as Joel Chandler Harris, Maurice Thompson, Sidney Lanier, George Washington Cable, and Charles Egbert Craddock, this course required the students to read and write essays and reports "on the chief epochs and masterpieces" of both English and American literature. In addition to German and the required course in physical training, Ransom enrolled in Mathematics 1, which surveyed the principles of trigonometry and analytical geometry and ended with a brief introduction to calculus.

During his sophomore year his program was much the same. He continued his study of Latin (more Cicero but mostly Horace), Greek

(Euripides, Sophocles, Aeschylus, and Aristophanes), and German. His English course, "Movements in English Literature," consisted of a "survey of the development of English poetry" and a study of "nineteenth century essayists and novelists." To replace the mathematics course he enrolled in History 1, which during the first term and half of the second concentrated on English history from its beginnings until 1689, and during the remainder of the year, on the American colonies, with the purpose of studying "the development of English political principles under American conditions."

Motivated, perhaps, by reading William Malone Baskerville's biographical and critical studies of southern authors, which Richard Jones used as one of the texts in the freshman English class,[47] the editor of the *Vanderbilt Observer* began an article, entitled "Literature and the Student," published in October, 1903, with the statement that he and his fellow students lived in an "age of literary activity," which in some respects "may be called the renaissance of American literature, particularly in the South." In order to convince those who had just enrolled in the university to take full advantage of their years at Vanderbilt, he reminded them that literature is not only a "source of knowledge and instruction, it affords much pleasure and amusement as well." With this statement he reached the central point of his essay which he underscored by citing some of the authors his fellow students should read and contemplate:

He is to be pitied who does not enjoy an evening with the sacred songs of Tennyson or a stroll with Ruskin in the "Queen's Gardens." Who is there who does not have to hold his sides for laughter when he picks up Mark Twain or Joel Chandler Harris? He is lead [*sic*] away into enthusiastic delight who reads the stories of Thomas Nelson Page or the quaint sonnets of Whitcomb Riley. Are we not thrilled with holy rapture, inspired with nobler purposes and loftier ideals . . . after having communed awhile with Frances Havergal or read the rhymes of John G. Whittier?[48]

What the unidentified writer of this essay could not have known, of course, was that a southern literary renaissance would occur within the next few years, and that among the hundred-odd freshmen he was welcoming and advising was a quiet and unobtrusive youth who less than two decades later would provide intellectual and aesthetic leadership to a group of poets and critics who would usher in the new southern literature. But before this young man and his associates, since known as the Fugitive poets, could revive a literature, which had "expired, like any other stream whose source is stopped up," they first had to discover what had impeded its flow.[49] Ransom would later contend, with the complete agreement of most members of the group, that the kind of poetry that would command the attention of the perceptive modern reader was not the "act of a child," as was that of most of the poets cited by the writer of this *Observer* essay; instead it was the "act of an adult mind."[50] If poetry is to provide the kind of knowledge one can get almost nowhere else and thereby justify its existence in an age of science and technology, he would insist, it must not be the soft, simple kind of verse recommended here. Rather, it must be of the quality produced by the really great poets—Chaucer, Spenser, Shakespeare, and Milton—all of whom knew how to put their "whole mind and experience to work in poetry." But how was the writer of the *Observer* essay to know in 1903 that this provincial university, with its few brick buildings and "its more than 150 varieties of trees," would attract the most articulate and influential group of writers the section has ever produced, writers who would not only unclog the stream of southern literature but for three decades would direct its flow. Among the probable readers of "Literature and the Student" was a reserved, self-assured lad, a few months past his fifteenth birthday, who would get it all started.

Mostly Nurtured from England 1905-1912

DURING THE FALL of his second year at Vanderbilt, John Crowe Ransom thought seriously about dropping out at the end of the spring term. His plan was to find a teaching post, in or near Nashville if possible, so that he could earn enough money to pay his own expenses in his last two college years. In October, 1904, his father was assigned the church at Fayetteville, Tennessee, at a salary of eight hundred dollars a year.[1] Although John's brother Richard was away teaching and earning his own living, his sisters Annie and Ellene were still at home. Annie's music lessons took extra money and would require a great deal more if she went away to receive professional instruction. Ellene would be at home for a number of years yet, but there was still her education to consider. All in all, Ransom was convinced that the cost of keeping him at Vanderbilt was more than he should expect his father to pay; consequently, during the Christmas break, which he spent with the family in the parsonage at Fayetteville, he sought and received his father's permission to begin searching for a suitable position.[2]

When he returned to Nashville in early January, he discussed his plans with Angus G. Bowen, headmaster of his preparatory school, and together they selected about two dozen schools to which Ransom should apply. For the most part these were secondary schools which were preparing students for admission to Vanderbilt and other similar colleges. Probably included in this list were the following Tennessee schools: the Webb School at Bell Buckle, Branham and Hughes

Academy at Spring Hill, the Wallace School of Nashville, Ware Seminary at Columbia, and the McFerrin Training School at Martin. He also made inquiries at the Cobb and Nichols School at Town Creek, Alabama; the Louisville Male High School in Kentucky; and the McTyeirie Institute in Baldwin, Mississippi.[3] Despite the fact that Ransom would be only seventeen years old when school opened in the fall, Mr. Bowen encouraged him to present his qualifications to teach in the upper and middle schools. At the Bowen School he had earned the highest academic average in his class, and at Vanderbilt he had maintained the position at the top of his class even with a demanding course composed of Latin, Greek, English literature, mathematics, German, history, and physical culture.[4] In his letter of recommendation Mr. Bowen indicated that Ransom was well prepared to teach mathematics, history, German, English, and the classical languages in the upper school and the entire range of subjects in the middle school. In addition, he could supervise elocution, debate, and dramatics. His final asset was his sound religious background, which would make him an active and valuable member of the church in the community where he taught.

In spite of Ransom's perseverance and the excellent references from Mr. Bowen, not to mention those from his professors at Vanderbilt and from several ministerial friends of his family, it soon became apparent that positions of the kind he sought were much harder to locate than he had supposed. When no definite offers had been received by mid-March, he asked his father to enroll him in the placement bureau operated by the Methodist church. Just before the end of May he received an offer to teach the sixth and seventh grades in the Taylorsville High School, located in the southern part of Mississippi. The position would pay, according to the letter Ransom received from the superintendent of education for Smith County, only forty dollars a month. At this salary neither Ransom nor his father saw how he could save, in less than three or four years, the eight hundred dollars needed to complete his degree at Vanderbilt. Consequently, and without his son's knowledge, Mr. Ransom responded to the offer with a telegram reading: "Professor Ransom requires sixty-five dollars a month."[5] Maybe Mr. Ransom was surprised that the demand was met immediately; John surely was, he recalled sixty years later, when he learned he was to receive half again the salary he had expected.

In late August, only four months past his seventeenth birthday, Ransom boarded a train in Nashville's almost-new Union Station for Birmingham, where he waited overnight for the Southern Railway train to Laurel, Mississippi. In Laurel he waited almost three hours for a train on the tiny Gulf and Ship Island Railroad to take him the final twenty-odd miles to Taylorsville. The almost flat, cut-over pine land of southern Mississippi, with an occasional bare hill on which the sparse, coarse grass had already lost its battle with the almost-endless days of ninety-degree summer sun, was far different from the lush greenness of his native Tennessee, which he was leaving for the first time. Ransom found life in Taylorsville crude, "even for a young man who had grown up in the small towns of middle Tennessee."[6]

In 1905 Taylorsville was a settlement of about five hundred people who lived in rambling, dog-trot houses built of raw, unpainted pine by carpenters new to their trade. These houses came at each end of a business district composed of general stores operated by the Eaton brothers, J. P. Myers, J. G. Hughes, J. T. Ford and Company, and Ainsworth, Mayfield and Company.[7] Mr. and Mrs. Arthur Houston and Mr. and Mrs. Peter Robinson operated hotels or boarding-houses, both of which were maintained primarily to accommodate the drummers who came from Hattiesburg or Laurel, to take orders from the general stores, and to furnish temporary lodgings for persons associated with the lumbering industry that supported the town. At each end of the little village was a sawmill; on the eastern side was that of Pat and Cliff James and on the western, that of the Turner brothers. During daylight hours throughout the year eight-wheeled log wagons pulled by four mules hauled the lumber from these mills along the unpaved streets to the railroad yards near the southern edge of the village, and in the fall the road was filled with smaller wagons loaded with cotton on their way to one of the two gins that processed all the cotton grown in the county.

All the stores were built along the north side of the main street and four times every day everyone in these establishments came out on the porches to watch the trains as they struggled along the narrow-gauge railroad on their way to or from Laurel, with stops at Soso, Guitano,

Summerland, Service, Mize, Wisner, Cooley, Abel, and Low. Between the stores and the station was an area, given to the town by the Eaton brothers, which served as a hitching post and wagon yard. This area, especially on Saturdays, was completely filled with the wagons, buggies, surreys, and saddle horses of the farmers who came in from the surrounding countryside to sell fresh vegetables, corn, sugarcane syrup, and other farm products, or to buy their weekly groceries and supplies. On Saturdays, if Ransom walked downtown near noon to collect his mail from the post office near the Eaton store, he could observe the families gathered around the artesian well that flowed in the middle of the wagon yard, eating the fried chicken, pork chops, and baked sweet potatoes they had brought from home, or the sardines, cheese, and salmon they had purchased in one of the stores.[8] Often several families would spread their lunches together, the grown-ups eating from the back of one wagon and the children, under the watchful eyes of almost-grown sisters, from another. Ransom found this spirit of neighborliness and hospitality amply demonstrated in his students. "I marvelled at the friendliness of my pupils," he recalled; "they brought me many stalks of sugar cane, which were good for peeling and sucking, if you liked."[9] One experience he remembered most vividly many years later was the afternoon he accompanied three of his students to a cane mill and observed the process by which the juice was extracted from the cane stalks and converted into syrup. He pitied the plight of the mule forced to walk around and around all day as it turned the rollers that pressed the juice from the stalks of cane. The odor of the cooking syrup he found "most pleasant" and the juice itself "cold and good, but a little too sweet for my taste."

After one night in one of the boardinghouses, Ransom moved into the home of Mrs. Walter Carr, who lived a few hundred yards from the school. At Mrs. Carr's, he shared a room with a fellow teacher, A. A. Mooney from Arkansas, who was beginning his first year as the third principal in the "new school house." The one-room school had been replaced in 1902 with a new building which was the pride of the community and a show place for the entire area. This two-story frame structure provided classrooms on the first floor for Miss Florence Weatherby (first, second, and third grades), Miss Alma Ainsworth (fourth and fifth), Ransom (sixth and seventh), and Mr. Mooney (eighth, ninth, and tenth); upstairs was an auditorium large enough to accommodate the entire student body of 110, their teachers, and as many of their parents and friends as could come to the weekly "concerts," at which debates, dramatic productions, drills, and songs were presented.[10] Each room was expected to contribute to these productions, although the principal burden naturally fell on the older children in Ransom's and Mooney's rooms.

In the classroom, despite his extreme youth, Ransom soon established a reputation as a strict disciplinarian and a demanding teacher. "He was dignified, sober, serious-minded and seemed to us very mature," one of his students remembers; "none of us could believe him when he told us on his birthday he was only eighteen."[11] He taught all the subjects required of sixth and seventh grade students—English, mathematics, health, geography, science, spelling, and history—and took particular pride in the programs he presented as his part of the concerts. He encouraged his students to memorize poems and "declamations" and introduced them for the first time to the proper means of addressing their opponents and the audience at the opening of a debate. "Mr. Chairman, Honored Opponents, Ladies and Gentlemen" did not fall naturally from the lips of eleven- and twelve-year-old Mississippi boys and girls, but they learned to use such formal means of address "because Mr. Ransom insisted on it."[12] Although he was empowered and instructed to do so, he did not follow the usual custom of the time in maintaining discipline. He did not cane his students, nor did he send them to Mr. Mooney to have the punishment administered. Instead those who "talked during books," as his students expressed it, who failed to bring in their assignments or created disturbances while others were "saying their lessons," were kept after school and made to memorize poetry and Bible verses, or to write two hundred times the words they had misspelled in the daily spelling drills. Some of the students instructed "to remain after school" attempted to anticipate their assignment by writing their misspelled words during the school day. Those "caught in the act," as they often were, had to write their words an additional four hundred times each. To discourage inattention and misbehavior, Ransom posted on the wall behind his desk a schedule of assignments, the times at which specified pupils would be allowed to perform the tasks they all wanted to do—bringing in wood for the huge Franklin stove with which the room was heated, dusting the erasers and washing the chalk board, sweeping the floor and arranging the benches in the recitation area, and, the most cherished of all assignments, operating the navy-blue calico stage curtains on the days when the sixth and seventh grades were responsible for the weekly concert. Any student required to stay after school for any reason also lost his assignments on the "special duty roster" for a month.[13]

Ransom was popular and well liked in the boardinghouse and in the community. One day soon after school began Mrs. Carr called him into the kitchen where she was cooking supper and told him that rather than fifteen dollars, the amount agreed upon for room and board, she was going to charge him thirteen dollars a month and do his laundry free.[14] He never knew what motivated this act of generosity, particularly since it was not extended to his roommate, unless, as he speculated later, Mrs. Carr was irritated by Mooney's inclination toward overfastidiousness. Each time he came to the table he brushed his chair off with his handkerchief; then, after grace was said, he carefully examined his plate and rubbed it thoroughly with his napkin. This ritual, Ransom remembered much later, was often followed by this exchange: Mrs. Carr: "Is it clean, Mr. Mooney?" And Mooney: "Yes, of course it is, Mrs. Carr."[15]

The community was particularly pleased to find that both Mooney and Ransom were Methodists and regular attendants at the weekly services held in the new church building completed less than three years before. The minister, the Reverend Mr. R. A. Gale, asked Mooney to teach the adult Sunday school class. He accepted, as he knew he was expected to do, and Ransom was one of his most reliable students. He was present every Sunday, except for two he missed while at home for Christmas holidays; and he always prepared his lesson, read the assigned chapters in the Bible, and responded readily to the many questions Mooney directed to him. Obviously Ransom was no stranger to a Methodist Sunday school class, and his performance there each Sunday convinced the fathers whose children he taught that the training of their sons and daughters was in the best hands possible.[16]

As soon as they moved into the community, both Ransom and Mooney attracted considerable attention. Since they were members of the faculty, young ladies regarded them as most acceptable escorts to the Sunday school picnics, ice cream suppers, and other social occasions. But neither of them completely fulfilled the ladies' expectations. Soon after the school session began, it became apparent that Mr. Mooney was "sparking in earnest" Miss Alma Ainsworth, whom he married the following summer. Although Ransom was polite—a little withdrawn perhaps, but certainly appreciative of all the attention he was receiving—he never actually sought "the company of any particular girl."[17] The girls were extremely pleased, however, when he walked with them back from church on Sunday nights or from prayer meetings on Wednesday evenings, as he often did, though usually in groups of three or four. The biggest social event of the season was the box supper held each autumn to raise funds to purchase books for the school library, to acquire "scenery" for the stage, or to be used for other worthy purposes around the school. Each of the young ladies brought a brightly decorated box filled with dainty finger-sized sandwiches of pimento cheese, fried chicken, bananas, homemade cookies, and other delicacies. The young men would examine the boxes carefully as they were brought into the auditorium for auction, trying to determine which they wished to buy in order to share its contents with the owner. On this late October night one recent graduate of the school, with the help of some tenth-graders, discovered which box belonged to Miss Ainsworth and kept the bidding going until Mr. Mooney had to pay two dollars (the usual price was twenty-five to fifty cents) to have supper with his fiance. Much to the disappointment of many of the young ladies, Ransom acquired very early in the evening, and for a modest sum, the box of Bertha Eaton, the postmistress and a maiden lady of approximately twice his age. For the remainder of the year he escorted her to any social occasion to which he was expected to bring a partner.[18]

In late March the trustees met to "elect teachers" for the following year, and Ransom was invited to return at a salary of seventy dollars a month. He was delighted at this demonstration of confidence in him and particularly pleased by the flattering comments he received from the parents of his students and the members of his Sunday school class, but his desire to return to Vanderbilt remained as strong as ever.[19] In spite of the care with which he had saved his salary, however, he had considerably less than half the amount required to complete his final two years. Typically, he wrote his father for advice; Mr. Ransom advised him that if he had to teach another year before completing his degree, he should attempt to get a position closer to home. Ransom informed Mr. Mooney, therefore, that he would not remain at Taylorsville and immediately wrote all the school officials with whom he had corresponded the previous year. For a time it seemed he might have acted rashly to resign his position with no prospects of another, but in mid-April, while he spent the summer in Fayetteville with his family, his father assured him that if no suitable post was available, he should return to Vanderbilt for his junior year, even though they would have to borrow money to supplement his savings. Just when Ransom had decided to go into Nashville to complete arrangements for returning to the university he received a letter from M. M. Summar, principal of the Haynes-McLean School in Lewisburg, asking him to come over to discuss a position on that faculty. He went to Lewisburg and talked to Mr. Summar, a man Ransom liked immediately and who remained a close friend until his death. Summar's friendliness and engaging informal manner did not conceal his sincere dedication to his profession. The section badly needed college-educated men and women, and he was willing to devote his time and his considerable energies to providing the kind of educational experiences gifted young people needed to insure their admission to the best universities in the country. Ransom's impression upon Summar must have been equally favorable because he was offered a position in the upper school. He would teach both Latin and Greek and earn a salary of ninety dollars a month for a nine-month term. He accepted immediately and returned to Fayetteville, he remembered many years later, "as pleased with my prospects as I have ever been."[20]

The next year passed rapidly. Haynes-McLean was much like the Bowen School that Ransom had attended in Nashville. Vanderbilt encouraged the establishment of these preparatory schools by offering supervision and guidance in establishing and maintaining adequate academic programs. The university also sent its graduates to important posts on the faculties of such institutions and admitted their graduates into its academic departments. Ransom found his teaching most satisfying. He taught Latin and Greek to students in the fifth and sixth forms and was sponsor of the debating club. To be able to prepare thoroughly the assignments he gave his students was a definite advantage to Ransom because he was required to review in detail the fundamentals of both Latin and Greek, exactly the kind of review he needed to be prepared to reenter the university in the fall. He was asked by Mr. Summar to be host to Dean F. W. Moore and other officers of Vanderbilt when they made their official inspections of the school, visited its classes, and conferred with its faculty. The proximity of Lewisburg to Fayetteville encouraged frequent visits home, and, best of all, through frugal living and strict budgeting he was assured of having sufficient money to complete his education with a minimum of assistance from his father.

In late September, 1907, when Ransom reenrolled in Vanderbilt, he was justifiably proud that he could pay in advance the required fees: $100 for tuition, $20 for fuel and light, and $54 for a quarter's room and board in Kissam Hall.[21] It was his first year in the dormitory, and he was impressed, he wrote his mother, with the facilities of the five-story building constructed eight years before with a special appropriation from W. K. Vanderbilt and named for his mother, Maria Louisa Kissam Vanderbilt. Ransom was assigned to Suite 29, consisting of two single bedrooms separated by a study, which he shared with his cousin Joe Ransom. All of the students in the building, as well as those in the six brick cottages on nearby West Side Row, took their meals in the dining hall located in the basement.[22] To complete the requirements for his bachelor of arts degree, he was required to take a year's work in philosophy, physics, and chemistry; the remainder of his program could be elected from a list of courses in the arts and science curriculum. During his junior year he completed the requirements with deductive logic and psychology, general physics, and inorganic chemistry. As electives he took Greek 3 (Aeschylus, Theocritus, Plato, and Thucydides), Latin 3 (Tacitus, Seneca, Martial, and select plays of Plautus and Terence), and English 3 ("*The Drama*: an interpretation of representative plays of Shakespeare, with collateral study of other dramas and with some consideration of the theory

of the drama"). The following year he completed the degree requirements by enrolling in the following electives: inductive logic, ethics
and practical philosophy, the principles of economics, Old and Middle English language and literature—only four students registered
for this course and when all except Ransom dropped it, it was can-
celed and he was allowed to replace it with a second unit in Greek. His
final course was a seminar in Roman satire: Horace, Juvenal, Persius,
and Petronius. During both years he also took the required noncredit
courses in physical training.[23] It was a demanding course even in the
classically oriented liberal arts college of the time; however, Ransom
was elected to Phi Beta Kappa during his junior year, and in his senior
year he was student president of that society, even though he devoted
a considerable amount of time to nonacademic interests. Upon
graduation he was awarded the Founder's Medal, which is "conferred
upon the graduate who shall attain the highest average grade of distinction in the final year in each of the schools embraced in his degree."[24] With such a record, it is no wonder that John Murray, his
tutor at Oxford a few years later, would write that Ransom "came into
residence" in Christ Church "much better fitted, both in ability and in
training, than most Rhodes scholars to read the Honour School of
Literae Humaniores."[25]

In the spring semester of his freshman year Ransom had contributed two or three brief essays to the *Vanderbilt Observer*, and the following year he was elected to membership in the Calumet Club, the most
exclusive organization on the campus. Membership was limited to
twelve, and from its inception the club had followed the principle
that election was solely on the basis of literary merit, as demonstrated
by publication in the *Observer*, and that places in the club would be
kept vacant if there were not enough students of merit to fill its small
quota. "The Calumet Club is a literary organization," Ransom wrote in
1909, "in which merit alone secures admission. They are leading literary thinkers; it is their purpose to encourage literary activity. They
want cultured men who are gaining distinction in their departments.
Every year a small number of new men are admitted to membership.
Every man who wishes to do his best should aim at the Calumet
Club."[26] From the beginning this club, which had the obvious purpose of encouraging serious literary activity on the campus, operated

in a manner very much similar to that followed by the Hermit Crabs established by Ransom and a few of his closest friends at Oxford a few years later, and both of these anticipated the Fugitive group in several important ways.

The members of the Calumet Club decided upon a modern author whose work they wished to discuss—two of those chosen in Ransom's day were Browning and Hardy—and at each meeting one member volunteered, or was asked, to bring to the next session a paper discussing some aspect of the particular work under consideration. The member who led the discussion would read his paper and the other members would give their reactions to it. At the biweekly meetings some original poems and stories were interspersed among these critical papers. That the students took their appearances before the Calumet Club seriously is demonstrated by the fact that Ransom worked harder on an essay on Hardy to be presented there than on anything else he did at Vanderbilt.[27]

During the fall semester of 1907, members of the group undertook a project to combine with similar organizations on the campuses of the University of the South, the University of North Carolina, and the University of Georgia. A meeting of the representatives from these institutions was called, and Sigma Upsilon, a national literary fraternity, was founded. Within a year seven other institutions had joined.[28] Ransom was a "little surprised and very much pleased," he wrote home in the spring of 1908, to learn that he had been elected editor of the *Observer* for his senior year because "it really is a very great honor." There was no way, he concluded, that he could more wisely spend his time except, perhaps, on the regular classroom assignments. During the summer he wrote the persons he wanted to serve as his six associate editors, and so many of his first choices accepted that he could conscientiously begin his first editorial the following fall in this way:

In the staff of associate editors named above the editor believes that the best possible selection has been made from the large number of good literary men at Vanderbilt. The editor and business manager of this magazine hold office by virtue of their election last spring by the Dialectic and Philosophic Literary Societies, under whose auspices the magazine is published. In the selection of his staff, however, the edi-

tor has not considered membership in either society as a requirement. Nor has he considered membership in any fraternity, club, class
or department of the University as such. To do so would be a pre-
sumption on his part, inasmuch as this magazine, the organ of literary
societies, exists as the means of encouraging and honoring literary
effort on the part of all of the men at Vanderbilt. The *Observer* staff
may be supposed to be representative of the best literary talent of the
University, and nothing more.[29]

Ransom's editorials throughout the year covered a broad range of
topics. He encouraged the writers at Vanderbilt to compete in the first
short-story contest sponsored by Sigma Upsilon, which carried a first
prize of thirty dollars and a second prize of twenty dollars. The *Observer*, he wrote, "hopes that this honor will fall upon a Vanderbilt
man. The prize itself is the lesser consideration in the face of the fact
that the leading universities of the South will compete for the honor."
What has become of the college poet? he asked on another occasion. A
lovely autumn is "slipping away unhonored and unsung. Indian
summer, frosted pumpkins, golden harvests, ruddy fruits and rosy
cheeks—has nobody around here noticed these things?" He expressed his delight that hazing was no longer common at Vanderbilt
and his complete agreement with the faculty regulation, in force for
the first time, requiring every freshman and sophomore to "pledge
himself that he will neither take part in nor instigate hazing or class
rushing of any kind." He attempted to assuage the feelings of students
not elected to membership in a social fraternity by pointing out the
deficiencies of the process by which members were chosen: "The objection of a single member of a fraternity has weight enough to cause
the rejection of any name brought up for consideration, regardless of
the wishes of other members of the body. Again, the hasty spiking
season, beginning as it does immediately upon the matriculation of
new students, is responsible for the overlooking of some of the best of
the new men in favor of others whose attractions are but superficial."
He repeatedly urged support of the magazine through subscribing to
it, patronizing its advertisers, and contributing to its pages. To any
student who could not afford the cost of a subscription, he offered
copies free and invited them to give their names to the business manager. "You can then support it," he concluded, "by simply reading it."

He argued strongly against the common practice of selecting important campus officers through fraternity politics, and he entered freely into rather heated discussions of the two most controversial issues on campus that year. The first of these was a proposal from the student forum that the Negro waiters in the Kissam dining hall be replaced by student waiters. Although he saw some merit in the suggestion, he felt compelled to raise important considerations on the other side. In fairness to the 250 students paying for the service, he wrote, the students should not be paid more than the Negro waiters were receiving. The change should not be effected until there was some assurance that student waiters could provide equally efficient service. The most important consideration, he argued, would be the way the student waiters were accepted by other students. No one can "dismiss at will even the most groundless of his prejudices," and it is reasonable to assume that the "education of the Vanderbilt student body in common sense is not yet so complete but that the student who waits on table to get a college education will put himself under some disadvantages socially." Finally, if the new system were to begin during the current year, opportunity should be provided for those who did not approve the change to get their meals elsewhere. If these problems could be solved, a system of student waiters should be adopted because it could well "mean a college education for some who have not otherwise the means to get one." The new system was approved by the members of the West Side Association, the students living in Kissam Hall and West Side Row, and it went into effect at the beginning of the spring term. The editor of the *Observer* was the first to proclaim it a complete success: "Student waitership works with fine relish and dispatch. The service is much quickened and otherwise improved; and everybody enjoys the new order of things. Nobody has suffered social ostracism for waiting on table. Nobody has shown any disposition towards the student waiters except one of consideration and forbearance."

The stand he took on the second issue almost certainly was not warmly received by many of his fellow students. The student forum seriously debated a proposal under which students who had maintained a daily average of 90 percent or above would be exempt from written term examinations. Although the proposal was strongly supported by many students, it was "heartily opposed" by the *Observer*. "There is no substitute," its editor argued, "for the written examination," the basic justification of which is that it requires a "comprehensive review of the subject." This kind of review requires the student to go back over the details he has learned "piecemeal and bind them into a logical system." From a "jumble of miscellaneous facts he must construct a science." He who argues that he should be excused from examinations because his examination grades are always lower than those received on daily assignments should have more examinations, not fewer. "The student who cannot collect his knowledge sufficiently well," Ransom wrote, "to stand a creditable examination is not entitled to a degree from this or any other university. The university proposes to develop men of larger outlook and clearer insight than the ordinary man is capable of. It cannot do so without training their power of classification and analysis." The best of all possible systems is one that combines required daily preparation and a rigorous and complete examination, the grading of both activities to be so exact that they are "an absolute test to the student's present grasp of his subject." [30]

The editorship of the *Observer* gave Ransom his first opportunity to develop his prose style by reacting to a fairly broad spectrum of subjects and to an audience whose sympathies often did not agree with his. His participation in the Calumet Club demonstrated to him in a way he would never forget the values to be acquired from a personal and direct approach to the masterpieces of literature. His awareness of the additional benefits accruing to a small group of dedicated and enterprising students and teachers discussing and analyzing a literary work together surely encouraged him to assist in forming the Hermit Crabs and the Fugitives.

On June 16, 1909, when he received from Chancellor James H. Kirkland the first diploma given that year by the Academic Department of Vanderbilt University, Ransom thought he had definitely decided on his future vocation. Almost three months before commencement, M. M. Summar had come from Lewisburg to Nashville to invite him to return to the Haynes-McLean School. His one year there had convinced Summar that Ransom was "one of the best school men of my acquaintance," that he was not only popular with "both pupils and patrons" but that he was a most effective teacher since he "can do with the boys about what he pleases"; consequently, if Ransom would return, he would be promoted to senior master and coprincipal.[31] He would teach Latin and Greek to the sixth form and have complete control of the academic program of the school. Mr. Summar would be responsible for finances and for the operation and maintenance of the physical plant. As a partner in the operation of the school, receiving a share of the profits, Ransom stood to earn at least twice as much as he had two years before. These benefits, plus the fact that he had thoroughly enjoyed his previous year there, convinced Ransom that he should accept this most generous and flattering offer. After discussing the matter with his father, he did. Mr. Ransom knew that the financial prospects of the offer were unusually good, particularly for a young man who would not reach his twenty-first birthday until April thirtieth, and the entire family was pleased that John would be settled so well and so near the towns in which they could expect to live as long as Mr. Ransom held an appointment in the Tennessee Conference of the Methodist Church. For the past two years he had been presiding elder of the Murfreesboro District and could reasonably expect to remain there one or two more years. Even when he was given another assignment, the new station would likely be within fifty miles of Lewisburg. On the morning after graduation, then, Ransom went to the family home in Murfreesboro, secure in his conviction that without hesitation or doubt he had moved directly into his life's work.

He enjoyed his summer in Murfreesboro. His Aunt Mary and her family lived on a farm encompassing two square miles of beautiful rolling land a few miles from town and very near the site of his father's birth. Except for two or three extended visits to this farm, the entire summer was spent in the comfortable, two-story brick parsonage located at 337 East Main Street. All of the family was there, including Dick who came in for a long visit while his school in Senatobia, Mississippi, was on vacation. During his days in town Ransom played tennis, visited, read, and enjoyed his mother's excellent cooking, and in the evenings the family often gathered in the parlor to hear Annie play the piano or to read together a novel by Dickens or Thackeray. On the evenings when Mr. Ransom was home, he usually read aloud and the others listened, interrupting occasionally for comments or questions. Since all members of the family could not be present for every session, each reading began with a summary of what had been read in the previous session (this was usually Ransom's assignment) so that everyone would have all the information he needed to follow the development of the complicated plots of those Victorian novels. On some evenings, usually when the girls were away for some reason or when Annie was busy with one of her music students, Ransom and his father would sit on the front porch and discuss religion, politics, philosophy, or literature. Often these discussions became so animated that Mrs. Ransom would caution them to hold their voices down; otherwise, she would say, the "neighbors will think you are quarreling."

Early in August, Ransom moved to Lewisburg, where he and Mr. Summar began immediately the many tasks necessary to insure an orderly opening of the fall session. While Mr. Summar was supervising the general care of the building and grounds, Ransom checked carefully the schedule of recitations, the availability of texts and other teaching materials, and the registration of students. The "honor of the new assignment," Ransom said many years later, "gave me a new momentum." After the fall term got underway and he became immersed in his sixth-form Latin and Greek classes, he could not have been more content. But about midway through the fall he had an unexpected letter from H. C. Tolman, who had taught Ransom five years of Greek at Vanderbilt and who for many years would serve the university with distinction as academic dean, notifying him that he had been nominated by a faculty committee for a Rhodes Scholarship. If he were able to accept this honor—one of the highest, Professor Tolman assured him, that the faculty could confer upon one of its students—he should submit a formal application and be ready to come to Nashville for interview if and when the regional committee called him. He prepared the application, filed it, and waited for the call, which came shortly after Christmas. A few weeks later he was notified of his appointment. In spite of his satisfaction with his position and his unwillingness to disappoint Mr. Summar, who "released him with great reluctance," Ransom knew he must accept the appointment, a conclusion enthusiastically supported by his family and

his professors and friends at Vanderbilt. At the end of the school
year, therefore, he returned to Murfreesboro to make final plans for
his years abroad.[32]

For a family as close as the Ransoms the prospect of a three-year
separation—and no one saw how the money could be raised for a visit
home before his course was finished, even for the best of reasons—
was definitely unpleasant. It was with strongly mixed feelings, therefore, that he bid his family goodbye in the early morning of September 27 and made his way to Nashville, where he caught a train for
Philadelphia and from there a ship for Southampton. During the
twelve-day passage on the *Haverford,* he spent considerable time with
a fellow Rhodes Scholar, William Alexander Stuart from Virginia,
who for the next two years—before Stuart had to withdraw for a year
because of ill health—would be one of his closest associates. One of
Stuart's first impressions of Ransom was that he had a speaking
knowledge of German, a fact he could recall fifty years later because
in "those days it was a rare Rhodes scholar who could speak anything
but English."[33]

In Oxford Ransom enrolled in Christ Church College and Stuart
in Balliol, but these two fellow southerners, both of whom felt some
lack of confidence in their ability to complete successfully the course
they were undertaking, saw a great deal of each other, especially in
these early days. Stuart was very much surprised, he said later, to
learn that Ransom had chosen "to read the Greats" because this
"School of pure learning was the most prestigious" of all the programs
offered anywhere in the university. Most Americans of that time were
unwilling to undertake this area of concentration because of their
"inadequate grounding in classical literature" and "their insufficient
facility in Greek and Latin."[34] The *Student Handbook* of Christ Church
in the year of Ransom's enrollment described this course of study
thus: "The Final Classical School, or the School of *Literae Humaniores* is
the oldest and is admitted by all hands to be the premier school in
dignity and importance. It includes the greatest proportion of the
ablest students, it covers the widest area of study, it makes probably
the severest demands, both on examiner and candidate, it carries the
most coveted distinction."[35] The course was divided into three parts:
1) The Greek and Latin languages, 2) the development of philosophy,

and 3) a period of Greek and a period of Roman history. Rather than reading about the philosophers, Ransom was expected to read their works in the original language.

Although Ransom had studied both Latin and Greek for eight years (and taught them for two) and had completed all of the undergraduate courses offered in philosophy at Vanderbilt, he soon doubted the adequacy of his preparation, especially in the latter field:

I'd had Collins Denny in Philosophy, and so I appeared to my appointment—the students had individual appointments, at the beginning of the term, to march down the great hall to meet the Dean of the College who would then shift you to your tutors. I was shifted about to five people altogether, and each of them raised the question of whether I ought to take "Greats," or understood what I was trying. And I was very confident, and I finally got to my philosophy tutor who was a very eminent philosopher named Blount. And he said, "Have you read any philosophy?" And I said, "Yes, I had two years of philosophy at college." "What did you take?" And I said, "We took a course in deductive logic—Aristotelian logic." And he said, "Whom did you read?" And I said, "We had a book by Noah K. Davis." And he said, "Ah, I don't know that name; but did you take anything else?" And I said, "Well, we had a course in inductive logic." And he said, "What did you read?" And I said, "We had a book by Noah K. Davis." And he said, "A most ubiquitous man." And then he said, "Did you take any other courses?" I said, "Yes, then we had a course in ethics." And he said, "Whom did you read? But please don't say Noah K. Davis." I said, "Noah K. Davis." And he said, "My education is faulty. I don't know Noah K. Davis. But did you take any other courses?" I said, "Yes, then we had a course in psychology." And he said, "I can't bear it, but I feel that you had Noah K. Davis." I said, "Yes." And it was perfectly true that we had had Noah K. Davis, and no other philosopher, living or dead. And so he said, "Come to my rooms next Thursday evening at eight, and bring me an essay entitled " 'What is Thought?' " [36]

What Ransom did not tell his tutor was that Noah K. Davis was a professor at the University of Virginia under whom Denny had studied and who had written or edited all the textbooks used in the philosophy department at Vanderbilt while Ransom was a student there.

In this way Ransom began his work in Greats, but in subsequent conferences he came to understand more precisely what was expected of him. During the fall term he was to read, in Greek, one major work by Aristotle and one by Plato. From ideas and impressions derived from this reading, he was to prepare two essays each week. For his period of Greek history he chose that from 776 to 403 B.C. and began a reading of "the complete works of Herodotus and Thucydides, a number of Plutarch's Lives, a number of Greek historical inscriptions, and some miscellaneous writings." Later he would begin his study of Roman history from 43 B.C. to A.D. 117. "As the source of this history," he wrote later, "I was required to show detailed knowledge of the complete works of Tacitus, some of Pliny's Letters, some Roman historical inscriptions and some miscellaneous Latin literature." [37] From the very beginning he impressed his tutors. In Greek history Mr. Robert Dundas found his work "unusually thorough and solid, and his judgments sane and well-reasoned." [38] Mr. John H. Murray, his first tutor in Greek literature and philosophy, was aware immediately of "his genuine interest and capacity in all sides of his School, Ancient Philosophy and History and Classical Scholarship." Especially in philosophy, Murray was impressed from the first with Ransom's ability to sense the "vital points of a problem," as well as with his "ordered thinking" and his ability to write "as he thinks, with clearness and conviction, and in agreeable English." [39]

His determination to do well and, if possible, to excel in the rigorous discipline he had undertaken required Ransom to spend most of his time on specific assignments. On a few occasions, however, he accompanied some of his fellow Rhodes Scholars to the American Club on Cornmarket Street to read from the ample stock of American magazines and newspapers in the reading room there. Sometimes in the afternoon he went there with Stuart or with McDougall Kenneth McLean, whom he had known at Vanderbilt but who was now the Rhodes Scholar from Texas, for afternoon tea, which, he wrote his mother, "is a very civilized custom indeed." [40] In spite of the unusually stringent demands upon his time, he attended as many of the weekly debates held in the American Club as possible. These debates, which were modeled very closely after those held by the Oxford Union Society, soon became one of his principal interests and, except for tennis and team sports, almost his only diversion. On these occasions he met most of his fellow Rhodes Scholars and with some of them he formed friendships that lasted long beyond their time at Oxford:

Christopher Morley of Maryland, Roy Loomis Lange of Oklahoma, Roger Sherman Loomis of Massachusetts, Howard Alfred Taber of Rhode Island, William John Bland of Ohio, Elmer Holmes Davis of Indiana, Edward Henry Eckel of Missouri, and Joseph Washburn Worthen of New Hampshire.

So diligently did he work during the term, Ransom wrote his father from Hawarden, where he was spending the Christmas vacation, that he was "somewhat bagged out." The two essays a week and the constant study had made a "very severe term indeed" and now he looked forward to a month-long vacation of reading and relaxation. The only reason he objected to the heavy snowfall—which started the day after his arrival, fell without interruption for thirty-six hours, and reached a depth of two feet—was that it forced a cancellation of the golf match he and Bland had scheduled with two of their English friends. He hoped the snow would soon melt so that he could play some golf, for as soon as he could improve his skill he was certain he would like that game better than any other he had ever played. But now, he was concerned that the snow would not melt in time for him to return to school, for this "is the most snow I have seen since Trinity" when it was "piled so high I could just see the cows' backs as they went down the lane."[41]

He was able to return to school without trouble, however; and since the comments his tutors had written on his essays had made him confident he could do a "creditable job," he was encouraged to spend more time on the tennis court and golf course. He even went out for rowing and with no previous experience at all made the team. "I have a flash of recollection," Stuart wrote much later, "of a small young man in the bow seat of an 8-oar racing shell. This was Ransom pulling vigorously in one of the Christ Church boats in the races known as 'The Torpids.' In rowing, bow was where they would place a little man if he was strong and would pull with fervor."[42] Sometime during the winter Ransom adopted a schedule which he followed for most of his time there. After arising in a cold room (there was no heat and sometimes the temperature would fall as low as twenty-five degrees), he took a cold bath and went to breakfast at 8:30. After breakfast he worked until 1:15, then took a light lunch, after which he had some form of physical exercise. On the rare days when he was not rowing (and almost every day after he left the crew), he played tennis or golf, increasingly more of the latter when he had time, for he had never found "any finer physical enjoyment than playing 18 holes of a good golf match." About 4 or 4:30, he returned and had a "long leisurely soak in a warm tub." Afterwards, he had tea and worked until dinner at eight in Hall. After dinner, unless he had an appointment with his tutor, he went to a concert, lecture, dramatic production or he read in his room.[43] Some of the authors mentioned most often as occupying his time in these after-dinner hours were Shakespeare, Emerson, Carlyle, Hardy, Browning, Meredith, Thackeray, and Whitman. Although he tried to reserve his evenings for these leisure activities, sometimes they had to go if he needed to work on one of the two essays required each week.

As soon as he was settled in Peckwater Quadrangle, he began for the first time in his life to collect a personal library. He bought, first of all, Grote's *History of Greece* (twelve volumes), a complete Shakespeare (in six volumes), Emerson's *Essays,* and the complete works of Thomas Carlyle. Gradually he acquired, he wrote his family near the beginning of his second year, "a small German library (mostly philosophy)," an encyclopaedia, "texts and reference books in Greek history," a "good many philosophical books," and "several miscellaneous books from Everyman's."[44] Although the amount of required reading and writing at Oxford kept his work within fairly definitely prescribed limits, he thoroughly enjoyed what he was doing. There were about the proper amounts of freedom and direction, he thought; and he was constantly aware, he wrote his father near the end of his first year, of how fortunate he was to have this experience. During the year he had written a number of essays, both historical and philosophical, and just before leaving for a month-long walking trip through Scotland and the Lake Country, he selected two for his father to read so that "you can know," he wrote in a short accompanying note, "what I am thinking." One of the essays was on Plato, which he said was "too short and inadequate"; and the other, on logic, had "encountered considerable opposition from my tutor." Both of them are significant to Ransom's intellectual development because they demonstrate some views which contribute to a "theory of knowledge that has occupied my attention for some time."[45]

After his walking tour, he made a brief visit to London, where he listened for a whole afternoon to the speeches in Hyde Park and witnessed demonstrations by the striking dockworkers and suffragettes. While he was in London he completed an essay on British education and sent it to his father with instructions to read it with care and when he was satisfied with it to send it on to the editor of the *Methodist Review*. "If there is any money," he wrote, "it should go to Dick." For several weeks, too, he had been writing an essay on Ibsen, and when it was completed he expected to send it on to his father for his reactions and for possible inclusion in a future issue of the *Review*.[46]

Toward the end of July he made his way to the Continent, where he was to join some of his Oxford friends for a leisurely tour of Germany. The Channel crossing was rough, and for the first time in his life he was seasick, "an unpleasant episode of only a few minutes," he wrote Annie, "after which I turned over and went to sleep."[47] The train ride from Le Havre was not altogether pleasant because the third-class coach on which he was traveling was so crowded that he could not get a seat by the window. Since he could not get a clear view of the scenery, he observed as closely as he could the other passengers in the coach, particularly the Germans. "I have not seen in either English or American faces, though possibly in French," he wrote his family, "anything like the great proportion of coarse and brutal expressions that strike one very forcibly when traveling in Germany."[48] His train made many stops, nonstop service being limited to first- and second-class trains, but he enjoyed his visits to Brussels, Heidelberg, and Freiburg. He had tea in Cologne, then went up the Rhine by moonlight and reached Manneheim by 12:30. In Manneheim, and "on Sunday no less," he attended a performance of *Carmen*; and later at the Royal Bavarian Opera House he heard Wagner's *Tannhauser* and Caruso singing in Verdi's *Aida*. Although some tourists stood in line for twenty hours to get seats costing five marks or more, Ransom and his friends had relatively little difficulty because they were willing to take standing space for one mark. The following day he went on to Heidelberg. "I have never seen finer hills, and prettier streets," he wrote home, "nor a more impressive old castle." The university gives the town an "air of wealth and culture." He spent two days there, and enjoyed a brief reunion with some of his Oxford friends, before going on to Freiburg, where he expected to stay at least a month. This city, he wrote his mother as soon as he arrived, "is located in the black forest and is surrounded by the most splendid wooded mountains." A "flourishing and up-to-date city," it has "no end of handsome streets and public buildings and pretty houses. After the dirt of English cities it seems very clean and new. Then there is plenty of shade so that some of the streets are as fine as Main Street, Murfreesboro." He was impressed with the "German genius for citizenship, which gives them the finest municipal and state advantages that a government has ever secured for its members."

At the end of August, Ransom began making his way back toward England because he wanted to get in a few days of golf before going on to London to do some work in the British Museum. When the term opened on October 13 he had to present a long paper on Greek history; his weeks in Germany, though most pleasant despite the almost constant rain, had contributed little to that project. When he arrived at Hawarden, about ten miles west of Chester and the home of William Ewart Gladstone until his death in 1898, he found his luggage and books had not been put off the train. But he was able to get everything he needed from St. Deiniol's Library, which had opened in 1908 and contained Gladstone's entire collection of books. His greatest disappointment, perhaps, was the fact that although the rain had let up, it was still too damp and chilly to put in much time on the golf course. On Sunday, October 1, he went down to London for ten days before the opening of term. Back in Oxford, he found that all four of the "Greats" tutors in Christ Church were ill with influenza, but Mr. Blount, to whom he was assigned again, was well enough to give him a brief appointment and together they decided that this term Ransom should concentrate on logic and metaphysics.[49]

Before the term was far underway, Ransom himself came down with the same disease and was pretty much confined to his room until the end of October. While he was still recuperating, he wrote his family that next term he would take up a new sport, either hockey or lacrosse, because he was convinced that his illness was, in part at least, the result of his having so little outdoor exercise during the summer and early fall. He had decided not to accept the invitation to row again because the training was so strenuous and time-consuming that it interfered with his studies. Although he did play a little hockey, he was never good enough at the game really to enjoy it; consequently when he had the opportunity to join a small tennis club, which had one of the few gravel courts in England, he decided to stick to that sport. At Halloween, he and McLean went over to Sunnyside, the home of Sir William Murray and his family, and Ransom won the prize for apple bobbing. The Murray family, which included two unmarried daughters, "are fine Scotch people," Ransom wrote his mother, "who make visitors feel at home." [50]

During his confinement with influenza, particularly after he began to recuperate, he got a great deal of work done; after he was able to go out again, therefore, he had more time for social activities. In early November he and William M. Rogers, the Rhodes Scholar from Mississippi, had Miss Evy Lee Palmer from Nashville and Miss Ann Hefley, daughter of a Methodist minister from Memphis, over to the Junior Common Room for lunch and a week later he and McLean had tea there with the two Murray girls. Before Thanksgiving he went into London to visit Willard Steele, who had been a member of Ransom's fraternity at Vanderbilt, and his new bride, the former Miss Kate Hinds of Lebanon, Tennessee.

Shortly after the meeting of the annual conference in October, his mother wrote that John James Ransom had been assigned to the Arlington Methodist Church, located on the Murfreesboro Pike a few miles from Nashville. Ransom responded immediately that he was sorry he had not been there to help move the books and that he was delighted the family would be in the country again and able to have a cow and chickens as well as a vegetable garden. "I like the country," he wrote, "although I am aware of the inconveniences." Now that he had been away from Tennessee for more than a year, he was more convinced than ever that "it is the best place I have ever seen." [51] A week before he had been told that as the president of the American Club he would be expected to say a few words at the annual Thanksgiving program, at which the Reverend Dr. Len K. Broughton, formerly of Atlanta and now of London, and Price Collier, "author of books on England, Germany, and other subjects," would speak. At the dinner, at which there were a hundred and fifty guests, a typical American meal was served—including turkey, stuffing, sweet potatoes, corn, mincemeat pie, and plum pudding—Ransom thought his "little speech went very well." Arranging this program and preparing his few remarks had turned his thoughts back toward America. "Oxford is a good experience," he concluded, "but I cannot imagine Americans being satisfied there for a long period. The differences are more than surface deep. Americans are said to be practical but they are the only nation of idealists I know anything about." To the Thanksgiving dinner he escorted one of the Murray girls, and a week later he and Miss Hefley attended a Paderewski concert at which the master played Chopin's "Opus 37," "The Funeral March," Liszt's "Campanella," Beethoven's "Opus 109," and Mendelssohn's "Jagerlied." The performance, he wrote Annie, "almost disturbed my conviction that I preferred violin to piano music." [52]

Ransom's pleasant congeniality, his witty and agreeable manner, William A. Stuart remembers, made him a favorite among the Americans at Oxford. This popularity and his inclination to turn any subject under discussion into a question for formal debate had induced his closest friends to support him for treasurer of the American Club. He served in this capacity for one year and as secretary for almost another before he was elected to the presidency. "I remember that in our periods of leisure," Stuart wrote on March 6, 1972, "Ransom manifested a growing tendency to lead the conversation into debatable subjects. His opinions were well developed and strongly maintained. The resulting arguments, while not acrimonious, often tended to develop seriously conflicting schools of thought in our group. The subjects ranged widely over many fields of speculation. It was noticeable that Ransom usually incited arguments on subjects which he knew more about than the rest of us." One of the topics that aroused much discussion, Ransom wrote his father, was philosophy versus science. In these sessions Ransom took the side of philosophy against McLean or H. A. Taber of Rhode Island. Soon their rooms became a meeting place for the undergraduates who liked such discussions. "People hereabouts have become afraid to express any positive opinions nowadays," he wrote, "due to the outstanding menace of philosophic criticism." [53] And these discussions were just extensions of those he was carrying on with his tutor, John Murray, for whom he was preparing an essay attempting to reconcile determinism and free will. His interest in philosophy had become so absorbing that he was afraid he was neglecting other aspects of his program, particularly Roman culture. As soon as the term was over, he promised himself, he was going to undertake in earnest a systematic study of his period of Roman history.

During that fall and spring his club activities were extended even further. In late October he was elected secretary of the Twenty Club, the social and debating club of Christ Church which he had joined the previous spring. "The club is an extremely nice affair," he wrote home, "and the meetings are usually very pleasant. The English speakers are very entertaining. . . . I don't think it can be said fairly that they have no sense of humor. They are very sarcastic and use fine language, though their delivery is rather painful to behold."[54] The following spring he organized the Hermit Crabs, patterned after the Calumet Club which had meant so much to him at Vanderbilt. It was a literary club designed to have a maximum of twelve members, of which no more than half could be Americans. The original plan, adopted by the nine charter members—which included William A. Stuart and Christopher Morley—called for weekly meetings and for each member to present at least two papers each term, these papers to be either original poems or stories or analyses of specific aspects of the works of selected authors. "The literary club I started," he wrote El-lene, "has had a very flourishing infancy." The first four authors selected for study were Ibsen, Wilde, Stevenson, and Synge. The contributions for the first three terms of the club's existence were about equally divided between the original and the critical. For his project Ransom first attempted some poetry but soon became discouraged and settled on a study of "The Ethics of Ibsen."[55] Stuart presented a "fable in the style of Robert Louis Stevenson," which Ransom liked so much that he asked that it be read again. "However," Stuart remembers, "there was no general demand, and hence no re-reading, leading me to think that his request was not taken seriously by anyone but me."[56] Ransom thought well enough of his own essay on Ibsen, which he read in the spring, to send it to the *Atlantic Monthly* and, when it was refused there, to ask his father to see if the editor of the *Methodist Review* would like to publish it. At the end of the year he was convinced that the Hermit Crabs was the best literary club in Oxford; and Stuart, when he returned to the university in the fall of 1913, after a year's absence, was surprised that the club no longer existed. Ransom would later say that this experience turned his attention toward literary criticism, his essay on Ibsen being his first serious effort in the genre, if not toward the writing of poetry.

That Ransom took his club participation seriously is indicated by the tone of his many references to the activities of the three major ones to which he belonged. On several occasions he complained that the American Club was not doing as well as it should because the members were not taking the programs seriously enough. Once while he was president, following the usual custom, he chose the question and assigned the speakers. But some of the members, Stuart recalls, "decided to have a 'nag' debate instead of the assigned question and speakers. At the meeting we charged the administration, particularly the president, with usurping dictatorial powers, declared our independence, and assigned our own speakers on the question chosen by us, which was: 'Resolved that in the opinion of this House, life at Oxford produces a subtle deterioration of the moral fiber.' Ransom let us have our fun, but at the end he imposed a fine on each of us." [57] Once when the American Club was holding a joint debate with one of the regular college societies, he set a topic in which he was particularly interested and assigned himself as one of the speakers. The topic was: "That this House welcomes the prospect of the return of Theodore Roosevelt to the Presidency." He and his partner took the negative side, which represented a conviction he strongly felt. Several weeks before, when the campaign was just getting underway, he had written his father that Wilson was the best possible choice because "Teddy Roosevelt is not quite safe and Taft is too safe." Although his team was defeated, he was not convinced the judgment was based entirely on the arguments presented.

He was invited to spend the Christmas holidays with Sir William Murray and his family, but he decided to go back to Hawarden, because, as he wrote his father, "it is splendid for reading, walking, and playing chess and golf." Also, he concluded, "it is rather dangerous to accept entertainment in an English home where there are marriageable daughters." [58] By December 17, he was settled in the lodge and already developing a routine. During the mornings he read Plato's *Republic* in Greek and Kant's *Critique of Pure Reason* in German (despite his best intentions, he could not bring himself to do the work in Roman history he felt he needed); and in the afternoons he hiked, played golf, or explored the nearby countryside on the bicycle he had borrowed from McLean before leaving Oxford.⁵⁹ The evenings were spent playing chess with the warden of the lodge or arguing pragmatism with a young Oxford graduate who was spending the holidays there. He had developed a genuine fondness for British life and manners, he realized, particularly for the manner in which many of the men and women he had met "arrange their afternoons." ⁶⁰ "In England," he wrote his mother, "the period from luncheon to tea, with all people having any leisure at all, is saved for walking, riding or playing something, bathing and dressing for tea. It is almost impossible to live properly in this climate without using that arrangement." The weather was the best it had been for fifty years, according to the paper, and the ten days before Christmas were about as satisfying as any he had ever spent. During the evenings leading up to Christmas the town "resounded with Christmas Carols," and on Christmas Eve many groups of choristers appeared and sang in the brilliant light of a full moon; the first band, which appeared while he was at supper, was followed by many others so that visitors at the lodge were "seldom without music until midnight." The good cheer aroused by this traditional Christmas ceremony was further stimulated at three o'clock the next afternoon by a Christmas dinner "with all the expected ingredients except cranberry sauce." ⁶¹

After Christmas he was joined by Blount, and together they went into Chester, explored the ancient walls, visited the cathedral, and attended rugby and association football matches. Around the first of the year three inches of snow fell, but the golfers merely substituted a red ball and played on without interruption. But soon the typical winter rain set in, and except for an excursion into Liverpool to visit the art gallery, Ransom stayed inside and concentrated on Kant's *Critique*. "I am also doing some thinking on my own on the problems on which he pronounced," he wrote his father. "My waking hours are concerned with thoughts of space and time. I have a few ideas which seem to me original and more or less sound; but I shall submit them to my tutor before I advertise them." As he prepared to return to Oxford for the new term, he was reminded that at this time next year he would be searching for a position in some college as near Nashville as possible, teaching philosophy and Greek. He was thinking of teaching, for three or four years at least, until he could make "some financial headway for the family's sake" as well as for himself.[62] If he could find the kind of position he wanted in the right location, he might "teach some years longer, and perhaps indefinitely," because he was planning "to embark on some publishing ventures and teaching is most closely connected with that sort of enterprise."

As soon as he returned to Oxford, he arranged to do some work in psychology. Although he was dubious of the value of experimental psychology because all "it has managed to do so far is to elaborate the obvious," he felt he needed some knowledge of the field if he was to teach philosophy.[63] So he undertook a program requiring three weekly essays rather than the usual two. The demands of his academic work and of his three clubs left little time for anything else, and he was becoming seriously concerned about his neglect of Roman history. He had chosen as his area of concentration the Empire period beginning with the death of Julius Caesar, and his authorities, therefore, were Tacitus, Pliny, and Cicero.[64] He was very much interested in the material, and his tutor, Mr. Andrews, was an eminent historian. Why, then, he asked his father, was he forever putting Roman history behind everything else? One reason for his indifference, he believed, was his tutor's lack of interest in rhetoric or literary style. "I am sorry for this," he wrote, "since it seems to me that Roman history is the finest literary and dramatic material I have ever found in history." A month later, realizing he was still not giving the subject the time it deserved, he speculated further: "I am much interested in the personalities and the political developments of history, and I enjoy the texts from a literary standpoint, but I have no enthusiasm for the intricate details, such as the organization of an army and the problem of dates, which take up such a large part of the attention given to the histories." His dissatisfaction was not with the reading he was doing, which he found most rewarding, but with the kind of essays he was forced to prepare. Only after the searching, probing process of expressing in writing his reactions to a subject was he ever sure of his own thoughts, and the essays he was asked to prepare in history, he was convinced, were so restrictive that the writing was unproductive.

In order to get the physical exercise he needed he rejoined the tennis club so that he could use its all-weather gravel courts two or three times a week. He continued to arise at 7:30 and take a cold bath, though the temperature in his room was often below freezing, before rushing off to a chilly service in the College Chapel at 8:00 o'clock. He returned to a breakfast of fruit, tea, and toast, which he shared with McLean, then he took a quick look at the newspaper before settling down to a morning of work. (His schedule was so demanding that he almost completely gave up lectures, which he had never found very stimulating anyway.) After lunch, which usually consisted of fruit and soup in his room at 1:00 o'clock, he took his exercise—which, weather permitting, was usually tennis—then he came in for a bath and tea, after which he worked until dinner in Hall at 7:30. His evenings were devoted more and more to work, though he continued to attend his clubs regularly and on occasion he went to a concert or to the theater. Unless he was out too late, he always had guests in his room, or visited theirs, for a pint of beer before retiring. His leisure reading was relegated to Sundays and his favorite authors were Shakespeare and Browning, although he once became so engrossed in Meredith's *Beauchamp's Career* that he forgot to go to church. "Not many pleasures," he wrote his mother, "are superior to observing a new author."[65]

He was so intent on honoring the strenuous schedule he had set for himself that he had some difficulty making up his mind to accompany John Murray and a small group of British students who had formed a reading party to spend the spring vacation in Brittany. Even after he had decided to go, he asked that he be allowed to join them later, and he went to an inn called Hill View, five miles from Oxford, for two weeks. There he met three third-year students who were preparing for their "Schools," scheduled for a few weeks later. In the little leisure he allowed himself, and that which the others could spare from preparing for their examinations, they played a little golf, on a course "better than either of the three in Oxford," and rode their bicycles into "some of the fine old villages nearby."[66] On April 9 he left for Brittany, so pleased with his work, he wrote Annie, that he planned to spend a lot of time reworking his Ibsen essay. The Channel crossing from Southampton to St. Malo took thirteen hours; the wind was high, the sea rough, and everyone on board was seasick. From St. Malo he went twenty miles inland to Dinan, where he joined John Murray and six British undergraduates. Dinan, he soon discovered, had many medieval homes and "splendid old churches," and, best of all, the inn where they were staying had "two gravel tennis courts in perfect condition." [67]

He thoroughly enjoyed his discussions with the British students, in which he was often called upon to defend America; his task became more difficult, he wrote his mother, after he and three of the students met in the inn one night an American who explained "in greatest detail how much each of his several considerable possessions cost." What amused Ransom most about this encounter was that he talked to the American, a Colonel James from Washington, for an hour or more and the Colonel never suspected "he was addressing a fellow American." There were many parties and, as he had suspected, not much studying. In the time he could steal from social activities, however, he read some philosophy, continued to revise the Ibsen essay, and even did "some good work in Roman history." The most memorable experience of the vacation was his observation of one of the weekly market days:

Market day (Thursday) is the finest sight that Dinan affords to my way of thinking. The country people bring in their produce and fill the streets all day. They wear the old fashioned Breton peasant costume, which means for the women black dresses and tiny white bonnets with long stiff iron[ed] strings hanging down behind. The peasants in this section are really fine-looking specimens physically. The women seem to do more than their share of the farm work; they drive in their pigs and calves, done up in a sort of harness . . . and seem to do most of the buying and selling. The pigs are all white and evidently household pets. I have seen the women, when their pigs refuse to go, stop and scratch their backs for a few minutes, after which the pigs would become perfectly obedient. [68]

He returned to Oxford at the end of what the papers assured him was the "driest April in a hundred years." Soon after his return, however, the rains came. "Peckwater Quadrangle, where I live," he wrote home on May 8, "looks as if it is dropping to pieces with age and is most impressive in the cold rains." Some of his friends, he knew, would think it strange that even in bad weather he liked to walk around Christ Church meadows, but even in the rain he thought it the prettiest walk in Oxford. "The meadows are just back of one part of the College which Ruskin built," he wrote his mother, "and are in the form of a circle, enclosed by the famous 'Long' and 'Broad Walks,' the Isis (which is the classic Oxford rendering of the Thames), and the Cherwell (pronounced Char). It is a twenty minute walk and much frequented by the American tourists who are beginning to arrive." Soon after he was settled in, he became involved in the activities preparatory to "Eights week," the "social event, as well as the athletic event of the Oxford calendar." [69] Just south of Folly Bridge the Cherwell joins the Isis and together they flow through a narrow channel into the flat lands. Here, between Folly Bridge and Iffley Lock, each May the "bump races" called "Eights" are held. Each crew attempts to bump the boat in front of it until the winner holds "pride of place at the head of the river." To provide a fit setting in which to receive all the visitors who come to witness this great event, all the undergraduates in Ransom's time were required to grow geraniums in the window boxes outside their windows. Those who did not respond to this "persistent request" were likely "to have their windows smashed." Ransom's flowers, he happily reported, "are the best I've seen." He was personally involved in many "socials, teas and river picnics," but his happiest assignment was providing entertainment for the niece of Whitelaw Reid, the American ambassador in London. For this young lady, whom he described as "18, very pretty, and fond of dancing," he arranged a river party, attended also by McLean, Stuart, and the Murray sisters, a breakfast in the Junior Common Room, in which the silverware "embossed with my initials was prominently displayed," and other "pleasant occasions." [70]

Although he thoroughly enjoyed these social functions (a few weeks later when he received an invitation to a tea and garden party to be held at the home of the American ambassador on July 4, he strongly suspected it came as a result of his hospitality to Mr. Reid's neice), he also regretted that for weeks he had done no real work. After a conference with Mr. Dundas, his tutor in Greek history, "who assured me of his satisfaction with my work in that subject," he decided that he should now devote his time to the Roman historians. In a letter to his father written just before he left to join William S. Hamilton of Kentucky, Edward H. Eckel of Missouri, and Stuart for a few weeks in Switzerland, he outlined his work plans for the summer. In addition to the Roman history, he expected to read again, and this time with greatest care, Aristotle's *Ethics*, "the most important single book for my course," and, "of course, some more philosophy because I can use in Schools all the philosophy I can digest."[71] In his spare time he wanted to work some more on Ibsen and try his "hand at some short stories." He also acquired ten new books—including "David Hugh Cecil's *Conservatism*, Smith's *English Language*, and a psychology book by my tutor McDougall"—which he intended to read for a specific purpose. If he could possibly find the time, he was going to submit an essay in the competition for the £20 prize offered for the best essay written on any one of these ten books. He had not tried for any prizes previously because most of those offered in Greats "require more fluency in making Latin and Greek verse than I possess." After he had finished the ten books required for the "Home University Library prize," if he was not stimulated to write an essay, he would try for the Shakespeare prize—the "most profitable one at £55"—or if he developed "any poetic gifts" in his work for the Hermit Crabs, he would try for the poetry prize. At any rate he had planned a full schedule and expected his last summer in Europe to be "the most profitable one yet."

During the last week in June he went to London and took a room in a small hotel off Russell Square.[72] On his first day in the city he walked over to St. James Park to watch the "great folk on daily parade" and came back by Hyde Park and listened to some of the speeches. Listening to these speeches and observing the demonstrations supported the conclusion he had stated two months before in a letter to his father, that significant social and political change was imminent in England, if not in all of Europe. "The coal strike continues," he had written on March 26; "coal is higher than it has been since the close of the Franco-German war. It now sells at 46/per ton, or over $11.00. A million strikers and about twelve hundred thousand workmen other than coal miners are out of work. The train service is much disorganized. Many poor people are starving. There is no prospect of an early settlement and matters are likely to get worse. It seems that hard times are about for England." [73] At the parties he attended, preceding the main event on July 4 at Ambassador Reid's residence to which more than two thousand guests came, he must have seen other evidence of the changes that were sweeping Europe. At private gatherings, as well as in public halls, one could observe couples doing the tango; one newspaper of the day referred to "the contortions of this immodest dance" and another to the "horrors of American and South American negroid origin." [74] On any day he could have seen the activities of the suffragettes, whom he referred to in his letters home as "the new women" and whose exploits, often described in detail in the papers, would reach a tragic climax the following June at Epsom Downs when Emily Davidson brought world attention to the cause by rushing out on the track in the middle of a race and being trampled to death as she tried to grab the reigns of the king's horse. [75]

His awareness of these concentrated "attacks on the ruling class" who were desperately and unsuccessfully attempting to maintain a "sense of pageantry" is obvious in his comments to Ellene about his visit to Windsor Castle, Eton, and Stoke Poges. [76] The castle, he reported, " is an enormous affair and contains many wonderful things in its rooms, including some fine Rubens and Van Dyck pictures." That the British continued to support the royal family he found praiseworthy, "though baffling to most Americans." He was disappointed in Eton because the boys were "scattered about in small houses," but the "playing fields and the stretch of river are as pretty as rivers and fields get to be." His final impression was that "it is a dreadfully aristocratic place. Boys wear black coats that don't quite come down to their waists, white ties and high silk hats; the little boys are fitted out like this, as well as the sixth form who are ready to 'go up to Oxford and Cambridge.'" In order to get to Stoke Poges he took the bus and walked the last two miles. In spite of his best efforts he could find only two monuments going back to Grey's time; the "lea was cut up by iron fences and asphalt," but the old yew trees were still there.

On his way back through London he heard *Il Trovatore* sung in French (he thought it not as good as the German version he had heard the previous year), and he was pleased that even at the London Opera House, "built by Mr. Hammerstein of New York and run in opposition to Covent Garden," good student seats were available for a shilling.[77] Then he went on to the Villa Sylvia, a pension at Vevey on Lake Geneva, where Hamilton, Eckel, and Stuart were already in residence. For the next "several weeks," Stuart remembered in 1972, the mornings were spent "among our books" and the afternoons "along the lake or in the Alps or on the tennis courts." One experience remained firmly fixed in Stuart's mind: "One day Ransom and I rowed across the lake in a small row-boat to the Italian shore. On our return, filled with pride over our physical prowess, we were informed that it was a risky venture in a small craft because the lake was subject to sudden changes of surface level causing dangerous currents."[78] Near the end of their stay the group was joined by McLean, who after a few days set out with Ransom on a walking tour through Switzerland. One day, much to McLean's distress, they made twenty-seven miles. Although he was disappointed that the fog limited the visibility, Ransom enjoyed the walk, even in the rain, because the "pine forests were fragrant and paths were firm underfoot." As soon as they moved from the French-speaking to the German-speaking section of Switzerland, he thought he could detect a difference in the inhabitants. Like the Germans, they had none of the "stiffness of the English" and they struck him as a "very sound and strong people."[79] At Freiburg, he settled down in the hostelry operated by Frau Kircher, where he had spent some time the previous summer, to get in a few weeks of good work before returning to Oxford for the opening of the fall term of his final year. His devotion to duty was such that recreation was limited to a daily walk into the countryside or up to Louisenenhofe for coffee and apfelkuchen, which he found good but "inferior to Mama's peach cobbler." Here, he read the *Scottish Philosophers* by Pringle-Pattison, worked on Roman history, and finished his essay for the Home University Library competition. He chose to write on conservatism and in spite of the amount of time and energy devoted to its composition, the final result was most unsatisfying. Although as usual the actual writing had helped "greatly to clear up" his ideas, upon rereading the essay he found too much "evidence of haste and undigested ideas, though the thought in the main seems . . . correct."[80] His summer program had gone well, he decided; he had done a great deal of writing, even trying his hand at fiction. But even though he had devoted an inordinate amount of time to two stories, neither was good enough even for his father to see. He was pleased, however, with the beginning he had made on some "studies in literary theory," and if he could spare the time from preparing for his examinations he was certain he could have one essay, in addition to the one on Ibsen, ready for his father's consideration before Christmas.

He was so tired of the "metaphysical existence" he had been living for the past few weeks, he wrote his father, that he decided to return to England a few days early in order to have two or three weeks on the golf course before the opening of the fall term.[81] The realization that he was on the verge of beginning his final year had made him "most intensely American" and for several weeks he had been able to read Walt Whitman "with more appreciation than ever before." On September 22, he arrived in Hawarden to find all of the rooms, except his, occupied by "Church of England parsons," but he enjoyed their company, he wrote his mother, because "they are sociable people and well supplied with good stories." In fact, they reminded him of the "assemblies of Methodist ministers," except that these smoked and appeared "intolerant toward members of other churches." Since the weather was warm and mostly dry and he was able to find an "ample supply of willing golfing companions," the days passed pleasantly. In the evening he played chess with the warden, or with one of the Anglican ministers, and gave the remainder of his time to Tacitus and other Roman historians.[82]

When he arrived in Oxford at the end of the first week in October, another pleasant surprise awaited him. Although he met neither of the stated requirements—he was not twenty-five and he did not have an Oxford degree—he was permitted to live in "unlicensed digs." Along with Davis, Lange, and McLean, he moved into a very comfortable apartment, consisting of four bedrooms and two studies, at 126 Walton Street. This arrangement gave him more freedom and was much less expensive than living in Hall. For his private bedroom and a study, which he shared with McLean, he paid only thirty shillings a week, including "food well cooked and served in the best style." The food was particularly good, the best he had had in England, because

Mrs. Thompson, the landlady, "is a good cook and gets a plentiful supply from her husband's fish and game shop." [83]

The first major assignment confronting him was his "Collections," or college examinations, but, he wrote his father, he did not fear them because "the past summer is the best I have had for the amount of work done." Too, he realized, the "results don't really matter much for they have nothing to do with the University examinations next June." After he had written the six required papers, he was pleased with his performance, particularly in Roman history. His confidence was confirmed a few weeks later when he was informed by John Murray that his examiners thought he was "likely to distinguish himself in the examinations next summer." [84] Such a remark was ample recompense for the many hours of hard work he had devoted to meeting the severe demands of the oldest, the most prestigious of all the "Schools" at Oxford, the one in which he had been urged not to enroll two years before.

But his years in England had affected him in ways much more fundamental and significant than those that came as a direct result of the knowledge he had acquired from the rigorous academic discipline to which he had so eagerly subjected himself. Convictions were forming in his mind that would not be fully articulated for almost a quarter of a century: ritual and ceremony, form and pagaentry are ingredients essential to the development of a formal tradition; and the proper function of such a tradition is, as he would later describe it, "to instruct its members how to transform instinctive experience into aesthetic experience." [85] This indoctrination into a foreign culture accentuated his natural inclination toward a formality of manner that became so pronounced that often in the future some of his best friends would accuse him of indifference and aloofness. Often the polite, urbane manner, the pleasant smile, and the soft, somewhat Anglicanized southern speech would be thought to constitute a barrier that few were allowed to penetrate. One of his students at Vanderbilt a few years later would think him distant, withdrawn, unapproachable and would say that many of his contemporaries were "put off" by Ransom's "affected English way." After twenty years or more of close friendship, Donald Davidson would complain in a letter to Allen Tate: "I have never been able to understand that man"; and

Tate, in one of the soundest of the early evaluations of Ransom's poetry, would describe this enigmatic quality as "a mind detached from the American scene and mostly nurtured from England." Undoubtedly, Ransom's concern for what he would later call the "kingdom of the aesthetic life" was first aroused during these years. This concern and all of the related activities it stimulated would produce within the next two decades the mature attitudes included in the credo: "In manners, aristocratic; in religion, ritualistic; in art, traditional."[86]

III   **A Slow Fire**
1912-1913

As HIS FINAL YEAR at Oxford approached, John Crowe Ransom turned his attention to the not altogether pleasant duty of deciding upon his future vocation. On March 26, 1912, he wrote his father that he was thinking of going into journalism rather than returning to teaching. "Journalism calls for more enterprise than teaching," he wrote; "I could without much effort devote myself to scholarship, especially philosophy, in which I think I might win some recognition." At the moment, however, he felt the need for a more active life than the teaching of philosophy would allow and a vocation that would "serve a more useful purpose."

In addition to what one of his Vanderbilt instructors had described as "an unusual power of expression as a writer," Ransom was convinced that he had "other qualifications." [1] He had demonstrated his interest in writing throughout his career at Oxford, for, as he wrote his family on September 6, no other activity so assisted him in clearing up his ideas on whatever subject he happened to be "considering at the moment." Consequently, he had done some reporting for his favorite tutor, John Murray, who was editor of the *Oxford Magazine*. In a letter of November 4 he wrote Ellene that on the night he attended a performance of "The Speckled Band," which he had been assigned to review, he sat in the same row with the Prince of Wales. At least one article on his Oxford experiences had appeared in the *Methodist Review*. The reactions of his family and friends to this article, and the fact that the editor of the *Review* had asked him to prepare a lengthy feature story on Wesleyan education in England, encouraged him to consider seriously a career in journalism.[2] He wrote his friend Christopher Morley, informing him of this interest and indicating that he was revising his essay on "The Ethics of Ibsen," prepared the previous year to read to the American Club, with the hope of publishing it in a magazine "such as the *Atlantic.*"[3] When this essay appeared, he continued, Morley could use it as he made the rounds of editors and publishers attempting to find a suitable position for his fellow Oxonian. Then on his own he wrote to the Hearst publications, soliciting their interest in a series of articles he proposed to write on his experiences during the long vacation he planned to spend that summer in Germany.[4] During the two months in which he heard nothing, his hopes were high, but on July 5, 1912, he wrote Ellene that he was "disappointed and dejected" because his proposal was not accepted.

That he had some misgivings about the suitability of a career in journalism or that he was doubtful of the prospect of turning up the kind of position he wanted is suggested by the fact that on September 6 he stated his intention to teach for two years in order to "pay off some old obligations" and to have time to do some "studies in Literary Theory." He had been encouraged, also, by one of his philosophy tutors to continue "some investigations" into moral philosophy. He wrote his father on February 2, 1913, that "Mr. Blount has complimented me by suggesting that I have gotten on to some original points." He continued to think about these things and to read as much as his schedule of preparing for his "Schools" would allow, and he anxiously awaited the time he could "write an attempt at the analysis of morality and later a higher affair on the restatement and the relative importance, under the theory, of the conventional virtues."

In spite of the tremendous pressure he was beginning to feel because of the impending examination, he became increasingly impatient, during the winter and spring of 1913, to know what he would be doing the following September. But he had decided when he wrote home on February 2, that he would not accept the flattering offer of M. M. Summar to join him in beginning a new preparatory school. Such an assignment, he decided, would not allow him sufficient leisure for reading and writing. "I am beginning today," he wrote the following week, "to canvass the Southern state universities," and he hoped to be invited "to join the faculty of the University of Georgia." During the past week he had also written W. R. Cooper, a Rhodes Scholar from Alabama, about the possibilities at the university of that state and to Max Souby "at the Normal School in Murfreesboro." Although the latter institution would not be satisfactory in many respects, it would have the distinct advantage of allowing him to be near his family again. In addition to his investigation of employment possibilities in a great many of the southern colleges and universities, he had made inquiries at Amherst, at some other places where he "would like to be," and at Groton, Phillips-Exeter, and one or two other "good preparatory schools" suggested by his Oxford friends.[5]

As he was writing these two or three dozen colleges and preparatory schools, he was attempting to collect letters of reference from his former teachers and colleagues. The endorsements he received were most impressive. M. M. Summar wrote that Ransom was the "best all around school man" he had known in more than twenty years of preparatory school teaching. Bishop Collins Denny, who before his elevation in the Methodist church had taught philosophy at Vanderbilt, wrote that during his four undergraduate years Ransom "was marked by an ability far beyond that shown by a majority of students," and W. L. Dudley, professor of chemistry at Vanderbilt, remarked that he was "a painstaking student of the highest grade." Although all the persons he asked to recommend him responded with highest praise, including Chancellor J. H. Kirkland and Dean H. C. Tolman, with whom Ransom had taken Greek, he must have been most pleased with the responses of his Oxford tutors. Robert H. Dundas wrote, "Mr. Ransom's work was unusually thorough and solid and his judgments sane and well-reasoned: it is not his habit to wear his learning on his sleeve, but I believe it will be available when required; and he has the caution of the true scholar." Particularly gratifying was the unqualified endorsement of John H. Murray, the tutor Ransom knew best and who for the rest of his life was Ransom's good friend.[6]

In spite of what he must have realized were impressive credentials, response to his many inquiries was not promising. Although everyone appeared "pleased with my qualifications," he wrote his mother on February 26, 1913, "there seems to be no immediate prospect of a vacancy." He had had an affirmative reply from Groton, but he was reluctant to go there because he had "heard that it is the last word in snobbishness for American schools"; if the actual situation was as bad as the rumors suggested, he would certainly hate "to enter an enterprise like that" and would "save it for a last resort." He was pleased that his father had enrolled him in the Methodist Placement Bureau, the agency through which he had secured a position at the Taylorsville (Mississippi) School eight years before; and he hoped to find a position near enough to Murfreesboro to allow him frequent visits home.

As the weeks passed and his college examinations drew nearer (his preparation was now so earnest that he was studying eight or more hours a day), no offer came except one from Hotchkiss, a boys' preparatory school in Lakeville, Connecticut, and that was a one-year appointment to teach Latin while the head of that department was on leave.[7] Since he needed some relief from his present anxiety and was almost assured of a position at the Phillips-Exeter Academy for the year following the appointment at Hotchkiss, he wrote, on April 9, that he would join that faculty if, in addition to the salary of $1,500, he could be furnished rent-free an apartment on the campus. Although the response from Hotchkiss was not immediate, he informed his mother on May 10 that "they have accepted my offer and gone some better, offering room, board, laundry and $1500." He was extremely pleased to have the matter of employment settled so that he could devote all of his attention to the examinations, the outcome of which seemed to concern him more and more. Although he continued to work six to eight hours every day and thought he should have his "work up pretty well by the time of Schools," he was anxious that his family not be disappointed if his performance on the examination was less than outstanding. "It is problematical whether or not I can earn a first," he wrote, "and I warn you not to set any great hopes for that event. Success in Oxford examinations is very much a question of style and of the psychology of the examiners, and it is almost barred to an undergraduate with American ways of thinking. Only one American has ever gotten a first in the Greats."[8]

Although he knew his parents would share his disappointment at not being able to return to the South, he was pleased with the position at Hotchkiss for several reasons. First of all, the liberal salary and allowances would enable him to settle the most pressing of his financial obligations and to assist Annie, who wanted and deserved, he thought, the opportunity to continue her study of music in one of the good conservatories in the East. He was convinced, and rightly so it turned out, that Hotchkiss would offer leisure for study and writing because the "faculty is large and the discipline light." His course assignments, two classes of Caesar and two of Vergil, pleased him very much, as did the fact that H. A. Taber was joining the faculty as instructor in physics. Ransom was convinced that this year would be particularly important to him, because it would provide an excellent basis for deciding whether to continue teaching in a college preparatory school, to seek again a position in a college, or to give up teaching entirely and seriously try to find an acceptable position in journalism.[9]

Now that he did not have to keep such a diligent watch on the mails, he decided to return to Boars' Head, a small village five miles from Oxford, where he was able to work without interruption, in order to make a last all-out effort to "get his subjects up for Schools." On May 27, only two days before the examinations, he relayed to his family his concern that he was not able to complete the ambitious study schedule he had set for himself. He was least confident of his knowledge of Roman history, but, he concluded, "the tutors are encouraging and I have no nerves." Immediately after the examinations were completed he expressed his dissatisfaction with his performance. While they were in progress he felt particularly composed, and in every instance he was impressed with the fairness of the questions. But now that they were over and he looked back over the experience, he knew that he had "turned in a long series of very mediocre papers." Although his doubts of earning a first were firmer than ever, he was too "washed out and useless" to worry now. Anyway, he was pleased to have his three years' work done and could think of little except his imminent visit home. Since Hotchkiss did not begin its fall semester until September 17, he would have more than a month at home, if he could depart, as he planned, around August 1.[10]

He had not forgotten, certainly, that only the written portion of the examination was over, and his *viva voce* was scheduled for July 20.

Since he believed it was useless to attempt to prepare for this examination, he decided to accept a long-standing invitation to visit an Oxford friend who owned a Scottish estate not far from the home of John Murray's family. On June 30 he wrote his mother that he was well settled and really enjoying the hunting, fishing, golf, and tennis. Since it was still light enough to walk around at 11:30 and daylight came at 2:00 A.M., no one seemed to have either the time or the inclination to sleep much. Every night between 8:30 and 10:30 there was a shooting party, and he had killed nine rabbits. He was disappointed that he never saw a roe-deer and his luck was poor while fishing for salmon. Much of his time was spent with golf and tennis, his skill at which was greatly improved because of the new racket he had acquired just before leaving Oxford, and now he was able to "defeat all comers." He described the village where the group played tennis as "one of the prettiest towns" he had seen. "It . . . strongly suggests Switzerland," he wrote, and "is surrounded by hills of heather which are usually about half covered with clouds. The tennis courts are wonderfully good and the road home across the wild moors is still better. . . . As we came back from Grantown, we got the sunset and the new moon in our faces. Sun sets at eight something but the effect lasts at least two hours." [11]

He returned to Oxford on July 17 and three days later was subjected to a "very thorough and very severe" oral examination, one which, he realized immediately, exposed all of his weaknesses. Two of the examiners, he was told, wanted to give him a first, but three were opposed, and he had to settle for what he was assured by his committee was the "best of the seconds." On July 31 he cabled his parents: "I have just missed my first and that is about all there is to say. It is the first time I have ever failed at a critical moment and it will be a good lesson for me. I consider it a moral defeat rather than intellectual; bad enough but still one that can be remedied." [12] He could only speculate that one of the reasons for his failure was that he had been mistaken about the kind of examination to expect. Instead of the broad questions that would allow him considerable freedom of choice and provide him the opportunity to demonstrate the grace and clarity of his prose style, there were too many instances in which specific information he did not have was obviously wanted. As he looked back upon his months of preparation, he realized that though he had worked hard, his review had not been "methodical and thorough enough." In spite of his present disappointment, he knew his three years at Oxford had been of tremendous benefit to him, and he did not want this temporary setback to undermine the genuine affection he felt not only for Oxford but for England, and its people and institutions. "Oxford," he ended his last letter from England, "is very lovely now, though rather deserted, and I shall take away a fine taste of English life." [13]

He was so anxious to get home, after an absence of three years, that he could hardly wait for his graduation on August 2. Three days later he boarded the *Laconia* in Liverpool and docked at Boston on August 12. He spent a day there before going on to Hotchkiss to check on his living quarters, to see that the 275 books he had shipped from Oxford had arrived, and to meet any of his future associates who might be around the campus. Then he headed for home, with two other brief stops along the way. In New York he made some preliminary inquiries concerning the prospects of Annie's continuing her musical studies there, and while he was in the city, he reassured Christopher Morley of his continuing interest in a career in journalism. On the next lap of his journey to Nashville he stopped off in Abingdon, Virginia, for a brief visit with his old friend William A. "Jeb" Stuart, who had accompanied him on the twelve-day voyage from New York to Southampton three years before. Nearly sixty years later Stuart could still remember that visit with much pleasure, recalling particularly that Ransom "won golden opinions from my parents" and that his tennis game was the best that "many of my friends had seen." [14] When he boarded the train for the final stage of the journey home, he must have recalled his mother's promise, in the last letter he received from her before leaving England, that all of the family would be at home to receive him, including his brother Dick, who was bringing his wife and daughter, neither of whom Ransom had ever seen, up from Florida to greet the returning scholar.

Four weeks later, after getting settled in the cottage of the man he was replacing at Hotchkiss for a year, he recalled with much pleasure the three and a half weeks he had spent at home. He was much pleased, he wrote his father three days after the opening of the fall term, with Dick's appearance, and he thought his marriage had given him "steadiness and perseverance [the lack of which] "was his only serious defect." [15] He was delighted that Ellene was doing so well at Vanderbilt, but as soon as possible he would like to help her transfer to Columbia or Radcliffe, where she could "learn to work for herself." Annie must come east to study as soon as possible. "I think she has fine ability for music," he wrote, "and it is wonderful how well she plays, considering how little stimulus she has had from first-rate teachers. She ought to have the chance of acquiring a fresh stock of ideas, especially if she is going to find worthy meanings for her music." He planned to send her some books immediately, so that she could interest herself in some problems not musical, because at present he suspected that she was "in the position of having to interpret her music by means of a very insufficient set of ideas."

He lived in his comfortably furnished cottage with twelve students and took his meals in the dining hall. He had two rooms, a bedroom and a sitting-room–study with "elegant white book cases" of exactly the size to accommodate his library. Although his days were rather full—his teaching, proctoring, and class preparation left him just time enough for a little golf or tennis—lights were out at ten o'clock, and after the boys retired he could devote two or three hours to his own work. Immediately after he was settled, he wrote his father, he resumed work on an essay exploring the ethical bases of government, "especially of democratic government." [16] This task he expected to consume all of the leisure he could devote to it for three or four years. First of all, he felt "obliged to outline the main ethical systems," and as soon as he completed his work on T. H. Green, he planned to move on to a systematic rereading of Kant.

As much as he appreciated the natural beauty of his surroundings and the physical comforts provided by the school, he grew restive under the rather severe restrictions imposed upon the educational process by the elitist boys' preparatory schools. First of all, with one notable exception, he found the young masters completely oblivious to "what is going on in that part of the world not contained within the textbooks and recitation rooms of their particular subject," and his hopes for intellectual stimulation from his colleagues were for the most part frustrated. "Even where they are fine scholars, and that is usually true," he wrote his father, "they regard their special departments as closed subjects, to which they have the key." Because their primary aim was to prepare their students to do well enough on entrance examinations to insure their admission to one of the Ivy League colleges, all of these "really intelligent and beautifully educated" young teachers were completely tied down to the textbook system. "It is distressing," he complained, "to have to hurry through Caesar, for instance, with barely enough time for translation and the more important constructions and no opportunity to teach a boy to approach the subject as a scholar. I can't call for any original work in strategy or geography or ethnology, or even grammar or history, simply for lack of time; to do the assigned work and to allow for the other teachers doing theirs, I have to teach Caesar in the most mechanical way; and the sum total of all the teachers' efforts is to confirm a boy in the habit of second-hand thinking."

Even in his middle twenties, however, it seems that Ransom was aware of the distance between the ideal world of the heart's desire and that in which man must live; consequently, his disenchantment did not prevent his enjoyment of the creature comforts that surrounded him. The meals in the dining room were superb, the best he had been served since he was forced to leave his mother's table. He wrote his family that, despite his daily games of golf or tennis, he was concerned that he not gain too much weight. "There is always plenty of rich cream at breakfast, good butter at all meals, and milk whenever wanted."[17] The New England countryside, which reminded him a great deal of Scotland, with the "same degree of hilliness and, just now, the same sort of haze over the hills and the lake," was the prettiest he had ever seen. Around the campus were acres of pear and apple trees heavy with fruit, and every Saturday during that autumn, alone unless he could persuade one of his colleagues to accompany him, he took long walks into the rolling hills around Lakeville. One of his favorite hikes was to Bald Peak, six miles away, from which he could get an excellent view of the Berkshires and the Catskills. The brilliant colors of the leaves, the clear days, and the briskness of the cool autumn weather were a pleasant change from England. His weekends were always full, too full, he soon found, for him to honor the rather strenuous schedule of reading and writing he had set for himself when he first arrived. The six or eight married masters always kept open house for their bachelor colleagues, and the headmaster entertained lavishly and often. As the year moved nearer to Christmas, he found that not only were the afternoons and evenings of the weekends filled with social engagements but he was receiving two or three invitations to attend functions, many of which were semiofficial he thought, scheduled for nights during the week. Although he had to admit, he wrote Ellene, that he enjoyed this attention, he was not at all pleased with the amount of work he was able to do.[18]

One of the young masters at Hotchkiss had a direct and immediate influence on Ransom as he was attempting to decide, finally, upon his teaching field. In the fall of 1913, Samuel Claggert Chew, a fellow southerner and a bachelor of Ransom's age, joined the English department. The previous spring he had received the Ph.D. degree from Johns Hopkins; and when he called on Ransom during their first week of classes, he had already begun the systematic examination of English literary history that would establish his reputation as one of the most highly respected scholars in his field. After their first meeting, Ransom wrote his father: "He is new here and young and one of the few men really alive to what is going on" outside the specific demands of routine daily assignments. Ransom quickly found that Sam Chew was the only person at Hotchkiss to whom he could look for the kind of intellectual excitement he had always received from animated discussions with friends and associates. These informal but often heated sessions of give and take—first with his father, then with the closest of his friends at Oxford, and finally with his fellow Fugitives at Vanderbilt—were always tremendously stimulating to Ransom and undoubtedly assisted him in formulating and refining his attitudes and convictions on any subject, be it political theory, art, or the proper attitude of man toward nature or God. Even after they had been expounded and debated in these oral discussions, many of Ransom's best-known social and aesthetic theories were tested thoroughly and repeatedly in letters—at this time mostly to his father but later to Allen Tate or some of his other friends—before he was willing to release them in the urbane, witty, and apparently spontaneous style of the published essays.

Although his interest in Bergson, whom he had read since his undergraduate days, continued and he was still determined to "write one or two articles showing it is a false lead he is giving us," he was terribly disappointed that he had accomplished little on the proposed book on ethical theory. He had to give too much time to "some detailed work on faculty committees," and he had a great many more enticing social distractions than he had anticipated. And, his discussions with Chew, and the reading he felt compelled to do to "keep up my end" of these discussions, were pushing his interests in "three or four directions at once."[19] He was still convinced that Bergson "is not concerned with ethics primarily but with the metaphysics of knowledge" and that he "is an original genius and has a fascinating doctrine," but he had neither the time nor the specific motivation to do the reading and study required to support his ideas in print. What he did not write his father was that Samuel Chew had strengthened his interest in English literature, especially in literary theory, an interest that had first been aroused by discussions in the Hermit Crabs during his second year at Oxford.[20]

Chew was reading the Victorian novelists and at his suggestion Ransom again read Hardy and Meredith. As a result of his reading and what Ransom described as his "prolonged and heated, though friendly," arguments with Chew, he was convinced that he had something to say on "the theory of the novel." He outlined for his father's reactions a "theory of poetics" which Chew had found "most impressive." Although imprecisely phrased and barely half formulated, these speculations show Ransom struggling toward some of his best-known and most-influential critical statements:

I recognize a good translation of Vergil with no difficulty and I like it because even the translation is poetry. Yet it lacks meter. Everybody knows that poetry (in its complete form, at least) employs meter: but what else poetry contains no one has yet formulated. The place to study that question is in a Vergil class, or wherever else we get poetical translations of poetry of another language, for we no longer have the meter; and all we have saved is those less tangible elements that are not mechanical. The question then is how does the translation that satisfies good taste differ from correct and formal prose? What is unique in the good translation, as a result of a comparison, will be the x, the unknown quality of poetry.

A little analysis discovers x. What the susceptible translator avoids like the plague is the smoothing out of the obscurities in the original. Though it reads strangely out of the artificial atmosphere of rhythm, the good translation preserves the discontinuities, ellipses, the failing to attain preciseness and perfect connection. It deliberately prefers, at times, the words that are not the most appropriate, those which mean the given thing yet involve it in accidental associations that provoke the imagination and enrich the logical process of following up the point, yet come perilously close to leading the mind altogether astray. This kind of selection in words and phrases, coupled with a proper disdain for fullness of expression and for the clear statement of logical connections . . . this procedure means, with malice aforethought, to induce the mode of thought that is imaginative rather than logical or scientific. It does not stick so strictly to the point: it bridges chasms and doesn't tell what its bridges are made of; it deals in terms that are enveloped with a wealth of color, rather than those that pin the attention to the point, and it is not averse to running riot in this color at its own sweet will. So dreams, the extremity of the imaginative process, differ from scientific argumentation.

So much seems plausible when I try to analyze tasteful translations of Vergil. But the convincing stroke is delivered when I reflect on the nature of meter and find *a priori* that the imaginative rather than the logical mode is precisely what the exigencies of meter might have been calculated to induce. Words have a double nature: they stand for things and are associated inseparably with thought; they also have definite second values, like the notes on the piano. Ordinary speaking prose (and perhaps ordinary writing prose) is unconscious of the sounds of its words. Poetry is invented when men see this double nature. Poetry prescribes first a musical arrangement of words; and, second, fits into it what meaning it can. But, given the musical requirements, the choice of words to convey the ideas is vastly limited. On a more refined scale, the great poet is only the school boy using his rhyming dictionary and choosing from six words three when he might have had five hundred in prose. And so the poet *has* to use words (even if he did not wish it) which fail of precision and introduce extraneous color and distract the attention and suggest beautiful enterprises to the imagination. His meter requires him to throw away his connectives at many points, to abbreviate his verbal expressions, to pass from object to object over zig-zag trajectories that no stud but Pegasus can follow. Finally the poet acquires the sure touch for his art so that he no longer accepts the conscious dictation of his mechanical standard but welcomes these aerial ventures for themselves and guides his steed as much as he is guided.

And so my theory of poetics aims to show an inevitable union between poetic form and what is called poetic imagination.[21]

This letter deserves to be cited at such length because it not only demonstrates the strong intellectual relationship between Ransom and his father but it also contains the first written statement of some of Ransom's most important critical principles. His definition of a poem as a "loose logical structure with an irrelevant local texture" in *The World's Body* (1938) is certainly a development of this rudimentary discussion of the dual role of words in the poetic translation, and his insistence that poetry attempts to induce the "mode of thought that is imaginative rather than logical" suggests his defense of poetry as a means of cognition not of instruction. Both of these theories, given immature and incomplete statement in late 1913, received public expression in several essays published in the *Fugitive* and elsewhere in the early twenties; they were further developed and refined in an important correspondence with Allen Tate in the middle and late twenties before they were broadly circulated in the provocative and influential critical essays of the thirties, forties, and fifties.

The more he read in English literature, particularly Shakespeare, Spenser, Milton, and Hardy, the more certain Ransom became that he should attempt a "large book of poetics with exhaustive illustrations from English poetry" and the further his interest strayed from the "big work on ethics and political theory." At any rate, he wrote his family a week or two later that he had decided to try for a place in the English department of a southern university because he thought more positions were available in that discipline than in either philosophy or classics. Because of his deepening interest in English literature and because "publications on that subject are lighter, easier, and more profitable," he was inclined, he concluded, to neglect philosophy for the moment.[22]

How much Ransom's desire to be near his family influenced his decision to seek a position in English literature is difficult, if not impossible, to determine. His Christmas at home, the first in four years, he remembered with much pleasure. On December 8, just nine days before he left for the two-week Christmas break, he awakened to find four inches of snow on the ground, and the exciting prospect of a real New England winter delighted him as it also turned his thoughts

toward Christmas at home. "I picture some fine scenes on the Murfreesboro Pike," he wrote his father; "I will undertake to brew the tea
toward the dark of the day. Then we should have some games and
some literary amusements. I think we ought to read some more-
than-usually good books, you being the reader in chief. Of course we
shall have to call upon the musicians of the locality for their services.
But I am continually congratulating myself upon belonging to the
Ransom family, and don't see the necessity of going very far from
home for entertainment."[23]

Everything turned out even better than he had planned. After
staying overnight in New York on December 17, he left by train at 6
P.M. the next day and arrived in Nashville at 8 P.M. on December 19.
From the station, where his father met him, he went directly home to
be greeted by the entire family, except for Dick and his wife and
young daughter, who could not afford the trip to Nashville. Annie
was delighted with the prospect of spending the winter and spring in
New York, and Ransom was very proud that he was able to make the
down payment on her tuition, as well as to provide the $100 due on
Ellene's winter-quarter tuition and fees at Vanderbilt. Not only did
the fact that he was able to help his talented sisters make him enjoy his
homecoming more than "at any time" he "could remember," but his
happiness at being with his family again and the memory of his three
Christmases away from home made him more than ever determined
to find a teaching position as near Nashville as possible.[24]

When he returned east on January 4, he brought Annie along to
study music in New York. After she had played Bach's "Ninth Prelude
and another piece" for the director of the conservatory, that gentleman concluded that "she undoubtedly has music quality but her technique seems superficial" and advised her to take two hour's instruction each week from "Mme. Conrad, Stojowki's assistant, at a cost of
$100 for ten weeks, and harmony with Mr. Rice."[25] Ransom followed
her progress closely and went to see her every four or five weeks. On
one of these visits he attended a Vanderbilt University dinner, where
he was "greeted pleasantly" by Mr. Whitefield Cole, chairman of the
Board of Trust, and more than just pleasantly by Chancellor Kirkland, who "quite properly," Ransom wrote his mother, "referred to
me as a source of pride to the University."[26]

Almost immediately after his return to Lakeville, motivated undoubtedly by the desire to be near his family and able to assist them
financially, as well as to pursue his recently discovered interest in
English literature, he wrote letters to the southern universities that
had expressed an interest in him the previous year. Both Georgia and
Alabama, the places where he thought his chances were best, responded encouragingly but made no definite offer. Then he decided
to apply "for something at Vanderbilt without much chance of succeeding," because the severity of the winter, with snow "at least a foot
deep" and the temperature hovering between fifteen and twenty degrees, "can get right depressing."[27] When, as he expected, the prospects at Vanderbilt did not seem particularly promising, he naturally
began to look elsewhere. (He addressed his inquiry to Chancellor
Kirkland, who wrote that "our English faculty meets our present
needs." Apparently Kirkland did not inform Edwin Mims, who was
chairman of the English department, of Ransom's interest in a position at Vanderbilt.) The headmaster offered to recommend him as
chairman of the English department at Hotchkiss, and despite the fact
that some of the older members of the department objected because
of his relative inexperience, he was offered the position at a salary of
$1,650 plus room, board, and laundry. While he had this offer under
consideration, another came from the Loomis Institute, a boys' preparatory school scheduled to open in the fall of 1914 with an endowment of three million dollars. This latter offer was particularly attractive because the trustees also proposed to appoint a "physical director"
at a salary of "$1,500 plus living." Ransom immediately recommended
his brother Dick for this position and wrote his mother that if "that
place goes to Dick, I'll go to do English and Latin."[28]

As the end of the school year drew closer, Ransom naturally became more concerned about his situation for the next year. His applications to Harvard and Princeton for fellowships to support him while
he completed requirements for the Ph.D. degree were "under consideration," he was informed, but no definite offers had been made. On
his return from New York, where he had spent the weekend with
Annie and attended a reception given by one of her teachers, he
wrote his mother that he was "committed to Loomis if Dick lands the
physical position." Impressed no doubt by the guests he had met at

the reception, at which "lots of German and other languages were in circulation," and by the "informal tango" for the young people that followed the reception in spite of the fact that it was Sunday, he wrote that if the Loomis position for Dick did not develop he might try again for a position in journalism.[29]

Several months earlier he had written that Annie "should be aware of Tennessee myopia" and that she should "keep her soul open and clear" and attempt "to maintain a consistent outlook upon the widest possible expanse of this humanity whereof we are all members." During his year in Connecticut he had passed through New York three times on his way to and from Nashville and, upon invitation, had spent several weekends with friends who were studying or working there. After a visit with E. H. Eckel, who was studying at the General Theological Seminary, he had written his father that Tennessee "was incomplete on its artistic and dramatic side" and that his years in Europe had convinced him he would be happiest near a metropolitan center like New York. When his father responded, giving instances from his experience intended to illustrate the dramatic possibilities of rural life, Ransom's reply, though motivated in part by his willingness to debate almost any issue, shows that the strong force of family affection, which was always pulling him toward Nashville, was to some degree neutralized by the persistent feeling that New York offered opportunities he could find nowhere else.

Country conditions operate to produce in country people the qualities of stability, conformity, mental and spiritual inertia, callousness, monotony.... The country community is very small; very native or inbred and therefore very homogeneous, and very well fortified against the intrusion of ideas from without. No one is required to undergo any tremendous intellectual exertions.... Instead of a star, he hitches his wagon to the placid family mule and feels very virtuous and deserving if he can attain a comfortable dog trot.[30]

Morality and art, as well as intellectual development, are adversely affected by an isolated rural environment. Because there are so few "contrasts and surprises" in the country, its inhabitants must always "fail to attain a very high degree of morality." If "I seem to be using artist and moralist interchangeably," he wrote, "I am not guilty of a mental lapse because I think the two fields are closely related." The artist, he continued, "is preeminently a man to play upon the strings of human nature; he is interested in humanity, its vivid passions, its subtle refinements, its slow fires; he communicates the fascination of the study and thereby becomes a moral precepter." So that he would not be misunderstood completely, he would undertake—for the first time in his life, he wrote—to define morality. First he would indicate what it is not: "It cannot consist in a man's reading of his own narrow special brand of humanity as the standard of all human excellence." This definition is an early statement of his recurring argument for the importance of form and ritual: "Morality . . . means the subjection of the natural man with its animal cravings into conformity to some ideal standards." Later he would state specifically what he barely inferred in this letter—that this "conformity to some ideal standard" can best be attained through acceptance of traditional patterns of behavior. But lest his father conclude that he "is scornful of Tennessee," he admitted that he did not "know any land more delightful for climate or landscape or people or cooking."

With a divided mind Ransom faced his uncertain future. Upon the recommendation of Elmer Davis, a former Rhodes Scholar from Indiana then living in New York and editor of a very "livid magazine," the first and only issue of which Ransom had seen during his last visit with Annie, he was determined to consider seriously any opportunity in journalism that developed. In the meantime his situation became slightly less complicated. When he learned on April 3 that Dick would not be offered a position at Loomis, he immediately withdrew his application. His prospects of "honorable employment," he wrote his mother on the same day, were not depressing, even though they were not "too exciting." He could remain at Hotchkiss in the English department, a position he preferred to the one he then occupied, or he might receive an appointment in the Latin department of Phillips-Exeter. He had been in correspondence with the headmaster of the latter institution for several months, and he thought an offer might be forthcoming. If he should receive an offer of the kind he expected, he had made up his mind to take it so that he could meet "some outstanding financial obligations" as soon as possible. He needed to complete payment of the loan he had made to help pay for Annie's musical training in New York, and he had also signed with his father a note for $400 to assist Dick, who for many years moved from one financial crisis to another. These obligations were in addition to the regular payments he was making on the money he had borrowed while at Oxford, and he had also promised his father that he would continue to assist with Ellene's Vanderbilt expenses. If the Phillips-Exeter position turned out to be as lucrative as some of his colleagues had suggested it might, he had decided that he must accept it. In the meantime he awaited a response from Harvard and Princeton, both of which had promised to respond to his request for fellowship assistance by May 1.[31]

On April 9, however, he wrote that he had decided to accept the Hotchkiss post, if his father did not object, because he had heard nothing from Phillips-Exeter, and he doubted that the offer, if one came, would be better than the one he had. The company at Hotchkiss had never been exciting, and he knew he would miss Sam Chew, who had decided not to return. During the last six months of the school term he and Chew had seen each other everyday, had had many of their meals together, and had discussed literature and philosophy many nights, several times until almost dawn. After they both left Lakeville in June, however, there is no record of their ever seeing each other again, except for a few chance meetings at the annual conventions of the Modern Language Association. His relationship with Chew established a pattern that would recur in his life. For brief periods Ransom was very close to a person or a group of persons, usually because they were involved with ideas or causes that happened to interest him at the moment. At Oxford he established firm personal relationships with his fellow Rhodes Scholars, one or two of his tutors, and the members of the Hermit Crabs. Except for Christopher Morley—with whom he corresponded frequently for a few years after their graduation, particularly while Morley was trying to find a publisher for *Poems About God*—these attachments were dissolved almost as soon as Ransom returned from England. During the middle twenties he and Robert Graves exchanged a good many letters (most of them concerned *Grace After Meat*); almost as soon as the book appeared, however, the letters became less frequent and soon stopped altogether. Except for Allen Tate, and to a lesser extent Donald Davidson, Robert Penn Warren, and Andrew Lytle, none of the friendships established during Ransom's long tenure at Vanderbilt lasted very long after he left Nashville. His interest in people just did not go far beyond the members of his family and a very small circle of close friends. After each phase of his career, therefore, he turned his back on it and the people involved.

Since he was well settled in Lakeville and had established an agreeable routine there, he felt that next year he would have even more time for his own work. The essay on poetics had reached seven thousand words and would soon be ready for the typist. Before the end of May he expected to send it to either the *North American Review* or the *Yale Review.* Since he still had much to say on the subject, he was determined to complete, over the summer if possible, a book-length manuscript; he was especially eager to illustrate the value of his theory "by discussing Whitman and other poets on the ragged edge of conventional meter and then some of the drawing room poets like Tennyson and Swinburne and some of the prose poets like Carlyle." [32]

When he wrote his father on April 24, he was badly in need of advice. Rather than no offers at all, which had been the situation two months before, he now had too many. Although he did not receive a fellowship from Princeton—the department chairman had written that they had "too many good men of their own"—Professor James B. Greenough of Harvard had offered him an assistantship at a stipend of six hundred dollars plus remission of tuition and fees. The only requirement of the position was that he "correct and supervise the themes of sixty men"; therefore he could undertake almost a full course of study leading to the Ph.D. degree, and he could supplement his income, by as much as four or five hundred dollars he hoped, by tutoring some of the many preparatory-school boys seeking admission to Harvard and other Ivy League colleges. He still had not responded to Hotchkiss, and just that day he had received a "disappointing offer" of $1,500 to teach Latin at Phillips-Exeter. He was inclined to accept the Hotchkiss position because no other institution offered as much, and he was reconciled to the fact that for one more year at least he must remain separated from his family. Apparently his father advised him to accept the fellowship at Harvard because on May 13 he wrote: "My inclination for Harvard was reinforced by your handsome letter written on my birthday. It is true I am sadly in debt. But another birthday made me think about the bad economy of spending year after year in uncongenial fields. I think I may be able to do something worthwhile in English, perhaps in literature as well as criticism. I undoubtedly can get a good start in the latter at Harvard."

With his immediate plans made, he could turn his attention back to his essay on poetics. In the same mail that carried one copy of the essay to the *North American Review,* he sent another to his father and requested not only "emendations and corrections" on specific points but general comments on the merits of the theory. When his appointment came from Harvard, he was surprised, he wrote his mother, to find it was a joint appointment to Harvard and Radcliffe because he "had not bargained for any dealings with the new women." [33] Next year would not be a financial disaster, he reasoned, because he had just reached an agreement with a "tutoring school" in Roxbury, Massachusetts, assuring him of all the outside work he could do at $2.00 an hour. When he left for Nashville on June 18, he was looking forward to a long summer in which he could engage his father in many "a discussion of style or something else on which we don't wholly agree." Before he had to return to Cambridge in late September, there would be much leisure for "reading, writing, golf, tennis, and dining out," but best of all he was to have three months at home with his family, the longest period they had been together since his departure for Oxford nearly four years before. Annie had returned to Nashville on May 13, after four months in New York; Ellene would be free from her studies at Vanderbilt; and if Dick and his wife and daughter could only come up from Florida for an extended visit, there would be "much joy and happiness on the Murfreesboro Pike."

What he did not know, of course, when his train pulled into Nashville in the late afternoon of June 20, was that he had come home to stay for almost a quarter of a century. In late August, when he was offered a position in the Vanderbilt English department, he gave up his plan to study at Harvard and returned to his alma mater, where except for an enlistment of almost two years in the United States Army during World War I, he remained until he left for Kenyon College in the fall of 1937. Here he found his true vocation, and the creative spark, first ignited in Oxford and barely smoldering since, would burst into full flame during the next ten or twelve years. He not only provided intellectual and aesthetic leadership for a group of young poets, some of whom would become the most influential men of letters the South has ever produced, he wrote lyric poetry of the highest order and developed theories to justify the existence of this and all other good poetry in an age growing increasingly skeptical of a commodity unable to demonstrate its value in the marketplace.

A Kind of Centering
1913-1918

THE THREE YEARS Ransom spent in England, with long school vacations and summers on the Continent, gave him a new regard for the South, and his year in New England convinced him that he was happiest within his family circle. His decision to accept the position at Vanderbilt was influenced by his desire to return home and by his conviction that teaching English literature, particular at the college level, would provide the intellectual climate out of which he could carry on his speculations and writing on poetics. "In going back to Vanderbilt," John L. Stewart believes, "Ransom acted upon a conviction and an impulse, both a bit hazy at the time but no less strong for that; together they comprised his earliest intellectual recollection and were to become a significant force in his thinking throughout his adult life."[1] Ransom's conviction was that man "is crippled by a dissociation of the reason and sensibility," and he felt that the prime function of art and the artist in the twentieth century was to restore the balance between reason and sensibility so that man could know and enjoy what he was later to call the "concrete particularities" of the world in which he lives.[2]

His readings in English literature, particularly in the poetry of Shakespeare, Milton, and Spenser, as well as conversations with Samuel Chew during their year at the Hotchkiss School, had convinced him that English poetry was more concrete and less dogmatic than the classical literature he had studied so enthusiastically for almost ten years. In spite of the fact that the salary offered by Vanderbilt was much less than the one he would have received had he remained at Hotchkiss, other considerations made the position most attractive. As chairman of the English department at Hotchkiss, he would have earned $1,650 plus room, board, and laundry. At Vanderbilt he earned $1,200, out of which he paid $100 for a two-room suite in Kissam Hall and $13 a month for meals in the dining hall. This loss of income was more than compensated for by the attractiveness of the teaching schedule, the fact that he would have more time to devote to his own work, and the realization that if he wished he could spend every weekend with his family.

His colleagues in the department of English were Edwin Mims, who had earned his Ph.D. degree at Cornell and had taught at Trinity College and the University of North Carolina before returning to his alma mater in the fall of 1912 to head the department, and S. N. Hagen, a philologist who had been educated in the graduate program of Johns Hopkins and who taught half-time in the German department. Many years later Mims commented on why he had employed a young man who did not appear to be "qualified to teach English because he had never had any courses in the subject":

My policy was to find young men who knew Southern conditions and who had been trained in the best universities in this country and abroad. In the summer of 1914 I met on the campus John Crowe Ransom, who was visiting relatives in Nashville. I had often heard him spoken of as one of the most brilliant of the recent graduates of Vanderbilt and who had as a Rhodes scholar from Tennessee studied three years at Oxford, specializing in the classics and in philosophy.... When I asked him if he would accept an instructorship in English at Vanderbilt he readily accepted. There was never any doubt that he was the man particularly adapted to teach composition, and I soon gave him a course in creative writing. Later as the demand for graduate courses increased he offered a course in contemporary literature and later still one in Milton and Spenser.[3]

During his first year at Vanderbilt, Mims had completely reorganized the English curriculum. The first course in English composition met for two hours each week with either Ransom or Hagen—in the fall of 1914 they had 148 students between them—for instruction and practice in writing. For a third hour all of the freshmen met in one section to hear Mims lecture on English literature. As sophomores, all Vanderbilt students enrolled in a course that traced the development of English literature from Beowulf to Kipling by reading and discussing the selections in the *Century Readings in English Literature.* All three members of the department offered this course and required their students to become acquainted with the names, titles, and facts of English literature, and, in Mims's sections at least, to memorize the five thousand or so lines that in the opinion of their instructor were most representative of their literary heritage. During the junior year all English majors, and any others who might elect the course, studied American literature for two quarters, concluding with a survey of southern writers in which Mims used *Southern Prose and Poetry,* a text edited by him and Bruce Payne, one of his former students. The third quarter of this course was devoted to a study of Shakespeare's plays, and here Ransom began almost immediately the practice of teaching literature in the manner later made popular by Robert Penn Warren and Cleanth Brooks in *Understanding Poetry* and *Understanding Fiction.* Rather than attempting to read and lecture on all, or nearly all, of Shakespeare's plays, as Mims and Hagen did, Ransom concentrated on four or five plays, reading those closely and analytically and emphasizing particularly the poet's use of language. The English offerings were completed with courses in Victorian and Romantic poets, Chaucer, the Arthurian legends, and an "English Literature Seminary," the last of which was offered only on specific demand.

Ransom's teaching methods were in obvious contrast to those of Mims. Donald Davidson, who returned to Vanderbilt in the fall of 1914 to begin his sophomore year, enrolled in courses with both men. "For me," he wrote forty years later, "there was excitement in Dr. Mims' courses, partly from the stunning revelation that English and American literature offered subjects to study, not just books to read." Although he had read almost everything he could lay his hands on and had grown up listening to his father, a Middle Tennessee school teacher, quote long passages from his favorite poets, it had never occurred to him "that one studied Poe or Lowell or Johnson *at college.*"[4] If Mims made him aware that "English and American literature *had a history,*" Ransom made him conscious of poetic techniques and devices besides music and sound. For the first several weeks in Ransom's class, Davidson was not impressed. In contrast to Mims, one of the great reciters and readers of poetry, Ransom read poetry in a voice flat, quiet, and almost inflectionless. Although Davidson changed his mind before the term was over, at first he considered Ransom a dull teacher because he almost never summarized, synthesized, or uttered pronouncements about the greatness of the selection under consideration. Instead, quietly, patiently, and almost pedantically, he analyzed the plays, sometimes devoting the whole hour to one scene or, more frequently as the year advanced, to a few lines. Although Ransom never assigned specific passages to be committed to memory, as Mims and many other teachers of the time did, Davidson was surprised to learn years later that he could not only quote many of the passages Ransom had discussed but that he remembered Ransom's specific comments about them.

Some of his students thought Ransom was too much affected by "the English way" and one said that a professor in another department told him not "to pay any attention to that fellow."[5] His usual method, even in his freshman composition sections, was to read a story or poem to the class and then ask questions about what he had read. Most of the questions were concerned with craft or atmosphere rather than plot or theme. One student remembers his "dapper and fastidious" dress, his subtle wit, and his informal manner in class. Dorothy Berthurum, the distinguished medievalist, studied both freshman English and the sophomore survey with Ransom. She recalls that in the beginning she thought he was coming to class without adequate preparation. His manner was so informal and his assertions so tentative that he seemed unsure of himself and uncertain of what he expected to achieve. "There was something there," she remembers, "that was not quite native, some kind of—what shall I say?—brushing away of the conventions, of the superficialities, which I didn't recognize until I knew something about Oxford myself. And then I thought that was it, probably. Some kind of centering."[6]

This kind of centering, his informal manner, and the personal attention he gave to any student who wanted to talk about literature or writing were his most effective characteristics as a teacher during these years. William Yandell Elliott, a distinguished political scientist, recalls that Ransom's relations with his students "were those of an absolutely first-class tutor" and in a "warm, personal sense" went far beyond those normally associated with student and teacher.[7] Allen Tate, who was Ransom's student in the early twenties, recalls his ability to point directly to the specific weakness in a student essay: "I remember John used to take something I had written and put his finger on a certain word and say, 'Why is that there?' It was done so casually and with such great disinterestedness. You see, he had no animus about him; he was detached, and that's how we learned from him."[8]

His informal classroom manner and his personal interest in his students might have been a carry-over from his Oxford experience. "There was," Cleanth Brooks suggests, "a continuing man-of-letters tradition there, even a kind of rich amateur tradition, which by-passed pretty much the Germanic seminar business that came over in the 1880's and 1890's." What Ransom brought to Vanderbilt was finally the "tradition of talk," the tradition of the "talented amateur" as opposed to the "professionalism of the German seminar."[9] Certainly he was less formal and, perhaps, not as professional as some thought he should be. One student mistook his natural reserve for boredom and commented that he never had a teacher with less enthusiasm for what he was doing. Another accused him of never preparing an assignment and presented as evidence to support this conclusion the fact that he often came to class and read, with very little comment, a story or a poem. But, apparently describing the same technique, another said that the most impressive aspect of Ransom's classroom manner was his ability to provoke a thoughtful response from his students, to get them to ask appropriate questions, to involve the more perceptive of them in the procedure of reading literature in a way "Dr. Mims never could."[10]

Surely Mims must have had some doubts about employing a man who did not have a degree in English literature and who had never gone through the rigorous discipline of a single graduate course in the subject. One source maintains that Mims was so doubtful of Ransom's ability "to keep order" in his classes that for the first six weeks he sat just inside the door of his office, which opened upon the room in which Ransom was teaching. One day after Ransom had finished a class, Mims motioned him into the office. "I'm going to close my door and get on with my work," he said, "for I'm satisfied you can keep order. But, young man, I'm afraid you aren't a very good teacher."[11] Allen Tate's response to this story was, "If Dr. Mims had heard John forty years later, at the end of his brilliant career, his opinion would have been the same." Even though Mims did not approve of all the methods employed by his young instructor, whose approach was too casual and whose opinions were rendered with less than an air of final authority, Ransom was not an ordinary teacher and his chairman quickly recognized this fact. "He showed an uncommon ability to attract students to his courses," Mims wrote years later, "and by 1921 he had about him a group of students who in and out of his classroom were writing poetry and fiction and other forms of literature."[12]

As soon as Ransom was settled in his two-room suite in Kissam Hall, arranging one room as a study to accommodate his rapidly increasing collection of books, he began to put together an essay for which he had made extensive notes the previous year. Since his return from England in the spring of 1913, he had been concerned, as all thoughtful people were, about what seemed to be an inevitable war between England and Germany. All of his associates, and even his family, seemed to feel that only on England's side lay right and justice. One notable exception to this general rule was Herbert Charles Sanborn, who had replaced Collins Denny as chairman of the philosophy department. After studying at Heidelburg, Berlin, Halle, and Leipzig, Sanborn had received his Ph.D. from Munich.[13] Davidson's impression of Sanborn at this time suggests why one of Ransom's temperament would be attracted to him: "One could but be awed and obedient when Dr. Sanborn strode vigorously to his desk, cloaked in all the Olympian majesty of Leipzig and Heidelburg, and, without a book or note before him, delivered a perfectly ordered lecture, freely sprinkled with quotations from the original Sanskrit, Greek, Latin, German, French, or Italian, which of course he would not insult us by translating."[14] Sanborn, Mims later wrote, had "absorbed the technique and the spirit of German scholarship" at its most "flourishing period"; to him German thinkers were the "heroes of thought," and he openly and enthusiastically stated his German sympathies.[15] Encouraged no doubt by the discovery of such a formidable ally and by the conviction that in many important respects the German national character was nearer that of America than the British was, Ransom set out to state a principle, of which some Americans, he thought, should certainly be aware. Since the Civil War was little more than fifty years in the past, all southerners should realize that "right is seldom univocal."

Following his usual custom, he wrote out a first draft on his essay and gave it to his father for comment. Although John James Ransom was understandably concerned about the reception the essay would receive in Nashville, where sentiment was so obviously pro-British, he did not advise his son not to publish it: he merely indicated a few points at which the argument might be clarified or strengthened, or the style improved, and returned the essay. Ransom mailed it to the *Yale Review*, where it was immediately accepted and published in the issue for July, 1915.[16]

"The Question of Justice" became, then, the first of Ransom's essays to reach print, except for those that had appeared in college- and church-related publications. He was excited and anxious to have reactions from Professor Mims and his other colleagues, especially from Professor Sanborn, whose prompt response that the "argument was sound" encouraged Ransom tremendously.

Although almost all of America is on the side of England, the essay begins, there is "moral dignity" on both sides, and the tragedy is that "two good ideals should prove so irreconcilable." As Ransom saw it, the world was again involved, as it had been in the Civil War, in a conflict in which there was "right on either side." In that war the North "was fighting with the loftiest military zeal to emancipate an oppressed class and the South was fighting for political freedom." In order to prove that right and moral dignity were with both Germany and England, Ransom reminded his readers that there are two kinds of justice. In the first of these, which he called static justice and attributed to Aristotle, power is used to preserve the status quo through (1) distribution of new goods among the "members of a community in the ratio of their present holdings" so that no change shall "be brought about in their relative standing" and (2) restoration, by violence if necessary, to their former owners the goods that have come into the hands of new owners ("The violent act must be reversed to restore the old status"). The second kind of justice is hinted at in Plato's *Republic* but never fully worked out. Ransom called it creative justice and defined it as "that justice which gives to each man in the proportion that his strength and effort merit." This kind of justice does not try "to perpetuate any distribution," is "sensitive to change," and is "continually wiping out the old distribution." In the world of 1915, he maintained, creative justice was best expressed in the Socialist doctrine which proclaims "that ownership goes with use and need and not with priority of possession." In the beginning man's holdings are "proportionate to his strength and enterprise," and in a capitalistic system the law defends an individual's acquisition as long as one individual does not forcibly take what belongs to another. But an inequity soon develops because, though the constitution "remains fixed," the "balance of merit among actual men is always shifting." After a while, therefore, the distribution is not in accord with the merits of the holders.

In the present confrontation, Ransom continued, England is operating under the concept of static justice and Germany under that of creative justice. Germany wanted territorial expansion and resorted to war because she knew of no other way to achieve her desired ends. Germany favors a new distribution of territory "because under the present distribution" her "genius and enterprise" are not allowed to get that which she justly deserves. She has provoked the war so that she can get what creative justice would award her. England, on the other hand, fights as a threatened nation. She is defending not only her own possessions but those of weaker nations in distress. She is "committed to the furtherance of static justice, which never looks back on existing titles." What confronts the American, Ransom concluded, is the "necessity of accepting two conflicting points of view, both of equal propriety, so that he will not be stampeded into a defense of one side or the other." In this essay, then, Ransom presents for the first time his view of a world composed of inexhaustible ambiguities, one in which choice is at all times difficult and often almost impossible.

During the fall and spring of 1914–1915 several of Ransom's students began to stop by his rooms in Kissam Hall, sometimes to borrow books, more often to continue a discussion interrupted by the end of the class hour, or, increasingly as the year advanced, merely to talk about literature or philosophy. A favorite topic in those discussions, as one participant remembered them forty years later, was the extent to which the higher criticism of the Bible had undermined the elements of Christian faith.[17] Included in these discussions, in addition to Donald Davidson, were several other persons who later would be members of the group of young poets known as the Fugitives—Alec B. Stevenson, William Yandell Elliott, and Stanley Johnson. With this group, and at Davidson's special invitation, Ransom began to visit Sidney Mttron Hirsch, who lived with his parents on Twentieth Avenue, only two blocks from the Vanderbilt campus. Like the talk in Ransom's rooms, these discussions usually followed a topic that one of the participants was particularly interested in at the moment. The talk might begin with a short story, a poem, or a novel someone had just read before moving into various individual preoccupations, like Stanley Johnson's interest in Borden P. Browne's philosophy of personalism or Hirsch's in Rosicrucianism and Cabalism. In a letter to Alec B. Stevenson, who was spending the summer in Canada, William Yandell Elliott described one of these meetings:

Nat Hirsch, Stanley Johnson, Donald Davidson, John Ransom and Sidney Hirsch were the company last night and it was Olympian. I am living in rare altitudes this summer, though I haven't gone to Monteagle yet. We get together often and I can feel myself grow. . . . Out on the Hirschs' porch, with cigar ends glowing occasionally, a debate always insured from the nature of the company, it is the *Happiness.* Last night it was the vanity of being that was under discussion, Johnny maintaining a dualism at least—*Elan Vital* and Material Expression, I, admitting a logical duality, maintaining a pluralistic Individuality of Being, but a Metaphysical unity.[18]

All of those evenings were not spent in what Davidson once called "heady conversation." Sometimes the group sang to Davidson's accompaniment on the piano, and on other occasions they went on brief excursions up the Cumberland River or took the streetcar downtown to the Vendome theater to see a touring group do the *Merry Widow, Madame Butterfly,* or *Hamlet.* [19] But usually Ransom and Johnson took opposing sides in animated metaphysical discussions, or Hirsch's rambling etymological monologues would evolve into a declaration of the necessity of poetry's occupying a central position in any civilized society. Davidson describes the almost unique quality of those evenings:

[We] fell silent and became listeners when—as always happened—
Sidney Hirsch picked out some words—most likely a proper name like
Odysseus or Hamlet or Parsifal, or some common word like *fool* or
fugitive—and then, turning from dictionary to dictionary in various
languages, proceeded to unroll a chain of veiled meanings that could
be understood only through the system of etymologies to which he
had the key. This, he assured us, was the wisdom of the ages—a
palimpsest underlying all great poetry, all great art, all religion, in all
eras, in all lands. All true poets possessed this wisdom intuitively, he
told us, solemnly, repeatedly. Furthermore he proved it later on,
when we began to forsake philosophy for poetry, by pointing out that
some image that had crept into our verses, no matter what we intended it to mean, revealed exactly the kind of mystic symbolism he
had traced from the Ramayana to Homer to Sophocles to Dante to
Shakespeare to William Blake. Probably no group of poets ever before received just this kind of assurance.[20]

Surely Ransom must have realized how fortunate was his choice to
return to Vanderbilt. In spite of a rather drastic reduction in salary,
he could still meet his most pressing financial obligations. Not only
was he able to assist Ellene with her Vanderbilt expenses, he met on
schedule the payments on the loans he had made, with his father's
endorsement, at the bank, and on more than one occasion he was able
to give his mother small gifts to supplement the meager salary of a
Methodist minister. Best of all he could visit his family as often as he
liked. His classes were also most productive. The reading he had to do
to prepare to teach them encouraged him to read closely and analytically a great deal of the English literature he felt he must know in
order to test some of the aesthetic theories he was developing. Class
discussions and their continuation in his rooms at night or at the
Hirsch apartment gave him the opportunity to defend his theories, as
did his reading and analysis of individual poems before a very perceptive and articulate group of colleagues, students, and other friends.
Some of Ransom's critical ideas began to solidify. "He had come to
believe," Stewart points out, "that modern man is crippled by a dissociation of the reason and sensibility which results in an imbalance
whereby the reason, armed with abstract principles which have been
spectacularly successful in supplying the material needs of the body,
tyrannizes over the sensibility and restricts its innocent, profitless delight in the vividness and variety of the world. With this conviction

went a 'fury against abstractions' and a desire to restore the sensibility
to its proper eminence in man and his society and to enable it to enjoy
the harmless indulgences."[21] He was convinced that his decision to
teach English literature was a wise one, for here he could find the rich
particularity, what he was later to call the world's body, that philosophy lacked. Not since Oxford, and perhaps not even then, had he
been so intimately associated with a group of young men who could
hold up their end of an argument and start his head "buzzing with
new ideas" and Ransom was delighted, as his first year at Vanderbilt
neared its end, that the members of this little circle were spending
more and more time together.

By early 1917 the atmosphere on the Vanderbilt campus had notice-
ably changed. Almost as soon as America entered the war, Chancellor Kirkland appeared before students and faculty to make a formal declaration of the university's new policy. "Up to this time," he
said, "there has been much discussion in America of both sides of the
great war. We have been divided into two camps which are designated
as pro-German and pro-ally. Now the time for academic discussion
has ended. The voice of America has been heard." He immediately
began to explore ways by which Vanderbilt could assist in her country's idealistic efforts "to save the world for democracy."[22] Although
all regular classes would be continued at least to the end of the current
semester, all intercollegiate athletics were immediately suspended and
students were encouraged to participate in the military drill that
would begin as soon as supervisory personnel could be supplied by
the United States Army. Within a month almost all the students and
some of the younger faculty members were drilling daily from 4 to 6
P.M. on the athletic fields.

At the same time Kirkland called Professor Sanborn, the most
outspoken German sympathizer on the campus, into his office and
reminded him again that the "voice of America has been heard" and
that all members of his faculty were patriotic Americans. No longer,
apparently, was Ransom concerned that "right and moral dignity"
were on both sides of the conflict. A few months later he knew, as he
wrote Charles Cason, editor of the Vanderbilt *Alumnus,* that "Germany must be whipped as soon as possible" so that the world could

return to its normal pursuits. Along with many of his young colleagues and some of the junior and senior students, Ransom applied for admission to the Officers' Training Camp. He was ordered to report to Fort Oglethorpe, Georgia, on May 12, 1917.

The night after Ransom checked into Training Company Fifteen he wrote his mother to send his bathrobe because although his company was "just next to the bath houses, we have to go in costume and it means an extra dressing if we have no bathrobes." Apparently he enjoyed the strenuous life of the army camp, if not the crude living conditions. Arising at 5:15 each morning, he found himself constantly and completely occupied until taps sounded at 10 P.M. Never in his life, he wrote his father, not even as a child, had he spent days and nights so completely void of any kind of mental exertion. The nearest thing to intellectual engagement was furnished by the required lectures on such subjects as military discipline, government, and courtesy, or at the speeches made by celebrated military figures intended to arouse patriotism among the prospective officers. That the latter did not always accomplish the desired result is indicated in some of Ransom's letters to his family:

I listened to addresses last night by General [John T.] Wilder and Mr. H. Clay Evans. The first of these was a prominent general in the battle of Chickamauga and the last is the well-known Republican carpetbagger, Congressman of the United States, and Consul-General at London. . . . All of us young soldiers have noticed how hard it is to get accustomed to the Union point of view. . . . General Wilder and Mr. Evans devoted much time to proving that Chickamauga was a victory—meaning a success for the Union troops—and spoke a little disparagingly of Bragg, Forrest, and other Confederate champions.[23]

Also in the audience that evening was Donald Davidson and his reaction was even more negative:

One summer evening in 1917 when I was among the trainees at the First Officers Training Camp at Fort Oglethorpe, Georgia, the fifteen training companies were marched into a grove to hear a guest speaker. He was Federal General John T. Wilder, who had commanded a unit of mounted infantry in Rosecrans' Army of the Tennessee and had waged deadly war against our Confederate forebears, under Braxton Bragg, on the very battlefield of Chickamauga where we were then encamped. With great pride the old General told of his part in that other war. He dwelt long and, it seemed to me, with vicious exultation upon the fact that his mounted infantry were armed with Sharp's repeating rifles, and therefore did bloody execution upon the Johnny Rebs opposite him, who had only single shooters. It did not seem to matter to General Wilder that the young men before him were descendants of the Confederate soldiers whom he had so gleefully slaughtered in 1863 with his Sharp's repeating rifles. Quite the other way, in fact. Rising to a fine oratorical climax, he made his patriotic point, which was that even as he, General Wilder, had killed Johnny Rebs in great number in 1863, so should we in 1917 proceed to kill Germans in equally great numbers.[24]

As in everything else in which he was engaged, Ransom put his best effort into learning to be a soldier. The instruction in horseback riding, which took up a large part of the afternoons, he particularly enjoyed, and the other assignments he accepted cheerfully and attempted to complete as nearly perfectly as he could. He adjusted to a new routine with little apparent discomfort. "They still seem to think," he wrote his sister Annie on June 3, "there are a good many things for us to learn around here, judging from the rate they expose us to new branches of soldiering every day." Just when they had mastered one method of communicating with flags, for example, they were introduced to another; the expectations of the commanding officers were very high and he had heard, he wrote his mother near the end of July, "that only one third of the cadets will actually receive a commission." But he had at least two reasons, he reported, to maintain some confidence that he would be among the few fortunate enough to get their "bars and be sent immediately overseas." First of all he belonged to a good unit, the only one among fifteen singled out and complimented for the way it executed the manual of arms during an inspection by the commanding officer and his senior instructors, one of whom commented in Ransom's presence that "it was as good as a performance of old regulars." The second reason for his optimism was an occurrence that had disturbed him very much when it happened. At the half-way point in their training his commanding officer had arranged a conference with every member of Training Company Fifteen except twenty. Ransom wondered why this group was exempted, and he was really alarmed when the company sergeant explained to one of this twenty, "The C.O.'s done made up his mind about you, one way or another." Ransom was concerned, he wrote his mother, because he did not know how his "captain could know anything about me at all." Later the captain told the entire company that he had not interviewed some of the men because he was satisfied with the progress they were making.

As intent as Ransom was on retaining the good favor of those who would finally pass judgment on his competence to serve as an officer in the United States Army, he managed, after he became familiar with the training routine, to find some time for other activities. He was able to revise the poems he had been writing for more than a year and to read some of these reworked versions to Davidson before sending them on to New York so that Christopher Morley might help him find a publisher for them. There was time, too, near the end of his training, to visit with some of his relatives in the area. When his cousin Joe Ransom, who was now second in command of Training Company Thirteen, received orders to report to New York for shipment overseas, they went into Chattanooga for lunch at the Paul Campbells', who, Ransom explained to Annie, was "a cousin of mother's nephew." While in town they saw a "double header between the Knoxville Smokies and the Chattanooga Lookouts" and had dinner at the Hotel Patton.[25] Ransom also discovered *Pearson's Magazine,* edited by Frank Harris, a "socialist and anti-British but a good patriot and a mighty fine writer." Ransom sent a copy to his father with the offer to give him a subscription if he liked it.

He received his commission in August, 1917, and almost immediately he was sent to New York and assigned space on a troop carrier for shipment overseas. On September 22 he wrote his father that his passage was "quite free from submarine menace" and so smooth that he had not "missed a meal." In France he was assigned to the Field Artillery Training Base, and he immediately entered his advanced training with enthusiasm. On October 21 he reported that he was the only person in his unit who "scored perfect" on the previous week's work and his only complaint was the scarcity of news from home. He was particularly concerned, he wrote his mother, about the enrollment at Vanderbilt and the appointment his father would receive at the Annual Conference of the Methodist Church. On November 2, he reported that he was writing from the room of

Morton Adams and Joe Thompson, two former Vanderbilt students who had been with him since he entered the army six months before. The stove in his room would not draw, and he had deliberately sought out a warm place because he had four long letters to answer, including one from Ellene which he was particularly glad to get, for she always "gives all the news going." To his father's offer to assist him with his financial obligations, Ransom responded, "I am pretty heavily involved, as you know. But I am in a position to let the other fellow worry, and I am not doing any of that business myself, but just attending to my obligations gradually as I am able." But he did send Mr. Ransom $185.00 with instructions to distribute it as follows: "Cole note $25.00; American National note $50.00; insurance payment $110.00."

The artillery school was located in Saumur, a town of twelve thousand in the west of France, on the Loire near Tours. The buildings used by the school were those formerly occupied by the French cavalry school, where, he wrote Annie, "the finest riders in the world were turned out and where our own army got its theory of horsemanship." Although it was "a little wearisome to keep on going to school," he found the work interesting and the level of required mathematics demanding. The young officers, as he later described the course he first took and subsequently taught, "had to be very conversant with Geometry and Trigonometry. Many problems had to be solved and rigid examinations taken. These under the head of securing fire-data, such as range, direction, etc., and overcoming problems of slope." To cope with the problems in ballistics, "higher mathematics was constantly in reference, if not positively required." The students also had to deal with problems of physics, such as "initial-velocity, air-resistance, windage and rifling." The mechanical requirements were scarcely less challenging for those who, like Ransom, had had no formal training in the field. There was, he wrote, "much independent work in topography, where students had to make and use accurate drawings on a leveled plane-table."[26] In addition to the ability to apply all of this theoretical knowledge under the pressure of combat, "students had to take apart the gun (the 155 Howitzer) and all its equipment, study all its features, and acquire a somewhat less expert knowledge of still other types of materiel—such as the 75 mm gun and the British and German types." All of the mornings during the ninety-day course were devoted to intensive instruction and training in the subjects described above and the afternoons were given over to exercises, under the direction of expert French instructors, in the fine art of horsemanship. All in all, he concluded, both the "teaching and the grading" were fully as exacting as in the work he had done either at Vanderbilt or at Oxford.

That Ransom underestimated neither the demands of the training nor the expectations of his superiors is indicated by the several references in his letters home to the fact that he was the only "member of my unit who made a perfect score on the quiz we had today." His performance was so good that at the end of his training he was the only one in his class to be recommended for promotion to captain; but, he wrote his mother, "that means nothing for the present" because "the army has decided to hold promotions to see how the officers perform in the field." When he was informed that he was to be reassigned to a unit at the front, despite a recommendation from his commanding officer that he be retained as an instructor at the school, he was delighted because "I didn't come to France to continue my pedagogical career. It has been 'school days' since I entered the training camp in May and I am anxious to try my hand at managing and instructing the men."[27]

Since Christmas Eve and Christmas day were free of duty, he was able to have a "nice vacation by the fire and that means more to a man in the army than elsewhere." In these moments of relative freedom he always regretted that he had not brought more books with him because he found that he could not drop his "literary interests." "I have a little billet," he wrote Christopher Morley on December 27, "with a bed, a table, and a stove and I have large black cigars in store, so I'm quite happy. It's cold and snowy now, and Christmas was a bit depressing, but we have little work to do and I look forward to long evenings with my books and papers without dismay." He had his orders for reassignment, which allowed him four days in Paris, and he planned to buy some books against his "next period of leisure" and, as a delayed Christmas present for his father, some gloves "of a make whose merits I have thoroughly tried out." He reported to his new unit, the Fifth Field Artillery, early in the new year and on January 14 wrote that he was "still with the heavy guns and beginning to feel more or less at home with them."[28] They were horse-drawn and the "preparation and conduct of fire is based upon the same mathematics as that used with the 75's." His particular duty was assisting in the care and maintenance of the horses. He was responsible for acquiring grain and hay from local French merchants and farmers—an assignment that required him to polish up his French, because he had some trouble explaining to his interpreter what he wanted interpreted. But he was issued a "pretty good horse," and he thoroughly enjoyed the rides he had to make across the beautiful French countryside, though he always had to be alert because the horse "floundered around mighty badly" on the icy roads. Despite his happiness at having finally become involved in combat, he missed some of the comforts he had almost come to expect. He had not been paid for two months; neither had he received a letter from home or had time to write long letters home. Until he had more leisure, he wrote his father, he would have to send brief notes to his parents with the hope that they would share them with Ellene and make appropriate explanations to Annie and Dick, both of whom were living away from home.

His mail finally caught up with him on February 17, when he received a letter written on his mother's fifty-fifth birthday; and in his answer, the first letter of any length he had written home in almost two months, he commented on the "balmy spring days—good sunshine and no snow for three weeks," on the "good chow" served in the officers' mess, and again on the nature of the duty in which he was involved. Obviously, he could see the irony of the army's assigning the top man in his class, the one who was best informed on the operations of the weapons employed by his unit, to "giving instructions in the care and use of horses to a bunch from the wild west," although he was somewhat surprised at how little these westerners knew about horses. But all branches of the service were not unimpressed by his mastery of the assigned materials in the Field Artillery School, because by April 28, after a little less than four months at the front, he was back at Saumur, this time as an instructor.

Although he was sorry to be away from the front, he was flattered that the commanding officer of the training school had requested his transfer because of his outstanding achievements as a student. He was soon comfortably settled in a three-room apartment on the ground floor of a small apartment building in Saumur, and he took his meals at the best hotel in the city. He was faring, he wrote his mother on May 12, "a little better than I ever did in my life except at home itself." He was assigned "the best horse I have ridden, named Hola," and since his teaching was not to begin for four or five weeks, he had time for long rides into the countryside. He was even able to get "cigars and candies at prices a good deal below what you are paying at home."[29]

Following the practice of many American fathers, John James Ransom had published several of his son's letters in the local newspapers and in some of the church publications. As soon as he learned what his father had done, Ransom wrote in an uncommonly stern tone that he was "afraid ... to say anything in my letters home that might stand the remotest chance of being considered worthy of the paper. It's a pleasure to write private letters home thinking they are for very particular consumption, but not to make every letter an essay for the paper."[30] That he was concerned about the quality of his writing which appeared in the paper is demonstrated by his reaction to Edwin Mims's giving a letter of his to the Vanderbilt *Alumnus*. Although there was nothing in the letter of any great consequence, Ransom wrote his father that he would never write Mims again (and apparently he did not), because his colleague had violated a confidence in publishing without his knowledge and consent a letter "which contained private matter for one thing and sentiments almost unpatriotic for another." The private matter to which Ransom referred evidently was a statement regarding his continuing literary interests. "As for my literary efforts," he wrote, "I find it is not possible to dismiss interests of that sort from my mind. I have written a few efforts myself and I am always blaming myself for not having brought more books with me." The reference to sentiments "almost unpatriotic" must be to his rather guarded statements concerning army life. The thought of remaining in service for an extended period was distasteful to him, and he had feared for several months that he was "in for a life sentence but now prospects look normal again with better news from the Italian front."

Ransom's insistence that personal correspondence remain private is evident in his relationship with Charles Cason, editor of the *Alum-*

nus. After repeated invitations to submit a statement for publication so that all of his Vanderbilt friends and former students would know where he was and what he was doing, Ransom sent in an "essay for the paper," the tone of which is much more formal and impersonal than the hundreds of warm, personal letters he wrote to his family and close friends during his months overseas. Any one of the six paragraphs indicates quite clearly what First Lieutenant John C. Ransom considered suitable for the public print:

War would not be tolerable under any circumstances by finely-organized creatures, I suppose, if it were not regarded as the one means and hope of a return to reason and peace. The strange thing about war, however, as I see it, is that it does not grow more tolerable to its victims, like other calamities, as it drags on and on. When the first ardor of war has burnt out, there is only a cold fortitude which keeps it going; and it operates against an ever-mounting war-weariness. It is horrible to see how war, as a regimen, a regularity of life, can fasten itself upon a people like a disease which it does not seem possible to cure. Our veterans of the Civil War may have seen something like it before their tragedy was finished, but the younger generations must come to Europe before they can understand what a disaster these long and bitter wars can be. I am not speaking here of the loss of life, which is appalling, nor of the material cost, which is frightful. I mean the effect that such war has on the temper, the spirit, the religion, the sanity and health of the whole mobilized population.[31]

Not only did the indiscriminate use of private correspondence violate his highly developed sense of decorum, but, as he wrote his mother on March 12, Ransom detested the kind of "advertising one gets by being put in the paper, even though it is meant in a kindly way. I know from many conversations that it is quite embarrassing to the soldiers over here to hear of the heroics that take place in their honor in the home-towns . . . while hundreds and thousands of Frenchmen and Britishers are doing their duty without fuss."

As much as he wanted to get back to the front, he remained at Saumur to the end of the war; and he continued to instruct, in groups of approximately twenty, his "fellow officers in the use of the 155 gun."[32] Among those who came through the school while Ransom was there were Alec Stevenson and William Frierson, both of whom would later join the group of young poets who, with Ransom, would produce the *Fugitive*.

When Stevenson arrived in Saumur, he found among the officers in training there ten other men whom he had known at Vanderbilt.[33] It was here, too, that Ransom first saw printed copies of *Poems About God*, a project to which he had given as much time and thought as his duties would permit during the two years of his overseas assignment. Almost from the time he arrived in France he had had frequent correspondence with Christopher Morley, who kept him informed of his persistent efforts to find a publisher. On September 30, 1917, he wrote Morley: "If the publishers are the big fools I know they are not and take my ms., I'd like dearly to read proof and make a few vital corrections." Although Morley was following every lead he knew, the information he sent Ransom was not encouraging. He wrote on October 31 that the *Independent* had taken a poem, but three weeks later he reported that the collection of poems was "still on the road: both Husbsch and Doran have gotten out from under." In spite of this depressing news, he assured Ransom that soon he expected to "bear happier tidings"; in the meantime, he concluded, "rest assured . . . that I will try to follow up your interests as faithfully as one of my faulty and unsystematic disposition can do."

Although Morley had sent the manuscript to several publishers and individual poems to at least a dozen different magazines, his letters during the fall and winter of 1917/18 reveal how difficult it was in this war year to place with a New York publisher a book of poems by an unknown poet. However, Ransom was not dejected. After spending a lonely Christmas reading and writing letters home, he assured his friend that he understood the difficulty of the task he had undertaken. "I fear you will take the vicissitudes of P about G more seriously than I do. Have become very distrustful about the merits of them myself and am not a bit sore at the poor publishers who don't see them. Just let them wait awhile, my dear Chris. At present I have no chance at composition—next to none, that is. Can't even consider the matter. I'd really prefer to let the things alone a while."

His military duties allowed few opportunities to write verse or even to revise that already written, some of which pleased him much less than it had in those happier days before the war. Even with more time to write, his motivation was slight because the news from New York did not improve. On February 13, 1918, Morley wrote that poems had been returned from the *Atlantic Monthly,* the *Yale Review,* and the *Independent* and that his only advice was "to hold off until a few pieces can be included and then get Henry Holt to reconsider." About two months later, after Ransom had been returned to the rear and "to a position of comparative luxury," he began to write the "few new pieces" that Morley had requested. On April 29 he reported that he "turned in and finished off a couple of efforts that had been in the back of my head some few weeks." He cautioned his friend not to be depressed by the repeated rejections. "I'm not the kind," he wrote, "to be discouraged by editors as long as my bread does not issue from them. Too thick of skin, I suppose. . . . But I find myself hoping that in the early summer you may think it well to make another attack on Henry Holt, after I can make a few revisions and additions."

He was surprised to learn that during his months at the front he had not been as far from poetry as he had thought. Not only was his mind cluttered with new poems but his dissatisfaction with the old ones was so pronounced that he was almost persuaded to withdraw the poems and start anew. If he was ever to let *Poems About God* go, he knew that he must release it now; therefore on May 13 he wrote Morley: "The old book is clean done, I think now. That is, it's big enough as far as volume goes, and I've outgrown it until it's becoming a bit artificial with me. Hence my desire to wind it up if possible." In this letter he enclosed, along with an introduction indicating his dissatisfaction with the volume and hinting at its future suppression, four new poems and many suggested changes in the old ones. As soon as Morley received this revised manuscript, he sent it along to Holt with his strong endorsement. Surely one of the more fortunate coincidences in modern literary history is the fact that at the time the manuscript arrived in the Holt offices that firm had Robert Frost on a small retainer with the understanding that he would read and evaluate any poetry manuscripts the company was considering for publication. Frost read the poems, which some of the reviewers would suggest owed a great deal to him, and, as he expressed it later, found that the young poet "had the art and . . . the tune"; he recommended publication. This recommendation, along with that of Morley, apparently persuaded the publishers to assume the considerable financial risk of bringing out the volume even though the sale of poetry was very slow indeed. The book appeared the next year without Ransom's seeing the proof sheets and being able to make any of the dozens of changes he had begun considering almost as soon as he sent the manuscript to New York.

At the Fugitive reunion in Nashville in May, 1956, Robert Penn Warren gave an account of Ransom's actions when after many months of waiting he held for the first time a copy of *Poems About God.*

I encountered in California some years ago a man named McClure, who edits the paper at Santa Monica. . . . Well, he was in France at the same time that John was as a soldier. And when I was living out there, he wrote me a note—I had never met him or knew anything about him—and said, "I am a friend of an old friend of yours. Won't you come to dinner?" So I went to dinner at his house and had a very pleasant evening. And he said that he was walking down the street with John Ransom, who was a good soldierly companion of his during that period, and they went to get the mail at the battery mail distribution. And they got a few letters, and John got a little package. And he opened the little package, and there were two copies of *Poems About God* in it. And he said John hadn't seen the book before, and he opened it and inspected it with composure, and then turned to McClure and said, "I'd like to give you a copy of this." [34]

When the war was over, the government suddenly found itself in a situation that was potentially explosive. With more than two million officers and men in Europe, no way to keep them practically employed, and no means of getting them home for months, there seemed to be all the ingredients for real trouble. One of the most successful of the several projects the government sponsored to keep the "men occupied and out of trouble," as Ransom wrote home, was to allow those qualified and interested to enroll for special courses in selected universities. Ransom immediately enrolled at Grenoble, and later at Nancy, where he first became aware of the Symbolist poets. "Several nice young ladies introduced me to the poetry of the nineteenth century of France," he said at the Fugitives' reunion, "and I came back with a lot of volumes, and I know that the French Symbolists attracted and perplexed me a great deal." [35] Although he did not talk about them very much in those early important meetings of the Fugitives at Vanderbilt immediately after the war, they were "very much in my consciousness after 1919." What impressed him most was "their great gift of phrasing," their "great boldness of metaphor." This interest in the Symbolists might help to explain the difference in style between the poems in *Poems About God* and those which he began writing soon after his return from France. In early 1922 Ransom read "Necrological" at a Fugitive meeting, and Allen Tate "marveled at it because it seemed to me that overnight he had left behind him the style of his first book and without confusion had mastered a new style."[36]

As the time approached for Ransom to return to America, he realized that he was again faced with an important decision regarding his future. He was not assured of a position at Vanderbilt, even if he decided he wanted to return to teaching. The official policy of the Board of Trust, as announced on June 10, 1918, was that the university would "favor" the returning veterans with "such positions as can be kept open for them or may be open at the time of their return; but that there be no guarantee of future employment."[37] (But Ransom had been informed by Mims that he would likely receive an offer from Vanderbilt.) During the past year, first at Saumur and later at Grenoble, he had had more time to himself than at any time during the previous ten years. As he read back through *Poems About God,* he was convinced that he could write poetry. Now with his discovery of the Symbolists and his intensive reading of some of the contemporary poets, he felt he knew much more about the use of language than he had known when he wrote that earlier volume. At no time during his enlistment in the service had he been able to dismiss his consuming interest in writing, and the more he thought about his future, the more certain he became that he should think again about a career in journalism and free-lance writing. "I love English literature," he wrote to Charles Cason on March 5, 1919, "and if I am left alone I would love to teach it in my own way; as well as always, whatever happens, to do a certain amount of scribbling fatigue of my own." But, he concluded, he would soon be thirty-one years old, and he felt that if he expected to try earning a living from his writing, he had to make the decisive step soon.

After a five-day visit in Pornic with some friends, Ransom left Nancy for Brest on July 9, 1919, to await passage to America. From there he wrote Christopher Morley, who since their Oxford days had encouraged him to try a career in journalism, that he hoped to have time for a visit with him in Philadelphia when he came through New York. Morley would understand, he wrote, that his visit would combine business with pleasure and that he would welcome any suggestions his old friend might have about employment. In Brest, Ransom unexpectedly ran into Alec Stevenson, also awaiting passage to America, and they spent an evening together, drinking wine, reading some of the poems in *Poems About God,* and talking. Ransom was particularly interested in getting some practical advice about journalism from Stevenson, who before his enlistment had served for a brief period on the staff of the Philadelphia *North American.* At any rate he wrote his mother that before the end of the third week in August he expected to visit his family in their new home, the parsonage at Brentwood, the church to which his father had been assigned in October, 1918. Although he was not at all certain where he would settle permanently and how he would earn his living, he knew he wanted to write, and for the first time in his life he knew he wanted to write poetry.

V   **Without Rank
or Primacy
1918-1924**

AS RANSOM dutifully boarded the Saumur train in
Paris at 8 P.M. on Sunday evening, November 10, 1918, he knew that
peace in Europe was imminent.[1] Although he badly wanted to see
Paris *en fete,* for the first time in four years acting in a manner "worthy
of herself," he made his way slowly back to his army post, happy in the
knowledge that he could begin to make definite plans to resume the
career interrupted by the war. Convinced now that his real vocation
was that of man of letters, he realized that he must decide soon where
and how he could best practice his profession. As soon as the armistice
was signed and the excitement had abated somewhat (Even in "little
Saumur," he wrote Christopher Morley on November 12, "the people
almost went mad."), he inquired of the Nashville *Tennessean,* for
whom he had written a few editorials, if there were any prospects of
an opening in the editorial department. On the same day he wrote
William Cross at Yale, "with special reference to the subject of Advanced Composition." Within the next day or two he intended to send
a similar letter to the department of English of the University of
California in Berkeley. His first stop when he arrived in the States was
to be in Philadelphia so that he could elicit the assistance of Christopher Morley in obtaining a position on one of the large eastern
newspapers or in the editorial offices of one of the New York publishers. "I'm open-minded," he wrote Morley; "that means, I haven't
got a job and want one. Vanderbilt isn't quite big enough for my
peculiar tastes."

On March 17, 1919, from the University of Nancy—where he was "dabbling in letters, reading and writing (reading French and writing English)"—he wrote Morley again, advising him that he had decided to return to teaching unless some unusually attractive position was available when he arrived in the East. "I've put out some feelers at Yale and Brown, and I still have some standing probably at Vanderbilt. I'm interested mainly in Advanced Composition, mainly around the Literary Club idea with which I had some success at Vanderbilt." When he learned, on June 17, 1919, that he was to report to Brest about July 1 for "transportation to America," he wrote to Morley, again soliciting his "sage advice about the future." Although he had had letters from Charles Cason and Edwin Mims, both of whom wrote encouragingly of his being able to return to Vanderbilt, his response had been noncommittal. For, as he wrote Morley, he had definitely decided that his career would profit if he were able to settle in the East.[2]

When he arrived in New York in mid-August he went to the Bretton Hall Hotel at 86th and Broadway, where he had asked Morley to write him, to see if his friend had been able to make any appointments for him.[3] During the next three days he had interviews with several publishers, but the best offer he could get was from Putnam's, "a 25 or 30 dollar a week job" to learn the business. His interviews at Columbia and the Massachusetts Institute of Technology—he made a hurried visit to Boston to see Professor Frank Aydelotte—were much more encouraging. Almost certain that he would be returning to one of these places within a few weeks, he decided not to stop in Philadelphia to visit Helen and Chris Morley, as he had promised, but to go directly to Nashville to see his family.

When he arrived at the parsonage in Brentwood, he was surprised and saddened to see how much his parents had aged in the two years he had been away.[4] A part of their trouble, he realized immediately, was that they were lonely. For the first time since their first child was born, they were alone. During the summer the house had been full—all of the children but John had been there—but by mid-August they had all departed. Dick, his wife Lucille, and their daughter Ella Crowe, had returned to Long Beach, California, where he was teaching science in high school. Annie had gone to the North Carolina

Woman's College in Greensboro to teach music and Ellene to Athens (Alabama) College to teach English. So it was with mixed feelings, surely, that Ransom wrote Morley on August 27: "You will see from the address that I've reneged, reverted and fallen flat. Yes, I shall be at Vanderbilt this year, as Assistant Professor in English." He had wanted to be in the center of things, to be near the literary capital of the country so that he could form associations with other poets and critics, for he felt that only through direct confrontation with those who shared his interests would he receive the stimulation he had needed so badly during his years in the service. But he had found his "mother and father getting old and somewhat lonely, and thought it best to spend the year with them." The decision was for one year only, he assured Morley, and before this time next year he would need his help again.

The circumstances of Ransom's returning to teach at Vanderbilt were similar to those of his first employment there five years earlier. Early in May, when it appeared certain that the enrollment for the fall would reach or exceed that of the year just before the war, Mims had recommended that Ransom be invited to return to his alma mater. In conference with Chancellor Kirkland, he had proposed that Ransom be promoted to assistant professor at a salary of $1,700.[5] They both agreed that to give him the rank that Walter Clyde Curry, who for physical reasons was not able to serve in the war, had achieved the year before and the salary Curry was scheduled to receive for the current session was only just. Both had come to Vanderbilt at about the same time, and Mims argued that one should not be penalized for serving his country. Just before Ransom left France, Mims had notified him that such an offer would probably be made and was disappointed when Ransom replied that he was not certain he would return to teaching. Before he made a final decision, he wrote, he wanted to see what other kinds of positions were available. Both Mims and Kirkland thought the position should be filled as soon as possible; consequently, Kirkland recommended that Alec B. Stevenson, whose father taught Semitic languages at Vanderbilt, be offered an instructorship at $1,400 a year.[6] As soon as Stevenson returned to Nashville, however, he notified Mims that he had definitely decided to search for a position in business. At about this time Ransom called to pay his respects, and Mims asked him if he would be interested in his old position at the terms mentioned in his letter of the previous summer. Knowing how disappointed his parents would be if he left almost immediately to accept one of the positions in the East, he told Mims he would like to stay in Nashville. With this response Mims wrote an enthusiastic letter to Kirkland:

John Ransom . . . [has shown] up again, much to the delight of all his friends. I asked him if he would accept the position that you suggested when we had the matter up in May . . . and he has given a decided affirmative. He has good prospects of landing a position at Columbia or Mass. Tech., but would prefer Vanderbilt to any other place, especially for next year. I know that your reaction will be that he ought not to have been so definite in his demands in the first instance, but I think we can afford to reject this aspect in view of his remoteness from the scene of action. Under the circumstances I think we are most fortunate to get him. I felt all along it was a pity to have to come down to the choice between two men as young and inexperienced as either Aleck [*sic*] or [William Yandell] Elliott. . . . Ransom strikes me as finer than ever. His experience has been a rare one. He will make a most desirable member of our auxiliary community. He will be an indispensable aid to the *Alumnus,* having already served as Cason's right-hand man. He is on the verge of a decided literary reputation and will bring prestige to the department. He is splendid in Composition and brings to the department what we most need.[7]

If Ransom were appointed and Elliott given a part-time position at $800, Mims concluded, "the English department will hum next year. We shall be in a position to do the best work we have ever done. It will be a matter of pride to all of us." To make up for the difference in budget, he offered to raise the necessary funds "without asking a single man in Nashville on the Board for a cent." Kirkland agreed to Mims's proposal, informed him he would not have to raise any money, and Ransom immediately accepted.

Within the week Ransom had moved back into his old two-room suite in Kissam Hall, but he took his meals with his parents. He reached home the "later part of August," Ella Crowe Ransom wrote Aunt Belle Crowe in Sheffield, Alabama,[8] "as sound and well as when he left for France." The best news of all, she reported, is that "just a short walk brings him home three times a day." He and Curry, who also lived in Kissam, enjoyed frequent discussions of literature and

philosophy, and together they visited Sidney Hirsch, who now lived
with his brother-in-law, James Frank, at 3802 Whitland Avenue. Ransom's dissatisfaction with *Poems About God* had intensified his interest
in poetic form and for two years he had been experimenting with the
sonnet, sending his best efforts to Christopher Morley for comment
and criticism. Some of these suggest the basic attitudes, if not the
precise techniques, of the sonnets written ten years later and included
in *Two Gentlemen in Bonds*. The one enclosed in the letter of May 19,
1918, is a good example:[9]

The House

With such strong arms I shut my Love about,
She rested there; which was to me a token,
This was a house she could not walk without,
Securely bricked, and never to be broken.
Alas, the tight imprisonment was vain,
'Twas much too wide and physical for hearts;
When we had come most near, and scarce were twain;
We had not met; some soul and secret parts

Escaped the snare; and most unperjured lips .
That bargained sweetly for our soul's exchange
Must lie, and love be blocked with this eclipse,
That she and I would live and still be strange.
    And as for Death, whose stroke disservers men,
    What fool would make a firm possession then?

Although Curry was not committed to poetry, he could "write
good lines," as Allen Tate said twenty years later, and he and Ransom
began to exchange sonnets, some of which were discussed in the informal sessions out on Whitland Avenue.[10] When Donald Davidson
returned a year later, he was shocked to find that Ransom was dissatisfied with *Poems About God*. Copies of some of these poems Davidson had carried around in manuscript and read over and over during
his two years in France.

He had taken a new turn and was writing sonnets—mostly in the
Shakespearean form. In fact he and Curry had been engaged in a
kind of sonnet *flyting*—firing strings of sonnets back and forth at one
another in typescript. Ransom was apparently in the lead with what
almost amounted to a sonnet sequence. Later, I believe, Ransom, still
discontented, destroyed these numerous sonnets. I saw no more of

them after a while, except the one or two that appear, remodeled, in his *Chills and Fever*. [11]

When Ransom returned to Vanderbilt in the fall of 1919, his career as poet, though of less than five years duration, had already undergone some drastic changes. During the summer and fall of 1915, Ransom had become less intent on pursuing abstract philosophical discussions and more interested in talking concretely about a specific poem, often one assigned to one of his classes. Although Davidson could not have known then that he was observing the beginning of an approach to literature that Ransom would later give the somewhat misleading name of the New Criticism, he recognized his teacher's new and compelling interest in poetry:

One day of days I remember well. My teacher, John Ransom, beckoned me aside and led me to a shady spot on the campus near the streetcar stop called "Vanderbilt Stile"—though the stile had long since yielded to an open entrance. Ransom drew a sheet of paper from his pocket. Almost blushingly, he announced that he had written a poem. It was his very first, he said. He wanted to read it to me. He read it, and I listened—admiringly, you may be sure. The title of the poem was "Sunset." [12]

Shortly thereafter—and encouraged no doubt by the fact that some of his early verse had been accepted by the *Independent*, the Philadelphia *Evening Public Ledger* (on which Christopher Morley was a columnist), *Contemporary Verse*, a little magazine published in Philadelphia, and the *Liberator*—Ransom began to think of bringing out a volume of poetry. Although most of the poems were completed before he went overseas, many of them were revised while he was on active duty. The introduction, written in France, gives the basic plan around which *Poems About God* was organized:

The first three or four poems that I ever wrote (that was two years ago) were done in three or four different moods and with no systematic design. I was therefore duly surprised to notice that each of them made considerable use of the term God. I studied the matter a little, and came to the conclusion that this was the most poetic of all terms possible; was a term always being called into requisition during the great moments of the soul, now in tones of love, and now indignantly; and was the very last word that a man might say when standing in the presence of that ultimate mystery to which all our great mysteries reduce.

Wishing to make my poems as poetic as possible, I simply likened myself to a diligent apprentice and went to work to treat rather systematically a number of the occasions on which this term was in use with common American men.[13]

The introduction also reveals the author's discontent with his verse and hints at its early retraction:

Most of these poems about God were complete a year ago, that is at about the time when the great upheaval going on in God's world engulfed our country too. Since then I have added a little only, and my experience has led me so wide that I can actually look back upon those antebellum accomplishments with the eye of the impartial spectator, or at most with a fatherly tenderness, no more. In this reviewing act I find myself thinking sometimes that the case about God may not be quite so desperate as the young poet chooses to believe. But it is not for that reason that I shall ever think of suppressing a single one of his poems.[14]

Although the reader of the mature poetry may well sympathize with the poet's wish to suppress this early verse, its careful study is rewarding to one interested in observing Ransom's development as poet. As different as these poems are from the almost perfect lyrics that he would publish between 1922 and 1925, definite hints of that sophisticated poetry are here. These early efforts are fables, anecdotes, or simple little narratives concerned with the fleetingness of youthful energy and beauty, with man's dual nature and the vast disparity between what man wants and needs and what he can reasonably expect, or with mutability, decay, and death. The poet's dissatisfaction, it would seem, is not with the basic attitudes presented in the poetry but with the manner, the techniques, employed in their presentation. The scene of this first book is obviously Middle Tennessee, where Ransom grew up, and the speaker is the poet himself. Never again would Ransom write poetry with such an unmistakable autobiographical bias. But even more unpleasing than this obvious lack of aesthetic distance are the many instances of amateur craftsmanship: the flat and conventional diction, the sentimental tone, the awkward and ineffective uses of meter, the heavy-handed irony.

Although most of the reviewers missed completely the principal thrust of the book—a sensitive young man expressing his amazement, his wonder and awe, and his concern for the ways in which God makes himself manifest in the world—Ransom must have been pleased when he read the reviews, which his sister Ellene and Christopher Morley had saved for him and which he had not examined carefully until his return to Nashville. Although everyone found some features of the verse objectionable—several reviewers thought the poet's use of God was sacrilegious—it was reviewed by two or three well-known critics in prestigious journals. The reviewer for *Poetry* called Ransom a "brittle" poet and said he seemed to have a kinship with the Georgians because of a "deliberate child-like method of presentation."[15] He was complimented for his "terse phrasing" and his "sensitive perception of the psychology of a mood," but blamed for his "sincerity," which seems strained rather than real. Readers would have to wait for Ransom's second book, this reviewer concluded, to get an acceptable impression of his art. If the poet repeated himself, he would "pass into oblivion"; if he moved on to something different, he would likely "do it much better." Writing in *Bookman*, Maurice F. Egan thought Ransom was "groping for a new expression of the Infinite" because observation and experience have made him abandon the God of Calvinism.[16] Though some of what the poet said would be shocking, nothing was meant merely to shock; the poet was meticulously trying to give an honest impression of the world we live in. Not only was it an "honest book," it had a "really poetic and original charm." In the *Yale Review*, Charles W. Stork included *Poems About God* among six books of contemporary poetry given brief notice.[17] Whereas Conrad Aiken had "no story to tell and no ideas to express" and Witter Bynner attempted to be "cleverly cryptic," Ransom was a "voracious realist," had an "anti-social bent," and found the religion of "uneducated folk . . . ridiculous." The verse he described as "crabbed doggerel" and concluded that the poet needed to know a "bit more about life and a good deal more about poetic form."

The reviewer in the *Nation* gave brief notice to *Poems About God* in a review of seven books of modern poetry, including Rudyard Kipling's *The Years Between*, which naturally got most of the space. Other poets whose works were mentioned were Scudder Middleton, Clement

Wood, Geoffrey Whitworth, Aline Kilmer, Thomas Thornley, and Keith Preston—all of whom seemed to the reviewer to have about the same amount of poetic talent as Ransom. His comments on Ransom were primarily on the introduction:

Mr. John C. Ransom reviews his compositions, in a preface, objectively considering them as the works of a young antebellum poet, none of which, because of their honesty, he has the heart to suppress. One knows what a rag to the bull such a preface would have been in the days when the *Quarterly Review* was lying in wait for young poets, and we confess that it has given us a consciousness of how a Quarterly Reviewer felt. We seem to find ourselves (say) in Lockhart's seat, though without his memorably acid pen, writing somewhat as follows: "Freed from the prejudices of friendship, we should not have been quite so tender to these poems as the writer of the preface. We should have excised without a qualm the malodorous narrative of the death of the hired man, despite its ingenious *grotesquerie*, together with some trivialities, some blasphemies, and a few poems where the author has the advantage of us in being presumably able to understand their purport."[18]

The only poem this reviewer liked was "Noonday Grace," which he called "a country-life study full of character and flavor, touched with ironic reflectiveness." He concluded his brief notice by placing Ransom, along with Frost and James Stephen, in a group of young poets experimenting "in the colloquial manner."

In his review in *Dial,* Louis Untermeyer placed Ransom among the young poets reacting against "purely decorative literature" by establishing some previously neglected attitudes toward a "free but earth-planted naturalism."[19] The members of this school—J. M. Synge, W. W. Gibson, John Masefield, Rupert Brooke, Siegfried Sassoon, Carl Sandburg, Edgar Lee Masters—insisted upon a "return . . . to brutality." Although Ransom's range was small, his manner was varied, according to Untermeyer. "The lines run from the surprisingly powerful to the incredibly banal, from epithets that are forceful to phrases that are both flatulent and flat." Untermeyer concluded by saying that he hoped the "growing sophistication" hinted at in the introduction would not "over-refine a gift that has, for all its rawness, individuality, strength, and the promise of stronger things."

As Ransom read through these reviews, some of which were more than a year old, he must have been pleased that what he now described to Davidson as "my feeble, juvenile efforts" had been noted in such journals as *Poetry, Dial,* and *Nation* and that they had received the tentative approval of Louis Untermeyer, who was establishing a reputation in certain circles as the authority on modern verse. But he must have been disappointed that his intentions in the poems had largely gone unnoticed. Even Davidson, when he first read the poems, was uncertain of what his former teacher was aiming for. "The meaning of Ransom's poems," he recalled in 1958, "came to me dim and distorted like shapes glimpsed at the bottom of a Tennessee creek—clear yet wavering, most incalculably shaken just at the point of perception."[20] But after repeated readings while he was on active duty in France, though they "still blurred" his "exploring, eager eyes," he came to see in them the Tennessee country he had left. Davidson was coming to perceive what Ransom was attempting to accomplish, as the anonymous reviewer in the Vanderbilt *Alumnus* could not, although in some respects he was closer to the mark than Untermeyer and the others. That reviewer noted Ransom's realistic details of Tennessee country life: "The old swimming hole, the plain living and somewhat stern piety of the parsonage, the fields of corn and wheat, the forests, the country church and school."[21] But Ransom's purpose was not, as that reviewer suggested, that of the local-color writer; he was not trying to present the eccentric behavior, the peculiar beliefs, or the odd customs of the folk of a region in order to demonstrate their individuality, to prove that they were really unlike the residents of other sections of the country. Ransom was attempting, with much less certainty than he later achieved, to show the fullness of individual experience, to reveal in its rich and varied particularity the world's body. In a letter to Allen Tate a few years later, Ransom briefly explained his intentions.[22] He was searching, he wrote, for the experience that is the "common actuals"; if he could find it, he wanted to make that experience, through the natural associations it evoked, provide for the reader the "dearest values to which we can attach ourselves." Finally he wanted "to face the disintegration or nullification of these values as calmly and religiously as possible." *Poems About God* was Ransom's first battle in his continuing war against abstractionism, his first suggestion that all the knowledge man needs and desires cannot be obtained by reason and communicated by scientific discourse, that through proper study the duality of man's experience becomes apparent.

Throughout the 1919/20 academic year Ransom continued to live in Kissam Hall and take his meals with his family on Sixteenth Avenue. Although some of his father's clerical friends thought Ransom's poems advanced beliefs contrary to those of the Methodist church—and one had even said that the Reverend Dr. Ransom would not "even allow the book in his house"—all available evidence clearly shows that every member of the Ransom family was extremely proud of the young poet.[23] Ellene, with Annie's help, carefully collected all the reviews they could find and proudly presented them to him shortly after his arrival in Nashville. Ella wrote Aunt Belle Crowe in August, 1919, "We are very proud of . . . [John's book] and proud of the fine criticism it has received. We were very indignant recently at an article headed 'John Crowe Ransom's Poems not Orthodox.' . . . We were all indignant and justly so at this piece of *Yellow Journalism* and we are going to see what we can do about it." Before Ransom arrived in Nashville in August, 1919, his father had read the poems carefully and obviously more than once. In his copy, which he showed to Ransom, he had made copious marginal notations. As always, Ransom valued his father's reactions to his creative efforts and studied his suggestions with great care.

Ransom's life quickly fell into its prewar pattern. In addition to the regular lower-division course in composition and literature, he resumed his teaching of advanced composition, which he now described for the bulletin of the College of Arts and Science as "a practical course in writing various types of prose, including the short story, accompanied by extensive reading from contemporary books and periodicals." In addition to Curry, whose conservative literary taste Ransom valued, he found other stimulating companions, among whom were William Yandell Elliott and William Frierson, a senior English major. Although both of these brilliant young students would soon leave Nashville to take up Rhodes Scholarships, during this year and in subsequent summers they attended the meetings at the Frank house. Ransom's promotion to assistant professor gave him a feeling of accomplishment and made him think for the first time that he might be able to achieve his professional goals within the English department at Vanderbilt. Because he had been able to apply a large portion of his army pay to his prewar debts (during a long period at Saumur and later he lived largely on his poker winnings and sent most of his regular pay home), his present earnings were enough for his needs. And the money he gave his mother for the meals he had at home gave her the little extra money she badly needed.

When Mims notified Ransom in the spring of 1920 that Chancellor Kirkland had approved for him an increase of $300, bringing his salary up to $2,000, he was tempted to cancel his plans of going to New York in June to check again on employment possibilities there. But again he was noncommittal, and Mims returned to Kirkland with a strong plea that Ransom's salary be increased as far beyond $2,000 as possible. Because of his contributions to the department, Mims argued, particularly in creative writing, and his growing reputation as a poet, he was a very valuable man. Mims was delighted by Kirkland's response, and as soon as he received the letter stating the best offer the university would make, he called Ransom into his office and read a paragraph to him. "I have your report and have carefully considered all the arguments made therein," Kirkland wrote; "I have concluded finally to recommend a salary for Mr. Ransom of $2200, with the privilege of sharing the annuity fund if he desires. This is the utmost point I can bring myself to reach. I think it represents a very liberal advance on his present salary."[24] Ransom agreed and immediately told Mims that he would remain. The idea of "sharing the annuity fund" particularly appealed to him because for the first time in his life he had a position he could regard as permanent, one which increasingly during the next fifteen years he came to believe he would leave only at the end of his academic career. At least two developments contributed to this conclusion. The first of these was the fact that during the year the discussions at the Frank house turned from philosophy to literature, and with Davidson's return to Nashville in the summer of 1920, more and more of the conversations were concerned with technique, with the details of composition employed in an individual poem, often a sonnet Ransom had just completed. The other was his meeting Robb Reavill, a vivacious young lady from Colorado whom, on December 22, 1920, he would marry.

Early in January, 1920, Elizabeth Kirkland, the chancellor's daughter, invited three friends who had been at Wellesley College with her to be her houseguests for ten days so that they could participate in the activities associated with her formal introduction into Nashville society. One of these young ladies was Robb Reavill, who though born in Logan, Utah, had grown up in Sweetwater County, Wyoming, and Denver, Colorado. She had grown up around horses and had become an expert rider almost by the time she was able to walk. At Wellesley she played field hockey and later was amateur women's golf champion both in Nashville and in Gambier, Ohio. The other two girls were Harriet McDaniel, Mrs. Kirkland's niece from Atlanta, and Helen Huntington Holiday from California. As soon as the young ladies had accepted her daughter's invitation, Mrs. Kirkland informed the young bachelors on campus—Ransom, Curry, Alec Stevenson, and Madison Sarratt, then a member of the mathematics department and later vice-chancellor of the university—that she did not want these girls to be idle while they were guests in her home and that she expected them to be escorted to the various official functions. Not knowing what to expect, Ransom's acceptance of this invitation was less than enthusiastic.[25]

On the evening of the girls' arrival, the young men met them all at dinner in the Kirkland home. No attempt was made to provide specific escorts for each of the girls, but the group was congenial and got along well together. Although she saw Ransom and chatted with him briefly before dinner, Robb Reavill spent most of her time with Madison Sarratt and Alec Stevenson. When her breakfast was brought to her room the following morning by the Kirkland servant, it was accompanied by a sonnet signed by "The White Knight." She naturally thought it had been written by either Sarratt or Stevenson. When she made some allusion to the poem later that afternoon, however, she got no spark of recognition from either of them. The next morning another sonnet accompanied her breakfast, this one signed by "The Green Knight." Knowing now that the author of these formal love notes must be Ransom—she had already excluded Curry from consideration—she sent a present, a stalk of bananas, to his apartment, bought a copy of *Poems About God,* memorized a poem, and quoted it to him when next they met. The sonnets continued to arrive with each breakfast tray and she retaliated with a present—once she sent him a live duck—until finally she wrote a poem of her own (her first and last effort of this kind) and sent it by special messenger to his rooms in Kissam Hall. The next morning there were two poems on the tray. The first was hers, in the margins of which were extensive comments pointing out errors in spelling, grammar, and syntax, noting awkward diction and inexpert uses of rhyme and meter. Although he did not assign it a definite mark, she certainly realized, she recalled fifty years later, that he "thought it less than perfect." Her natural resentment of this rather unchivalrous treatment of her creative effort was relieved by the second poem on the tray. This one vowed lasting affection and promised "my heart and hand and all my punctuation."

The only time the two were alone together was once when Miss Reavill walked with Ransom the four hundred yards between the Kirkland home and Kissam Hall so that he could pick up a book out of which he wished to read her a poem. She waited out front for him to go in and get it—and did not even look toward the dormitory because she "knew boys lived there"—then went with him immediately back to the Kirkland residence. On Friday afternoon, after having been in Nashville for almost two weeks, all four of the girls went to Atlanta to visit in the McDaniel home for a few days. The following Sunday Ransom suddenly discovered that "things were rather dull in Nashville"; therefore he got the early train, arrived in Atlanta shortly after noon, and took a streetcar out to the McDaniel residence.[26] When he got there, he was told that the girls and some other guests were on the back lawn. After receiving their expressions of surprise at seeing him again so soon and assuring them one and all that he had come to tell them how much he had enjoyed their associations in Nashville, he invited Miss Reavill to show him around the grounds. On this walk, which lasted no more than half an hour, he assured her of his interest in continuing their relationship.

During that winter and spring they wrote each other frequently, and Robb Reavill's first impression was confirmed. This man for whom she felt such a definite attraction was far from ordinary. His letters were clever, interesting, and stimulating, and they clearly demonstrated that his interest in her was strong and personal.[27] After the spring term was over at Vanderbilt, he went to Memphis to spend the summer as a reporter for the *Evening Scimitar*. There he was assigned to write copy for the editorial page, most of which appeared unsigned or over the initials of one of the senior men on the staff. Although the assignment was considered full-time by the newspaper, this kind of writing came easy to Ransom and he soon found that he could spend almost every afternoon on the golf course. He had a pleasant summer, and he welcomed the extra money which would allow him to complete a plan that had been forming in his mind since January. For some time he had wanted to visit his brother Dick, who had accepted a position at the Grubbe Vocational College and moved to Arlington, Texas. In mid-July, therefore, he decided to go to Denver to visit Miss Reavill and meet her family, after which he would make the long swing down to Arlington, spend a few days with Dick and his family, and meet his nephew Stephen for the first time. When he returned to Nashville, he would bring his niece Ella Crowe for a long visit with her grandparents.

He thoroughly enjoyed the long train ride to Denver and spent most of his time in the observation car, as he wrote home, "looking at a part of the country I had not seen before."[28] When he arrived in Denver he was graciously received by all the Reavills, whom he liked immediately. Robb's father, a successful lawyer and a prominent leader of the Democratic party in Colorado, had been graduated from DePauw University and later studied law there.[29] A kind and generous man, extremely devoted to his family, he was most favorably impressed by the formal and courtly manner of the young professor-poet from Tennessee, as were Robb's mother and her brother Tobey, a 1916 graduate of Harvard.[30] Robb showed him the beautiful countryside around Denver and they took many long horseback rides together. Almost every day they played golf, and although he had played as often as he could for ten years and very regularly during his summer in Memphis, Ransom found he could defeat his charming companion only infrequently. Later, when he saw how well she really could play, he was convinced she had let him win occasionally to bolster his masculine ego.[31] During this week they made definite plans to marry, and soon after his return to Nashville, Robb set the date. They were married on December 22 and moved on January

1, 1921, into an apartment at 1918 Twenty-First Avenue, South, close
to both the Vanderbilt campus and his family's apartment.

During the fall and winter of 1920/21 the meetings at the Frank
home, which had become even more regular, were supplemented by
more informal gatherings at the Ransoms' or at the Davidsons' small
apartment on Adelicia Avenue. By the time Stanley Johnson returned
in September, 1921, to begin work on his master's degree, the meetings had come to follow the definite pattern described later by Davidson in his *Southern Writers in the Modern World*:

First we gave strict attention, from the beginning, to the *form* of poetry. The very nature of our meetings facilitated and intensified such
attention, and probably influenced Fugitive habits of composition.
Every poem was read aloud by the poet himself, while the members of
the group had before them typed copies of the poem. The reading
aloud might be followed by a murmur of compliments, but often
enough there was a period of ruminative silence before anyone said a
word. Then discussion began, and it was likely to be ruthless in its
exposure of any technical weakness as to rhyme, meter, imagery,
metaphor and was often minute in analysis of details. Praise for good
performance was rarely lacking, though some excellent poems might
find the group sharply divided in judgment. But even the best poems
might exhibit some imperfection in the first draft. It was understood
that our examination would be skeptical. A poem had to prove its
strength, if possible its perfection, in all its parts. The better the poem,
the greater the need for a perfect finish. Any inequality in technical
performance was sure to be detected. It was not enough for a poem to
be impressive in a general way. Poems that were merely pleasant, or
conventional, or mediocre did not attract much comment.[32]

In November, 1921, Davidson brought Allen Tate to one of the
meetings and again the nature of the discussions changed and in a
way that proved tremendously stimulating to Ransom. Since his introduction to the Symbolist poets during his last days in France, he
had been interested in literary form, in the use of meter and rhyme in
poetry, as he had since Oxford in the nature and function of poetry
itself. In Tate he found an unsettling influence that was most provocative, for Tate's interest in modernism was more intense and his
knowledge of contemporary writers broader and deeper than Ransom's. Although Sidney Hirsch presided at the meetings, usually from

his place on the chaise lounge, from the very first both Davidson and Tate recognized Ransom as the leader of the group. Not only was he six years older than Davidson and twelve years older than Tate (he had taught both of them), but he had published a book of poems and had moved much further in mastering his craft than either of them. "John Ransom," Tate recalled in 1942, "always appeared at the Fugitive meetings with a poem (some of us didn't), and when his turn came he read it in a dry tone of understatement. I can only describe his manner in those days as irony which was both brisk and bland. Before we began to think of a magazine John had written a poem which foreshadowed the style for which he has become famous; it was "Necrological," still one of his best poems. . . . We all knew that John was far better than we were, and although he never asserted his leadership we looked to him for advice." [33] Davidson's description of Ransom's role in the early meetings of this significant group of young poets is equally definite and convincing, as is his explanation of the reasons why Ransom was sometimes given too much credit outside Nashville for the work of the group:

His performance was authoritative, and so was his criticism. It was natural that some of the prominent public notices we received should single out Ransom, the already mature and published writer, as the leader of a coterie in which the rest seemed in greater or less degree satellites. It would be more correct to say that Ransom, the most advanced, was the first to choose his orbit; then others, one by one, found theirs, exerting great mutual attraction, with perhaps some repulsion here and there, upon one another. [34]

Sometime in March, 1922, Sidney Hirsch suggested that the group had written enough poetry of sufficient quality to begin thinking of publishing a magazine. Although, as Tate later said, it seemed to almost every member in the group, "a project of utmost temerity, if not of folly," the next month the first of nineteen issues of the *Fugitive* appeared. [35] To this first issue Ransom contributed three poems and a brief foreword, the latter proclaiming that "the *Fugitive* flees from nothing faster than from the high-caste Brahmins of the Old South. Without raising the question of whether the blood in the veins of its editors runs red, they at any rate are not advertising it as blue." He added that the phenomenon sometimes "known rather euphemistically as Southern Literature has expired, like any other stream whose source is stopped up."[36] One of the poems Ransom contributed under the name of Roger Prim (in the first two issues all of the poets used pseudonyms) was "Ego,"[37] which, though in the voice of the poet of *Poems About God,* does demonstrate Ransom's awareness of the importance to his poetic development of his associations with this group of young poets:

> You have heard something muttered in my scorn:
> "A little learning addleth this man's wit,
> He crieth on our dogmas Counterfeit!
> And no man's bubble 'scapeth his sharp thorn;
>
> "Nor he respecteth duly our tall steeple,
> But in his pride turning from book to book
> Heareth our noise and hardly offereth look,
> Nor liveth neighborly with these the people."
>
> With reason, friends, I am complained upon,
> Who am a headstrong man, sentenced from birth
> To love unusual gods beyond all earth
> And the easy gospels bruited hither and yon.
>
> So I bring hurt upon mine own sweet kin,
> And on my scholars, the young simple snails,
> Treading their tumuli to holy grails:
> I make reproach, and then these griefs begin.
>
> For no man loves to seem so small of grace,
> And I could wish me too born dull, born blind,
> If I might not estrange my gentle kind,
> Nor brag, nor run a solitary race.
>
> Friends! come acquit me of that stain of pride:
> Much has been spoken solemnly together,
> And you have heard my heart; so answer whether
> I am so proud a Fool, and godless beside.
>
> Sages and friends, too often have you seen us
> Deep in the midnight conclave as we used;
> For my part, reverently were you perused;
> No rank or primacy being hatched between us;
>
> For my part, much beholden to you all,
> Giving a little and receiving more;
> Learning had stuffed this head with but lean lore
> Betwixt the front bone and the occipital;

Anatomy, that doled these dubious features,
Had housed within me, close to my breast-bone,
My Demon, always clamoring Up, Begone,
Pursue your gods faster than most of creatures;

So I take not the vomit where they do,
Comporting downwards to the general breed;
I have run further, matching your heat and speed,
And tracked the wary Fugitive with you;

And if an alien, miserably at feud
With those my generation, I have reason
To think to salve the fester of my treason:
A seven of friends exceeds much multitude.

In its first issue Ransom wrote that the magazine would "appear at intervals of one month or more, till three to five numbers have been issued. Beyond that point the editors, aware of the common mortality, do not venture to publish any hopes they may entertain for the infant as to a further tenure of this precarious existence."[38] Actually during 1922 four issues of the magazine appeared, to which Ransom contributed fourteen poems. Eleven of these poems would be included in his next collection *Chills and Fever,* but only "Necrological" would continue to meet the increasingly stringent demands he made on the poetry that was reprinted in his later collections. But several other poems published during this year demonstrate that Ransom had made definite progress toward the disciplined structures associated with his mature verse. The occasional lapses into inexact and inappropriate diction, as well as the often amateurish use of subject, indicate that Ransom's mastery of his craft was not complete, but in almost all of the poems there are evidences of his development as poet. "In Process of a Noble Alliance" shows his effective use of a carefully conceived and almost perfectly executed dramatic situation, and some of the other poems bear the unmistakable stamp of the mature manner. In "Boris of Britain," "The Vagrant," and "Fall of Leaf," to choose some obvious examples, one can detect the poet's experimenting with such techniques as the oblique approach, the dramatic point of view, and the creation of a precise attitude toward his subject through the ironic and witty use of language. The subject matter of some of this poetry is that which has always interested Ransom: the dual nature of the universe, the transience of human life, the decay of beauty and energy, and the awful certainty of death.

Among the most important benefits accruing to Ransom because of his early association with the Fugitives, all of whom were much less mature as artists than he, were the opportunities he had to contemplate the *ars poetica* with a talented and serious-minded group of young poets, two of whom—Davidson and Tate—were as dedicated to their art and as intent upon learning their craft as he. In the formal meetings, as well as in the informal discussions between meetings and the frequent exchange of letters when someone was out of town, Ransom could present his theories on the nature and uses of poetry. He could demonstrate the validity of these theories when applied to individual poems, usually poems written by a member of the group, and he could always expect a candid and sensitive reaction to his own poems. This frank exchange of reaction and opinion Ransom always found enormously stimulating. As a younger man he had submitted his speculations on a broad range of subjects to his father and later, during his year at Hotchkiss, some of his earliest formulations about art to Samuel Chew. From Davidson and Christopher Morley he sought comments about his earliest verse. Now Davidson and Tate, and to a lesser extent some of the others, not only gave him the frankest and most helpful comments he was ever to have on his poetry, but they seriously challenged and made him defend his theories of art. The fact that his poems would be published in the *Fugitive* and read by discriminating readers both in the United States and in England surely encouraged him, as Davidson said later, to make the study and writing of poetry "the conclusion of the whole matter of living, learning, and being."[39] Through the pages of the *Fugitive* such important literary figures as Witter Bynner and Louis Untermeyer were first introduced to his mature poetry, and older literary acquaintances, such as Robert Graves and Christopher Morley, were able to follow his development.

As Ransom wrote Robert Graves on August 31, 1922, he was "more devoted to poetry" than he had ever been, although he had been able to write very little during his honeymoon year. The academic year 1922/23 offered, it would seem, even fewer opportunities to pursue the muse. During the fall term Walter Clyde Curry was given leave to continue his studies of medieval English literature in the British Museum, and Mims was away during the spring, teaching at the University of California. So that both of these men could continue to draw all or part of their salary from Vanderbilt, the other members of the department took over their classes. Throughout the year Ransom had sixteen hours in class each week. With his regular freshman courses, an additional section each term, and his two sections of advanced composition, he had more than a hundred composition students. With a load of this kind during the regular year and the necessity of having to teach wherever he could during the summer to meet his financial obligations, it was no wonder he wrote Graves that he was "growing a bit stale" in his "present unrelieved monotony" and that he had to seek a leave of absence so that he could get some of his own work done.[40]

During 1923, nevertheless, he published twenty-one poems (all but three of these in the *Fugitive*) including "Philomela," "Conrad at Twilight," "Agitato ma non Troppo," "Spectral Lovers," "Spiel of the Three Mountebanks," and "Vaunting Oak." He was rapidly moving into the period of his best poetry. During this year he was struggling, as Davidson has pointed out, to unite form and myth, to discover the "religious concepts and symbols that alone can validate the merely literary concepts and symbols and establish them as poetry in a realm impregnable to the attack of skeptical science."[41] He found himself, he wrote Graves in midsummer of 1922, "hampered and tortured" as he looked for a form to carry his themes.[42] He had tried the "modern irregular forms effected over here by some clever people" but had found they just did not function for him. His themes, he feared, too, would make him unpopular in some quarters, because he had to be honest in his poetry and he usually created the impression that he was a "rebel and a poor admirer of our beloved world." Ransom was telling the English poet that he was attempting to write poetry depicting his view of reality, pointing up the disparity between the actual world and the fantasy world of the idealists. He wanted to find the form that would represent with the greatest possible accuracy and precision the inexhaustible ambiguities, the tensions, the paradoxes and ironies that make up the world man must live in.

Through William Yandell Elliott, Robert Graves had been introduced to *Poems About God,* and he was so impressed that he wrote Ransom a letter of warm praise. Since he did not know Ransom's address, he wrote him in care of Henry Holt. When he received no response, he wrote again, this time sending the letter to Ransom's Nashville address, which he had gotten from Louis Untermeyer. In this letter he indicated again his willingness to help Ransom find a British publisher for his poems. Ransom responded immediately to this second letter, apologizing for not having answered the first by saying he must have mistaken it for a publisher's circular and thrown it unopened in the waste basket. He thanked Graves for the "kind things" he had said about *Poems About God* but expressed his dissatisfaction with the poems in that volume, finding them now "very juvenile in spots." [43] He enclosed a number of more recent poems, one of which was "Philomela," so that Graves could form an idea of the "sort of thing that interests me now." He concluded with a statement expressing his agreement with Graves's theory of poetic origins, at least as that theory had been explained to him by Elliott. "When a poet does something he likes," he wrote, "I'm sure it is usually because he has turned on one of his subliminal selves and let it do most of the work."

On August 31 he answered Graves's request that he be allowed to try to publish some of the more recent poems in a magazine while he was seeking a British publisher for the entire manuscript. "You have my permission," Ransom wrote, "to use anything of mine anywhere and at any time. And to retitle anything, or to edit as you please." He also enclosed a manuscript, which he was then calling *Philomela* and which he said was a "compilation from *Poems About God* and my later stuff." He could use, Ransom wrote, any part of this manuscript, which contained forty-six poems and ran to slightly more than a hundred pages, because it had just been returned by Henry Holt, who did not "raise the question of merit so much as that of market: 'in view of the continued low state of the demand for poetry.'" Although he intended to send the manuscript to Harcourt, Knopf, or Doran, he assured Graves that he would prefer an English publisher. The material had been arranged in order of composition, and if Graves could find a publisher he hoped this arrangement would be followed, because he thought it would show a "regular progress in technique."

Graves liked the new poems very much indeed and intended to use all of them in the revised manuscript he would submit to the publisher. The title, however, did not strike his fancy and he suggested that rather than *Philomela* the book should be called *Grace After Meat*.[44] Ransom immediately objected to this title since it emphasized "Grace," a poem he did not like because it was "too raw." At about the same time he sent a copy of the manuscript to Graves, he had mailed another to Christopher Morley, who had promised to find him a New York publisher. During the spring, summer, and early fall Ransom sent Graves new poems as they were completed and revised versions of some of those which had appeared in *Poems About God*. The discussion about the title continued and in almost every letter Ransom submitted alternatives to *Grace After Meat*, because, as he said in one letter, he thought " 'Grace' an artistic offense" and he would rather "pass for an artist than exhibit my history."[45] Some of the alternate titles he suggested were "Vaunting Oak," "Under the Locusts," which he particularly liked because it emphasized "about the best thing in the volume," and "Mortal Oak."[46] He insisted that Graves use revised versions of the old poems—"Cloak Model" and "Resurrection" because they "seem to need this revision"—and as many of the more recently written ones as possible. "Winter Remembered" was reduced from six stanzas to five because the form of that poem had never satisfied him. What now remained of it had once been three separate sonnets.

Just before Graves, with some help from T. S. Eliot, had convinced Hogarth to bring out *Grace After Meat*, Morley had lived up to his promise to get Ransom a publisher for *Chills and Fever*.[47] In high spirits, with prospects of almost simultaneous publication on both sides of the Atlantic, he wrote Graves: "You and Morley . . . are birds of a feather and a credit to ornithology." He also agreed to Graves's publishing "Grace" because "if you would like to have written it, my judgment is all wrong." No longer, he said, would he attempt to "prosecute my grievances against the Grace poem over your magnanimous protests. I've been extremely inconsiderate in bothering you about the title, and I bow to your judgment entirely." He assured Graves that the title he liked, and the one Leonard Woolf agreed to, would not "spoil the book" for him.[48]

Both Graves and Christopher Morley assisted Ransom at a time when even the slightest encouragement was a tremendous stimulant. On April 24, 1924, Ransom wrote Allen Tate that Morley had sent him "the most effusive letter of praises I have ever had, about my manuscript, and then spilled a little of it in his column in the *Post.*" Ransom quoted him as saying, "Have no fear: beyond the possible probable shadow of doubt I will get you a good publisher for your really glorious farrago." Within the month the manuscript was accepted by Alfred Knopf. Since during the spring and summer of 1924 Ransom was writing some of his best-known poems ("Blue Girls" appeared in the *Fugitive* for June and "Parting at Dawn" and "Tom, Tom, The Piper's Son" for August), as well as completing extensive revisions of some of those published earlier, he immediately advised Knopf of his desire to include in the volume some new poems and a later version of some of the older ones. Knopf's response that he would accept any changes approved by Morley pleased Ransom at the time, although this arrangement later proved slightly embarrassing. In his desire to make his poems as nearly perfect as possible, he could never refrain from what he later would call "tinkering" with them; consequently he made some changes almost on impulse—many of these he later retracted—and sent these revised versions to Morley along with some new poems. Unlike Graves, as demonstrated by his insistence on using "Grace" in the collection he was bringing out, Morley accepted uncritically any suggestion Ransom made. In late April, Ransom had sent copies of a poem which he was then calling "Religio Medici Kentuckiensis" to both Morley and Allen Tate, asking for Tate's reactions and requesting Morley to consider the possibility of including it in the collection. Tate responded immediately that the poem was in quality far inferior to Ransom's recent poetry and should be put aside for a while. Ransom assured him that the poem "has been consigned to oblivion," that Tate had merely confirmed his suspicions about it, and that it would have been retired long ago except that "Steve chose to praise it as a masterpiece." When he wrote Morley that in his opinion the poem was "unworthy" of publication, however, he was informed that it had already been sent to the printers. "I learn today," he wrote Tate, "that 'Religio Medici' . . . has been inserted and is therefore committed to posterity instead of oblivion."[49]

On July 4 he finished reading proofs for *Chills and Fever* and wrote Graves while he was still under the impression created by reading through all the poems at one sitting. "I like the looks of the book, in fact felt weakly tender over it," he admitted, and then added in an uncharacteristically cynical tone: "Then I thought of what the public would think; or rather, how they wouldn't be able to think anything; it would be for them a hopelessly hard nut to crack. For odd as it may seem to you, I can assure you that my simple strains will not find in Nashville, not even among fond relatives, nor well wishers more frequent than I deserve, more than two persons who will guess what I am after (I make loyal exception to my Fugitive brethren of course); and in the whole United States I should imagine there are not fifty who *could* read it with sympathy and not even ten who *will*." There were times when he wondered why he "should sweat for such an unessential cause."

These periods of depression could not long prevail over his feelings of accomplishment with individual students in and out of his classes, nor over the strong bonds he was establishing with the Fugitives and the lasting friendships he was making with some of them. He was developing a sense of belonging to a geographical place, a community, and he was happy to be among friends and relatives. But he was beginning to have serious doubts that poetry was the medium through which he could best express himself. Living as he was in an age of religious skepticism, in one of pragmatism, empiricism, and materialism, he wondered if he could not best serve art through a systematic investigation of the nature and function of poetry. Donald Davidson would later argue that no great civilization had ever existed without poetry and that reasonable men could not expect the modern age to be an exception. That conclusion could have come from the thoughts going through Ransom's mind, as those reflections were expressed in conversations with his friends and in his letters to Tate, Graves, and others. Someone must justify the existence of poetry in an age of science and technology, attempt to convince a people becoming more and more dependent upon reason that poetry is an invaluable means of cognition, that through it man can acquire knowledge he can get almost nowhere else. It is ironic that at the time he was writing his best poetry, when he was creating those almost perfect lyrics that would establish his reputation as one of the most enduring poets of his generation, his interests were already turning from poetry to literary theory.

Chills and Fever appeared in New York in August and *Grace After Meat* three months later in London. Both books were well received by the critics, most of whom recognized them as important volumes of poetry and many gave a fairly accurate account of the poet's intentions and accomplishments. All in all Ransom had much more reason to be pleased with the reaction to these books than he had to the reception of his first one. *Grace After Meat* includes twenty poems— nine were taken from *Poems About God,* ten had appeared also in *Chills and Fever,* and one, "Ilex Priscus," was previously unpublished. *Chills and Fever* contains forty-nine poems, thirty-six of which had first appeared in the *Fugitive,* and includes a large portion of Ransom's best-known verse; certainly it is an adequate representation of the years in which he was writing his best poetry.

Writing in the *New York Times Book Review*[50] Herbert Gorman calls Ransom a definite modernist and finds Christopher Morley's phrase about his "pretty and intricate savagery" an apt description of the tone of the verse. He also comments on his "sardonic humor," a "twist of thought that is phrased in measures that cleverly escape colloquialism and yet suggest it." Although he is certain Ransom would not like the comparison, he finds Ransom's poetry similar to that of T. S. Eliot in "a sophisticated obliqueness" and in "the delicate and slippery nuances of phrasing." E. A. Niles finds it "curious, charming, and irritating."[51] He quotes the closing lines of "Conrad in Twilight" to show the poet's characteristic manner: "an occasional sharp suggestion of Frost, a nice use with a sort of stilted grace of stately Latin derivatives, and a (generally less obvious) flavor of the King James Version." The best poem in the collection, he believes, is "Captain Carpenter," which appears to be nonsense but is the "most ferocious and lovely, and the most heroic, humorous and stirring" selection in the volume. He concludes a generally favorable review with the statement: "Mr. Ransom has plenty to say, and few words to say it in; he is not easy reading. He knows his business; it is not through lack of the word he wants that he will irritate those of us who like our rhythm or *vers libre,* prose or poetry, straight. And a little irritation may provoke mental activity; read him."

Rolfe Humphries is certain that many readers will object to Ransom's language—"clomb, concumbent, chymist, halidom, ogive, frore, springe, thole, fumiter, tumuli, litten—such precious antiquities as these make him a shining target for those who profess the virilities of the Fleshy Schools."[52] He has his own manner, a distinguished one; he writes "the long line" better than anyone else and has "a deft ear for the eccentric rhyme." *"Chills and Fever,"* Bernice L. Kenyon insists, "is a find to enrich any bookshelf."[53] It has "more substance" on any page than some books "contain in their entirety." Ransom is "daring of thought, dramatic, civilized . . . erudite . . . and esoteric." His verse is characterized by its "lyrical sophistication," its "whimsical agility in thought and words," and an ability to "say the most unsayable things."

In his introduction to *Grace After Meat* Robert Graves had commented on the similarities between Ransom's poetry and that of Robert Frost.[54] "In their manner," he had written, "we find an extremely fastidious art disguised by colloquialisms and a pretence of 'every-which-way' (to borrow Frost's own word)." In their matter they both are spokesmen for the "rebellious 'poor whites.'" Ransom, he concluded, is doing for Tennessee what "Frost has done for New England, Vachel Lindsay for his Middle-West, and Carl Sandburg for Chicago." In his review of *Chills and Fever* he continued very much in this vein, asking if Ransom's hometown of Nashville were not a "byword in the States for comic provincialism."[55] This kind of provincial self-consciousness accounts for the "occasional obscurantist quality" in the poetry, as well as for his "choice of ink-horn and feudal imagery" and an "attachment to the classics." His "provincial sensitiveness" will not allow him "to abandon himself" to the "spell of the nightingale" and his "self-conscious ironic habit" will not permit him to "go on any emotional debauch." He concludes with a "summary of his Ransomness": a "humorous turn of speech," a "muscular quality of both metre and thought," and the "periodic denotation of most unlikely and effective phrases." Both Davidson and Tate objected to certain qualities of Graves's review. Davidson thought his air of British superiority was "disgustingly obvious," that he had praised

Ransom at the expense of the South. Tate objected to the "poor-white" phrase and wrote Davidson: "I daresay John is quite as civilized as Graves."[56]

In his literary column, "The Spyglass," which was appearing regularly in the Nashville *Tennessean,* Davidson announced the appearance of the book and later gave it a full-scale review; in the review his antipathy to Graves's approach is obvious.[57] The philosophy of the poems, he wrote, is not a "growth of disillusionment or a maze of abstractions; it is an expression of a personal attitude toward the world, evident throughout his poetry—generous and inclusive acceptance of life for what it is, humility in the face of perplexing issues; a serious wish, essentially religious, to find truth; the creed of a fine-spirited gentleman, sensitive to physical and spiritual wonders." There are, he continued, fewer resemblances to Frost in Ransom's poetry than to Edmund Spenser. As the title of Tate's review of the book indicates, he placed *Chills and Fever* squarely in the classical tradition.[58] After an opening jab at Louis Untermeyer's putting *Poems About God* into a growing cult of brutality ("the cult hasn't been heard of since"), Tate stated Ransom's poetic intentions:

Now, as in 1919, John Crowe Ransom is a poet orientating his perception of the field of the Immediate—not the *petite sensation,* but under the conviction that the proper study of man is man, classically proper; but he is encumbered with the properties of an outworn and, for his purposes, irrelevant Romantic tradition. . . .

Yet there is no other verse in America just like John Crowe Ransom's. If one put aside the attempt to relate his work categorically to one of the two main streams of literature—an attempt slightly out-of-date but perhaps still serviceable—it is easily distinguished for subtlety of wit, ranging from a seemingly naive irony to impatient satire, and for a personal idiom flexible enough to carry these qualities to a variety of effects, often brilliant and always individual. . . .

Altogether, "Chills and Fever" evinces a mind detached from the American scene and mostly nurtured from England, indifferent to the current mania of critics for writers who "express America." If it articulates no deep essentiality of experience, it is a lucid commentary, whose properties aren't very detectable critically, on the shifting surfaces of experience. And it points, throughout, to a performance, more fundamental in vision and purer in method, yet to come.

Louis Untermeyer called Ransom "an imaginative poet, a technician of brilliance, a story-teller of power, whose flavor is as individual as that of any American writing today." [59] His music, which is "half-soothing, half-acrid," sounds a "new note in our lyricism"; yet Ransom, for all his talent and potential for greatness, would never be a popular poet. His vocabulary was "over-elaborate," his utterance often pedantic, and his speech too "elegant." Untermeyer concluded his review with what may be called the general estimate of a group of almost universally favorable reviews: " 'Chills and Fever' seems the best volume of American verse which has lately come to this reviewer's table. No book of the year—and not many of the last decade—has revealed a finer craftsman, a more sensitive musician, a richer personality. In short—if I may be allowed the uncommon extravagance of the capital—a Poet." But the most complimentary statement, perhaps, came from John McClure, associate editor of the New Orleans *Double-Dealer,* in which Ransom, Davidson, and Tate had all published poems. [60] "Mr. Ransom," he wrote, "has developed the intellectually expressive cadence to a point probably not excelled by any American—not even by Eliot, Pound, or Stevens, and certainly not by Frost."

Since *Grace After Meat* was published in England and review copies were hard to get in America and because it was compiled from the two previously published books of poetry, it was not nearly as widely reviewed as either *Poems About God* or *Chills and Fever.* Nevertheless it did not go unnoticed. Babette Deutsch included it and *Chills and Fever* in a review of four other books of poetry, collections by John Drinkwater, Edwin Muir, and Robinson Jeffers, as well as George Moore's *An Anthology of Pure Poetry.* [61] Although Ransom's name was misspelled throughout, [62] the review was generally complimentary. She disagreed with Graves; the most obvious influences on Ransom's poetry come not from Frost but from T. S. Eliot and Jules Laforgue. A poetry "highly wrought and deeply thought," it has both wit and sustained emotion. As poet, Ransom is "as strict, as difficult, and as rewarding as the noble game which is said to have been invented by the Indian Buddhists as a moral equivalent for war, and which may outlive a diversion that modern inventions have rendered somewhat tedious."

Edwin Muir discussed *Grace After Meat* in the new *Saturday Review of Literature,* [63] and although he found much in the little book to displease him, he called its publication the second most important literary event in recent weeks, the most important being the appearance of Edith Sitwell's *Troy Park.* Ransom, Muir wrote, has received adequate recognition from only one American critic (he obviously had not read the reviews of *Chills and Fever*), and a part of the reason for his neglect may be found in the kind of poetry he writes. If one looks among his British contemporaries to find the poet Ransom resembles most, he must inevitably conclude Robert Graves: "their ways of apprehending life and handling experience, their preoccupation at the same time with quite ordinary facts and metaphysical problems, their serious attempts to come to terms with themselves and their surroundings, their assumption of intellectual detachment as a means to this." Despite these similarities, however, Muir maintained that Ransom did not imitate Graves and doubted that Graves had seriously influenced him. Muir considered Ransom "bolder both in thought and technique" than Graves, as well as colder. For Muir, Ransom had what Graves did not, a "heraldic quality," which Muir defined as the "ability to translate experience into something which is half myth, half philosophic fable, and in doing that to chill and clarify it." But the strength of the poetry is also its weakness. This "heraldic quality," which makes Ransom's verse distinctive, is attained neither by the eye nor by the heart but by the intellect. The appeal of the poetry is therefore very limited; it misses greatness because the truly "great poet gains freedom from his sufferings by realizing them completely, in a living act of the imagination; Mr. Ransom tries to gain freedom by realizing them intellectually, with the passion of the intellect; but the means are too easy and the relief not complete." The kind of intellectual poetry Ransom writes had rarely been done as well since the seventeenth century, according to Muir, and he is "undoubtedly one of the most interesting poets of our time."

One can well see why immediately after reading this review Ransom wrote Graves [64] that Muir's was the most useful commentary on the book he had read, "the most philosophic statement of my position that I have seen, though not the most favorable." Not until Allen Tate's review of *Two Gentlemen in Bonds* two years later would he feel that a critic had come so close to identifying the main thrust behind his poetry. But he must have been pleased with the reaction to *Chills and Fever*. Not only had it been widely and favorably reviewed by most of the important commentators on modern verse, but many of these reviewers had made a serious attempt to identify his principal themes and to evaluate the technical qualities of the verse. Almost everyone saw the publication of this volume as an unusually significant literary event and Ransom as an important young poet. An indication of the kind of reception the volume received is revealed in a remark Ransom made to Graves: "By the way, you won't mind my saying what I would by no means publish to the general public: I barely missed the Pulitzer Prize ($1,000) for 1924, being defeated in favor of Robinson (who had already won it in 1922) because my work was offensive to one elderly committeeman who wouldn't budge to suit the others' wish, and who had his way because the decision had to be unanimous."

During 1924 Ransom continued to devote a lot of time to the duties associated with the publication of the *Fugitive,* as did most of the other members of the group. "It was the last year," as Louise Cowan has noted, "in which editorial tasks were performed in an amateur fashion, with the whole group still taking an active part in the magazine's affairs." [65] Ransom's explanation, in the third issue, of how necessary functions of editing and publishing were performed was certainly a characteristic understatement. "The procedure of publication is simply to gather up the poems that rank the highest, by general consent of the group," he wrote, "and take them down to the publisher." [66] Such a statement does not take into account the hours spent in meetings trying to decide which poems should be included, or the time consumed in reading and marking proofs and in addressing labels and mailing copies to subscribers. There was also correspondence to be answered and subscriptions to be sold. All of these activities took time which few of the members could afford to give, and a disproportionate share seemed always to fall upon the same few members.

Some of the Fugitives were also reluctant to have their joint efforts regarded as the work of one man, as had happened several times during the magazine's brief existence. Others were aware that Ransom was the only poet in the group with anything like a national reputation and were most diligent, therefore, in their efforts to avoid imitating him. As Louise Cowan has pointed out, however, "with his dry good sense, his cutting irony, Ransom was a difficult influence to resist and . . . all of the Fugitives acquired something of his manner and a few of his turns of phrase as well as some of his keen and original ideas."[67] In the third issue of the magazine the poets had dropped their pseudonyms because, as Ransom stated in a brief editorial, they were "startled and chagrined" when "two notable critics had concluded that all the poems had come from the same pen." When David Morton in the *Bookman* for March, 1923, referred to Ransom as editor, Tate wrote Davidson that he thought Ransom should make a public statement correcting the error. That Ransom chose to remain silent was especially irritating to Tate when a few weeks later Christopher Morley, writing under the pseudonym of Kenelm Digby in the *Evening Post,* had referred to "John Crowe Ransom's *Fugitive.*" From Greeley, Colorado, where he was teaching in the summer school of the State Teachers' College, Ransom sent the column to Tate and remarked: "Friend Digby has done it again, has put my foot into it, as you will remark from the enclosure. I send it in order to protest my innocence, and, with the hope that Sidney will not compel me to sign another retraction. Also, with my name left out, I should think these few words of his constitute about the best single exhibit from the press that we can boast of."[68] But Tate was not appeased and wrote Morley immediately that the *Fugitive* was not Ransom's "nor mine even, nor truly anybody-else's." In his next column Morley corrected his error.

This kind of misunderstanding undoubtedly prompted the members to draw up a plan whereby an editor and an associate editor would be elected each year. A slate composed of Davidson as editor and Tate as associate editor was proposed and approved by everyone except Merrill Moore and Ridley Wills, who did not vote because they were out of town, and Ransom, who expressed his disapproval of the plan both to Davidson and to Tate. "Every member knows," he wrote Tate, "we have no editor in the dictionary sense of that term; then we have no business publishing on a false basis."[69] His response to Davidson was more extensive:

Am this A.M. in receipt of a long letter from Jesse [Wills], with an outline of our new masthead and a copy of your modest and manly letter "to the Fugitives" dated August 14. A former letter from some Fugitives also contained a cryptic reference to "Don's book," which I have not seen fully explicated as yet, but I feel that I have basis enough for forthwith extending to you my heart-felt congratulations upon the accession of a publisher for your poems and to all Fugitives my felicitations upon securing you to run our affairs for another year.

At the same time I am not satisfied with our masthead, and must declare my intention of agitating for a change as soon as I can attend a next meeting; but in doing so, I cheerfully engage to abhor "strife and recrimination," to conserve my weak arsenal of "tomahawks and war-whoops" against a more appropriate occasion and to approach the question "with a feeling of good will."

I think our leader's title should be "Managing Editor," with the utmost deference to the happy selection of the person that has just been made. In a previous letter to the group by way of casting my vote, I said the same thing but too briefly out of a lack of time.

The new masthead, if Jesse has furnished me an accurate draft, is to show a list of thirteen "Editors." Beneath that appears the name of an "Editor of the Fugitive." I fail to see an accurate distinction there. It occurs to me that with thirteen "Editors," the only additional editor must be either (1) an Editor-in-Chief, or (2) a Managing Editor. I consider that the former is not the correct designation of the office whose duties were so carefully defined in The Resolutions, since those duties do not include what to the world and in the dictionary are the chiefest editorial functions, namely, a responsibility for the contents. The latter title I would think falls exactly into place but has the disadvantage of being somewhat the less a worldly honor and therefore may not appeal to an incumbent as worth the onerous burdens of the office; that is a perfectly fair question which the incumbent would have the perfect right to settle for himself.

If that is not a strong argument, it is at least reinforced by the fact that we have advertised extensively that we have no chief. Personally, I have written three editorials, some by command, and two personal letters, these I believe both by request and voluntarily, to make this point. More recently the official announcement was conveyed to Digby, who last week inserted in his column a notice concluding: "It seems that *The Fugitive* has no Editor, and is never likely to have, but is published by some thirteen Editors of whom one has as much to say as the others. . . .

In stating my personal and selfish attitude, I mean to pose only as an example of what I had heretofore conceived as the universal (or nearly so) Fugitive opinion. From the professional point of view, we all (with the possible exception of Curry) regard poetry as a potential source of profit. As an associate professor specializing in composition,

I know that *The Fugitive* is of direct professional importance to me. It is for that reason that I resent (if one can resent without feeling a personal grievance) a misrepresentation of the facts which permits the assumption that my own part in the magazine is one of less importance than that of some other.[70]

He concludes that this is "as systematic a statement" as he can make in the time he has. As always, Ransom's argument was reasonably conceived and persuasively presented. Obviously his objection was not against the person chosen but a matter of principle. In explaining why he felt he should not be relegated to what he considered a subordinate position, he demonstrates what Davidson means by his "literal mindedness." It was "a term he used," Davidson said, "just before rending to bits with calm, analytical pincers some too airy fancy that one of us had bounced into in a mere fit of rhyme."[71] Here he defended a most unpopular position with the same kind of persuasive earnestness that he would employ a few years later to present the case of agrarianism before largely unsympathetic audiences in Richmond, Chattanooga, and New Orleans.

That Ransom was seriously concerned about his prospects in the academic world is revealed through the many references in letters, conversations, and interviews to his being a "home-made scholar" with no graduate degrees and very little formal education in his discipline. He was well aware, too, that he sought promotions in rank and increases in salary through the publication of poetry and criticism rather than scholarship. So strong was his conviction, therefore, that he must have full credit for all of his efforts, even his contributions to the *Fugitive,* that he was willing to risk offending both Tate and Davidson, his closest friends. For a time, particularly early in his career, he had felt he must have an advanced degree if he were to achieve a satisfactory position in the academic community; consequently during the early and mid-twenties he made several rather half-hearted attempts to return to school. When he came back to Vanderbilt after World War I, he explored the possibilities of combining teaching and study toward the Ph.D. In his petition to the committee on graduate instruction, he requested that he be permitted to complete residence requirements in one year, at the end of which he would prepare a "thesis satisfactory to the Department of Philosophy" and stand the required examinations. To support his request that he be relieved of one year of the residency requirement, he cited that he had had a course in Anglo-Saxon poetry with S. N. Hagen in the fall of 1914 and one in medieval literature the following year. As work related to his area of concentration, he offered Greek and listed in detail the readings he had done in this area, both at Vanderbilt and at Oxford. Although his petition was approved, he never entered the program. As late as the fall of 1925, when he was preparing to submit an application for a Guggenheim Fellowship, he wrote Robert Graves that although he was applying for the fellowship so that he would have time to complete a book of criticism he also wondered if he might not "accomplish some kind of degree at the same time." [72] William Yandell Elliott, who had spent some time in Nashville the previous summer en route from California to Harvard, had told him that he could get a D.Litt. at Oxford. "The notion astonished me," he wrote Graves. "Is that likely? I'm sure I could do a Ph.D. at Paris and without any French residence to speak of, too."

One may well doubt the reasonableness of his fears or wonder how genuine they really were. He had been promoted to assistant professor and then to associate professor at about the time Curry had (and Curry had a Ph.D. and was producing important scholarship); so maybe he was becoming more confident of his training, interests, and performance, or perhaps he was reluctant to plant an idea in Chancellor Kirkland's mind. At any rate, when he wrote Kirkland informing him of his intentions to apply for the grant and outlining his plan of study if he received the award, he did not mention working for an advanced degree. Instead he indicated that he would complete a book that he had been working on for some time and which would complement "several detached pieces which I published several years ago." [73] The year's release from teaching would give him time to do some individual reading and study that would enable him to complete more satisfactorily his assignments in the English department. "I feel," he wrote Kirkland, "that I ought to take the chance of a year of leisure and foreign study.... At Oxford I worked at philosophy and the classics entirely, and my knowledge of English literature is home-made; I need a chance to do some study under guidance in my professional field, though I do not think I would care to exchange my

Oxford equipment for the usual kind of preparation made by teachers of my subject." He was not successful in his application for a Guggenheim grant for the 1926/27 academic year, but he was given leave by Vanderbilt, and he spent the summer and fall of that year in Colorado working on the first draft of "The Third Moment," his first attempt at an extended essay in literary criticism.

Even without the advanced degree and the bibliography of literary scholarship, Ransom could be pleased with his advancement in the profession. Not only was he making definite progress at Vanderbilt, where, as Randall Stewart has pointed out, the farsighted policies of Mims were setting a pattern for other institutions to follow: "It is interesting and I think unique at that time, and very much to the credit of Mims, the department head, that he passed Curry and Ransom, *pari passu,* through the various grades; that is he allowed equal 'credit' for a scholarly article in PMLA and a poem, for 'The Horoscope of the Wife of Bath' and 'Antique Harvesters.' This was a remarkable situation at a time when George Lyman Kittredge dominated practically every English department in the country."[74]

Ransom's associations with the *Fugitive,* the publication of *Chills and Fever* and *Grace After Meat,* and the favorable reactions they received, had brought him to the attention of the chairmen of other departments across the country. For the past four years he had been offered positions on the summer-school faculties of several colleges: among others, George Peabody College for Teachers, West Tennessee Teachers College, and the State Teachers' College of Greeley, Colorado. Although he felt he had to accept some of these offers, he resented the fact that financial necessity would not allow him to keep his summers free. In the summer of 1924, Professor Jay B. Hubbell of Southern Methodist University in Dallas, Texas, having read some of Ransom's poetry and seen references to the *Fugitive* in the *Literary Review,* offered Ransom an associate professorship, with promotion after one year, and a salary of $3,100, which could be supplemented by teaching in the extension division of that university at the rate of $300 a course.[75] At first glance this seemed to be exactly the kind of situation Ransom wanted. The basic salary, $500 dollars more than he was earning at Vanderbilt, supplemented by the income from two extension courses, would free his summers for writing at the same time it prevented the prolonged absences from his family. His brother Dick had recently joined the faculty there, and Ransom was delighted with the prospect of the two families getting to know each other better. The two brothers had not been together, except for occasional short visits, since before the war. Dick and his wife Ella had two children; and Dick's family was scarcely acquainted with Robb and their children—Helen (born January 17, 1922) and Reavill (born September 14, 1923).

There were attachments, however, that made him reluctant to leave Nashville. Strongest of all, probably, were the associations with the Fugitives and the deep and lasting friendships he had formed with some members of the group, particularly with Davidson, who already regarded Nashville as his permanent home, and Tate, who although he had left Nashville could be expected to show up again at any time. Ransom and Robb had also formed some warm friendships in the city itself. Robb continued her riding and golf, and she and Ransom had found a number of pleasant companions to accompany them to one or another of the excellent golf courses in Nashville. They had both become avid bridge players and had joined a club that played twice a month. In addition there were many informal visits among the members of a group of attractive, convivial, and social-minded business and professional men and their wives. At these meetings bridge was the usual game, but sometimes the group played charades, a game at which Ransom gained a reputation for stumping his opponents with clever imitations of characters or incidents from classical literature, legend, or myth. Ransom was also aware of his parents' increasing age and of the fact that they had come to regard him as head of the family, not only his father and mother but Ellene and Annie as well. And there were other, even more compelling considerations. "I decided to stay at Vanderbilt," he wrote Mims who was out of Nashville for the summer, because "I don't feel with my lack of orthodoxy I would be playing fair in accepting Southern Methodist University retainers. It might mean unpleasantness for me and injustice to my employer. So I am still here, and feeling grateful for the personal freedom we enjoy which has not been brought to my mind so forcibly before."[76]

Although he had already made up his mind to remain, he warned

Mims that he could not feel himself "a fixture" at Vanderbilt as long as he was certain that his "market value, even in institutions not open to the same objections as Southern Methodist University," was considerably above the salary he was getting at Vanderbilt. What disturbed Ransom most was the reception he received from Chancellor Kirkland, with whom he had talked in Mims's absence, while trying to make his final decision. Kirkland had told him rather brusquely that the executive committee of the Board of Trust "would not reopen the salary question at this time" and that he "wouldn't care to consider my promotion without consideration of the promotion of others." Even more disappointing to Ransom was the fact that Kirkland would make no promises about increases either in rank or salary for the future. "On the contrary," he wrote Mims, "as to rank [Kirkland] was sure at no early date could there be three professorships in English; rather [he] indicated that if revenues held up a salary increase of $200 annually (as for the past two years) would be likely." Although Kirkland had urged him to stay if he could, he had almost insulted him, Ransom thought, when he concluded the conference with the statement that if Ransom decided to go he "would get an instructor for my freshmen classes and parcel out the rest among other members of the Department!" It was hard to stay, Ransom concluded, "after such a blank reception," but for the time being at least "you may count on getting my most loyal efforts at Vanderbilt, and my warmest appreciation of your own liberality and support—a thing everyone of your subordinates is gratefully aware of." [77]

The next summer Mims took the occasion of an attractive offer for him to join the faculty of Duke University to explore the future prospects of both Curry and Ransom in the department at Vanderbilt.[78] The offer was so "favorable from the standpoint of salary and other personal considerations," he wrote Chancellor Kirkland, that he could not dismiss it as he had "other propositions in recent years." He was happy at Vanderbilt and for some years he had felt that he would complete his academic career there; but now, before he could respond to Duke, he felt he must know the chancellor's plans for the future of the English department. There are some indications already, he wrote, that the medical school and the sciences are to be emphasized at the expense of arts and letters:

When I think of the situation in my own department, I am frankly discouraged. As I understand, you do not see any chance for more than one full professor, and you hold out no hope either to me or to Curry and Ransom that they may expect any substantial increase in salary or promotion in rank. I am in grave danger any moment of losing one or both of them. Ransom is simply not able to make ends meet and would be forced to accept almost any position that pays more money. I wonder if you realize how valuable a man he has become in the University and how well established he is in the literary world. His work in composition can scarcely be duplicated in an American college. Curry feels under special obligation to the University for generous treatment last fall and two years ago and would not go away without very decided promotion, but it is only a question of time when we shall lose him. What I should like to know is whether these men may expect the maximum salary as associate professors next year and whether they may look forward to full professorships in say two years.

Kirkland's response to this request is not available, but he must have been reassuring. At any rate Mims remained at Vanderbilt, and within a reasonable period both Curry and Ransom were promoted. As Ransom completed his seventh year at Vanderbilt and his fourth since his return from France, he could be justly proud of his accomplishments. With no advanced degree beyond that from Oxford and little formal training in his discipline, he had received two promotions and several offers to join the faculties of other institutions. He and his family were comfortably settled in a roomy apartment at 1610 Seventeenth Avenue, South, only a short walk from the campus. With the "seven of friends" he had initiated and established the small magazine that now, with its editors numbering fourteen, was receiving national recognition and would in time become known as one of the most distinguished and influential publications of its kind to appear in America in the twentieth century. He had produced three volumes of poetry, the second of which had been very well received and had come very near winning the most cherished American literary award available to a poet at that time.

But, although he little suspected it, one phase of his career was rapidly closing. Within a year the last issue of the *Fugitive* would go to the printer and much of his best poetry was already written. Increasingly during the next year, and in the three or four following, his interest and his creative energy would go into a defense of poetry, not as an instrument through which one can "improve" or "idealize" the world, but as a means through which one can know that which he can know in no other way. Development of his most influential theories concerning the nature and function of poetry lay immediately ahead.

Richard P. Ransom, John Crowe Ransom's
grandfather, *ca.* 1885.

John James and Ella Crowe Ransom,
John Crowe Ransom's parents, *ca.* 1930.

Ransom's fraternity picture at Vanderbilt, 1904. Ransom is fourth from left.

Staff of Vanderbilt's literary magazine, 1908–1909.

Ransom in 1910, shortly after his appointment as a Rhodes Scholar.

Robb Reavill, at the time of her marriage to Ransom, 1920.

Ransom and his daughter Helen, 1922.

Ransom with Helen and his son Reavill, 1924.

Home of James M. Frank, where many of the Fugitive meetings were held.

Ransom in Colorado, where he wrote "The Third Moment," 1926.

Robb Reavill Ransom, *ca.* 1930.

Philip Blair Rice, Ransom, and Norman Johnson, at the founding of *Kenyon Review*, 1939.

VI The Ultimate Mode 1925-1927

IN MARCH, 1925, the *Fugitive* began its last year of publication with Ransom as editor and Robert Penn Warren as associate editor. The first issue clearly demonstrates Ransom's increasing interest in criticism, beginning a series of book reviews and brief critical pieces that would be continued throughout the year. But Ransom's speculations on the nature and function of poetry did not represent a major shift of interest. More than ten years before, during his year at the Hotchkiss School, his conversations with Samuel Chew had diverted his attention from philosophy and the classics to English literature. From that time on, his letters to his father and, a few years later, those to Robert Graves and Christopher Morley indicated Ransom's absorbing interest in aesthetic theory and particularly his conviction that only through poetry and the allied arts could one realize completely certain important aspects of human experience. This was the period, from 1922 to 1928, in which Ransom was engaged in what he would later describe as "preparation for criticisms,"[1] and these "preparations" consisted of his never-ceasing attempts to allow his knowledge of classical literature and philosophy to illuminate the systematic study of English literature in which he was engaged for the first time. His readings in the writers of the English renaissance were so broad and deep that by the end of the decade he was offering graduate courses in the poetry of Spenser and Milton.

Ransom's associations with the Fugitives, particularly with Tate and Davidson, were of inestimable value to him. In formal discussions at Fugitive meetings, as well as in conversations between meetings and in the frequent exchange of letters, he had the opportunity to give definite expression to the ideas he was forming from his extensive reading and, best of all, to defend these ideas before friendly antagonists who had the ability to detect any error in logic or weakness of expression. Ransom's letters of the time, and apparently his conversations as well, were filled with references to Aristotle, Plato, Plautus, Kant, Coleridge, Schopenhauer, Bergson, Freud, Jung, and Santayana. Many of the ideas given final expression ten or more years later were first extracted from this list of thinkers; then they were formulated and individualized in discussion and letter before they were given formal shape in a brief essay in the *Fugitive*. In October, 1922, motivated in part at least by the interest Robert Graves was taking in his career, Ransom published in the *Fugitive* a brief review of *On English Poetry*. Although he agrees with Graves's theory of the "social function of poets" and thinks the Englishman's study of the "psychological origins of poetry" is both legitimate and significant, the book, Ransom suggests, hardly touches the most important problem confronting the modern American poet. The question the contemporary poet must answer before he can seriously engage his art, he insists, is whether the poet can abandon his poetic tradition. Although Graves "accepts the limitations which prosody puts about his speech," most young American poets tend to give up meter before they have made a fair effort to use it. "They abhor the thought of changing the considered phrase that perfectly expresses them, in the interest of an irrelevance called meter." Upon this point Ransom would take exception with his countrymen. "It would seem at least likely," he points out, "that the determinate mathematical regularities of meter which are imposed upon the words have as much to do with the total effect of a poem as, in a sister art, the determinate geometrical regularities of outline which are imposed upon the stones have to do with the total effect of a work of architecture."[2] Although this analogy lacks the precision and appropriateness so characteristic of the devices Ransom would use in later essays, it does present most emphatically his conviction that traditional literary form is an essential part of the poet's art.

The next issue of the *Fugitive* carried a brief essay, "Whose Ox?," in which Allen Tate indicates that Ransom's concern that the contemporary poet has given up meter and rhyme does not represent the extent of the modern revolt against traditional form.[3] Modern artists are revolting against the "tyranny of representation" and like the modern painter, the poet feels justified not only in rearranging the images that represent "the constituted material world" but in "remaking, remolding" in a strictly subjective order the materials of the world he must work with. This essay and Tate's poem "Nuptials," which appeared in the same issue with a dedication "To J.C.R.," initiated a correspondence which allowed each poet to articulate in detail the theory of poetry he was developing and to defend each of its tenets against the objections that the other was sure to raise. Unfortunately only half of this correspondence is preserved; following a lifelong habit, Ransom disposed of the letters he received as soon as he had thoroughly read and digested them. In these letters and in an unpublished manuscript, which he always referred to as "The Third Moment," Ransom worked out his "general aesthetic of poetry, a kind of Prolegomena of Any Future Poetic."[4] These discussions convinced him, as he later expressed his obligations to Tate publicly, that he shared his friend's "views of poetry . . . with fewest and slightest reservations."[5]

In the first of these important letters[6] Ransom takes the occasion of the publication of Tate's "Nuptials," which he says antedates Eliot's *The Waste Land* and contains "most of its effective devices," to comment on Fugitive poetry generally and, through it, upon certain tendencies in most modern verse. "I think that most of us . . . are like jewellers' apprentices," he wrote; "we invent nothing; we hardly see the whole, but we are good at cutting the individual stones. Our patterns that we make out of all our treasures are either nil or they are perfectly standard. . . . Would it be painter's parlance to say that we can paint but we can't compose?" Then he comments derogatorily upon *The Waste Land*, which Tate had encouraged him to read; this reaction, when expressed publicly a few years later, provoked a temporary but serious breach between the two poets. "Waste Lands [*sic*] doesn't satisfy me," Ransom wrote, "though it is amazing. Do you recall that chapter in his prose book when he laments the absence of a form, from which void comes all this waste of the modern spirit unable to use its strength?" Herein, Ransom thinks, lies the weakness of Eliot's poetry. Although he tries for the form in poem after poem, he does not have it. In order to explain his precise meaning he gives Tate some "scattering (if not glimmering) generalities about a work of art," and presents the kernel of the critical theory he would develop during the next ten years:

The art-thing sounds like the first immediate transcript of reality, but it isn't; it's a long way from the event. It isn't the raw stuff of experience. The passion in it has mellowed down—emotion recollected in tranquillity, etc. etc. Above all things else, the core of experience in the record has been taken up into the sum total of things and in its relations there discovered are given the work of art. That is why the marginal meanings, the associations, the interlinear element of a poem are all-important. The most delicate piece of work that a poet has to do is to avoid a misleading connection in his phrasing. There must not be a trace of the expository philosophical method, but nevertheless the substance of the philosophical conclusion must be there for the intelligent reader. The artist can't stay off this necessity—can't hold aloof, be the impartial spectator, the colorless medium of information, the carrier of a perfectly undirected passion, the Know-Nothing from Missouri. I can't help believing more and more (it must be the trace that the classical pedagogy has left on me) that the work of art must be perfectly serious, ripe, rational, mature—full of heart, but with enough head there to govern heart.

It is obvious that Ransom is moving directly toward the description of the creative process outlined fully for the first time in "The Third Moment" and presented in final form in the essays written in the 1930s and collected in *The World's Body* (1938). The disagreement over the artistic merits of *The Waste Land* almost resulted in a complete break between Ransom and Tate, and although a reconciliation was finally effected—primarily because of Donald Davidson's dedicated efforts to bring the two friends back together—no letters were exchanged for more than a year. During the winter of 1922 Ransom had written Tate of his amazement that Eliot shows "so much wisdom in his prose while he favors a poetic vernacular that is utterly irrationalized,"[7] but Tate was not at all prepared for the almost completely negative review of Eliot's poem which his old teacher published in the *Literary Review* of the New York *Evening Post* for July 14, 1923.[8]

Ransom begins his review with an extended comment upon the nature of the creative process and how it works. "At one moment we are conscious," he points out, "but at the next moment we are self-conscious, or interested in the moment that is past, and we attempt to write it down. Science writes it down in one way, by abstracting a feature and trying to forget all the rest. Art writes it down in another way, by giving the feature well enough, but by managing also to suggest the infinity of its original context." There are advantages to both of these methods: that of science is economical because it attempts to record only the abstraction; that of art is more nearly complete because it records, along with these abstractions, the "tissue of the concrete in which they were discovered." The perceptive observer is well aware of the deficiency of the scientific record because—as the work of F. H. Bradley, Bergson, Kant, and John Dewey abundantly demonstrates—science cannot record the stream of consciousness, which is the "source of all that is." Art "fishes out of the stream what would become the dead abstraction of science, but catches it still alive, and can exhibit to us not only its bones and structure but many of the fine unaccountable motions of its life." Science often fails man, who comes repeatedly to the point where his intellect will not supply him with answers he wants and needs. At these times he must "abandon his problem to mysterious powers within him." If his abandonment is complete, he will find his answer. "It is a kind of revelation. He submitted facts and he receives them related into truths." For this process to be effective, the artist must rely on his imagination. He must not expect a predictable solution; he must abandon his causes. To perform his function adequately, a critic must have a theory of inspiration because his purpose, finally, is to expose failures of the creative imagination. The very future of art depends upon the critic's willingness to expose bad art.

With this last statement Ransom moves from a recapitulation of his general theories of art—none of which could have surprised or shocked Tate, to whom all of them had been recounted before—to a consideration of The Waste Land as a work of art. There can be no doubt, Ransom begins, that the author of The Waste Land has unusual creative powers or that the effect of the poem on certain readers is powerful. And the poem is definitely modern, its most obvious characteristic being its disconnection. It has many parts but no bridge to connect them. Even the interiors of each of these parts do not use the normal means of connection, "grammatical joints" and punctuation. It would seem that the poet's intention is to "present a wilderness in which both he and the reader may be bewildered, in which one is never to see the wood for the trees."

Against this tendency toward expository discontinuity the critic must stand fast; he must insist upon an art in which the imaginative vision has fused its disparate elements. Eliot was never able to combine the disjointed components of his poem because the fragments were "at different stages of fertilization." They come from many different tongues and are expressed in many different meters. Some are "emotions recollected in tranquillity and others are emotions kept raw and bleeding." Because this collection of impressions comes from so many different stages of the creative process, synthesis is impossible. Ransom also objects to Eliot's use of quotation. "There is not a single occasion," he argues, "where his context is as mature as the quotation which he inserts into it." Like many other modern poets Eliot is trying for novelty. His disregard for traditional literary form makes *The Waste Land* inferior to such early poems as "Prufrock," and "Sweeney," which seem to come from a disciplined and genuinely creative talent. One of the most "surbordinate" and "unequal" poems in the language, *The Waste Land* will not live. The English language cannot accommodate at the same time "two such incompatibles as Mr. Wordsworth and the present Mr. Eliot."

As soon as Tate had read Ransom's piece he wrote a letter to the *Literary Review* and sent a copy to Ransom in Greeley, Colorado, where he was teaching a summer term at the State Teachers' College.[9] Tate's letter clearly demonstrates his conviction that Ransom had used the most important poem of the decade merely to support his own theory of creativity. "John Crowe Ransom's article, 'Waste Lands,' in the *Literary Review* of July 14 violates so thoroughly the principle of free critical inquiry and at the same time does such scant justice to the school of so-called philosophic criticism, to which one supposes he belongs," Tate wrote, "that it may be of interest to your readers to consider the possible fallacy of his method and a few of the errors into which it leads him." First of all, Ransom builds up a "rather thorough-going schematism of the origin and process of artistic creation" and he argues that the critic "needs a theory of inspiration" so that he can "trace error back to its source." But Ransom has given nothing of the "psychological origins of art as a standard of aesthet-ics," about which he obviously knows little; what he has done is to offer "an abstract restatement of superannuated theories of consciousness." But the real weakness of Ransom's position, Tate argued, is revealed when he tries to comment on specific aspects of *The Waste Land.* Be-cause Eliot is a pluralist, he has not "achieved" a philosophy; therefore he is immature and his poem is of little consequence. Ransom's real difficulty is that he fails to see the form of the poem. Because it "presents meters so varied and such a load of grammar and punctua-tion and such a bewildering array of discrete themes," Ransom cannot believe it is one poem. The inability to see the reason for using quota-tions from other poems Tate can only attribute to naiveté. Does Ran-som believe Eliot used the quotations to achieve a beauty he could not achieve for himself? The effect created by the use of quotation is ironic and Tate ponders why Ransom would confuse parody and irony. Tate's final objection to Ransom's essay is that it dismisses Eliot without proper concern for his merits as a poet and, he concluded, "Mr. Ransom is not alone. He is a *genre.*"

On July 30, at about the time Tate's letter reached the offices of the *Literary Review,* Ransom received his carbon copy; he was so taken aback that he sat down and responded immediately. "Your carbon copy of the letter to Editor of *Lit Review* was a sock-dolager," he began. "Don't misunderstand me—I don't mean your argument—but the tone. You shouldn't do these things. Your duplicity is charming from an intellectual point of view, but there's also a sentimental one." What startled Ransom most was that the position Tate took was so far differ-ent from the one he had developed in previous talks and conversa-tions, and, it pretended "to such a topological state of erudition!" But rather than writing his reactions to Tate personally, as he had pre-viously done, he gave release to his feelings by writing a full-scale reply to the editor of the *Literary Review.* He sent a copy of the letter to Tate, with an inscription across the top saying that by the time it arrived in Nashville, it "may or may not have been sent" to the *Review.* (It was sent in time to be published on August 11.) One would think, Ransom began, that Tate's letter was written by an enemy bent upon destroying "such scant reputation for scholarship as I might have laboriously accumulated, but the truth of the matter is that the author and I have enjoyed a long and peaceful acquaintance." In fact, he said, Tate "sent me a copy of the letter with certain waggish additions for my benefit." Then Ransom described their relationship in a manner that completely infuriated Tate. For two years Tate had "suffered the damning experience" of being a student in Ransom's classes and the letter is but a "proper token of his final emancipation, composed upon the occasion of his accession to the ripe age of twenty-three." Ransom had always been impressed, he wrote, with the rate at which Tate's mind traveled, and he knew of no better illustration of this quality than his reference to "my superannuated theories of art, having as I do the most definite recollections which enable me to say that this superannuation, so far as Tate is concerned, has entirely taken place in the last three months." He closed the letter on a more serious note, but one no less damaging to Tate's ego. Why Tate had attributed to him a comment on the coherence of Eliot's prose, Ransom did not know, since he did not mention Eliot's prose in his review (although he had in letters to Tate). His opinion of Eliot's critical prose was that it is "vitiated by precisely the same quality that marks in greater degree the prose of Mr. Tate's letter—and the work of a whole sodality of younger critics—it abhors the academic (i.e. the honest and thorough-going) method, and is specious, after all, using its glittering scraps of comment and citation without any convincing assurance that the subject has been really studied."

That Ransom was provoked is evident from the bitingly satiric, almost sarcastic, tone of this letter. When Tate read it he wrote Davidson, objecting to its *ad hominem* cast and vowing to sever the relationship completely. In his role of conciliator, Davidson responded: [10] "I deprecate John's letter in the *Literary Review* very grievously,—yet I hope you will take the letter as not serious, rather as jocular, and either not reply (which would be preferable) or reply in a conciliatory and not controversial tone. The first sentence of John's second paragraph, which I myself first overlooked ["To the point of his letter I have only one thing to say seriously"] does indeed give ground for a nonserious interpretation." After Tate had had time to cool off, he notified Davidson that as far as he was concerned the matter was closed; nevertheless he would feel better if he had a note of apology. Ransom apparently wrote no such note, but when he returned in late

August the relationship, Davidson happily noted, was apparently cordial. For almost a year after Tate left Nashville in the late fall of 1923, the correspondence was not resumed and even then the first few letters have a tone of rather guarded formality. By mid-1924, however, both men were again reacting candidly and openly to points of literary theory presented in the critical pieces they were publishing in the *Fugitive* or to those raised in the letters, which again were frequent and richly detailed. Never again would these two friends engage in open critical controversy in print.

In February, 1924, Ransom published in the *Fugitive* a brief essay in which he admits that poetry must face up to modernism, a difficult assignment indeed because no one seems to know what modernism is.[11] It is a term too long allowed to go undefined. In formulating their program, the Imagists, who some would say represent the most significant traits of modernism, argued for "honesty of theme and accuracy of expression." Even a poem of a single image, if honest and accurate, was better than the most ambitious effort if the "conception of the diction came second-handed out of the schools." They also made their meters more elastic to accommodate the "spontaneity of the Word." In fact they almost gave up meter, and herein they comitted their gravest error. For, Ransom argues, it seems that poetry has to play a dual role with words; "to conduct a logical sequence with their meanings on the one hand, and to realize an objective pattern with their sounds on the other." Since there is no relationship between the meanings of words and their sounds, it appears almost miraculous that "words which make sense can also make a uniform objective structure of accents and rhymes." The total effect of poetry, he concludes, is the "sense of miracle before the union of inner meaning and objective form." The future of poetry depends upon the poet's ability to create, and the public's willingness to accept, a formal art in which an accommodation is effected between the "inner thought and the objective pattern" to which the artist has committed himself.

Tate carried the dialogue on with an essay in the next issue of the *Fugitive*.[12] Although free verse has lost its appeal, the explanation for this development cannot be found, as Ransom had argued, in the fact that the poet is able to derive meaning in spite of the "nearly uncompromising fetters of a self-imposed metrical system." If this were true, poetry would differ from prose only as a spectacle in which extreme difficulties had been overcome. What Ransom's theory fails to note is that poetry, unlike expository prose, is not concerned exclusively with logical statement; rather its intent is always bound up in "the pure presentation of intuitions or ideas." The language of poetry differs from that of prose, not because of the demands of prosody but because it must be "flexible enough to accommodate a presentation of the entire fantasy of sensation." One may conclude, therefore, that the obscurity of modern verse is not the result of the poet's attempt to make both sound and sense out of the same words; it is a natural reflection of the times. The modern poet lives in an age characterized by individualistic intellectualism. There is no longer a "common-to-all-truth" and poetry can no longer rely on "a harmonious firmament of stage-properties and sentiments." Modern poets have no experience with such things; some of them insist, therefore, that the only possible themes for poetry are their own perceptions. The breaking up of traditional idiom has come because much of this poetry is not based on spontaneous expression, spoken language; instead it attempts to embrace the "entire range of consciousness." To demonstrate this principle Tate refers to Baudelaire's "Theory of Correspondences," in which an "idea out of one class of experience" is "dressed up in the vocabulary of another."

Ransom's response to this argument was immediate. Within a week after the essay appeared he wrote Tate that he had read the article with much care and had finally "elicited from it some of the fine ideas which you have so precariously and prodigally therein hinted at." We agree, Ransom wrote, on free verse since we both admit that some writers, Carl Sandburg for example, may use that form if they choose because their "stuff is good enough to go down in one way or another." But since you admit that certain "paraphernalia" is necessary in the composition of verse how will you "escape my dualism?" You have not, he continued, confronted my basic point, which simply stated is that the "poet must (a) make sense and (b) with the same words make meter." No amount of investigation has revealed to him the poets who, as Tate had argued, "make sound patterns only to break them down again for a greater illusion of freedom." This statement cannot be supported "among the poets of the tradition" because those poets, even including Pope, look on rhyme and stanza as a "pretty definite, determinate pattern, and although they may hate their bondage, they realize that supplying the patterns is a condition of their art. The experimental poet will test to see how far he can go and still conform sufficiently to remain in his art"; some may even convince themselves that their poetry is good enough to stand as free verse. Although he likes Tate's discussion of the unavailability of great themes for the modern poet, the "Theory of Correspondences," Ransom protested, is the "most fantastic dogma" ever presented: "Shakespeare has a lot of correspondences; I daresay the Imagists have; if they (*vers librists*) don't, suppose they should—would they then be *vers librists* or moderns? And chiefly don't you imagine that I can cite you scores of modern poems wholly acceptable as such, which haven't a scrap of correspondences about them? This is really a most nonsensical differentia, my fine Allen!"

Tate must have responded immediately, for within a week Ransom had written him another letter. Some of his remarks, particularly his reactions to the Theory of Correspondences, Tate must have found offensive, for Ransom's opening remark is that his letter did not say "what it intended," that he is "staggered at the monument of discourtesy" which he has erected.[13] "I wasn't at all consciously in any belittling attitude," he wrote, "as I surveyed your article and tried to collect my fugitive thoughts." He realizes now, he continued, that his emphasis was too negative, that he failed to comment sufficiently on the many points of merit the article contained and, above all, he failed to point out, as he certainly was aware, that Tate had undertaken a subject "of which the inherent difficulty made a full exposition impossible in the limits assigned you." Ransom wanted, he insisted, a free and candid exchange of opinion because he badly felt the need to give his "aesthetic theories an airing" and he had no other "victim." "It is possible," he concluded, "that I am one of the most accessible responses you yourself can find when you are similarly engaged." Ransom, it would seem, was trying to avoid a repetition of the "Waste Land" controversy, even in their private correspondence.

From Lumberport, West Virginia, where he taught in the high school for a term before going on to New York, Tate was carrying on a regular correspondence with Ransom, Warren, and Davidson. From the latter two, particularly Davidson, he was able to keep informed of the activities of the Fugitives, and from Ransom, to receive a prompt and intelligent reaction to his speculations on the purpose and function of artists and the arts in the modern world. For Ransom this correspondence with Tate, who was virtually the only person Ransom continued a friendship with over the course of a period longer than a particular stage, was undoubtedly the most fruitful of his career. During the twenties and thirties if Ransom were away from Nashville for an extended period, as he was in most summers, he and Davidson corresponded about Fugitive and Agrarian matters. Most of the letters he exchanged with Andrew Lytle were written during his Agrarian phase, and those with Warren or Cleanth Brooks usually concerned affairs related to the *Southern Review* or the *Kenyon Review*. But the correspondence with Tate continued with few interruptions over a period of fifty years. One can only speculate on why this relationship was one of the most permanent of Ransom's life. In the first place their feelings for each other, based firmly in mutual respect, developed into warm affection. They found very early, too, that their discussions of aesthetic theory were tremendously beneficial to both of them. Both were convinced that the commonly held belief in scientific knowledge as final authority was the supreme enemy of poetry and the allied arts; and as each struggled to develop his theory of the nature and function of poetry, he found the other his most reliable critic, the one person from whom he could always expect a candid and well-reasoned response to any argument, no matter how speculative. In the preface to *The World's Body* Ransom described how he thought this exchange of ideas affected both of them: "When the talk was at a certain temperature," observations came to the surface "in a manner to illustrate the theory of anonymous or communal authorship." After the critical theories of both men were fully developed, other motivations emerged to complement friendship as a stimulus in keeping the correspondence going. Ransom valued Tate's opinion on a very broad spectrum of matters related to the *Kenyon Review*, ranging from basic editorial policies through prospective contributors to means of raising funds to keep the journal going. When he was asked many years later to speculate on the reasons for their long personal relationship, Tate said he felt that after a while his range of acquaintance in the literary world was so wide that Ransom had a selfish interest in continuing the correspondence. Through him, Tate was convinced, Ransom could keep up with what was going on in the literary world with a degree of ease and thoroughness that he could not otherwise accomplish. Although this kind of behavior was self-serving, perhaps, and in a way cruel to others, it was, Tate insisted, "part of the man's logical system and done unwittingly in large part."[14]

In some of his letters of the middle twenties, like the one of May 6, 1924, Ransom assured Tate that his presence was sorely missed at the Fugitive meetings, that "he was a priceless value to a dull and stodgy group," and that so far as he could determine there seemed to be little inclination to discontinue the magazine. But this kind of personal detail is almost always subordinated to the points of literary theory, which each letter carefully presented and which were always scrutinized and answered in detail. Through these letters it is possible to trace step-by-step the development of some of Ransom's most important critical ideas. After a careful reading of "The Future of Poetry" Tate had indicated his conviction that twentieth-century poetry can be understood only after a close study of three characteristics: the formal, the philosophical, and the rhetorical, the last being another way of referring to what he had previously called the "correspondences." Ransom was primarily concerned in his article with the formal aspects of poetry, and he thought that Tate's "One Escape from the Dilemma" was concentrating on the same area. He could not see, therefore, how Tate's suggestions regarding the "Theory of Correspondences" could be of much help in addressing the problems confronting the poet who is trying to make his words conform to a predetermined pattern of sound at the same time that they must carry along a consciously developed meaning. "I thought your performance," he wrote, "was dialectical and a priori; you wanted to establish a mode of compromise which would escape an ugly dilemma." Even now, when he understood that Tate was referring to a specific group of poets and identifying their "several distinguishing marks," Ransom still insisted on the significance of literary form. The traditional poets have always agreed on a "common conception of form," he argued, and it is this form which the modern poet is disregarding. Although "philosophies and rhetorical modes may come and go," the artist must always be mindful of form because "an art defines itself as an adventure in a given form."

These letters, too, were sprinkled with extensive comments on matters of style, from which one may get a clear impression of why some of Ransom's writing students have said he was their most helpful instructor. The following passage from the same letter is just one of many such examples:

I feel that you are in contact with red-hot truth, for you continually drop glowing and impressive sparks whenever you wax critical. But you tend to rely successively on the sparks, when you want a continuous blaze. In other words, you get hold of a beautiful intuition and immediately antagonize your followers by founding a Church thereon; when the probability is, you have stopped considerably short of the core of truth and are naming some accidental relation or other as *The Fundamentals.* I should think you ought to get your own consent to a little subordination among your (seemingly) perfectly insubordinate ideas. It is poetic, modern, and pluralistic to exalt each in turn to the pinnacle; but the net result is confusion, which I feel is not really your purpose in prose, at any rate. Why are you not more provisional, tentative, qualified, disparaging, as you contemplate the Stream of your Ideas? It may be my expectation is quite commonplace and pedagogical, but I have been expecting all these years to find from you a piece of critical prose that has a single leading idea, one that lends itself to a rather plain statement, and treated at a length which will allow for about a thousand brilliant excursions hither and yon, but with so much resolution that from everyone of these excursions you can effect your safe return.

During the last year of its existence the *Fugitive* provided Ransom the opportunity to express for the first time formally the critical ideas that he had been slowly developing for more than ten years. In the first of these essays[15] he confronts the problem of the complexity of modern verse, its tendency to veer toward the obscure and the esoteric. Many modern critics, he begins, follow Plato's erroneous example of excluding all but the pure and simple modes of art. Those who adhere closely to this doctrine will miss much of the best of modern verse, for many present-day poets are trying to refute the idea that poetry is the act of a child. The easy poetry of the past century is often thought to be the English tradition. In spite of dexterous craftsmanship, Tennyson's poetry is simpler than most readers believe, and Browning's is complicated only by its grammar and syntax, not to mention the "nonsense melodies of Swinburne and the sinister naiveté of the pre-Raphaelites." Neither Byron, Keats, nor Shelley ever really grew up, although Keats missed writing the second English epic because he undertook that formidable task when he was too young. In retrospect we can see that no one in that entire century was able to put his whole mind and experience into the writing of poetry, as Chaucer, Milton, Shakespeare, and Spenser had.

Because of this shortened view and a mistaken conception of what constitutes the English literary tradition, Ransom continues, some commentators still insist that youth is the age of poetry, and some poets, if not young, cultivate "an ingenuous and callow simplicity." As a consequence many mature readers no longer read poetry—H. L. Mencken says its only purpose is to put him to sleep and Maxwell Bodenheim assigns the same attitude to the entire modern public— and the poets who are interested in "stating their own minds" are labeled "willful and obscure." We must rise up against the romantic notion that "wisdom comes out of the mouth of a child" and proclaim the truth: the mind is an entity of slow growth and its "deliverances are profitable only when it is mature, wise, and sincere." If poetry is to be an activity of sufficient value to engage the mind of an adult, the "poets must report their own mixed modes" and not attempt "to simplify or purify them." This attitude Ransom would express nearly fifteen years later in the preface to *The World's Body*, where he calls for a "post-scientific" poetry, one that will engage all of the faculties of men who "have aged" in the "pure intellectual disciplines."

In the next issue of the *Fugitive* Ransom published "Thoughts on the Poetic Discontent," the most influential of these early essays.[16] Here he is concerned with dualism, which he will continue to argue is the essential nature of the world in which man must live. Since the dualist is said to be a "practical man whose mind has no philosophical quality," not many poets are satisfied with dualism. Nevertheless, Ransom suggests, it may be that man begins his life as a dualist, realizing the difference between the spiritual world within and the objective world without. In this first stage he does not regard the world as particularly sympathetic, he sees it as fairly plastic to his will and believes that through special attention and diligence he can have it minister to his happiness. He looks upon the world as "a wilderness which may [be] transformed into a garden, a habitat which has the makings of a home." When it becomes apparent that he cannot control the world, he turns to philosophy and metaphysics. Seeing that he cannot "impose his will upon Nature," man comes to the conclusion that his "personal identity" will be annihilated by superior forces. He then enters the second stage of his development and surrenders "the idea of his own dominating personality in exchange for the more tenable idea that he is in some manner related by ties of creation to the world, and entitled to some share in the general patrimony." In this stage, Ransom argues, man finds a mystical community, one in which God has placed both man and nature in a strictly controlled universe. The poet begins to "note every sign of understanding on Nature's part, and his songs are filled with 'pathetic fallacies.'" He is forever trying to escape an isolation which he finds unendurable.

Fortunately, he does not remain content in this state for long and the "romantic constructions of his mysticism" do not last. As his reason develops, he falls under the "sober observations of his science" and his illusions are punctured. Since he can no longer accept his own romantic treatment of nature, he realizes his songs are filled with pathetic fallacies and advances to the third stage of his development. Although there is a reaffirmation of dualism, it is not merely a return to his first position, for now he is "a dualist with a difference." Now he is "reluctant, speculative, sophisticated rather than ingenuous, and richer by all the pathetic fallacies he ever entertained." His state now is one of a matured and informed dualism.

Much poetry has been composed by poets who never advanced beyond the second of these three stages; for example, nearly all that of the nineteenth century. Byron's return to dualism was characterized by an almost completely destructive bitterness, and Wordsworth, Shelley, Tennyson, and Browning found "sufficiency in their romantic escapes." The earlier and greater poets—Chaucer, Spenser, Shakespeare, Donne, and Milton—all had their share of romantic adventures, but they "turned back to the stubborn fact of dualism with a mellow wisdom which we may call irony." Irony is the "ultimate mode of the great minds" because it "presupposes the others";

it implies, first of all, a "strenuous period of romantic creation," then a rejection of all romantic forms. This rejection is not easy and it is not complete:

[It] is so unwilling, and in its statements there lingers so much of the music and color and romantic mystery which is perhaps the absolute poetry, and this statement is attended by such a disarming rueful comic sense of the poet's own betrayal, that the fruit of it is wisdom and not bitterness, poetry and not prose, health and not suicide. Irony is the rarest of the states of mind, because it is the most inclusive; the whole mind has been active in arriving at it, both creation and criticism, both poetry and science.

This essay and "A Doctrine of Relativity" (which appeared in the *Fugitive* for September, 1925) clearly demonstrate that Ransom is very near to establishing critical positions he will never abandon.[17] In the latter essay he argues that a poem embodies many meanings. There is more to it than its fable, which may not be as innocent as it looks, for as one reads through it there will likely be a dozen or more terms to "take the mind away into passionate excursions." It is at this point that the differences between poetry and science are most obvious. Poetry uses the "widest possible" terms, science the narrowest; and these poetic terms attempt to "evoke in our memories the deepest previous experience." Unlike the scientist the poet's processes are not restricted to the rational; his references are always "free and personal," those of the scientist "fixed and ideal." For this reason a poem often connotes something different to various readers and something different from what it meant to the poet. Though the poem may look innocent, it records an "intricate historical experience," and the poet can hope for it to be intelligible only to those "whose history is tangled in just the same way as the poet's." The poet who tries to appeal to the widest possible audience generalizes and simplifies his experience until it becomes trite and useless. Although there are no universal standards by which poetry may be judged, it is saved from being chaotic because its form and content are based on tradition. "It is a familiar art, and we all know what to look for and how to read it when we see a fresh specimen."

As Ransom worked steadily toward the aesthetic principles upon which he would establish the ontological theories that would influence an entire generation of critics, he gave less and less attention to his own poetry, but his teaching career at Vanderbilt developed surely and steadily. His courses, "Advanced Composition" and "The Literature of Our Own Age," were well attended; in fact there were always many more students in the writing class than he could accommodate. Although he had allowed as many as thirty students to enroll in a class, he had been forced to add a second section. In addition to these upper-division classes, he continued to carry a heavy schedule of freshman composition. Every term he had from fifty-five to sixty students in the freshman writing class, all of whom were expected to submit an original composition each week; and in certain instances, when some member of the department was on leave or when there was an unexpected resignation in midyear, he was asked to take on another section of twenty-five or thirty freshman students. He also served on several important university committees. During this period he was a member of the Rhodes Scholarship selection committee for Tennessee and every third year, when the committee met in Nashville, he made all local arrangements and entertained the group on the Vanderbilt campus. As Vanderbilt prepared for its semicentennial celebration, many faculty members, Ransom among them, were given time-consuming committee appointments. Ransom's specific assignment was to chair the committee on publicity and invitations, in which capacity he was expected to send official letters of invitation to all guests from outside the university and to prepare appropriate announcements, news items, and feature stories for the *Alumnus* and other news media. With these heavy demands upon his time and energy during the academic year and his summer visiting assignments at the Colorado State Teachers' College, it is no wonder that he wrote Andrew Lytle that he needed some "loafing and gentle leisure"[18] or that he complained to Robert Graves that he was getting a "little bit stale in my present unrelieved monotony."[19]

During the Thanksgiving break Ransom read proofs for the final issue of the *Fugitive,* including the long editorial he had prepared explaining the reasons for the discontinuance of the magazine. "This action is taken," he had written, "because there is no available Editor to take over the administrative duties incidental to the publication of a periodical of even such limited scope as the *Fugitive.* The Fugitives are busy people, for the most part enslaved to Mammon, their time used up in vulgar bread-and-butter occupations. Not one of them is in a position to offer himself on the altar of sacrifice."[20] Unlike most little magazines of that time, and indeed of all times, the *Fugitive* was in no particular financial strain. As a matter of fact, because of the generosity of a list of patrons—including the Associated Retailers of Nashville, Ward Belmont College, and Joel Cheek, a wealthy local financier—the financial condition of the magazine was sounder than it had ever been, except during the period when Jacques Back had "conducted the entire business management." Of even more importance, and here Ransom seems on safe ground, was the fact that there was no evidence that the members of the group were any "more bankrupt in creative energy than in money." The quality of the poetry in the last issue, in fact, is very high (including, among others, Ransom's "Lost Lady," Hart Crane's "LaChrymae Christi," Robert Graves's "The Corner-Knot," and Laura Riding's "Sonnets in Memory of Samuel"), and there was enough material on hand for several more issues. The truth of the matter was, as Ransom admitted, he was more reluctant than ever to give to the magazine the amount of time required to produce and distribute it; and this attitude was shared by Davidson, who, with both Tate and Warren out of town and with Ransom's interest lagging, would have to bear the principal burden of editing and publishing the magazine. Of even more significance, perhaps, was the fact that Davidson, like Ransom, was no longer interested in using the *Fugitive* as a means of publication. He was no longer writing the kind of brief lyric the magazine could publish, and Ransom's creative energy was going more and more into philosophic and aesthetic inquiry.

Since his marriage five years earlier, Ransom had planned a trip to England so that he could introduce Robb to a people and a culture he much admired. Now that his friendship with Robert Graves was well established, he wanted to get near enough to Graves so that the two of them could discuss some of the literary theories that were boiling in his head. "I've given a lot of thought—mostly of an unsystematic, recurrent kind—to the poetic problem these last few months," he wrote Graves on June 12; "I have noticed that you and I don't entirely speak the same language in aesthetics." Since he had just begun to do "some very severe writing on these matters," he was beginning to realize the "profit in handling the thing in new terms." He was convinced that he could learn much from Graves and he badly needed the leisure to get his ideas down in publishable form. Another person he wanted to meet was T. S. Eliot, whose critical prose he was now reading in earnest. He had just finished *Homage to John Dryden* and gave it an enthusiastic endorsement, but as he read Eliot he was more concerned than ever that he did not have more time for his own work. "He confirms many of my own ideas," he wrote Graves, "or beats me to them."[21]

As the summer passed he continued to talk about a year abroad, and Robb became so sanguine that she began to read all the travel books about England she could get her hands on. They were "both anxious to try country life and take things quietly." If possible, they would like to find a place near Oxford where Ransom could study for an advanced degree, if the necessary details could be worked out, but most of all he wanted to write and do a "lot of cycling, tramping, boating, and golfing."[22] After as much investigation as he could do from Nashville and an extended discussion with Christopher Morley by letter, he decided to apply for a Guggenheim Fellowship, if he could get leave from Vanderbilt and the support of Morley and Graves. On September 23 he wrote Graves:

I have in mind a year in England, contingent to a considerable degree. If things look right I'm going to try to get a Guggenheim Fellowship for the school year 1926–27. That is like the Rhodes Scholarship a little, but much better in terms, and quite elastic in purpose. The Board invites you to submit your subject and plan of study; you must be specific and they decide whether your thesis is a valuable looking one and whether you are the man who could work it out. They profess to give special consideration to those who practice the creative arts. Probably I could get one; I know some of the Board, but I'll need to have (a) a good plan of work and (b) some strong letters about my capacity. If your conscience doesn't titillate too readily, I'm wondering if you might do me one of the latter. I'm sure you could help me with the former.

Apparently he decided that "things looked right" for on January 2, 1926, he wrote Chancellor Kirkland that he had applied for the fellowship and had submitted his name among his references. After informing him that if the fellowship were granted he would request a year's leave, he gave a brief statement of his proposal. He intended a book-length essay that he was tentatively calling "The Gothic Principle in the English Literary Tradition." A month earlier he had outlined the proposed plan in a letter to Graves. Although he was interested in pursuing any number of subjects—"Mixed Modes," "Poetic Irony," "Nature in Poetry"—he had finally decided to concentrate on the Gothic principle in English poetry:

It is, I feel, a thesis after your own heart—touches your own interest at many points. But it is especially timely for an American to do; our need is greater than your need. With us, our whole education, our culture is intended to spoil the youth with Euphemisms—it's directed against the uncouth pioneer instincts that linger in us, and ought to linger so far as literature is concerned. Hence the enormous weight of social responsibility, falsely conceived, that rests upon the shoulders of our writers. For I shall have a chapter on the Nature of Genius; and I understand that to be essentially the kind of mind that has access to the solid inherited folk-stratum underneath his conscious accumulation of culture; or in figurative language, it's the mind of the low man, like Chaucer and Shakespeare, who got themselves into society, wrote in the fine style like their betters for a while, and after they found it quite too easy to speak that language, developed the idea of giving vent to their low natures, to the great enlivenment of the impoverished literary forms of society. And I have a chapter on Shakespeare called Thinking in Gothic: there I propose to analyze a huge number of specimen passages to show his theory of poetry; it consists in smooth classical coherence only up to a certain point, where he lets out a tremendously unexpected crude misfit phrase, which miraculously gives all the vitality to the passage. . . . And a very fine chapter, I think, on Religion and Gothic, in which I show that all religions that are vital are a folk product first, and contain sensational and obscene features in plenty: but get themselves taken up by the higher critics, theologians, and Liberals, who try to emasculate them of their Gothic quality—whereas they cannot survive this process if they are to stay the religions of the whole society. And a chapter on science as anti-Gothic, which makes this point: the scientists are exactly like Plato; they would deny the poets a place in the State, because the poets deal with imitations; the true reality is the Idea, in Platonic language, or the type and generality, in scientific language, and the concrete persons and things are only imitations. The whole interest of science is to classify and generalize and it has no patience with human personality or even the stubborn familiar thinghood of things; and art and religion between them save this sense of existence to the people. My hardest chapter will be on the relation of Gothic and classical; and undoubtedly it will come to this: Classical is more intellectualized, more philosophical; both are comprehensive and fair statements of the whole of life; Gothic gives undigested facts, concrete reality in all its stubborn identity, while classical presents these facts as already on the way to being integrated into a system, as already half-abstracted.[23]

That Ransom's proposed project contains the basic idea of both *God Without Thunder* and *The World's Body* is evident from this extended summary. But Ransom was never to complete the plan in the form outlined here because he did not receive the Guggenheim grant. On June 14, 1926, Davidson wrote Tate that Ransom was bearing up bravely but could hardly conceal his dejection. Although he and Robb were disappointed that their prolonged visit to England must be delayed (for four years as it turned out), some of the developments of that spring pleased Ransom enormously. First of all, Knopf had accepted *Two Gentlemen in Bonds* with the promise that it would be released early the next year. It was with a feeling of accomplishment, almost with a sense of having completed an important segment of his life, that he turned his attention more and more toward criticism and away from poetry. Never again, except very late in life when he was under a compulsion to revise his early poetry, would the writing of verse receive a major part of his creative energy. With his mind "occupied more and more with literary theorizing" he must have been particularly pleased when Chancellor Kirkland approved his request for a term's leave. In early June he left for Memphis, having already sent Robb and the children on to Denver. He was delighted with the prospect of having four months of freedom from teaching, the most extended period of leisure for study and writing since his release from the service. As soon as he completed a six-week term of teaching at the West Tennessee Teachers' College, he planned to go immediately to Denver and from there to the Colorado State Teachers' College for three weeks, after which he and Robb hoped "to park the babies with the grandparents and go down about Sante Fe" where they expected to stay until he had to return to Nashville for the beginning of the January term at Vanderbilt.[24] The entire four months, he wrote Tate, would be spent in trying to "put together" some "scraps of aesthetic doctrine and whip a book into shape."

During his six weeks in Memphis he was as unhappy as he would allow himself to become. Not only was the weather more humid and unpleasantly hot than he could remember it being during his previous summers in Memphis, but he also missed Robb and the children. More than ever he regretted that his incessant need for money required him to teach during the long summer vacations and thus precluded his doing his own work. His students, most of whom were primary and secondary school teachers who had to return to college each summer in order to receive enough credit to renew their teaching certificates, were neither stimulating nor demanding. The chairman of the department of English, he wrote Donald Davidson on July 1,[25] "had given me such a boosting preliminary to my arrival that crowds registered for my simple courses, and they have all along shown a disposition to regard me as the wise young Jesus; I do not know whether they can be fooled these two more weeks or not, now that the hot weather has at last come upon us." His living quarters, a room in one of the dormitories, were rather primitive, he wrote, "which serves me right considering I have been such a professing primitivist—the grub is pretty bad and the coffee unspeakable." To add to his discomfort was the fact that he could get little of his own work done. Not only was he recovering from an extracted wisdom tooth, but, as visiting celebrity, he had a large number of official, often boring, social commitments.

It was in this state of near depression that he learned that Allen Tate had received a letter from Laura Riding leading him to believe that Ransom "had been publishing abroad" an "unfavorable and certainly meddlesome opinion" of Tate's "person, character, and mentality."[26] Again Ransom attempted to reassure Tate. "I have been most scrupulous," he wrote, "in every possible public expression that I [have] ever made about you. I have possibly made unfavorable comments about you to a few intimate friends, which I know have never gone any further." During Laura Riding's visit last fall he had talked to her for about an hour about all the Fugitives but only about literary matters. "Her impression," he concluded, "that I was busy offering disparagements at your expense, whether to her or anybody else, is manufactured out of the virgin cloth of her mind." Tate apparently agreed that "she was simply up to mischief," for a few days later Ransom wrote Davidson[27] that he had had a letter from Tate, "in which he repudiated Laura's letter and all . . . responsibility therein, but felt a little hurt (very naturally) at the state of mind which Laura appeared to impute to me." Ransom had informed Tate immediately that "Laura was stringing us along or trying to embroil us." Ransom had just received, he wrote Davidson, Tate's response: "The hatchets are all buried, at least till Laura gets back, when they are to be resurrected for the purpose of chopping her head off." The incident caused no further comment, and Miss Riding's name was seldom mentioned in the frequent exchange of letters during the next few months.

Ransom had missed the children so badly during his weeks in Memphis that when he arrived in Denver he proposed that they not leave Helen and Reavill with their grandparents while he and Robb went off to live in New Mexico; instead he suggested they find a place near enough Denver that the family could stay together and the children see their grandparents as often as they wished. Robb agreed to the plan immediately; she had allowed herself to consider a lengthy separation from the children only to give Ransom a better opportunity to complete his book. By early September, therefore, all four of the Ransoms were settled in a small mountain cottage about forty-five minutes from Denver. It is "a tight cabin," Ransom wrote Tate, "fit for fall weather at least and best of all, just a hundred yards above the grocery store. First we meditated parking the children with either pair of grandparents; but I'm glad we didn't, as the little cusses are pretty good company, and I have a sanctum in which they can't enter when I sport my oak."[28]

Ransom's letters during that summer and fall demonstrate the intensity with which he was considering the principal points of his literary credo. "Frankly, I expect to discount your criticism," he wrote Tate; "I do not see with you when it comes to poetry; I accept almost every specific criticism, without having in the least the same scale of comparative values."[29] His dissatisfaction with Tate's poetry, he wrote, was surely an indication that he was not in sympathy with

Tate's intentions.[30] He was convinced that Tate overdid his idea of "perfect contemporaneity," for to him being contemporary, if not accidental, must surely be spontaneous. Tate's attempt to find a new means of expression was futurism, really an attempt to anticipate the turn language would ultimately take; therefore he was not content to be contemporary but was consciously seeking to be ahead of his time, which was "as bad as being archaic." What "I am trying to do," Ransom continued, is not "to let the question of the old and the new get into my mind at all but to keep up a certain heat of composition in the faith that the imagery will be sufficient unto the day and unto the nature of my subject." He also questioned Tate's belief that the modern poet lived in a bad time. "I think," he wrote, that "the fundamental life-history of individuals is about the same in all periods . . . the practical subjects to me are peculiarly individual interests, which I cannot see as particularly different for any reasons of time or space."[31]

Tate's publication of a foreword to Hart Crane's *White Buildings* (New York, 1926) and of "Poetry and the Absolute" (*Sewanee Review,* January, 1927), gave Ransom an excellent opportunity to continue their discussion of the nature of poetry and its function in the modern world. In the latter essay, which is, in part at least, an answer to Ransom's "Thoughts on the Poetic Discontent," Tate argues that Ransom's "warily skeptical dualism" explains the conditions "under which a poet may know anything." But Ransom's description, Tate says, is of "general intelligence, not specific poetic intelligence," and his explanation of the "relation between the poet and his world" does not include the "relation between the poet, or the reader, and the poem." Since this relationship, that of the poet or reader to the poem, "conduces to an absolutism," Tate concludes that Ransom's distinction between monism and dualism, so essential in the "metaphysical enquiry into the nature of reality," just does not apply. The necessity for art, he explained, rests in the "irresistible need of the mind for absolute experience," a need which cannot be "satisfied in ordinary, cursory experience." Poetry is the fusion of "an intensely felt, ordinary experience, an intense moral situation, into an intensely realized art," and, properly read, the poem can furnish the reader the opportunity to participate in an absolute experience, one he certainly could not have assembled for himself.

Ransom began a long letter of response on April 3 but did not complete it until April 13. He thanked Tate for encouraging him to read Hart Crane. His impression of Crane's poetry was so favorable that he was almost convinced that it was about the "most important work done in these days." He was thinking, he wrote, of doing a critical article on Crane, whom he believed to be the "freest mind" among modern poets, maybe since Blake—that is, he was "most free from abstraction, from qualification . . . from conceptualism." Ransom's primary interest was not in Crane's poetry, however, but in the basic shift he thought he had detected over the past year in Tate's critical position. If Tate were writing this review now, Ransom thought, he would be less free in praise of Crane's poetry, as he would be less severe on Ransom's dualism if he could rewrite "Poetry and the Absolute." For, Ransom argued, in his most recent letters Tate not only had accepted his "warily skeptical dualism" but had gone him one better in "requiring for a major poet . . . a system of fixed values in which to seek the flag of quality." Now, Ransom speculated, Tate would agree with him in seeing in Crane a "deficiency . . . in judgment." In spite of some misgivings about Crane's final worth as poet, however, Ransom greatly admired some aspects of his poetry. First of all, he wrote, there is his "total addiction to the literal metaphor as opposed to the simile. The general poet keeps his logical subject intact while mentioning and correlating all the alternative subjects. Crane actually leaves the logical subject and commits himself with great rapidity to its alternates." His greatest gift is not his technical dexterity but his ability to think qualitatively in an age that places so much emphasis on conceptualism. Although Ransom found some of Crane's poetry "tractarian" because it was "aesthetics first and poetry second," Ransom would not minimize his greatness as a man "whose capacity for vision, mobility of mind, deliverance from the fixed tracts of contemporary thinking, must be a mortification to all the other living poets."

In turning to Tate's discussion of the poetic absolute, Ransom repeats his belief in the dual nature of poetry. "It must do more than one thing at the same time," he wrote; "its basis is a . . . logical substrata, but that must consist with a rhythmical development of sounded words, and with one or more, often many, secondary and 'associational' meanings which may be systematic as in an allegory, but must at least have a very high frequency. . . . Poetry is more than prose but it must first be prose." For this reason one cannot make a "formula out of an unqualified Absolute." Tate's insistence that a "finished poem" must be treated as "an ultimate finished absolute" does an injustice to the art because a "poem is hot not cold, living not dead, a source of constant fresh experience, not a page that has been turned." It is an "unpredictable source of energy," which is composed of two components: the "container, which is the relative and quantitative, and the movement, which is the free and contingent and qualitative." If poetry is an absolute, it is one which consists in infinite relativity. Whatever the poet beholds, Ransom concluded, the thing beheld is "capable of furnishing two separate experiences: a quantitative and systematic suggestive experience and a quantitative 'absolute' objectified experience." Art, finally, is the "meeting place of the individual and the universal, the absolute and the relative."

During the summer and fall of 1926 Ransom devoted all his energies to getting down for the first time in systematic fashion his critical ideas, and this correspondence with Tate forced him to give these ideas definite focus and concrete form. Both mornings and afternoons of those pleasant days in Indian Hills, Colorado, were consumed in the writing of a long essay, which, he wrote Mims, was currently going "under a fancy title: *The Third Moment*,"[32] a first attempt to treat formally "a great mass of observations I have to make about literature." For the present he had decided not to pursue his notion of the Gothic element in literature—that would come later; for now, he would attempt to prepare for more specialized studies by presenting a "technical philosophy of aesthetics." His first task, he realized, was to complete a kind of introductory chapter, intended "to show the drift" of his ideas and "to give an easy abstract" of his position. After that assignment was completed he would get some reactions to it before attempting to fill in the details.

As soon as this introductory chapter was completed he sent it to *Harper's* and was delighted to get a prompt reply. Although the editors could not decide immediately on the appropriateness of the essay for publication in the magazine, they asked to see the entire manuscript when it was completed. This indication of definite interest in the book, added to that already expressed by Knopf, who had published *Chills and Fever* and had *Two Gentlemen in Bonds* in press, encouraged Ransom to try to complete a manuscript before Christmas. "*Harper's*, by the way," he wrote Mims, "has taken quite a fancy to me; Wells, the editor, wrote saying that every time he went to England people asked him why he didn't feature my work, and requesting a group of poems; and out of my leftovers he chose four, to go into a group for single publication."[33] He must have felt his career was taking a decided turn for the better, for at about the same time he was asked to do a book in the American Men of Letters Series, and Oxford University Press wrote to see if he would "do a volume for them on Southern literature." The first of these offers he considered, but asked for some time to make up his mind; the second he declined immediately, citing his lack of specific preparation for the assignment and recommending Donald Davidson.

Now that he could devote his days to writing—except for the long daily hikes he and the family took along the trails leading into the mountains and those best of all times when he taught Helen and Reavill trout fishing—he felt he would have a manuscript ready for the typist when he returned to Nashville in late December. As he gathered his thoughts and "meditations over many years" to prepare the introductory chapter of his critical book, he wrote Tate that "a little further elaboration" of his "aesthetical ideas" seemed definitely in order. Since for the first time in his life he had "official status with my authorities as composer *in absentia,* professional," he had a "certain feeling of pretentiousness"; nevertheless his work went well and he brought with him when he returned to Nashville a typescript of more than two hundred pages. During the opening weeks of 1927 he carefully revised this manuscript and sent it to Harper and Brothers, who kept it several weeks before returning it with recommendations for extensive revision. For several years Ransom kept this essay on or near his work table and attempted to make the suggested changes. But finally he realized that it was hopelessly abstract, that such a study could "scarcely afford to be pursued in any way except in the constant company of the actual poems"; therefore he "had the pleasure of consigning [it] to the flames."[34] Since no copy of this manuscript exists, its contents can be reconstructed only from a careful reading of the letters Ransom wrote during the period of its composition, particularly those to Allen Tate. On September 5 he gave Tate a detailed summary of the ideas he hoped to present in the book.[35] This letter deserves to be quoted at length, for it reveals the state of Ransom's mind at this particular moment. It also provides an excellent summary of his long-germinating critical ideas and anticipates many of the critical principles he would ultimately present in *The World's Body* and *The New Criticism* (1941):

The three moments in the historical order of experience are as follows:

I First Moment.
Bear in mind that the moments as I shall describe them are immensely simplified and ideal. The first moment is the original experience—pure of all intellectual content, unreflective, concrete, and singular; there are no distinctions, and the subject is identical with the Whole.

II Second Moment.
The moment after. This moment is specific for human experience as distinguished from the ideally animal experience. Biologically man is peculiar in that he must record and use his successive experiences; the beasts are not under this necessity; with them the experience is an end in itself, and takes care of itself. In the second moment cognition takes place; never mind the fact that cognition is always recognition, and presupposes *two* moments,— for we can say that the first moment must be *repeated* before the time arrives for the (qualitatively) second moment. The feature of the second moment is it is now that the record must be taken of the first moment that has just transpired. This record proceeds inevitably by way of *concepts* discovered in cognition. It is the beginning of science. Its ends are practical; but its means are *abstractions*; and these, it must be insisted, are subtractions from the whole. Now what becomes of the whole in this operation? A feature, or several features, are taken up and spread upon the record; let us say, they are written down on lasting tablets; at the least, they go into the Ready Memory where items of knowledge are constantly in use, and constantly available. The rest goes somewhere and is preserved, else we could never miss it; it goes, according to Bergson, into Pure Memory; according to the modern school of psychologists, into the Unconscious, where it is far from idle, and whence it somewhere, sometime, will

come up again. So experience becomes History, conceptualized knowledge, in respect to a part, and Unconscious Knowledge, lost knowledge, in respect to the vast residue of the unconceptual. So also is generated the cognitive or scientific habit; which is that which disposes us to shorten the subsequent First Moments of our experience to the minimum, to dwell upon our subsequent fresh experiences only long enough to reduce them as here; and which is so powerful when formed that many of us unquestionably spend most of our waking lives in entertaining or arriving at concepts.

III Third Moment.
We become aware of the deficiency of the record. Most of experience is quite missing from it. All our concepts and all our histories put together cannot add up into the wholeness with which we started out. Philosophical syntheses do no good—the Absolutists are quaint when they try to put Humpty-Dumpty together again by logic—they only give us a Whole which, as Kant would say, is obtained by *comprehensio logica* and not by *comprehensio aesthetica*— a Whole which it is only necessary to say fails to give us satisfaction. The world of science and knowledge which we have laboriously constructed is a world of illusion; not one of its items can be intuited, we suddenly appear to ourselves as monsters, as unnatural members of humanity; and we move to right ourselves again. (The scientific world, as seen on these terms, quite clearly appears as an artificial or *phenomenal* world, and so our objection is quite regular and eclectic.) How can we get back to that first moment? There is only one answer: By images. The Imagination is the faculty of Pure Memory, or unconscious mind; it brings out the original experiences from the dark storeroom, where we dwell upon them with a joy proportionate to our previous despair. And therefore, when we make images, we are regressive; we are trying to reconstitute an experience which we once had, only to handle and mutilate. Only, we cannot quite reconstitute them. Association is too strong for us; the habit of cognition is too strong. The images come out mixed and adulterated with concepts. Experience without concepts is advocated by some systems, and has some healing power, but it is not an adult mode; it cannot really produce images without concepts, but only an imageless and conceptless state; as in the Dionysian state of Nietzsche or the Orientalism of Schopenhauer. What we really get, therefore, by this deliberate recourse to images is a mixed world composed of both images and concepts; or a sort of practicable reconciliation of the two worlds. Therefore we are not really opposed to science,

except as it monopolizes and warps us; we are perfectly content to dwell in the phenomenal world for much of our time; this is to be specifically human; we would not be babes or beasts; we require merely the fullness of life, which is existence in the midst of all our faculties. And our Aesthetic can never deny science wholly, which would be wildly romantic, and not reasonable, if not suicidal. This leads us to a distinction between *Romantic* or *Pure* tendencies, *Gothic* or *Mixed,* which is like the distinction between the *East* and the *West.* Science is a kind of blindness, but necessary and useful; exactly as the typical successful mercenary appears blind to the poet. . . . An important detail is to show why, with our formal cognitive habit or apparatus, we cannot have fresh experience of first moments; because they disintegrate as fast as they come. And this corollary: In Nature as compared with Art, our sense of Wholeness is extremely vague and unsatisfying; the artistic contemplation of nature is better, a very advanced state, in which we are conscious of the scene as we might have conceptualized it, and at the same time of the scene as we actually do persist in intuiting it. But this is quite like art: a mixture.

After this lengthy and particularized discussion of the theory itself, Ransom lists the "five different states or operations" in which man attempts to "reconstitute the fugitive first moment": dreams, fancies (or daydreams), religion, morals, and art. Then he suggests the specific approach he will make in the body of his book, which will concentrate on poetry as a representative of the arts as they attempt to recreate the first moment of human experience. The essence of his discussion centers around the nature of poetry, which he defines as "always the exhibit of Opposition and at the same time Reconciliation between the Conceptual or Formal and the Individual or Concrete." The "obvious fact" which years before had started him on this line of inquiry was his realization that the requirement of meter in poetry, an obvious example of the formal, "does not seem to impair the life and effectiveness of Concrete Experience. They Coexist." Without too much difficulty one can find in this summary a rudimentary statement of many of Ransom's mature critical ideas: his insistence that aesthetic theory should have a firm ontological basis, that the material object is the "stuff" of poetry, that the essential nature of poetry resides in its dualism, that the poem can reconstitute the "fugitive first moment," the world's body, through a combination of image and idea, and that the view of human experience presented by science, with its practical ends and abstract means, is less than complete. Only through art can one realize completely all aspects of human experience.

In the fall of 1926 another project was completed and for a short period at least Ransom had to turn his attention from criticism to poetry. The last issue of the *Fugitive* carried a brief statement from Ransom promising future publications by the group, and almost immediately Davidson had begun to investigate various possibilities of getting the best of Fugitive verse between hard covers. Even before the magazine ceased publication he had suggested to Tate the possibility of a yearbook and Tate, although he liked the idea of a volume of Fugitive verse, indicated his preference for an anthology which would give "the best of the past and a sample of the present." While he was collecting verse from each of the Fugitives, Davidson began to canvass publishers to see if he could discover any interest in the proposed project. In response to Davidson's request, on September 30, 1926,[36] Ransom sent him a list of his poems to consider for inclusion in the volume, Davidson having the right, of course, to exclude any which "space or any other reason might dictate." From *Poems About God* he recommended "The Lover" and "Under the Locusts"; from *Chills and Fever,* "Judith of Bethulia" and "Captain Carpenter"; from the soon-to-be-published *Two Gentlemen in Bonds,* "Dog" (or if the files of the small Philadelphia magazine in which this poem appeared were not available in Nashville, "Eclogue"), "History of Two Simple Lovers" (later called "The Equilibrists"), "In Mr. Minnet's House," "Hilda," and "Man Without Sense of Direction." His choice from *Chills and Fever* was "scanty," he wrote, because he understood he would have to pay Knopf for any poems used from that collection. But, he concluded, he knew he had listed more poems than Davidson could use and he was "quite content with their quality as being as good" as he could furnish. Two weeks later, however, he learned from Knopf that he would not have to pay for the poems from *Chills and Fever* and, very wisely, sent Davidson an alternate list:[37] "Agitato ma non troppo," "Bells for John Whiteside's Daughter," "Winter Remembered," "Necrological," "Judith of Bethulia," "Captain Carpenter," "Old Mansion," "Tom, Tom, the Piper's Son," "Philomela," and "The sonnet about the encounter of two mariners." But, Ransom concluded, "if your preference is otherwise, go ahead." Davidson's final selection included some poems from both lists and some from neither.

Ransom's thoughts did not wander completely away from his own verse, as indeed they never would, because as soon as he had finished with the selection of poems for *Fugitives: An Anthology of Verse,* he had to read proofs for *Two Gentlemen in Bonds,* a task he completed before returning to Nashville in mid-December. Released In January, 1927, the contents of this volume are arranged in three groupings: The Innocent Doves (fourteen poems), The Manliness of Men (sixteen poems), and Two Gentlemen in Bonds (twenty sonnets). The first two groups contain some of Ransom's best poems ("Vision by Sweetwater," "Dead Boy," "Piazza Piece," "Blue Girls," "Janet Waking," "Antique Harvesters," and "The Equilibrists"); but the last—a sonnet sequence presenting the inevitable clash between two brothers, one worldly and the other ascetic—was allowed to go out of print until the poet selected twelve of the twenty sonnets for inclusion in the revised and enlarged third edition of his *Selected Poems* (1969). Upon its appearance in January, 1927, *Two Gentlemen in Bonds* was even more widely and seriously reviewed than *Chills and Fever* had been. The reviewers—beginning with Davidson's notice in the *Tennessean* for January 23 and including full-scale treatments by Conrad Aiken, H. S. Gorman, John Gould Fletcher, Allen Tate, and Edmund Wilson—all regarded the book as a major achievement by one of the most important poets of the era.

In his brief note—the "unexpected early appearance of the book" did not "permit a full comment" and he wanted readers in Nashville to know about the book immediately—Davidson set the tone for the more detailed evaluations to follow.[38] Saying that "Mr. Ransom has refined and perfected his art into an instrument flexible and apt to all demands put on it," he found the poetry in this volume "satisfying in the clear, warm and beautiful finality with which it touches its subjects" and Ransom "unique, not merely among American but among all poets." Among contemporary American poets, he concluded, Ransom "is one of the few who will meet the ultimate tests." Edmund Wilson was a little less extravagant in his praise, but his review was definitely complimentary, saying that Ransom's poetry had "much charm" and a "certain amount of originality."[39] The section of the book which he liked least was the sonnet sequence. Though "prettily done," its "sweetly wise" ironic tone echoes too closely that of E. A. Robinson. But Ransom's verse can be read with the "same sort of pleasure" one derives from reading that of Edith Sitwell or Wallace Stevens. "He is not a great poet, but he is a delightful and distinguished writer" and the best of his verse has the "light and translucent, but deliciously satisfying, loveliness . . . of the finest watercolor."

In an omnibus review of eight books of poetry, Herbert S. Gorman proclaimed *Two Gentlemen in Bonds* the best of the volumes by Americans under consideration; the others were Langston Hughes's *Fine Clothes to the Jew,* James Rorty's *Children of the Sun,* and Hart Crane's *White Buildings.* [40] Ransom's "satire, irony and a realism of phraseology" give his poetry a "flavor peculiar to him alone." An excellent book, it is a "fit successor" to *Chills and Fever.* Conrad Aiken thought Ransom and Archibald MacLeish the most "exciting" poets to emerge since the "days of the so-called 'poetic renaissance.'" [41] Like Siegfried Sassoon, whose *Satirical Poems* was also under review, Ransom was an "ironist and satirist," according to Aiken; he takes "an inordinate delight in stating the simple in terms of the complex and in droll elaboration," but Ransom has what Sassoon lacks, the "ability to make ideas and feelings march together" and a "really exquisite sense of word values." This critic's final estimate must have given Ransom particular pleasure, for although he did not approve of Aiken's disregard for literary form, he regarded him as an unusually gifted poet. *Two Gentlemen in Bonds,* Aiken concluded, is one of the best books of poetry to appear in many years, and it proves Ransom a "match for any poet now writing."

Babette Deutsch compared Ransom to Ezra Pound, finding both poets "erudite and sardonic, with a liking for the tart and a rare virtuosity of technique." [42] But, although Robert Herrick and Sir Thomas Browne "jostle each other here," Ransom's "cadences are peculiarly his own." No poem in this volume is as "fine as some of the metaphysical pieces in *Chills and Fever,*" but any reader who "savored that volume should not miss this one." Writing in *Poetry,* Marie Luhrs commented on the "freshness of Mr. Ransom's style" and on his ability to "achieve sharp new rhythms and fantastic pictures." [43] Although his "technical tricks are violent"—rhyming, as he does, "heavy words like

dissolved and *intervolved* and *subtraction* and *transaction,*" composing peculiar verse forms and "encrusting them with brutal expressions"—he
achieves "delicacy and emotion." Some of the sonnets in the title
poem, particularly "Epithalamion of a Peach," are "hard, heavy, and
cruel"; they have "cadences . . . brewed in bitterness." Such poems
reveal Ransom's "dangerous originality," in which he is "often tempted to astound with a phrase rather than with a thought." It will be
interesting, therefore, "to watch Mr. Ransom to find out whether the
extreme cut of his poetic clothes will make him or break him." John
Gould Fletcher found Ransom's distinguishing characteristic his "definite sense of geographic location"[44] and his "praiseworthy determination to grapple only with themes that arise from that location." A
"more urbane Frost," Ransom is an artist whose poetic thrust comes
from the region that produced him, the American South where "*noblesse oblige,* a tolerant mellowness made slightly bitter by defeat and a
sane and rational humour . . . still prevail." His final estimate is that
Ransom "is a distinguished and highly individual addition to American poetry."

The review Ransom said had done him the "honor of more inward
examination" than he had previously "secured from any source" was
written by Allen Tate and appeared in the *Nation* for March 30,
1927.[45] "The fourth volume of John Crowe Ransom's poetry," Tate
begins, "is not the equal in brilliant variety of technical effect or in
range of subject matter of *Chills and Fever,* issued in 1924"; nevertheless on the whole it is "the qualitative equal of anything else he has
done." In fact this collection "precipitates the particular essence which
is Ransom." That essence Tate explains as follows:

Mr. Ransom is the last pure manifestation of the culture of the
eighteenth-century South; the moral issues which emerge trans-
figured in his poetry are the moral issues of his section, class, culture,
referred to their simple, fundamental properties. . . .

Two of Mr. Ransom's qualities in especial connect him with the
culture which in its prime registered its genius in politics and law;
rationalism and the code of *noblesse oblige.* These qualities, informing
every poem, dictate the direction of his artistic vision from all
starting-points whatever. Rationalism, not in the sense popularized by
the *philosophes,* but in the older and purer sense of the humane tradition, a tradition lying at the very core of the old Southern order,

stiffens his poetry with an irony and lucidity, and a subtlety, which elevate it with a unique distinction in the present American scene. His rationalism is the evaluating instrument of the code of honor; it gives the code profundity and edge; it is the weapon of casuistry. The system of casuistry appears in a kind of solemn dandyism, but back of the dandyism lurks a profound stoicism, and an immovable detachment which feeds upon an intellect always sufficient unto itself. All the emotional crises of Mr. Ransom's poems, even the occasional essays into sheer lyricism like "Vision by Sweetwater," hinge upon the single conviction—*noblesse oblige*. There are, of course, two sides to the medallion; in poems like "The Equilibrists" and "Dead Boy," more vaguely if not more subtly in the sonnets "Two Gentlemen in Bonds," Mr. Ransom can render a beautiful commentary upon his tragic personal vision because he accepts the code within which the characters struggle; elsewhere, when he cannot accept their code, as in "Amphibious Crocodile," he pours out the meager yet venomous acid of his satire. In every poem he is either the satirist or the ironist; and as a fine minor artist he has always the same thing to say, in new and unpredictable images.

It may be that the phrase "always the same thing to say" explains Tate's prophetic statement "that further additions to the testament complete now with this volume would cry out redundancy." At any rate with this volume Ransom's career as practicing poet was almost over. After 1927 he published only a half dozen new poems, and most of the creative energy devoted to his verse went into rewriting some of his earlier poems and into the apparently endless process of revising others. Many of these new versions have not pleased even the most sympathetic of his readers.

Before his review appeared in print, Tate followed his custom of sending a copy to Ransom, who wrote and mailed immediately a carefully composed letter of appreciation.[46] He expressed his intense pleasure with the review but indicated his inability to determine if the sentiments expressed therein were the result of Tate's "habitual honest reflections" or the "fruit of your generosity as a friend." Whichever the case, he continued, "I find pleasure, and perhaps would as soon have it one way as the other." Although, ironically enough, Ransom realized he was unable to perceive the central thrust of Tate's poetry, Tate was the only critic who had "come near the heart of the matter" as far as his own verse was concerned.

I am obliged to see that in rationalism and *noblesse oblige* you have picked out two cues that penetrate very deep into my stuff. . . . George Bond has just reviewed me in the Dallas paper along the usual lines: my Southernism is suspect, it is far less than 100 per cent; whereas the Southernism he has in mind is a recent feminized (or, as you say, sentimentalized) vulgarism that represents a terrible declension if I know anything about the values. Anyhow, I don't write consciously as a Southerner or a Non-Southerner. It is perhaps for that reason that I am not willing as yet to confess that I shall not write any more poetry, or that when I do it will be a redundancy along the old lines. If I am not mistaken, I shall be compelled to keep on writing poetry for the very consideration that makes me believe that that way lies health and sanity; but I have a notion that it will become more and more radical and fundamental and less and less local.

Tate's response to this letter stimulated Ransom to consider again with great care the principal points of Tate's review.[47] This time he came back to Tate's discussion of rationalism and *noblesse oblige,* as means of understanding his poetry. Although he was honored that Tate had made him the "mouthpiece of a very noble culture," he wrote, this was the "questionable" and least important feature of the interpretation. What he considered to be most significant in Tate's comments he expressed in some detail:

What is important in your witness was that my stuff presents the dualistic philosophy of an assertive element *versus* an element of withdrawal and respect. Your terms *rationalism* and *noblesse oblige* are nearly as ultimate and pure as could be stated in discourse. If you are right, I am happy—I've put unconsciously into my creative work the philosophy which independently I have argued out discursively. I write this in no arrogance, of course—understanding well that the aesthetic quality is always a specific quality and is not guaranteed by the philosophy under it—a matter of practice, not theory. But what rather astonishes me is that having given me such a gorgeous dichotomy of interest you now seem to take it all back by saying that I rest on a couple of specific concepts (casual, local little things?) and exhibit a fairly simple and coherent (and special?) coherence. (Viewed now in your sentence as not a dichotomy at all, merely two chance concepts out of many.) If your original diagnosis were right, then I raise the dualistic issue which is fundamental and not special; I do a variety of what we all must do. And as for the simplicity of my product, you know I have always been offensive in talking about maturity and seeming to make it a personal advantage of my own that I have achieved maturity by comparison with others who might be mentioned. Well frankly, and no offense intended, I have found it mighty hard to get my simplicity—have had to fight off a lot of counter tendencies—simplicity is not to be regarded as a beginning but a goal—it's a purification and abnegation. What I miss nearly everywhere in poetry is this simplicity. I haven't really got it yet. The mind with its defensive apparatus sets up a thousand false goals and objectives to keep us from simplicity: all of them meant to disguise the fact that we don't really want to face the music and confront the Pure Fact which is in the aesthetic situation. My object as a poet might be something as the following, though I won't promise to stick by my analysis: (1) I want to find the Experience that is in the Common Actuals; (2) I want this experience to carry (by association of course) the dearest possible values to which we have attached ourselves; (3) I want to face the disintegration or nullification of these values as calmly and religiously as possible. That's a simple program hard to realize.

He concluded his letter saying that, like Tate, he was unwilling to allow Hegel to "solve a pair of contradictions with a triad." So the artist must fight certain tendencies in modern philosophic thought, as well as many of the basic assumptions of modern science. His fundamental belief in duality as the essential nature of poetry remained unshaken. He closed with a slogan: "Give us Dualism, or we'll give you no Art."

What Ransom is defending here, in part at least, is what Tate will later describe as the "deliberately minor" mode of his verse. Tate had long insisted, in letters to Davidson and Ransom, that "there are no important themes for modern poets"; hence the modern poet must write lyrics; he must be subjective. Davidson described this kind of poetry as that which "is content with narrow limits of form, few subjects, in order that it may perfectly succeed."[48] Ransom's exploration into the nature and function of poetry convinced him that he could perform best in this minor mode. Through a combination of concepts and images, poetry can present the concrete particularity of an object's being; and in a small number of what Randall Jarrell called perfectly realized poems, Ransom reiterated his basic themes: man's dual nature—the conflict of body and soul and the inevitable misery that follows man's unwillingness to accept this basic condition—and the disparity between the world as man would have it and as it actually is, between what man wants and needs and what he can reasonably expect to receive. The most sensitive and perceptive man is destined to know the tension of attempting to hold two opposing ideas in the mind at one time. These occasionally almost perfect poems, which Ransom characterizes as deliberately minor, are composed in what has come to be known as his mature manner: the subtle irony, the nuanced ambiguities, the wit, the oblique approach, the use of simple narrative to present dramatically a character in a moment of crisis from which he will emerge with a fuller understanding of his nature and the nature of the world in which he must live. Almost the whole of Ransom's poetic career falls within an eleven-year period, from 1916 to 1927. In his entire career he published fewer than 160 poems, only 80 of which he included in his *Selected Poems.* Almost all of those he chose to preserve were written between 1922 and 1925, the years in which the *Fugitive* was published.

Soon after *Two Gentlemen in Bonds* appeared, Edwin Mims anticipated his annual report and wrote Chancellor Kirkland to inform him of an emergency that might occur in the department of English.[49] Ransom's reputation as a poet was such, he wrote, that he would no doubt receive attractive offers to join the faculties of other universities. To acknowledge their awareness of his excellence as a teacher, as well as his "superior work as scholar and critic," the administrative officers of Vanderbilt should recommend his immediate elevation to the rank of full professor.

I think that justice demands that Ransom be made full professor on as large a salary as the budget will allow. Permit me to say that you are wrong in your idea that he wants to leave Vanderbilt or would welcome an invitation elsewhere. If there is a frank, honest man in the world, it is John Ransom and I am confident he prefers to stay here for personal and other reasons. After thirteen years of service—and may I say of distinguished service—he is entitled to a full professorship. He cannot remain in a subordinate position nor can he live on what he is now getting. His promotion would keep him here for a period of years when we most need him and when he is at his best in the creative and critical work he is doing.

Mims's letter had the desired effect. At its spring meeting the Board of Trust approved Kirkland's recommendation that Ransom be promoted. And for the first time since coming to teach at Vanderbilt in the fall of 1914, Ransom regarded his position there as permanent. Now that he could "make a decent living" he was happy, he wrote Tate, "to live on where and how I have been living these ten years and more." At about this time, as Tate recalled later, he received a different kind of letter from Ransom, who wrote that for the past few weeks he had been revising an old essay, first called "Pioneering on Principle," which he was sending out for publication under the title "The South—Old or New?" It soon became evident that the exchange of letters between Ransom and Tate would have a different focus and that Ransom's literary career had taken a new turn. "I've attacked the South for the last time," Tate wrote Davidson on March 1, 1927, "except in so far as it may be necessary to point out the chief defect the Old South had was that in it which produced, through whatever cause, the New South." In a letter to Tate written a few months later,[50] Ransom commented on their "joint Southernism" and indicated that his belief in "something ineradicable in Southern culture" was reinforced by the fact that Tate and many other southerners who "exhibit the same stubbornness of temperament and habit" go North but cannot bring "themselves to surrender to an alien mode of life."

During the next ten years a major portion of his time and energy would be expended in attacking the New South program of industrial progress and defending the principles of the Old South. Ransom had always valued certain characteristics of the culture of his region: its code of gentility, its manners, its emphasis on family closeness and loyalty, and its demonstrated belief in ceremony and ritual. Now that he was convinced that this culture was in danger of immediate extinction, he undertook, along with eleven other southerners, to inspire a "genuine and powerful revival" of southernism among the young people of his region. Immediately ahead lay the controversial Agrarian symposium *I'll Take My Stand* (1930), for which he would write the introduction and the lead essay. In the 1930s he would write more than two dozen articles, including "The South Defends Its Heritage," "The South Is a Bulwark," and "Modern with a Southern Accent." No reader of these essays can fail to see Ransom's dissatisfaction with a society whose principal goal is material progress, one in which art is merely another mass-produced commodity.

VII	**A Prescription To Live By 1926-1930**

FROM HIS hotel room in Greeley, Colorado, in mid-June, 1926, Ransom wrote a letter to Donald Davidson which indicated an unmistakable turn in his literary career. Davidson had suggested a resumption of the *Fugitive*, the printing of an annual volume, or some other kind of joint publication to keep the group of young poets in touch with each other. Although he had no "official reservation of any sort," Ransom replied, he did have misgivings which he asked Davidson to keep in confidence: "These concern mostly our vanishing personnel. I'm just afraid I may be a non-contributor, to start with the least first. I get my *ms.* into Knopf for the printer next week, and then I'm in for a season of prose, which may quite envelop my quick spirits." Others of the group were equally unreliable. Robert Penn Warren was no longer in Nashville, Alec Stevenson and Jesse Wills were devoting full time to business interests, and Allen Tate's most recent verses "destroy any allusion that we are a 'school of poets' with unity."

The "season of prose" referred to by Ransom was "The Third Moment," to which he devoted all of his creative energies during the summer and fall of 1926 and every other spare moment he had for the next two years. As he prepared to join his family in Denver, he wrote Davidson: "I do believe I've got some good doctrine to work into shape. Have reinforced myself with a lot of philosophy books which seem to give me moral support. All I crave now is expert consultation; I'll have to work the whole thing out and submit the results to you and Curry at New Year's." [1]

When he returned to Nashville, with more than two hundred manuscript pages, he was not entirely satisfied. He had got down some concepts of literary theory, but he knew they were not stated sharply enough; he could not contain his tendency toward vagueness and abstraction. For a time, he had to content himself with reconsidering and rewriting those two hundred pages. Although he could not finish the manuscript, he could not put it aside. Eighteen months later he wrote Tate: "The opus of mine advances. It is about thought out now and largely written (indeed rewritten) and I hope it can be finished this summer." [2] He was in Colorado again that summer and worked on the manuscript there and continued to fret about it after his return to Nashville in early autumn. Shortly after the opening of the fall quarter, he had a letter from Chancellor Kirkland asking about the progress of the manuscript. Since he had been granted official leave to work on the book, Ransom felt he should prepare a full and formal report. The only reason he had not given such a report earlier was that he thought "the completed work would be forthcoming and the letter was unnecessary." [3] Although the basic ideas he was expounding in the book had "weighed upon ... [his] mind for more than ten years" and he "had devoted to it about all the spare time" he had had for thinking, he was more "interested in it than ever" and felt "more assured of its justice and worth."

Because he could not present his entire thesis in a few words and because he doubted that the "good chancellor would want to be added to the list of victims" on whom he had tried out his "doctrines in advance of publication," he did not offer a complete explanation, but he did attempt to show Kirkland the drift of his mind. Although he assured Kirkland that he hoped to have a complete manuscript by the end of the school year, he pointed out that the *Saturday Review of Literature* had just accepted an article which "is a condensation of some of my arguments" and that the chancellor might wish to consult that piece when it appeared in order to assure himself that "I have not been completely idle."

The article to which Ransom referred is "Classical and Romantic," which was published on September 14, 1929. [4] In it he concentrated, as he had indicated he would, on the "antipathy between art and science," a conflict he would reiterate many times in his mature critical essays.

Science, he begins, is the "mind devoting itself exclusively to the attainment of a practical purpose," a strictly intellectual technique by which such goals are attained. Since science always "fixes narrowly on the road to some special goal," its reach is very limited. Science can satisfy only a "minority of our wants," the "simplest and most material" of our desires. To satisfy our deepest and most compelling needs, we must move into the province of art or religion. The experiences contained in viewing a work of art or in worshipping God are quite different from those that come from science. Unlike science, aesthetics and religion do not exercise "our minds towards any productive accomplishment." Later Ransom would borrow a term from Schopenhauer and identify the particularized kind of truth we get only from art as "knowledge without desire," which, of course, is the essence of the distinction he makes here when he insists that works of art are "psychic exercises" and represent the most formidable reproach a perceptive man has to a scientific way of life.

The article makes this distinction between art and science even more definite in the discussion of the two kinds of literary art, the classical and the romantic. The term *romantic*, he begins, connotes that "rare and simple attitude which we call the love of nature," or the "love of anything for itself." Being pragmatic, science is interested only in using nature. To think of science as the only way to knowledge, one must anesthetize himself and "become comparatively insensible." Only when the senses are freed and one comes to "contemplate those infinities of particularity," the "landscapes, the people, the flora, the merest things," is he able to participate in the "purest aesthetic experience." The images, which are "representations by imitation," or romantic art, aim at being "representations which, short of the actual objects themselves, are the fullest possible, and are indeed of infinite fullness." Classical art, on the other hand, is "the criticism of science by science's own standards," since it always witnesses to the failure or success of science in "attaining the purposes at which it aims." Classical art speculates on the practicality of the "very ardent practical desires" which the human being entertains, but romantic art presents the "par-

ticularity of things," through which one may "feel . . . [a] joy of restoration after an estrangement from nature."

In spite of his inability to express his theories of art as precisely
and concretely as he wished, Ransom did not abandon the ideas which
had been slowly forming in his mind; but sometime in late 1928 the
emphasis was temporarily directed from art to religion. In shifting his
attention from poetry to religious myth, however, his concerns remained unchanged. Two years before he had insisted in a letter to
Tate that man attempts to recapture the fullness and completeness of
actual experience through religious myth as well as through art.[5] For
years he had been appalled at how "roundly the world . . . of late [has]
been disabused of the most and the best of its myths," and he decided
finally that he must point up the resulting "poverty of mind and
unhappiness of life."[6] This turn of interest was expressed in a letter in
which Ransom complimented Tate on his essay "The Fallacy of
Humanism," which had appeared in the *Criterion* for July, 1929. "It is
as you say," he began; "religion is fundamental and prior to intelligent
(or human) conduct on any plane."[7] Even in some of the political and
social essays he had been writing lately, Ransom pointed out, he had
suggested that religion was the "only effective defense against progress," the "only guarantee of security and—an item that seems to
me to carry a good deal of persuasive power—the enjoyment of life."
After this introduction he summarizes the "background of thought"
that had gone into "a hot and hasty book on religion" which he had
been writing "since last February" and hoped to complete during the
summer:

The fear of the Lord is the beginning of wisdom; a big beginning, but
only a beginning, of which the end is the love of the Lord. Substitute
nature for the Lord and he won't feel aggrieved. The Jews knew all
about that in their Old Testament; the New Testament was a temptation which the soft-headed western world couldn't resist; in the N. T.
it seems (to the soft-headed W. W.) that the love of the Lord is the
beginning of wisdom and it's the kind of love a world bears to a
faithful slave population, or public service that never sleeps; better
the kind a scientist bears to the gentle, tractable elements in his test
tubes which so gladly yield him up their secrets and work for him.
The N. T. has been a failure and a backset as a religious myth; not its
own fault, as I think but nevertheless a failure; it's hurt us.[8]

This book, which he was calling temporarily "Giants for Gods," was only an interlude, he assured Tate, in his aesthetic interests, and "far from being disconnected with them." In his present circumstances—with his mind pulled both toward the purer kind of aesthetic speculation, which had almost completely absorbed his interest for four or five years, and toward the political and social essays, which were demanding more and more of his creative energy—he knew he could not write a "really finished and permanent book," but it was a "sincere book" and one "that somebody ought to write."

The point is that so many myth-systems (doubtless all of them) have contained myths (many in the Greek system) of Giants, or earth-born super-men (in Nietzsche's myth), who were not Gods but only demi-Gods, yet *thought* they were Gods and behaved themselves accordingly. Prometheus, for example; whom the Greeks with all their intellectualism could not quite endorse. (Please read, if you haven't already, S. T. Coleridge's paper on *Prometheus Bound*; the most philosophical piece of literary criticism an Englishman has ever uttered.) Shelley's Prometheus is quite innocent of anything Greek in its spirit. Satan is the Hebrew Prometheus and so conceived is Milton's P. L.—he is Lucifer the Spirit of the Renaissance, the Zeitgeist of Milton's own age of science, very boldly displayed and only rejected after a proper hesitation. But then Jesus is Lucifer again; all the saviors in the myths are Giants, and the problem is in what sense they can save, and for what purpose they are to be worshiped. Of course they are all earth-born or half-human and half-God; the whole matter of the myth is to ask and determine the question, what is man's destiny, what is his proper relation to the God of nature? The function of Jesus in setting up as a Giant was to decline to set up as a God. But he may have wavered in his purpose; or the myth-makers in theirs, if you prefer. So the western world raised this Giant to a God. . . .

Little by little the God of the Jews has been whittled down into the spirit of science, or the spirit of love, or the spirit of Rotary; and now religion is not religion at all, but a purely secular experience, like Y.M.C.A. and Boy Scouts. Humanism in religion means pretending that man is God.[9]

This book, which became *God Without Thunder* (1930), was very important in Ransom's literary development, because it gave him the opportunity to crystallize, formulate, illustrate, and defend some of the ideas he had been struggling with. The central thesis of the book is man's need for an inscrutable God, one that cannot be comprehended by his reason or explained by scientific fact. Just as man cannot know the nature of the world in which he lives through relying solely upon scientific abstractions, he must resort to religious myth if he is to perceive the true relationship which exists between the physical and metaphysical realms. Through myth, which employs the supernatural to "represent the fullness of the natural," such truths are expressed and the most fundamental values are affirmed. What Ransom attempts to do, he says in his preface, is to explain the "function of the myths in human civilization" and to point out "why one myth may be better than another." His intention, in short, is to show how and where the mythology of modern America is wanting.[10]

Historical orthodoxy was, he argues, an accumulation of supernatural stories or myths which revealed a God who was mysterious, one who was the author of both good and evil and who was worshiped with burnt offering and sacrifice. He was so great that finite man knew he could not be fully understood, and he appeared to prophets in visions. Even those to whom God revealed himself could describe him only in mystical or fantastic terms. The new God is nature, and herein lies one of the great deficiencies of modern religious practice. To poets and men of religion, nature is "feared and loved," but to the scientist it is "studied and possessed." The scientist blinds himself to all aspects of nature which he cannot formulate, understand, and control. His God is one who rules through law, through a nature that can be depended upon, a universe of "consistency, orderliness and the beauty that goes with order." The old religion never asserted that God (or nature) was dependable, or orderly, or that he "would surrender himself to laws formulated by man." The old God was a whole God because he ruled over the entire universe, not just that part which is intelligible to man; the new God, because of the limitations placed on him by man, is a half-God or demigod.

Because of the change in attitude toward the deity, the new God is no longer worshiped with sacrifice and burnt offering. The only sacrifice now offered is that which can be accounted for in terms of human welfare. Such an attitude, Ransom was convinced, marks an end to religion as a significant influence on human attitudes and beliefs, for no sincere religious institution can be effective without ritual and sacrifice. The mysteries behind the universe must be retained and respected so that man will not "become brutalized, conceited and blinded." Ancient man believed, too, that from their inscrutable, contingent, mysterious God came everything, both good and evil. But the new religionists pretend that evil does not exist or if it does, it is the kind that secular science can cure.

Modern man denies the validity of myth. He is interested in facts, those phenomena which have been registered by one or more of the senses of an honest and reliable observer; therefore it is difficult for him to account for any remarkable or miraculous event. Through his reliance on science, he must regard such occurrences as false because they cannot be substantiated by any acceptable method. He regards the myths of orthodox religion as failed attempts to be scientific and historical. He cannot accept the myth that is frankly fable, one that alleges a miracle or miraculous occurrence. Because his attempts to explain an event never go beyond its natural history and because they employ only a part of that history, man cuts himself off from an important area of human experience. What he refuses to accept, and what he must accept if he is to achieve his full potential as man, is the myth which reveals the totality of human experience by giving the natural a supernatural background, by attempting to imply the whole of history by leaving altogether its natural dimensions. Only through myth can man know a God who embraces the whole of a universe indefinite in terms of space and time and of a magnitude beyond its own natural history.

The positivistic beliefs of modern man declare that one can know nothing but nature and that there is nothing else to know. Because physics is possible, it is true; because metaphysics is impossible, it is untrue. "Nature is for history," Ransom argues, "the aggregate of observed facts. Nature is for science the aggregate of facts arranged in groups, or displayed as instances of types, or classified under headings" (GWT, 74). Such a view, however, leaves many more questions unanswered than it answers: What lies beyond the immediate limits of visibility? What lies before and after the period of time which dates the observations? What makes any object much more complex than all the formulations history and science can give it? The answers to these questions must be based on assumptions that can never be proved through demonstrable facts. A religionist "knows that nature is made and kept natural," he writes, "only by the virtue of a supernatural being that compels it; or, that one cannot account for the facts except by appealing to something not fact" (GWT, 75). The names which the mythmaker has given to these metaphysical entities are God, Satan, Heaven, and Hell. They are not meant to be understood; they are not phenomenal and cannot be used. The myths in which they are contained are "enjoyed, repeated spontaneously and as an act of ritual, professed, practiced, believed, and held firmly ... as a guide to conduct, passionately defended from competition, meant intensely and fiercely" (GWT, 85).

Only through myth can the existence of evil in the world be adequately presented. The mythmaker, the "wisest man of his day," perceived that his myth—carrying the most profound truth ever conceived but one so intricate that its significance was not available, even to the most devout of believers—must have concrete details, and it must be vividly and energetically presented. Thus he created the fable of the Garden of Eden, of Adam and Eve, and of Satan and the Fall. This myth, as Ransom reads it, presents the conflict of science and religion for the human mind, and from the victory of science comes the first sin. After they had eaten of the forbidden fruit, Adam and Eve knew they were naked, and they immediately set about fashioning garments out of fig leaves. God knew, of course, of their guilt and pronounced sentence: for woman, subservience to her husband and the pain of childbirth; for man, toil and suffering; for both, death. The forbidden fruit was science, or the secular attitude which "scorned the simple, animal-like adaptation of man to his environment, and suggested that man ought to possess nature as he was entitled to." The myth deals with man's attempt to rise above his origin and, thus, with the fact that he must return to dust; with his ascent to power by estranging himself from the earth; with his fall from an economic status in which "he picked his living off a tree to one in which he kills animals and raises crops." The myth of Cain and Abel deals with the agricultural economy which replaced the pastoral one. The Fall was man's choice to turn away from "the idyllic simplicity of life, to seek to improve the human position at the expense of nature as an enemy." Man built an artificial environment, one much simpler than the natural one, and produced a false illusion regarding nature's simplicity.

The Adam-Eve-Satan myth is similar to that of Prometheus, the demigod or man-God who attempted to alienate mankind from Zeus. He offered the blessings of science to man by stealing fire from Heaven and suggesting that man could and should be independent of Zeus. This action, its consequences, and Zeus's punishment of Prometheus are the subject of much Greek drama. Through *hybris,* man's unbridled ambition, he often comes to grief. The Greek mythmakers depicted many warnings against man's belief in the preeminence of science, against the establishment of a false or unnatural relationship between man and God, between man and nature: Ixion, who was bound to a revolving wheel for attempting to defy Zeus, may be interpreted as man's inability to escape the consequences of adopting an artificial, oversimplified view of nature such as that proposed by the applied scientist; Sisyphus, who had to roll a stone uphill to watch it roll down again, is surely a comment on the modern view of work merely for the sake of work. The Hebrew Lucifer is equated in *Paradise Lost* to the Greek Prometheus. Surprised that God has forbidden the taste of knowledge to his creatures, Lucifer makes a strong argument that this lack be rectified, but Milton "repudiates Lucifer's dangerous and specious services" and "things are as they are in the Genesis myth." Shelley goes against the myth, frees Prometheus, and proclaims that happiness on earth can come only through the powers of secular science.[11]

Satan, then, is a demigod who wanted to set up as God and rule the world. Another demigod is Christ, a man-God "who represents the highest human development" and who offers man hope (GWT, 140). Although he refused to try to be a God, his disciples would not accept his self-imposed limitations and made him assume the throne of God. Christ demonstrated through his actions on earth that man can "refuse to secularize himself," but Satan is not "out of business" and since the death of Christ he has won many victories, the most extensive of which has been Occidentalism—"the polity by which men have assumed self-sufficiency, and undertaken to effect the conquest of nature by their sciences" (GWT, 144–45). Even Christ, the man-

God who always subordinated himself to the true God, has "been represented as claiming to be that God." Through the person of Christ an important aspect of God's nature was revealed—that God is "warmly and tenderly human"—but "it was a frenzied leap of faith" that made some believe that the universe must be intelligible, that God, the true father of his children, would sooner or later be understood. This misconception of the true nature of God and of the relationship between God and man is a prime example of Occidentalism, of science usurping the role of religion: in spite of modern man's pretensions, he knows little more than Abraham about how to adapt himself to the total universe and will not acquire this knowledge, which is essential to his well-being, until he can differentiate between the functions of science and religion. "Religion is an order of experience," Ransom wrote, "under which we indulge the compound attitude of fear, respect, enjoyment, and love for the external nature in the midst of which we are forced to live." But science, on the other hand, is "an order of experience in which we mutilate and prey upon nature; we seek our practical objectives at any cost, and always at the cost of not appreciating the setting from which we have to take them" (GWT, 136). Only through the system of myths which constitutes religion can one discover "a working definition to the relation of man to nature (GWT, 156). Religion must join together two different and apparently contradictory views of this relationship: (1) that nature is devoted to man's welfare, was created by a benevolent God to be of service to mankind; (2) that nature is unintelligible and contingent, that its order is neither humane nor ethical. The first view is of course Occidental; the second, Oriental.

What can man do if he does not believe that God is limited to the good only and that evil is limited to human ignorance and will be conquered as soon as science can overcome ignorance? What recourse does the man have who feels the need of a sustaining orthodoxy? Ransom's answer is clear and emphatic:

With whatever religious institution a modern man may be connected, let him try to turn it back towards orthodoxy.

Let him insist on a virile and concrete God, and accept no Principle as a substitute.

Let him restore to God the thunder.

Let him resist the usurpation of the Godhead by the soft modern version of the Christ, and try to keep the Christ for what he professed to be: the demigod who came to do honor to the God (GWT, 327–28).

God Without Thunder appeared in the fall of 1930 and for a book of its kind was widely, if not always well, reviewed. Too many of the reviewers did not follow the thread of Ransom's argument; only two of them—Scott Buchanan and Francis Fergusson—saw the book's true value, and they both disagreed with some of its basic conclusions. One of the book's first notices came from Lloyd C. Douglas, the popular author of *The Robe,* who adopted a half-serious, mocking tone to do what he called some "labored spoofing." [12] The author of this book on religion, he begins, is a man "who cherishes words as an old maid loves her cat and geraniums" and well he might because he is a professor of English at Vanderbilt, a "job that is not to be sniffed at by anyone who has ever eaten hog-jowls and hominy with the savants of Nashville." Confessing that he has given this information because he believes an English teacher "will forgive almost anything that a critic may say about his thesis so long as it is conceded that his diction is top-hole," he proceeds to a consideration of the book itself. It is a book which will please nobody. The number of prominent people whom Ransom cites as missing "whatever mark they were aiming at" is phenomenal. Although there may be need for such a book in an age "whose emotions have been overstimulated until its heart-muscles are flabby and its valves are leaky," Douglas cannot agree that the solution to modern problems is a "reversion to a God who ordered and did not plead." But he proclaims it "a stirring book" and advises his readers to buy it and "think up a workable synonym for 'thunder.'"

John S. Middleton calls his review "Thunder Without Light" and says Ransom's book should be called "Thunder Without God." [13] Any reader of the book will certainly agree, this reviewer begins, with Ransom's admission that he lacks advanced scholarship in science and religion, the two branches of learning he proposes to discuss. The best he can do by the book, Middleton confesses, is to quote some "typical passages chosen at random to indicate the many inaccurate and absurd conclusions which help fill this volume." The most unusual review, and the most unsatisfactory to John J. Ransom who saved a copy for his son, was that of James Rorty, which appeared in the *New Freeman* for December 10, 1930. Assessing correctly Ransom's criticism of applied science and finance capitalism, Rorty says "Mr. Ransom's listing of the available communions" is incomplete. If he had looked further he might have found what he was seeking: "The religion of Russia is communism, a form of human polity which receives scriptural endorsement, even in Mr. Ransom's exegesis. Its instrument is science—communist science, applied not to the making of profits, but to the easing of man's ordeal on this earth, subject always to the irresponsible rule of the thunderer." When Ransom read this review he must have been amused, for many of the arguments presented in *God Without Thunder* are included in the essays that comprise *I'll Take My Stand,* and some of the contributors to that symposium wanted to call it "Tracts Against Communism."

A part of Ernest Sutherland Bates's confusion after reading the book, he said, was that he could not tell who Ransom's enemies were: modern science, the "Higher Criticism" of the Bible, the anthropologists, the mathematicians, or the philosophers.[14] But the book does have a thesis, "such as it is": the latent conflict between the two functions of God—"God as the transcendent cause behind phenomena, and God as the ideal of perfection." The best chapters of the book are those showing the "inadequacy of science to deal with the full reality of the concrete individual and its inability to handle the problems of the infinite and the surd." But, Bates concludes, Ransom's search for the tribal God of power points him toward the "American Big Business God whom he set out to reject." John Gould Fletcher, one of the contributors to *I'll Take My Stand* and at this time closely associated with Ransom and the other contributors to that symposium, had a much clearer conception of Ransom's intentions in this book than most of the other reviewers.[15] The book, he wrote, should be divided into three sections: in the first Ransom attempts to prove that the God of the Old Testament is "a more sensible and acceptable God than is generally supposed" by most moderns; in the second "he offers proof that the God towards which most modern scientists in England and America are tending, is an inadequate substitute"; in the third, he "proposes to state a case for the reality of suprasensible objects." Because of the limitation of space, Fletcher could only discuss the first two of these sections, and the second only briefly, because with this section, "which is closely analysed and extremely cogent," he was in almost complete agreement. With the first part he took some exception because he thought Ransom's approach to religion, despite his thesis, was too rational; his "handling of the magic process inherent in religion" was unsatisfactory.

William S. Knickerbocker, who would later oppose the Agrarian views of both Ransom and Davidson from the public platform, entitled his review "Theological Homebrew," calling the book the "second phase of the Fundamentalist campaign," the first being the Scopes trial in Dayton, Tennessee.[16] The first campaign concentrated on the biological theory of evolution; the second was aimed at mathematics and physics. One of the "most challenging books of the moment," it poses the question which all reflective people must answer, "not only with the head but with the heart," for it is concerned with the "most vital of all themes: the inscrutable mystery of God." Ransom, the poet, has shown the world that he is a "brilliant philosopher with an intimate acquaintance with modern thought" and an "acute reasoner." After presenting the thesis of each of the three sections briefly, however, Knickerbocker could only conclude that religion "is not what Mr. Ransome [sic] thinks it is, nor is orthodoxy what he defines it to be." Although Ransom is very religious his "theological homebrew" is too much like the irreligious concoctions of Herbert Spencer, not to mention those of David Hume, Immanuel Kant, Sir William Hamilton, and Henri Bergson. Not only does Ransom "fumble" with the most familiar terms of science, theology, and philosophy, he simply does not understand the movement in progress "to integrate science and religion." The remedy he prescribes is worse than the disease he diagnoses. Ransom has no notion of the "Old Testament being fulfilled in the New"; nor can his "emphasis on the inscrutability of God be found in any of the creeds of Christendom." In essence *God Without Thunder* is a "repudiation of the Christian religion" and a much better title for the book "would have been 'Thunder Without God.' "

The unsigned review in the *Times Literary Supplement* is generally favorable, pointing out that Ransom's "criticisms are nearly always of American rather than of English writers" and that although he claims to be a fundamentalist, his insistence that the stories of the Old Testament are to be accepted not as fact but "as myths with an allegorical meaning" makes him a very unusual one.[17] The principal thrust of the book, this reviewer believes, is its attack upon science for the formation of the modern industrial regime. Although "unorthodox not in its defence but in its orthodoxy," the book is written with "great ability and no little feeling, and maintains the reader's interest even when he cannot agree with its logic."

Both Francis Fergusson and Scott Buchanan comment on the book's seminal qualities.[18] Fergusson points out that Ransom's poetic sensibilities make "him almost unique among American writers" on the topics which concern him here and says it is "most heartening to find an American poet so firmly grounded that he can claim a stake in his country's institutions." The writer's purpose in this work, Fergusson recognizes, is to present a religion "with the sanctions of his own natural society behind it . . . with a God he may love and fear and whose commandments represent for him the deepest wisdom." Buchanan focuses immediately upon the essence of Ransom's argument in a way few other reviews of the time did:

The argument begins with the God of Israel. He was mysterious, and not fully understood; he was worshipped with burnt offerings and sacrifices; he was the author of evil as well as good. All these propositions are heresies for the modern mind. . . . Together they say that God the Father is forever above and beyond any of our formulations, whether of science, economy, or morals.[19]

Although *God Without Thunder,* as the first prose book of a poet with a fairly well-established reputation, was commented on in a reasonable number of reputable journals, both in the United States and in England, few of the critics apparently were aware of the area of Ransom's primary concern, and most of them did not approve of the conclusions they thought Ransom had reached. They did not comment on the relevance of the major thesis of the book to his social and political essays which were just beginning to appear, and they could not foresee, of course, that his defense of religious myth incorporated many of the attitudes and beliefs of the essays on literary and cultural topics he would continue to publish for the next thirty-odd years. This thesis Robert Penn Warren dealt with at some length five years after the book was published:

The myth of rationality is deficient, because science "drives too hard after its objective, and pays no attention to the setting." It provides a form of knowledge concerned, not with the concrete, but with the abstract; not with quality, but with quantity. It professes to fit its items into a system, but any one item, in its richness of being, may defy the system until Doomsday. Science provides only one type of chart for the experience of man in the world; in so far as this becomes the basis of education, that is, the basis of interpretation for other charts, a violence is done to human sensibility, which likewise has an appreciative concern with persons, objects, and events of this world—a concern called, in its formal aspect, art. . . .

The way of life congenial to the terms of the myth of rationality is called industrialism. The God of Reason has offered a machinery, a technique, and a gospel of production which provide, theoretically at least, a maximum of efficiency in the gratification of desire. . . . This superior efficiency separates man from brute creation, but a sensibility which the exercise of reason in this fashion would destroy or impair might differentiate him even further. . . . In a system dedicated to the gratification of appetite by the most competent, the most reasonable, process, effective action becomes the ideal of human conduct: Progress, or the perpetual violation of nature. But to be human at all, "we have to have something which will stop action, and this something cannot possibly be reason in its narrow sense."[20]

It was upon these principles, as Warren points out, that Ransom supported agrarianism.

The Dayton "anti-evolution" trial of 1924, Donald Davidson wrote in 1957, "broke in on the literary concerns" of him and some of his friends "like a midnight alarm." About this time he, Ransom, Tate, and Warren "began to remember and haul up for consideration the assumptions that as members of the Fugitive Group, we had not bothered to examine." One of the assumptions which they began to examine closely was that "the South still possessed at least the remnants, maybe more than the remnants, of a traditional, believing society."[21] A little later, perhaps in 1926, Allen Tate wrote Ransom a letter far different from the ones he had been sending down from New York for the past three or four years. "I told him," Tate recalled in 1942, "that we must do something about Southern history and the culture of the South. John had written, on the same day, the same message to me. The letters crossed in the mail."[22] On March 21, 1926,

Davidson replied to a letter from Tate saying that he enthusiastically endorsed the idea of a "symposium on Southern matters." Early the next month Ransom wrote Tate proposing specific areas of southern thought and culture on which they should concentrate.[23] The activity that would result in the publication of *I'll Take My Stand* was underway.

During 1927–1928 Ransom and Davidson had many long informal conversations in their offices at Vanderbilt about the projected book. At least by the late spring of 1927 these discussions included Frank Lawrence Owsley and Lyle Lanier, both members of the faculty at Vanderbilt, and, on the frequent occasions when he visited Nashville, Andrew Nelson Lytle, a 1925 graduate of the university who in his last year there had attended some of the Fugitive meetings. On June 25, 1927, Ransom wrote Tate of the interest and enthusiasm engendered by these meetings:

About our joint Southernism: two considerations occur to me as bearing on the hopefulness of the cause: one is yourself, and many other men who exhibit the same stubbornness of temperament and habit; men of my acquaintance born and bred in the South who go North and cannot bring themselves to surrender to an alien mode of life; this fact, many times repeated within my own knowledge, argues something ineradicable in Southern culture. The other one: Croce (with one or two others) appears to have inspired a genuine and powerful revival of Italianism (in a most advanced aesthetic sense) among the younger generation of Italians. Why can't we? Look at the Vanderbilt crowd; the candidates are always there, just waiting to be shown what their cause is.

Although Tate went to France in the fall of 1928, his interest in the yet-incompletely defined project, fed no doubt by the many letters he got from his friends at home, remained high. Early in 1929 Lytle wrote that as soon as Tate completed his biography of Jefferson Davis, they and their friends "ought to devote the next three or five years to a lucid and forceful re-statement of our philosophy, for when the industrial powers dictate, there will never be the chance." On February 5, Davidson wrote that "Ransom, Wade and I have been trying to get up a Southern symposium." In the meantime Ransom had published "The South Defends Its Heritage" and "The South— Old or New?"—both of which presented rather straightforwardly some of the attitudes held by those who were engaged in the lengthy conversations in the faculty offices on the Vanderbilt campus.[24] The second of these, excerpted from a lengthy unpublished manuscript called "Pioneering on Principle," emphasizes an aspect of the acquisitive American materialistic system he would continue to find unsavory throughout his Agrarian period. There is, this essay begins, a rumor that the South is being industrialized and brought into line with the rest of the country. If this rumor is true, and Ransom sees evidence to support its validity, he hopes and believes it will not be an easy task. The greatest contribution the South can make is to demonstrate "how an American community can really master the spirit of modern industrialism rather than capitulating to it." To accomplish this objective, the South must remain "Southern in the pure, traditional, even sectional sense." The southern culture is the only one in America based on European principles, and for this reason it should not be disturbed. Unlike England, America has never advanced beyond her pioneering stage and has not developed stable customs and institutions. In a traditional society, the citizen attempts to acquire material necessities with as little effort as possible so that he can put the principal share of his energy "into the full life of the mind." For most Americans, particularly those living in the industrialized Northeast, such an attitude "appears stupid," only because they are "given over to materialism," because they are "in a state of arrested adolescence." America must be made to see that it is normal for a mature civilization to give up "pioneering on principle," to renounce its materialistic dreams. The ambitions of a man's youth take two forms: the masculine, such as the applied scientist who attempts to control nature, to harness its power; and the feminine, in which one looks enviously at his fellow man, trying to acquire more than he has. The first of these is hallowed by Americans under the name of progress, which is the concept of man's increasing command over nature and which "enhances too readily our conceits, intoxicates us and brutalizes our life"; the second, under the name of service, seduces "laggard men into fresh struggles with nature." The latest form of pioneering is industrialism which feeds on both kinds of ambition and does not foster in man the "deep sense of beauty" and the "sublime religious feeling" that are dependent upon man's realization of his humble state. The South must not capitulate and become just "another instance of the ordinary industrial community"; it must resist the "novelties of progress and service" that are trying to destroy its traditional way of life.

These two essays were an announcement to all who read them of the intentions and the basic concerns of the Agrarian group. The characteristics of modern America that Ransom and others viewed with increasing distaste and alarm were mentioned in the conversations at Vanderbilt and in the frequent exchange of letters. "Our cause is, we have all sensed this at the same moment," Ransom wrote Tate in the fall of 1927, "the Old South. Lytle wrote me the other day from Yale, for instance, on the poor quality of the men up there. . . . I walk a great deal and throw fits over the physical beauty of this place. Our fight is for survival: and it's got to be waged, not so much against the Yankees as against the exponents of the New South."

As soon as Tate read "The South—Old or New?" in the *Sewanee Review* for April, 1928, he wrote Ransom that he had seen "some traces of the profound" in it, and Ransom responded that it was only as profound as he "dared to make it." The title under which the essay had been submitted was "Reconstructed but Unregenerate," which Ransom later used for his essay in *I'll Take My Stand*, but William S. Knickerbocker, the editor, had found that "too stiff" and had given it an "antebellum title in the tone," Ransom wrote, that "I detested and tried to avoid." Shortly after the essay appeared, Ransom enclosed a copy of it in a letter to E. P. Dutton offering to prepare a monograph entitled "Dixie: The Future of the South" in that company's Today and Tomorrow Series. Although the publisher expressed interest in the proposal, after two months it was rejected. On July 5, 1929, from Yaddo, where he was spending a month, Davidson wrote Ransom of a "series of earnest conversations" he had had with Gorham B. Munson. When Munson asked about the Fugitives, Davidson had told him of the "projected enterprise in the way of a partisan volume about Southern matters." Seeing that Munson appeared genuinely interested in the symposium, Davidson recommended "The South Defends Its Heritage" as "the best exposition in brief of our present stand." Munson read the article that night and the next morning presented Davidson with a lengthy memorandum of "shrewd and sympathetic comment," which Davidson sent along to Ransom. David-son was particularly gratified, he wrote, to learn that Munson thought more highly of the plan of the southern group than he did of the one at Harvard, which included Paul Elmer More, Irving Babbitt, and others and was bringing out a volume entitled "Humanism in America." What these humanists lack is coherence, he wrote; "there is no coherent body; whereas we form a unit of mutual understanding and actively are in touch with a specific cause."

After some delay, the result apparently of a heavy schedule of summer teaching, Ransom responded to Davidson and sent his letter on to Tate suggesting that they should get their southern collection together as soon as possible so that they could profit from the interest raised by the "Babbitt-More volume."[25] To Davidson he wrote that he was "flattered" by Munson's "detailed attention" and that he "agreed in the main with his points." Tate, he reported, had written "in rather glowing terms" about "The South Defends Its Heritage," and Ransom was convinced that Tate would be "a valuable resident worker in some definite Southern movement such as we have been projecting." By the time Ransom wrote this letter, both he and Davidson had received invitations from Howard Mumford Jones, at this time a member of the faculty of the University of North Carolina, to contribute to still another symposium on southern culture. (This one became *Culture in the South,* edited by W. T. Couch.) "I replied vaguely," Ransom wrote Davidson, "saying that you and I had a similar project underway and that all my opinions and energies were already commanded." He would not have been too eager to contribute under any circumstance, he pointed out, because the prospectus Jones sent him seemed most conventional and he was convinced that though that volume might compete with "ours for attention, it will be distinctly out of our field."

In spite of Ransom's unconcealed enthusiasm for the project and the fact that he was publishing essays that prepared both publishers and readers for the appearance of the symposium, Davidson, for some reason, thought he was less than totally committed. "For several months," he wrote Tate on July 29, 1929, "with the partial and some-what hesitating encouragement of Ransom, I have been agitating . . . [for] a collection of views on the South, not a general symposium, but a group of openly partisan documents, concentrating closely around the ideas that you, Ransom and I have in common." He enclosed a tentative prospectus and the comments by Munson, which Ransom had already sent, and indicated that he had tentative feelers out to three publishers: Macmillan, Scribners, and Doubleday-Doran. He ended with a definite request for Tate's support of the project. He admitted an "uncertainty of mind," as well as a lack of knowledge of possible contributors. These problems, added to a "certain hesitancy on the part of Ransom," made him unsure that the project could get underway as quickly as it should.

Tate's response of August 10, which Davidson shared with Ransom, did much to give the project the impetus it needed. Not only did he indicate his full agreement with the views expressed in the letters he had received from Ransom and Davidson and with those in Ransom's southern essays, he also reported that he had solicited Robert Penn Warren's assistance in the endeavor. To Warren, who was then a Rhodes Scholar, he had suggested the establishment of a "society or an academy of *positive* reactionaries," the composition of a "philosophical constitution" to be signed by all members of the academy, and the acquisition of a magazine or newspaper to argue the principles advocated by the group. He had outlined his idea of an academy to John Gould Fletcher, he wrote, and "he is with us all the way." To show that he thought the symposium could and should be done immediately, Tate submitted a list of essay topics and prospective contributors. At the top of his list was "The Philosophy of Provincialism," which should be done by Ransom; then "The Southern Way of Life," which Stark Young might be invited to do, "if he can be prevented from including anecdotes of his grandmother"; or if Young will not, this assignment should go to Warren. He suggested "Contemporary Southern Literature" for Davidson, because "he knows and understands it better than any of us," and indicated that he would like to write himself on "Humanism and the Southern Tradition." Other topics he mentioned were "Religion and Aristocracy in the South," "Harper and Dew: Philosophers of the Old South," "Politics," "Economic Issues," "Education," and "Literature."

Assured of Tate's active participation, the group at Vanderbilt met even more frequently and the excitement generated by the animated discussions of concrete proposals, many of which were suggested directly or indirectly by Tate's letter, was most evident. Davidson vigorously supported the establishment of a magazine or "the capturing of the *Sewanee* [*Review*], and urged that they explore immediately ways of "recruiting young people from college campuses."[26] He begged Tate to return home as soon as he could because he needed his support to keep up the intense interest necessary to insure the complete dedication of other members of the group. "Ransom," he wrote Tate, "you know was never a man to push anything. He will give moral support, he will write, he will be a strong man in conference, but he does not energize." But Adrew Lytle is "terrifically interested." He, Ransom, and Lytle have had many conversations on the topics mentioned in Tate's letter, Davidson reported, and they are "all in a stound, but not the kind of stound that lays people flat. Rather we are raised up—but all we are able to do for the time being is talk."[27] These talks continued throughout that summer. Warren came home for a visit and joined in some of them. When he returned to England, he wrote Tate: "I spent a few days in the midst of the Nashville brothers, and they are on fire with crusading zeal and the determination to lynch carpetbaggers."[28] No doubt, as Davidson wrote Tate on August 20, "your letter solidified the thoughts that had been rattling around in our heads."

By the end of the year a great deal had been accomplished, almost an unbelievable amount in the light of the fact that no editor had been appointed, and all decisions, even those involving the smallest details, had to be agreed upon by a group scattered over two continents. The list of contributors was almost set: Ransom, Davidson, Tate, Lytle, Warren, Frank Lawrence Owsley, and John Donald Wade had agreed to write on fairly well-defined topics. Herman Clarence Nixon, Stark Young, John Gould Fletcher, Lyle H. Lanier, and Henry Blue Kline had been approached and were being considered seriously as contributors. By mid-spring all had accepted and had agreed on general topics for their essays; they hoped to have everything in the hands of a publisher by early fall. The lack of an editor, however, presented two immediate problems: producing a credo or manifesto to acquaint the contributors with the general aims of the symposium and finding a publisher willing to bring out the sort of book they proposed. To satisfy the obvious need of the credo before the individual contributors got too far along with their assigned essays, Ransom, Lytle, and Davidson began work on such a document before the end of 1929. "We'll send it to you," Davidson wrote Tate on December 29, "as soon as it's ready in its tentative form, and you, no doubt, will either want to compose one of your own for comparative study or to make amendments and suggestions in extensio, or both." They expected the credo to be used as a foreword to the volume. On January 5, 1930, the day Tate returned to New York from France, Ransom wrote him that the immediate problem was to make certain that all of the contributors are "properly indoctrinated"; therefore the credo or manifesto should be drawn up and distributed immediately as "our tentative articles of faith." If this document were available, everyone could use it as a point of reference as he prepared his essay, thus increasing the "unity and force of the essays as a whole."

Discussions of the importance of the immediate availability of the credo continued. Ransom, Davidson, and Lytle agreed to produce separate documents, then to combine the strengths of each into a really strong statement to be circulated among the contributors. Ransom was the only one to complete such a document, and he was very much dissatisfied with it, he wrote Tate, because it demonstrated all too clearly his inclination to be "rather abstract and philosophical about such matters." Before he sent the manifesto on to New York for Tate's reactions, however, he incorporated the suggestions of Davidson and Lytle. Tate went through the document with great care, and Ransom assured him that they would give his "points" thorough study.[29] Tate suggested the omission of one of Ransom's articles and the addition of two or three others. "My impression just at the moment," Ransom wrote, "is that the two that deal with Humanism ought to be one; and possibly that it ought to be incorporated into the one I have about the helplessness of the educational institution or the cultural program to accomplish anything. . . . The article you give dealing with the two spirits in recent Southern letters is excellent and timely."[30] On February 15, generally discouraged that everybody seemed to be procrastinating, Ransom wrote Tate that there had been another session on the manifesto and "with every discussion this work becomes more formidable and its dimensions increase." Everyone thought it must be worked through again very carefully before it was ready for publication.[31] The document, he was now convinced, should be completely recast and converted into a "statement of principles." The manifesto, he said, was "too bulky and too difficult and too various in its topics"; its chief fault was that it was "too dogmatic, and not sufficiently tentative in its tone; not that exactly but brash, personal." He intended to rewrite the "Articles of an Agrarian Reform," as the document was then called, into a statement of principles, "rather miscellaneous but more full and leisurely than in their present form." This complete revision might not make the articles available for separate printing before the book was published, but at least it would be ready for the members to sign before the book appeared. This general scheme, he felt, was agreeable to the six contributors in Nashville,[32] a conclusion with which Davidson apparently agreed, for on February 17, 1930, he wrote Tate:

After the discussion here ... it seemed almost hopeless to get the articles into a final presentable shape at once; the more we work with them the more complicated the problem becomes. And to pull and haul at them indefinitely would be to sacrifice our real project, which is to get a book ready. I think it would be wholly wise to wait on the articles until we have a book ready, or nearly so. Then we can shape them for separate publication, if it seems wise to do so, revising them in the light of the chapters of the book itself, and even in that case we can use them as a joint, signed statement, publishable by itself. You cannot imagine what difficulties attend phrasing, scope, etc.; we keep running into new views, obstacles, ideas, and have just about concluded that what we intended at first as a scheme for practical information ... [for] contributors has developed into an endless debate, and amounts to putting the cart before the horse.

Ransom spent considerable time during the spring and summer of 1930 revising the manifesto, converting the "Articles of an Agrarian Reform" to "A Statement of Principles."[33] The extent of his revision is evident after the most rudimentary comparison of the two documents. Although they do not vary significantly in doctrine, in form they are strikingly different. The articles were set up with a formal preamble followed by seventeen points, which Henry Blue Kline had felt had a religious or revolutionary tone. In his revision Ransom tried to correct this defect, as well as the dogmatism and brashness to which he objected, by eliminating the use of the pronoun *we*, by dropping certain debatable and argumentative points, and by making the language more specific and concrete. Any reader of Ransom's essays of the late twenties, and of *God Without Thunder*, was surely prepared for the major principles included in the statement—for the attack on the promises of science, technology, and the New South, as well as for the insistence on the necessity of man's establishing and maintaining a proper attitude toward nature if he was to have a full aesthetic and spiritual life. During the spring Ransom let Davidson see several different versions of the revised "Statement of Principles," and he took the latest form of the document with him when he went to teach the summer term at the West Tennessee Teachers' College. From Memphis he wrote to Davidson on June 23 that he had almost completed another revision and would send it the next day. He had struggled with it more than a week, for all the "principles" were not "as easy to fit in" as they would seem to be. He had finally settled, he wrote, on a new form, "an essay of separated paragraphs, part of them prefatory, part of them stated principles." The next day he sent the document but indicated that although he was fairly well satisfied with the form, the "wording and selection of items" did not please him. He had had to do such a rush job, he wrote, and his teaching was so demanding that he was afraid his mind was stale; but if Davidson would examine the document closely, make suggestions, and return it, he would take "another stab" at revising it. The manifesto came back to him on the evening of July 3, and he spent most of the next two days and nights going through it again; on July 6 he mailed the final revision back to Davidson, saying that it would need a "little more patching" but that "this can be done in the proofs."

The fact that there was no editor of the volume resulted in some confusion in the selection of a publisher and some rather heated discussion about the title. For some time Davidson had been corresponding with Lewis H. Titterton, an associate editor of Macmillan's, regarding his own publishing plans and for the past several months about that firm's possible interest in bringing out the symposium. For about the same period Tate had been writing Eugene Saxon, an editor at Harper's, about some of his projects, and after the symposium was fairly certain of being produced, he had inquired of Harper's interest in that book. After Tate returned to New York in

January, 1930, Ransom, who thought Tate was in a better position than any of the others to secure a publisher, wrote him to try to place "a symposium by eight or ten men, for fall publication if the manuscript must be submitted by April 30; or a symposium by 10 or 12 men if it may be submitted as of July 1 or 15." Ransom suggested that Tate follow up the cordial reception he had received at Harper's. If he did not find sufficient interest there, he should try Coward-McCann because Jesse Carmack, who held a responsible position in that firm, "is a Tennessean and has expressed interest in a book from this section"; Macmillan, because Davidson had opened the door there; and Doubleday-Doran, because Munson worked there. During the early months of 1930 negotiations were carried on simultaneously with two companies, Tate with Harper's and Davidson with Macmillan. Both firms agreed to take the book at about the same time. On February 18 Tate wired that Harper's had agreed to terms, and a contract came from Macmillan three days later. In a quandary Tate asked how he should respond to Saxon, and on February 22 Ransom replied:

The Harper's-Macmillan situation is amusing. If Don had not been Hamlet, he would not have written his indefinite letter of last Sunday or Monday to Macmillan; still less would he have written, after receiving your telegram, to extend to Titterton further hopes of getting into our plan. He could have retired with ease and honor from his Macmillan commitments at either time, and he could do so now. He's just not built that way.

Don't weaken on the Harper's proposition. I haven't expressed myself particularly and don't intend to. Don likes to think he's managing. But I would say and will say if we have to act as a group that Macmillan had best be let down as firmly but gently as possible, and we have no more time to worry about it.

Three days later Ransom wrote that Tate was authorized to sign with Harper's:

We had a group meeting and this is to say confidentially what may or may not appear in Don's letter: *We authorize you.* Don takes things hard and makes difficulties at every turn. But he's not consciously of an ugly spirit and we are met in good humor. His error was in not letting Titterton down the moment he got your letter about the contract. He has got himself into the position which he refers to as "discredited." The only graceful way out that he can imagine, I think, would be not to give the contract to either publisher.

On the same day of Ransom's letter to Tate, Davidson wrote Titterton: "When I first began to communicate with you on the subject of this book, I could speak to a large extent both for myself and for the book, without any violation of the proprieties: for during a great part of this time only three people were interested—Ransom, Tate, and I—and of the three perhaps up to a certain point I took the greatest interest. But since this early stage the project has gone through a series of changes. It is now more distinctly a group project." Davidson went on to explain that the group had recently asked Tate to act as its representative in negotiating a contract. It was only then, Davidson said, that "our plans for publication became definite."

Even after the contract was signed, at terms which pleased the entire group,[34] there were other editorial problems to settle, and Davidson wrote Tate that someone should be appointed as editor "to act as a clearing house and prodder so that things will not get mixed up."[35] As he had done so often during the days when the *Fugitive* was being published, Davidson apparently assumed many of the duties and responsibilities of an editor. Many of the contributors sent their essays to him with the request that he make whatever changes he considered necessary in order to fit them into the overall plan of the book. From Oxford Robert Penn Warren sent his essay on the position of the Negro in the South, one of the most controversial subjects discussed in the symposium. After Davidson read the essay, he thought it much too "progressive" and doubted that it agreed "with our ideas as I understand them."[36] Davidson wrote Tate that the essay "doesn't sound like Red at all," and he doubted that it "ought to go into the book." Tate assured Davidson that he thought the essay good, that it certainly should be included, and that Lytle's reactions to the essay were much the same as his; but Davidson replied that Ransom's "feelings are mixed." The writing he thought very good and agreed that it was better "on the whole that Red assumes a kindly attitude toward the Negro than otherwise," but he also felt that the essay "could bear considerable amendment."[37] There is evidence to indicate that it underwent some editing before it appeared as "The Briar Patch" in *I'll Take My Stand*.

Even the selection of a title for the work indicated the need for an editor, someone to make decisions on basic details. Sometime in late

March, John Donald Wade recalled years later, "Donald Davidson and I were talking, I believe. . . . Possibly each of us suggested a dozen titles. When I said, 'I'll Take My Stand,' he said he thought it would do."[38] To this statement, taken from the song "Dixie," was added the subtitle "The South and the Agrarian Tradition" and the book was named, but not to the complete satisfaction of many members of the group. At least six of them expressed disapproval of the title before the book appeared on November 12, 1930. In May, Warren wrote Tate: "I think the title . . . is the god-damnedest thing I ever heard of; for the love of God block it if you can."[39] A little later, when Davidson and Lytle visited Tate at his farm near Clarksville, Tate reported Warren's reaction to the title and indicated his agreement. Lytle concurred, and Davidson was asked to report the discussion to Ransom and get his reaction. Lytle felt years later that Davidson had not understood the seriousness of their objection; therefore he had merely reported that "Tracts Against Communism" had been suggested and had "left the impression that it was just another title." Nevertheless the choice of title was mentioned in many of the letters exchanged among members of the group during the summer.[40] H. C. Nixon thought the "suggested title appropriate"; Henry Blue Kline wrote that although his first reaction was "unfavorable," he could not "think up a better one." In June, Lytle wrote Tate that he wished the matter of the title could be discussed with the publisher and in July, Davidson suggested that Tate find out from Saxon if the title could be changed; at the same time he indicated his satisfaction with *I'll Take My Stand*. "So far as I am personally concerned, and I think Ransom feels the same way, I'd be quite content to have you title the book," he wrote; "and I don't think any other contributor would raise any substantial objection. Why not, then, just go ahead and fix it?" But, he continued, "Ransom thinks the present title a pretty good one" and indicated his own preference "for the present title over any other suggested."[41]

The discussion continued throughout the summer. On July 21, Davidson wrote to Tate that Harper's southern agent, who had recently visited Nashville, reported that the "Harper people are quite taken with the present title" and that he thought Lanier and Owsley were willing to withdraw their objections. But Tate was not appeased. In fact he was so disturbed that for a time he thought of withdrawing from the project entirely.[42] Finally, he decided to leave his essay in the book, but requested and received permission to add a footnote expressing his disapproval of the title. Even then, the discussion was not concluded. On September 3, Tate wrote a letter to Saxon to see if the title might still be changed. He sent a carbon to Davidson and asked if a vote could not be taken. Ransom and Davidson responded immediately in a joint letter to the whole group:

> We favor the title on its merits. To us it does not connote the same ideas that it does to you. It means: "A statement of convictions by Southerners; take them or leave them; specifically, we unite Southernism with agrarianism, on grounds both historical and philosophical." We are not startled by the consideration that the phrase is lifted from a song named "Dixie," and that in its immediate context appears the expression "to live and die for Dixie." The full title is: "I'll Take My Stand: The South and the Agrarian Tradition." Observe that the colon is one of the subtler marks of syntax that could not possibly occur to a frenzied and uncritical patriot—there is infinite protection for us in that colon.... The title-phrase is strong, clear, homely, and mostly Anglo-Saxon from the point of view of language and historically apt.[43]

Along with this official response both Ransom and Davidson sent personal letters. "You urged me—I take it, quite humorously and a little teasingly—" Davidson wrote, "not to faint on reading the proposed letter to Saxon. You must surely have anticipated then, the astonishment that I naturally felt. I was quite taken aback; and so was Ransom." Tate's reply indicated quite clearly that although the title would have to stand he remained unconvinced of its appropriateness:

> I was very much astonished at the high seriousness of your reply. We didn't take the matter half so seriously, and we were amazed that you all should enlist the cosmos behind you, making the proposed letter to the publisher an affair of good and evil, honor and dishonor....
>
> I say we didn't take it seriously, but of course we did—only in another way. Your Official Letter brought up a very good point—that as historians we know that movements have failed because their groups couldn't work together. It is obvious, of course, that we haven't worked together, and it is also obvious that my protests, and Red's too, have been efforts to work together. For the title was never

submitted to a formal vote, and the two attempts that I have made to get the group to work together on the title have been blocked.

It seems that you and John have been defenders of the title, Red and I the opponents. Your position was not backed by a formal decision of the group, or by a quorum of the group, and in the face of this, since we stood two against two, we felt that it was our privilege to test your position in the hope that we might vindicate our own. . . .

It is over now. Your title triumphs. And I observe that Alexander today on the basis of the title defines our aims as an "agrarian revival" and reduces our real aims to nonsense. . . .

My melancholy is profound.[44]

Writing in 1962, Louis D. Rubin, Jr., says that since its appearance *I'll Take My Stand* has been the "center of constant controversy" and that "not a single writer about the modern South has failed to mention and discuss it."[45] Twenty years earlier, Donald Davidson had said that the book "has this unique distinction: it has been refuted by more people who have never read it—or even seen a copy—than any other book in American history."[46] At the time of its appearance, it was widely reviewed; newspapers in cities in all sections of the country carried comments, though most of them were perfunctory notices and few seemed to be aware of what the writers of the essays were aiming at. Virginia Rock lists more than twenty-five southern newspapers that carried reviews, and almost that many from outside the region, including five New York papers as well as some in St. Louis, Buffalo, Detroit, Hartford, Boston, Chicago, Omaha, and Des Moines. Although one might well argue that the book has never received a completely fair and unbiased hearing, many of these early notices were far from unfriendly. William S. Knickerbocker, who would later confront both Ransom and Davidson in public debate, called it the "most audacious book ever written by Southerners," and the "most challenging book published in the United States since George's *Progress and Poverty*."[47] John Temple Graves said the book was a good antidote to the "platitudes of progress."[48] Another reviewer indicated that the writers of these essays reminded one of the "pleasures of the husking bee, the dance with real violins" and showed how one might avoid the "goading, selfish ambitions which drive his city brother into despair, neuroticism or an early grave."[49] A reviewer in the Des

Moines *Register* predicted that these writers "are very likely to form a nucleus for hundreds of more writers, who will be encouraged by the call of these men."[50]

Even though John Peale Bishop wrote Tate of his agreement with the major premises of the book and T. S. Eliot announced in the *Criterion* that "it is a sound and right reaction which impelled Mr. Allen Tate and his eleven Southerners to write their book," not everyone, of course, was convinced by the soundness of the book's argument or by what many regarded as its futile attempt to disregard a hundred years and more of progress. A columnist in the Macon *Telegraph* labeled the volume "a high spot in the year's hilarity,"[51] and the Nashville *Tennessean* reported the reaction of Chancellor Kirkland of Vanderbilt: "You can't get back to the agrarian scheme of things. There are arguments on both sides as to the virtues of each system of living, but it's an entirely academic discussion because the anti-industrial plan is impractical."[52] Henry Hazlitt, who entitled his lengthy attack in the *Nation*, "So Did Canute," argued that the Agrarians would be no more successful than that ancient king in stemming the tide of progress.[53] "This book," he wrote, "is in the main, the rationalization of a nostalgia for ancestral ways rather than a rational approach to real problems." H. L. Mencken attacked the book in both the *American Mercury* and the *Virginia Quarterly Review*. "The South," he wrote, "can no more revive the simple society of the Jefferson era than England can revive that of Queen Anne. The mills and factories are there to stay and they must be faced. Nothing can be done to help the farmers who still struggle on. . . . They are doomed to become proletarians and the sooner the change is effected the better." Reaction to the book, to say the least, was mixed. It was, as Rubin points out, "ridiculed, condemned, championed," everything "except ignored."[54]

Certainly Ransom was not surprised by the charges that he and his fellow contributors were neo-Confederates, poets, fugitives, and escapists, romantics unwilling to face the realities of modern life. It could be argued, in fact, that he, and they, were pleased with the controversy the book aroused because at least it was noticed; and, as it happened, this kind of reaction provided several opportunities for the Agrarians to present their case directly to the people.

While the essays were being prepared and collected, Ransom shared with all who would allow him to his interest in projects to follow the symposium. The first acquisition of the group, he wrote Tate on January 5, must be a county newspaper. "Both Don and I are very discouraged about the good of academic employment," he wrote, and "I would gladly get out at a little sacrifice; so would Don if his wife would let him." He suggested that the income from the symposium be used for acquiring a paper and was irritated when Davidson said half-jokingly that the $300 advance from Harper's would "come in handy for summer expenses of the contributors." He feared Davidson was "trying to break up the idea of acquiring a paper"; perhaps he was "afraid of the decisions involved." Ransom expressed his intention to oppose very strongly "the divisions of the spoils now or after the volume has been on sale." Although he became convinced that Davidson could not break loose to run the paper, he was delighted that Lytle and Owsley approved of the project, and he assured Tate that he would edit a paper for the group, if he did not have to make too much of a financial sacrifice.[55] "That I can't do," he wrote, "since I have not only my acquired family, but my original one, that is, my parents, in part to look after. But I will make some sacrifice anyway. As far as that is concerned, a county paper couldn't furnish much less of a living than does a minor professorship in a college. My wife and I are quite willing to take a chance if it doesn't look too much like suicide." Although nothing definite came of the project, the seriousness of Ransom's intention was demonstrated by the fact that when Lytle said in midsummer that a good crop would enable him to make a downpayment on a paper, Ransom made definite inquiries about several Tennessee county papers which were thought to be for sale. His attitude for several years continued to be that expressed in a letter to Tate on January 25, 1930. "We must," he insisted, "get a county newspaper.... The book itself is scarcely worth doing if we don't follow it up, and if, in short, we don't get a press and put it to work."

All of the Agrarians were eager to defend themselves against such charges as "unreconstructed rebels," "typewriter agrarians," and "tower-of-ivory agrarians," and their first opportunity came even before the book appeared. In the October, 1930, issue of the *Virginia Quarterly Review*, Stringfellow Barr, a young historian who had been

considered as a possible contributor to *I'll Take My Stand,* argued that
the South must recognize that industrialism is already established in
the section. Rather than ignoring this fact, the leaders of the region
should enact appropriate regulatory statutes so that the "new industrial experiment" will "rehabilitate her economically without wrecking
her spiritually." Exactly a week after this essay appeared, the Nashville
Tennessean carried an open letter, signed by Ransom, Tate, and
Davidson, accusing Barr of having abandoned the southern tradition
whose "virtues were leisure, kindliness, and the enjoyment of the
simple life . . . virtues which thrive in an agrarian climate but do badly
in an industrial." The associated press picked up the letter and circulated it throughout the South. Five days later, Lambert Davis, managing editor of the *Virginia Quarterly Review,* proposed in a letter to
Donald Davidson a public debate between Barr and a member of the
Agrarian group, the debate to be held either at Charlottesville, at
Nashville, or at some neutral city like Richmond.[56] As soon as Davidson received the letter, he discussed the proposal with his colleagues,
who were immensely pleased to have an opportunity to present their
argument to a live audience, many of whom their book would not
reach. However, no member of the group felt he could pay his own
expenses to go to Richmond or Charlottesville, and there were no
prospects of raising the funds necessary to hold the debate in Nashville. Davidson was instructed to express these reactions to Davis.

Ten days after Davidson had written that to him and his fellow
Agrarians the idea of a public debate seemed "excellent from every
standpoint," if the required financial support could be found, Davis
sent a telegram saying the Richmond *Times-Dispatch* had agreed to
sponsor the debate in that city. Davidson sent a telegram accepting the
proposal and naming Ransom as spokesman for the group. On October 16, Allen Cleaton, managing editor of the *Times-Dispatch,* issued
the official invitation for November 14, two days after the book was
formally released. In his telegram Cleaton stated the topic for debate
as "Regulated Industrialism versus Agrarianism," to which Davidson
responded: "Take pleasure in accepting your fine-spirited offer for
debate November 14. Speaker for our group will probably be John
Crowe Ransom. We dislike use of the word regulated in question for
debate. Prefer sharp statement Industrialism vs. Agrarianism or sim-

ply Shall the South Go Industrial. We do not of course propose a
return to stone age but ask for a fair field for contrasting arguments."
The next few weeks were filled with activity. Many details had to be
taken care of in correspondence, invitations were issued to distinguished southerners, many of whom were invited to sit on the platform; and in an attempt to stimulate interest in the debate, publicity
releases were sent to all the newspapers in the area. One such release,
printed in the *Times-Dispatch,* gave a succinct statement of the two
opposing positions:

Both Mr. Barr and Mr. Ransom agree that there was once an agrarian
economy that defined the Southern way of life and created the Southern tradition.

Both Mr. Barr and Mr. Ransom agree that the new industrial
economy, which dominates most sections of the union, is now beginning to grip the South, belated as its appearance is. What is the South
to do?

At this point Mr. Barr and Mr. Ransom differ sharply.

Mr. Barr considers that industrialism of the South is now inevitable.... Agrarianism has lost the fight.

Mr. Ransom argues that the Southern economy is still largely
agrarian and that the fight of the agrarian tradition to maintain itself
is not lost in advance....

Mr. Barr finds that industrialism is, on the whole, advisable for the
South, if only the proper precautions are taken....

Mr. Ransom considers that industrialism for the South is, on the
whole, more deplorable than desirable.... He considers that, even
under the best regulations conceivable, the life of industrial labor is
unworthy. He would have the South fight for its agrarian economy.[57]

Almost all the final details were settled by October 30, when Davis
informed Davidson that Sherwood Anderson, then living in Trout-
dale, Virginia, would serve as chairman. "I think, all things considered," Davis wrote Davidson, "the selection of Anderson a very wise
one.... Anderson has the advantage of being a good person from a
publicity point of view and also a man who has first-hand experience
of both the industrial and agrarian regimes."[58] During the next two
weeks many of the distinguished men and women given special invitations to sit on the platform accepted, and many of those who could
not attend sent commendatory messages. Among the latter group
were Stark Young, Heywood Broun, and Walter Lippmann.

On Friday morning, November 14, Ransom arrived in Richmond accompanied by Allen Tate, Caroline Gordon, and Donald Davidson, the last of whom had been commissioned to cover the debate for the Chattanooga *News*. A little before 8 P.M. they arrived at the Richmond City Auditorium and found many of the 3,500 seats already occupied. After greeting some of their many friends already in the audience, they made their way to the platform. Among the distinguished guests on the stage and in the audience were the governor of Virginia, the president of the University of Richmond, and such literary figures as Ellen Glasgow, James Branch Cabell, Henry Seidel Canby, and H. L. Mencken.[59] When Sherwood Anderson arose to introduce the speakers, every seat in the auditorium was filled, and some of the Boy Scouts who had served as ushers, as well as a few latecomers, lined the back wall.

Before presenting the speakers, Anderson gave some of his reactions to the subject to be discussed, declaring his desire to be a "worm in the apple of progress" and indicating his pleasure at seeing a "movement of young people in favor of the dignity of life on the farm and in small communities." Although Ransom was surely pleased to receive such an obvious display of support from the master of ceremonies, he must have been taken aback to hear Anderson anticipate one of the principal points of his argument: industrialism leads inevitably to communism. Each of the speakers was allotted forty minutes, but Ransom took almost an hour to read his carefully prepared, closely reasoned, and unimpassioned address. Anyone familiar with Barr's published writing on the subject, Ransom said, would know that he used the southern tradition merely "as a gardenia to stick in his buttonhole when he goes traveling in New York." The section needs, Ransom insisted, leaders who will use this tradition as "a prescription to live by." The kinds of checks Barr recommends for the regulation of industry would take many years to develop, and all of them—collective bargaining, workmen's compensation, unemployment insurance, and old-age pensions—are serious breaches of individualism and self-sufficiency, both integral components of the southern tradition. The laborers who come off the farm to enter the factory never dream "that any sort of economic life in a peaceful country" will "require them to surrender their individualism and join an army in order to get a decent protection." What they do not realize is that when they become "industrialists" they cease to be persons and become "units of industrial power," "factors in something called mass production." Near the end of his address, Ransom moved boldly into the point for which Anderson had prepared the audience:

By the least construction we can put upon Mr. Barr's language, he stands for the strongest unionism. And since he wants state action, he is a laborite—he is prepared to let labor become a political party and run the government as in Great Britain. But let us go further yet. Socialism of the variety practiced in a half-way house like Great Britain is a program of regulation which is merely temporizing. It approaches everyday closer to communism . . . and the grand finale of regulation, the millennium itself, is Russian communism.

Neither Mr. Barr nor anyone else, Ransom insisted, "will ever succeed in regulating into industrialism the dignity of personality, which is gone as soon as the man from the farm goes into the factory." Just before Ransom sat down to what Davidson described as "loud applause," he reminded his audience of the virtues of the agrarian life —"fresh air and sunshine, and contact with the elemental soil, and the enjoyment of labor"—and encouraged southern leaders (here he directed his remarks to the distinguished platform guests) to form a political bloc to support the agrarian way and to return to the farm themselves "as object lessons to their respective communities."

Ransom had evidently attempted to make his argument as simple, direct, and concrete as possible, and his delivery of the prepared paper, though quiet, dignified and perhaps too formal, was persuasive because his sincerity was immediately evident to all who heard him.[60] Barr's presentation was a complete contrast at every point. He did not read a manuscript but spoke from notes in a fiery, epigrammatic tone and sat down abruptly after twenty minutes. He had from the very first, Davidson reported, the complete attention of the audience. The system of agriculture in the South, he began, had been established because it was the best way available at that time to make a living. Almost everyone would agree, he continued, that the South had achieved an admirable culture upon this economic foundation, but he could not advise a return to the soil. There is nothing to be gained from "creating out of the farm a mystic lost cause." The southerner must live *now*. Anyway, he observed, the farmers did not reject Jefferson's new and improved plow "because God had a special fondness for the old model and resented the innovation." Progress is inevitable, he concluded, and the South must develop controls so that the industrialism that is here now and that which is sure to come can be used for the good of all the people of the section. What Ransom had called "communism," he preferred to call "paternalism." That "bogey doesn't frighten me. The history of our government shows that we have adopted many paternalistic features and grown used to them, and if paternalistic features should be eliminated from our government, the whole modern system would have to be wiped out." With this statement he reached the climactic conclusion for which he had skillfully prepared the audience: "When problems are complex, you ought never to cry 'I'll Take My Stand' but 'Sit Down and Think.'" With that he sat down to "thunderous applause and roars of laughter."

The rebuttals were animated and the debate ended shortly after 11 P.M. The stage was immediately filled with supporters of both speakers. No winner was declared but Davidson noted: "During the course of the debate, Mr. Barr's stringent sentences won him at times perhaps a bit more applause than Mr. Ransom's very solid and systematic argument got." The several reporters in the audience went off to file their stories, some of which were picked up by press associations and for the next few weeks news stories, feature stories, cartoons, and editorials appeared in newspapers throughout the southern and eastern United States. The *Times-Dispatch* reported that the Agrarians "are not children crying for the moon or sentimentalists weeping for a lost generation."[61] Writing in the Baltimore *Evening Sun*, Virginius Dabney pointed out that the debate in Richmond was just one battle in an extensive campaign: "By means of books, magazine articles, and public debates, the Nashvillians and their allies plan to carry the war into the enemy's country and bring a halt to the industrialization of the Southland."[62] A few days earlier, he had said, "They are still talking here [in Richmond] about the debate on the industrialization of the South."[63] Apparently Ransom was in complete agreement with Davidson's statement in the Chattanooga *News*, that the debate suggests "infinite possibilities of free and honest discussion before local audiences." The impact of this initial debate and its broad coverage in the press resulted in the scheduling of three similar discussions within the next few months, a development which pleased Ransom and the other Agrarians very much, because they felt these public debates were the best possible means of carrying their argument from academe into the marketplace.

Soon after Ransom returned to Nashville, he had an invitation from President Alexander Guerry of the University of Chattanooga to debate Barr in early February. Although he accepted immediately, Barr was not available at that time so the debate was set for January 9, 1931.[64] In the meantime H. C. Nixon scheduled a debate between Ransom and William S. Knickerbocker, editor of the *Sewanee Review,* for December 15 in New Orleans. On December 4 Ransom wrote Tate of his travel plans. He was going to drive down on Thursday, December 11, leaving Nashville before daylight and arriving in New Orleans about midday on Friday. Aside from a speech to the Round Table Club on Saturday and the debate with Knickerbocker on Monday evening, he had no plans, he wrote Tate, "except to study the loyalty of our Southern people and a plan to return to these headquarters about Thursday night." On the day Ransom mailed his letter he received one from Tate expressing his sorrow that a previous commitment would prevent his going to New Orleans and asking if Knickerbocker would definitely be his opponent. The next day Ransom responded:

Yes, Knickerbocker is my opponent, and he came into the office here Wednesday, after first asking me if I had a gun. He is a cheery fellow, friendly, bright and foolish as ever, but I do not find it in my unmilitary nature to continue to feel sore at him. Perhaps I'll have a reversion about the 15th inst. We discussed the debate and decided that he would lead off on the ground that he *attacked our book*; and I would defend. Ten-minute rebuttals. I expect to enjoy this bout, having out-grown my first greenness. I expect even more to enjoy New Orleans and Louisiana and will bring back you and Lytle the fullest report.

He did enjoy his visit to New Orleans. Nixon had made excellent arrangements for his stay and after the talk to the Round Table Club at noon Saturday, which went well, he thought, because his audience appeared attentive and the questions they asked afterwards seemed to indicate they understood what he had said, he had plenty of time to see some of the local points of interest. After dinner Saturday evening in one of the many excellent restaurants there, followed by some interesting conversation with Nixon and some of his friends, he drove around the city on Sunday and enjoyed particularly the many lovely old homes in the Garden District near Tulane University. On Monday evening at 8 P.M., Knickerbocker arose to address an audience of approximately one thousand persons. His delivery was not as impressive as Barr's had been at Richmond, but his message was about the same. If the South is to maintain its rightful position in regard to the other sections of the country, it must develop a diverse economy based on carefully regulated industry, commerce, and agriculture. Ransom had relaxed his style of presentation a little, relying less on a prepared text and more upon his informal but effective classroom manner. In his report of their meeting, which appeared in the *Sewanee Review* for April, 1931, Knickerbocker said that Ransom's lament for the plight of farmers, "who had become little more than robots as mill workers screwing on bolt no. 47 day after day, won the audience vote for agrarianism." In his "subtle employment of sentiment" lay "the seductiveness of his appeal." There was no doubt in the minds of Nixon and many others who listened to the debate that agrarianism had won the day. Ransom left New Orleans in good spirits, ready for the next encounter with Barr, who he was convinced had given him a "thorough trouncing" in Richmond.

On his way down to New Orleans, as he was traveling through Meridian, Laurel, and Hattiesburg, Mississippi, Ransom realized that he was passing near Taylorsville, where he had taught almost twenty years before. He decided then that when he had finished in New Orleans he would drive by there if he had time, to see if he would recognize anyone or anything. After an early lunch in Laurel, he drove along the recently constructed gravel highway through a village with the unlikely name of Soso and into Taylorsville, looking to see if there were any familiar sights.[65] Most of the virgin pine timber, he noted, was gone and on the gently rolling hills and in the valleys where it had once stood were fields in which the previous summer's corn, cotton, sugar cane, and watermelons had grown. In the town, which was not much larger than he remembered it, he could recognize many of the stores. Although cars had replaced the horse-drawn vehicles on the single main street, now paved, he found his way to the Methodist church he had attended and finally to the school. There in the newly consolidated high school, a large one-story brick building which housed more than five hundred students and their twenty-odd teachers, he found that the senior high school English teacher was Miss Dorrence Eaton, who had been in A. A. Mooney's room when he taught there. Her younger sister Corinne had been one of Ransom's students. He was flattered, he said much later, to learn that Miss Eaton not only remembered him but had followed his literary career and owned a volume of his poetry. As he drove back down the highway toward Meridian, where he would spend the night, he was convinced that the farmers in this remote Mississippi county were practicing the kind of subsistence farming he and his colleagues were advocating.

The debate in Chattanooga on January 9, though well attended, was a relatively tame affair. Ransom's success in New Orleans had restored his confidence in his ability to reach a general audience. With the main points of his argument within easy recall, he decided to discard his prepared paper and, like Barr, to speak from notes. Although Ransom's manner was much more persuasive than it had been in their previous meeting, Barr's was not so pugnacious. He was less witty and more conciliatory, Davidson reported; consequently there was no real clash of personality, no obvious contrast in styles of delivery, and a much less exciting debate.

The fourth and last of Ransom's debates was not so mild. Held on February 11 at Emory University as a part of a program sponsored by the Institute of Citizenship, Ransom debated William D. Anderson, president of the Bibb Manufacturing Company of Macon, Georgia, on the question: "Shall the South Follow the East and Go Industrial?" Before an audience reported to be "more than a thousand," Ransom repeated the main points of the argument he had given three times before in a manner that was becoming more relaxed and informal with each presentation. "Industrialism has but one genius," Ransom proclaimed, "and that is the genius of production, in which it makes no provision for emergencies. As a part of the genius of production, it developed advertising and salesmanship to overcome the natural good taste of the people and their natural thrift." [66] After stressing the dangers of a one-crop system, the evils of overproduction, and the attempt to create false need through high-powered advertising techniques, Ransom reached his climax. The South "must go agrarian," the factory workers "must go back to the land," for only in this way can "the menace of unemployment be halted." Only by a return to the land, a movement that should be assisted by the state, can the South "return to and maintain a permanent prosperity" and its citizens retain a quality of life superior to that in other sections of the country. "A man gets poor food in industrialism," he concluded; "machines, streets, and noise are abstractions. He needs actually to touch stone, earth and wood, and to know the infinite variety of nature."

William Anderson's argument emphasized the expected points. Ransom, he insisted, is living in "an age of romanticism now gone forever." Although it is true that the old civilization to which he wants the South to return "developed a fine life for those in the big house," it did not do so much for the less fortunate. "Our nation," he said, "is moving toward a greater conception of universal brotherhood, and if industry has done this, I say give us more industry." The only possibility for the farmer to know the good life is "by an increase in the industrial development." To demonstrate the peace, harmony, and good feeling between labor and management that can exist in a modern industrial establishment, Anderson brought with him a group of young girls trained in the schools of the mill. They entertained the audience with recitations and songs, one of the former, according to Sherwood Anderson, went as follows:

"Who do you love?" a leader asked.
"Anderson! Anderson!" they shouted.
"Who is the greatest man in the South?"
"Anderson! Anderson!" [67]

The last of the debates was held in Columbia, Tennessee, May 21, 1931. This time Ransom was in the audience, not on the platform. The Ransoms, the Tates, and the Lyle Laniers left Nashville about midafternoon in Ransom's car and stopped outside Franklin for a picnic lunch before driving on to Columbia. The debate, sponsored by the Columbia *Herald,* was held in the auditorium of Central High School, which was filled almost to capacity when the Nashville delegation arrived at 7:30, a half hour before the announced starting time. At 7:55 the two debaters, Donald Davidson and William S. Knickerbocker, mounted the platform. Like Ransom's in the Richmond debate, Davidson's argument was presented in a written statement and was a closely reasoned analysis of the evils of industrialism, regulated or not. An industrialized state would lead first to socialism and finally to communism. The absurdity of arguing for controlled industrialism was presented in an analogy near the end of his presentation:

Those who would argue pro and con on the issue as thus stated are like the people who let a dragon into the house and then set about a wild speculation as to whether the dragon should be required to eat in the dining-room or the kitchen, and what his hours of feeding, and his diet should be. And all the time the real argument should be: How shall we get the dragon out of the house in the first place, and back into his den where he will not devour us? I want to get the industrial dragon out of the house, where he never belonged, and back in his proper place, wherever that may be.[68]

Although there is no account of what Knickerbocker said on this occasion, apparently his argument was very much similar to the one he gave in his debate with Ransom in New Orleans—*i.e.,* Anyone familiar with the studies of the modern social scientists knows that the standard of living in the South is the lowest in the country, and the only way the section can rise from its position at the bottom of the statistical table is through an economic system that combines commerce, industry, and agriculture.

Many years later Ransom referred to these debates as larks which he thoroughly enjoyed because they gave him and his colleagues a very pleasant way of presenting their views directly to the people. He had always been interested in public debate and hoped with Donald Davidson that these five occasions on which important issues had been discussed before interested and often enthusiastic audiences were illustrative of the revival in the South of "its old and nearly vanished genius for honest and forthright public argument." The excitement of appearing before a not completely sympathetic audience led him to make regular appearances before Rotary clubs a few years later in England and sometimes on these occasions to make his talks more provocative and controversial than the assigned subject required.

Although Ransom surely had deep convictions regarding the social and economic principles to which he devoted a major portion of his creative energy during the late twenties and early thirties, this was not the happiest period of his life nor the most productive of his literary career. He published four poems between 1927 and 1929, but he seemed to realize that most of his best poetry was already written. On several occasions Tate asked Ransom for poems—in 1932 when he was guest editor for a southern issue of *Poetry* and several times while he was southern editor of *Hound and Horn*—and always Ransom's response was similar to that of January 31, 1932: "I have nothing so far; have never finished that poem of which I showed you a part; have not succeeded . . . in writing the kind of poem I wanted to and have not tried it yet very extensively. Nothing whatever. The best I can do is to say I'll give the muse a chance and will send you anything I can do that seems up to the mark; but doubt whether that undertaking is good for performance. Don't count on me." He did try but the muse would not respond and the appearances of poems were further and further apart. There are other indications that he was not entirely pleased with the turn his career had taken. Although he thought *God Without Thunder* a "sincere book" and one he "had to write," he also knew it was "incomplete," that he had rushed into print before he was altogether in control of the material it contained.

During this period more and more of his time and effort went into the production of manuscripts on political, social, and economic subjects, many of which were never published. Either they did not meet his always exacting standards or he could never cast them in a form acceptable to the publishers. The truth of the matter is that Ransom's political and social ideas are neither as novel nor as arresting as are his provocative and highly original speculations on literary theory. And the statements of these economic arguments lack the precision, the concreteness, the clarity—and thus the force and conviction—that one finds in the best of the essays of this type written by some of Ransom's fellow Agrarians, particularly those of Davidson and John Donald Wade. This never-quite-stated dissatisfaction with his literary career was reflected in his personal life. His willingness to give up his position at Vanderbilt to become the editor of a county newspaper was not only a result of his dissatisfaction with teaching, but it was also an indication of a general unrest, his conviction that something was wrong with what he was doing and how he was living. What he needed, he concluded, was a complete change of scenery. When a chance came, therefore, to spend a year in England—a sojourn which he and Robb had talked about and planned for many years—he was so excited that he could hardly make the definite arrangements required for a family of four to take up an extended residence in a foreign country.

VIII Patriotism Eating at Lyricism 1931-1937

THE EXTENT to which Ransom was committed during the late 1920s to the defense of the southern tradition is clearly indicated in his contribution to *I'll Take My Stand*.[1] In this essay, which comes first in the collection, he issues a call to arms and defends the southern habit of looking backward, which he defines as antique conservatism. Such a habit, he argues, is the best way to resist the current American gospels of progress and service. Although the South cannot escape industrialism completely, in the inevitable change that will come the region should attempt to retain as much of its traditional way of life as possible. Only in the South is there preserved the European art of living, and the residents of the area must realize that the apostles of industrialism would willingly sacrifice the quality of life now possible in the South in order to attain an abstraction usually referred to as an increased standard of living. What can the region do in the face of mounting pressure to industrialize, to be modern and progressive? It can, first of all, resist "the salesmen of industrialism," those foreign invaders who are capable of doing more damage than Sherman did in his infamous march to the sea, those apostles of change and progress who would destroy the southern way of life. Of even more practical cost to the region, perhaps, is his second suggestion, that the South defend its heritage in the political arena by "combining with other minority groups" which are "circumstanced similarly." The principles to be preserved, he concludes, are agrarian, conservative, and anti-industrial. The process through which this preservation may occur is very simple: the citizens of the section must practice the southern anachronism of looking backward until they become a "force the nation must reckon with."

Ransom's letters of the period reveal his disenchantment with the academic life. In spite of what he regarded as his "frugal tastes," after ten years of marriage, he did not own his home. In fact, he had to continue teaching during the summer in order to meet current living expenses. He could never save enough during the academic year to pay rent and buy food during the two summer months that he did not receive a check from Vanderbilt. His writing suffered, he was convinced, because he was forever involved in the process of earning a living. His interest in acquiring a county newspaper was genuine, because he thought that it would provide a tangible means of advancing the agrarian cause, as well as allow him more time to devote to his own work. Moreover, the city of Nashville was too crowded, dirty, and noisy for him; consequently Robb began an organized exploration of the outlying countryside to see if she could find a farm near the university from which he could drive in each day. Even if he should acquire a newspaper, he wanted to remain near Nashville because the area continued to hold strong attraction for him. His mother and father still lived on Sixteenth Avenue, near the university, and his sisters and brother returned to visit as often as possible. His mother, who was in excellent health for a woman of her age, was still the center of a family that remained very close in spite of the fact that most of the children were away from home for a large part of the year. Although his father was becoming frail physically, he remained intellectually alert and active. Since his retirement in 1922, he had continued to contribute regularly to church publications; and in spite of failing eyesight, he had devoted much time to translating into Portuguese J. M. Huddlestone's *Essentials of New Testament Greek* and James Moffatt's *Life of Jesus for Everybody,* the latter much the more difficult of the two, he often said, because he made "a special effort to reproduce Moffatt's English peculiarities in idiomatic Portuguese."[2] Ransom was very much aware, too, that his oldest and closest friends lived in or near the city. Davidson, Owsley, Lanier, and Wade were at Vanderbilt; Tate and Lytle, nearby.

A part of Ransom's discontent was certainly the result of curricular and other changes at Vanderbilt with which he was almost completely out of sympathy. When the college faculty, under what he believed to be strong administrative pressure, adopted a pattern of degree requirements allowing large blocks of elective credits, he was convinced that the traditional basis of a liberal education, one founded on classical languages and learning, was being undermined. In the fall of 1930 he was appointed chairman of a committee to recommend to the faculty some minimum requirements for the degrees awarded by the College of Arts and Science. After several meetings the committee was ready to make its recommendations to the faculty, but, since it was aware of the real center of power at the university, some of its members asked Ransom to make an informal report to Chancellor Kirkland. Shortly after the opening of the winter term, therefore, he wrote Kirkland setting forth the several recommendations of the committee and explaining in detail the rationale for each of them.[3] The committee, Ransom reported, "is primarily concerned about the decay of Ancient Languages and Philosophy, which have in the past been the staples of the Arts tradition in the colleges. Our proposal is intended to remedy that." The committee agreed, he wrote, with the basic concept that a student's time during his first two years should be consumed primarily in fulfilling general or distribution requirements so that he "can make his acquaintance with the leading branches of knowledge before he is allowed to commit himself to any one of them intensely." The committee proposed, therefore, that during his first two years the student take ten courses, of which six would be distributed as follows: two from the natural sciences, two from the social sciences, and two from the humanities. In addition he would take a year of expository writing. One of his language courses would be Greek or Latin; one of his natural sciences, mathematics; and one of his social sciences, formal logic. Ransom justified the last requirement by saying that he thought the study of logic "the best discipline in abstract thinking." It was once required of all juniors at Vanderbilt, he pointed out, and "it is still required at Oxford for Preliminary Examinations before a man may enter upon his intensive final Schools." The only recommendation for the student's final two years, in which he would be primarily concerned with an area of concentration, was that his "course of study would be strictly subject to the approval of his department."

Certainly neither Ransom nor any member of his committee was prepared for Kirkland's response to their proposal.[4] "It is not without some feeling of regret," he began, "that I see your committee taking up the whole question of college curriculum as if it were a new problem now inviting full discussion, just as if we were starting to establish a new institution." Pointing out that he had already gone through many such campaigns during his long tenure as chancellor, he indicated his reluctance to go through another, especially since "I see you are proposing to fight the same battles." It is evident that the members of the committee are not sufficiently well informed, he continued, of the "amount of work required to collect the minimum amount of information upon which such sweeping recommendations must be based." What is the place of Latin, Greek, or logic in the modern curriculum? "Is there no better reason for requiring them than the fact that they once were required or that they are at some other institution? I can see, therefore," he concluded, "no particular contribution that your scheme makes in the matter of concentration, and in the matter of distribution . . . your scheme presents nothing new." Instead of going back over the "same barren and familiar territory," he suggested some topics for the committee's consideration: the comprehensive examination, honors courses, the "remedy for snap courses." Examination of these and similar problems would be much more productive than "calling for a return along the path which every institution in America has traveled and reinstating regulations that have been universally abandoned." The realization that Chancellor Kirkland would actively oppose their recommendations must have discouraged the committee, for apparently it made no report to the faculty. Although they met a few times after receiving Kirkland's reaction, the members prepared no new report; and the next year, while Ransom was on leave, the committee was quietly dissolved. From this confrontation Ransom surely learned one fact: his conception of what constituted a liberal education differed considerably from that of the man who had been the principal administrator of Vanderbilt University for more than a quarter of a century. This difference would become even more obvious and alarming to Ransom in the immediate future.

His year of leave, the first release from full-time teaching for more than a single term since his return from France nearly fifteen years before, was something of a surprise and it could not have come at a better time.[5] During the fall of 1930 Ransom had received an invitation to apply for a Guggenheim Fellowship, but, remembering his disappointment five years before when his application was not approved, he could find little enthusiasm for the project. In fact he first thought he would not bother to get together the required information. Encouraged by Tate, to whom the Guggenheim Foundation had been especially generous by extending his grant for an additional six months, Ransom finally prepared a more refined version of his previous proposal. His ideas were coming even closer to those expressed in the essays included in *The World's Body* (1938). Even with Tate's assurance, reiterated by Davidson, that the foundation could hardly refuse to support a writer of his established reputation, Ransom was not at all convinced that even if his application were approved, he would receive a grant large enough to support him and his family for a year in England. To get his family to England and back, and support the four of them there for a year, would require, he knew, a minimum of $4,000; consequently he requested that amount, fully aware that the grants usually awarded by the foundation were for far less.

What he suspected would happen almost did. The amount of his request was more than the committee of the foundation felt it should grant to one applicant and "only the admittedly high quality of Mr. Ransom's creative writing" made it "willing to make an exception in his case provided it does not cost too much money."[6] Since Ransom was somewhat older and had a "larger family to support than the usual applicant," the committee didn't doubt, as Henry Allen Moe, secretary of the foundation, wrote Kirkland, that the amount requested was reasonable. But the fact remained, that this amount was $1,500 greater than that usually awarded. If the foundation could provide $2,500, Moe asked, "would Vanderbilt be able to make up the $1,500 difference?" After all, he concluded, it would seem "to be the duty of institutions of the standing of Vanderbilt to make provision for the studies of their full professors."

Kirkland's response indicates quite clearly that Moe's suggestion was not acceptable to him. In the first place he apparently did not appreciate Moe's blatant attempt to remind him of Vanderbilt's responsibilities to its faculty. "We recognize," he began, "our obligation to make full provision for special studies of our full professors," but he was just as much aware of many other legitimate requests, such as leaves of absence for professors whose health would not permit them to teach. During the current academic year in the College of Arts and Science alone, the university was paying more than "$11,000 for teachers who are doing no work whatever." He pointed out that Ransom had been given a term of leave at full pay only five years before, and indicated his hope that the foundation could "make arrangements to carry Mr. Ransom without appropriation from Vanderbilt." If Kirkland's purpose was to try to persuade Moe to increase the award, he succeeded, because on March 16 Ransom was informed that the John Simon Guggenheim Memorial Foundation had awarded him a grant of $3,000 and that it hoped "Vanderbilt will be able to assist you also." Two days later Kirkland wrote Moe that he would recommend to his Board of Trust that "Vanderbilt add $1,000 to your appropriation so as to make Professor Ransom's total remuneration $4,000, which was requested." This recommendation was approved by the executive committee of the board two weeks later, and Ransom was informed that he was granted leave for the academic year of 1931/32. When she received this information, Robb brought up to date the collection of maps and other information about the British Isles she had begun to assemble five years before and, with her husband, started to think seriously about where in England they would spend their year. From the first Ransom had thought they would find a house somewhere near Oxford, but all of these plans were changed when he received a letter from John Murray, who had been one of his tutors at Oxford but who was now principal of the University College in Exeter, offering him £200 for part-time tutoring and lecturing during the fall and winter terms. The opportunity to renew his friendship with Murray, with whom he had done little more than exchange Christmas greetings since he left Oxford, the enticement of the extra money, and the attraction of the "personal acquaintance in a College community" made the Ransoms decide on Exeter.

The summer was filled with the many details required of the family preparing to spend a year abroad. In addition to shopping for appropriate clothing and arranging for the physical examinations and innoculations, there were also the arrangements for the children's schooling. Because of a heart murmur revealed by his physical examination the previous spring, Reavill was to be given a year's rest; and after consultation with the officials at the Peabody Demonstration School, where Helen was enrolled, it was decided that she could be given a program of reading and study, under Robb's supervision, so that she would not have to attend a British school. Each of her teachers prepared a list of books to be read and other assignments to be completed, one of which was that she keep a diary giving a detailed account of each day's activities.[7] As soon as Robb had completed as many of these arrangements as possible, she took the children to visit their grandparents in Denver. Ransom was unable to accompany them, because long before he knew he would receive the fellowship he had agreed to teach a summer term at the West Tennessee Teachers' College, a commitment he felt he should honor now in order "to meet the expense of steamboat passage."

When he acquired tickets for the passage over, he arranged to have his car transported on the same ship. In mid-September the family drove to New York and saw the sights there before boarding the *Britannia* in the early morning of the twenty-sixth. "It is a fine boat and a steady one," Ransom wrote Davidson at the end of their second day at sea, "and there has been no sea sickness at all." Soon after docking in Southampton a week later, he collected his car, got all the "luggage back in by the hardest," and set "about prospecting for a place to live." First he checked some of the residential hotels near Exeter and found that the kind of accommodation he wanted would cost about two pounds ten shillings a week for each member of the family, a little more than he could afford. On the second day, however, they found a place they thought acceptable. "We have pleasant lodgings," he wrote Andrew Lytle, "in a middle-class home by the seaside in Devon, and that's bound to be good enough."[8] For six pounds, or about twenty dollars, a week he had acquired two bedrooms and a big sitting room, and, he wrote Tate, "the food is excellent, and we are comfortable. The beach is very fine; so is the country.

The golf course has gorse and heather and sea, the perfect combination."[9]

As soon as they were settled, Ransom made the ten-minute drive into Exeter, conferred with his old friend John Murray, and learned that for the time being his duties at the college would require his coming in to the campus three mornings each week for tutorial sessions. Sometime later in the year he would be expected to give two or three lectures on subjects of his choice. Family life soon fell into a most agreeable routine. On the mornings when he did not have to go to the college, Ransom worked upstairs in his and Robb's bedroom until lunch; then, weather permitting, he and Robb played eighteen holes of golf (she usually went out alone for practice rounds in the mornings), after which there was more "work upstairs" until time for the family's daily walk on the beach before supper.[10] They liked the sea and soon Helen's diary had several such entries as this: "Daddy, Reavill and I went to the beach to see the tide come in. It was not full but very pretty and the spray dashed over the rocks." After the children had had their supper and were ready for bed, Ransom would come to their bedroom and tell them a story, usually concerning the exploits of a character he had created and named Uncle Podger. Then he and Robb had a leisurely dinner, after which John Murray often came over for chess or sometimes brought along a colleague for a few rubbers of bridge.

After a few weeks Ransom wrote Davidson of his satisfaction with his experience as a writer "still on the payroll" but with no assigned duties.[11] "My lot at present," he wrote, "is almost wholly satisfactory. I eat well, I drink a few liquors, I live at ease, though rather cold, I have many pleasant acquaintances, I discharge some light duties in a sound educational institution, I golf, I read largely, and I write." A few weeks later he wrote Tate, "I can't say I'm studying or writing much. Just sittin' and smokin'." But there is "just one fly in the ointment: I miss my friends."[12] Each day he read the *Times* "right through and other more trifling journals from time to time and sometimes I have the feeling that these are almost the days of the end of Europe." Much of the reading he had been doing was in economics, and he often wished he could share some of the ideas that kept racing through his mind with his Agrarian friends back home.[13] Since he could not as-

semble that group for afternoon tea in his room "to take account of
the whole existing damned situation," he had to content himself with
giving his "variation" of the Agrarian doctrine to "one or two good
men at the College" and in a talk entitled "An American View of the
Economic Situation," which he gave to a half dozen or more Rotary
clubs.

The talks to the Rotary clubs, which he began early in January
with the encouragement of John Murray, served much the same purpose as the debates in which he had participated the year before. He
found the public appearances exciting and satisfying, because they let
him test publicly some of the ideas he was trying to incorporate into a
book-length manuscript, which he was calling *Land!* and which had
received the major portion of his creative energy for almost a year.
The English audience was polite and attentive; the clubs served good
food and drink and never expected more than a twenty-minute
speech.[14] The ideas around which Ransom built his talks, because his
audiences seemed to like them, were that it "was evident that the war
debts could not be paid," that "the American tariff wall would probably stay up" (they did not like this point too well), and that "America
had better keep out of Europe and work the garden at home."[15] At
Plymouth, his last talk, he spoke to the largest group he had had.
"They had the Stars and Stripes hoisted in my honor," he wrote Tate,
"and the American Consul at my right hand, which sorter cramped
my style, but I decided to hit out anyways and did about as usual.
They were the best audience I've had."[16] All in all, he said, everyone
seemed pleased with his performance; the English because they "like
plain talk" and John Murray because of the public relations value of
his appearances before audiences "who raise a great deal of money for
the college."[17]

Most of Ransom's writing time was given to the economic treatise
from which his Rotary talks were taken. Just before leaving the States
he had sent Harper's a 25,000-word manuscript, about a third of the
proposed book called *Land!*, with a request for a $500 advance and a
promise that he could have everything in their hands by January 15.
Because he had heard nothing since a brief note acknowledging receipt
of the manuscript, he suspected all was not well and wrote the publisher to send the material to Tate in New York if they could not

publish it. He needed the advance to make a payment on a note that would soon be due in Nashville. To Tate—whom he had notified that he was making "so bold as to add a little to your literary burdens and my obligation to your kindness" by requesting that he act as a kind of literary agent—he wrote requesting that if the manuscript were returned to "please serve it to another publisher," adding that Harcourt and Scribner's had already declined it.[18]

Throughout the fall he wrote almost everyday. On December 13, he informed Davidson: "As for my writing, which I was supposed to send to you, I've still been scribbling away at that book. It will be completed by January 1, a better book than it started out to be, though nothing like a great book; nevertheless I think you will approve it altogether so far as it goes. Harper's has about half of it now, and should have reported before now as to whether they want it; and if they don't it goes to Allen, whom I have asked to act as my literary agent. I think it will go through; it's good enough for that." During October and November, pressed for ready cash, Ransom lifted two articles from the material he had just written. The first he called "A Lion in Distress" and sent to *Harper's* magazine. Although he thought "it sound but not too hot in some ways," since he tried "both to be kind to England and to prophesy doom," it was declined. The editor wrote that they had recently published an article that "partly overlapped" it. The second, entitled "On Being a Creditor Nation," he sent to *Scribner's* magazine, from which it came back with a curt note saying, in Ransom's words, "that while hell is popping in the camp of our French and other debtors, there's no use writing theoretical theses on the subject."[19]

Although the publishers' obvious lack of interest in this writing was a matter of genuine concern, Ransom still thought he had "a pretty good book." Before he left Nashville he had delivered speeches based on its central thesis before the Faculty Club, where it was well received, and before the Coffee House Club, where "it almost got an ovation." He had discussed the economic principles from which it was derived with members of the economics departments at both Vanderbilt and Exeter, and he "was encouraged" by what "seemed to be its immunity from annihilation by the professionals."[20] But by Christmas he was saying that he was unwilling to push the book without "doing it

over on a plan" that would "make it more timely"; on January 3 he
asked Tate to return the "76 odd pages" that Harper had had so that
he could try to "get the thing in still better shape" for fall publication.
"I now propose," he wrote, "to make a really good book (pretty good
at least) out of the thing. This is because my conviction has deepened
and my rested brain cells are capable of a livelier presentation. The
Harper's people—Bissell and Saxon—evidently didn't think much of
my economics; said something about their need of a 'really authentic
study'; but I'm damned if I will believe their judgment." Three weeks
later he again asked Tate to return the manuscript so that he could
revise it. "I've two or three weeks work yet to do," he wrote, "and the
thing will be complete, and I'll send it back to America as an all-ready
manuscript for early fall publication. It will be . . . jazzed up somewhat
and I think it ought to place."[21]

The early months of 1932 were considerably brighter because
portions of the book were accepted for magazine publication. *New
Republic* took, and published almost immediately, a piece called "The
State and the Land," and *Harper's* accepted "Land! An Answer to the
Unemployment Problem,"[22] which Ransom described to Tate as "a
pretty strong agrarian pronouncement."[23] On May 19, however, he
received a letter from Harcourt turning down the revised manuscript.
This rejection apparently suggested rather strongly to him that something was basically wrong with the book; consequently that same evening he asked Tate to withdraw the manuscript, at least for the time
being. "This is too far-away a point to negotiate from," he wrote, "and
the economic subject matter shifts so rapidly that an utterance becomes an anachronism before it gets to print."[24] Maybe he would put it
aside for awhile and work on it some more after he returned to the
States, but "on the other hand maybe my kind of economics won't do
and I had better stick to poetry and aesthetics." This last point he
developed in some detail. Although he knew he had learned a lot of
economics in the past three or four years, he confessed a lack of
confidence in his ability to write an effective and convincing economic
treatise; maybe, he mused, "I haven't the economist's air, flair, style,
method or whatever." The following month he expressed some doubt
that he had any new or significant economic ideas to express. "The

more reviews of books I read," he wrote Andrew Lytle, "the scareder I get that my book has already been printed."[25] Apparently a book just published by Harper's "is mighty nigh my own gospel." When he returned to Nashville the following fall, he read back through the entire manuscript and apparently reached a definite conclusion. "My poor book is nearly a total loss," he wrote Tate on October 25, 1932; "I don't like it. It would have been a passable book published a year ago. Several publishers nearly took it. Within these next ten days I will have kicked it into the incinerator or else taken a grand new start and started over on a new outline altogether." Apparently he took the first course of action, because *Land!* is not mentioned again in any of his correspondence. This was the beginning of the end of Ransom's writing on agrarianism.

Although *Land!* claimed a great deal of Ransom's time during this year of comparative freedom, he was able to devote some attention to the "aesthetic studies" that had interested him for so long. During the fall, when his work on the economic treatise had been most intense, he wrote Davidson that he looked forward to January, when he expected to have the book finished, because he had begun "to feel active again on the inside" and looked forward to "some real freedom for creative writing."[26] A week later he wrote that he was unwilling to give his "economics book" the complete revision he knew it needed because "some other projects have now preceded it."[27] The nature of these "other projects" he outlined in some detail:

I've started on a very old project of mine, "minor poems" of a major poet—Milton. I now think I see the drift of my thinking, and it's part of the true gospel. I'm arguing for the Formal Tradition in literature; I'm saying the form of art is as important to a traditionalist as his religion, or his state, or his values anywhere. You've no idea how voluminous the exhibit is, nor how it applies to our day and time. I'm finishing in a few days a longish article on *Lycidas* alone, which as Milton's most daring excursion into modernity and formlessness, gives me a sort of epitome of what the whole little book will be.

His plan was to finish this essay and send it to a publisher, proposing it as the first in a series of aesthetic or critical pieces under his general editorship. Following his article on Milton, he would recommend an essay by Warren, one "nearly ready," in which he "illustrates the major thesis with examples from Restoration Criticism," after which would come essays from Tate and others.

Although this project never materialized, Ransom's interest in the "formal tradition in literature" prompted the "longish article" on Milton to become two: "A Poem Nearly Anonymous," (*American Review,* May, 1933) and "A Poem Nearly Anonymous: A Poet and His Formal Tradition," (*American Review,* September, 1933).[28] With this introduction Ransom moved directly into the composition of some of the critical essays collected in *The World's Body.* In the fall of 1931 he sketched out the principal ideas of "Poetry: A Note in Ontology," an essay essential to an understanding of his theory of the nature and function of poetry. In a letter to Tate, as in the essay, he discusses three types of poetry: 1) physical, or poetry of things; 2) Platonic, or poetry of ideas ("allegory, Victorian verse, etc."); and 3) metaphysical poetry, which to define will give "me all the pain of this particular essay."[29] Only in this third type is there the "beautiful union" between perceptions (things) and conceptions (ideas). Only through metaphysical poetry can one depict the actual experience, that "elusive first moment" which only art can reproduce. The ontological view of poetry which he had tried unsuccessfully to present five years before in the unpublished manuscript "The Third Moment" has been refined so that now only one kind of poetry can present that specific kind of knowledge which is unique to literature.

His use of *metaphysical,* he wrote, was in the particular application first given the word by Dryden. "I am back at my old God-without-Thunder thesis. The poets must animate the barren ideas and relations; but they have been intimidated." In such poems as "The Mistress," in which he tries to use "current scientific concepts," Abraham Cowley started the modern weakness of making the poem didactic, and he was following his master Thomas Hobbes, who was of the "common-sense school strictly." Since Hobbes, poets have been neither "bold" nor "quick and terse." Only "mere things" strike the nineteenth-century poets as a "safe recourse." Shelley writes, for example, "Thou Young Dawn, turn all thy dew to splendor." But dew is a "thing" and splendor is a "Platonic idea." The metaphysical poet would have said: "Turn thy dew, which is water, into fire, and accomplish the trans-substantiation of the elements." In metaphysical poetry there are both the "large-scale" effects, such as those found in *Paradise Lost,* and the "small-scale effects," such as those almost always present in the metaphors and conceits of the good poetry of the early seventeenth century.

He was, as he said at the end of the letter, "all het up over this topic and not yet entirely articulate." But he continued to work on the essay during the spring and early summer of 1932, while he was still in England; he completed a draft, which he sent to Tate for his reactions and recommendations, shortly after his return to Nashville in early September. As usual Tate read the essay closely and carefully, returning it with detailed comments. That Ransom studied Tate's reactions with great care as he revised the essay for publication is revealed by the letter he wrote after that task was completed. Naturally he was unable to accept some of the suggestions. "As to the definition of conceit as 'meant metaphor,'" he wrote, "I decided after all not to change. For it is not put forward exactly as a formal or sufficient definition; and it carries my sense in an easy popular way." He has used many of the recommendations, however, and others caused him to reconsider some of his arguments and to rephrase many individual statements. He first sent the essay, along with "Happy Farmers," to *Hound and Horn,* which refused them; both first appeared in the *American Review.* [30]

The year in England passed most pleasantly for the Ransom family. At Christmas they entertained Louise Herron, an English teacher from Ward-Belmont College in Nashville, who came down from London, where she was studying for a year, to spend three days with them. The children hung up their stockings for Father Christmas on Christmas Eve and after breakfast the next day—Helen and Reavill had already been up for hours—Ransom handed out presents for everyone, including Mrs. Blakemore, the landlady, who spent the day with them. After a traditional dinner, Mrs. Blakemore showed the children how to pull Christmas crackers. The next day she took the whole family to see the "start of a hunt," and the children petted the hounds and had their picture made with the master and the hounds. But although he was pleased that the children enjoyed the holiday so much, Ransom "missed being near friends and family."[31] "I thought often," he wrote, "of the Tate manor and its yule logs. A trip to furren parts for a man of my age is bound to be something of a disillusionment. I'm no longer prepared to make the proper allowances for the strange ways of strange folks. I'm set in my own."

In addition to the daily rounds of golf and the chess and bridge two or three times a week, the Ransoms had a fairly full social calendar. They dined out, usually with friends or colleagues from the college, three or four times a week, and often on Friday afternoons the entire family went into town for tea at Deller's, a place the children particularly liked, and once they stayed to see Laurel and Hardy in "Jail Birds" at the local cinema. Although Ransom wrote Tate that he had made no effort "to crash the literary gate," he did meet some interesting people.[32] With some of his colleagues at Exeter, he entertained Walter de la Mare when he came to read a paper. In late November, Christopher Dawson, who lived two miles away, came by to see the Ransoms one Sunday afternoon while they were on the golf course. A few afternoons later Robb and Ransom returned the call and soon they were visiting each other regularly. Ransom was much impressed with the young Englishman's erudition, and since Dawson liked to talk about religion, philosophy, and economics as much as he did, the two spent many long winter evenings together, often talking in the Ransoms' sitting room until nearly dawn. On January 3, 1932, Ransom wrote Tate that "Chris Dawson knows more religion and philosophy and economics than any young man I have ever met." Like you, "he is a good friend and a great admirer of Eliot's." Some of the meetings became very heated, because Ransom would never accept Dawson's argument that "Romanism is prepared to accept collectivism." That cannot be the destiny, Ransom argued, of "any religion that is truly Catholic." Even the Mohammedans, he had learned from some Egyptian students whom he was tutoring, have religious instructions against socialism. "Although he hates the modern world, the Mohammedan thinks the church can whitewash (or redeem) it without hurting it," Ransom wrote; "in which case the road to salvation won't be like the eye of a needle, for the rich man will get by without divesting himself." All in all, he concluded, his time in England had convinced him that the "landed life" was the "only life possible to sensitive people" for only there could one establish a proper relationship to his fellow men and to God. When he returned to Nashville, he must get him a place somewhere outside the city.

As the year advanced, he announced with some pride that the children had "gone English." [33] "Helen is fairly gone on English dress, English speech, and English table manners, but Reavill is about the hottest American I've seen. He's sorry for the English but has nothing to give them." One of the things he appreciated most about his year in England was that it gave him more time with the children than he had ever had. With Helen he discussed *Mill on the Floss* and *Moby-Dick,* which she had to read as a part of her English assignment from the Peabody Demonstration School. Because of his heart condition Reavill had to rest a great deal and often while Helen was outside exploring the countryside with Jane, the puppy she got for her birthday, he sat in the room while Ransom worked, reading or drawing. "I think he has talent," Ransom wrote on one occasion. "He has never had instructions, nor even seen the animals and Indians that he does. He always draws action. But then I suppose a man that draws action is not exactly a man of action, so I hope he's not a heathen." [34]

As spring approached, the family began to look for a place in the country where they could spend the remainder of their time in England. On the afternoon of April 19, Robb saw an announcement of a farm for rent about ten miles inland, and they all went out to investigate. Helen and Reavill liked it immediately because in addition to "a pony, baby chickens, 3 dogs, 7 cats and 3 rabbits," which they found in the house and back garden, they discovered pigs and calves in the barn. After they moved to Blackmore Cottage two days later, the children spent much of their time "watching the pigs eat or rubbing the noses of the pretty blue-eyed calves." When they tired of this, they could always engage in more active pursuits—such as riding around the farm lot on Molly, a pony so gentle that they could both get on her at once, playing hide-and-seek in the huge garden, or romping in the hay loft. Helen usually took Jane for a walk before breakfast to check on her new-found friends, and on May 1, when she was up before the sun, the entry in her diary begins: "As Daddy would say, 'Old Sol is peeping forth from his Eastern Chambers.' I get so tired of hearing him say that I could bust his nose." Robb and Ransom were as pleased with their new home as the children were. "We get good air, infinite pleasure, and pleasant service," he wrote Tate, and "all for a little less than eight pounds a week."[35]

Soon after moving to the farm, they learned that Caroline Gordon had won a Guggenheim Fellowship for the following year and that the Tates would be coming to Europe in midsummer, a full month or six weeks before the Ransoms would have to begin their return to America. Immediate plans were made for a reunion of the two families and the Lyle Laniers in Paris in late July. Robb made arrangements for a live-in maid to keep the children at the farm for a week just before they were to sail to New York, but as the time to go up to London to get the boat train to Paris approached, neither parent was at all enthusiastic about leaving them. Instead they took the children to London for their last week in England. "We were mighty sorry to miss the reunion in Paris," Ransom wrote Tate after they were settled back in Nashville; "we were in London all that time, wishing it was Paris, though glad that if it wasn't Paris, it was really London. The children were pretty homesick but managed to like London pretty well. Lyon's Corner House more than Westminster Abbey and American movies more than Buckingham Palace."[36]

Another reason for Ransom's canceling the Paris plans might have been the ever-present shortage of money. Before he left Nashville the year before he had known he had to supplement his $4,000 grant by at least $1,000 or $1,500 if he was to meet his obligations at home and support his family in England. Although he had earned slightly more than $600 tutoring and lecturing and had sold two essays for $300, he was still at least $500 short; consequently, he wrote Chancellor Kirkland on June 2, 1932, to inquire if Vanderbilt would advance him $500 on his next year's salary.[37] Kirkland responded on June 14 that "no one has any authority to make a loan out of university funds to be paid out of your salary next year." Since he realized, however, that Ransom "must be helped in some way," he enclosed a note for $500 with the request that it be signed and returned immediately. When he received the signed note, Kirkland endorsed it personally and had the money deposited in Ransom's account in Nashville. Although this note would have to be renewed in October, and some amount paid on the principal if possible, at least sufficient cash was available now to get him and his family back to Nashville. Ransom did warn Lytle in late June, however, that he had better be careful about inviting the "Ransom brood" to visit him at his Alabama farm "to eat off your garden because we mought come. Victuals promise to be mighty scarce this summer, August and September, waiting until payday comes."[38]

When he arrived back in Nashville, he was pleased to learn that Davidson, who was spending a year's leave at John Donald Wade's place in Marshallville, Georgia, was being replaced by Warren, who was well settled in a cottage on a large estate in east Nashville, his "rent consisting of the fixing of the house and living in it . . . an idyllic spot, a cabin in a bower." But he was saddened to find Davidson, who had lost many of his personal possessions in the Wesley Hall fire the previous spring, in such low spirits.[39] "He had terribly hard times here last spring," Ransom wrote Tate on October 25, 1932, "and is still one of the most intransigent spirits incarnated since Saul of Tarsus kicked against the pricks, but I believe he will pull through. You know, our rebel doctrines are good for all of us but Don, and very doubtful there, because they are flames to his tinder." This chance to get to know Warren better was the best homecoming present Ransom could have received. "Red's as good a head and heart as I've known, and it's a pleasure to be with him," he wrote; "I haven't really passed time with him since the great Fugitive days and doubtless never knew him then as you did."

A few days after the Ransoms were settled in the country place Robb had found for them near Ridgetop, Tennessee, about six miles from the campus, Andrew Lytle came to town to spend a few days. With the Warrens and the Laniers as guests, one Saturday evening there was the first of many poker games that winter, and Ransom was delighted to find that his luck or skill, which had served him so well in those long-ago army days, had not deserted him. On Sunday afternoon, after their first game, the Warrens returned and stayed through supper, giving these old friends an opportunity for long and leisurely conversation. They talked about Cleanth Brooks, who was still at Oxford and who had come to visit the Ransoms during the previous spring in Devon; Ransom commented on how closely Brooks had read *I'll Take My Stand* and how much he seemed to be in agreement with its principles. Both Ransom and Warren agreed that he could make an excellent contribution to the next symposium. What particularly pleased Ransom was the fact that apparently he and Lytle were in perfect agreement regarding some aspects of agrarianism that had troubled him. "Andrew is moving in the same direction I am, mentally," Ransom wrote Tate. "I hope you won't be too disgusted. He's prepared to accept *some* industrialization in the South to keep our farmers from feeding out of the hands of the Yankees; for they have to have commerce with somebody though that is not to be their prime object of existence. I guess I've gone off even further. In England last year I got so used to defending America that I forgot there were two or half a dozen Americas; I'm trying to see if we can't save the whole business, as Abraham tried to save all Sodom, though it was a wicked city." Ransom was delighted to be home so that he could see his family and friends almost every day, even though he missed the Tates. Most of all he was pleased to get back to familiar surroundings so that he could "tackle some writing" which he feared was already too long delayed.

The latest of his economic essays had argued that the soundest economic foundation for the American farmer was self-sufficiency, and his distaste for industrial capitalism included industrialized farming.[40] The advantages of a live-at-home economy were self-evident:

It is tempting to write like a poet, philosopher, or humanist about the aesthetic and spiritual deliverance that will come when the industrial laborers with their specialized and routine jobs and the business men with their offices and abstract preoccupations become translated into people handling the soil with their fingers and coming into direct contact with nature. . . . But there is enough merit in an agrarian movement if it will perform the pure economic service of restoring the superfluous men to livelihood.[41]

The farmer, he insisted, must be his own "carpenter, painter, road maker, meat packer, forester, wood-cutter, gardener, landscape gardener, nursery man, dairyman, poulterer, and handyman." Farming is not a seasonal occupation, he argued, for the man who enters into the vocation as he should will be fully engaged throughout the year. There will be few of the lay-offs so prevalent in industry, but if the farmer should have a little free time during the winter, no one will

"begrudge him a little hunting, fishing, and plain country meditation." Only the farmer who fully understands his role in the economic
order will be truly happy:

The destiny of our broad acres is not to be the simple feed-bowl of the
Western world, filled and steaming; nor even the simple feed-bowl of
the United States, absurdly big for the job, and half-filled. It is to be
hoped that its destiny is to support an excellent order of citizens, who
will be economic dualists, men of unusual integrity and freedom even
while they perform a professional function; farmers with more room,
and more heart, than most of the farmers of the world; happy farmers.[42]

The farmer cannot help himself by applying capitalism to the land.
He must not conceive of his land as a factory producing goods for
sale, because the return on the investment is too low. Only after he has
made a living for himself should he offer produce for sale. He must
regard his farm primarily as a means of subsistence.

Being home did seem to make Ransom more prolific; during the
academic year of 1932/33 he completed the two essays on *Lycidas*,
about which he had written Allen Tate the previous year, and wrote
three of his best-known Agrarian pieces. In "A Capital for the New
Deal," he described a plan for ending the worst depression in the
nation's history. The proposal, which he called "daring, simple, and
brilliant," was not his, he admits; it was suggested to him by Sidney
Mttron Hirsch, a friend since his Fugitive days. The most significant
economic problem confronting America then was finding a cure for
this devastating depression. Since a "depression is a condition marked
by too much productive energy stored up in the economic body,"
it cannot be alleviated until some stimulus releases this energy. Only
stimuli with great force and power can accomplish this objective:
war; natural catastrophes such as storms and fires, if destruction is
great enough; engineering projects, such as dams, roads, public
works, calling for sufficient outlay of capital and labor; a new discovery of natural wealth, such as gold or oil; or an extension of the
frontier. This time the nation cannot wait for nature to takes its
course; the economy must be artificially stimulated. Ransom's recommendation for releasing "the stored up energy in the economic body"
was to "erect a new capital city ... deep in the interior where our

capital city ought to be." Certainly now, as few times in its history, the nation needs a noble effort to "unify our country and concentrate our energies." Such a project would be to build on the banks of the Mississippi a capital city large enough to support fifteen million people. If the government would secure the land, construct the streets, bridges, and public buildings, and then sell land for homes and buildings, the city would support itself. Even if it did not, the cost of the project would be inconsequential when compared to the gains that would accrue to the nation: "Our national energies could scarcely find a field for prouder expression than in raising a national city which would stand henceforth as the object of veneration and the symbol of our unity in diversity, our power, and our peculiar character."[43]

Since he had to teach somewhere during the summer of 1933, Ransom was pleased when an offer came from the University of New Mexico, because it would give him an opportunity to see a part of the country he knew very little about. As usual, the heavy work load and the social demands on the visiting celebrity took most of his time; and the fact that he had no car—having left his for Robb and the children who were spending the summer in Nashville—prevented his getting about as much as he would have liked. What he was able to see, however, started him thinking on a slightly different tact. "I'm keen on Spanish cooking, music, language and general outlook," he wrote Andrew Lytle, "although it's all rather debased as it comes down through the Mexicans; the average Spaniard here is mixed Indian and Spanish. But as far as that's concerned the Indians here are not so bad. These Indians were not killers, they raised corn, had beautiful handicrafts, and built pretty good adobe cities; they still do and have; and it's a pity they're going in for the white man's radio and whiskey."[44] In late July, just before the term ended, he received a letter from Lytle inviting him and the family to spend an extended vacation with him at Cornsilk, the Lytle family plantation near Guntersville, Alabama. "I guess we'll go," he wrote Tate; "I'll be back in Nashville probably the 2nd." He was delayed a few days because just as he was preparing to leave New Mexico a letter came from John Gould Fletcher, who was living temporarily in Santa Fe, asking him to come by for a visit. He welcomed the opportunity, he wrote, "to talk with him and get the inventory of his ideas for a book." All of the contributors to *I'll Take My Stand* to whom Ransom had written were enthusiastic about the prospects of a sequel to the first symposium. There was "such a universal resolution on that project" that he was convinced there could be "a fine book for next spring."[45] An idea was beginning to form in his mind for an essay, he concluded, and he was anxious to get back so he could begin to work on it in earnest.

After a brief few days in Nashville, the entire family drove down to Cornsilk, and Ransom and the children stayed on for a week after Robb had to leave to participate in a golf tournament. When they returned home, about September 1, Lytle came with them, and he and Ransom went on to Benfolly to talk to Tate about the proposed second symposium. As soon as he was settled again in the new place Robb had rented for them on Glendale Lane, off Granny White Pike and near the home of Merrill Moore's parents, he took up the essay "Poetry: A Note in Ontology," which he had left unfinished when he went to New Mexico. When it was completed he turned to an essay that would incorporate some of his impressions of the Southwest, but it had to be put aside almost immediately because of the opening of the fall term at Vanderbilt. "The melancholy days are come, when we have to go to work again," he wrote Tate on September 28. "It makes me surly every morning to have to leave the country place." With this letter he returned an essay of Tate's he had read and sent him a draft of "Poetry: A Note in Ontology." Although he had "an alternative set of terms to account for the types and values," he wrote, he was astonished to find "how close is our agreement in many departments of thought," an agreement "so deep that it is probably permanent." The best news in the letter was Ransom's report that he had gone "so far as to have one mild poetic frenzy and perpetrate an effort." He enclosed a copy of "Prelude to an Evening," which Tate kept to include in the group of poems by southerners he was collecting for the May, 1934, issue of *American Review*.

In the spring of 1933 Seward Collins had written Donald Davidson that he proposed to found a new magazine to be called the *American Review*, the primary purpose of which was to publish the works of four groups of writers, all traditionalists or conservatives: the Humanists, the Neo-Thomists, the Agrarians, and the Distributists.[46]

The response from Davidson was so enthusiastic that Collins decided to come down to Nashville to talk to him and any other Agrarians he could assemble.[47] After the discussions in Nashville, the group retired to Cornsilk, and the conclusions reached there were, as Davidson said later, "almost an answer to a prayer." The Agrarians had finally secured a national outlet for their essays and other writings, and Collins must have been pleased with both the quality and the quantity of the material he received as a result of his commitment to open the pages of the *American Review* to members of the group. In its first three issues Davidson, Tate, Warren, Owsley, Fletcher, Lytle, and Ransom published fifteen articles and book reviews, and during the four and a half years of its existence the southern Agrarians published more than sixty essays in the *Review* (Ransom published eleven essays and a poem). Every Agrarian except four—Young, Kline, Lanier, and Nixon—contributed at least one essay. The realization that he and his fellow Agrarians now had the kind of relationship with a journal which all of them had sought for five or six years renewed Ransom's interest, which was beginning to wane just a little, and during the academic year 1933/34 he published seven essays, four of which were in defense of Agrarian principles.

An invitation to deliver an address to the graduate students and faculty of Louisiana State University encouraged Ransom to complete the essay he had begun after his return from New Mexico the summer before. After it was delivered there, it appeared in the *American Review* for January, 1934. In New Mexico last summer, the essay begins, he had made two acquisitions: a scene and a story. The scene was of the bleak and desolate country the train passes through on its way from Albuquerque to the East, a land so "dry and scrubby" that visitors often think it "incapable of supporting human life." But there is life there and on a rather large and impressive scale; the culture of the Indians persists despite the efforts of the traders, the missionaries, and the government to "enlighten" these "backward" people. The Indians continue to get from this sparse and infertile land many of the benefits a culture can provide. There are, first of all, the economic benefits. By practicing subsistence farming and not worrying about the price their products will command in the marketplace, they live where the white man cannot. Of even more importance than the economic security of this simple life is its aesthetic quality. Their way of life is not only "pleasant"; it "feels right." The impression that this scene made upon him was strengthened by a story he heard while he was visiting in Albuquerque. For several years during a severe drought the Indians could not grow enough food to support themselves. Seeing their plight an Indian agent offered to distribute among them the grants of money he had received from Washington. After conferring with his tribal counselors, however, the chief had refused the white man's money because he feared the effect these unearned gifts would have upon the young men. Since his youths were unaccustomed to money, had not been taught to live by it, the chief knew the introduction of this unessential commodity would corrupt his people and undermine their way of life. Any culture will decline, he realized, when a people "grow out of living from their own products."

Again Ransom refers to the American misconception which assumes that if a people are to be successful they must devote the major portion of their energies to economic pursuits. A traditional society does not continue what he had earlier called "pioneering" beyond a very early stage of its development. Like the Indian, the white man should adapt his life patterns to the geography of his region. As these patterns become "perfected and easy," they will cease to be economic and will become aesthetic. In the beginning they are adopted because they are efficient; but if they are retained, it is because they are enjoyable. The pioneer settler must be driven by economic motives; but as his society begins to assume a definite shape and its citizens to develop specific patterns of behavior, a truce develops between man and nature, "economic actions become" a people's art, and finally there develops a natural piety. This final development can hardly occur in a machine economy, in which there are few opportunities for aesthetic attitudes and experience, because contact is with machines, not nature. Products made by machine can only be used, not really enjoyed, because they have little aesthetic character.

One traveling from Tennessee to Louisiana, he concludes, is well aware of the different kinds of regions he passes through. As he comes through the Mississippi Delta, he can see a region that has accepted a machine economy and note the miserable conditions of the "black man on this black land." As he comes into Louisiana, his senses immediately take in the vast change: the live oaks, the moss, the sub-tropical flora, the waters, and the soft air. In Baton Rouge one sees everywhere evidences of the struggle domestic architecture has undergone in its fight for survival. On the university campus there is an obvious division in the style of the buildings. The older structures are "simple, genuine, and moving"; the new, although of a "modified Spanish" design, blend well with the "harmonious plan," which suits the region's landscape. There is one edifice in the city, however, which appears "altogether foreign to the regional history":

The visiting regionalist in Baton Rouge cannot escape its most famous feature: the State Capitol. It is nearly 500 feet high, bold in design, sumptuous in detail and finish, perfect in appointments, costing doubtless more money than a State Capitol ever did before—and extremely disconcerting to the sense of regional proprieties. It denotes power and opulence, and this is fitting for the architectural symbol of the State of Louisiana. But the manner of the expenditure of the millions of dollars that went into it was peculiarly unimaginative, like the manner in which money is inevitably spent by new men who have made their pile. The State of Louisiana took its bag and went shopping in the biggest market; it came back with New York artists, French and Italian marbles, African mahogany, Vesuvian lava for the paving. The local region appears inconspicuously in some bas-reliefs and statues, and in the alligators, pelicans, magnolias, sugar canes, and cat-tails worked in bronze in the gates and the door panels. They are so ineffectual against the shameless eclecticism of the whole that the Louisiana State Capitol could almost as easily stand in Topeka or Harrisburg or Sacramento as in Baton Rouge.[48]

This "magnificent indiscretion," Ransom said, is a most conspicuous and alarming "symbol of the aesthetic torpor and helplessness" of a people whose leaders are dominated by the economic motive, whose sense of value is distorted by material grandeur.

In the autumn of 1933 Ransom became involved in a minor critical controversy that led some critics to proclaim that the Nashville group did a great disservice to the critical reputation of a fellow southerner. In August, 1933, shortly after Aubrey Starke's *Sidney Lanier* appeared, Tate wrote a blistering review for the *New Republic* in which he said that Lanier's poetry, lacking "precision of statement" and combining a "blurring of images in a random kind of verbiage," had little to say to the poets of his generation either "in substance or in technique." The inference is that Lanier represented the kind of poet from whom Ransom and his fellow Fugitives were fleeing. A little later, in the pages of the *American Review*, Robert Penn Warren addressed himself to Starke's assertion that Lanier was the precursor of the Southern Renaissance. Warren accused him, instead, of representing all that "was dangerous in Romanticism: his theory of personality, his delusion of prophecy, his aesthetic premise, his uninformed admiration of science, his nationalism, his passion for synthesis, his theory of progress." But Warren's assessment of Lanier's poetic achievement is even more damaging than the denunciation of his thought. The poetry has almost all of the qualities associated with mediocrity: didacticism, vague and artificial figures of speech, arbitrary and secondhand allegory, vague perception and diffuse execution, sentimentality, unoriginal and second-rate ideas. Warren lent Ransom his copy of Starke's biography and let him read his essay before he sent it on to the *American Review*.

Starke reacted to the reviews exactly as Tate had expected he would. He wrote a full-scale response to Warren's essay, and included references to Tate's in passing, and sent it to Collins. Before publishing the essay, Collins sent it to Warren to see if he or any other member of the group wished to make an official response. Warren consulted Tate, who said that Starke's charges could not go unchallenged and that since both he and Warren were already involved, the official response should be written by Ransom or Davidson. Since Davidson was then preparing an essay for the southern poetry section of the *American Review*, which was to appear under Tate's editorship the following spring, it was decided that Ransom should reply to Starke.[49] Ransom's reaction to the invitation is expressed in a letter to Tate. "Since I'm feeling pretty mean today with a cold," he wrote, "I feel agreeable to undertaking it." Besides, he continued, writing this essay would give him an opportunity to do something he had wanted to do for sometime, to dissociate himself "from certain aspects of Southernism" by defining those which he believed in.[50] Starke's essay "The Agrarians Deny a Leader" and Ransom's "Hearts and Heads" both appeared in the *Review* for March, 1934.

Ransom opens with the statement that he is entering this controversy because Starke has done "a bold and interesting thing"; he has moved the discussion from literary theory to political and social doctrine. Although Warren and Tate, "restricted by the canons of the literary review," had concentrated almost entirely upon Lainer's poetry, they have been accused of attacking a fellow southerner, one who was also an agrarian. As Tate and Warren had argued that Lanier was not "their kind of leader in poetry," Ransom now asserts that he was equally not "their leader in economic and philosophic ideas." With less than his usual restraint, Ransom accuses Lanier of being "one of the Platonists, in love with big abstract ideas," but about the only supporting evidence he offers is that in the war Lanier was a perfect soldier because he "had no thought of his own"; after the war he wanted "to play the flute and write verse." Then, as he grew into first maturity he evolved a "curious philosophy of art," which Starke states as "the art of any age will complement the thought of that age." Such a theory argues that in a scientific age, such as the one we live in, art will not be concerned with reality but with an escape from reality. Although one could not expect Lanier to know as much about the nature and function of poetry as the critic who was aware of the "vast experimentation in poetry" or about the "body of criticism" which had appeared since his death, the poet who regards his verse as significant only because it provides an escape from the harsh realities of a materialistic age has an incomplete conception of the role of poetry in any age. Lanier had no sense of belonging anywhere, of being rooted to any one place. He regarded nature as an abstraction; he never knew that "sensibility to nature is an acquired faculty" and depends to a large extent upon having the right "working relation with nature," the right economy, and not upon having "tours and picnics."

In his "Centennial Ode" Lanier represented the Civil War as a joust between two noble knights representing the Heart and the Brain. All of this makes little sense to Ransom, because even if one will accept the inference that brain power was concentrated in the North, why should the South furnish the love to reunite the country? In the war Heart had been defeated and, in its aftermath, humiliated by the Head. Naturally the Heart became surly. To react otherwise would be a "very fancy Platonic attitude" of the sort that Lanier exemplified in his own life when he "did not react personally to the tyrannical treatment of his section by the North." Rather than offering love he should have given resistance so that the section would not lose its "national voice" and its "sectional integrity," so that it would not run the "risk of disintegration by crumbling." Lanier's kind of agrarianism was totally inadequate to meet the needs of the twentieth century. He argued for a kind of abstract humanism, not against trade but against some of its evils. He did not say that man should stay on the farm but that working conditions should be improved and hours shortened so that people would have time "to picnic over the hills or spend their time in cultural pursuits." His objection to the factory system was not that "it subtracts the dignity from human labor and the aesthetic value from the product" but that it had unpleasant conditions that should be improved. Ransom had often repeated his own attitude toward controlled industrialism as a solution to the South's problem, not only in his published essays but also in the public debates with Stringfellow Barr, William D. Anderson, and William S. Knickerbocker. Lanier's worst offense was that he regarded favorably "mechanical products and the new applications of science"; in his innocence he never realized that "a taste for the mechanical is a taste for the abstract." Although Sidney Lanier may have "devoted his life to the elucidation of pure agrarian theory," he cannot furnish the kind of leadership the modern southerner needs because he could "never tell his friends from his enemies."

During the time Ransom was writing his most avid defenses of agrarianism, he, Tate, Davidson, Warren, Lytle, and others were planning for a second symposium. On October 29, 1932, Davidson wrote Tate a letter outlining in some detail the kind of book he thought it should be: "The book should make full use of the present trends toward the farm and small town; of regionalism in art and economics; of what is best in the Humanist and other anti-liberal movements. We should be careful to present ourselves as the advance-guard of the new dispensation, not as our critics tiresomely say—'reactionaries.'" A little later Andrew Lytle reported that he and Lyle Lanier had been working on a plan to return five million people to the land and commented on his conception of how the second book should be organized. "This book," he wrote, "should deal with the basic matters of an agrarian culture, the farms and the farmers themselves. Its different phases can be divided up amongst us, and we can write it off in no time."[51] The discussions continued during the summer, and immediately after Ransom returned from New Mexico, where John Gould Fletcher had assured him of his continued interest in the project, Ransom and Davidson began to think seriously about a publisher. Because of Macmillan's interest in *I'll Take My Stand,* Davidson opened negotiations with that firm, and early in the new year, Ransom reported to Tate that Davidson had had a favorable response. "They want a table of contents and a description," Ransom wrote, "but not a *ms.* to pass on."[52] A little later, however, he had to report that "after some debate" Macmillan had chosen not to do the book, and that several of the potential contributors had suggested they try the University of North Carolina Press, whose interest in southern matters had been demonstrated in the fall of 1933 by the publication of W. T. Couch's *Culture in the South,* to which Davidson, John Donald Wade, and H. C. Nixon had contributed. (Lytle's essay was rejected.) Ransom had thought this an important book when he first read it and was pleased to find that *I'll Take My Stand* was mentioned by at "least half of its contributors, with all shades of approval or disapproval." When Collins asked Ransom who should review the book for the *American Review,* he had consulted Davidson, Warren, and Lytle, all of whom agreed with him that Tate was the man. Tate agreed to do the review and Ransom advised him to be "wise, fixed but not repelling," for he thought the "enemy is coming reluctantly over to our side," a conclusion he had first expressed in an essay published a few months earlier. In "Regionalism in the South," he had written: "There are strong signs of a *rapprochement* between Chapel Hill, North Carolina, and Nashville, Tennessee, as to policy and aims."[53] Although the bias of *Culture in the South* was more liberal than conservative, Tate's review indicated that he held some hope for a closer relationship between the two important groups who were trying to interpret the fundamental issues of southern life.

That the hoped-for *rapprochement* between the two groups never occurred was the result undoubtedly of the fact that the difference in attitudes on basic issues was too broad to be bridged even by considerable good will and effort. But the question of whether the University of North Carolina Press would or should publish the second symposium soon became academic, because the book Ransom and others were planning at this time was never completed. As a result of a series of developments in the fall and winter of 1933/34, a book took shape that was far different from *I'll Take My Stand* and not a little unlike the volume initially planned as its sequel. In the fall of 1933 Tate reviewed Herbert Agar's *The People's Choice* for the *American Review*.[54] He was so much impressed by the manner in which Agar had treated certain agrarian themes that he wrote Agar, who was then serving as London correspondent for the Louisville *Courier-Journal,* inviting him to contribute to the second symposium. The frequent essays Agar wrote for the *American Review* over the next eighteen months convinced Tate more than ever that he was a kindred spirit. From the relationship that subsequently developed between the two men came *Who Owns America? A New Declaration of Independence* (1936), a volume to which eight of the Agrarians contributed, but one which was far different in character from that which they had envisioned.

The first reason for the difference, Davidson complained sometime later, was that this one was "planned" by its two editors, Agar and Tate, and the kind of "group consultation" that had gone into the formation of *I'll Take My Stand* was completely absent from it.[55] In their attempt to present more points of view and attract a wider audience, Davidson was convinced that the editors had tried to bring together too many groups, some of whom were basically incompatible: the Agrarians and the Distributionists—Protestants, Catholics, agnostics, southerners, northerners, and Englishmen. The unity and consistency of some new point of view was definitely missing, as was the dedication to a single, coherent, and definable cause.[56]

Ransom's contribution, which had earlier appeared in the *Virginia Quarterly Review,* reveals a definite shift in some of his basic attitudes. In fact the view expressed here is not far different from that defended by Stringfellow Barr in their public debates six years earlier. "Now there is nobody," Ransom suggests, "even in the economically backward South, who proposes to destroy corporate business. Least of all, it may be, in the South, which wants to see its industries developed, so that it may be permitted to approach closer to its regional autonomy."[57] Ransom even outlines the kind of special assistance he would expect from the federal government: the provision of good roads, a free domestic market, first-class educational facilities, cheap electricity.[58] When he presents the sort of regulations he expects, one can see how far he has moved from the position he had defended in the debates with Barr. There he had argued, as Davidson had later expressed it, that trying to regulate industry was similar to arguing about whether the dragon, which would surely destroy the house he had been allowed to enter, should be permitted to eat in the "dining-room or the kitchen and what his hours of feeding would be." But now Ransom's argument is:

> The tenure of the job should be secure; that is, if the job fails, there should be a fresh source of income, a fund in reserve, to fall back upon. In other words, the South is entirely sympathetic with our incipient national and State program in this direction.
> The houses and premises, so far as they are provided by the company ... should be brought up to a standard of decent habitableness ... the section should be paved, planted in trees and flowers, provided with playgrounds and parks. ...
> There must be adequate medical and hospital services, and provision for good education.[59]

The book, which was released on April 30, 1936, was received cordially both in the United States and in England, but it created much less reaction, particularly in the South, than had *I'll Take My Stand*. The occasion of its publication did provide the opportunity for a convivial gathering of the Agrarians and some of their friends in Nashville. On the day *Who Owns America?* appeared in the bookstores Allen and Caroline Gordon Tate, the Herbert Agars, and Andrew Lytle came into town to join the Ransoms, the Davidsons, the Warrens, the Owsleys, the James Wallers, and George Marion O'Donnell at a party given in their honor by the local booksellers, Stokes and Stockell. Attended by more than fifty guests and marked by a performance of "Brother Micajah" by Andrew Lytle, this gathering was followed next day by an autograph party in the firm's downtown store. Attended by eleven of the contributors "amid photographers and interviewers and purchasers," this three-hour session was followed by a lecture by Herbert Agar at Vanderbilt. Later that evening there was a party at James Waller's house, at which, according to George Marion O'Donnell, "everyone from John Ransom on down was reeling and rocking."[60] At lunch next day the Tates, O'Donnell, and Ransom, who ate together at Petrone's, were a little subdued by all the excitement and the excesses of the evening before, but an afternoon at the Ransoms' country place and a cocktail party, hosted by Tom Walsh of Scribners, revived everyone for the last event of the day, "a very dry but very pleasant party" at the Davidsons, at which they all sang "old songs in a somewhat wavering chorus."

A few months earlier George Marion O'Donnell had written Richmond Croom Beatty of a meeting of the Agrarians at which Ransom had revealed to him a conclusion he had reached after several years of indecision. "We had a veritable convention of the Agrarian group around a table in Petrone's on the 2nd," he wrote; "the Tates were there, Warren, Lytle—with his sister—Ransom, Davidson, James Waller, and the Owsleys. Great was the gaiety of the assemblage, particularly after Warren had finished his fifth bottle of ale. . . . Ransom and I were scheduled to attend an English 20 class at one o'clock. Well, we went but Ransom dismissed the class in short order so that we could get back to the session. In dismissing the class, however, he made a slight blunder, for he said, during the course of his remarks: 'I've been down with a group of friends drinking lunch.'" Before the group disbanded, Ransom agreed to write a note on a selection of O'Donnell's poems scheduled to appear in the spring issue of the *Southern Review*. O'Donnell was delighted, he wrote Beatty, "because I know of no one whom I'd rather have write about my stuff than Ransom."[61] At some time during this afternoon, Ransom confided to O'Donnell a decision he had reached after months of thought; he was "determined to write no more economic essays," a conclusion with which O'Donnell agreed for reasons he thought he shared with Ransom: "My own feeling about the business is that I have had my say—that I have taken my stand—and that since I'm primarily a creative writer and not an economist I'd better stick to my creative writing. Moreover, it seems to me that Agrarianism or Distributism is now passing into a second phase—the political. The philosophical groundwork is complete with the publication of this last book." The work yet to be done can best be accomplished, he had concluded, by organizers, publicists, and politicians.

Ransom's determination "to write no more economic essays" was now apparently well fixed in his mind, for on September 17, 1936, he wrote Tate:

In Sunday's *Banner* you will see my review of *Mediterranean*, if you think it worth a dime, which it hardly is. Excuse the performance in view of the medium. However, it has started me on an exciting excursion of thought which I want to bring before you. I say there is one place that *patriotism* is eating at lyricism. What is true in part for you (though a part that is ominously increasing) is true nearly in full for me: *Patriotism* has nearly eaten me up and I've got to get out of it.

Since he was convinced that the "modern artist needs an objective standard to replace that one supplied by the church for certain planes of experience," he suggested that he and Tate found an American Academy of Letters. Its purpose would be to "supply public recognition" to living American writers whose works exemplify "solidity, completeness, flexibility, and background." The qualifications for membership were explained under the following headings: Dignity, Productivity, Scope ("the purely literary workman who performs in several fields with distinction is highly eligible"), Positive Traditionalism ("this eliminates artists who exploit a novelty or a revolutionary device and do not assimilate and use the literary tradition"), and Style ("the symbol of personal individuation which is the real objective of the American tradition and of any literary tradition"). He proposed that after the election of twenty-five charter members, no more than two new members would be elected in any one year. Ransom's list of proposed charter members is most interesting, as are some of his marginal comments: James Branch Cabell, Willa Cather, Ralph Crom, W. S. Dodd, Theodore Dreiser ("with reluctance"), John Gould Fletcher, Douglas Southall Freeman, Robert Frost ("We're almost obliged"), Ellen Glasgow, Joseph Wood Krutch, Sinclair Lewis ("After all he's a Nobelist"), Robert Morss Lovett, Archibald Mac-Leish, Marianne Moore, Paul Elmer More, Ezra Pound, John Crowe Ransom ("?"), George Santayana, Gilbert Seldes, Allen Tate, Mark Van Doren, John Donald Wade, Edith Wharton, Yvor Winters, Stark Young. Such names as T. S. Eliot, William Faulkner, Ernest Hemingway, John Dos Passos, and Wallace Stevens do not appear even on his list of those "*nearly*" qualified."[62] Although it was hard to "reject the brethren and sistern," he would not want the list "confused with a Fugitive or Agrarian organization," and he wished "old Ford" were an American citizen so he could be included. The group, he realized, was "pretty catholic" but any attempt to remove all the "alien persons" would result in a "Southern Academy," which is "too close to our peculiar variety of patriotism" to "do us any good."

A few days later he wrote Tate again, expanding the general plan and developing some of the divisions in more detail. He would definitely favor a "select national organization over a Southern" one, and he presented a number of alternate names for the organization: the College of Letters, the Institute of Literary Autonomy and Tradition, the Institute of Independent Letters, or the Institute of Living Tradition." He indicated, too, that he would revise his statement of qualifications in order to include "the main thing which I omitted: the purity, autonomy, anti-Platonism of the poetry." He would also insist that the election procedure be such as to avoid: "(1) The kind of writing which is merely specialized and lacks implications and background. (2) The ostensible pure art which is hired out to causes." The basic intentions of the academy would be two, which on the surface might appear to be contradictory: "to have our literature created by persons of philosophical capacity; to have its pure forms without taint or explicit philosophy."

That his interest and energy, once devoted to the Agrarian cause, were being diverted to other endeavors is supported by many references in letters written during the spring and summer of 1937, the last few months of Ransom's long tenure at Vanderbilt. On April 6 he wrote Tate: "I enclose a last act of patriotism. I'm signing off but a little by degrees. Perhaps this one had better never been written because it will seem to Don like treason and unfriendship. It's been on my conscience a long time. I can imagine it is a line you yourself might not care to take, feeling that our Agrarian position is stronger if we just urge it single and pure, without reference to politics. But I've felt uneasy a long time over that." The essay Ransom referred to as his "last act of patriotism" was not published, but the cast of Ransom's thinking is revealed in a letter he wrote to Edwin Mims on June 8, 1937, as he was considering an offer he had received from Kenyon College. The differences between his position at Vanderbilt, he began, and the offer he had received from Kenyon were greater than salary. Kenyon would allow him much more time to do his own work, and so many of his projects had fallen through in recent years because he had neither the "time nor the strength to work at them" that he was annoyed and dismayed. He badly felt the need to have the opportunity "to pursue the kind of writing which is peculiar or individual with me." He concluded the letter with an explanation of why remaining at Vanderbilt would be of no particular advantage as far as his literary career was concerned:

It is true that if this kind of writing were on regionalism or agrarianism, I would be going into foreign parts. But I have about contributed all I have to those movements, and I have of late gone almost entirely into pure literary work. My group does not need me; in fact we are not an organized aggressive group anyway. Among the literary labors I would like to do are poems; but it takes more peace and contentedness to do them than seems possible at Vanderbilt, where I have found my obligations and natural extensions of interest increasing all the time of late years. At my time of life it seems legitimate for me to work at literature a little more single-mindedly than I have been doing.

A few months later, after he had moved to Kenyon, he was even more explicit in a letter to Tate detailing where his primary interest now lay.[63] The following year he sent a flyer to Davidson announcing the establishment of the *Kenyon Review* and asking for some contribution to the new journal, for which he would pay "$5.00 a page for prose" and "a higher rate for poetry," the specific amount to be determined upon receipt of the poem. In a personal note penciled in at the bottom of the page, he wrote: "I do want things from you—poems, critiques, reviews (I'm sorry we won't be in the field for patriotic and agrarian things)—and the sooner the better."[64] After what would appear to be a careful and almost systematic attempt to inform his closest friends and associates of his changing views, one can well wonder why his public statement of the position he had reached in several stages over ten years or more appeared to some as a sudden and unexpected reversal. In the mid-1940s Ransom gave his reaction to two essays which appeared in the *Kenyon Review*, both of which comment on a topic that has "a great urgency for us: the unhappy human condition that has arisen under the modern economy, and the question of whether religion or art can do anything about it." In an editorial he summarizes the argument of W. P. Southard's "The Religious Poetry of Robert Penn Warren," one of the two essays under discussion:

We are far gone in our habit of specialized labor, whether we work with our heads or our hands; it has become our second nature and nearly the only human nature that we can have, in a responsible public sense. We have fallen . . . and henceforth a condition we might properly call "decadence" is our portion; guilt and repentance, guilt followed by such salvation as can be achieved. In the forms which this salvation takes, we do go back into our original innocence, but vicariously or symbolically, not really. We cannot actually go back, and if we try it the old estate becomes insupportable; a little trial will show that. It was the estate of good animals opposing nature with little benefit of rational discourse, therefore of abstraction (the splitting off of the concept from the total image) and special effectiveness. We would not like it now. So we manage as we are with the help of salvation, an excellent thing though only for a guilty species. Salvation is simple as picnics, or games, it may be; but for superior sinners it must take a higher form, such as individual works of art, or religious exercises which are works of art institutionalized and rehearsed in ritual. All these are compensatory concretions—they return to primitive experience but only formally; by no means do they propose to abandon the forward economy.[65]

Anyone familiar with *God Without Thunder* and the published essays on literary theory and practice that had been appearing for almost twenty years will recognize immediately that Ransom's summary of Southard's thesis includes nothing that had not previously appeared under his own name. It is no wonder, then, that he says he finds himself "in the fullest sympathy with Mr. Southard's argument." The only surprise comes when he accuses Southard of taking an "unexpected jump" near the end of his rational and convincing discourse, for this "unexpected jump" is a proposal with which many of Ransom's closest associates thought he was in complete agreement only a few years before:

It seemed that we had taken our constitutional and predestined development, and our progress was irreversible; but suddenly Mr. Southard proposes to found an agrarian community within which innocence may be recovered. I can reproach him for his fantasy with the better conscience inasmuch as I have entertained it too, as one of the Southern agrarians. And it seems to be in order to offer a brief notice about that, though I will not pretend to be representing Mr. Warren, or Mr. Tate, or others of that group.[66]

That innocence is irrecoverable Ransom had argued since the middle twenties when he was writing the unpublished essay "The Third Moment," but now he moved considerably beyond that position, Donald Davidson and others thought, in his insistence that the division of labor of the modern industrial society is a part of the postscientific world that twentieth-century man must accept:

For without consenting to division of labor, and hence modern society, we should have not only no effective science, invention, and scholarship, but nothing to speak of in art, e.g., Reviews and contributions to Reviews, fine poems and their exegesis. . . . The pure though always divided knowledges, and the physical gadgets and commodities, constitute our science, and are the guilty fruits; but the former are triumphs of muscular intellect, and the latter at best are clean and wholly at our service. The arts are the expiations, but they are beautiful. Together they comprise the detail of human history. . . . On these terms the generic human economy can operate, and they are the only terms practicable now.[67]

The southern Agrarians have not returned to the soil nor can they rationally advise those in business and industry to insulate themselves from the division of labor and find security in "their garden of innocence." The recent judgment of the Potsdam declaration, that the German people should return to an agrarian economy, Ransom can now only regard as a "heavy punishment," though he once would have thought that no sentence could have brought "greater happiness for a people." This essay was read, needless to say, with consternation and disappointment in Nashville and elsewhere.

When Ransom told Mims in the summer of 1937 that he was "annoyed and dismayed" that he did not have time and energy to "pursue the kind of writing" he felt he was best qualified to do, he was undoubtedly referring to the essays on literary theory and practice which had been appearing regularly for almost ten years, a group of which he at that moment was preparing for book publication the next year. Between May, 1933, and January, 1938, Ransom published all fifteen of the essays collected in *The World's Body*,[68] and now that he had discovered that literary theorizing "can scarcely afford to be pursued in any way except in constant company of the actual poems," he was eager to move beyond this initial effort, which he regarded as a "sort of apprenticeship with his general principles," so that he could make further explorations into and applications of what he had come to believe was a "fairly single and coherent doctrine." He informed Mims in the summer of 1937 that he wanted to write more poetry, but he would write little additional verse, although he would spend an increasingly large portion of his time as he grew older recasting the poems of the 1920s. Just ahead of him lay the period of his greatest influence as critic and man of letters. As editor of the *Kenyon Review*, which quickly became one of the most important critical quarterlies that America has had, he published the works of many of the established writers of the English-speaking world and introduced to serious students of literature everywhere some of the most significant of the promising new writers who were just beginning to publish after World War II. In the pages of the *Kenyon Review* would also appear some of the most informative and provocative of Ransom's own essays, clear incisive arguments, emphasizing the need for professional literary critics who would insist upon the necessity of an approach to literature that is primarily concerned with formal and aesthetic values, one always centered upon the world of art itself. Before he could move into the next phase of his literary career, however, he must undergo the excruciating experience of leaving the university with which as student and teacher he had been associated for more than thirty years and the section of the country where, except for relatively short periods, he had lived all of his life. His leaving Vanderbilt was not nearly as painful as it might have been but for certain developments over the past several years that had made him more and more aware of the growing distance between his conception of the function of a liberal arts college and that of some of the administrative offices of his university.

In the fall of 1935 he had been appointed to a five-man committee, chaired by Dean O. C. Carmichael (who most faculty members knew had been selected to succeed Kirkland as chancellor), to study the curricular structure of the College of Arts and Science, including such specific areas as requirements for admission and graduation. This committee, which also included W. B. Jewell, E. J. Eberling, and Lyle H. Lanier, met at least twice a month during the academic year, often with the chairmen of the academic departments, a few times during the summer, and almost every week during the fall of 1937. Since every man on the committee had been assured that its charge was one of considerable importance, its business was undertaken with a seriousness that made it more "time consuming than any other such appointment" Ransom had ever had.[69] After reading all the relevant literature Dean Carmichael and his staff had collected, each member was assigned to study in detail the practices of institutions comparable to Vanderbilt in one of the regional accrediting associations. After this comprehensive study and the subsequent reports to the committee, as well as the hours spent in meetings listening to these and other reports, the committee carefully drafted its recommendations, which went to a review board—composed of the chancellor, the deans of the senior and junior colleges, the dean of the school of engineering, and the chairmen of three divisions of the college: humanities, social sciences, and natural sciences—before it was presented to the faculty. The report of the review board which went to the faculty on April 13, 1937, was somewhat different from that prepared by the committee. Ransom believed that certain important functions traditionally performed by the faculty were being surrendered to the administration. After the document had been presented by Chancellor Kirkland, Dean Carmichael's motion that it be adopted was seconded by Professor Madison Sarratt of the mathematics department. Ransom arose immediately and proposed as a substitute motion, which was seconded by Professor Jackson of the German department, that "the report of the Board of Review be committed to further study." The motion was "vigorously debated" by Ransom and others, according to the minutes of the meeting, and at one time Kirkland gave up the chair to urge the defeat of the substitute motion. After more than an hour of discussion, the question was called—the chairman cautioning the auditors not to count the vote of anyone below the rank of assistant professor—and Ransom's motion lost by a vote of 26 to 27.

George Marion O'Donnell, who as an instructor was not allowed to vote, wrote Richmond Croom Beatty that the "curriculum revision scheme (principally prepared by Lanier and Ransom) was crushed by fiat." A majority of the faculty, who really favored the original proposal of the committee, were "reprimanded almost insultingly by the Chancellor" and everyone on campus is "in a stew over it." [70] Davidson thought that the whole exercise was "an insult to the faculty" and that the proposal, passed only after the most "blatant and obvious coercion" by Kirkland, would not have received a "half dozen votes ten years before." Ransom's reactions to this situation are not definitely known. If he was much upset, he did not reveal his feelings even to his closest friends. He kept his composure and there are no references to the incident in his letters, not even in those to Tate in whom he confided most. But at the end of the summer, after he had already decided to go to Kenyon, he told a reporter in Boulder, Colorado, that he thought in the smaller college he would have time to do more writing, that in a university too much of a professor's time was spent in such unproductive activities as "committees and curriculum reform and all that." One thing seems certain, however: Ransom did spend a lot of time on this committee assignment, time which he would have much preferred to devote to his own work. All of the time and effort he and his colleagues devoted to the project seemed to affect the outcome little, if at all. He must have been disappointed, if not disillusioned and disgusted, and this attitude must have made him more receptive to an offer that would provide a different academic environment, even if he had to give up his "familiars" and his "known corners and places down in Tennessee."

His Own Country
1935-1937

BY THE mid-1930s John Crowe Ransom thought he was settled for life. Since 1903 he had spent all but eight years in Nashville and had been in continuous residence at Vanderbilt, except for three academic leaves and numerous summer appointments in other colleges and universities. In June, 1927, he wrote Allen Tate, who had just rented a farm near Patterson, New York: "I am glad to hear that you are going to the country. I'm going to do that myself one of these days. We shall buy a little place somewhere out of Nashville to live, I suppose, perpetually. Have this June got my professorship at Vanderbilt; I suppose I can make a decent living and I am quite happy to live on where and how I have these ten years and more."

Although he had not been able to buy the country home he so badly wanted, after several moves he had finally rented a large house with two acres of land. After a year in what Ransom called the "most pleasing surroundings we have had," the owner returned and the Ransoms were forced to seek another home. This time they moved even further out, almost ten miles from the university, to a place on the Couchville Pike. Here, for a very modest rent, Ransom was able to live closer to his agrarian ideals. With four acres of land he could have a vegetable garden, and Reavill and Helen could have goats, guineas, bantam chickens, and a pet pig. For a time they even kept a cow. From here Reavill wrote his Aunt Ellene that his mother had given him a "program of self-improvement" which included his assuming responsibility for the following: "1. Feed pigs 2. Empty trash 3. Turn cow out 4. Read a book every week 5. Be punctual at appointments 6. Plus good manners."[1] The children became so attached to the pet pig that they could not bear the thought of parting with him, despite Helen's embarrassment when he ran through the legs of the young man who came in his best suit to take her to her first formal. Finally Robb had a professional butcher slaughter the pig. The next afternoon or so when Reavill returned from school and peeked into the cardboard carton on the kitchen table, he found among the neatly packaged cuts of pork the feet of his pet. Despite his father's gentle encouragement, he steadfastly refused to eat any of the meat.[2]

For the first time in many years Ransom started attending church again. Later he would declare that he had "backslid from my father's faith . . . even before I came upon Kant the Transcendentalist," that he had moved irrecoverably toward the system of belief formulated in *God Without Thunder*. He always referred to his faith as Unitarian, but now that he was living near the Arlington Methodist Church, which his father had once served as pastor, he began to attend the Sunday morning services. In the true spirit of agrarianism he wanted to become a functional member of the community to which he belonged. For a time, therefore, he not only went to hear the sermon and to meet and discuss politics and the New Deal with his neighbors, but he allowed himself to be persuaded to teach a Sunday school class. One of his students remembers that his teaching method did not vary much from Sunday to Sunday. After reading from the Bible, he talked for a few minutes about the background of what he had read; then he conducted a discussion by asking and answering questions, a procedure much like the one he used in his classes at Vanderbilt. The students were impressed by his knowledge of the Scriptures and thoroughly approved of his attempts to focus the discussions always on specific passages from the Bible. A rather unpleasant situation arose, however, when several members of the class observed that Ransom did not join in the recitation of the Apostle's Creed. When he was pressed for an explanation, he admitted that he did not accept the trinitarian concept of the deity embodied in the creed; consequently he chose not to recite any of it. Some members of the class were disturbed by this revelation, and when he conveniently could, Ransom withdrew from teaching and soon stopped attending any of the other services at the church. Immediately thereafter he reverted to the pattern he had established after his return from Oxford nearly twenty years before. As long as his father was an active minister, he sometimes went to hear him preach. As a general rule, however, Sunday mornings were spent at home or on the golf course. Never again was he a member of the congregation of any church.

Although some of the people in the community were shocked by Ransom's unorthodox religious beliefs, he and his family got along well with their neighbors. Helen and Reavill had many friends in the neighborhood, and Robb had an ample supply of golfing partners.

Not only were the Ransoms more content in this setting, especially in their rambling old house, than they had ever been before, but Ransom must have been pleased with some of the turns his professional career had taken. By earning his professorship at Vanderbilt he had demonstrated that a major American university would allow poetry and criticism to replace scholarship as a requirement for promotion and tenure. Although he had written little new poetry for more than ten years and his important critical essays were just beginning to appear (he had been deeply involved in agrarian activities for almost a decade), his literary reputation was increasing with each passing year. By the mid-1930s he could not accept nearly all the invitations he received either to speak or to read his poetry on college campuses. Almost every summer, in addition to participating in the writing workshops that were becoming increasingly popular, he was a visiting professor at some of the most prominent universities in the country. Over the years, too, he had received a number of very flattering offers of permanent appointments to other faculties, several at salaries considerably more attractive than his earnings at Vanderbilt.

But in the spring of 1937 Gordon Keith Chalmers, the recently appointed president of Kenyon College, asked Ransom if he would come to Kenyon "to write poetry and teach philosophy." Ransom told him, he said, "I can't come on those terms because I couldn't make a contract to deliver the goods in either respect, but I can teach some English, and if you want to see what I might do on the side, I will be glad to discuss the matter in more detail."[3]

The decision to leave his alma mater (the only university in which he had held a full-time position), to sever personal and literary associations reaching back more than twenty years and settle permanently outside the South, was one of the most difficult of his life. In the beginning it appears that Ransom did not consider the Kenyon offer any more seriously than he had the several others he had received in the past five or six years, but he was flattered that the president-designate of an established liberal arts college would come in person to make the offer.[4] Ransom was also keenly aware that fulfilling his academic duties at Vanderbilt demanded so much of his time that little was left for poetry and criticism.

His long-time friends and colleagues more and more had come to rely on his judgment, and he had become a leader in the faculty group attempting to maintain at Vanderbilt a traditionally oriented liberal arts curriculum. Ransom became restive under the pressures of the unpleasant and time-consuming assignments, and when a set of degree requirements much too liberal for his classical views of education was adopted, his disappointment was genuine, if not obvious. At this particular moment, the offer of a distinguished position on the faculty of a well-established liberal arts college—and one paying almost a thousand dollars more than he was earning, plus a rent-free campus house—could not be disregarded. Among his many friends who saw that this should not be treated as just another offer was Allen Tate, who was then living in his farm home, Benfolly, near Clarksville, Tennessee. When Tate heard that Edwin Mims, chairman of Vanderbilt's English department, had responded to the Kenyon offer with a request that Ransom "itemize his debts" so that Mims could "go about in Nashville" and solicit money to settle them, Tate was irate.[5] Convinced that Vanderbilt must meet the Kenyon offer "both in money and the dignity of the position offered," on May 24, 1937, Tate sent the Nashville *Tennessean* an open letter to Kirkland, and he mailed copies to some other newspapers in the area.

So that his letter would not come as the "intrusion of a stranger," Tate identified himself as an alumnus interested in the affairs of his alma mater. "My concern at the moment," he wrote, "is that after twenty-five years at Vanderbilt," Ransom is leaving to "join the faculty of a college in Ohio." Needless to say, even the thought of his leaving was repugnant to Tate; for an important southern university to allow its most significant man of letters to go to "a small college in the Middle West," he insisted, is simply another example of the region's lack of interest in the "notable revival of letters" in the South.

Mr. Ransom is, I fear, a little more famous internationally than locally. He is one of the most distinguished men of letters in the world today. Where Vanderbilt is known outside her alumni associations and similar groups of persons whose enlightenment of interest is not quite perfect, she is known as the institution where John Crowe Ransom profoundly influences, through his teaching and writing, the course of modern literature. I need not cite any of his more brilliant achievements, but I should like to bring to your attention two recent incidents that illustrate the far reaching character of his reputation. The Lowell family of Boston and Harvard University has just sent one of its sons to Nashville to study poetry with Mr. Ransom—I do not say to Vanderbilt, because Mr. Lowell will follow Mr. Ransom to Ohio. In the past few months a correspondent of mine at Cambridge, England, has informed me that his fellow students repeatedly express a wish to study under John Crowe Ransom.

Tate ended his letter with a statement that must have infuriated Kirkland, a man who prided himself upon his awareness of every aspect of the university from which he would soon retire after more than forty years as its chief administrative officer. College officials, occupied as they are "with organization and finance," Tate concluded, are often not in a position to judge the real value of certain members of the faculty. Boards of trustees, furthermore, composed usually of businessmen, are inclined to regard professors, even those of "first distinction as mere employees." Tate can suggest only one of two reasons for Kirkland's apathy: "If you are not aware of Mr. Ransom's distinction, which is of the very first order, the sources of your information have been faulty. But, if you, as the head of a great university, are indifferent to the grounds of this expostulation, then I can only pity you, and meditate upon emotions that I shall not easily get my consent to express. The literary historians of the future will express them for me."

Tate's letter appeared in the Nashville *Tennessean* for May 26, 1937, and Donald Davidson's response was immediate and enthusiastic. Lyle Lanier brought a copy of the paper by his office just before noon and before going home for lunch Davidson wrote Tate, "I don't need to tell you," he began, "how happy I am that you wrote that open letter to the Chancellor. You've struck a blow that needed to be struck, the Lord knows how much—and you're one of the few people, I think about the only one, really, who could have done it, because you have both an independent position, an understanding of the situation, and the ability to say the thing as it should be said. Also, you have the *right* to say it, as an alumnus, a Southerner, and a friend of John's."[6]

That afternoon when Davidson met Jack Nye, managing editor of the *Tennessean*, on a downtown street they stopped to exchange greetings. "Nye told me," Davidson said, "that few things in life ever had given him more pleasure than to publish the letter." But his pleasure in its appearance was, of course, not shared by Chancellor Kirkland; the night the letter appeared, a *Tennessean* reporter had called Kirkland to check some facts in a story he was preparing on a gift the Rockefeller family had given the university, and in his anger, "the Chancellor told the reporter that what anyone had done for the University was none of his business, properly seasoned with language suitable to the occasion."

The next day the *Tennessean* carried Kirkland's response to Tate, and its tone was typically logical and unimpassioned. "I do not know," Kirkland began, "why you chose a letter to the newspaper as a means of calling my attention to the matter of Mr. Ransom and his reported intention to join the faculty of a college in Ohio. I am not ignorant of Mr. Ransom's distinction in letters, and I am not indifferent to the grounds of your expostulations, so that I do not deserve either your censure or your pity." Concluding with the mild protest that his information has come "at second hand," Kirkland says he knows only that "the financial conditions attached to the offer in Ohio are so favorable that Mr. Ransom cannot afford to decline the invitation."[7]

The terms of this offer, so attractive that Ransom could not afford to decline it, have been for thirty-five years a closely kept secret. Ransom must have told Edwin Mims, his chairman, but Mims's references to the offer in his written communications with Kirkland are always indefinite. He informs Kirkland that Ransom and Davidson have been primarily responsible for the "rather unique contribution that we have made to English studies and to the life and thought of the country," that Ransom "does not want to leave the particular field of his interest and activity," and that he "would be a very difficult man to replace." If he leaves, "we shall have to start out on other lines perhaps, and the Department would not be so happily balanced as it now is." But Vanderbilt "cannot and should not match the offer."[8] Even the reporter sent by *Time* to investigate the situation filed a story grossly exaggerating the difference between Ransom's Vanderbilt salary and the one offered by Kenyon. Ransom told neither Tate nor Davidson any of these details, a characteristic course of action which Tate approved. Davidson always believed that the *Time* story was essentially correct.[9]

Never inclined toward a too-easy optimism, Davidson was skeptical that Tate's letter would achieve the desired resu'ts, because there "are plenty of people hereabouts (no doubt a large number of Vanderbilt alumni) who think that John is a negligible person in comparison with, say, the football coach."[10] But he was as hopeful as his temperament would permit, and he thoroughly approved of Tate's actions because, as he said, he loved a fight. What the "whole situation" has been needing, he wrote Tate, is some sort of public attention and this kind of attention has been difficult to get because the issues are too "subtle and involved." Now even the "dunderheads may begin to take notice if the outside world is heard from."

Tate's letter attracted the attention Davidson desired, both inside and outside the university. On the day Kirkland's response appeared in the paper, Mims came to see Davidson, who reported to Tate: "We had about a half hour of the warmest conversation we have ever had. He said, oh, if Allen had only written—if he had only talked to me first!—But this letter now makes it almost impossible to do anything! I told him with all the brusqueness that I could command, that he ought to be glad the letter appeared before and not *after* the case was closed. . . . He complained that the University could not possibly meet the offer; that even he, if he were Chancellor, could not (granted that the money should be available) give John a salary beyond the scale even of department heads."[11] Davidson assured Mims that he wouldn't hear the "last of it very soon if Ransom were allowed to leave" and that he must act decisively and soon. What action Mims took during the next two weeks, except for frequent consultations with the department, are not known; but Ransom continued to meet his classes, as his students, colleagues, and friends, under Tate's expert direction, mounted their offensive.

To be in a position "to know what was going on" and to keep up the pressure, Tate came in from Benfolly, and set up headquarters in the Nashville apartment of Brainard and Frances Cheney, where he was soon joined by Andrew Lytle.[12] Immediately after he received Davidson's letter, Tate wrote Mims that he had chosen to use the open letter, rather than coming directly to him, because if he had followed the latter course, he would "have had no status," he would merely have been "meddling in the internal affairs of Vanderbilt University." But since this issue is of public importance, "I do have status, that of a citizen, of a Vanderbilt alumnus, of a professional man of letters concerned with the cultural welfare of the South."[13] As a final thrust he addressed himself to the charge Mims had expressed to Davidson, that Tate's open letter to the newspaper had precluded Mims making a strong plea to the administration in Ransom's behalf: "I shall reprehend strongly and publicly any attempt of the authorities of Vanderbilt to place upon me the slightest degree of responsibility should John leave you, under the pretense that I have forced your hand and that the dignity of the University will not allow you to compete with Kenyon College."

On the same day Tate wrote Davidson congratulating him on the "fine and courageous" stand he had taken and commenting on Ransom's attitude toward all the activities in his behalf: "I know that John is embarrassed; I doubt if he is pleased. But, as I wrote him, this thing is a public issue and I am determined that it shall receive notice internationally."[14] Tate also brought Davidson up-to-date on some other important developments. Several journals, including the *Southern Review*, the *Sewanee Review*, and the *Virginia Quarterly Review*, had agreed to sponsor a dinner in Nashville for Ransom "to witness his great services to Southern literature," regardless of his decision concerning Kenyon. Undoubtedly Tate had several motives for arranging the dinner. Besides paying well-deserved tribute to his old friend, the dinner would probably press Kirkland into action and, maybe, embarrass him and other members of the Vanderbilt administration if they did not make every reasonable effort to keep Ransom in Nashville. With the help of Lytle and Ford Madox Ford, who was

Tate's house guest at Benfolly, negotiations were well underway for the dinner: "I talked to Red over long distance this morning. Morton D. Zabel, as the official representative of *Poetry*, has been persuaded by Ford Madox Ford . . . to come down for the dinner to witness John's service to American literature. Ford, as an international figure, will preside at the dinner. We will solicit telegrams and congratulations of all sorts of persons both here and in England."

The pressures became more intense as Tate got persons and agencies outside the university fully involved. In an extensive interview, appearing in the Chattanooga *Times* Thursday, May 27, Tate gave his reactions to Kirkland's response to the open letter: "Kenyon College, in Ohio, with an endowment of $2,000,000 can afford a special professorship of poetry; Vanderbilt with $20,000,000 cannot afford it for a distinguished world figure who has served them for exactly twenty-three years. One more distinguished Southerner is to be lost to the South. To use Chancellor Kirkland's phrase, Mr. Ransom could easily afford to decline Kenyon's invitation if he were extended a similar one by Vanderbilt." The same issue of that paper carried a lengthy editorial proclaiming that "Vanderbilt, with its large student body and great endowment wealth, should be eager to keep Mr. Ransom, rather than lose him to a small institution which, recognizing his attainments, offers a salary greater than Vanderbilt is apparently willing or able to pay." As this editorial writer pointed out, few colleges and universities in 1937 were bidding for the services of a professor of poetry, regardless of the level of his attainment; and this demonstration of the demand for a distinguished poet, critic, and teacher would strengthen the cause of letters everywhere. Nevertheless, "the alumni and friends of Vanderbilt University . . . join in the hope that all that can be done will be done to retain the services of Professor Ransom."

Whether all that could be done was done can only be conjectured; in fact it seems that some of the procedures basic to any successful negotiations were ignored. There is no evidence that Kirkland ever talked to Ransom or that Ransom and Mims conferred at all after Ransom told him that he had been "approached by President Gordon Chalmers of Kenyon." This failure of communication could well be the primary reason for Ransom's leaving because, as has been suggested, there seems to have been a great deal of confusion concerning the specific details of the offer and precisely what Vanderbilt was willing to do to counteract it. The confusion intensified as Tate and Ransom's other supporters executed further stages of their carefully formulated plan.

As Ransom performed his normal end-of-term duties of reading examinations and assigning final grades, a distasteful task for him in the best of times, he continued to hold his peace, not even confiding to his closest friends his grave concern as he debated the most disturbing decision of his professional career. Tate and Lytle, meanwhile, intensified their efforts to bring pressure on the Vanderbilt administration. The next phase of the plan developed on the morning of June 2, when Randall Jarrell and some of Ransom's strongest admirers in the student body presented Chancellor Kirkland with a petition signed by more than three hundred students urging him "to do everything in his power to keep Mr. Ransom at Vanderbilt."[15] Peter Taylor, who was in the delegation, remembers that Kirkland received the petition affably but gave no indication of what, if anything, he intended to do about it.[16] One of the local papers quoted Jarrell as saying that he could have obtained many other names "were it not for the fact that students have been busy with examinations for the past few days."[17] The petition, written by Jarrell, follows very closely the arguments presented by Tate: "Mr. Ransom is a poet and critic of the greatest distinction; he and the literary group he is so largely responsible for, have helped to make the name of Vanderbilt famous as a culture center; and for that he deserves the gratitude of the University. But more than this, he is a teacher who has faithfully and scrupulously served Vanderbilt for more than twenty-three years." The letter closes with the statement that many students, some of whom "have signed this letter," came to Vanderbilt to study with Ransom, that such students will not be attracted to Vanderbilt in the future, and that anything less than an all-out effort to retain Ransom will be a disservice to "the University's most celebrated teacher, to the students, and thus to the University itself."

At the same time Jarrell was preparing the letter and petition for the undergraduate students, George Marion O'Donnell was writing a letter representing the graduate students in English.[18] The prospect of Ransom's resignation is a matter of great concern, his letter begins, to him and to many of his fellow students, who chose Vanderbilt in preference to other universities, because "there was at Vanderbilt a creative intellectual movement more visible and more meaningful in contemporary life, than there was at any other American institution. This movement had its focus in the department of English, where John Crowe Ransom, Donald Davidson, John Donald Wade and Robert Penn Warren were setting out a new and healthy philosophy for America and at the same time producing creative work of a high order of excellence." Obviously, O'Donnell continues, Vanderbilt does not place a proper value on the services of the distinguished members of this group, for Warren and Wade have been allowed to leave and now there is the real threat of Ransom's following them. He concludes with a specific reference to Kirkland's response to Tate: "you have indicated . . . that for financial reasons Vanderbilt cannot afford to keep Mr. Ransom by meeting the offer that he has received from another institution." As Tate had done, O'Donnell expresses his bewilderment that Vanderbilt "with its $20,000,000 endowment" cannot afford "to compete with this other institution" with an endowment of $2,000,000.

Although Tate and Lytle were directing the overall campaign, they continued to keep Ransom's friends informed of developments and increased their efforts to secure assistance from anyone whose official association with Vanderbilt placed him in a position to have some influence on Kirkland. On June 1, Lytle wrote Frank Rand, who thirty years before had been a good friend of his parents and who now was chairman of the board of the International Shoe Company and president of the Vanderbilt Board of Trust. Beginning with the observation that he, "an entire stranger, would intrude into the busy life of so eminent a person only to bring to his attention" a matter of the gravest consequence to the university, Lytle goes on to say that after a "quarter of a century of devoted service to his Alma Mater," Ransom is on the verge of joining the faculty of a "small college in the Middle West." For Vanderbilt to lose the most distinguished member of her faculty to one of the wealthier institutions in the East, one that could come nearer than any southern institution to paying him what he is worth, could be tolerated; but to allow him to go to a "small and obscure college in the Middle West, which only has a tenth of Vanderbilt's endowment" is unthinkable. What Vanderbilt must do is place Ransom's salary on a level with that of the most distinguished member of the medical school faculty.

Lytle summarizes the reasons that Ransom must be retained: he is one of the most distinguished English professors in the country, "indisputably the best in the South"; he is a "public figure of the greatest weight in the world of letters"; he has for twenty years headed a literary revival in the South, "the strongest movement of its kind in the country." As the most distinguished member of Vanderbilt's English department, which before Wade and Warren left had been the "strongest in the country," Ransom must not be allowed to leave. For him to do so would "long reverberate to the detriment of Vanderbilt," and to some persons of distinction it would constitute irrefutable proof of the institution's indifference to her reputation as the "center of literary activity in the South." Even now, he concludes, some interpret Vanderbilt's attitude, not as one of indifference but as one of malevolent intent, for she is driving to other institutions the men who established her literary reputation.

Under the circumstances it is not surprising that Frank Rand's answer was noncommittal.[19] Lytle's letter was the first indication he had had of the "withdrawal of Mr. John Crowe Ransom from Vanderbilt," he wrote, but he expected to be in Nashville for commencement, and once there he could get "all the facts bearing on the contemplated move." That Rand did more than gather the facts is suggested by subsequent developments.

On the day Lytle wrote Rand, Tate sent letters to O. C. Carmichael, who would succeed Kirkland as chancellor, and to Charles Cason, director of the alumni association.[20] To Carmichael he wrote that he and his friends were "keeping in abeyance our plans for further publicity, until the action of Vanderbilt is determined," and he reiterated his fear that Vanderbilt's reputation "as a world-center of the humane letters is in serious danger and that nothing can save it if John Crowe Ransom is permitted to leave." Tate concludes by saying he has addressed Carmichael because he is convinced that nothing can convince Kirkland of the "consequences of his indifference," and he urges Carmichael "not to dismiss lightly so grave a question."

Tate is even more explicit in his letter to Cason:

In the past fifteen years Vanderbilt has won in literature a prestige so great that no other University in the country can equal it. This prestige was seriously impaired when Mims let Warren go to Louisiana, where he is now managing-editor of the most distinguished quarterly review published in English. (Even the best British journals acknowledge this fact.) Then Mims let John Wade go. He almost lost Davidson three years ago, and this year he promoted Davidson in spite of himself. Now Mims is about to lose Ransom. Curry will be left and Curry is a fine scholar, but these other men have given Mims' department its lustre.... If he [Mims] replaces Ransom with a mediocrity, as he is sure to do, Vanderbilt will never recover from the loss. John is the center of Vanderbilt's prestige—in spite of the fact that the Chancellor pets the medical school and probably sees John as just another English teacher—and with his going the best students will go, and Vanderbilt will sink to the level of an ordinary freshwater college.

In response to Tate's request for assistance in "turning on some heat down there," Bernard De Voto sent a telegram to Chancellor Kirkland, with a copy to the editor of the Nashville *Tennessean*, indicating his disbelief that Vanderbilt or any other university would "dream of letting John Crowe Ransom," a "distinguished scholar," one of the world's "foremost living poets and critics and a great teacher," go elsewhere. Although what Vanderbilt does about retaining its distinguished faculty members, De Voto acknowledges, "is not properly my affair," he feels that he must protest in this case because of his concern for American literature. "If Ransom is separated from the group of writers whom he has so long helped and inspired," he concludes, "the cause of literature in America will be immeasurably damaged and one of the strongest forces in our national culture will have its effectiveness enormously impaired." [21]

On the day the *Tennessean* carried De Voto's telegram, Tate wrote him, thanking him for the promptness of his response and inviting him to attend the dinner planned for June 10 to honor Ransom "regardless of what he does about the Kenyon offer." [22] Others responded almost as promptly. Every day for two weeks Kirkland received telegrams and letters protesting Vanderbilt's apparent indifference to Ransom's contributions to American letters. The day after De Voto's telegram, the *Tennessean* carried a plea from Louis Untermeyer that Vanderbilt not "lose prestige" by allowing "so distinguished an alumnus and teacher to leave the South." During the next three days the flow of incoming mail was heaviest; among the dozens of communications Kirkland received were letters and telegrams from Eleanor Carroll, Carl Van Doren, Clifton Agar, and Herbert Agar. Tate and Lytle could now afford, as Tate wrote De Voto, to "take the heat off for awhile" as they awaited further developments.[23]

What Ransom was doing during these days of suspense and uncertainty or what his attitude was toward his friends' efforts in his behalf can not be accurately determined. Characteristically, his sense of decorum would not permit him to interfere in a project which so many of his associates supported with so much enthusiasm. Apparently he remained as nearly aloof as possible, but his own decision remained difficult. He was not the kind of man who could easily dissolve a relationship of more than thirty years, and surely he did not want to separate himself from his oldest and dearest friends. Nevertheless there was, as always, the need to earn more money. His financial problems were surely no less acute than they normally were, and the Kenyon offer was the most flattering he had ever received. While Ransom awaited a formal reaction from Kirkland, Tate and Lytle continued to nudge appropriate persons and plan the Ransom dinner.

As Kirkland approached his final meeting of the Vanderbilt Board of Trust, he must have been aware of the repercussions that would inevitably follow Ransom's resignation. If so distinguished a faculty member were allowed to leave, many friends of the university, particularly those of literary interests, would surely criticize the institution's chief executive officer. But to retain Ransom's services, Kirkland must have realized, would require that he violate one of his most valued administrative principles: faculty members of equal rank and distinction should receive comparable compensation. At least twice before, as neither Tate nor Lytle was aware, salaries in the English department had been affected by his reluctance to violate this principle. Almost ten years earlier Mims had requested that Curry be given a raise to meet an outside offer, and Kirkland had responded with a salary $300 below the request and $1,000 below the outside offer. To pay Curry more, Kirkland wrote Mims, would put his salary completely out-of-line with others of equal rank and productivity. Since he could not raise all of the professors in Curry's salary range to the amount requested by Mims, he thought it unfair to raise any of them. On another occasion, after the board meeting in June, 1936, Kirkland had written Ransom: "Through some changes in the Department of English made necessary by the threatened resignation of certain officers, your salary was left lower than some of your colleagues. I asked the Budget Committee at our recent meeting to correct this inequality, and I am pleased to notify you that your salary for next year will be $3,822."[24] Acting only from his sense of principle, therefore, Kirkland gave Ransom an increase in salary to bring his earnings near those of Curry. In his communications with Ransom and Mims during the spring of 1937, Kirkland was reluctant, understandably, to violate his well-established procedures.

On June 3, Mims recommended Richmond Croom Beatty as a replacement for Randall Stewart, saying that he thought Beatty should be employed regardless of what "happens in the Ransom matter" and that the "other members of the Department concur" in this recommendation. But the next day he wrote again, to give "definite expression" to his views regarding Ransom and the prospect of his leaving. From the very beginning, he wrote, "I have taken the position that Vanderbilt can not, and should not, match the offer. I have said that no distinction should be made as to salary between Dr. Curry, for instance, and Ransom. The former has been every bit as valuable to the English department and to the University as the latter." Thinking that Ransom's salary was less than Curry's because of the outside offer Curry had received two years before (he did not know that Kirkland had corrected this inequity the previous year), Mims asked "whether the University in its generosity might correct what seems to me to be an error by granting Ransom a certain amount of what might be called back salary. I fully realize the danger of such a precedent, but circumstances may justify it."[25] He closed this letter with an evaluation of Ransom's distinction and an indication of his value to Vanderbilt:

Waving aside all that Allen Tate and his zealous friends have said— and I strongly resent their tactics and spirit—I should say that he has won a distinct place for himself among creative writers and critics in America and England. Furthermore—and this is of more importance from the standpoint of the University—he has had singular success in

inspiring some of our best students—graduates and undergraduates—to do creative and critical work. . . .

While I do not agree with many of the ideas and methods of the
so-called Agrarian group, I feel that they have had something to say
and said it well. The telegram to you from Bernard De Voto, editor of
the *Saturday Review of Literature,* which is the best literary review in the
country, expresses a point of view that is undoubtedly held by many
scholars and critics throughout the country. The movement led by
Ransom is wider than any set of ideas.

In the meantime the activities of Tate and Lytle—particularly Lytle's letter to Frank Rand—had achieved some tangible results. Kirkland could not accept Mims's recommendation that Ransom be given
a retroactive increase to bring his salary in line with Curry's, since
their earnings were approximately the same already, but he did have
a counterproposal, one suggested by Charles Cason. In addition to
the increase from $3,822 to $4,200, which Kirkland had already
communicated to Mims and, presumably, Mims to Ransom, an anonymous donor had made available to the alumni association a yearly
increment of $500.[26] Because of Kirkland's strong endorsement of
"balanced salaries," he was not willing to commit the university beyond the $4,200, but if Mims would write him "a special letter set-
ting forth exactly what offer . . . [Ransom] has received from Kenyon College and what in your opinion ought to be done by Vanderbilt
University in order to retain his services," Kirkland indicated he
would present Mims's recommendation to the executive committee
of the Board of Trust.[27] Apparently, if Mims were willing to recommend a salary not only unusually high by current Vanderbilt standards, but one even more unusual since it was to be paid jointly
from regular university funds and a restricted grant to the alumni
association, Kirkland was willing to present the proposal through the
committee to the board. Since the commitment for the annual supplement would far exceed his tenure, Kirkland naturally wished to
seek board approval. And since Rand was chairman of the executive
committee of the board, it appears certain that this important committee was aware of the special gift and approved of its being used in the
manner described by Kirkland.

Mims's next letter to Kirkland, written before he had received the chancellor's last proposal, concerned general recommendations for the next year and referred to the Ransom affair only in passing. "I have delayed making any suggestions with regard to the English department for next year," he wrote, "until we knew what Professor Ransom's decision would be." If Ransom decides to leave, Mims concluded—after recommending the appointment of Beatty to replace Stewart, the promotion of Davidson to professor of English, and the appointment of an instructor—"I shall recommend Claude L. Finney . . . as full professor and at a salary of $4,000." But on June 7, Mims responded formally to Kirkland's suggestion: "I have no desire or intention to present my suggestion with regard to Professor Ransom to the Board of Trust." His suggestion that Ransom be given a retroactive raise in a lump sum so that he could meet some outstanding obligations in Nashville was as an "alternative to the alumnus plan," and Mims repeated that he had "never thought that Vanderbilt should match the Kenyon College offer." When the board met on June 7, therefore, Kirkland made no recommendation and the *Tennessean* reported that "no action was taken" on the "possible resignation of John Crowe Ransom"; in response to a reporter's inquiry Kirkland indicated that "only routine business matters were discussed."[28]

As Vanderbilt was entertaining its Board of Trust at its annual meeting—honoring one of its most distinguished alumni, Justice James Clark McReynolds, and paying final tribute to Kirkland, who had served forty-four years as its chancellor—Lytle and Tate were busy completing arrangements for the dinner in Ransom's honor. On June 10 the *Tennessean* carried a brief article, supplied by Tate, announcing that the dinner, set for 7:30 at Hettie Ray's Dinner Club on Nine-Mile Hill, was not an invitation affair but could be attended by "any friend or admirer of Professor Ransom who desires to attend." Lytle was giving his personal attention to the menu and insisting that this meal must be the most famous Miss Ray had ever prepared. Consequently he was on the telephone several times during the day giving instructions on the selection and preparation of the food to be served. Among the special delicacies he insisted on was fresh corn, and, as he told Miss Ray, to be really fresh it should have come "from the field since noon today."[29]

By seven o'clock more than a hundred of the persons whom Tate and Lytle had invited by letter, telegram, telephone, and word of mouth, as well as by the newspaper notices, had crowded into the semienclosed pavilion where Miss Ray usually catered to the large crowds that came to dance to the music of Kay Kyser, Harry James, and the other big bands who broke the journey between Chicago and New Orleans or Miami with a night in Nashville. Ford Madox Ford demonstrated his enthusiasm for joining this protest against the "Establishment's disregard for the arts" by accepting Tate's invitation to serve as master of ceremonies. Dressed in "white duck trousers, a beat-up dinner jacket and shod in espadrilles," he opened the festivities with a fairly lengthy statement that no one, except those within a few feet of him, could understand. "I was perhaps," he said, "the first person in Europe to recognize what is taking place here. . . . I first came across Mr. Ransom's work many years ago in an English periodical; it contained two poems which struck me with that extraordinary force and personality and impressed me with their originality, tang, and flavor."[30] Between wheezes, as Tate wrote later, Ford introduced the celebrities who had been invited to render tribute to Ransom, and Tate read telegrams from such distinguished writers, editors, and men of letters as T. S. Eliot, Robert Hillyer, Edmund Wilson, Mark Van Doren, Carl Van Doren, Henry S. Canby, Stark Young, Carl Sandburg, Merrill Moore, Louis Untermeyer, Archibald MacLeish, Katherine Anne Porter, and Maxwell Perkins. Separate statements were made by Lyle Lanier, Andrew Lytle, Randall Jarrell, William Frierson, B. F. Finney (vice-chancellor of the University of the South), and Donald Davidson. Finally Ransom arose to announce the decision which by this time must have been known by everyone present. "Some of my friends," he began, "may regard me as a renegade to run away from my region for an indeterminate period of time." Although he suggested that his reasons for leaving were many and involved, one of the principal attractions of the Kenyon position was the promise of the opportunity to devote more time to writing. "It is a very sad thing to leave an institution where one has been so long. There are many reasons to stay . . . nearly 100 are here tonight."[31] The occasion, Ford told Tate later, "was a victory for the forces of the intellect."

On the morning after the dinner an editorial writer for the *Tennessean* proclaimed Ransom a practical poet, "one who can take the world as it is and realize, rather than idealize, it." [32] He was able to take a decisive step, despite his regrets at leaving so many close friends and associates, in order to give himself and his family more security. "His name and his presence would be an asset to any institution of learning in the country," the editorial concluded, and he should leave with the assurance that "Nashville and the South look forward to the day when it will be possible and profitable for him to return." In the Chattanooga *Times* for Sunday, June 13, appeared a second editorial, this one lamenting the fact that the "South does not make a real effort to keep in this section the distinguished men and women who are its natives" and reiterating the disbelief that Vanderbilt had lost Ransom to an Ohio college with one-tenth the university's endowment. On the same day that paper carried a long feature story summarizing Ransom's career and suggesting that the poet's Ohio address would be a paradox, for "Ransom is logical to the South. For all of his forty-nine years . . . he has lived in the South; he has given his brilliant mind to the consideration of the problems of the South; and he possesses a Southern citizenship that is both intuitively and insistently traditional."

Almost immediately after the dinner Ransom had to take a train for Gainesville, Florida, where on Monday, June 14, he had to begin a six-week term as a visiting professor at the University of Florida. Almost as soon as he arrived there, however, he wrote Tate at Benfolly:

The big dinner left me in a melancholy state, and, to tell the truth, mighty glad to get on the train and hurry away from the scene of so many friends and acquaintances broken off. . . .

I was mighty sorry to postpone my visit to Benfolly, but the press of things rather had me down. . . . Besides going to Ohio isn't what it might once have been, though it is pretty bad; the trails are good, and we will expect you all to visit us. [33]

Then, apparently for the first time, Ransom reacts to Tate's activities over the two or three weeks just passed: "I want to say this formally, too, before the subject is retired: I share fully in your notions about the principle involved in my relations to the University; at least, so far as I can be objective. I think I would have agitated with you if the hero had been somebody else than myself." Before leaving for Ripton, Vermont, for his regular summer assignment on the faculty of the Bread Loaf School of English, Davidson wrote Tate his formal response to "l'affaire Ransom": "First of all I need to go through some kind of purification ceremonies—after having my mind filled for so long with angry thoughts about evil people and things inhuman and monstrous."[34] Tate had done his very best, Davidson says, and can retire with the absolute assurance that "you have fought a grand fight in a good cause." Now Davidson urges Tate to turn his attention to other things, "write novels and poems and leave the Vanderbilt situation to sizzle in its own rancid grease for awhile."

After a term in Gainesville, Ransom went to the University of Colorado for a writers' conference. The stay in Florida had not been entirely pleasant; in spite of rewarding experiences with his students, whom he found of "fine and vital stock," the weather was "hot and languid," he wrote Tate, and the final work on *The World's Body,* which Scribners would bring out the next year, was a "big and not altogether congenial job," but it occupied his mind and was "enough to keep me going ahead and forgetting about the weather."[35] He was glad to see his family again (they had not accompanied him to Florida but had gone directly from Nashville to Denver to visit Robb's family), and he dreaded the return to Nashville to make final plans for the move to Gambier.

After a week in Boulder he was interviewed by a reporter for the *Daily Camera.* His students there, he is quoted as saying, though self-conscious, "have more ability than any I have yet encountered." Then he moved to the topic uppermost in his mind and the one which, the reporter indicated, had prompted the interview: "Why did you decide to leave Vanderbilt?" Ransom's answer was indirect. He approached the question by way of his lack of formal preparation to teach English literature. "I am what might be called a self-made scholar," he says; "in college I studied philosophy chiefly. Later I taught Latin. And then without actual preparation, I became an instructor in literature, teaching myself through reading all I know about it." The Kenyon position, he suggested, was nearer his training and interests; he was to be professor of poetry. Finally, he stated as specifically as he ever would his reasons for accepting the Kenyon offer: "I think in a smaller college I'll have more time for writing. In a large university there are so many demands upon a person's time—committees and curriculum reform and paper work and all of that." [36]

When the conference was over in Boulder, Ransom paused for a very brief visit with the Reavills before collecting his family and heading back to Nashville. In less than six weeks he would make his final break with the university and the city which had been his home for almost twenty-five years. Ransom's reluctance to discuss so personal a matter, even many years later, makes it virtually impossible to determine his reasons for making this move that not only was so unpredictable as to be almost completely out of character but one so extreme as to alter some of the basic patterns of his life. But, as the Kenyon *Alumni Bulletin* reported on August 20, 1937, in response to an article in the June 21 issue of *Time,* "salary could not have been a major consideration in the decision" because the amount finally authorized by Vanderbilt, though probably never actually offered, was certainly competitive. Regardless of the reasons for his decision, his leaving Nashville, as Allen Tate wrote many years later, was a *felix culpa* or a *felix crimen,* for almost immediately upon his arrival in Gambier—accompanied, as Tate had predicted, by Robert Lowell and Randall Jarrell (Peter Taylor followed the next year)—he became engaged in a series of activities that would profoundly affect the course of modern American letters. Shortly after Ransom's arrival, he and Gordon Keith Chalmers began to formulate plans for the *Kenyon Review,* the first issue of which would appear in less than two years. A few years later, the first session of the Kenyon School of English was held. Certainly these two developments brought together more distinguished and soon-to-be distinguished poets, critics, and writers of fiction than almost any other of this century, and every student of modern literature has benefitted from the achievements of an imaginative and resourceful man who came to the right place at the right time.

X   **Knowledge
Without Desire
1937-1939**

ALLEN TATE'S threat to Chancellor Kirkland that some of Ransom's best students would follow him to Ohio was prophetic. When Ransom left Nashville in late August, 1937, accompanied by Robb and the children, Robert Lowell, Randall Jarrell, and David McDowell were close behind. A recent graduate of Vanderbilt, Jarrell had completed all requirements for his master's degree except his thesis; he would be an instructor of English and the tennis coach at Kenyon. Lowell, who had planned to enroll in Vanderbilt only because Ransom was there, entered Kenyon as a freshman; and McDowell, who had completed a year at Vanderbilt, entered as a sophomore. A little less certain of his future plans, Peter Taylor withdrew from Vanderbilt and returned to his home in Memphis, but the following year he too enrolled in Kenyon.

The house to which the Ransoms had been assigned by the college was a large, white, two-story frame structure located almost in the center of the campus. As soon as the futniture was placed in the house, Robb returned to Nashville to enroll Helen for her senior year in the Peabody Demonstration School, and from there she went to Bell Buckle, Tennessee, to register Reavill for another session at the Webb School. Since their new home had four large bedrooms upstairs and a master bedroom and study downstairs, Jarrell and Lowell were invited to share one of the second-floor bedrooms, leaving a guest room and a bedroom each for Helen and Reavill when they were home on vacation.

After Helen and Reavill were enrolled in school, Robb decided to enter a golf tournament in Nashville before returning to Gambier. As the tournament was getting underway, however, she received word that her father was ill. Robb did not know the seriousness of her father's illness or how long she would have to be away, but she telephoned Ransom that she was taking the first train to Denver. Once in Denver, she learned that Mr. Reavill had suffered a massive heart attack and was on the critical list. She wrote Ransom that she would stay in Denver until there was some definite change in her father's condition. Robb had with her the Ransoms' youngest son John James (called Jack by the family) who had been born on April 12, 1935.

Without the family, Ransom wrote Tate, it "has been pretty lonesome in our big house," although "Randall and Cal [Robert Lowell] are good company."[1] They are "both good fellows in extremely different ways. Randall has gone physical and collegiate with a rush: tennis is the occasion. . . . Cal is sawing wood and getting out to all his college engagements in a business-like if surly manner." In spite of the fact that he was attempting to complete "Shakespeare at Sonnets" and get a collection of his critical essays ready for the publisher, Ransom was lonely. He missed his family and his Nashville friends. In an attempt, apparently, to fill all of his waking hours—he had not yet found a golfing partner nor had he discovered that his interest in poker was shared by several of his colleagues—he accepted an invitation from a group of students to offer a seminar in writing. This course, which was added to his regular teaching load of nine hours, met one evening a week in his living room. But despite all efforts to "keep as busy as I can," he could not overcome a feeling of emptiness that seemed to dominate his life. He wrote Tate soon after school opened: "This is a pleasant house physically but without much character spiritually. So far I have not found many literary students. The faculty are much better but evidently they don't expect much of their students."[2] A few days later he wrote O. C. Carmichael, the new chancellor at Vanderbilt, that he found "the lighter work a relief" and hoped to do more writing than he had been doing. What he missed most were the "advanced classes and the trained students" he had taught at Vanderbilt.[3]

There was time to work, however, and in early October he completed and sent to Tate a draft of "Shakespeare at Sonnets," the first essay he had done at Kenyon. After incorporating Tate's suggestions, which he knew would be "helpful as always," he expected to send it to the *Virginia Quarterly Review* and, if it was refused there, to the *Southern Review*. He would send it directly to the *Southern,* he wrote, except that he felt "a little resentful of the paying end of their arrangement down there." They paid a little better than the *Virginia Quarterly Review* but "infinitely later," and he needed the money. As usual, Tate returned the essay promptly, with detailed comments. To some of his specific questions about the structure of the essay, Ransom responded: "I remember starting in to work out this question: whether Shakespeare, by doing it often, doesn't make a convention of his own in the matter of pretending to have a third quatrain co-ordinate, but really tying it in with the couplet to make a kind of sextet; if he means it, it's good. Then I seem to have forgotten about finishing that study, or else felt too crowded with the rest of the material of that essay."[4] Although Ransom agreed that this matter ought to be handled "before abusing Shakespeare," he was convinced that the "sonnet is too little and too studied to permit variations of structure ad libitum; it's the most structural of all small forms; and there's always the actual Italian structure if you want to write that kind of sonnet."

As soon as he had completed "Shakespeare at Sonnets," the last essay he expected to include in the collection he was then calling *Poets Without Laurels,* he turned his attention to writing a preface, which he completed in late October, just before the deadline set by Scribners. He sent it to Tate with the question: "Is the tone too ambitious? Ambition is a tur'ble thing when you don't get away with it."[5] Again Tate's response was prompt and his suggestions very much to the point. "Your comments are so just and useful," Ransom wrote on October 29, "that I shall use them all. It's hard to get an objective view of your own stuff." As always, Ransom was reluctant to release the final copy to the publisher. The essays, written and published separately over the past four or five years, just did not have the power and coherence they needed to create the sense of unified purpose he wanted them to have. He saw so many deficiencies in them that if he had not had a contract in hand he would not have republished them. "The fact is," he concluded, "I see so much future for critical studies that my own are just beginning. It's the biggest field that could possibly be found for systematic study, almost a virgin-field. I want to wade right into it."[6]

Apparently he decided not to attempt to publish "Shakespeare at Sonnets" in the *Virginia Quarterly Review* because on the very day he wrote Allen Tate that the essay was finished he sent a copy of it to Cleanth Brooks with a request that it be considered for publication in the winter number of the *Southern Review*.[7] A later issue would be too late because Scribners planned to publish the book in the early spring. "I enclose the 'Shakespeare at Sonnets' about which I spoke to you last summer at Allen's," he wrote: "It is the last piece I felt necessary to do for completion of my *ms.*, which I have delayed sending in until this one was off." He felt he needed this essay because it illustrated the "general point" of the other essays, and he was afraid he had stated "the general point too much in the book" but had a "lightness on the side of actual criticism." He was aware that he was being a little rough on Shakespeare in a journal "edited by two great Shakespeareans" and requested suggestions for improving his argument. If the piece were accepted, he concluded, he hoped he could be paid for it immediately, for "finances are tight with me; will be throughout this year; afterwards, God helping, a little easier."

Acceptance was not immediate; instead Ransom received a response which he must have found disturbing, for he included the comments he received from both Brooks and Warren when he next wrote Tate:

The boys deal pretty pedantically with my poor paper, you will see; I thought when I read it I must have mistakenly sent it to the Yale Review and got back an epistle from Miss Helen Macafee. I wrote them a pretty warm letter but after thinking it over withheld it and wrote another. I also revised the thing, adding a bit, taking account of points of theirs which seemed to be worth anything, generally improving it. . . . I really stepped on their toes a little, come to think about it. For Red is a Shakespearean, and would not like my irresponsible knocks for the comfort of the Philistines; and Cleanth is an expert on metaphysical poetry, and thinks everybody ought to discuss the thing in his minute terms. They are a bit magisterial, or is it just my oversensitive imagination?[8]

Whatever their objections, Ransom must have taken care of them, for on November 17 he wrote Tate: "A nice note from the boys at Baton

Rouge says they're printing my piece. I suppose they felt aggrieved at my high tone, but they don't extend the argument further."

With this essay accepted he put aside the book, there being nothing else he could do with it until he began reading proofs, and went about the process of settling into a new place and a new home. "This promises to be cold climate," he wrote Brooks, "from samples of climate up to date. But it's pleasant here and will be pleasanter when my wife and little boy come back."[9] His house he found generally comfortable, "big, plain and nice," he wrote his mother, "but it has lots of cracks and chimneys and already we've had plenty of nippy weather, many frosts and cold wind, and some ice."[10] The part of the house he enjoyed most was "the side porch as big as a house" which "overlooks the best view of the place."[11] During that autumn he took long walks into the countryside around Gambier, which he found "just like Tennessee hill country" and "almost perfect" because the "autumn exhibit" was much better than he had ever seen it in the South.[12] Gambier, he soon discovered, was a "friendly place" and the faculty averaged "about as high as any place he had ever seen," fully up to the "Vanderbilt average in culture and solid learning, if not in aggressiveness."[13] The Ohio "human community," however, he felt in the beginning, though he soon changed his mind, was "nearly a dead loss: a flat, characterless race, a great loss here for a man moving from the South." But his duties were much lighter than they had been at Vanderbilt and this, he wrote Tate, seemed like a good place to work. Now that he had his manuscript off to the publisher he expected to start "composing again."

Some members of the faculty at Kenyon, a closely knit group of forty-odd when Ransom arrived in the fall of 1937, received him a little coolly. Although his reputation as a poet was not unknown to them, he was associated with the Nashville Agrarians, whom some regarded as southern reactionaries, if not downright fascists.[14] It was generally felt, too, that the contract of a very popular instructor was not renewed so that Ransom could be employed, and the inflated salary reported in *Time*, though the figure was accurately described in the Kenyon *Alumni Bulletin* as exaggerated, convinced some of the senior faculty members that his salary was inflated. But Ransom was not at all the man some of them had expected him to be. He was "genial and friendly," as one colleague described him, "such a gentle soul that no one could say a bad thing about him." He faithfully attended every faculty meeting, served cheerfully and effectively on faculty committees, obviously took his teaching assignments seriously, and soon convinced his colleagues that he fit neither the stereotype of the political agitator nor that of the reclusive poet. In fact he quickly established himself as one of the best liked and most highly respected members of the faculty, an image so soon fixed that the following year, when it became known that he would likely accept another position, the faculty council voted unanimously to encourage President Chalmers to use every reasonable means to persuade him to stay at Kenyon.

But his first autumn at Kenyon was not a happy time. Robb and Jack were in Denver for almost two months. Several times Mr. Reavill's condition improved sufficiently for them to make definite plans to return to Gambier, but each time it soon deteriorated. On October 28 he died. Although Ransom offered to come to Denver to help "close things up," Robb told him to stay in Gambier, that she would come there immediately after the funeral and, if possible, she would bring her mother with her. "It will be a terrible blow to Robb, who was devoted to her father," Ransom wrote his mother; "he was one of the finest men I ever met, and a mighty good friend of mine. He was as unselfish and uncomplaining as anybody could be. And gentle, too, except when he thought someone was abusing his children or his grandchildren."[15] Ransom was pleased, at any rate, that Robb's mother would come back with her because "bringing up Jack is just the sort of occupation that will suit Mrs. Reavill's tastes better than anything in the world." Robb and Jack returned just before Thanksgiving, but fear of the Ohio winter convinced Mrs. Reavill that she should postpone her visit until spring. Soon after Robb arrived in Gambier, she wrote Ellene that Mrs. Reavill had made a wise decision because "our house is cold as a barn. We wear overcoats all the time." A few days later, after a session with Jack who was just learning to read, she wrote again, this time in the style of the first reader: "We must go to town to buy a coal stove. Our house is cold in spots. Our house is cold in lots of spots."[16] After Robb and Jack returned, Ransom's spirits became much brighter. Soon the family would be together again, for Helen had written that she would be out for Christmas holidays on December 15 and Reavill three days later. In preparation for their first Christmas in Ohio, Ransom took Robb into Columbus to do some shopping. But, as he wrote his mother, she "looked around and found the day was gone before she had accomplished much in the way of purchases, which I thought made a very successful trip." [17]

During this first autumn at Kenyon, Ransom engaged in a series of conversations that not only influenced his own literary career but affected in a most tangible way the development of American literature in the next two decades. Even before he invited Ransom to come to Kenyon, Gordon Chalmers, encouraged by his wife, had wanted to start at Kenyon a really first-rate quarterly patterned after the *Yale Review* or the well-known British quarterlies of the nineteenth century.[18] In the spring of 1937, soon after his appointment to the presidency of Kenyon, Chalmers had tried to persuade Robert Frost to come there to serve as poet in residence and to edit such a journal; and Frost, who did not want to settle in the Midwest, recommended Ransom, with whom he had had the first of several all-night conversations during a visit to Nashville earlier that year.[19]

Shortly after Ransom was settled in Gambier, Chalmers called him into his office to discuss the project with him, a topic he had not wanted to present earlier because he had just then received final approval of the plan he had presented several months earlier to his board of trustees. He had not mentioned the prospective quarterly during his discussions with Ransom in Nashville because he wanted him at Kenyon as soon as possible, even if the journal had to be delayed for several years. Certainly, he told Ransom, he did not want to make promises he could not keep. Now he was convinced that plans for the quarterly should be started immediately, so that the first issue could come out the next year. His board of trustees had already agreed to finance it for a three-year trial period.[20] Since editing the journal would be a full-time job for one man and since he did not want to remove Ransom completely from teaching, Chalmers proposed that Ransom be editor and that another man be brought in as associate editor. Both Ransom and his associate editor would teach half-time. If Ransom agreed to the plan, he promised to consult with

him on the choice of the new man, and he wanted to attract someone
of highest quality, of the "calibre of Mark Van Doren."[21]

Ransom was surprised and delighted at the prospect of editing a
literary quarterly. "Yesterday," he wrote his mother on October 29,
1937, "the President called me in to talk about founding and editing a
Great Review here; that is more than I ever ventured to hope for and
the most interesting thing I could get into." But he realized, as he
wrote Tate on the same day, he had to proceed carefully in order not
to make some serious mistakes. The first important decision was the
choice of the associate editor and on this matter, he knew his candidate immediately: Tate, and if not Tate, then Warren. Tate, he was
convinced, was the "best in the business" for the editorial position, and
he must convince Chalmers of this fact.[22] To make the position attractive to Tate, he was prepared to urge that his title be coeditor, that the
two of them have equal responsibility and authority for the publication, and that Tate's "salary be at least as good" as his. The teaching
portion of the position he expected to improve almost immediately
because Chalmers had promised to provide a number of poetry
scholarships each year, and he hoped to go to "some good places like
Harvard, LSU, Vanderbilt, and Chicago and buy in that many good
writers at the end of their sophomore year, keep them through their
last two years, and invite the best of them to stay on for an M.A." The
strongest inducement, however, he saved until last. "I have an idea,"
he wrote, "that we could really found criticism if we got together
on it."[23]

For the next several months he devoted much time and energy to
the proposed journal. At every opportunity he talked to Chalmers
about Tate and even provided a list of persons to consult about his
reputation as man of letters. As these conversations continued, Ransom became more and more convinced that Chalmers was warming
up to the idea of bringing Tate to Gambier. "He knows you and I are
Agrarians," Ransom wrote Tate on December 10, "and I think felt
apprehensive over that (probably knowing nothing about it) until I
told him that I would not like to see the Review pinned to any economic or political program." In fact the introduction of this topic
allowed Ransom to present his argument on another matter that concerned him. Chalmers favored a general review, but Ransom wanted

to confine its interests to literature and the other arts. "It seems to me," he wrote Tate, "that our cue would be to stick to literature entirely. There's no consistent, decent group writing politics . . . [and] in the severe field of letters there is vocation enough for us: in criticism, in poetry, in fiction." Both on the choice of associate editor and the determination of the kind of journal it would be, Ransom received support from unexpected sources. In New York Chalmers, at Ransom's suggestion, talked to Gorham B. Munson, who "advised him to leave out politics." Later in the same month Chalmers was in Boston and consulted William Yandell Elliott, Ransom's friend from their Fugitive years, who insisted that "he must get a really eminent man to go in with me on terms of equality, that no half-baked youngster would do."[24]

Now his major task, he was convinced, was to "indoctrinate Chalmers with an idea of what *real* distinction for a periodical is" and to convince him that "Tate will add real distinction to the project." To support him in this climactic drive, he invited Lambert Davis, editor of the *Virginia Quarterly Review,* to visit the campus to confer with him and Chalmers. When he wrote Tate, early in December, he was optimistically awaiting Davis' visit because Chalmers "is converted 100% and is anxious to have you at Kenyon." But when Davis came, the strategy backfired; he reported that the *Virginia Quarterly Review* operated on a salary appropriation of approximately $4,500, including the entire staff—circulation, business, secretarial, and promotional. With this report now official, Chalmers was convinced, and Ransom agreed, that it "would be impossible to convince the Board" to give Tate a salary in the neighborhood of the one Ransom was receiving. So Ransom, with great reluctance, had to advise Tate to accept the position at the Woman's College of North Carolina, which he had had under consideration for several weeks, because the "prospect here is not of a kind to put up against the bird-in-hand there."[25]

In mid-December Ransom attended a Rhodes Scholarship committee meeting in Louisville and from there he went to give a talk in Indianapolis. When he returned to Gambier, he found the proofs for *The World's Body,* which he had to read over Christmas before going on to Chicago to appear on the program of the Modern Language Association. His experiences there made him more anxious than ever to get his journal started for the time was "ripe ... for some good critical studies." He wrote Tate, "The professors are in an awful dither trying to reform themselves and there's a big stroke possible for a small group that knows what it wants in giving them ideas and definitions and showing the way. But there's a real dearth of genuine leadership in the group." Ronald S. Crane spoke on the same program with him and although "he's the best of the lot, he's not quite up to the mark." If anything worthwhile was to be achieved within this organization, Ransom thought that more men like Carl Van Doren, Austin Warren, and F. Cudworth Flint must become involved, but the best strategy might be just to "let the professors alone."

Discussions concerning the magazine continued during the spring. On May 28 he wrote Tate: "The Review is right on the edge of getting started; just a little more work on the printer's estimates to make sure we shant start and then flop." He wanted it to be "a handsome thing and of the most distinction" he could make it, coming out "prompt and regular" and paying a good rate to the contributors. When the printer's estimates were received, Chalmers was convinced for the first time that the cost of producing a general review was more than they could afford. It was decided, therefore, that they would publish a magazine of approximately one hundred pages "devoted entirely to literature and the arts." With pledges of $15,000 already in, plus revenue from expected sales and advertising, financing a publication of this size was secure for three years. The remaining members of the staff were appointed: Philip Blair Rice came from the University of Cincinnati to serve as managing editor and to teach three classes each term in the philosophy department, and Norman Johnson, an honor graduate of Harvard, was to serve as secretary and to teach one section of freshman English. Ransom was explicit in his statement of the kind of periodical he expected to produce: "I want to see it solid but not dull. I think a good bet is to have a good deal of satirical or negative writing; there are enough deserving butts to pay our respects to; that is a popularizing feature, perhaps, but must not, of course, define the nature of the publication. I think also that we want to see new kinds of writing, that is critical writing; the less standard and conventional in shape and tone the better. We ought to make a little racket every time we appear."[26]

Three final matters concerning the review were settled before Ransom left Gambier for a busy summer of teaching elsewhere. The first concerned responsibility for the journal. He and Chalmers, Ransom wrote Tate, talked "quite officially and formally" about their relationships to the project. Although he recognized his responsibility to the donors and the trustees, Chalmers assured Ransom that he had full confidence in him and expected him "to keep a firm rein on the whole conduct of the publication." Most of all, he agreed that Ransom would have "final say on what was printed" and that the "success and permanence of the review would depend on our undertaking a publication on a professional level of distinction, with no reference to local setting whatever, and on ultimately securing some sort of public recognition which we can pass on objectively to the subscribers and donors." [27] On the question of a name for the new publication Ransom allowed President Chalmers to make the final decision. He and Rice had decided to call it the *American Critic* and were already referring to it informally by that name, but since Chalmers wanted the name of the college in the title it became the *Kenyon Review*. On the selection of advisory editors, however, Ransom stood firm. Chalmers wanted to include a "whole group of faculty editors," but with Rice's help Ransom convinced him that the persons named to this post should be known and respected in the field of letters.

When Ransom left Gambier in early June for two weeks of teaching at the University of Kentucky, therefore, the basic arrangements for publishing the *Review* were almost complete. With $15,000 already pledged and an annual budget of $6,700, the quarterly could run for at least two years, even if no subscriptions or advertising at all were sold. As long as they continued to receive an annual supplement of $5,000, Ransom and his staff would have to raise only $1,700 in subscriptions and sales each year to insure continuous publication. He prepared a general descriptive statement about the *Review* for Rice to mail to prospective contributors and subscribers as soon as he had acceptances from the persons he had invited to serve as advisory editors. The circular invited the "submission of critical essays and poetry" and promised to pay "$5.00 per printed page for prose" and for poetry a higher rate, "the particular payment" to be "estimated upon receipt of the poem." The first number, to be dated January 1,

1939, would be on sale in December, and the deadline for material to be used in the issue was November 1. "The *Kenyon Review*," the statement concluded, "hopes to carry on literary and aesthetic discussion in language of a rather severer economy than is usual, provided no sacrifice is required in warmth of style, or literary quality."[28] The circular could be mailed in the early fall as scheduled because by midsummer Ransom informed Rice that the "following have accepted posts of Advisory Editors: R. P. Blackmur, Paul Rosenfeld, Roberta Teale Schwartz, Allen Tate, Philip Timberlake, Mark Van Doren, and Eliseo Vivas.[29]

Ransom's schedule for the summer of 1938 was arduous indeed because, as he wrote Tate, he was "chasing the filthy dollar being at last about to emerge from insolvency, but faced with huge expenditure in the interest of Helen's education." Also he wanted to contribute something to the support of his mother, who since his father's death four years before had lived off a meager widow's pension from the Methodist church and whatever contributions her children could give her.[30] After two weeks at the University of Kentucky, he went to the University of Chattanooga for five days before going to the Murray (Kentucky) State Teachers' College for a similar period. In all three places he lectured, gave public readings of his poetry, conducted creative writing workshops, and conferred with aspiring but unpublished writers—mostly middle-aged housewives and maidenly secondary school teachers—about their poems and stories. Ransom always approached these assignments with absolute seriousness and spent many long evenings reading manuscripts he would discuss the following afternoon with their authors. Seldom did he discover anyone of genuine talent, but he felt that since he was being well paid for his services, his students deserved his conscientious and respectful attention. (Then, too, there was always the remarkable exception, as had been the case the previous summer in Boulder, when the "sanest and most charming girl there" had asked him to read a portion of a novel she was working on. The evening he devoted to reading that manuscript was "delightful" because he quickly discovered that this "beautiful lady" had "considerable creative talent." She was Jean Stafford and the unfinished novel she had asked him to read became *Boston Adventure*.[31]) But the demands on his time were such that he could not get down to doing any of his own work until after he arrived at the University of Texas on July 18.

As soon as he was settled there, he returned to work on an essay that would become a part of *The New Criticism* (1941). The previous spring Robert Penn Warren had asked him to do for the *Southern Review* a critical piece "taking up some of the questions [Yvor] Winters has raised and not settled."[32] As Ransom was thinking out this essay, he and Cleanth Brooks, whom he had seen during the summer, became involved in what he described to Tate as a "big argument"; consequently, to answer some of the objections Brooks had raised to his insistence on logical structure in poetry, Ransom turned from Winters to William Empson. By studying Empson's criticism carefully Ransom hoped to demonstrate how even the good critic, one with whom he was often in agreement, could "muddle his critical conclusions" by concentration on the textural particularities of a poem and neglecting its structural core. This essay he completed shortly after his return to Nashville on August 30, where he had a leisurely visit with his mother, his sisters, and his Nashville friends. In late September he mailed the essay to Brooks, who accepted it immediately and said it would appear in the fall issue of the *Southern Review*.[33] Soon after Ransom returned to Gambier on September 20, he wrote Tate to tell him his impressions of Tate's "Tension in Poetry," which he had just read in the summer issue of the *Southern Review*. "It's your ripest and deepest piece of criticism, I think. Again I reflect that it's exactly the piece I wish I could have done, and the piece toward which my thinking, though perhaps not my pedestrian writing, was tending. It will stand up as the best single specimen of our most advanced contemporary criticism." To call Tate's attention to the direction his critical thinking was taking, Ransom mentioned the Empson article, which he doubted his old friend would approve because it "may be a little reactionary, or on the Winters' side." It is doubtful that Tate, to whom for almost twenty years Ransom had been expressing his critical ideas almost as soon as they were formed, found anything startlingly new in the Empson piece. But the preparation of these two essays—the study of Winters, who devotes too much attention to the structure of poetry, and of Empson, who concentrates almost entirely upon its texture— surely provided the opportunity for Ransom to advertise the new kind of critical writing his age was producing. At the same time he was able to develop in greater detail the ontological theory of poetry he had been working on for more than a decade. The best and most nearly complete statement of this point of view is in the essays collected in *The World's Body.*

In April, when Tate received the copy of that book, which Ransom had had the publisher send him before the book's official release, he had written his sincere congratulations. Ransom's response was immediate and warm: "I was much rejoiced over your fine letter commending my book, it was the first reaction I had had at all and I fear it will be about the best one I shall receive."[34] Tate's letter was all the more welcome because he had been going over his copy, which he had just received, "wondering if it really came off." In response to Tate's comment on Ransom's acknowledgment of indebtedness to him, he replied that it was "you who insisted that the essays be collected" and, more importantly, "you who put in the determining word to Scribner's." But Tate's greatest aid to the book, he repeated, was his "having contributed, often unintentionally, in the preparation of the content." As always Tate's perceptive comments focused Ransom's attention on some of the weaknesses of the book:

Meters and mythology are indeed neglected in this book, which is excessively on the side of generality. I have much more I would like to say on the topic of meters. I don't know what to say about mythology; I feel that there is a subject of first-rate importance which I have scarcely scratched; it needs some hard work; I doubt if you and I would differ on it finally, but at the present stage it's very far from finality. That is one of the things we ought to confer about.[35]

Tate pointed out that to him the chapter "Poetry: A Note in Ontology" was the "central essay" in the collection and Ransom agreed, although his rereading of that portion of the book had made him more aware than ever of how far execution had fallen behind conception in the composition of the essays. He was not able to express his ideas as clearly and as completely as he wished:

The Note in Ontology is a central essay, and I'm glad you see it so. Unfortunately, after clearing the ground in my first two sections of it (the Physical and the Platonic half poetries) I don't denominate and define the true exhibit; it should be Integral Poetry, or Molecular

Poetry, or True Poetry, or Whole or Organic Poetry, or Absolute Poetry, or something; the Metaphysical poetry is just a variety, and it's a good variety to exhibit with, but its name should not have pre-empted the title and the general definition. I rather rode two horses in that essay, or tried to. I think I do have the right introductory matter in the last section, in leading up to the Metaphysical style, though I don't advertise it properly. I remember you once wanted the term Creative Poetry, and I demurred a little on the ground of something magical or mystical in the connotation.

The reviews of the book began to appear before Ransom left Gambier for the summer and continued throughout the fall and winter. Although it was noted or reviewed in many mass circulation periodicals, and commented on at length in the critical quarterlies, few of the critics were able to see it for what it was, one of the most significant theoretical treatments of the nature and function of poetry produced by an American critic in the twentieth century. One of its best reviews was among the first, that of Thomas Merton which appeared in the New York *Herald-Tribune Books* for May 8, 1938. Although Ransom has written "a distinguished book about poetry," Merton begins, "he has not attempted to give us any systematic theory of literary criticism." He has developed, however, "a definition of poetry in terms of cognition," presenting as it does a "knowledge that cannot be gained by any other means" and concerning itself with the "aspects of experience that can never be well described, but only reproduced or imitated." But few readers, Merton fears, will agree that Shakespeare's sonnets are "diffuse, self-indulgent pieces of emotionalism" or that Shakespeare is responsible for "most of the bad romantic poetry that has been written since his time." But what Merton dislikes most is Ransom's setting Shakespeare up as a metaphysical poet only to prove that he is not as good as Donne. "This attack is unfortunate," he concludes, "in its unnecessary and disproportionate violence, but that does not mean that it is uninteresting, or, especially, false."[36]

Henry S. Canby's review is complimentary but too general to be of much value. Not a "book for the general reader, nor the historical scholar," it is a "rare phenomenon nowadays" because it is a "book on poetry" and is concerned with what the "poet has been trying, and is trying, to do in poetry, rather than a monograph on influences and sources." The difficulty Canby has with the book is its lack of unity or a consistent point of view. What Ransom needs to do is to "give up essay writing for a while, and organize his interesting and valuable method and thesis into a book."[37] Until that book is written it will be impossible to judge his qualities as a critic. Frederick A. Pottle begins his brief review with an expression of his agreement with Ransom's statement that his is an age of criticism. "Whatever else its shortcomings may be," he writes, "the present age will rank high in the history of [the] theory of poetry." And Ransom is well prepared to make a valuable and lasting contribution to this field, being "deeply read in philosophy (including the philosophy of science) . . . a teacher of literature, and a professional critic, and . . . a poet." What Pottle likes best about the book, in addition to a "natural urbanity of style which one does not associate with the schools," is Ransom's delineation of Puritanism as the distinguishing feature of the modern mind. Now, since eating of the tree of knowledge, man insists on taking the world apart and analyzing each part separately, and science is the name we give to the "schemes by which we organize things generally in order to use them." Although the great portion of our lives must be devoted to collecting and organizing this type of knowledge, we must realize there is another kind, one that does not sacrifice "the body and solid substance of the world." In his greedy desire to control and use the world in which he lives, man pushes the world's body ruthlessly aside and it can only be recovered by the memory and the imagination, through a kind of poetry that is content to realize the world and does not attempt to idealize it. Pottle is not satisfied with Ransom's chapter on I. A. Richards and accuses him of sounding "something like Max Eastman," but he approves of the theory that criticism of poetry should be objective, that it "should concern itself with the nature of the object rather than with its effects upon the critic as reader."[38]

Although he believes the essays in the book provide a "clear esthetic attitude and point of view," Louis Kronenberger cannot accept what he thinks is Ransom's central thesis: "True poetry has no great interest in improving or idealizing the world, which does well enough." All of this sounds too "escapist" to Kronenberger because behind each poem is a poet and behind the poet is "that part of the man who is a citizen of the world." By accepting this theory of the function of art, Ransom "frees himself from all obligations of world-citizenship" and "leaves unsettled for others the most pressing problem of the day, which is what the role of the artist is to be in contemporary life."[39] For Michael Roberts, Ransom's "conclusions are usually negative and do not form a coherent body of doctrine"; what does come through—"a tendency towards confusion" and "a generalization in terms of dichotomies like 'compound and mixture,' 'universal and particular' "—sounds too much like "pure aestheticism." In the use of detail, however, Roberts finds Ransom nearly always enlightening and his own "handicap as a critic seems to be an odd insensitiveness to some suggestions and association of words, and a somewhat coarse ear for musical effects not covered by rules of prosody. The questions that he raises are always important, and he writes with energy and insight."[40] The author of the unsigned note in the *Times Literary Supplement* is convinced that Ransom is attempting "to make of literary criticism an intellectual discipline" and the result of such an emphasis is that often a "microscopic and pettifogging scrutiny of language usurps the place of an appreciation of style." The worst example of this technique in practice is Ransom's study of Shakespeare's sonnets, which appears to be "one prolonged essay in wrong-headedness." Such judgments as those in this essay come "not from regarding the study of English literature as an intellectual discipline, which it may well be, but from trying to manufacture an intellectual discipline out of it."[41] Percy Hutchison finds almost nothing in the book that he approves of. Its "chaotic nature" is the result of its being a collection "of random papers done from time to time by the author for various unrelated quarterlies." Everyone who reads the book closely will almost certainly, he believes, "differ from Mr. Ransom on almost every page."[42]

Even the reviews in the critical quarterlies, where one would expect the treatment to be most detailed and informative, do not deal adequately with the critical theories Ransom presents. R. P. Blackmur uses his space to contrast the approaches of Ransom, the "literary critic," and Edmund Wilson, the "imaginative essayist." Whereas Wilson always tries to "show what lies behind and about a body of literature," Ransom always goes directly to the literature and "proceeds from that vantage point to reduce, or heighten, his observations to the level of specific literary principles." The result of this basic difference—Wilson deals with ends, Ransom with beginnings—is that when the reader finishes one of Wilson's essays he often feels that he does not have to read the work which the essay discussed; it has been replaced by Wilson's discussion of it. But after reading one of Ransom's essays, the reader feels he has been "put in contact with the work itself"; the essay, not the work of art, disappears and the reader feels the compelling urge to get down the work of art and test the new knowledge he has acquired.[43]

Kenneth Burke points out that Ransom's work exemplifies the kind of criticism he himself most desires, that which "talks closely" about the work of art under consideration, and in doing this kind of criticism Ransom "writes with the lecturer's dialectical aptitude at pointing up a theme by the use of a counter-theme." He achieves an impressive effect by contrasting the work of Edna St. Vincent Millay with that of Donne or, in "Shakespeare at Sonnets," the romantic with the metaphysical poetry. But when he turns from discussions of poetry to speculations on poetics, the reader is likely to become confused, not to understand exactly Ransom's conception of the status of art. Specifically, Burke cannot follow Ransom's argument in his attempt to show that pure science is more "predatory" than pure art or that applied art is less "utilitarian" than applied science. Actually, Burke concludes, Ransom is "encroaching upon the field of sociology, without availing himself of the 'closer approximations' that the terminology in this field would make possible." The easiest way to misread the book would be to try to see "the fifteen chapters as systematized parts of one piece." Such was not the intention of the author; each chapter, read separately, is perfectly clear in design, and the book presents a consistent point of view, that of a critic "among the keenest in the appreciation of poetry's attainments, and among the ablest in bringing this keenness to poetry's defense."[44]

Arthur Mizener opens his review of a half-dozen or more critical books with his comments on *The World's Body* because "it is a book which should be done all the honor that any of us can do it." Not since *The Sacred Wood* has there "been a first book of critical essays equal to it for acuteness of perception" and "richness of ideas, or wit." Ransom's greatest merit as critic is a "kind of common sense" which keeps him always aware of the "two horns of the dilemma between which modern criticism must hesitate." He differentiates between imagination, the organ of knowledge which produces images and "presents to the reflective mind the particularity of nature," and another organ, which "working by a technique of universals" derives the facts of science. Both kinds of knowledge mean to be true. Not only does Ransom insist upon the cognitive function of art, he emphasizes the crucial importance of form. His purpose, finally, is "to place poetry on an equal footing with science by demonstrating that it is a kind of knowledge quite as important as science," and to make clear that literary form, "a committing of the feelings to their determination under the 'terms nominated,' is the only means to such knowledge."[45]

Considered together, these reviews do touch upon some, but not nearly all, of the critical principles developed and demonstrated in *The World's Body*, a collection of the critical pieces that had been appearing at the rate of two or three a year since 1933. But in many cases these essays are more detailed, more explicit statements of ideas and attitudes which had gradually evolved over more than two decades; some of them were first formulated in letters to Ransom's father, to Allen Tate, or to other friends, and some were presented in tentative form in the *Fugitive* before they were refined, enlarged, and restated in the essays of the early and mid-1930s. Ransom would remain the theoretical as opposed to the practical critic, but he never tired of recasting his ideas in an attempt to communicate them clearly and exactly. Many of the essays published during the last fifteen years of his tenure as editor of the *Kenyon Review*, the period of his greatest influence as critic and man of letters, only seem to announce an essential change in his critical position. Actually they often represent another attempt to clarify a misunderstood statement by supplying additional details or, in some cases, by merely changing the metaphor.

In the preface to *The World's Body* he indicates the kind of poetry to which he and his generation are attached, a "post-scientific poetry," the "act of a fallen mind," a poetry that tries to "realize the world," not to "idealize" it. Modern man has elected to know the world in which he lives only through the scientist's conception of it; and such a view is a partial one, for from it have disappeared its body and solid substance. If we are to know the world "which is made of whole and indefeasible objects" we must recover it through poetry from our memory to which it has retired. Poetry, then, is an order of knowledge quite distinct from that which one gets from science. It is the only means through which one can recover the world's body; therefore poetry is "the kind of knowledge by which we must know what we have arranged that we shall not know otherwise." This sort of argument is an obvious development from the kind of speculation that Ransom was engaged in when he attempted to set forth the three "moments" that comprise the historical order of experience.

Ransom's consideration of this mixed world leads him to discuss the nature and function of poetry, to differentiate among its several types, and to contrast its aims and purposes with those of science. Poetry attempts through images and ideas to re-create the rich particularities of the world's body. There are only two ways to transcribe the natural world, that of science and that of art. Science records through grafts and formulas "the universal relations, the cores of constancy in nature." The scientist is interested in universals and excludes individuals except to initiate new studies or to verify old ones. To him an individual item is of interest only to the extent that it serves to illustrate a universal law. The idealist philosopher, such as Plato, attaches no interest to mere particulars except as they demonstrate the "beginnings of a process destined to go 'higher,' 'behind,' or 'further.'" The scientist studies nature only to bring it under his control, to put it to some practical use. With his method and purpose, those of the artist can be contrasted at every turn. The artist attempts to imitate nature, to make full and complete representations: he "interests himself entirely in individuals, or he should." He strives to recover the "individuals abandoned in science, in business, and in affairs." To him "individuals are ultimate." [46] The artist, unlike the scientist, possesses "knowledge without desire." He wishes merely to know nature, not to know it so that he can use it. Art is superior to nature because it cannot be used, only known. The doctrine of mimesis "was the foundation of Greek aesthetic" and is "probably the best foundation of any aesthetic" because it recognizes the true purpose of art, that is, to assist the human being to know the particularity of his environment. The doctrine of catharsis, however, Ransom cannot accept because it seems ultimately to foster a scientific, not an artistic, purpose. It argues that art purges man of certain dangerous emotions, pity and fear, so that he can live the life of the good and dependable citizen. Art intensifies the aesthetic moment in order to minimize and localize it, and clear the way for the scientific moment.

Ransom's reflections upon the "mixed world of ideas and images" led him to define and classify three kinds of poetry. The first is physical poetry, the sort advocated by the imagist, which intends "to present things in their thingness" and in this intention stands "opposite to that poetry which dwells as firmly as it dares upon ideas." To present his concept more exactly he says the opposition must be phrased as image versus idea in order to be acceptable to the idealistic philosophers who argue that a thing does not exist but who mean the "equivalent when they refer to images." Their important concession is that "image is the raw material of idea," a "material cause" which "cannot be dispossessed of its priority."

It cannot be dispossessed of a primordial freshness, which idea can never claim. An idea is derivative and tamed. The image is in the natural or wild state, and it has to be discovered there, not put there, obeying its own laws and none of ours. We think we can lay hold of image and take it captive, but the docile captive is not the real image but only the idea, which is the image with its character beaten out of it. (WB, 115)

Science destroys the image not through refutation but through abstraction; in order to get whatever "value" an image has, the scientist reduces it, tames it, and destroys its freedom. It is by this process that man weakens his imagination to the extent that he is not able to "contemplate things as they are in their rich and contingent materiality."

We are compelled to poetry through memory and dream; thus art is "based on second love not first love." Through this means man attempts to return to something he has lost, to recapture that elusive first moment. Although Ransom values physical poetry for its attempts to circumvent the abstractions of science by its constant recourse to image, he points out that it deals only with a part of experience. To reconstitute experience in the totality of its individual being requires a combination of images and ideas.

The second kind of poetry is Platonic, a kind of pseudo-verse which tries to look like physical poetry by hiding its ideas behind its images. In this kind of poetry, which comes from the belief that nature is rational and can be possessed through the force of logic, things can always be translated into ideas. What the Platonist does not realize, or will not accept, is the basic principle of "The Third Moment": The world of ideas is not the original world of perception, as the view of the scientist is not of the whole and comprehensible object. This world, the original world of perception, must be "experienced and cannot be reported." But Platonists "practice their bogus poetry in order to show that images will prove an idea" and use images merely to illustrate ideas. If physical poetry is only a "half poetry," Platonic poetry is a false poetry. Although the only salvation for poetry is that man "recant" his Platonism and turn back to things, as he turns from his idealizing he must be aware that his mind has been affected by its excursion into Platonism. In "Thoughts on the Poetic Discontent," published in the *Fugitive* for June, 1925, Ransom had argued that the mature attitude of man is flavored with irony and poetry because he is reluctant to give up the "music and color" and the "romantic mystery" of his belief in the existence of a "mystical community," a union between subject and object, percept and concept, man and nature. Now the statement of this idea takes a slightly different form. When man recants his Platonism and turns back to things, it is not a complete aboutface: "If pure ideas were what these men turn from, they would have no poetry at all in the first period, and if pure things were what they turn to, they would be having not a classical poetry but a pure imagism, if such a thing is possible, in the second" (WB, 128). Out of this dualistic state, which results from man's being pulled in two directions simultaneously, comes the complex attitude which allows the aesthetic moment:

The aesthetic moment appears as a curious moment of suspension; between the Platonism in us, which is militant, always sciencing and devouring, and a starved inhibited aspiration towards innocence which, if it could only be free, would like to respect and know the object as it might of its own accord reveal itself.

The poetic impulse is not free, yet it holds out stubbornly against science for the enjoyment of its images. It means to reconstitute the world of perceptions. Finally there is suggested some such formula as the following:

Science gratifies a rational or practical impulse and exhibits the minimum of perception. Art gratifies a perceptual impulse and exhibits the minimum of reason. (WB, 130)

From this "adult mode" in which images and ideas vie with each other for the attention of the mature man comes true poetry. It is the state in which the imagination "brings out the original experiences from the dark store room" and attempts to reconstitute an experience which we previously had but allowed to become mutilated, abstracted, and universalized by the scientists or the philosophers. But this is a "mixed mode," one in which "images come out mixed and adulterated with concepts." In order to deal with this complex world in which perception and conception are irretrievably intertwined, the poet develops many devices to increase "the volume of the percipienda or sensibilia." Among these devices are meter (which regulates the material and appeals to the rational faculty), fiction (which is the device used by art to create "aesthetic distance" between object and subject), and tropes (which encourage "astonishing lapses of rationality beneath the smooth surface of discourse, inviting perceptual attention, and weakening the tyranny of science over the senses"). The most important of these tropes is the metaphor.

Out of this complex world comes true poetry, which Ransom calls in this essay metaphysical poetry, although he later thought the term too specialized and restrictive.[47] A distinguishing characteristic of this poetry is its use of the conceit, which Ransom says is a "meant metaphor," one that is "developed so literally that it must be meant, or predicated so baldly that nothing else can be meant."[48] In a metaphorical assertion, Ransom concludes, there is a "miraculism" or "supernaturalism" if the poet means what he says and compels the reader to believe what he has read. This miraculism occurs "when the poet discovers by analogy an identity between objects which is partial, though it should be considerable, and proceeds to an identification which is complete" (WB, 139). Since this kind of miraculism occurs more often in the lyric poetry of Donne than it does in that of Shakespeare, Ransom argues that Donne's is the better poetry.

It is from this kind of miraculism that poetry derives an ontological significance. "It is the poet and nobody else," he says, "who gives to God a nature, a form, faculties, and a history." Without poetry to give God a body and a solid substance, He would remain the "driest and deadest among Platonic ideas." Myths are "conceits, born of metaphors," and religions "are produced by poets and destroyed by naturalists." To conclude, however, that poets resort to miraculism in order to controvert natural fact or scientific data is to misunderstand the kind of knowledge with which poetry is concerned. As religion "pronounces about God" where "science is silent and philosophy is negative," the poet will concede that "every act of science is legitimate and has its efficacy" at the same time he is about his purpose of complementing science and improving discourse. Whereas "scientific predication concludes an act of attention," that of poetry "initiates one" and leaves the reader "revelling in the thick *dinglich* substance that just received" its representation through miraculism. This kind of representation is just as true as the generalizations of science, and it always reminds the sensitive and perceptive reader that the object so presented is "perceptually or physically remarkable" and one "had better attend to it."

In addition to the use of tropes, through which the miraculism of poetry occurs, Ransom writes of other technical devices the poet may employ, or controls he must exercise, in order to increase the "volume of percipienda or sensibilia." Basing his discussion on Milton's *Lycidas,* he demonstrates that "anonymity, of some real if not literal sort, is a condition of poetry," that through the assumption of a fictive personality the poet achieves "artistic distance" and announces that his art is not history. In order to write a poem about the death of a friend and poet, John Milton, "a scrivener's son and a rather finicky young master of arts from Cambridge," became a Greek shepherd mourning another shepherd, and he used a literary tradition in which he no longer completely believed because "the occasion demanded it." The use of this literary form restrains the natural man and allows the poet to come to the fore. Confronting an object in which he is interested, man's natural instinct is to react at once to that aspect of the object in which he is "practically interested," but the use of literary form removes the object from his immediate reach so that he cannot "disrespect it by taking his practical attitude toward it." Man's natural instinct is to possess an object, to convert it to his own use, to gulp it down, but his "instructed instincts" make him want to know the object for its own sake, "to enjoy life, to taste and reflect" as he drinks. The natural impulse, which is attended to by the scientist, is to study an object to see what physical satisfaction it contains, either for present or for future gratification, to bring it under control so that man may use it now or later. The controlled reaction of the artist is "neither to lay hands on the object immediately, nor to ticket it for tomorrow's outrage" but to conceive of it as having its own existence and as worth knowing for its own sake. This is the kind of knowledge one gets from art, what Schopenhauer called "knowledge without desire," and the characteristics of the object which are revealed by this kind of study are not those uncovered by scientific investigation. They have no practical value: "They are those which render the body of the object, and constitute a knowledge so radical that the scientist as a scientist can scarcely understand it, and puzzles to see it rendered, richly and wastefully in the poem, or the painting. The knowledge attained there, and recorded, is a new kind of knowledge, the world in which it is set is a new world" (WB, 45).

When the poet confronts an object to which he has a compelling desire to react, he cannot react immediately because his utterance must be cast into literary form. These "second thoughts" of the poet are always superior to the first, because in the process of composing the poem the "burning passion" has "been treated with an application of sensibility." The use of literary form places upon the poet a double requirement:

One is metrical or mechanical; but the measured speech is part of the logical identity of the poem; it goes into that "character" which it possesses as an ideal creation, out of the order of the actual. The other requirement is the basic one of the make-believe, the drama, the specific anonymity or pseudonymity, which defines the poem as poem; when that goes we may also say that the poem goes; so that there would seem to be taking place in the act of poetry a rather unprofitable labor if this anonymity is not clearly conceived when a poet is starting upon his poem, and a labor lost if the poet, who has once conceived it and established it, forgets to maintain it. (WB, 41)

Using Milton to represent the attitude the serious poet would have toward his art, Ransom presents a succinct summary of some of his basic assertions regarding the relationship of the artist to the art object:

He is never discovered except meditating an object which is formidable, with a scrutiny which is steady, like that of a scientist. . . . Milton is a strong man, and has intense economic persuasions, if we may bring under that term his personal, moral, and political principles. These are his precious objects; or the situations in which he finds them exercising are. But the situations in the poetry are not his actual ones; they are fancied ones which do not touch him so nearly, distant enough to inhibit the economic impulse, which would have inhibited the sensibility. The result is that Milton's poetry, broadly speaking, may be said always to deal with "important" or highly economic subjects. But the importance of the subject is not the importance of the poetry; that depends more on the sensitiveness and completeness of the experience. (WB, 46–47)

The essays in the collection which attracted most attention or aroused most comment were "Poets Without Laurels," "The Cathartic Principle," "Shakespeare at Sonnets," and "Criticism, Inc." In the first of these, the most-often anthologized of his essays, Ransom addresses the question of why "poetry as a living art has lost its public support." Why are poets no longer "bards and patriots, priests and prophets, keepers of the public conscience, and . . . men of importance?" One reason for the deterioration of the role of poet in modern society, he believes, is the invasion of puritanism into every area of human endeavor. The effect of this intrusion into art is that in attempting to purify his art the poet has developed a false conception of the nature and function of poetry. No longer able to accept Sir Philip Sidney's statement that poetry should both teach and delight, many modern poets write either "pure" or "obscure" poetry. The first of these is demonstrated by Wallace Stevens' "Sea Surface Full of Clouds," a poem of great technical competence but one of "no moral, political, religious or sociological values," one in which "the subject matter is trifling." It is a "poetry for poetry's sake," one from which no moral can be derived. The other, the obscure poem, is represented by Allen Tate's "Death of Little Boys"; in this kind of poetry an important subject is treated, but in order to avoid even the possibility of a charge of moralizing, the poet "builds up deliberately . . . an effect of obscurity." The public simply ignores the first kind of poetry, because it has no apparent usefulness, and hates the second kind, because it "looks important enough to attend to, and yet never yields up any specific fruit" (WB, 61).

The impact of puritanism on the modern poet has been to blur his vision; he cannot see that the "union of beauty with goodness and truth has been common enough to be regarded as natural." Their dissociation is what is "unnatural and painful." In their reaction against the pseudo-poetry in which "lumps of morality and image lie side by side and are tasted in succession," many modern poets have an imperfect conception of the nature of the product they are trying to produce. To demonstrate what he thinks is its true nature, Ransom takes an analogy from chemistry. Lemonade is a mixture of water, lemon, and sugar. After combining the three ingredients, one can change the mixture to suit his taste by adding more lemon or more sugar. Table salt, however, is a true chemical compound, composed of sodium and chlorine. These two elements make a well-known product with a distinctive taste, one that cannot be changed by the addition of more of one element or the other. Although everyone knows the taste of the product formed by the compound of sodium and chlorine, few would claim to know the taste of either of these elements taken separately. Is it possible, Ransom asks, that the "MA" (the combination of morality and aestheticism) in poetry "is not a drop of lemonade after all, but a true molecule, into which the separate M and the separate A have disappeared and out of which an entirely new taste is born?"

Ransom's interpretation of Aristotle's doctrine of catharsis, which Frederick A. Pottle said was "unorthodox, shocking and perhaps right" has attracted a great deal of attention over the years.[49] Although Aristotle expressed no theory of comedy, Ransom contends that by following his principles regarding tragedy one can determine his attitude toward this other kind of drama. The kind of modern romantic comedy, which begins as tragedy by exciting the worst apprehensions but weakens and at length permits the happy ending, Aristotle called incomplete tragedy because it produced no complete catharsis. To the Greeks, comedy was satire and lampoon; it dealt with the ridiculous. Because this sense, like pity and terror, unfits a man for the duties of good citizenhood, it should also be purged. In his comments about the effects of tragedy, as well as in his implied attitude toward comedy, Aristotle's reactions were those of a "man with a medical training" who insisted that "people had better make the best of a delicate situation," like the "point of view of a modern military authority legalizing prostitution in the neighborhood of the camp" (WB, 189). One of the weaknesses of the Greeks was that they were addicted to pity and terror and since it was important that they be relieved of this weakness, they might as well go to the drama, which they were likely to attend anyway, and get rid of it there.

Although some commentators would not permit Ransom to be called a good Aristotelean because of this essay, his reputation as an eccentric and irresponsible critic or as a modern rebel disrespectful of the reputations of some of the literary giants of the past is based in large part on "Shakespeare at Sonnets."[50] First of all, Ransom says, the sonnets are ill-constructed; their metrical pattern often clashes with their logical organization. Too often, also, the sonnets represent the qualities Ransom associates with "Romantic" poetry; that is, verse tainted with "subjectivism, sentimentality, and self-indulgence." Shakespeare wrote in the sonnets an "associationist poetry," one that is "rich and suggestive even while it is vague and cloudy" (WB, 280). In this kind of verse the "pretty words have pleasing if indefinite associations," and because the "associations tend rather to cohere than to repel each other" it appears to be a poetry of "wonderful precision, when logically it is a poetry of wonderful imprecision." The violence of syntax, as well as that of imagery, in Shakespeare's poetry often results in obscurity, making it resist paraphrase and destroying its structural integrity. In short Shakespeare is the "most illustrious ancestor" of those nineteenth-century British poets who furnished "such exquisite indulgences to the feelings and yet at the same time so little food for the intellect." In a final section designed to demonstrate that Shakespeare, in the sonnets at least, was seldom able to effect the kind of miraculism Ransom had earlier associated with the highest form of poetry, he contrasts Shakespeare's sonnets with the poetry of Donne. In Shakespeare's associationist poetry there is a "half-way action providing many charming resting-places for the feelings to agitate themselves," but in Donne's metaphysical poetry an elected line of action "goes straight through to the completion of the cycle and extinction of the feelings" (WB, 291). In other words Donne's metaphors are meant; the partial though considerable similarity between objects with which the comparison begins is developed until the identification is complete. But in Shakespeare's poetry there is a plurality of images, a succession of metaphors, which are individually sustained.

In the last essay in the collection Ransom undertakes to inform his readers of "the proper business of criticism." For too long critics have been amateurs without the specific qualifications to perform the highly specialized function they have undertaken. Readers of criticism in the past have looked to three sources for the kind of competence the critic needs, but the results have been disappointing: to the "artist, who should know good art when he sees it; but his understanding is intuitive rather than dialectical"; to the philosopher, who may be able to expound a theory of art but is usually not well enough acquainted with individual works of art to comment on their technical details; and to the university professor, who is the logical source of the kind of help readers of poetry need and deserve. But those who look to the professor of English for the kind of critical assistance they desire will surely be disappointed. Although the professors are learned, they are not critical; they "spend a lifetime in compiling the data of literature" and seldom if ever render a literary judgment. They are often good textual, philological, and historical scholars, but these activities, as important as they are, do not provide the precise, formal, and systematic literary criticism the world of art must have. He calls, therefore, for a "Criticism, Inc., or a Criticism, Ltd.," so that this essential activity "may be taken in hand by professionals" rather than continued as a part-time, avocational interest of amateurs.

Although an adequate assessment of Ransom's most significant and authoritative book of criticism was many years away, when he returned to Gambier in early September to see the first issue of the *Kenyon Review* through the press, he was entering the period of his greatest influence as a literary critic. During the next twenty years he would convert this quiet little community in the rolling hills of central Ohio into an important center of literary activity. But now, as he wrote Tate, he felt he would be able to contribute to the age of criticism, which he saw as just beginning in America, by publishing some of the close studies of literary texts that he had called for in "Criticism, Inc."[51] When the *Review* became established and the critics saw the kind of essays it carried, they would be encouraged to write analytical, formal criticism because the market for such works would be considerably expanded. Now, he concluded, the official learned publications on this side of the Atlantic "are unavailable for this purpose" and only the "*Southern Review*" offers any market." If the "younger breed of men" are to see "whether the generalities . . . they offer so glibly will really work," they must be encouraged to produce by having a means of publishing what they write. The *Kenyon Review* would be dedicated to the specific purpose of disseminating such criticism.

In his absence over the summer Ransom had left some of the final details of establishing the publication in the capable hands of Philip Blair Rice, a "natural born editor of the stern cold-natured variety," one who not only knew "all the young authors" but who also had definite "executive force." [52] While Ransom was away, Rice had mailed almost four thousand copies of the official announcement that publication of the first issue of the *Kenyon Review: A Quarterly of Arts and Letters* was imminent, and he had solicited and received several new pieces for Ransom to consider for inclusion in the first issue. Ransom felt that he, too, had made a real *coup* in following a suggestion by Tate and getting an excellent essay from Ford Madox Ford which, since he had not yet received the essay which John Peale Bishop had promised on Thomas Wolfe, would probably be the leading essay in this initial issue. Because there was so much excellent material to choose from, he increased the size of the first number from 96 to 112 pages, and in order to keep "a sort of relation between the thickness and flat area" he decreased the size of the margins.[53] By October 18 he, Rice, and Norman Johnson had finished reading proofs, and Ransom was convinced the issue would be "good, not great"—the best critical piece being Ford's, followed by Philip Rahv's essay on "the dead novelist Kafka and Bishop's on Wolfe," the last having arrived just in time to appear in the leading position. Ransom's only lament was that he had not been able to get a single poem by a major poet.[54] "A professional artist has designed us a beautiful cover," he wrote his mother on November 14, "and at the rate of payment of $5.00 per page to contributors, we will have about as good content as there is: reviews, essays, poems and a few choice editorial comments by J.C.R."

As soon as advance copies were ready, he sent one to each of the advisory editors asking for comments and advice. "Let me have the works, criticizing the contributors, the editor or editors, the printers, anybody for anything."[55] Although he protested that the response to this request was not critical enough, he must have realized that this was indeed a remarkably good first issue. In addition to the essays by Ford, Rahv, and Bishop, there was the first of Delmore Schwartz's several excellent critical studies to appear in the *Review*, this one on W. H. Auden's poetry. Ransom's intention to include discussions of some of the arts other than literature was met by Paul Rosenfeld's very competent treatment of American music.[56] Recent books of fiction, poetry, biography, and philosophy, as well as studies of Toulouse-Lautrec and George Gershwin and a selection of letters by Gerard Manley Hopkins, were reviewed by well-known critics, many of whom would be regular contributors: Howard Baker, R. P. Blackmur, Herbert J. Muller, Yvor Winters, and Rice. One of the surprises of this first issue is the quality of the poetry presented by two then-unknown poets, "The Winter's Tale" by Randall Jarrell, who during the next five years would appear in the *Review* as poet, critic, and reviewer, and "The Cities' Summer Death" and "The Dandelion Girls" by R. T. S. [Robert] Lowell, who as an undergraduate student demonstrates the use of language and image that would make him one of the most important poets of his generation.

As the subject for his "few choice comments" Ransom chose two books: *Shakespeare's Philosophical Patterns* by Walter Clyde Curry and *Understanding Poetry* by Cleanth Brooks and Robert Penn Warren. Curry finds more system to Shakespeare's philosophy than Ransom can in the several plays the book discusses; therefore, he encourages his old friend and former colleague "to re-examine the whole body of plays in order to determine when, and to what extent, he is a philosophical playwright, and when, and to what extent, he is not." The publication of the second book is of particular importance because it fills a genuine need. "It is the first textbook of its kind: a smartly varied anthology of 240 or so poems, richly furnished with analytical aids, and offering progressive initiation into the rare kind of knowledge indicated by the title." He is extremely pleased that as many old poems as new are analyzed because we "do not possess anything like a critique of our own major poets."[57] Ransom was obviously aware that this book, with its many demonstrations of how a poem should be read, was taking into the classroom the kind of critical commentary he had called for in "Criticism, Inc." Here was example after example of the appropriate manner of approaching the poem in order to gain the kind of knowledge one can get only from an intensive study of the art object itself.

In a brief editorial announcement Ransom includes a paragraph which can be regarded as a statement of the need he would try to satisfy with the *Kenyon Review*:

Now it is the Age of Criticism. I need only cite: Eliot, Richards, Empson, Tate, Winters, Blackmur—a list of intensive critics the like of which has certainly not been furnished in literary history at one time before. The living art decays, for that must be the impression of an editor reading faithfully through the manuscripts on the desk. But the love of it quickens, and taste becomes luxurious and demanding, and the rise of critical understanding places even heavier responsibilities than usual upon the already weakened impulse of the modern poets. These responsibilities may be almost greater than poetry can bear again, but I do not altogether see the need for acute alarm. We shall have other ages in which the criticism relaxes, and poetry spontaneously increases, but now our age is critical, and it has its own passionate enjoyments.[58]

Perhaps in suggesting that the "weakened impulse" of the poet cannot bear the heavy responsibility of a reading public with educated sensibilities, Ransom is unintentionally expressing the reasons why his best poetry was far in the past; certainly he wanted to participate fully in the "passionate enjoyments" of this age of criticism. The first issue of his quarterly announced its role for the two decades that he would edit it. Above all, it would provide an outlet for the best critical writing in England and America with the hope that the magazine would help to quicken the love of the creative arts among sensitive and perceptive readers everywhere. As "critical understanding" increased and taste became more "luxurious and demanding," perhaps the poets and novelists would make a serious effort to meet the more exacting demands of their enlightened readers.

The second issue continues Ransom's intention to represent all the arts—and the literatures of countries other than British or American—with Forbes Watson on American art, the conclusion of Paul

Rosenfeld's essay on American music, a translation of two of Federico Garcia Lorca's poems by Rolfe Humphries, and an essay on Lorca by William Carlos Williams. The reviewers were more impressive and the range of books reviewed was much broader than in the first issue: Allen Tate on George E. Whicher's biography of Emily Dickinson, Mark Van Doren on Delmore Schwartz's *In Dreams Begin Responsibilities*, Randall Jarrell on Yvor Winters' *Maule's Curse*, Joseph Warren Beach on André Malraux's *Man's Hope*, Robert Penn Warren on Lionel Trilling's *Matthew Arnold*, and Ransom on Merrill Moore's *M: One Thousand Autobiographical Sonnets*. There were also reviews of books on the American theater, the dance, philosophy, and new writing.

The most interesting and, to Ransom, the most significant essays in this issue were those contributed by Eliseo Vivas, Howard Dykema Roelofs, and Philip Blair Rice to "A Symposium on the New Encyclopedists." These essays and the encouragement of Rice made Ransom look carefully at Charles W. Morris' *Foundation of the Theory of Signs*, which he recommended immediately to Tate. It is "really brilliant," he wrote, "makes Richards look mighty small; his definition of designatum and denotum would have special bearing on your topic."[59] Tate read and discussed the book in several letters to Ransom before making extensive use of some of its principles in "Literature as Knowledge," as Ransom would in "Wanted: An Ontological Critic." In his comments on the symposium Ransom gives his first public notice to Morris and his fellow editors of the *International Encyclopedia of Unified Science*.[60] Although he is grateful that the editors and writers of these most significant studies are not bypassing the arts altogether, he is disturbed that they seem to regard them as quasisciences. The arts, which the scientists have relegated to the position occupied by science a century ago, are also in a state of disrepute with philosophy because that discipline is dominated by positivists and naturalists. What the scientists and philosophers do not realize is that science and literature are two different orders of discourse and use different kinds of language; one is literal and explicit, the other implicit and literary. This sort of misunderstanding is very old, going back at least as far as Hobbes, who regarded poetry as "science dressed in the costume of the period," and Hegel, who argued that art was a "*decora-*

tive or 'sensuous' version of science." Even in modern times I. A. Richards has advanced the theory that art is merely "an *emotional* version of science." The only way to correct these misconceptions is to insist that art has a language of its own, unlike that of science, and its semantical meaning cannot be rendered in the language of science. In an attempt to point up the differences between the order of knowledge provided by science and that available in literature, Ransom again refers to the basic principle of the theory advanced more than ten years before in "The Third Moment": "It would seem that science comes first, with its highly selective rendering of a given reality, which consists in attending to some single one of its aspects; art comes afterwards, in what mood we may imagine, and attempts to restore the body which science has emptied."[61]

The last two issues of the first year of the *Kenyon Review* furnished ample evidence that a critical quarterly of the highest quality had appeared. The essays in the number for Summer, 1939, have seldom been surpassed in one issue of a periodical produced anywhere at anytime. In addition to Philip Rahv's "Pale Face and Red Skin," one of the best-known articles ever published in the *Kenyon Review,* and Ransom's "Yeats and His Symbols," an authoritative study of a major aspect of the work of the greatest modern poet, the issue carried George Marion O'Donnell's "Faulkner's Mythology," a truly seminal essay; it begins systematic study of Faulkner's greatest novels. There were also essays by Randall Jarrell on A. E. Housman and by Kenneth Burke on artistic freedom and artistic responsibility. In this issue and in the one following it Ransom was able finally to publish some poetry by major poets: Dylan Thomas' "Poem," Allen Tate's "The Trout Map," and his own "Address to the Scholars of New England," his first poem in more than five years.[62] The final number for the year included a symposium on the state of poetry in England, France, and the United States, to which Herbert Read, Justin O'Brien, and Robert Penn Warren contributed, and an essay, "Science, Art, and Technology," by Charles W. Morris. Among those contributing reviews to these issues were Mark Schorer, Austin Warren, Lionel Trilling, Edgar Johnson, Christopher Isherwood, F. O. Matthiessen, Harry Levin, Roberta Teale Schwartz, and Randall Jarrell.

At the end of his second year in Gambier, Ransom could be right-fully pleased with what he had achieved. The publication of *The World's Body* and the reception of the *Kenyon Review* placed him, he realized, in a position to encourage the development of the kind of criticism he knew the world of letters needed and to direct its growth. The necessity of reading the unsolicited critical manuscripts was not an altogether unprofitable task because among the dozens he thought "absolutely useless and unbelievably bad" was the occasional provoca-tive one. From many of the established or soon-to-be established names in criticism he received essays which stimulated his thought and set him to work on some of the particularly knotty cruxes in his theories concerning the nature and function of poetry. These theoret-ical investigations of the grades of reality embodied in poetic dis-course commanded an increasingly large portion of his creative ener-gies in the decade following World War II.

But for the members of his own family and a very small group of intimate acquaintances, Ransom was not genuinely concerned about people. At different periods of his life, however, he was close to par-ticular persons because they were interested in and knowledgeable about causes and ideas in which he was involved at the moment. After his father, with whom he always had a close personal relationship—and between his fifteenth and twenty-fifth years an intimate intellec-tual one as well—there were his friends at Oxford; then Samuel Chew, Christopher Morley, and Robert Graves; and later, in Nash-ville, the Fugitives and Agrarians. His associations with each of these persons were of great value to him, for he discovered very early that he could develop and organize his thought best when he was able to test his ideas on able and sympathetic antagonists. Now at Kenyon the person to whom he turned most often when he needed an intelligent reaction to one of his critical concepts was Philip Blair Rice. A warm and pleasant manner, combined with a keenly inquisitive intellect and a deep interest in and knowledge of ancient and modern philosophy, made Rice the kind of close professional acquaintance Ransom needed to discuss his theories of aesthetics. With Rice providing an appropriate sounding board, as to some extent Randall Jarrell and

Robert Lowell did also, Ransom tested and refined many of the critical attitudes included in *The New Criticism* and in significant essays
published throughout the forties in the *Kenyon Review* and elsewhere.

One of Ransom's most pleasant surprises was his discovery that the
Kenyon students were better prepared than he had at first thought
they were. (Their quality increased rapidly, too, as students began to
come, particularly from the cities of the Northeast, to be a part of the
literary activity generated by the *Review* and later by the Kenyon
School of English.) He continued the practice, begun in his first year,
of holding his creative writing classes one evening each week in his
living room. Like Allen Tate, Ransom thought the most important
function of the teacher was to demonstrate to his students something
of the art of reading literature.[63] This approach is described by Laurence N. Barrett, who about this time had a class with Ransom at Bread
Loaf.[64] Ransom always "stood easily before the class," he wrote, and
taught "extemporaneously in a quiet voice" that just managed to
"compete with the lawn mowers outside the window." When he read
there was no rhetoric in his voice, none of what at that time was
popularly called interpretative reading. "He had too much love for a
poem," Barrett thought, "not to let it stand on its own, and too much
regard for his students to come between us and the poem. He simply
read with a quiet dignity, and beneath his restraint we could feel his
affection for the thing." He never tried to interpret a poem or to make
his students see the poem through him, but if his students chose they
were "welcome to watch him encountering the verse, not as a *magister*
but simply as another human reader, and not in order that we should
imitate his responses but, one level beyond that, in order that we
might work with them and against them." He taught the poem, then,
as he read it, "almost anonymously." But some of Ransom's best teaching, Robert Lowell recalls, went on outside the classroom. He made
himself available to his students, letting them know they were welcome to drop by the office or, after hours, to come by his house. He
would go on walks with them and talk about poetry or philosophy
between comments about the trees, the flowers, or the birds encountered along the way. "Somehow he made the calling of writing poetry
and criticism seem all important, but he did it with gentle balance.
Balance, serenity, gentleness—they were the words you associate with

him. He had a wonderful way of insisting that you do certain things, like studying classics and other things I didn't want to do. Yet he didn't over-direct." [65]

As Robert Penn Warren has pointed out, "teaching, editing and writing" were all "tied together" in Ransom's "game sense of life." His associations with his students, always an essential part of his life, at this particular time were especially important because they helped to ease the shock of transferring from Nashville to Gambier. He followed closely the progress of his students, particularly in these early years at Kenyon, those who had come with him from Vanderbilt. Robert Lowell "is a fine boy," he wrote Tate on April 28, 1938, "very definitely with great literary possibilities." Although he did not know if his potential was greater as poet or critic—he soon encouraged him to write poetry even if he had to give up criticism—he thought he "was making fast progress in both lines." Ransom also published in an early issue of the *Review* a poem by Peter Taylor; and David McDowell, who later had a distinguished career in publishing, served on the *Review* staff and wrote reviews for it. That Ransom recognized Jarrell's talent is demonstrated by the fact that in these early years he was one of the *Review*'s most frequent contributors. Ransom also appreciated Jarrell's facile critical brilliance and had many literary and philosophical discussions with him—during their first year in Ohio, Lowell said later, they talked of Shakespeare almost incessantly—but as a man Ransom found his younger colleague somewhat trying. "He and I don't talk together well; I have the feeling he can't generalize though he has taken a good deal of philosophy," Ransom wrote Tate; "but he is a very wise young man and learned, and good hearted."

The sudden break from the section he had lived in all of his life was made much less severe, too, by the fact that he and his family soon discovered that life in Gambier was not as "flat and characterless" as he had at first supposed. With Helen at Wellesley, which she had entered in the fall of 1938, Reavill back at Webb, and Jack in nursery school, Robb for a few weeks had time on her hands. But soon she found some golfing partners, and she and Ransom discovered that their interest in bridge and poker was shared by many other faculty couples. Ransom's companions soon found that he played with great skill and intense competitiveness, and if his winnings were to be kept within reasonable bounds, even with limited stakes, the game required one's closest attention. He quickly established a reputation as an expert gardener, and his vegetables and flowers, particularly his dahlias and irises, became the envy of the neighborhood. But, as George Lanning commented, in Ransom's garden everything was "separated according to its nature, and lined up firmly and confined squarely." One of his neighbors thought it strange to see him weeding the garden in the jacket and tie he had worn at school that day, and another complained, "I wish John would mix things up a little, and stop putting all his plants in *rows*. . . . It's not what *I'd* call a *garden*." [66] By 1939, then, the Ransoms had begun to feel perfectly at home in Gambier; work and play, as one quality, they found as possible there as in Nashville. Ransom was convinced that through the *Kenyon Review* he would be able to make his contribution to the age of criticism of which he felt so much a part. Within the next decade he hoped to assist in formulating and presenting the body of critical theory, as well as examples of its practice, which he thought absolutely essential if poetry was to regain its basic function of providing the kind of knowledge which civilized man must have and which he can acquire almost nowhere else.

Robb Reavill and John Crowe Ransom, 1945.

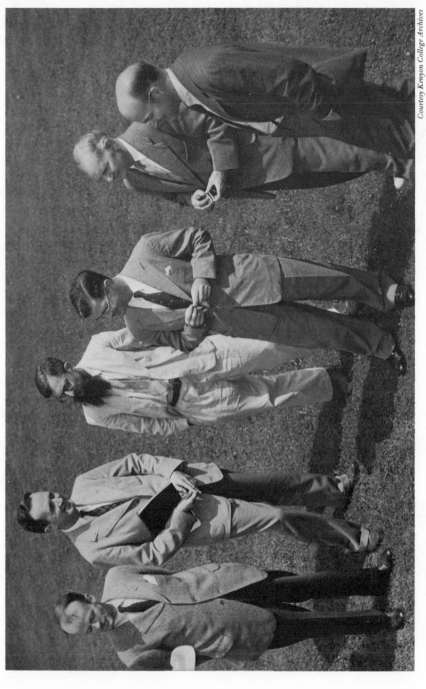

Kenyon School of English Fellows, 1948. Left to right: Allen Tate, Richard Chase, William Empson, Cleanth Brooks, Ransom, and F. O. Matthiessen.

Yvor Winters, Ransom, and Tate, at Kenyon, 1949.

Tate and Ransom, 1949.

At Kenyon College, *ca.* 1950. Left to right: Robert Frost, Ransom, Roberta Teale Schwartz (Mrs. Gordon Chalmers), and Robert Hillyer.

Fugitive Reunion, 1956. Left to right:

Front: Tate, Ransom, Davidson
Middle: Milton Starr, Alec Stevenson, Warren
Back: William Y. Elliott, Merrill Moore, Jesse Wills, Sidney Mttron Hirsch

Ransom's sisters, Annie and Ellene Ransom, *ca.* 1960.

Courtesy Kenyon College Archives

Ransom on his eightieth birthday.

Ransom's residence on Kenyon campus for almost twenty years.

Ransom with Warren, at Ransom's last public appearance, February 27, 1973.

Ransom Hall, on Kenyon College campus.

The Nature of Poetic Discourse 1938-1945

DURING THE summer of their first year in Gambier the Ransoms bought a "handsome second-hand stove" and installed it in the kitchen of their campus home. This room, Ransom wrote his mother, had felt "like the North Pole," but quickly became the center of family activity.[1] After dinner Ransom worked or read there; and on the coldest winter nights, when it was his turn to entertain, the weekly meeting of the poker club convened around the table on which the family ate most of its meals. With the luxury of a living area heated to Robb's satisfaction, the entire family urged Ransom's mother to spend Christmas with them and to bring Ellene and Annie with her. There is plenty of room, Ransom wrote on November 14, and a few extra guests would be no burden to Robb because they had just acquired a "live-in maid, a country girl" whose family lived out in the county about ten miles from the village of Gambier. Helen and Reavill had both asked for a family Christmas at home, a request Ransom looked upon most favorably, particularly if his mother and the girls could come up from Nashville. The expense of keeping Helen at Wellesley and Reavill at Webb was, as he wrote Cleanth Brooks, a "tremendous drain on the exchequer." Although Ellene and Annie decided they should not subject their mother to the hazards of an Ohio winter, the Ransoms in Gambier had a full house over the holidays. Cinina and Robert Penn Warren came by the day after Christmas, and Cinina stayed for five days while her husband attended the MLA meeting in New York. On his way back to Baton

Rouge, Warren came through Gambier and the two old friends had five days of what Ransom described to Tate as "the best conversation I've had since Tennessee."[2] They discussed Warren's first novel *Night Rider,* which had appeared during the autumn and which Ransom thought "one of the smoothest narratives" he had seen, although he wished the "material were *conventionally* heroic instead of being about the odd and isolated Kentucky night riders."

In fact there were so many guests over Christmas, Robb wrote Ellene, that some of them had to furnish their own blankets and "John and I didn't have a minute to ourselves."[3] As much as he enjoyed having the children home and being able to entertain the Warrens for the first time in Gambier, Ransom was pleased when the crowd thinned out shortly after the new year, because there was a very pressing matter he and Robb had to discuss. Allen Tate had written from the North Carolina Woman's College at Greensboro that the chairmanship of the department there was vacant and had urged him to apply. Tate had already talked about Ransom to the dean, who knew him and respected his work, and Tate was convinced he would receive the appointment if he would accept it. Ransom had responded that he was happy at Kenyon "except for one or two things." He had gradually become aware that he exceeded his colleagues more than he "had supposed in the matter of salary" and he felt "rather self-conscious about it." Also, there was no place nearby for Helen to attend college, and "she is a rather expensive article at Wellesley now." This problem could be solved either by getting more money—which was impossible at Kenyon, for President Chalmers could not afford to offer him an increase in salary and he would not accept one if it should come—or by his teaching in a school that Helen could attend. Since the Woman's College met both of these requirements so well, he could not be "other than interested" in an offer from there. Although he had been informed by the chairman of the English department at the University of Texas, where he had taught in the summer school, that he could have a definite offer from that institution as soon as he was in a position to consider it, Ransom preferred to join Tate because their being in close and continuous association, he was convinced, would result in a "series of fine critical books" which would be "a career for both of us" and "an objective to aim straight at."[4] After Tate had informed the dean of Ransom's interest, he was urged to come to Greensboro for a conference; and unless Robb had strong objections, he wrote Tate, he was ready to enter into serious negotiations, if the authorities there were.

When he was able to discuss the matter thoroughly with Robb, he found her not only willing but anxious to move south again. Consequently, he went into Columbus on January 12, he wrote his mother, to get a new suit to wear to his conference with the "Dean of the College and the President of the University of North Carolina College system," from whom he expected to "receive a very handsome offer" since he had already informed them he would not consider a "salary equivalent to that of my present position."[5] At Greensboro he was very much impressed by what he heard. "They want me to go on with my critical studies," he wrote his mother shortly after his return. He would be given complete freedom in the operation of the department because "North Carolina has produced plenty of social scientists and not enough literary men."[6] Although his teaching schedule was to be six hours each week, "you are the boss," he reported the president as saying, "and can do what you like." He was offered $6,000—$5,500 salary and $500 living allotment—and the opportunity to earn an extra $500 any time he wished to teach a term of the summer session. This offer, he realized, was most generous, "more than any professor in the South gets with maybe a handful of exceptions." Since Robb wanted "to go south again" and both Helen and Reavill could attend school at Chapel Hill "at no cost except board," he wrote Tate that he was "pretty certain" he would accept but he wanted to leave Kenyon "as gracefully as possible."[7]

As Ransom suspected, Gordon Chalmers did not make his decision any easier for him. When Ransom reported the offer, Chalmers immediately promised to extend the *Review* beyond its three-year trial period and to pay Ransom an extra $1,000 a year as its editor. Although he appreciated very much this expression of Chalmer's confidence in him and in the *Review,* Ransom was convinced that he should not increase further the discrepancy that already existed between his salary and that of other senior members of the faculty.[8] He agreed with Chalmers that the "dialectic as carried on with the girls" would not be very stimulating, but he and Robb were convinced that Greensboro would be a pleasant place to live, at least better than this "Ohio outpost." From the opportunity to associate closely with Tate he would receive intellectual stimulation; and the position, though demanding, would allow him enough free time to write. This combination would surely give him ample opportunity to see if "there's any performance in the old engine."[9] The response he received from Nashville, however, was not as enthusiastic as he had expected. Ellene, his mother reported, wondered if the Greensboro position might not be a "step down," since Kenyon and the *Review* were so well known that at a recent performance of the Nashville Symphony Orchestra she had heard two men, both of whom were complete strangers to her, in animated conversation about her "illustrious brother."[10]

He did not know, he wrote his mother on March 5, whether the new position was a "step-up" or a "step-down," because he was not interested in "prestige or prospects." It did seem to him, however, that Greensboro was "up, very decidedly," in the two things that count: the salary and the "possibility of Reavill and Helen getting a first-rate education at very little additional expense." His reaction to his mother's suggestion that he might have been "too much influenced" by Allen Tate was uncommonly firm:

I don't like to hear you abusing Allen, whose publicity in my behalf two years ago was what made my leaving Vanderbilt a matter of record at all; and when you mention the man's being told about Vanderbilt's mistake by someone sitting next to him at the Symphony, that was because someone had seen something about it in the papers, or had been told by someone who had seen the papers, and wouldn't have known about it in the long run but for Allen's generous indignation and plain talk in my behalf; nor would the dinner have come up if Allen hadn't got it up, nor would the "testimonials" have come in if he hadn't wired people for them. . . . I think it's mighty fine to have friends who will fight for you, and it's quite easy to point to what they have accomplished in this case.

The position, he concluded, "is ideal," better than he had ever "ventured to expect anywhere, at any time." The authorities there "want me to write and publish," and "I have a system of criticism and many projects to get on with, and I could edit a great many valuable studies, with the aid of the University of North Carolina Press, which they think would put the University of North Carolina on the map; they would also like for me to return to verse-writing if I chose." He liked everything he had seen about the situation there: time to write and the freedom and intellectual stimulation he needed to do the kind of work he wanted to do, not to mention a salary better than that of any other professor he knew and the "most liberal terms" to be found anywhere. When he went to see Chalmers on March 29, he was assured that no one wanted him to stay at Kenyon unwillingly, that no one felt he was under any moral obligation to remain; however, Chalmers did ask for more time and requested that Ransom delay a final decision for two weeks. Although he offered to release him from one class and to raise his salary to a level slightly above that offered by North Carolina, Ransom insisted that any increase he received must come from outside the college budget. "He doesn't have the money," Ransom wrote Tate, "and Greensboro is South and perhaps the Tates will be there and it's three times as comfortable in the South for a Southerner. Greensboro is secure, permanent, comfortable; Kenyon is not any of these things." [11] Although he promised Chalmers the extension of time requested, he thought the odds were at least five-to-one that he was going to North Carolina.

The following week he went into the president's office with his mind fully made up to resign, but Chalmers told him that he had an appointment with the director of the Carnegie Foundation, whom he was going to ask to endow the *Review* and its editor. Again Ransom delayed his final decision, but even after he learned that Tate had received a firm offer from Princeton he still felt that he was "committed toward Greensboro." [12] Aside from the *Review,* which probably "costs me more than its worth," he had "no literary interest at Kenyon" and he hated to feel that he was "on dress parade." Nevertheless the prospect of the Tates leaving was far from pleasant. "Would you be willing to stay," Ransom wrote, if you were "switched over to more conventional teaching?" If he should write Dean Jackson that he was coming, he would like to urge him "to give Tate enough to keep him there." As far as he was able, he would allow Tate to redefine his position to his own tastes. [13] Ten days later, when Tate wrote that he was definitely accepting the position at Princeton, Ransom responded that although the prospects of his going were far less inviting now that "the Tates are pulling out," the chances were still at least "ten to one I'll accept the Greensboro offer." But Robb was not so certain, for she wrote Ellene on April 6: "Our fate is not yet decided; it is about as bad as the Nashville decision." At the same time she assured her sister-in-law that she would not attempt to exert any special pressure on Ransom to go or stay. "While I'm a pretty poor manager and not much help," she wrote, "I've never asked him nor would I ask him to do anything he'd be ashamed of doing."

Just when he had definitely made up his mind to leave Kenyon, the unexpected happened. President Chalmers received a grant from the Carnegie Foundation and was able to meet all of the conditions Ransom had given him in their several conversations. Beginning with the fall term of 1940, Ransom wrote his mother on March 13, he would carry the title of Carnegie Professor of Poetry and would receive a salary of $5,900, an increase of $1,200. He would continue to edit the *Review* but would be expected to teach only one class. Since most of his salary would no longer come from the general budget, he did not feel he "stood in the way of the other professors."[14] Not until the very end of his teaching career did he again seriously entertain an offer of permanent employment elsewhere. For the next twenty years he lived in Gambier—teaching, writing, and editing, making this little village in central Ohio one of the most important centers of literary activity in the country.

During the fall of 1938 Ransom had begun work on the first poem he had undertaken for several years. Thinking a definite commitment would give him the stimulation he needed to return to poetry, he agreed to write some original verse to be read at the meeting of the Harvard chapter of the Phi Beta Kappa Society on June 23, 1939. Although he wrote part of a draft in the fall and was pleased with the progress he had made, he had to put it aside in early December to prepare a lecture. He did some revision over the Christmas holidays, but he was so deeply involved in the negotiations regarding the North Carolina appointment that he did not get back to the poem until mid-March. Then with the date at which it must be completed fast approaching, he began to fret about it. "What started out as a lark," he wrote Tate, "became a burden and I could have written several free

poems out of the energies I have spent on this occasional poem." [15]
Robert Lowell, who saw him almost every day during this period, said
he must have completely rewritten it at least twenty times. [16] Commenting a few years later on the creative process, Ransom seems to
be describing the procedure that Lowell observed during the winter
and spring of 1938/39:

Poetry comes in waves; that is, you have to work to a very high tension
before the stuff that comes out's any good. When you begin you have
some themes in mind; you know the thing you want to write a poem
about very well, but you're rusty; and it's entirely a matter of speeding
up—quickening—and giving a shock to your verbal talent so it'll be
quick, decisive, and bold. And the first day or two you write, it just
streams off and you think, "My, this is wonderful." You look at it the
next morning, early, and it's pretty bad. You throw it away, right
quickly, and try again; and day after day that happens. But finally you
see that there's something here: "I won't throw that away; that's got
the making of something." It's entirely the amount of language you're
using. It has to be absolutely new and fresh and in your own idiom
and not a recollection of somebody else's idiom; and not stilted, and
not sentimental, and with words used as much for their absolute values as possible, and it has to be rich. You can't forecast what the poem
is going to turn out to be. It always surprises you. [17]

Despite the fact that he might have been, as he expressed it, a
"little rusty" the poem was far enough along by April 20 to offer it to
Cleanth Brooks for the *Southern Review*. But it is "not finished yet," he
warned; "it's half done, about. I can't even tell just how long it will
run." He asked Brooks to give him an honest evaluation, not "to
accept it out of personal reasons." Above all, he wanted to know
"whether the first poem I've done in quite a while is any good. I'd like
to do more if the start is at all auspicious. I am quite prepared to hear
the truth that it isn't." [18] After the poem had been read at Harvard
and after he had already decided to publish it, along with Tate's "The
Trout Map," in the *Kenyon Review*, he sent it to Tate with this comment: "I'd very much like to have your word on it. The way that poem
looks in print to me, perhaps even more to my friends, will determine
my future avocations pretty much." [19] Perhaps he did not like the way
the poem looked in print, because it was a good many years before he
attempted another.

Later that spring, in reporting on the reasons for founding the *Kenyon Review,* he indicated the purposes it would continue to hold as long as he was its editor: "The Kenyon Review, A Quarterly of Arts and Letters has been founded for two purposes: to provide in America a magazine of interests and standards not found in any existing periodicals, that is, a strict and authoritative appraisal of all the contemporary arts and ideas; and to represent to the world at large in interesting and readable form, one of the major concerns of Kenyon College, the liberal arts."[20] In spite of the serious threat to any nonmilitary activity resulting from the outbreak of war in Europe and the ever-increasing certainty that America would soon enter that conflict, Ransom remained steadfast in his resolve to give an accurate and provocative evaluation of contemporary culture in a form intended to appeal to the most discriminating readers. The term "fit audience though few" seems to describe with a special aptness the readership of the *Review* during the next two decades. At the end of its first full year it had a paid circulation of 350, and at the end of its fifth year that number had risen to slightly more than 1,300.[21]

Despite the best efforts of Ransom and his staff, the *Review* could not support itself from circulation and advertisements; and early in the spring of 1941, as the time for the meeting of his board of trustees approached, President Chalmers warned that he might have difficulty securing its pledge of $5,000. During the previous summer Wilbur Cummings, the board member who had most enthusiastically supported the *Review,* had died, and Ransom wrote Tate that it was "more obligatory than ever to get on with the prospect of outside financing in whole or in part."[22] In spite of his "natural disinclination to pass the hat," he informed Chalmers that he was "ready to travel if I must." While he was awaiting some kind of action from Chalmers—who had assured Ransom that he "was not about to let the magazine fold" because it had "brought too much favorable comment on the college for that"—Ransom prepared a "short but comprehensive statement" about the status of the *Review* and the necessity for the proposed campaign to secure outside financing.[23] This statement he mailed to the advisory editors, to contributors and subscribers, and to other supporters, asking that they send him comments he could include in his solicitation for funds. Response to his request vastly exceeded his expectations, and he had some difficulty selecting excerpts to include in the published leaflet. When "The *Kenyon Review*: A Statement and Appreciation" was mailed in early June, 1941, it included endorsements from Clifton Fadiman, who said the *Kenyon Review* was the "most conscientiously edited literary periodical in the United States"; George Dillon, editor of *Poetry*, who called it "the most eagerly read and the most influential magazine of its kind"; Christopher Morley, who said it was "a sort of porcelain superstructure upon the gross prairies of living, but it does give a wide view"; Charles W. Morris, who said "it seems to meet a need that no other journal meets"; Philip Wheelwright, who maintained that the *Kenyon Review* "has come to occupy a unique place and fill an indispensable function in American intellectual life"; as well as statements from the Paris *Etudes Anglaises*, Frederick Prokosch, Justin O'Brien, Marianne Moore, Lionel Trilling, Richard Weaver, Charles Riker, Edonard Roditi, Theodore Greene, H. G. Owen, and Wen Yuan-ning, editor of *Tien, Hsia Monthly*.

Since the demise of Eliot's *Criterion*, the statement begins, the *Kenyon Review* is the only "modern" and nonacademic quarterly in English "devoted exclusively to arts and letters." [24] Anyone aware of present literary trends knows that we live in an age of criticism, a time when "many young writers are producing matter that deserves publication." There is certainly enough available critical writing to support a "Review of great distinction if its editors are capable." In its two years of publication the *Kenyon Review*, "under pressure of good material clamoring for publication," has increased its size from 112 to 128 pages; and if adequate financing were available, it could go to 160 pages without sacrificing the quality of the material printed. So far the journal has been published from gifts "amounting to more than $15,000" from "nine friends of the College." From the beginning it was felt that these friends would see the journal through its experimental stage and after that time it would try to get outside funding. Now that time has come, the statement concludes, and if the *Kenyon Review* is to continue publication, it must find five or six thousand dollars in each of the next five years.

As he wrote Tate, Ransom had "two or three leads" which he immediately followed up. In early May he went to New York and called on Henry Luce, president of Time-Life, Inc., Clifton Fadiman, and F. P. Keppel of the Carnegie Foundation. From there he went to Princeton, where he spent a pleasant weekend with the Tates and had a long conversation with Henry Church, heir to the Arm and Hammer Soda Company fortune. Although he had expected no immediate assistance from Henry Luce or the Carnegie Foundation, he was cordially received and, he wrote Tate, was convinced he had "made a strong investment for the future."[25] His meeting with Church brought immediate tangible results, although the amount he received was less than he had expected. When he was first preparing for the visit, he wrote Tate that he hoped to raise at least half of the $5,000 he needed from this one source; but because of other commitments and the fear of a vastly increased tax to support the military preparedness program, Church could pledge only $750. Apparently Ransom was not displeased with his efforts because he wrote F. P. Keppel, "We have succeeded in our campaign for funds and seem now on rather good footing."[26]

The entry of the United States into World War II had an unexpected effect upon the financial status and the entire future of the *Kenyon Review*. In a conversation with Robert Penn Warren during the Christmas holidays, Ransom was warned of the demise of the *Southern Review*; and on January 28, 1942, Ransom wrote Tate that, despite the success of the recent financial campaign, there was a strong possibility the *Kenyon* would also be discontinued. The faculty committee appointed by the president of the college to study the budget might decide, he feared, that the *Review* was a "luxury rather than an educational necessity." Whatever the decision of that committee, he knew he was confronted by the immediate necessity of decreasing by at least half the rate of payment to contributors, of having to employ a student secretary, and of being able to publish only three times a year. But the unfortunate suspension of the *Southern Review*, he reasoned, might work to his advantage. As soon as it was an established fact that that journal could not continue, he wrote Brooks and Warren to explore the possibilities of a merger. If such an arrangement were possible, he offered to use the cover of the *Southern Review*, to print on it the names of both journals, to publish all of the material already accepted, to honor all unexpired subscriptions, and to list on the title page their names and his as coeditors. "We'd make this joint editor-ship real in every workable sense," he wrote Tate, "and we could easily by arranging some sort of exchange, have one of them up here a part of each year, on the faculty and on the grounds."[27] Ransom's sugges-tion of a merger pleased both Brooks and Warren, they made the appropriate recommendation to the administration of Louisiana State University, who gave it a tentative endorsement, and the issue of the *Southern Review* for Spring, 1942, carried the statement that this was its last number and that "all unexpired subscriptions will be filled by the *Kenyon Review*." Although the merger was never effected, the *Kenyon Review* was paid $750 to fill the unexpired subscriptions by the *Southern*, and beginning with the Autumn, 1943, number the mast-head of the *Kenyon* named Brooks and Warren as advisory editors.[28] The subscription list and the "new editorial strength" which his jour-nal inherited, Ransom wrote Keppel, considerably increased the strength of the *Kenyon*.[29] By increasing the cost of a subscription from $2.00 to $3.00 a year, the price of the *Southern*, and by selling more advertising space to commercial publishers, there was a real possibili-ty, he believed, that the *Kenyon* could become almost completely self-supporting.

The financial pressure, however, got no easier. The following spring, as Ransom prepared a budget, he realized he must raise at least $1,500 if he was to remain in the black. Renewal subscriptions, particularly those from former subscribers to the *Southern Review*, were not coming in as fast as he had expected, and he knew the amount he had received from the publishers for advertising would probably decline because their business was hard hit by the war.[30]

Since he had to go to New York with Robb, who was going to see a specialist recommended by the Tates, he not only called Church but visited the offices of the Rockefeller Foundation and talked to David H. Stevens, director of its program to assist the humanities.

For some time Ransom had been concerned that despite her rigorous schedule of outdoor activities, including eighteen holes of golf two or three times a week, Robb had suddenly begun to gain weight and often complained of headaches. At Ransom's insistence she saw a local doctor, but he could arrive at no definite diagnosis, though he detected that her blood pressure was dangerously high and recommended a specialist in Columbus. Ransom encouraged her to see a Dr. Wolf in New York, who, Tate had written him, had done "wonders for John Peale Biship." Robb wrote to Dr. Wolf and although she informed him that she was "of the literary impecunious Ransoms" and not a "rich nouveau mid-western prospect" she was given an appointment for April 1. Six weeks after their return Ransom reported to Tate, on May 16, "Robb is just about at rights again. She had a fine series of meetings with Wolf and has had treatments which he recommended after she left New York. . . . Robb is down in weight and down in blood pressure too."

His fund raising venture in New York he thought also successful. Church renewed his pledge for $750 and Stevens received him cordially and expressed a more than casual interest in the financial difficulties involved in publishing a literary quarterly in war time. Soon after his return to Gambier, he received two very pleasant surprises. First of all, a trustee, one of the original supporters of the *Review,* unexpectedly gave $1,000; therefore, with Church's bequest, publication was assured for at least one more year. Even better news, as it turned out, was Stevens' request for more information about the *Review.*[31] In addition to data regarding its financing, he asked about possible growth of the journal both in size and circulation, the "spread of its contributors," and the amount of time Ransom devoted to editing it. Specifically, he wanted evidence to indicate that the journal and "its editor's reputation on a national scale" were attracting students to Kenyon. The "nature of my curiosity," he concluded, could be summed up "in the remark that I expect someday a college or university will gain a standing for having a strong school of criticism" and he suspected a journal "may be part of the prescription." To this end he asked what Ransom knew of other "centers . . . seriously concerned with this matter. The obvious ones are Iowa, Vanderbilt, Michigan and Princeton."

When the letter arrived Ransom was at Bread Loaf teaching for the summer, but he prepared a detailed answer as soon as he returned. Because of the generosity of Henry Church and 125 other donors, his four-page letter of August 27, 1943, began, the *Review* has started its fifth year with $2,500, which, along with its expected income of $4,000 from subscriptions and advertising, will pay its way for the current year. But for the war, which "is interfering with our subscription list," the journal, he was convinced, would be completely self-supporting. As it is, however, for the past few years the *Review* has received no subsidy from the college, except this year when one of the "former trustee-angels wanted to put in his $1,000 as of old." The *Review* has a "devoted public if a small and special one," with subscribers "everywhere in the country, though not many on any one street." Its greatest appeal is with "a certain section of the college enrollment," particularly with the "smart pupils and the younger faculty" in the "literary and fine arts departments." "The part of your letter which interested me most," Ransom concluded, is the "possible connection between the *Review* and a possible school of criticism." Because of the special interests of its editors, the *"Kenyon Review* is a semiphilosophical as well as a critical journal," and this interest has affected the curricular offerings of the college—the departments of philosophy, English, and classics having cooperated in arranging a program designed to make the "right students" into "literary philosophers, or else philosophical literary men and critics of the arts." If there were graduate work at Kenyon, he was convinced that "many admissions would be motivated by what we might offer as a 'school of criticism.'" The letter ends with the first formal expression of the idea that developed into the Kenyon School of English:

For more than ten years I have cherished a steadily mounting conviction that the next great strategical move of English studies would be a move toward the critical side. The old-line departments of English which still offer little but historical scholarship are losing ground in the competition for able male students. Very naturally; for they have brought the historical job to something like reasonable completeness, and it does not furnish an excitement to the creative men as it did. I believe these observations are now a commonplace. But as to *why* the departments do not turn to critical studies for at least a considerable part of their staple. It is not because of some viciousness in the personnel (and that would be a poor ground on which to approach them anyway) but, in my opinion, because the critical studies are still conducted by amateurs, and do not furnish a program that is basic enough and solid enough to go into a teaching program everywhere.

Ransom's experience during the past few summers at Bread Loaf had convinced him that "the brilliant students in English are intensely in earnest about critical studies and will sacrifice almost all other studies if necessary in order to get them."

On September 8, 1943, Stevens thanked Ransom for his informative letter and for the three accompanying copies of the *Kenyon Review*. At the first opportunity he promised to come to Gambier to talk to Ransom personally.[32] In the meantime he received Philip Blair Rice, who was spending the fall in New York working on a Guggenheim project, and recommended to his board of directors a grant of $7,500 to the *Review*, $3,750 in each of the next two years. As a consequence the journal on June 30, 1944, reported a surplus of $1,669.85.[33] With the income from advertising almost doubling the next year—because publishers were already anticipating the end of the war and the flood of returning veterans to colleges and universities—on July 1, 1945, the *Review* had a surplus of $3,474.30. For almost four years it had existed and flourished with no official help from the college except for salaries and office space.[34] At the end of the period covered by the grant, Ransom wrote a report to the foundation giving the details of how the funds had been used. In addition to employing a professional administrative secretary, the first the *Review* staff had had, the grant permitted an increase in the rate of payment to contributors, from $2.50 to $4.00 a page for prose.[35] He had also been able to increase the size of each issue and to publish more verse and fiction.[36] "As for the critical essays, which are our staple," he concluded, "I am confident we raised our standards steadily and at the end of the period had come to be accepted in the academic world, and with some outside readers, as perhaps offering the best example of what literary criticism should be." Of greatest significance, perhaps, was the fact that the *Review* had helped to establish a number of young writers with promising careers ahead of them. Among others, he mentioned Jean Garrigue, Robert Lowell, Marguerite Young, Walter Elder, Walter P. Southard, Richard Chase, and Eric Bentley.[37]

Despite the pressures of a wartime economy, the necessity of a constant search for funds to meet the ever-increasing cost of publication, and the inevitable distractions of the most disastrous war in history, Ransom and Rice (with the able assistance of their three advisory editors: Lionel Trilling, Cleanth Brooks, and Robert Penn Warren) were able to produce a quarterly of a quality seldom equaled anywhere in this century. To read the contents pages of the volumes of the *Kenyon Review* issued from 1940 through 1945 is to call the role of the most important American writers practicing their craft during this period. In an effort to give an adequate sampling of "what literary criticism should be" the *Kenyon Review* carried essays and reviews by, among others, Yvor Winters, John Erskine, Arthur Mizener, Delmore Schwartz, Austin Warren, Kenneth Burke, Cleanth Brooks, F. W. Dupee, F. O. Matthiessen, Jacques Barzun, Richard Chase, Eric Bentley, R. P. Blackmur, Robert Penn Warren, Mark Schorer, and Lionel Trilling. If critical essays were the journal's staple, and Ransom surely exerted more time and energy trying "to produce exhibits" in this genre than he did in any other, the poetry published during this period, though not always of highest quality, demonstrates very well Ransom's attempt to strike a reasonable balance between the work of established poets and that of the most-promising newcomers. After a decade in which he produced little poetry of significance, in the early forties Allen Tate went through a period of rich and intense creative activity, and almost all of the poetry he produced during these years was first published in the *Kenyon Review*. In addition to "Jubilo" and "More Sonnets at Christmas," which appeared there in the spring of 1943, his best poem, "Seasons of the Soul," was published in the winter of 1944. Among the other established poets whose work appeared in the *Review* were Louis MacNeise, Delmore Schwartz, Wallace Stevens, Robert Penn Warren, Mark Van Doren, and Randall Jarrell. Among the younger poets in the *Review* were Marguerite Young, Mona Van Duyn, Jean Garrigue, John Ciardi, Reed Whittemore, Howard Nemerov, Genevieve Taggard, Robert Lowell, Richard Eberhart, and Karl Shapiro.

With the assistance of a grant from Doubleday, Doran, and Company, the *Review* was able to offer during a two-year period (1944 and 1945) a first prize of $500 and a second prize of $250 for the best short stories submitted by a writer who had not published a book of stories; consequently the quantity of fiction received by the *Review* was considerably increased and the quality of that published obviously improved. In addition to "Alchemy," one of Andrew Lytle's most ambitious and best-executed stories, some of the better fiction published in the *Review* during these years was produced by younger writers, many of whom were then virtually unknown: Mary Lavin, Jean Garrigue, Walter Elder, Marguerite Young, Frances Gray Patton, John Berryman, and Mona Van Duyn.[38] The fact remains, however, that fiction was not as well represented in the *Review* as was either poetry or criticism, and the quality of the stories appearing there during this period was obviously inferior to those which Brooks and Warren had published in the *Southern Review*.

Soon after the appointment of the new board of advisory editors—the appointment of Cleanth Brooks and Robert Penn Warren was announced in the Autumn, 1942, number and that of Lionel Trilling in the next issue—Ransom had two of them to act as editors of special issues. The Autumn, 1943, issue was a special Henry James number celebrating the hundredth anniversary of his birth. Edited by Robert Penn Warren, it included essays by Katherine Anne Porter, Francis Fergusson, Jacques Barzun, F. O. Matthiessen, Austin Warren, David Daiches, Eliseo Vivas, and R. P. Blackmur. In the summer of 1944, the hundredth anniversary of the birth of Gerard Manley Hopkins, Cleanth Brooks edited a special issue dedicated to that poet, to which Marshall McLuhan, Harold Whitehall, Josephine Miles, and Austin Warren contributed essays. The Hopkins centennial tribute was concluded in the next issue with an essay by Arthur Mizener and notes by Robert Lowell and Austin Warren. To continue its attempt to give an "authoritative appraisal of all the contemporary arts," the *Kenyon Review* carried one or more articles on music, painting, or architecture in every issue, and the regular features included George Beiswanger's "Broadway Letter," a survey of the offerings of the New York theater, W. H. Mellers' "Music Letter from England," and Philip R. Adams' "Art Letter." In addition there were occasional pieces like Donald Stauffer's "A Letter from the Critical Front," Mellers' "American Music: An English Perspective," George Hemphill's "The Discourse of Music," and Friede Rathe's "Russian Music."

On November 14, 1940, Ransom wrote Tate that he would stay with him when he came to Princeton the following week to lecture. Although Ransom was looking forward to even a brief time with his old friends, he was worried that he might not have prepared carefully enough to give the kind of address his audience "expected and deserved." The explanation for his predicament was entirely reasonable, he thought, because all of his time had been absorbed in completing a draft of *The New Criticism*. "I am sweating gore," he wrote, "finishing off my book for New Directions." Although he thought he had some "pretty good stuff," he was not at all pleased with the writing. "I don't know how often I've looked at my stuff the next morning and thrown ten pages away." At any rate he was anxious to have Tate's opinion, "because I take some departures here, and I think you wouldn't entirely approve of them." When he wrote this letter he expected to have the manuscript off to Tate within the week, but it was still unfinished when he had to leave for Princeton. The week following his return he wrote Tate why he was not accepting the post of poet-in-residence at Princeton for a year. "The terrible bother and expense of moving for a temporary position which would be largely away from my center has dissuaded me from joining you." Ransom added that he was holding up the book manuscript because James Laughlin, president of New Directions, had asked him to add an essay to the book; consequently, he planned "to hold the *ms.* till Christmas and add a chapter of my own doctrine and almost save myself writing another book." [39]

On January 16, 1941, he informed Tate that the additional chapter was finished:

The Winters essay is the next to last one in the new book, would have been the last one except for the chapter which I wrote in November and added after sending the *MS* in. I owe the suggestion for that to Delmore. He said it was a pity I couldn't find an "ontological" critic; wished I might have made Tate or Blackmur or Brooks into one; I didn't quite do that but I wrote a Chapter IV entitled "Wanted: An Ontological Critic"; naturally I was telling on my own what an ontological critic would do. It would take off from the Winters chapter which gets the thing down to terms of structure and distinguishes the poetic from the scientific structure. When I look for what is 1) universal in all the works of art, including non-moralistic works, abstract works, and music, and at the same time 2) absent from the scientific discourse, it's texture; or the extra dimension; or particularity. I try to put this as precisely as I can. It's an ontological interest behind the art-work; a speculative one; I've stopped saying, because of possible ambiguities, a metaphysical. Outside of this new chapter, of which I don't have a copy, the thing nearest to it in my former writings would be my paper on Pragmatics of Art, Winter 1940, replying to Morris. But I might say that I'm not satisfied with my terms and definitions. The future of aesthetics is ahead of us, as the man said.[40]

When advance copies of the book were ready, in late April, Ransom had a copy sent to Tate immediately and awaited his reactions, which as always were not long in coming. As usual Tate's comments were instructive and provocative; this time they were so stimulating that Ransom began to think of a sequel. Although this work was never finished, the creative activity growing out of Tate's discussion of some of the weaknesses of The New Criticism prompted Ransom to continue to search for appropriate terms to describe the unique nature of poetic discourse. This effort would lead, a dozen years later, to his producing the first of his essays on "The Concrete Universal."[41] The deficiencies of the book, as Tate saw them, were two: 1) The worth of Yvor Winters' criticism was greatly inflated; 2) Through his reiterated insistences on the importance of poetic structure, Ransom had "played right into the hands of the Positivists, the Pragmatists, and the Naturalists." As always, Tate believed, Ransom had placed too much emphasis on the "importance of the argument of a poem."[42]

As soon as Ransom received Tate's letter, he responded in detail to each of the several objections. The chief fault of the book, he agreed, was that he "sacrificed the critics in order to get his own oar in," that he "tried to give some running account" of the critical doctrines of four major critics at the same time that he was attempting "to present his own doctrine in departure from them." Instead of the "systematic book on poetic theory" he should have written, "and the one I set out to write," he used these critics "to point towards one." In his attempt "to ride two horses," he has been unjust both to the other critics, particularly Eliot and Empson, and to himself. He should have waited for his own book to propose his theory of the nature of poetic discourse so that he could have developed in more detail the specific qualities of structure and texture and their complex relationships in the poem. He was depressed because he had failed, he could now see, in his efforts to point up "the unique qualities of poetic discourse, and this was a task that must be done." Few other critics, excepting those cited and discussed in this text, were attempting to deal with the problem. The positivists are "little boys dedicated to scientific or analytical principle," and to nothing else. He despaired, too, of the aesthetic principles of the "old-school philosophers" who are so indecisive they "tend to muddy the water" and merely make a "mystery of the things." Most of them are unwilling to admit that there is "any given distinction between poetic and scientific discourse except in subject matter."

If he had failed in his attempt to present his theoretical point of view, as he was convinced he had, he was hardly more successful in putting forward his more practical intentions. Because poetry is a kind of discourse different from science, there must be no "taboos," "restrictions," or "philosophical censorship" against those critics who are doing the kind of analytical, formal criticism essential to the delineation of the unique nature of the poetic discourse. He was also attempting to free himself of the "public reputation" that he was a member of a "close group or clique or gang or confederacy." If those of us—Tate, Brooks, and Warren—who are intent upon restoring poetry to a place of central importance in society are to accomplish our objective, he concluded, "we must develop our individual ideas; our community can be taken for granted now, or, if necessary, it can easily be made out afresh." His sense of failure was so acute that he knew he must get on to the new book of criticism immediately, although this theory had become a torment to him and he badly wanted to get back to writing poetry.

As soon as the book was available, Philip Blair Rice sent a copy to I. A. Richards asking him to do an essay "criticizing Mr. Ransom's general aesthetic position with specific reference to his comments on your writing," and assuring him he should "feel no obligation to be courteous to the editor of the *Review*."[43] Richards kept the invitation "under consideration" for almost a month before sending in his demurral.[44] His response left no doubt of his reactions to Ransom's evaluation of his critical theories:

After reading *The New Criticism* and some thought I've decided it will be better if I don't write any review or make any comment. Mr. Ransom seems to me to have just mistaken so much of the point and aim of my early books that to me it's as though he were shooting into a pool, not at me. And I do not think the attempt to clear these mistakes up publicly could be profitable to anyone. I suppose the cause is that "psychological" language I used to use; each reads it his own way, not mine, and frequently refutes me with observations which I thought I was somewhat insisting on myself. I am afraid though that Mr. Ransom may find others doing to his own formulations somewhat the same and I prefer not to join them.

Richards' fears were realized almost immediately. One of the first reviews *The New Criticism* received was by Louise Bogan,[45] who argued that Ransom's preference for "high, philosophic, and complete objectivity" congeals into prejudice. She mistook his insistence on the cognitive function in poetry for an attempt to remove from poetry all emotional content. Because Richards believes in the heresy "that emotion has something do with poetry," she wrote, he is completely overridden. She accused Ransom of demonstrating a new kind of snobbery, one which argues that "to think, and to express oneself in images," is vulgar. He is so "determined to haggle with his material" that his " 'objective cognitions,' " his " 'structures,' " and his " 'textures' " merge into a "confused blur." Ransom's "Wanted: An Ontological Criticism" [*sic*] is a classic example of the "treacheries of abstract language" and clearly requires an " 'ontological' literature to operate upon." After Ransom, Bogan concludes, it is a pleasure to return to Richards, "a delightful writer and a supremely clever man." Babette Deutsch's comments indicate that she at least had tried to read the book.[46] Although Ransom sometimes engaged in "rather abstruse discourse," his argument always ended in a plea for a "rather commonsensible way of looking at poetry," which should not be regarded as a set of documents to be studied by linguistic and historical scholars but as a means of securing a "knowledge of the world in which we live, as distinct from the world of scientific discourse." The importance of a poem is not that it produces "feelings, emotions and attitudes," but that it is a way of knowing the world. Although she would agree with Ransom that literary judgment should be made in cognitive, not psychological, terms and that the value of a poem is not measured by the worth of the moral it inculcates, she joins Miss Bogan in accusing Ransom of attempting to remove all feeling from poetry. "Granted that poetry affords a knowledge impossible to the skeletal constructions of scientific discourse, is it not precisely because in poetry, as in life, cognition is always colored by feeling, that this is so?"

Alexander Cowie found the book "provocative and useful" but "not completely satisfactory" because Ransom nowhere gave an adequate definition of the new criticism, although he did suggest that it is differentiated from the old by using psychology to assist in making "an extremely intimate analysis of the nature of esthetic experience and of the technique of producing such experience."[47] Ransom's views, "though often intuitively shrewd, are not sufficiently clear and coherent"; thus the book, with its "air of charming but somewhat indolent improvisation . . . sheds a good deal of light but fails to focus it." Richard Eberhart discussed the book, along with R. P. Blackmur's *The Expense of Greatness* and Allen Tate's *Reason in Madness*,[48] and concluded that all three were "a credit to criticism": Blackmur's the "most literary," Ransom's the "most logical and theoretical," and Tate's the "most direct, polemical, and political." Ransom attempts but does not succeed in dismissing "Richards, the producer (in our times) of the psychological approach" with his "logical structure-texture oppositions." His attempt to diminish Richards' stature as critic only increases our regard for him. The praise for Empson is excessive, Eberhart believed, the treatment of Eliot "easy and lucid," that of Winters "exciting" and "suggestive." Eberhart's final evaluation was that "honesty and charm appear throughout the book," that Ransom's "modesty is everywhere evident," and that although "he enjoys a good deal of philosophizing," he does upon occasion get "down to some excellent particular criticism."

Like most of the reviewers, Fred B. Millet commented on the inadequacies Ransom finds in the other critics whose work he reviews: Richards' overemphasis on the emotional elements in literature, Eliot's "theoretical innocence," and Winters' excessive moralizing.[49] The aim of the book, Millet argued, would be clearer if one read the last essay first, because Ransom's "judgments of other critics' theories depend directly upon his own and are completely consistent with them." Although Millet approved of Ransom's insistence on the importance of the "analytical study of literature," he saw limiting that study "to a consideration of structure and texture and their relationships" as "nearsighted" and "indefensible." Ransom's insistence that the function of poetry is the recovery of the world which we know through perception and memory, Millet contended, is a restatement of Aristotle's theory of representation, but Ransom does not indicate why the world "that already exists in a dense and refractory state" should be represented. "Poetry," Millet concluded, "is not merely form or structure or texture but an experience, an experience of the poet's representation and *interpretation* of his real or imagined world" and the value of this experience cannot be decided by "even the closest analysis of form or structure or texture."

Ransom's structure-texture formulation, for Kenneth Burke, is the heart of his argument.[50] But since these two terms are used not "positively but dialectically, they do not name two different 'things' but a *relationship*." What is "structure" in one situation may be "texture" in another. Burke did not believe Ransom's terminology adequate to represent the kinds of distinctions he was concerned with:

I think that Mr. Ransom could profitably round out his terminology by some such third term as the "structure of texture." Studies like Caroline Spurgeon's *Shakespeare's Imagery,* for instance, or Lane Cooper's treatment of the fascination theme in Coleridge's Mystery poems, remind us that the poem does have some principle of organization other than the mere logical structure (or situation or plot or development, or whatever may be the element in a poem capable of prose paraphrase). There is a general tenor discernible among the heterogeneities, something that limits the range of variations, or that points them thematically in the same direction. And if the term "structure" is reserved for the logical element which the poem's "texture" uses as its point of departure, then "structure of texture" could designate the element of consistency limiting the range or quality of these departures.

Even with its "technical limitations," and Burke was almost alone in this assertion, Ransom's theory is one of which every reader of poetry should be cognizant. His arguments for poetic realism, as opposed to the limited world revealed by positivism—for the important cognitive function of poetry, but not for a didactic assertion—constitute one of the most persuasive defenses of poetry in our time. He is not, as he wrote Tate on January 16, 1941, arguing that the "literal object matter" of the cognition one receives from poetry is different from that which he receives from other sources, but that it is "ontologically or structurally distinct," that it is a "different grade or level of cognition." What most reviewers failed to see, or to comment on, is that although

Ransom had maintained for more than twenty years an essential duality for poetry, he has only now developed the terminology to define the explicit roles of its two basic components.

Most of the critics Ransom chose to discuss had been publishing critical studies for a good many years, and the best work of some of them was already behind them. The title he used to justify his suggestion that in the loosest possible sense they might be thought of as a "school" had been used by Joel Elias Spingarn almost half a century earlier and was certainly not new. But the term the *New Critics* quickly gained currency and at the end of the war became a kind of slogan for the new breed of professors and their students in their reaction against the way literature was being taught in colleges or written about in the scholarly journals. Nowhere in the book does Ransom define specifically what the "New Criticism" is, but he insists that in spite of its eclecticism, much of the critical writing "done in our time" has a "depth and precision," as well as a "unity of method," beyond "all earlier criticism in our language." His reason for being less definite is that "this is a new criticism" and is, therefore, "unsure, inconsistent, perhaps raw." Among the critics whose works exemplify this "unity of method," and he regrets he cannot include in his study the criticism of R. P. Blackmur, he chooses to discuss the theories and practices of I. A. Richards (and "his pupil" William Empson), T. S. Eliot, and Yvor Winters. As much as he is impressed with the work of these critics, he finds it "damaged by at least two specific errors of theory." The first is the "idea of using the psychological affective vocabulary in the hope of making literary judgments in terms of the feelings, emotions, and attitudes of poems instead of in terms of their objects." The second is what he calls "plain moralism."[51] Here, then, he has identified two of the commonly held misconceptions about the nature and function of poetry, which he and other formal critics would later refer to as the "affective fallacy" and "the didactic heresy."

Ransom's method of procedure is similar in the first three chapters, the longest of which by far is that devoted to I. A. Richards. After an opening statement in which he gives a complimentary evaluation of each critic's contribution to modern criticism, Ransom examines the basic components of that critic's theory and its application by giving lengthy quotations from his work, on which, in the approved manner of the analytical critic, he comments at length. In this way he is able to judge the value of each critic's contribution by measuring it against his own theory of "the ontological critic." He approves completely of Richards' concentration upon the text of the poem and his close attention to its particularities. He thinks that Richards is one of the few modern critics whose assertions derive from a "complete aesthetic of poetry," an aesthetic system which with some adjustments "could pass over and become a system for the other arts, such as music and painting" (NC, 3–4). Early in his career, however, Richards insisted that the statements of poetry had no validity in themselves and were useful only as a means of expressing and arousing emotional states. Although he had moved away, in his later writings, from this "affective theory," he never fully accepted the cognitive function of poetry; therefore he was never able to perceive that art is a means of representing the dual nature of the world. Following the example of his teacher, William Empson reacts perceptively and sensitively to the textured details of the poem; he writes convincingly of the value of its apparently "irrelevant particularities" in determining the view of reality it represents, but his concentration on the "character of its local objects," often makes him deemphasize too much the value of the poem's basic argument. Nevertheless his *Seven Types of Ambiguity* is "the most imaginative account of readings ever printed" and he, "the closest and most resourceful reader that poetry has yet publicly had" (NC, 102).

As Richards represents the psychological critic, Eliot is the historical critic because he "uses his historical studies for the sake of literary understanding" (NC, 139). It is "likely we have had no better critic than Eliot," and his persistent efforts to find the "poetic practice which is standard in the sense that it is furnished by the main stream . . . of English poetry" is very valuable because he is able to look at the "poem against its nearest background to see what sort of criticism it needs" and then to come up "with a set of judgments which are comparative in the first instance, but critical in the end" (NC, 140). Although Eliot does not issue critical principles in his work—and Ransom finds him deficient in critical theory—he has a "critical sense which is expert and infallible" (NC, 145). The value of his critical judgments would be considerably enhanced, however, if he had a "philosophical habit" or the "philosophical will" to push through this critical sense "to definition." And Eliot, in one sense, has the deficiencies of both Richards and Empson. Like the early Richards, Eliot argues that poetry's basic function is to release emotion, thus devaluing its cognitive function. Like Empson, he deemphasizes the value of structure, not by ignoring it, as Empson had, but by the assertion that the poetic statement in itself need not be factual and command belief. Ransom comments at length on Eliot's celebrated statement of the modern "dissociation of sensibility." Although Ransom has studied closely the work of those seventeenth-century poets in whose writing Eliot believes the "modern dualism of thought and feeling" has been bridged, he has failed to find the "thing Eliot refers to" and is, therefore, inclined to "think there was nothing of the kind there" (NC, 183). He has tried to find some "description of poetry which would regard it as a single unified experience, and exempt it from the dilemma of logic," but he is still convinced that such an effort will never succeed because it attempts to fuse "two experiences that ordinarily repel one another." We cannot "feel a thought," but we can "conduct a thought without denying all the innocent or irrelevant feelings in the process." This insistence on the essential duality of poetry brings Ransom to a statement of what he called his "structure-texture formulation":

Such a formula indicates that we can realize the *structure,* which is the logical thought, without sacrificing the *texture,* which is the free detail—or if anybody insists, which is the feelings that engage with the free detail. For, again, Eliot's talk is psychologistic, or affective, but we may easily translate it into objective or cognitive terms. We recall his big emotion as attaching to the main thought, and translate that simply as the logical structure of the poem; then we recall the little feelings attaching to the play of the words, and translate them as its local texture.... I think we must waive the psychological magic involved in the act of feeling our thought in honor of something much tamer and more credible: the procedure of suspending the course of the main thought while we explore the private character of the detail items. We stop following the main thought, and take off in a different direction, as we follow the private history of an item; then we come back to the main thought. (NC, 184–85)

Ransom commends Yvor Winters for his conviction that effective poetry must command belief from its readers, but his concentration on the "moral ideas in a poem," to the sacrifice of all else, makes him a victim of the "moral illusion." Few poems offer "original moralities," and to the extent that Winters "has devoted himself disproportionately to this kind of moralism, his effect on the new criticism is to blight it." Unlike the other critics discussed so far, Winters "insists on obtaining from the poem a satisfactory rational content or logical structure," but he does not demonstrate how the rational content of a poem is different from that of a prose discourse (NC, 221). Although Winters does recognize the nuances of association, he does not observe sufficiently the "surge of feeling," the local particularity of meaning, the rich texture which carries an essential part of the poetic experience. On some occasions, too, Winters is guilty of the intentional fallacy:

The total intention of the poem is something, but not an intention known to the poet at the moment when he begins to work up his logical content into a poem. Total intention is the total meaning of the finished poem, which differs from the original logical content by having acquired a detail which is immaterial to this content, being everywhere specific, or local, or particular, and at any rate unpredictable. And what, precisely, is the poet's intention at the beginning? It is to write a poem, and that is, since he has written poems before, to turn his logical content loose to shift for itself in the world of fortuitous experience; to get out of the world of pure logical content. (NC, 224)[52]

Each critic studied has contributed something to the "unity of method," to the "depth and precision" that make the criticism of the present more valuable than that of any time in the past. All of them share the conviction that if one is to know the poem he must concentrate on it and not on its author's life or the age in which he lived. In a very real sense they complement each other. In spite of his tendency toward moralizing, Winters is the best of the critics at structural analysis; no other critic has done this essential task so well. Richards' attention to the particulars of a poem is commendable, as are Eliot's immense learning and his ability to make "half-truths or gnomic truths" about poetry. But none of them has attempted the "close studies of structure-texture relations" which must be done to represent the true nature of poetic discourse. "The best endowed critic in the world for this purpose," Ransom concludes, "might very well be . . . Mr. William Empson, the student of ambiguity," but his studies have all been "valuable diversions, a little to the side of the great critical problems." In an attempt to locate the "ontological critic," the one who could "define the structure-texture procedure of poets" and thereby "define poetic strategy," Ransom explores in his final chapter the theory of semantics advanced by the philosopher Charles W. Morris. Morris has gone further down the road which Ransom thought would lead to the discovery of the true nature of poetic discourse, but even he did not go far enough. Although he has never actually "denied cognition" and "often seemed to assume it, quite non-behavioristically, quite otherwise from Richards," and although he has demonstrated his fear of "Platonic universals" by indicating his belief that a "universal has a real correspondence of some sort," his theories do not differentiate sharply enough between the poetic and scientific discourse.[53] To make this distinction is the most significant function of the ontological critic.

In "Wanted: An Ontological Critic," Ransom begins, therefore, by asserting the necessity of the critic's being able to distinguish between the poetic and the scientific structure. A poem differs from prose not in "moralism," "emotionalism," or "sensibility" but in the kind of structure it has, an odd structure whose exact purpose is difficult to indicate. It is a structure which "is not so tight and precise on its logical side as a scientific or technical prose structure generally is" but one that "imports and carries along a great deal of irrelevant or foreign matter which is clearly . . . obstructive." From this kind of formulation, which is what the best critics give us, comes the realization that a poem is a "loose logical structure with an irrelevant local texture." That there is "revolutionary departure" in poetry from the "convention of logical discourse" would appear obvious, but the importance of this realization lies in the nature of the difference:

The structure proper is the prose of the poem, being a logical discourse of almost any kind, and dealing with almost any content suited to a logical discourse. The texture, likewise, seems to be of any real content that may be come upon, provided it is so free, unrestricted, and large that it cannot properly get into the structure. One guesses that it is an *order* of content, rather than a *kind* of content, that distinguishes texture from structure, and poetry from prose. At any rate, a moral content is a kind of content which has been suggested as the peculiar content of poetry, and it does not work; it is not really peculiar to poetry but perfectly available for prose; besides, it is not the content of a great deal of poetry. I suggest that the differentia of poetry as discourse is an ontological one. It treats an order of existence, a grade of objectivity, which cannot be treated in scientific discourse.

This should not prove unintelligible. We live in a world which must be distinguished from the world, or the worlds, for there are many of them, which we treat in our scientific discourses. They are its reduced, emasculated and docile versions. Poetry intends to recover the denser and more refractory original world which we know loosely through our perceptions and memories. By this supposition it is a kind of knowledge which is radically or ontologically distinct. (NC, 280–81)

Ransom is emphasizing again the differences between poetry and science, and again he is arguing that only through poetry can man recover the "body and solid substance of the world" which is composed of "whole and indefeasible objects."[54] As presented through the kind of data science can collect, the world appears "only as a scheme of abstract conveniences." Although Morris does not take the final step essential to an understanding of the unique nature of poetry, he comes closer than anyone else Ransom has found. There are, according to Morris, three forms of discourse: science, which emphasizes the syntactical or logical meaning; art, which presents the semantical; and technology, whose concern is the pragmatical. Whereas science is interested only in *knowing*, art is concerned with *making* and *knowing*. Although aesthetic discourse is "objective and knowledge-giving," as scientific discourse is, the kind of knowledge art represents differs from that produced by science because of the differences in the kinds of signs used to communicate that knowledge. Science employs mere symbols that have no function other than that of referring to other objects; but art uses icons, which not only refer to other objects but "resemble or imitate" those objects. The object symbolized by the scientific sign is an abstraction or a single aspect or property of the object represented, whereas that symbolized by the aesthetic sign or icon is the whole object. As a scientific sign might be used to refer to man, the icon would refer to a particular man. What the icon does, as Ransom had been insisting for years, is the proper function of art; it restores to an abstract item the "body from which it was taken."

With all of this Ransom is in essential agreement, but at about this point he and Morris part company. He agrees with Morris that aesthetic discourse is "objective knowledge" and that its "constituent signs are icons." But why, he asks, would one stop with Morris' statement that an "icon embodies some value property" and not go one step beyond to assert the "human significance or usefulness or pragmatic function" of the aesthetic discourse? Ransom moves beyond Morris to give his "ontological argument": (1) The validity of a scientific discourse depends on its semantical purity; each symbol refers to an object specifically defined and the reference of a single symbol is always limited and uniform. (2) The icons of aesthetic discourse refer to the complete and whole object and cannot be limited; not only do they embody the value property of the object represented, they are indefinable. When the icon is introduced to replace the scientific symbol, therefore, both the "syntactical and semantical dimensions of a discourse are imperilled." Since icons cannot function with the logical exactness of the scientific sign, the aesthetic discourse often digresses from its "logical pattern at many local points." Thus the poem moves beyond its prose paraphrase, which like the scientific discourse offers a single value system, into the "realm of the objects themselves, which are many valued." The world presented by the scientific discourse through its signs is predictable, limited, and restrictive; the actual world of art as represented through its icons "does not bear restriction" and includes "enough fullness of content, to give the sense of the actual objects."[55] Scientific knowledge and aesthetic knowledge should be considered as alternative knowledges, which should illuminate and complement each other.

In this way Ransom differentiates between scientific and aesthetic discourse and comments on the value of the loose and imprecise poetic structure with its clusters of "irrelevant or foreign matter." It is, he repeats, a means of acquiring knowledge which we cannot know otherwise. To define, finally, the unique nature of the poetic composition, Ransom says he must "abandon the framework of Mr. Morris' speculations," which have "provided considerable moral reinforcement" for his inquiry, and go even further back "in the ontological analysis of the poem." That is, he must follow the poet through the actual process of poetic composition.

Writing a poem, he begins, is a search for language that will make both sense and rhythm, and sometimes even rhyme. This poetic language must do "two hard things at once," for the "composition of a poem is an operation in which the argument fights to displace the meter, and the meter fights to displace the argument." To demonstrate how this process works he gives the analogy of the woman who tells her houseboy to bring up from the pantry a dozen of the biggest and reddest apples. The boy has to choose from a box that contains one hundred apples which vary in both bigness and redness. Since there is no correlation between these two qualities, the boy solves his problem in this way:

He ranges the apples first in the order of their bigness, and denotes the biggest as B_1, the next as B_2 and so on down to B_{100}. Then he ranges the apples in order of their redness, and denotes the reddest as R_1, the next reddest as R_2, and so on down to R_{100}. Then for each apple he adds the numerical coefficient of its bigness and the numerical coefficient of its redness; for example, the apple which is tagged B_1 is also tagged R_{36}, so that its combined coefficient is 37. He finds the twelve apples with lowest combined coefficients and takes them to his mistress. (NC, 296)

The apples brought to the mistress are probably neither the biggest nor the reddest. To get the combination of the two qualities, he has had to make sacrifices in each of them. But he may have found that having to sacrifice some deep red apples because they were small, has allowed him to select apples of color patterns more variable, unpredictable, and interesting.

The process of combining in a poem an intended meaning and an intended meter is illustrated in this analogy, although the composition of a poem is infinitely more complex than the "curious problem" that confronted the boy who had to select the apples. Words have both semantic and phonetic values; and those selected solely for their phonetic value are not likely to make sense, those for their semantic value may not make meter. The liberties a poet must take with the rational argument of a discourse when he sets it to meter are obvious.

The question, then, is what is the nature of a discourse that will permit such liberties. The argument of such a composition must be partly indeterminate because it will be altered by the meter; the sound must be partly indeterminate because at times it will be sacrificed for meaning. So the critic must understand that a poem contains not two elements but four: the *determinate meaning* (the "intellectual meaning" or as much of it as survives in the finished poem; the prose paraphrase of the poem); the *indeterminate meaning* ("that part of the final meaning ... which took shape under metrical compulsion"; the residue of meaning not included in the paraphrase); the *determinate sound-structure* (the meter); and the *indeterminate sound-structure* (the phonetic character the "sounds have assumed" unrelated to the meter). The distinction of these elements, and especially of the determinate and the indeterminate meanings is the "vocation *par excellence* of the critic."

Whatever the importance of the subject matter treated by the poet, his struggles to express his ideas in meter will be such that a better statement of these ideas could be made in prose. One should not go to poetry, therefore, for a really authoritative study of ideas. The critic does not concentrate upon that part of a poem which can be expressed in a prose paraphrase but upon the relationship between the determinate and the indeterminate meanings, the ideas and the indeterminate material in which they are developed. Only through this kind of study will he be able to discover the unique nature of poetic discourse, a kind of composition that does not worry too much about the perfection of its ideas but does bother "a great deal ... about the positive quality of that indeterminate thing which creeps in by the back door of musical necessity."

Although the meaning that comes into a poem because of the demands of versification may result only in inaccuracy and confusion, it may also open up new worlds of discourse. The most significant of the indeterminacies that come into a poem come from the imagination of the poet. He may at first resent the necessity of importing "unwanted irrelevance because of the violence it does to his determinate meaning," but soon he "comes upon a little irrelevance" that interests him and he proceeds to expand it and indulge it because he sees it as a definite asset to his meaning. Indeterminacy is made, too, when images enter the composition, and, like images, meter seems at first to "harm the discourse," but soon it "makes a radical innovation." As the poet comes to realize that sustained metrical regularity is "barren and restrictive," he adds to the poem's texture through metrical variations. He may roughen his meter as he roughens a "good, clean argument." The critic who would fulfill his role, therefore, must see that his primary function is ontological. He must give a satisfactory designation to the "essence" of poetry by delineating its basic qualities and differentiating between poetic and scientific discourse.

After publishing *The New Criticism,* with its assessment of the achievements and limitations of some of the most significant critics of his generation, during the war years Ransom wrote for the *Kenyon Review* a series of essays in which he attempted to demonstrate how he thought the ontological critic should react in his efforts to define the nature of poetic discourse and to justify its existence in a society more and more devoted to the quasiknowledge and the false promises of science.[56] Although he realized he was publishing a great deal in his own journal—once he asked Tate to tell him if it got to looking too much "like a personal organ"—these essays and many of the others carried in the *Review* quickly made it the most influential critical quarterly in the country. With the demise of the *Southern Review,* Ransom's journal carried more significant analytical criticism and serious comment on the world of arts and letters than any other American publication of the time. The reputation of the *Kenyon Review,* the quality and appeal of Ransom's critical essays, and the many readings and lectures he gave all over the country, as well as the reactions to *The World's Body* and *The New Criticism,* made Ransom by 1945 what one commentator called a "formidable shaping presence on the literary scene."

In spite of the fact that he must have realized he was contributing a great deal toward bringing about the age of criticism he had predicted, Ransom's dissatisfaction with his own work was extended into his other activities. "I can scarcely endure to think of my having no part in the war," he wrote Tate on January 5, 1942, "nor [of] my Review's having no part. A Frenchman of the noble tradition would not allow such a thing to happen; Eliot wouldn't." With the number of students in college becoming fewer each semester—at one time the enrollment at Kenyon was under a hundred students and only Ransom and Philip Timberlake were left in the English department—he became so despondent that he began to resent the endless hours he had to spend in "conferences, committees and faculty meetings," time-consuming activities that accomplished almost nothing at a time when he thought the whole system of liberal education was imperiled. In spite of his successful financial campaign the year before, the *Kenyon Review* was again on a reduced budget and was faced with discontinuation for the duration of the war, if not permanently; nevertheless, he was searching for some way for it to make a tangible contribution to the war effort. In the number for Autumn, 1942, Ransom announced that while its "editors await any call that might be made upon them for service, they go about their duty of editing and publishing." A few weeks later he wrote Tate:

I'd like your thought about this. I am feeling pretty patriotic (I'm a great sucker in a crisis), and I have the uneasy sense of having in my writings recently identified myself with an anti-topical kind of literature to a degree that doesn't represent me. So what about initiating at once in the Review a series or rather a sequence of studies bearing on the war in two senses (one or both): first, studies of the time and place, and the exact dignities and rights, of a crisis art; a philosophical bill of rights, largely defensive. Second, some actual miscellaneous applied literature or crisis literature, being essays about the war or its esoteric (political or artistic) ramifications, done by brilliant men who have hitherto been pretty "pure" in their exhibits; these writings would have to be good. The first category would continue very nicely, drawing forth reflections and oppositions from perhaps a stream of writers in other numbers; and we might really get further with the problem than the critics have ever done before.[57]

This plan was never put into effect. Although many of the contributions to the *Review* show the impact of the war on the creative sensibility—such as Tate's "More Sonnets at Christmas" and "Seasons of the Soul"—no feasible means of active participation occurred to Ransom. Early in 1943, however, Kenyon College was assigned 225 Army Air Corps Cadets for a part of their preflight training, and for the remainder of the war Ransom had a full complement of teaching.

Most of his summers during these years were spent in Middlebury, Vermont, where he was on the faculty of the Bread Loaf School of English. There he enjoyed his conversations with other faculty members, such as Theodore Greene of Princeton, with whom he discussed the nature of poetry ("whether poetry is a tight unified logical whole or a loose disorderly one").[58] With Greene and with Philip Wheelwright of Dartmouth, he offered a course combining English and philosophy, which he found most stimulating because he "could hardly pass a month without seeing the trouble with some doctrine of my own." In the courses he became thoroughly convinced of the attractiveness of literary study if it were properly conducted.[59] He also enjoyed his association with Robert Frost, who invited the Ransoms to live in his house during the summer of 1942. This arrangement pleased Ransom very much because his principal objection to teaching there was the living accommodations. During the summer of 1941 he had lived with the "Wilsons (two overpowering old Virginians to hear them talk), the George Andersons of Brown and the Joyces from Dartmouth with one common room and one bathroom." Meals were little more pleasant because then he was expected to preside "over little tables of old maid students in the dining room."[60] With a house of his own he could bring Robb and Jack— Helen and Reavill as well if they were home—and about the only unpleasant aspect of these profitable summers would be removed.

Although the entire family was saddened by Mrs. Reavill's death in December, 1942, there were happier developments. After Helen's almost disastrous year at Wellesley—one in which, as Robb wrote Ellene, "she didn't study; she cut classes and her grades are not gray; they are very, very black"—she enrolled in Vanderbilt.[61] There she began to apply herself and received good marks, "getting a relish for critical studies, while there's no limit to her desire to do some creative writing." After one term there, Ransom wrote Tate: "Helen received 4 B's and an E for attitude. I don't commend her attitude altogether, but it was respectful towards the teacher and as the subject was French, in which she is very good, I think the teacher was like Don [Davidson] who disciplined both Helen and Robb for my sake, with the result that he thought each was about the best in the course for that year and neither got an hour of credit for his course."[62] She was graduated in January, 1945, and became engaged the following month to Duane Forman, a graduate of the Vanderbilt Medical

School who was serving an internship at Johns Hopkins. "She inherits her father's literary gifts and her mother's athletic ability," a society reporter wrote in the engagement announcement, "for she has written a play dealing with Greek characters which was produced at Peabody Demonstration School, and is an excellent tennis player." [63] Reavill enrolled at Kenyon but withdrew in April, 1944, to enlist in the navy and after being trained at naval air stations in Washington and California, in the latter of which he won the 140-pound wrestling championship, he was home for a month's leave at Christmas, 1944, with his wings and a commission in the United States Naval Reserve.

As the end of the war neared, Ransom was approaching the period in which he would receive wide public recognition as editor, critic, and poet. Within the next decade the *Kenyon Review* would become known, as C. P. Snow once said, as far away as Moscow and Tokyo, "wherever people are interested in literature written in English." Within the year the first edition of the *Selected Poems* would be published, and based on the verse in that collection Randall Jarrell would proclaim: "Ransom is one of the best, most original, and most sympathetic poets alive; and it is easy to see that his poetry will always be cared for, since he has written poems that are perfectly realized and occasionally almost perfect." [64] But his more immediate reputation came not directly from his reputation as either poet, critic, editor, or teacher but indirectly from all of these. The generation that had grown up in the Depression and gone off to war was impatient with the trivial nature of much of the prevailing literary study, which seemed so far removed from both life and literature. These veterans would soon be home, and many of them were in a mood to allow Ransom to prove his claim that the proper study of literature merited the closest attention of the best minds of their generation. Almost before they had a chance to settle into a routine after their discharge, Ransom had received sufficient financial support to open the Kenyon School of English so that he could offer "proper courses in English literature" under instructors who have "published distinguished critical writings." The purpose of this venture was to attract the "brilliant students in English who are intensely in earnest about critical studies" so that they could obtain instruction and practice in the appropriate processes through which one can make an "intimate possession" of a work of literature.[65] The persons selected to study in Gambier would share their experiences with their students in schools and colleges throughout the country. One of Ransom's colleagues, who wondered if there would be enough interest in the serious study of literature to justify such a program, must have been astounded by the reaction to the proposal. Among those recently discharged veterans were more than just a few, as one expressed it later, who regarded Ransom as a Moses who would lead them "through the desert to the promised land of poetry."[66]

XII **Symbols of Major Decisions 1945-1950**

DESPITE the fact that Ransom had written only five poems in the eighteen years since the publication of *Two Gentlemen in Bonds, Selected Poems* (1945) was given the sort of respectful reception usually reserved for the appearance of a book from an artist whose reputation is already established. These poems, one critic wrote, represent, as the "work of few other contemporary American poets do, a triumph for integrity, patience and discipline."[1] Another proclaimed him "one of the dozen or so poets in this country who have a distinct and original voice."[2] The contemporary poets with whom he was most often compared were Wallace Stevens ("Ransom shares with Wallace Stevens . . . a rather quizzical and quaintly conceived vocabulary")[3] and T. S. Eliot (As "compared with Eliot," Ransom "has not so broad a scope, nor so deep a look and feel").[4] In an attempt to show Ransom's relation to the English literary tradition, many commentators pointed to the poet's widely known preference for the poetry of the seventeenth century and suggested that his choice of subjects was reminiscent of the Cavaliers, but in a few "highly mannered poems" a preciseness in wit and a delicacy of feeling remind one of Marvell and Donne.[5]

The "high excellence" of the best poems in the volume, one critic asserted, "reminds us again that he occupies an enviable and special place, a permanent place, in contemporary American poetry."[6] This secure position among twentieth-century American poets is "rather precariously achieved" through poems that are sometimes "merely minor," verse "delightful to read and to listen to" but so mannered that "language ultimately becomes its own subject-matter."[7] One feels, this critic maintained, that Ransom "could write beautifully about almost anything," but he sometimes has trouble "making his themes and characters important." This book, however, is a "monument to craftsmanship"; not only are there no bad poems in it, there "isn't a single embarrassing line."[8] When Ransom is at his best he blends subject—"an ironic and unresolvable conflict between the ideal, the romantic or intellectual dream of perfection . . . and the actual, everyday life of the world and the flesh"[9]—and manner—subtle irony, wit, a detached but sympathetic tone—to create a poetry not only of a very high quality but one that is obviously original:

T. S. Eliot once remarked that the business of the poet was to "focus the word and practise the incantation," and the individuality of a good poet obviously consists in doing these two things in his own special way. When Mr. Ransom is at his best his words are admirably focussed—an unexpected noun or adjective refracts the light of his thought in a surprising, often refreshingly colloquial, fashion. . . . The incantation, the rhythm, of Mr. Ransom's best poems is equally effective; the contrasting of masculine and feminine endings, the checkrein rhythm of the well-known "Captain Carpenter" which is so appropriate to its theme, the use of extra syllables to make the lines waver, all these devices help to create a poetry that is individual and stylish, and which in one poem, at least—"The Equilibrists"—can stand "with Landor and with Donne."[10]

Many reviewers were concerned, as Richmond Croom Beatty had expressed it the year before *Selected Poems* appeared, that "the luxuriant stream of Ransom's poetry has dried up, during the past fifteen years, into a thin and turgid trickle."[11] Whatever the reason, "this drying up of the sources of Mr. Ransom's poetry," Arthur Mizener wrote, "is a great misfortune, not only because his poetry was so good, but because, as the five new poems show, the wonderful command of the means of poetry—and I do not mean mere technical facility—is finer today than it ever was."[12] Not everyone agreed. In his review of *Two Gentlemen of Bonds* nearly twenty years before, Allen Tate had suggested that Ransom might have used up his talent for writing verse, that "further additions to the testament" might "cry out redundancy—that Mr. Ransom had overwritten himself."[13] In the first systematic study of Ransom's achievement as poet, Robert Penn Warren had argued that the sonnet sequence "Two Gentlemen in Bonds" was less satisfactory than the other poetry in that volume because these sonnets were not in Ransom's characteristic ironic vein.[14] Some seemed to fear that the "poet has been swallowed up by the critic." Others insisted that his "mannerisms," so "perfectly suited to his subject matter" in the earlier poetry have become obsessive, that in his later poetry the "material tends to fade out," leaving only a kind of "verbal eloquence."[15] Whatever their merits, these last poems were written in a new and denser style, one in which the "images are more closely crowded, the rhythms are heavier, the meaning more indirectly and obscurely conveyed."[16]

The same critics who were aware of the smallness of Ransom's poetic output were not oblivious to what Richard Eberhart called his "search for perfection." Although he had produced few new poems since the publication of his last volume, his attention was not completely divorced from his poetry. Over the years he had been engaged in an activity which he referred to as "tinkering with my verse," and almost all of the poems included in *Selected Poems* had been altered in each of their several appearances in print. Of the forty-two poems in the collection, all but six had first appeared in magazines, some as far back as 1920. Twenty were included in *Chills and Fever* and seventeen in *Two Gentlemen in Bonds*. Since seven of the poems had also been used in *Fugitivies: An Anthology of Verse* and six in *Grace After Meat*, some were being published for the fourth or fifth time when they were included in *Selected Poems*, and many of them had been revised with every appearance. To be sure, most of the revisions were minor—word changes and adjustments of punctuation—but many were certainly major. One of the poems, "Blue Girls," was so completely recast that a new poem was produced. Only one line, the second, from the version which appeared in the *Fugitive* for June, 1924, remained unchanged when the poem was reprinted in *Selected Poems*. No one can fail to see that the first version is vastly inferior to the second:

Blue Girls

If I were younger, traveling the bright sward
Under the towers of your seminary,

I should get a look and a thought, or even a word;
But I am old, and of aspect too contrary
For you who are less weary.

For why do you bind white fillets about your tresses
And weave such stately rhythms where you go?
Why do you whirl so lovingly your blue dresses,
Like haughty bluebirds chattering in the snow
Of what they cannot know?

Practice your beauty, blue girls, if you will;
The lean preceptress, she of history,
Showed you the manifold of good and ill,
And all you saw was princes crooking the knee
To beauteous majesty.

Do you think there are thrones enough, one for each queen?
Some thrones are chairs, some three legged milking stools,
Or you even sit in ashes where thrones should have been;
And it is for this, God help us all for fools,
You practice in the schools.

Practice your beauty, blue girls, nevertheless;
Once the preceptress, learned bitter one,
Printed the sward in a flounce of purple dress
And was a princess pacing as to her throne;
But now you see she is none.

It is obvious to anyone familiar with this poem as it appeared in *Selected Poems*—and it has remained unchanged since—that the actual process of creation occurred in revision. To study these two versions carefully is to get a clearer impression of the creative process, a better understanding of a poet's use of language, rhyme, and meter:

Blue Girls

Twirling your blue skirts, traveling the sward
Under the towers of your seminary,
Go listen to your teachers old and contrary
Without believing a word.

Tie the white fillets then about your hair
And think no more of what will come to pass
Than bluebirds that go walking on the grass
And chattering on the air.

Practice your beauty, blue girls, before it fail;
And I will cry with my loud lips and publish

Beauty which all our power will never establish,
It is so frail.

For I could tell you a story which is true;
I know a lady with a terrible tongue,
Blear eyes fallen for blue,
All her perfections tarnished—yet it is not long
Since she was lovelier than any of you.

Although none of the other revisions was quite as sweeping as this one, many of them would certainly be classified as major. "Winter Remembered" had first appeared in the *Sewanee Review* for January, 1922, as an English sonnet. Before it was reprinted in *Grace After Meat*, the concluding couplet was dropped ("Which world you choose and for what boot in gold,/ The absence, or the absence and the cold?") and three new quatrains added, making it a twenty-four line poem divided into six four-line stanzas. By the time it appeared in *Selected Poems* one of the quatrains added in *Grace After Meat* had been dropped,[17] leaving it very near the poem as it has appeared since.[18] "Dead Boy," which was published in the New York *Evening Post* for February 24, 1920, as "Sonnets of a Selfish Lover" and in the *Sewanee Review* for April, 1924, as "The Dead Boy" underwent an almost complete transformation before it was included in *Selected Poems* (1945). The version included in *Two Gentlemen in Bonds* (1927) was considerably different from that in the *Sewanee Review*. Nine lines were changed and four were added,[19] and in *Selected Poems* five of the lines altered in *Two Gentlemen in Bonds* were revised again.[20]

First published in the *Fugitive* for December, 1923, and reprinted in *Chills and Fever* and *Grace After Meat*,[21] "Vaunting Oak" was altered a little each time it appeared and extensively revised before it was included in *Selected Poems*. Four lines changed in *Grace After Meat* were restored in *Chills and Fever*, leading one to speculate that Robert Graves might have taken seriously Ransom's suggestion that he make any emendations he wished. Since Ransom did not read the proofsheets of *Grace After Meat* (Ransom requested that they not be sent to him), he could not have reacted to Graves's alterations until he was preparing copy for *Selected Poems*. For *Chills and Fever* Ransom made only one minor alteration in the poem, changing a phrase in line 39 from "a girl discovering her dread" to "a girl remembering her dread," but in the *Selected Poems* (1945) he made some major changes, dropping a six-line passage and revising twenty-three other lines. The deleted passage is repetitive and therefore unnecessary to the development of the argument of the poem, and many of the line changes are obvious, and usually successful, attempts to improve rhythm or meter or to provide textural richness.[22] Some of the changes apparently were made in an attempt to express more exactly a specific meaning—line one, for example:

1. He is a tower unleaning. But he may break (CF)
1. He is a tower unleaning. But how will he not break (SP)

Although meaning was altered in some of the other changes, the poet seems to have been striving for other effects:

9. Ecstatic around the stem on which they are captive (CF)
9. In panic round the stem on which they are captive (SP)

2. If heaven in a rage try him too windily (CF)
2. If heaven assault him with full wind and sleet (SP)

5. Of timeless trunk that is too vast to shake (CF)
5. Naked he rears against the cold skies eruptive (SP)

23. Who had sorely been instructed of much decrease (CF)
23. Who had been instructed of much mortality (SP)

29. But thinking that she had lied too piteously (CF)
29. But, that her pitiful error be undone (SP)

Some of the other poems underwent major revisions. Between its appearance in the *Fugitive* (June–July, 1923) and its reprinting in *Chills and Fever,* "Spectral Lovers" was subjected to only three line changes, all of which were minor. But the version in *Selected Poems* contains sixteen altered lines, including two of those revised in *Chills and Fever.*[23] Before its inclusion in *Selected Poems* "Necrological" had appeared in the *Fugitive* (June, 1922), *Chills and Fever* (1924), *Grace After Meat* (1924), and *Fugitives: An Anthology of Verse* (1928) and had undergone twelve significant changes. Apparently Ransom was satisfied with the poem as it had evolved through these rather extensive revisions because only two additional changes were made for *Selected Poems,* and both were minor: line eleven was changed from "In defeat the heroes' bosoms were whitely bare" to "In defeat the heroes' bodies were whitely bare"; and line 17, from "The lords of chivalry were prone and shattered," to "The lords of chivalry lay prone and shattered." During this period Ransom began the major revisions of "Tom, Tom, the Piper's Son" and "Conrad in Twilight," which he continued through every publication of these poems.[24] Before "The Equilibrists," which was first printed as "A History of Two Simple Lovers" in the *Fugitive* for September, 1925, was reprinted in *Two Gentlemen in Bonds*, Ransom had omitted a stanza which contained a statement of that poem's theme given too early and too overtly:

> The beauty of their bodies was the bond
> Which these incarnate might not pass beyond;
> Invincible proud Honor was the bar
> Which made them not come closer but stay far.

For *Selected Poems* he made only two additional changes. He substituted *which* for *whence* in line 6 ("From *whence* came heat that flamed upon the kiss") and added *Epitaph* as a heading for the last four lines.

Although almost every poem in the collection was revised, many of the changes were not significant. Ransom's inability to create many poems that through the years would remain completely satisfactory to him is demonstrated in this volume. Many of the poems have been improved through revision. "The alterations," as David Mann and Samuel H. Woods, Jr., have written, often show "shifts toward a simpler diction, smoother meter, and greater clarity."[25] But Ransom's basic techniques did not change. Those he worked out during the years of the *Fugitive,* those which constitute what critics have called his mature manner, have not been radically altered. Except for the differences already noted in the poems written after 1927, the tendencies that would concern Robert Buffington years later were just beginning to emerge at the time Ransom prepared this book for the press. The pervasive irony of the early poetry is evident in that written after *Two Gentlemen in Bonds,* but the intellectual concerns seem to differ. Ransom was beginning to doubt, apparently, the advisability of attempting to carry "two opposing ideas" in the mind "at the same time" in "cosmic irresolution." Attempts to provide a synthesis of the polarities that keep one suspended in a "torture of equilibrium" would become increasingly evident in the changes Ransom would continue to make in his poems throughout his life.

Despite his inclination "to tinker with" the poems, "especially towards tightening up the meters," a few of them he never wanted to change very much. Many of his best-known poems, particularly those which were already becoming established as anthology pieces, he allowed to stand virtually untouched. Among those, only "Janet Waking," in which line 10 was changed from "Running on little pink feet upon the grass" to "Running across the world upon the grass," could be thought of as undergoing significant change. In "Bells for John Whiteside's Daughter" punctuation was made to conform to current practices by adding a comma, dropping one, and changing a semicolon to a comma. In "Here Lies a Lady," the word *Aunts* in line 3 becomes *Aunt,* and a phrase in line 10 is changed from "as a thin stalk" to "like a stalk white and blown." Several other poems undergo alterations equally minor: a semicolon becomes a dash and the first letter of *Sir* is capitalized in "Piazza Piece"; *ladybird* becomes *lady bird* and *earth* is substituted for *world* in "Lady Lost"; one semicolon is changed to a comma, another to a period, and a comma is deleted in "Emily Hardcastle, Spinster." The only emendation in "Survey of Literature" occurs in couplet 8, which is changed from "The flatulence of Milton/Came out of wry Stilton" to "The influence of Milton/Came wry out of Stilton." Most of these poems will not be affected by the almost constant retouching, or in some cases the complete recasting, to which much of the other verse was subjected before each new collection appeared.

By 1945, then, all the poetry on which Ransom's reputation as poet must rest had been written, and most of it belonged to a period at least twenty years in the past. Although many of the reviewers commented on his limited output—he published only 154 poems—and lamented the fact that the poet had been overcome by the critic—the important poetry was written over a period of eleven years, from 1916 to 1927—no one discussed another kind of limitation he had placed on himself. In the early 1930s, when his career as poet was virtually over and he was writing the essays that would be collected in *The World's Body,* he gave a convincing defense of "minor poetry," a kind Allen Tate said in 1963 his old friend had "deliberately" set out to write.[26] Ransom comments on "minor poems" in "Shakespeare at Sonnets":

The virtue of formal lyrics, or "minor poems," is one that no other literary type can manifest: they are the only complete and self-determined poetry. There the poetic object is elected by a free choice from all objects in the world, and this object, deliberately elected and carefully worked up by the adult poet, becomes his microcosm. With a serious poet each minor poem may be a symbol of a major decision: it is as ranging and comprehensive an action as the mind has ever tried.

In his description of minor poems Ransom is concerned with those qualities of verse which T. S. Eliot discussed in some of his important critical essays. Modern poetry, Eliot wrote in "The Metaphysical Poets," must be complex because "our civilization comprehends great variety and complexity, and this variety and complexity, playing upon a refined sensibility, must produce various and complex results. The poet must become more and more comprehensive, more allusive, more indirect, in order to force, to dislocate if necessary, language into his meaning."[27] The mode of the poet, then, must be ironic and the essential ingredient of his verse, wit. This combination, Eliot asserted, has been absent from poetry since the seventeenth century. Properly used, as in the poetry of Andrew Marvell and some of his contemporaries, wit is a "structural decoration of a serious idea" or an "alliance of levity and seriousness."[28]

In Fugitive meetings, private conversations, and, particularly, in letters Ransom, Davidson, and Tate had discussed this and related subjects many times and in great detail. "I'm afraid Eliot is about right in saying there are no important themes for modern poets," Tate wrote Davidson on May 14, 1926; "hence we all write lyrics."[29] In an essay published in the *Fugitive* for December, 1922, Tate had addressed the question of obscurity in modern verse:

The poet's individuality, his peculiar way of viewing the world, his "genius," informs the poem, although neither he nor anyone else can explain the *ens realissimum* of that genius. And it is pretty well decided beforehand that his finished product must *represent* some phase of life as ordinarily perceived, and that he must look for his effects in new combinations of images representing only the constituted material world. It is possible that this notion, unlike the question of technique, is somewhat gratuitous and inadequate; and I believe that the unique virtue of the contemporary revolt is its break, in a positive direction, with the tyranny of representation.[30]

Ransom agreed that a strong reaction against nineteenth-century poetry was in progress, but he insisted that the revolt against that poetry was much broader than a break with "the tyranny of representation." The modern poet's disaffection for the poetry of his nineteenth-century forebears was the result of a fundamental difference in his view of reality.[31] Much of the poetry of the nineteenth century is characterized by a kind of immaturity because it was written by poets whose intellectual development was incomplete. Man should move through three stages in his progress toward maturity. In the first, his intellectual attitudes are dominated by a kind of naive dualism and he is convinced that he controls the world in which he lives. Then he moves into a second stage, a sort of optimistic monism based on the conviction that a benevolent God is personally responsible for assigning both man and nature appropriate places in a system "where not a sparrow falls without effect." Romantic poetry is immature because it was written by men who never moved beyond this "naive and uninformed" stage of their development.[32] The best of twentieth-century poetry is postscientific because it is created by poets whose attitudes and convictions have been partially formed by the "sober observations" of modern science. The illusions of the Romantic poet are punctured, and many modern writers, like those of the seventeenth century and earlier, return to the "stubborn fact of dualism with a mellow wisdom which we may call irony." This dualism is not a return to the first position, for "too much history has intervened"; now the writer is a "dualist with a difference—reluctant, speculative, sophisticated rather than ingenuous and richer by all the pathetic fallacies he has ever entertained." This final stage of man's development, which few if any in the nineteenth century reached, is the "ultimate mode of great minds" because it presupposes all the others:

It implies first of all an honorable and strenuous period of romantic creation; it implies then a rejection of the romantic forms and formulas; but this rejection is so unwilling, and in its statements there lingers so much of the music and color and romantic mystery which is perhaps the absolute poetry, and this statement is attended by such a disarming rueful comic sense of the poet's own betrayal, that the fruit of it is wisdom and not bitterness, poetry and not prose, health and not suicide. Irony is the rarest of the states of mind, because it is the most inclusive; the whole mind has been active in arriving at it, both creation and criticism, both poetry and science.[33]

In the earliest of the important essays on Ransom's poetry, one written ten years before the appearance of *Selected Poems,* Robert Penn Warren identifies wit and irony as the "two properties most generally ascribed" to Ransom's poetry and demonstrates how these two qualities operate at the very center of his verse.[34] First of all, wit in Ransom's poetry is more than a "poetic attitude"—the term is George Williamson's—it is a "functional aspect of the general state of mind from which the poetry is written," an insrument whose use can best be understood by comparing it to that of metaphor. Metaphor implies a comparison which strictly speaking makes little sense and according to science is not defensible, but is justified in terms of the "emotional enrichment of a poetic theme, or more ambitiously sometimes, as the vehicle of its communication." But wit gives the poem another kind of enrichment. Contrary to the opinion of many readers, whose tastes were formed from nineteenth-century verse, wit represents a serious attempt to fuse the emotional and intellectual qualities in poetry. In Ransom's verse wit is employed in "incidental imagery," in a "certain pedantry of rhetoric," and in the "organization of the entire material," and it is "usually directed to a specific and constant effect."[35] Irony, like wit, is often used specifically for effect, but Ransom's irony has "ethical reference" and is not "one of irresponsible contrasts and negations." With wit it is used to define the "center" of his poetry, "that sensibility whose decay Ransom, along with various other critics, has bewailed."[36]

The kind of poetry Ransom favored is no secret to anyone who has read his criticism. Only in metaphysical poetry, he argues in "Poetry: A Note in Ontology," is there a perfect fusion of image and idea, intellect and feeling. As critic Ransom expresses approval of the kind of poetry he himself presents in *Selected Poems,* a poetry of logical rigor, structural discipline, and textural richness. But Donald Davidson, who thought one of the functions of poetry was to evoke the past and remind the reader of his rightful tradition, accused Ransom of writing in what he called a "guarded style." Eliot's defense of minor poetry, and Ransom's as well, Davidson believed, is an attempt to justify poetry "that is content with narrow limits of form, few subjects, in order that it may perfectly succeed."[37] Davidson agreed with F. Cudworth Flint when he complained that although many modern poets write excellent short lyrics, they do not supply "an artistic focal point," a "center of unity" and a "credible mythology," because their qualities cannot be presented in short poems but could be embodied in poems of epic magnitude.[38] Davidson's objections to the defense of minor poetry were given full expression in a letter to John Hall Wheelock:

> Their procedure was to seek out ways of making the "small" poem carry a tension that would charge it heavily with meaning. Implied in their practice—though not clearly stated in their critical pronouncements—was the belief that the poem of large meaning and extended dimensions was impossible for the modern to execute. Therefore they did not attempt narrative verse of any but the smallest possiblie scale and in general avoided any sustained efforts in verse.[39]

In spite of Davidson's objections, Ransom was convinced that he, and perhaps any other modern poet, could work best in a minor mode. Only through a combination of images and concepts, can poetry present the concrete particularities of experience and show the reality of an object's being in a way that science cannot. But the modern poet has been instructed in the "pure intellectual disciplines, and cannot play innocent without feeling very foolish"; therefore his poetic stance—his relationship to and his attitude toward his subject—are very important. Poetry is a "communication of minds of the same order" and the poet whose work suggests that it "is something we can engage in without our faculties" will produce a "heart's desire poetry" which will try either to improve the world or to idealize it. The mature poet will realize that although no poetry is true in the way science is, it does accomplish the "sort of representation that it means to." Properly executed, a poem can make us aware, in a way no other medium can, that an "object is perceptually or physically remarkable, and we had better attend to it."[40] If we may judge from Ransom's actual practice, he was persuaded he could best present the "concrete particularities of an actual experience" in poetry of a certain kind, that which he called minor poetry.

Although the protagonists in many of Ransom's poems suffer

from the modern disease of the dissociation of sensibility, from the schism between reason and imagination, between science and faith, the recurring themes in the poetry are those which have concerned man as far into the past as history reaches: man's dual nature, the conflict of body and soul, mutability, the passing of youthful beauty and energy, and the awesome certainty of death. If the subject matter is typical and commonplace, the style of the mature verse is unusual, if not unique, and the distinctive relationship between the two contributes a great deal toward establishing the tone of the poem and giving Ransom a poetic voice unlike that of any of his contemporaries. The ironist realizes, as Miller Williams points out, "that every statement contains its own contradiction, that every human act contains the seeds of its own defeat."[41] This is the "mellow wisdom which we call irony" and it is always present, but never obtrusive, in Ransom's best verse: in the polarity of statement; in the tension between the way things are and the way we think they ought to be; between the sentiment that naturally belongs to a situation and the inappropriateness of the language used to develop it; between the maudlin sentimentality inherent in a relationship and the classical restraint used to describe it; between a violent, ugly content and the bloodless language used to present it. A part of the distinctive tone of the poems is the care with which both sides of a situation are presented so that the reader sympathizes with the efforts of reconciliation at the same time that he realizes their futility. The irony is not only Socratic in that it accepts human limitations so that man may move through ignorance to knowledge; it is also Schlegelian in that the poet's subjective self is revealed through the objectivity of his work.[42] In these poems, along with the persuasive irony and its constant companion wit, there are always what Graham Hough describes as those "massive and ineluctable facts" presented in the most unlikely and delicate settings:[43] a young friar walks on a battlefield after a battle and is left to contemplate reality as a puzzling maze of irreconcilable opposites; a young girl is made to face the reality of death, the most painful fact of human existence, through the death of her pet hen; a little girl dies and the man next door is left to ponder the inscrutability of the world. Some of the poems in this collection will surely be read as long as poetry is regarded as a serious art because it contains all of those poems which Randall Jarrell has said are "perfectly realized" and occasionally "almost perfect." [44]

On January 13, 1945, while Ransom was getting the final copy of *Selected Poems* ready for the publisher, Eric Bentley, who had just completed a term as a *Kenyon Review* fellow under a program sponsored by the Rockefeller Foundation, made a formal report to David H. Stevens, the director of the foundation's Division of the Humanities. Bentley's duties on the *Review* "ranged from details concerning a particular article to matters of general policy." Although he devoted a great deal of time to his assignments—particularly to assisting Ransom and Rice in securing contributions in music, art, and contemporary foreign literature—there was ample time, he wrote, for informal talks with the editors of the *Review* and with other members of the college community. These conversations, he was convinced, were most beneficial to him, and he hoped the "enrichment was not wholly one-sided." On February 22, Ransom wrote Stevens his reactions to Bentley's tenure at Kenyon. "Bentley is a brilliant specimen," Ransom began, "of a certain tough-minded sector of the younger generation which is likely to play an important part in our future culture." Although he is "learned academically" and capable of the "most intensive thinking," he is "determined not to inhabit an ivory tower." In spite of strong political convictions, he does not "bother much about current political issues" and puts almost the whole of his considerable energy into literature." In the office of the *Review* he did "whatever was asked of him," attended to some routine but necessary assignments, and "made studies and suggestions for the conduct of our periodical." His greatest value to the *Review* was in establishing contact "with a number of emigre Europeans who write on literature and other arts." Some of the persons with whom he corresponded, Ransom concluded, have already submitted acceptable essays and stories. Obviously Ransom was much pleased with the way Bentley had conducted himself during his semester on the campus and was prepared to welcome Harold Whitehall, who would replace him for the next term.

A few days after Ransom's letter was mailed, Bentley responded to

Stevens' request for "recommendations as to the future of the *Kenyon Review*."[45] Bentley recommended that the *Review* make a concerted and serious attempt to raise its subscriptions from 2,000 to 10,000, an achievement that could be effected without sacrificing quality "with a little more money in the till and a little more cunning on the editorial board." The *Review* must launch an extensive advertising campaign and attempt to produce a more diversified appeal, by making deliberate efforts to attract a broader circle of readers "through musical, artistic, linguistic, political interests, as well as literary interests." Bentley pointed to the "accessibility" of so many Europeans now living temporarily in the United States. "After the war the *Kenyon Review* must be swift," he wrote, "in contacting Europeans in Europe. Here a certain commercial slickness is required if the *Kenyon Review* is not forever to be beaten to it by very canny slicksters like Mr. Allen Tate and Mr. Philip Rahv." (At this time Tate was editing the *Sewanee Review* and Rahv, the *Partisan Review*.) Ransom has said, Bentley concluded, that he would like for his review to be "as good as the *Nouvelle Revue Francaise*. . . . But before that ideal can be reached, the organization of the *Review* would have to be expanded. In my belief, to double the size of the organization would be to quadruple its circulation."

Certain that Ransom would approve of his suggestions, for all he had "done was show the need for more money," Bentley sent him a carbon of the letter. But when Ransom read it, he was disturbed; he saw that Bentley was recommending a basic change in the nature and intent of the *Review*, a recommendation which, he was convinced, was based on a false assumption. After consulting Rice and finding him in complete agreement, Ransom wrote Stevens his objections.[46] Since Bentley "is so obviously devoted to our interests," he began, "I should not care to reproach him," but Ransom "felt morally impelled" to write dissociating himself from Bentley's "high powered plans." Although Ransom would like to attract high-quality contributions from wherever he could get them, he did not think the *Review* "must stand or fall upon the fullness of its reports of the writings of the foreign men of letters." Not to attempt to keep up with major European writers would certainly be unwise; nevertheless, the "moral of our College auspices, under which we publish, and our provincial location" would surely argue that the *Kenyon Review* should remain "substantially a voice of American literature and opinion." He could not agree, furthermore, that the significance of the journal's contribution to the world of letters must depend on its ability to reach a circulation of 10,000. As editor his major emphasis should be on attempts to maintain and improve the quality of the magazine. Although the "effort to increase circulation should not be perfunctory," it should not be the "main effort; otherwise we are just journalists."

Bentley was followed by three other fellows, all supported by the Rockefeller Foundation: Harold Whitehall, Charles Riker, and Robert Penn Warren. In a letter to John Marshall, associate director of humanties for the foundation, Ransom expressed his appreciation and that of the college for the "very substantial benefits" the *Review* had received from that organization. The Rockefeller fellowship program he proclaimed a complete success. Each of the four fellows "who came and stayed with us, giving and receiving intellectual stimulus," left evidence in Gambier of his tenure there; at the same time he took away something of value to him. Bentley has moved so rapidly "from triumph to triumph," Ransom began, it is hard to realize his career was so recently founded. A "forthright journalist by instinct," he has needed all the help he could get "to keep his bright clean style and yet handle subtle and difficult materials." With his tremendous energy "he initiated many projects for the magazine," and he has been placed on the permanent staff as an advisory editor. The needs of Harold Whitehall were different. His "devoted service to the academy" had infected him with the academic point of view, and the "best thing we could do for him was to enforce the literary tone upon his attention, as it prevails in a magazine like ours, and I believe that came about in the course of the sessions we had with our manuscripts." The *Review* profited from his many excellent business suggestions and his linguistic discussions. The third fellow, Charles Riker, had had much "less literary performance than any of the other men," but he is destined, Ransom wrote, to be a "musical critic, and teacher of musical criticism, who has a language far more precise than the one ordinarily used in that game." He greatly aided the *Review* with his expert advice about writers on music and art. Already an established writer and an experienced editor, Robert Penn Warren, the last of the fellows, was "much further along" when he came to Kenyon than the others were. But while he was there he gave "an accumulation and concentration of advices," and since a "literary man is never finished with his own development" he must certainly have received "in the course of much literary talk" during his term there "something of value from persons of different temperament from his own."

During the same year the *Review* received important benefits from a supplementary grant of $7,500 from the foundation. "We employed a professional secretary," Ransom wrote, "and put our business office in order. We paid a little better rates to our contributors, we increased the size of the issues, so that they have a more rounded content. We brought up to the highest current standard, as I have been pretty well informed, our department of original fiction, and we printed new verse on a more liberal scale." Ransom concluded his discussion of the benefits that had accrued to the *Review* from the generous gifts of the Rockefeller Foundation with an indirect reference to the next project for which he would receive support from that source. "I judge that it was entirely in my capacity as editor," he wrote, "that last spring I had letters from half a dozen heads of English departments asking where young men were to be found who could give instruction in critical writing." Meeting this need was one of the major reasons Ransom gave two years later in his request for a grant to support the establishment of the Kenyon School of English.

In the spring of 1946, after Tate's resignation as editor of the *Sewanee Review* had become definite,[47] Ransom inquired about the fate of that journal. He was convinced, he wrote, "that it is finished without Tate as editor," and although he did not want to embarrass his old friend in any commitments he had made, he was very much interested in "materials which you may have had brought to your attention or even have accepted, so far as they are negotiable.... I scarcely dare to think we might inherit from you as we did from the *Southern Review*, by taking over unexpired subscriptions. But any help you can extend in a literary sense will be more than welcome."[48] Tate responded immediately that he had been assured by the administration of the University of the South that the *Sewanee Review* would be continued and asked Ransom to recommend someone to succeed him as editor. Ransom suggested two names. The first was Marshall McLuhan, whom Cleanth Brooks had recently recommended to him and whose essay on Gerard Manley Hopkins had impressed him most favorably. "He's one of us," Ransom wrote, "though he's Catholic." But "a still better man is Austin Warren of [the] University of Iowa. He has been unhappy there at that awful place since Foerster went out. . . . He is a genuine man of letters, I think; of gentle nature but uncompromising taste. He might like the peace of Sewanee with a Review to run."[49]

The *Sewanee Review* was continued under J. E. Palmer, who did well enough to be appointed editor of the *Yale Review*. This exchange of letters, however, did revive regular correspondence between Ransom and Tate, now in its twentieth-odd year, which had lapsed temporarily, perhaps because of Tate's despondence about the failure of his marriage. Soon Ransom and Robert Penn Warren, who was spending the summer in Gambier as the Rockefeller fellow, had decided on a project to get Tate more definitely involved again in the *Kenyon Review*. To commemorate the fiftieth anniversary of William Faulkner's birth, Ransom wrote on July 17, 1946, he and Warren had discussed the idea of a special Faulkner number and had agreed that Tate should edit it. Their discussions had included such items as "a new story by Faulkner, two or three essays on Faulkner by Americans, one or more each by Englishmen, Frenchmen, and Italians. Apparently F's *literature* is not *engagee* enough for New York critics, so that he is in the position of a prophet who will not be honored at home till the visible honors come from abroad." Five days later Tate replied that he was "all for the Faulkner number in the *Kenyon Review,* and you can count on me to help you in any way you may find me useful."[50] During the next several months the special issue was planned in elaborate detail. At Warren's suggestion Malcolm Cowley, "who has come over to Faulkner now," agreed to see if any unpublished story might be available. A few weeks later in conversation with Cowley in New York, Warren learned that Harold Ober, Faulkner's literary agent, had reported that "F. has a fine Indian story not yet placed, very dear to himself."[51] Ransom promised Tate, "We'd try to pay out pretty well (for us) for such a story." Among the American writers consulted about contributing to the issue, in addition to Warren who promised an essay on "Faulkner and Nature," were Caroline Gordon,[52] Malcolm Cowley, Katherine Anne Porter, Francis Fergusson,

William Troy, and F. O. Matthiessen. To represent the English attitude, Tate invited essays from D. S. Savage, Geoffrey Grigson, and Herbert Read. Using his broad acquaintance with writers from other European countries, Tate attempted to make the issue truly representative of the European attitude by inviting contributions from French, Italian, and German critics. He also recommended to Ransom that Wightman Williams, "the most gifted illustrator in this country," be commissioned to do a "sketch of Faulkner, as a frontispiece." After the "issue is pretty well shaped up," he concluded, "I will see what Holt may be able to do about it as a book." [53] Ransom was enthusiastic about Tate's plans and wrote him "to go ahead—you have the final decision at every point. We'll even splurge, spend money, as you require, in order to do something of unusual distinction." [54]

Despite the enthusiasm of Tate, Ransom, and Warren, and all of the time and energy they devoted to the project, the Faulkner number was much less successful than other special issues undertaken by the *Review*. Because of other commitments, many of the persons invited by Tate to contribute to the issue had to decline. Others who agreed to contribute did not deliver their essays at the time promised. After more than a year of almost continuous effort and "God knows how many letters," Tate wrote that he thought the Faulkner number was off, that he had rather not do it than to do it with second-rate critics. Ransom concurred, thanked Tate for his time and effort, and expressed his regrets that "we gave you a false lead." [55] But all was not lost, he wrote, because he thought he had collected enough Faulkner material "for a small feature next fall." He had a "very good essay" by Lawrence Bowling, a close study of the technique of *The Sound and the Fury*, with "cross references to techniques in other novels." Also, there was a paper by Richard Chase "on the *substance*" of *Light in August*; "and now I wonder," he concluded, "if we couldn't get a new story by Faulkner himself . . . and I do wish you yourself would consent to write a general paper on Faulkner, or a paper on some other novel, critical in the widest sense." But Ransom's intentions were never completely realized. He could not get the Faulkner story and neither Tate nor Caroline Gordon, who was also invited to do a "general paper," was able to contribute an essay. His plan to honor a prophet at home before "visible honors came from abroad" [56] could produce no more than the essays by Bowling and Chase, in spite of his desire to present a more adequate tribute to one of our "finest, original talents," whose writing though a "personal homemade affair" is "wild and strong."[57]

As the period for which the Rockefeller grant for general operating expenses of the *Review* neared its end, Ransom wrote John Marshall thanking him for past generosity, explaining how the funds had been used, and demonstrating an urgent need for additional assistance.[58] The previous grant, he said, had been used to increase payment to contributors, for secretarial assistance, and for office expense and promotion.[59] As much as he valued the ability to pay his contributors the higher rate—and he knew "popular writers" still earned much more for "work far below the literary and critical standards of this Review"—there was a matter of even more importance, he pointed out, both to him and to the journal he edited. He hoped that the foundation's willingness to assist in increasing the rate of pay to contributors would not preclude its consideration of a renewal for a general assistance grant. "So far as we are concerned," he wrote, "the two requests are vitally related. Without the general one I am not at all confident that we shall be in any position to administer increased payments to contributors, since we may very easily be out of publication and have no contributors to pay."

Ransom's urgent plea did not evoke the expected response. When he concluded his letter with the statement that "editorially we are better than we have ever been" but "we cannot continue operation without further outside assistance immediately," he undoubtedly expected prompt approval of the request for the general assistance grant he and President Chalmers had submitted at the end of July. Instead, Marshall responded that he did not understand the intent of Ransom's letter. Although he appreciated the "materials basic for a request for assistance" to enable the *Review* to "raise its rates of payment to contributors to the equivalent of 2-1/2¢ a word for signed prose material and 50¢ a line for verse," he felt the necessity of using the phrase "material for a request" because Ransom's references to the uncertainty of the journal's continuation had raised a question "of whether or not any such request can be considered." Such a question had not come up in "similar discussions with the editors of the *Partisan Review*," he wrote, and Allen Tate had assured him that the *Sewanee*

Review would not be discontinued. "All this seems to us to suggest," he concluded, "that a reappraisal of the situation of the *Kenyon Review* with the college administration may be in order."

Ransom sent a copy of this letter to President Chalmers, who immediately called him in for an "urgent conference." At the end of this discussion, Chalmers gave Ransom a statement which included the promise: "The College will not let the *Review* die, but it is difficult to see where, in this and the next three years, the necessary supplementary funds are to be found to balance the *Review* accounts."[60] After his conversation with Chalmers, Ransom wrote Marshall that "the College will in no case fail to secure the *Review*, and will provide out of its general budget for that purpose if necessary." He could now enter an "unqualified request" for funds to increase "the rate of payment to our contributors."[61]

With the immediate future of the *Review* assured, Ransom was able to get back to a project that had interested him for a number of years. For the past several months, with the encouragement of John Marshall, he had been preparing a formal request for the Rockefeller Foundation to support "an Educational Project in the Humanities." He had conferred in Gambier with Chalmers, Phil Rice, and Charles Coffin, chairman of the English department; he had made two trips to New York to talk to Lionel Trilling and F. O. Matthiessen, who had come down from Cambridge; and now he was ready to draft a plan for the Kenyon School of Criticism, a proposal for what *Time* would call a "precedent-smashing course in English for advanced students of literature" and one that would make the department of English of Kenyon College nationally famous.[62] After the basic scheme of what was to become the School of English had been approved by the authorities at Kenyon and by Matthiessen and Trilling, who would join Ransom on its board of senior fellows, Ransom sent a rough outline of the proposal to Allen Tate, Robert Penn Warren, and a dozen or so other established critics and men of letters who would become fellows of the school. In the early winter of 1947 a final draft of the proposal went to the foundation. Many first-rate students, the statement began, have indicated their sense of the shortcomings of advanced English courses by electing not to enroll in them. These courses "do not have a proper regard either for the literary interest of their maturing students or for the possibilities of their subject." The academic scholarship to which they are devoted is "admirable within limits, but beside the point when it goes too far." The bulletin of the Kenyon School of English, first printed in the summer of 1948, described in explicit language the deficiencies of these courses:

For a long time it has been noticed that their appeal to the abler and more spirited students has been lessening. It is not a novel impression that this is because their devotion to their texts commonly stops short of the stage at which the texts are taken as literature. They expend very nearly their entire energy upon disciplines which are philosophical, historical, biographical, bibliographical, and ideological. But the able students become too well aware that the imperative and exciting activity of literary criticism is going on outside the academy. They are not being trained, and perhaps not even being encouraged, to form literary judgments, and they are not content with the recital of facts which are important but largely sub-literary, and which are not being consistently employed with intelligent purpose.[63]

The disaffection of the English students, Ransom argued, is understandable and just. They are aware that the age in which they live has produced critical writing of "such integrity, seriousness, and public importance" that it has been called "an age of criticism." They know these critical studies are very much different from the academic studies with which they are familiar, because the "critics have a deeper and more enlightened interest in the creative process as a human adventure; they are prepared to study the work as a composition, involving materials, devices and powerful motives." The School of English proposes, he concluded, to "bring literary criticism into the academy more rapidly, by teaching it to those who are going to be teachers." The Rockefeller Foundation approved the project and awarded a grant of $40,000 to fund three summer sessions of approximately forty-five days each.

At the registration for the first session, which was held on June 24, 1948, seventy-nine students and twenty-three auditors enrolled; twenty-three official visitors attended one or more of the daily discussions, and many others came out for the Wednesday evening forums. One of the students who attended this first term was so "astounded" to see so many "literary giants" brought together on one small campus that he "could hardly function" for more than a week. It was a distinguished faculty: Eric Bentley, Cleanth Brooks, Richard Chase, F. O. Matthiessen, William Empson, John Crowe Ransom, Austin Warren, and Allen Tate. Ransom's only regret about this first faculty was his inability to get T. S. Eliot to join the group. He had offered him a stipend of $2,500—other members of the faculty received $1,500— and promised to schedule at least three lectures at $500 each at nearby universities. Tate had added a cordial note to this invitation, telling Eliot of the pleasant company he would find in Gambier and suggesting other possibilities for lectures, principally in the East. Eliot's response was "so cordial" that as late as mid-January Ransom was sure he would come. When he had had no definite word by the end of the first week in February, he sent a cablegram, to which Eliot replied that "he must regretfully decline the generous offer this time but hoped he would be invited again." [64] In spite of this disappointment, Ransom was pleased with the result of many years of planning and hoping. "The courses were there, and the students were there," he was quoted as saying, "How could we fail? Everything has worked out according to plan—only better than we expected."

Since Kenyon College did not have a summer session, the School of English had pretty much the run of the campus. The men students lived in the middle division of Old Kenyon, the principal residence for men in the regular session, and some of the fellows and male auditors lived in the west wing. Women students and auditors were housed in Bexley Hall, the building of the Divinity School of Kenyon College. All students, auditors, and many of the fellows ate together in Pierce Hall, the college commons. Classes, which met for three two-hour sessions each week, were scheduled between 8:30 and 12:30 each day, Monday through Saturday. [65] Afternoons were left for work in the library, reading, writing the numerous required essays, or for informal discussions. All of the fellows held regular office hours, and students and auditors were invited to come by to discuss whatever they had on their minds. Everything was very relaxed and informal—although both men and women students were advised that "shorts should not be worn at academic appointments"—and each afternoon students and fellows shared the recreation facilities— swimming pool, tennis, badminton, and croquet courts, gymnasium, and softball diamond. Although tea was served each afternoon between 4:30 and 5:30 in Pierce Hall, almost everyone preferred to go to Dorothy's, a hamburger restaurant and a popular student meeting place in the village of Gambier, for a cold glass of beer. Special films were shown some evenings in Rosse Hall, and a public forum was held each Wednesday at 8:00 P.M.[66]

The atmosphere on the campus at Kenyon during the three sessions of the School of English was not that usually found on a college or university campus. The students who attended, according to George Lanning, a visitor in 1948 and a student in 1950, were very "much New Critical," and they brought to Gambier more enthusiasm than they had ever given to the study of literature before. Although they did not conceive of themselves as "pioneers"—the pioneers, they were convinced, were on the faculty—they did "feel as early settlers":

We had come to help make order in the wilderness of literary criticism. Perhaps we were like the early Beats—as improbable as that yoking may at first appear. But I mean that we possessed the kind of exhilaration that they had to start with. And we knew, too, that on every side, even in our midst, was the Enemy, the woolly headed Beast of primitive criticism in whose territory we proposed to settle. He was fighting back hard—very hard, just then. Vigorously, we "explicated" in and out of class; we got so we could spot a Precious Object at a thousand yards; and where we couldn't find an ambiguity we made one. It was all tremendous fun, and if we were often foolish our elders let us take our heads. And we learned a great deal—as much, of course, from informal association as from lectures. Those lectures, I'm afraid, were sometimes too much of a challenge. This was the year when William Empson was working on complex words and Kenneth Burke was lecturing on poetry as symbolic action. Though I didn't have a class with either man, I gathered that some of their students were following them imperfectly—though with all their hearts.[67]

Although attendance declined slightly each year the school was in session—sixty-seven enrolled in 1949 and sixty in 1950—the enthusiasm of the students did not wane, the quality of the faculty remained high, and the course offerings most attractive.[68] To name the senior fellows and fellows, most of whom taught in one or more of the sessions of the School of English, is to give an almost exhaustive list of the Americans, and some of the British, who were writing significant criticism in the forties: F. O. Matthiessen, John Crowe Ransom, Lionel

Trilling, Jacques Barzun, Eric Bentley, R. P. Blackmur, Cleanth Brooks, Kenneth Burke, Richard Chase, William Empson, Alfred Kazin, L. C. Knights, Robert Lowell, Arthur Mizener, Philip Rahv, Herbert Read, Philip Blair Rice, Mark Schorer, Delmore Schwartz, Allen Tate, Austin Warren, Robert Penn Warren, René Wellek, Basil Willey, Yvor Winters, and Morton D. Zabel.

Everyone was so well pleased with the School of English that when the three-year Rockefeller grant neared its end, Ransom and Charles Coffin began preparing a request for its renewal. On the evening of November 29, 1949, the senior fellows met with John Marshall in New York. Ransom had written Tate on November 17, "We are applying for a renewal of our School of English grant, and probably for a new feature, a Resident Fellow to stay through the year at Kenyon and give a seminar course to a group of School of English students so that they can take an M.A." After the meeting, Ransom reported that "Marshall was enthusiastic about our schemes." When he returned to Gambier he and Coffin prepared a final draft of a proposal intended to insure the continuation of the school for another three-year term. In early December John Marshall came to Gambier to discuss the details of the proposal, and things went so well that Ransom was most optimistic. "It is certain to be approved," he wrote at the end of the conference, but less than a week later his tone was near dejection. "I have a morsel of bad news," he informed some of the fellows, "which you are entitled as members of the Party to know at once." [69] He had just received a letter from President Chalmers saying he "had 'changed his decision' about one of the two halves of our petition to the Foundation: the one about a Resident Fellow and the MA work." Everyone had seemed so agreeable at the meetings in which the final terms of the proposal were approved that Ransom was unable to determine the reasons for this abrupt change of attitude, which came after a "long session of the Senior Fellows at which not an ugly word was said." He did recall, however, that the "president (perhaps in a panic but pleading he was weary with travel) did ask to be excused from the business part of the session." The only reason Chalmers offered for changing his mind was in a somewhat cryptic one-sentence memorandum: "From our discussions of the last several years with respect to the Review and the School of English," Chalmers wrote, "you will remember that I am necessarily concerned that the College itself as it deals with literature shall not be predominantly one thing." Ransom could only assume that Chalmers feared the point of view Ransom represented would come to dominate the English department of the college. "After [Robert] Hillyer's appointment to the College (without the benefit of consulting with the English staff)," Ransom wrote Tate, "he had felt that other literary interests besides my own ought to be represented in the College staff and curriculum."[70] Perhaps, too, Chalmers felt that the method proposed to select the resident fellow—upon the recommendation of the three senior fellows—would "dispute his legal right to make a Presidential appointment." Everything considered, and from the vantage point of hindsight, Ransom could only conclude that Chalmers had left the meeting between the senior fellows and the officials of the Rockefeller Foundation because he "must have decided that he couldn't dictate [to] the School without running into resignations from all the Fellows."

Chalmers' reaction to the request for the renewal of the grant produced several results, some of them immediate. First of all Ransom requested and was given a year's leave, which he spent at Indiana University. "They've been after me for some time," he wrote Arthur Mizener on June 2, 1949, "and I've been there and have some friends, and find this sort of thing the closest to a free sabbatical year I can get." But, as he wrote Tate, there were other reasons.[71] With Philip Blair Rice editing the *Review* for a year so that Ransom would know what life would be like without that assignment, he wanted to get into a large university with an active graduate program in English to see how he "could make out there." Also, as he had expected since he had to withdraw the "more attractive half of our proposal," the Rockefeller Foundation "turned down the plea of the School of English for a renewal," giving as its only reason for denying the request that "this special concentration of critical courses is no longer needed now when the type of thing is so widespread and so universally authorized."[72] Although Chalmers seemed to "want to approach other angels," Ransom knew of no others who were really approachable. Tate suggested the Bollingen and the Old Dominion foundations and Ransom passed the information on to Chalmers, who vetoed the first of these for a "very special reason." "The special thing which C[halmers] wants from Bollingen," Ransom wrote on June 3, 1950, "is to endow my own chair at Kenyon." The amount given by Carnegie, not a "capital fund but an aggregate to be spent," would be exhausted at the end of the 1950/51 academic year, and unless another donor could be found, the college would have to assume the full cost of Ransom's salary, which was considerably greater than anyone else's in the college.

In the spring and early summer, then, Ransom was confronted with two crises. The solution to the first of these seemed easy, for Indiana University had issued a formal invitation for the School of English to come to that campus. Although Ransom personally approved of this move (for he liked very much the people he had met during his year there), he was acutely aware of his responsibilities to the fellows of the School of English; and he felt a deep and abiding sense of loyalty to Kenyon College, especially to its board of trustees, and, despite their personal differences, to President Chalmers. His own future was also complicated by these recent developments. As soon as Chalmers had learned that Carnegie would not renew its grant "to fund the Chair of Poetry," he had assured Ransom that his situation would remain unchanged. But Ransom was disturbed, he wrote Tate on June 3, because he felt he had no business getting more than "my share of salary from the regular Kenyon budget." In a letter to Tate three weeks later, he returned to a more explicit discussion of this subject:

I am very much at sea about my own course. It is embarrassing to know that my salary is more than $2,000 better than anybody else's here, to the best of my information, and that the college budget is extremely straitened now. I wouldn't want to stay, I think, unless I can be taken off the budget, and I won't wait this time so long as I did when the offer from Carolina Woman's College, which you will recall, was up. I have told them at Indiana that I will give them a reply this fall. Having lived a year at Indiana I know I can make out there. In fact it is very nearly a virgin field for building up creative literature and critical studies, and one likes to think he is doing good, especially when one gets well paid for doing it. They gave me a good welcome. And the Graduate seminar was stimulating; I should get a good deal of writing done there, whereas it is easy to slack down at Kenyon. I shouldn't mind dropping the editorship in favor of doing more writing at this stage, though it is not an objective. I suspect that your own teaching and lecturing in new places these past few years has had something to do with your intense activity in writing. Going on here would be nice, I will admit, for this is the best place I have ever lived, but I won't endure very long the consciousness of waiting on while the President is passing the hat to get support for me. I might add one other item, not of extreme importance: at Indiana they retire their professors at 70, at Kenyon 68; and it looks as if I would hold out pretty well to that advanced old age.[73]

Ransom's unsettled state of mind continued through the summer, and he wrote letters to each of the fellows outlining a procedure for determining the fate of the School of English, which by the end of August almost all of them had approved. After much thought he had concluded that the best course of action was as follows: "When Gordon Chalmers says Kenyon can't keep the School, Indiana University will invite all the Fellows to carry on under *their* auspices; no School will exist till the Fellows indicate that they want to go on under Indiana University."[74] At the end of the third session of the school, which Ransom reported as "very fine," Charles Coffin announced "it would open next year in all probability, though not necessarily at Kenyon." When Chalmers returned in early September from his summer in New England, he responded immediately to Ransom's letter, written in late summer,[75] urging him to make his decision on the school as soon as possible "so that if it's not to be at Kenyon the other institution can take over in plenty of time for next summer's arrangements." Chalmers moved so promptly and so decisively that Ransom was afraid, he wrote Tate on September 6, that he might have acted, if not unwisely at least too hastily:

Yesterday the President returned to his office, and called me in for a conference at once; the first time in many years that he hasn't sat back and waited for me to break through the dragon's guard to call on him. I should say he's had a change of heart, somewhat, over the summer; I don't know what has happened. He is apparently anxious to retain me and the School of English too. Wanted to know how long I thought he could decently withhold decision on keeping the School, without imperiling its continuance next summer at Indiana. I said I thought six weeks. . . . I told him that I had the same mind as you did in the matter, if I understood it: I wanted to keep the Review going by remaining at Kenyon if possible, but I was satisfied that the School could be kept going anyhow, either here or at I.U. He seemed much pleased that you wanted me to stay on here with the Review, and very grateful in advance for any move you might make in favor of that event. So should I be; for I am of the same mind as he is in a few events, it would appear. I really am fixed in the determination to leave Kenyon if my salary, in order to remain at its present figure, has to encroach on the general College budget; and I don't know what prospects are. There will have to be an angel, so far as I can see.

Three weeks later, when Chalmers had made no further report, Ransom wrote Professor Richard Hudson of Indiana University that he should have President Herman G. Wells of that institution write immediately asking when a final decision would be reached. By this time Ransom found himself hoping the school would go to Indiana because "GKC is so foolish, and it's too hard for me to be amiable when he discusses the educational idea." On October 27 Chalmers announced that the School of English would not remain at Kenyon, and Ransom went immediately to Bloomington to confer with a "lot of officials and friends" and to reiterate his conviction that the "identity of the school consisted essentially in the commitment of the Fellows to be associated with it." He was much pleased with the reception he received. President Wells immediately promised a $15,000 supplement for the summer of 1951,[76] and the chairman of the English department assured him there would be no change in the management of the school.[77] As soon as he returned to Gambier, he wrote each of the fellows that the Kenyon School of English was moving to Indiana University to become the School of Letters, but the "educational ideal and operation" and the "personnel of the staff" would undergo as few changes as possible. He announced that Austin Warren was replacing the late F. O. Matthiessen as senior fellow and that he and Lionel Trilling would retain their present positions. Already the three senior fellows and President Wells were arranging a "very strong program of courses" to "inaugurate the new tenure of the School at Indiana," and all of the fellows were invited to retain their appointments. The calendar would remain unchanged—a term of forty-five days beginning in mid-June—and the stipend would continue to be $1,500, as it had been for the past two years.[78]

By early November all the fellows but eight had accepted their appointment to the School of Letters, and Ransom was fully engaged in arranging the schedule and employing faculty for the summer of

1951. Richard Hudson came to Gambier for a conference with Charles Coffin, whom he was replacing as director of the school, and he discussed with Ransom the faculty and courses for the first session in Bloomington. The winter issue of the *Review* announced the change of location. Because the "original funds secured for the School of English at Kenyon College," have been exhausted, the notice read, "the College has turned over its interest to Indiana University," which will operate the enterprise as the School of Letters and will maintain the "educational ideal and plan of courses" and the "staff of Fellows and Senior Fellows" that were "in effect at Kenyon." Correspondence with Tate, Mizener, Francis Fergusson, and others indicates that Ransom remained very much in charge of the operation. "What about giving another course in 1951?" he asked Tate on November 20; "I guess I'll be back with a course, I have to be if a Senior Fellow is to be on hand. Fergusson will give a course and Mizener. Bentley wants to come in; and really I'd like to wait to hear from you before answering him; if you will come for 1951 we'd leave him out, and it would be better for us if you should come." Ransom was well pleased with the way "things are shaping up," particularly with the fact that "Dick Hudson really has things in hand at I.U."

During the Thanksgiving holidays Tate telephoned Ransom to accept the appointment and to discuss possible course offerings. Since Tate was very much involved in the speculations that would result in his distinction between the "symbolic" and the "angelic" imaginations, he proposed a course in Dante and Poe. At first Ransom could see no significant relationship between these two poets, and his reaction to Tate's suggestion was not enthusiastic. Tate immediately sent a detailed explanation of his idea, to which Ransom responded: "Upon reading your letter and thinking things over, [it] seems to me we'd want exactly the subject you preferred: Dante and Poe; and your sub-title explains what might not at first thought appear to be a connection between these authors." [79] A few weeks later, when Austin Warren agreed to offer a course, Ransom wrote Tate that since only one senior fellow was required for each session he thought he would "withdraw for this year," engage Eric Bentley, and attempt to do some writing. By midwinter Richard Hudson sent out official notices announcing the first session of the Indiana School of Letters with a

faculty composed of Eric Bentley, Francis Fergusson, Arthur Mizener, Philip Rahv, Philip Blair Rice, Delmore Schwartz, Allen Tate,
and Austin Warren.[80]

At the end of the 1951 session, Ransom asked each of the teaching
fellows to report his reactions to the first summer at Indiana. Before
leaving Bloomington the teaching fellows met and appointed Tate
their spokesman. On August 7 he sent his formal report to Ransom.
"The School was a great success," he wrote; the "morale of the students was high." The "staff worked beautifully together," and "we may
well feel satisfaction with the general results." The criticisms he and
the others had to make came in three areas: 1) As director, Richard
Hudson was not nearly as effective as Charles Coffin had been. "Not
even the minimum of the daily routine went off well. . . . The weekly
public lectures and forums seemed entirely too much for him; the
announced lecture room was invariably changed at the last minute,
but no effort was made to notify the students; and the air-
conditioning was not turned on for the first four lectures." Because he
had employed his wife, "an amiable and intelligent woman," as his
secretary, the "daily routine of the School" was not properly super-
vised; out of loyalty to her husband she was so much "concerned with
his situation" that she could not discharge efficiently those responsibilities that logically fell to her. 2) If possible, Ransom should be
present at every session. As senior fellow, Austin Warren was not as
effective as he might have been. His criticisms "were almost always
good, but his manner was deplorable. He buzzed all over the place
performing his 'apostolic' duties. . . . All his activities were conducted
in a cloud of ecclesiastical analogy." 3) The third area of discontent
probably accounted in large part for the first two. Everyone at the
school, both faculty and students, was very much aware that Bloomington was not Gambier. At Kenyon the School of English was about
the only activity of the summer, and almost the whole of the administration's attention was devoted to that enterprise. But the School
of Letters was only one of many educational programs on the
crowded schedule of a summer session of a large state university.
Since the "situation at Bloomington is wholly different from that at
Gambier," the "simple organization" which had operated the school
must be "somewhat elaborated." Rather than three senior fellows,

there should be five, with Ransom being the "senior Senior Fellow" and bearing "title of Provost or at least Chairman." One senior fellow should be in residence during each term so that he and "small committees," to be appointed by the senior fellows from the fellows in residence at a specific time, could assist the director in his routine dealings with the department of English and appropriate officials of the university administration. This committee could also function in other areas, such as recruiting students, organizing forums and public lectures, and attempting to secure funds from foundations. This recommendation would reduce "Hudson's work to that of registrar; this seems highly desirable."

Ransom knew that Tate's suggestions were offered for the purpose of improving the School of Letters, and he acted upon them immediately. "I'm going to Bloomington shortly," he wrote on August 18, "to go right into the matter of Hudson's conduct of office, though I think the way to do that is frankly and unsparingly but at the same time as a friend." Ransom did talk to him, and with the approval of Lionel Trilling and Austin Warren, had Allen Tate and Philip Rahv appointed to the board of senior fellows. The following summer Ransom was himself in residence at Bloomington, and Hudson's management of his responsibilities was so much improved that he wrote Tate he did not know "another man there who can equally handle the office." Consequently, when Hudson's term expired and he was appointed for another term of two years, Ransom indicated his enthusiastic approval.

The excellent arrangements he was able to make for the continuation of the School of Letters and the assurance he had from Gordon Chalmers that the *Kenyon Review* would not cease publication convinced Ransom that he should remain in Gambier. "We are especially benefitted, I believe, by the willingness of the agents of foreign writers to deal with us now.... Formerly the ... returns from publication here did not attract them." [81]

With his own future settled and the continuation of the *Review* assured, Ransom turned to his "small symposium of selected expressions on the general topic of criticism."

After Ransom's review of Stanley Edgar Hyman's *The Armed Vision* [82] was completed, he showed it to Phil Rice and a few others around the office. Rice requested permission, which Ransom granted, to send it out to a few critics for their reactions and for additional comments on the state of criticism generally. "Mr. Ransom's statement," Rice pointed out, "has seemed provocative to several people who have seen it," and as a part of its tenth birthday celebration the *Review* "is inviting half a dozen persons to send ... 1000 words or so ... on the topic" for the winter issue. Ransom had opened his assessment of Hyman's reaction to the "New Criticism" with a statement that "criticism of such intensiveness and earnestness" as that discussed by Hyman "did not exist on any substantial scale in our language till now." What we call tradition is the "aggregate of the secrets," the "skills" and the "know-hows," and the motivations behind the "primitive and largely unconscious behaviors which men practised before the industrial revolution." Unlike R. P. Blackmur, Ransom had concluded after much thought and indecision, that psychology, sociology, and anthropology are the most effective means of studying the plight of man in a mechanized society. When sentiments, those "warm quick responses to certain 'precious objects,'" decay, or when they are received with cynicism or suspicion, techinical sociology is invented. There was no need for the New Criticism until "the sentimental and primitive bases of literature" had become so badly deteriorated that they could not function. A new kind of criticism is essential today, however, because the modern writer has no idea of "what he can build on" and present-day readers have no understanding of the old literature.

Four critics responded—William Barrett, R. P. Blackmur, Richard Chase, and Allen Tate—and their statements were published in the next issue.[83] During the past twenty years, Barrett argued, criticism has sought a new autonomy. Attempting to "cut out clearly his own province within literature," a certain kind of critic has begun to "cut himself off from literature." The result is that some criticism is written for its own sake and not as a means of sharing with the reader the experiences of creative literature. The "New Criticism," which Ransom "has gathered together and firmed up in the *Kenyon Review* over the last ten years," Blackmur said, has dealt with "what could be felt at work in poetry, and has done so by a variety of methods with an eye on a variety of values." In the decade ahead he would like to see the same kind of attention given to fiction. One way to understand the intentions of the New Critic and to appreciate the values of his work, Richard Chase wrote, is to contrast his performance with that of the "Ordealist Critic," such as Van Wyck Brooks, or the "general culture" critic, such as Edmund Wilson. Both are more interested in presenting the "suffering or failure of the artist and his estrangement from society" than in evaluating the books he has written. Allen Tate commented on the contributions made by Ransom and the *Kenyon Review* to the critical revolution of the past two decades. Not only did Ransom "create its myth by giving it a name" but some of the best examples of formal criticism to appear in the past ten years were published in the review he edited. Ransom's "great and actual service" to the critics of his generation, however, was "his own restless exploration of the grounds of criticism and his hospitality to other writers of various points of view who have produced evidence of being seriously engaged." If there are sides to take, in Ransom's controversy with Blackmur, however, Tate would take Blackmur's, since he seemed committed to no particular method. "There can be no end," Tate concluded, "to the permutations of the critical relation to literature, philosophy and religion." The New Criticism offers "as many permutations as criticism in the past has offered." There are many of the so-called New Critics and the work of each is unlike anyone else's. As interesting as these four statements are—and they all make an important point in limited space—their major significance, perhaps, is that they serve as a prelude to a more ambitious series entitled "My Credo (A Symposium of Criticism)," to which ten critics would contribute, in three issues of the magazine the following year.

The Summer, 1948, issue of the *Sewanee Review*, which under the able editorship of J. E. Palmer was stronger than it had ever been, was primarily devoted to a tribute to Ransom on his sixtieth birthday. Any doubts of his place in American letters should have been dispelled by this gesture—one of the most distinguished literary quarterlies in the country devoting an entire issue to assessing the literary merits of a living writer. The stature of the men who contributed and the quality of their comment were equally noteworthy.[84] Although almost everyone noted Ransom's contributions as poet, critic, and editor, most of the essays were primarily concerned with the poetry. Before moving to his primary interest, a conviction that Ransom's meager output had denied his poetry the attention it deserved, Donald A. Stauffer attempted to place the "gentleman from Ohio" among his contemporaries. A "cartoonist, making a literary-critical map of the United States," he contended, "would undoubtedly draw in the suave, white-haired, self-contained figure of Mr. Ransom sitting on his hill at Kenyon. This geographical region would allow the artist considerable room to outline a portrait, and justice would compel a good-sized figure if he wanted to sketch the state of our criticism and poetry in fair proportions."[85] Although Ransom's primary interest in criticism is in the "metaphysics of aesthetics," he carefully avoids "swollen systems of thought" and even "phrases in technical jargon." His thought often seems easier and simpler than it is because of the clarity and simplicity with which it is expressed. Because of the "selective precision of his approach to literary criticism," Ransom clearly "deserves an order of merit." As well known as his criticism is (and it has received only a portion of the "attention it warrants"), Ransom is best known, perhaps, for his "long performance of one of the most arduous, unrewarding, and necessary jobs in the field of literature: the editing of a thoughtful literary quarterly."[86] It is as poet, finally, that Ransom has not been "rightly valued." His poetry offers "excellent material to help a young poet learn his art," for although "inspiration cannot be taught . . . craftsmanship can." The poems, in spite of textual richness, show an unusual stability, and, like objects, they are solid and fixed so that if one looks long enough and hard enough, he can sometimes "see some of the strokes that make them."[87]

Although their focus was on specific qualities of Ransom's verse, both Cleanth Brooks and F. O. Matthiessen commented more generally on his achievement as poet. In the finest of his poems, Brooks wrote, there "is a triumph of tone, a special ordering of the poet's attitude toward his material, a liberation of the elected poem from the particular and accidental emotions of the poet as man rather than as artist." In contemporary poetry there is nothing like this quality of Ransom's. Even the method of Wallace Stevens, that "special master of perspective and of tone," is "perhaps much more special and more limited than Ransom's." None of his contemporaries has produced a "poetry so fine grained, so agate hard, so tough minded."[88] After discussing the usefulness of "good minor art" and indicating that Ransom's poetry was an "almost perfect instance" of what is implied by the term, Matthiessen defended the severe limitations Ransom had placed on his production. His *Selected Poems,* Matthiessen said, contain all of his principal themes, but several of the poems omitted from the collection "could take their stand with the best work in any representative modern anthology." In his critical pieces Ransom has argued that a "poem must be an act of knowing" and all of his best poems "afford us a singularly whole experience." What he wanted to say, maybe all he had to say, he has said "in a form uniquely his own."[89]

Wallace Stevens placed Ransom in mythical Tennessee, a place characterized chiefly by its vitality, its "raciness."[90] Ransom's poetic response to such a place is not from acquired knowledge, from "the books he has read," the "academies he has seen," the "halls and columns and carvings on the columns." Instead, his approach is defined by an awareness of this reality as "an affair of fundamental life," and his response is as far removed as possible from learned analogy and acquired metaphor. In short, Ransom is a successful fictionist, a poet capable of creating out of the flux of existence a reality of things "not as they are, as we should like them to be." But no one in this special *Sewanee Review* issue came closer to identifying the highly individualized tone of Ransom's poetry, than his former student and colleague, Randall Jarrell:

Ransom seems in his poems, as most modern poets do not, sympathetic and charming, full of tenderness and affection, wanting the light and sorry for the dark—moral and condemning only when he has to be, not because he wants to be; loving neither the sterner vices nor the sterner virtues.He has the personal seriousness that treats the world as it seems to him, not the solemnity that treats the really important things, the world as everybody knows it is. His poems are full of an affection that cannot help itself, for an innocence that cannot help itself—for the stupid travelers lost in the maze of the world, the clever travelers lost in the maze of the world.[91]

There is no doubt, Jarrell concluded, of the position Ransom should and will occupy among American poets: "It is only fair to say that Ransom is one of the best, most original, and most sympathetic poets alive; and it is easy to see that his poetry will always be cared for, since he has written poems that are perfectly realized and occasionally almost perfect—poems that the hypothetical generations of the future will be reading page by page with Wyatt, Campion, Marvell, and Mother Goose."

As he neared the end of his active career as editor and teacher, surely Ransom was aware that he was held in highest esteem by his fellow artists throughout the country, although his natural modesty precluded any acknowledgment of this fact even to his closest friends. He was best known, perhaps, as editor of the *Kenyon Review,* which was regarded as one of the most significant literary quarterlies ever published in this country. By the end of World War II this journal, as Howard Nemerov has said, "was there—so solidly there" that he and others of his generation thought "it had been there since at least the Civil War." To appear in its pages was regarded as irrefutable proof that the young poet or critic had genuine talent, if not pure genius. Many students, younger teachers, and novice poets, novelists, and critics were convinced that the literary center of the country was Gambier, not only because of the *Review* but because there in one or another of the sessions of the School of English everyone they regarded as important was sure to appear. After the publication of the special issue of the *Sewanee Review,* who could doubt that in the opinion of his peers Ransom possessed a poetic gift of unquestionable merit, one almost completely realized? Had not some of the most highly respected critics and men of letters in the country argued most convincingly that neither the meager quantity of poetry produced nor the limited circulation it had received should be regarded as a measure of its excellence? Anyone at all familiar with the development of American criticism over the two decades just past—two of the richest in American literary history—would know, too, that Ransom's speculations on the nature and uses of poetry were both original and valuable; his inquiries into the "place of the work of art in the total moral and psychic experience," as Tate has pointed out, were unlike those of any other American critic. Now, after a five-year lull in which he had published little because of the demands of the School of English, Ransom was entering his last decade of teaching and editing, a period in which some of his finest criticism would appear.

An Important Force in Human Affairs 1950-1959

By THE LATE 1940s Ransom was convinced that the age of criticism which for the past twenty-five years had produced critical writing of "unusual quality" and "extraordinary quantity" was in a state of crisis. Perhaps the interest in literary theory and practice which for more than two decades had attracted the "best minds in the academy" was declining because the critical writing, "more intense than a language has ever known," had served its purpose and the literary world awaited another great creative surge like that which followed World War I.[1] Much of the best critical writing of the thirties and forties was the result of the fact that the literary artists of the twenties were so "far ahead of their public that they employed critics for a whole generation before the public could have comfortable possession of them." The literature produced in that decade, and the years immediately before and after, was both "ingenious and sophisticated," and almost "discontinuous with the literature to which we were accustomed." Through "devoted industry," however, the critics had defined and mastered most of the literary masterpieces of this extraordinarily rich period and made them available to the entire literary community.[2] If one need had been met, at least temporarily, two others—of equal importance if literature were to remain an important force in human affairs—were very much evident. The critics must continue their evaluations of the older literatures in the light of modern standards—the series of "Reconsiderations" Ransom had run in the *Kenyon Review* during the mid-forties is an example of the sort of thing he had in mind[3]—and they must intensify their studies of the "structural techniques of fiction," the "diction and tropology of poetry," and the "metaphysics of literature." The critic should assist the general reader in understanding the human purpose that drives him into the literary world of fantasy and imagination. To accomplish this essential purpose, the critic must help the reader to perceive the reality of literary form, to become aware of the unique nature of the poem or story, of how the "precious object" really functions.

In spite of the undeniable accomplishments of this new criticism, which had achieved a linguistic revolution in the reading of poetry with its emphasis on the total connotation of words, it had not fulfilled all the expectations it aroused. In an attempt to derive from a poem all the meanings that it could possibly embody, the critic had discovered that it had a "kind of centrifugal energy, whereby its meaning expands with a little encouragement, and can be followed by the sympathetic imagination":

The detailed phrase is honored with the spread of its own meaning, though this meaning may be away from that of the poem as a whole. And the critic goes straight from one detail to another, in the manner of the bee who gathers honey from the several blossoms as he comes to them, without noticing the bush which supports all the blossoms. The poem is more generous than the bush in its capacity for bearing blossoms which are not alike but widely varied, in size, fragrance, hue, and shape. So poetry has waited for our age to recognize and publish a sort of irresponsible exuberance in the energy of its materials, which constantly imperils its sober order.[4]

Some of the modern critics have tended to create an impression of poetry's disorder because they are "careless of the theoretical constitution of poetry." They have made their readers aware of many "exciting turns of poetic language," but they have not revealed the poem's true nature. The new criticism has discovered additional meanings in the poetic texts, but it has not insisted on poetry as the source of "perennial human values."

Perhaps, as George Lanning suggests, Ransom's enthusiasm for the kind of criticism he had called for ten years before had waned, or "the pleasure in victory had palled";[5] nevertheless he was eager to publish in the *Kenyon Review* an adequate tribute to this age of criticism, for which he and his journal had been primarily responsible. In the Winter, 1950, number, therefore, he announced an important new series to complement the symposium on "The Critic's Business" which had appeared the previous year. "An important series of critical pronouncements [is] to begin shortly," the announcement began; "leading critics who represent diverse points of view will write essays defending their respective credos." Since the editors think "it will be a public service for the critics to write without restriction upon the basic values they find in literature" and, especially, to present their conception of "the critic's business," the critics' responses will not be restricted by previously submitted sets of questions. About the only instructions Ransom gave to the critics invited to contribute to the series, therefore, were that the credo be composed "with great scruple" and that it make "philosophical (ethical, social, aesthetic, formal, etc.) commitments about the demands" each critic makes on literature and the "proper and improper varieties of criticism."[6] His plan, he wrote each prospective contributor, was to run the series to a dozen or so entries and then to turn all of the essays over to a book publisher. He was thinking of a volume to complement *The Kenyon Critics,* a selection of the best critical pieces from the *Kenyon Review* which Ransom had compiled the previous year. The publishers were already asking him for a sequel, and he was convinced that specific and concrete statements of principles and beliefs by the leading critics of England and America would be both timely and important.

Almost everyone whom Ransom invited to contribute submitted an essay, and the number for Autumn, 1950, carried the first four pieces: Leslie Fiedler's "Toward an Amateur Criticism," Herbert Read's "The Critic as Man of Feeling," Richard Chase's "Art, Nature, Politics," and William Empson's "The Verbal Analysis." Although Ransom was pleased with this beginning, he was concerned that the views of the New Critics be adequately represented. Ransom wrote Tate as soon as copy for the autumn issue had gone to press: "You will see that we much need some old-line new-critic credos, and most of all that means you, as I see it. We have credos coming up immediately from Northrop Frye and Cleanth, promised from Trilling and Rahv, whom I will jog right away. I think also of asking Spender (who has turned conservative enough, and is a sort of Shelley when it comes to his view of poetry, with emphasis on spontaneity and creative imagination); he's finished as a poet, I should think, but has a distinction in his prose, always something fresh." [7] Ransom planned to solicit essays from Randall Jarrell and/or Arthur Mizener, and Francis Fergusson, if he will "expound his sense of literature as proceeding under religious auspices, in which he is pretty close kin to Eliot." Although the papers Ransom had received so far were "very serious," "carefully composed," and "much beyond our expectations," he urged Tate "to set about a credo of your own, if you will, and as soon as you can." [8]

Brooks's essay, which arrived just in time to be included in the issue for Winter, 1951, must have relieved Ransom's fear that the New Critical point of view would not be adequately represented. Entitled "The Formalist Critic," the essay opens with an attempt to present the basic principles upon which this loosely knit group of critics would agree: literary criticism is a "description and evaluation of its object"; its primary concern is with unity, "the kind of whole which the literary work forms or fails to form," and the relationship of the parts to the whole; the formal relations in a literary work may include, but will certainly exceed, those of logic; form and content may not be separated; literature is metaphorical and symbolic; the general and universal are reached in literature through the concrete and particular. In the same issue the point of view of the historical scholar-critic was represented by Douglas Bush's "The Humanist Critic" and that of the mythopoeic critic by Northrop Frye's "The Archetypes of Literature." The series was concluded in the following issue with Stephen Spender's "On the Functions of Criticism," Arthur Mizener's "Not in Cold Blood," and Austin Warren's "The Teacher as Critic."

These brief critical pieces, as well as the exacting standard Ransom set for the essays the *Review* normally carried, moved the *Times Literary Supplement* to proclaim on August 29, 1952, that in "American literary life today the critic has a dominant role." In Great Britain there is no equivalent for the literary magazine like the *Kenyon Review* which devotes at least three quarters of its space to criticism. These quarterlies (others mentioned are *Sewanee* and *Hudson*) "keep up a very high and serious standard," and are "receptive to new trends in creative writing" as well as in criticism. Because they represent the "cultural tendencies of the various contrasting regions in the United States," they serve to prevent a complete concentration of literary and publishing activities in New York. Ransom and the other contributors to the *Kenyon Review* have attempted to vindicate the "fruitful obscurities and complexities" of twentieth-century literature and to "create a model for the American literary sensibility." In both of these undertakings, the article concludes, "Mr. Ransom and his colleagues have succeeded admirably." [9]

One reason, and perhaps the most significant one, that Ransom was able to maintain the quality of the essays he published in the period immediately after World War II was the fact that he paid reasonable rates to contributors. His hopes of continuing to publish this kind of magazine were destroyed, however, when the Rockefeller Foundation refused to renew the grant out of which he had supplemented payments to contributors. With great reluctance, therefore, he was forced to invite all the authors whose work he had accepted for future publication "to recover their *MSS*" if they wished. "We want the Poe," he wrote Allen Tate on March 18, 1952, "but don't hesitate to take it elsewhere if you need the money. Our feelings can't be hurt under the circumstances." Three weeks later, however, he wrote that he and Phil Rice had misunderstood a communication from Charles B. Fahs, director of the Division of the Humanities of the Rockefeller Foundation. What had been "regarded as a final brushoff" by everyone at Kenyon, including Gordon Chalmers, was not intended thus. "They have given us a broad hint," he wrote, "to make them another proposition which won't involve direct subsidy to contributors but will give us the money, which we then spend on contributors." [10] All accepted manuscripts could be paid for at the usual rates because the foundation had given a small "tide-over grant" to assist in this area until a new request could be approved.

The preparation and presentation of the new proposal were expedited considerably because Edward F. D'Arms, a friend of Phil Rice from their Oxford days and now an associate director of the humanities division of the foundation, indicated the "kind of proposition" likely to receive support. The new program, one of the most successful administered by the *Review* under Ransom's editorship, was announced on October 1, 1952. For each of the next three years a *Kenyon Review* fellowship would be offered to a poet, a writer of fic-

tion, and a critic. The purpose of the fellowships, the official announcement stated, "is to free some distinguished younger writers, at
least in part, from the burden of working for a livelihood while they
develop fresh literary projects of their own." A fellow would receive
$2,000 if single and $3,000 if married. No publication was required
and the fellow could work on his project as and where he pleased. In
addition to the stipends to the fellows, the foundation awarded $4,800
each year for administrative expenses. Since it is understood, a footnote to the 1952/53 budget of the *Kenyon Review* explained, "that we
can assimilate the expense of administering the new Fellowships without much extra cost . . . the bulk of the gift will be devoted to maintaining the rate of payment to contributors."

The qualifications of the fellow were specifically stated. Although
it was conceivable that a fellowship would be awarded to a writer to
permit him "to continue a work which he has already perfected and
with which he is publicly identified," the selectors would likely be
more favorably impressed with the project of the "writer who has a
great deal to his credit already" and "is entering upon a new phase of
his literary career." The committee could not "foresee the possibility
of considering the writer who has little or nothing to show in print"
because it would "want solid evidence that he is an able writer in the
first place and then consider his new program on its own merits and
more informally." Following his usual procedure, however, Ranson
did not depend upon the formal announcement to achieve the results
he desired. Although an official notice appeared in the *Review* and
several hundred circulars were mailed, many with handwritten messages from Ransom, he also wrote personal letters to Allen Tate,
Caroline Gordon, Cleanth Brooks, Robert Penn Warren, Lionel Trilling, Arthur Mizener, and dozens of others, asking that they make
specific recommendations. Many of those finally selected were
suggested by these persons—Flannery O'Connor, for example, was
proposed by Caroline Gordon and Andrew Lytle by Robert Penn
Warren.

The first *Kenyon Review* fellows were announced on January 20,
1953, and this group, like all succeeding ones, included some of the
most promising young writers in America. The fellow in criticism was
Irving Howe, whose books on Sherwood Anderson and William

Faulkner had already appeared and who proposed to work on the
political novel in America. In fiction the award went to Flannery
O'Connor, whose novel *Wise Blood* had just been published but whose
short stories had been appearing in the literary quarterlies for six or
eight years. She proposed to work on a second novel. The fellowship
in poetry was given to Edwin Watkins, a 1945 graduate of Kenyon
whose career was just getting underway. The *Review* was honored to
be the first magazine to sponsor fellowships designed to free a few
writers from the burden of earning a living while they pursued literary goals, and Ransom was extremely pleased with the first recipients,
anyone of whom "may become a top figure in American letters of our
time."[11]

Subsequent awards under this first grant were given to persons of
equal promise and distinction,[12] and the foundation thought the program so successful that it was renewed for a second term and the
number of fellows was increased to four. The stipends were raised to
$2,700 for an unmarried and $4,000 for a married fellow, and grants
were made to establish similar programs to be administered by the
Hudson Review, the *Sewanee Review,* and the *Partisan Review.* For a
period of three years, then, these four quarterlies participated in
a nationwide program of literary fellowships which contributed in a
most tangible way to their common goal of maintaining literary standards and encouraging and developing new talent. A list of the names
of the young writers who participated in this program includes many
of those who were considered most prominent in the sixties.[13] For six
years (1953–1958), nearly twenty-five of the most gifted young
writers in America could devote extended periods of time to their
writing because their stipends as *Kenyon Review* fellows freed them
temporarily from the necessity of having to earn a living. Many
of the productions coming out of this newly acquired leisure went
to the *Kenyon Review,* to which the writers might have felt some obligation, though none was even remotely suggested by the terms of their
grants.[14] Contributions from those sources, added to others attracted
by the rate of pay, enabled Ransom to maintain during the last years of
his editorship a journal unsurpassed either in England or the United
States. If the criticism seemed to have lost some of the vigor that had
established it as the most significant appearing in English, the reason,

perhaps, was that the New Criticism had accomplished its purpose. The New Critics' basic attitudes toward literature had been so widely diffused that by this time they were being expounded in literature classes across America. The quality of the fiction was as high as it had ever been, and although there was little poetry as good as that published by Wallace Stevens and Allen Tate a few years earlier, some of the most significant poets a generation or two younger than they were establishing their reputations by publishing regularly in the pages of the *Kenyon Review*.[15]

During the last days of Ransom's editorship the *Review* still occupied rooms in the basement of Ascension Hall, an old building which then also contained offices for most of the administrators of the college and classrooms for the liberal arts courses. George Lanning describes what he calls the "squalor from which the magazine emerged":

The business office was on the east side of a hallway that transected the floor from north to south, and looked out on a parking lot.... The editorial office was across the hall and down two doors. Because the basement was below ground level on that side of the building, Mr. Ransom's windows faced into a mossy stone well [*sic*]. The room was dark and cheerless, and on gloomy winter days oppressive.... Along one wall of this office was a blackboard on which the contents for the next issue were written out, together with reminders, notes on assignments and possible projects, and so on....
Across the hall from Mr. Ransom was the office of the philosophy department, and here his managing editor, Philip Blair Rice, had a desk. I suppose, then, you might say the *Review* had two and a half rooms for itself.
They were terrible rooms. In winter, heat passed without pause through the overhead pipes, and in summer damp and mustiness prevailed. The whitewashed pipes clanked and shook in the cold, and in warm weather were beaded with moisture. To stay in either office for long was to collect so many flecks of whitewash that you appeared to have unmelted snow in your hair. In both offices were double desks whose drawers had to be wrenched open in wet or humid weather— that is, from April to November—and often stayed shut despite the most profane and enraged tuggings.[16]

It was in this setting that Ransom received the hundreds of manuscripts from which the poems, stories, and essays, except those com-

missioned in advance, were selected for each issue of the *Review*.
Many of these manuscripts he gave a preliminary reading, and those
he thought worthy of consideration for publication he passed on to
Phil Rice for his reaction. Those obviously unsuitable for his needs
were returned with a printed rejection notice. These notices sometimes
provoked reactions which Ransom thought worthy of depositing in
the "crank file" he kept in a cabinet behind his desk, even though he
did not always have time to respond to them personally. "You mean
despicable snobs," one disappointed would-be contributor wrote on
the back of the notice and returned it to Ransom; "I send you 6 poems
that took 8 months to compose and this is all you can write. Did it take
you 5 minutes to peruse these 8 months of travail? Don't you Philistines have any feelings at all? Please answer." Another, who signed
himself the Poet Laureate of South Carolina, responded: "I . . . realize
you are adverse [*sic*] to anything traditional. Thirty-three of my books
of poetry have been published and all have been swiftly sold. I confess
a tendency to communicate with my reader." One man was so dis-
gruntled when he received the rejection slip that he bundled everything up, poems and notice, and returned them to Ransom with this
message: "Let's forget the whole thing. If you guys are willing to
pretend I never sent you a manuscript, so am I. I have a rule of my
own, which is never to buy round-trip tickets for my work. If you
don't want it, neither do I."

Many of the rejected manuscripts were returned with a personal
note, copies of many of which were kept, especially during the years
when with the help of foundation support the *Review* was able to
employ a professional secretary. Although many of these responses
were phrased in language that was at best ambiguous and at times
very nearly double-talk, the contributor usually had little doubt that
his manuscript had been rejected, though he might not always know
exactly why. "Thank you for sending us these terse and strong little
poems of character and situation," Ransom wrote to one poet; "sometimes they get a little difficult to follow. . . . I hope you will send to us
again." To another, he wrote: "Here is a poem you sent us sometime
ago. It's nice but not definitive, in the sense that it makes us acquainted sufficiently with the poet or his way of working." And to
another: "You have a fine gift of tongues but some of these poems

have a little epical 'crisis' or miraculous feature in them, which is a little hard for me to take in a small poem."

Much of the correspondence of the years of Ransom's tenure was destroyed by later editors of the *Review*;[17] that which remains clearly demonstrates, however, his desire to respond personally to all serious writers who sent him material to consider for publication. Some of these rejections were certainly difficult for him since he was declining to publish material from writers whose ability he respected, many of whom were his closest personal friends. On February 18, 1950, he wrote Caroline Gordon that he was returning a story to her. In spite of the fact that it was "well constructed and had a great deal of force and vividness," he had decided not to publish it because he had showed it to a "couple of veterans," one a younger member of the faculty, who agreed with him that the two main themes of the story had been overworked: "the recurrence of wartime violence in a veteran's conduct under stress, and the contrast between a man's adequacy to the demands of combat and his inadequacy to the situations of civilian life." His younger colleagues had also pointed out that "your picture of student life, and some of your dialogue, is more suitable to the Fitzgerald era than to this queer one." At about the same time he returned a chapter of a novel to Brainard Cheney with this explanation: "I think it too brief and summary by itself to make a good unit of narrative. I have the feeling that the attitudes and emotions of the lady, in being presented so briefly, have necessarily been exaggerated, or at least presented too harshly to make her a sympathetic character for the reader to adopt. The moral seems somehow too cut and dried."[18] When he returned "A Circle of Fire" to Flannery O'Connor, she responded in the manner that one aware of the seriousness with which she regarded her art would expect. Ransom had suggested that the action appeared to ramble, that "Mrs. Pritchard seemed too dominant and completely overshadowed Mrs. Cope," but that "you have the makings here of one of your best stories." O'Connor revised the story and returned it, thanking him for sending it back and commenting that although she had not "completely overhauled it" she had "reduced Mrs. Pritchard's remarks, shortened the action and tried to realize the character of Mrs. Cope better."[19] She was convinced that she was returning a better story, but if he was not pleased with it she hoped he would send it back again for "this is the only way I'll ever learn anything." In fact while revising this story she had discovered something that concerned her and she asked his advice. She was rather isolated, she wrote, as far as having someone to give her technical advice about her stories, because Robert Fitzgerald was in Siena, the Tates in Rome, and "nobody in Milledgeville [has] read anything since 'Eneas Africanus.'" She had noticed, she wrote, that at one point she had gone into Mrs. Cope's mind, and she "had been trying not to get in anybody's mind but to use the child once in a while for an observer, the rest of the time leaving it to the omniscient narrator." Ransom thought the story much improved, accepted it for publication with no further changes, and O'Connor apparently forgot the inconsistency in point of view.

The next year, in response to an inquiry from Andrew Lytle, Ransom asked to see a portion of *The Velvet Horn,* the novel on which Lytle was working at the time; Ransom also encouraged Lytle to have his students submit their good fiction, for the *Review* had difficulty getting "fiction of any distinction." Some of the stories it received "aim at distinction" but "that's about the best we can say for them." A remarkable exception, he wrote, is Miss O'Connor's "A Circle of Fire" in the issue for Spring, 1954, which he thought "first-rate" and "almost as good as the one we published from her last year, the best story I've seen in years." Lytle sent a long section of the novel, which Ransom reluctantly rejected and which subsequently appeared in the *Sewanee Review.* [20] When the book appeared, dedicated to Ransom, he read it and wrote immediately: "I should say, editorially, that our 1956 Fellow in Fiction has just about proffered as the fruit of Fellowship the finest achievement we have had. I can see now how mistaken I was in not using that magnificent section we had a chance at, in the course of the composition a good while back. I'd say that your novel is a series of lyrical and dramatic achievements, on a base of philosophic attitude founded on the sense of nature and the paradoxes of sex, and grounded firmly in history and the old (and maybe timeless) South." [21]

The most difficult letter of rejection he had to write, he informed Tate, was one to Robert Penn Warren declining a section of *Band of Angels* and the response he had from Warren, which was both temperate and respectful, did not completely relieve his feeling that he had acted out of personal bias and had not exercised good literary judgment. He was reluctant to send the manuscript back, not because of friendship for he knew Warren "would not be affected by that angle of the matter," but because he felt so uncertain in judging fiction since "I've done so little in that field myself." Warren attempted to reassure him:

You have to go by such lights as are in you, and I should be the last man to deny it since I have gone so much by your lights, as I was able to read them. Naturally I'm sorry that you can't use the chapter. But thank you for the quick decision. I have done a little toning down this week before the thing goes to the printer at Random House, but not enough, I am sure, to affect your feelings—verbal for the most part, and taking out one or two of the most shocking details. . . . But, of course, in the early draft I had toned down the facts so much it was already looking as though a flock of leeches had been working on a consumptive with leukemia.[22]

Ransom's reaction to *Band of Angels* really represented a dissatisfaction with Warren's fiction that had begun with *All the King's Men* and become more firmly entrenched with each subsequent novel. After reading *World Enough and Time,* he wrote Tate:

When Red and Cleanth were together, it was clear (as we many times felt) that Red supplied the ideas; but now it becomes clear, I think, that Cleanth supplied good stern moral principle, and that both of them suffer now that their relationship has been broken up. I think Red's book is pretty horrible. It's like Tom Wolfe except that it's less consistent. Red's philosophy seems now to justify the guilt of his heroes (he never had much heroines) on the ground that they are implicated in the Universal Guilt. It makes him philosophize sententiously about Truth, Innocence, Justice, and what not. All that I feared from the ambiguities of *All the King's Men* has come out strong and clear in this volume, where there's no ambiguity at all. It's most depressing. How can Red be the soul of honor personally (as I still feel sure he is) and dally with the themes he does in his fictions? . . . I can't but think that Red is going to take a serious panning from the serious critics.
There's just one honest man in Red's book, the one who assisted with the defense of the hero at court, and he isn't *realized.*[23]

A few months after this letter was written Ransom was in Washington for a meeting at the Library of Congress. One evening after a particularly busy day he and Warren met in the bar of the hotel where Ransom was staying and talked until 1:30, when, as he wrote Tate from Gambier, "they put us out. It was the best talk I've had with him in ten years. . . . In his personal convictions, 'philosophy of life,' etc., Red is all right, and better than his books. I think it's not quite in Red to assume responsibility for his books. But I was mighty pleased to find him in private unchanged." A part of Warren's difficulty, he was convinced, was that fiction was not his best genre, and Ransom was unhappy that his old friend and former student was neglecting poetry to bring out novel after novel. As the poems later collected in *Promises: Poems, 1954–56*, appeared in the quarterlies, Ransom read them and praised them in letters to many of his correspondents. In the winter of 1952, Warren came by Gambier on his way to Kentucky to visit his father who was ill. While he was there, he showed Ransom a section of *Brother to Dragons*, on which he was working at the time, and Ransom was delighted. "Red is in very fine fettle," he wrote Tate; "he is doing a long poem, a real epic of Kentucky; better, I think, than any of his novels unless the first one."[24] Before it appeared in book form, Ransom published more than a hundred pages of the poem in a single issue of the *Review*, and he broke down the dummy of a later number after it was set and at the printer's in order to be able to use a section of *Promises: Poems, 1954–56* before the book was issued.

As Ransom's long tenure at Kenyon neared its end, he and Robb continued to live quietly in the rambling old eleven-room campus house they had occupied for nearly twenty years. Although the place was a little large now that the children were away, the extra space was very handy, particularly when the children and grandchildren visited at Christmas and in the summers. There was ample space for Ransom to hold his writing classes in the living room one evening a week, for him to have a large study in which he did almost all of his writing, and for him and Robb to entertain their friends with bridge, charades, and the occasional meeting of the poker club. Members of the family—Ellene, Annie, and Robb's brother Tobey—as well as old friends and former students, visited frequently and some of the children or grandchildren were often there. Jack entered Ohio State in the fall of 1954 but he was home every weekend. After earning a master of fine arts degree from the State University of Iowa, Reavill had gone to Vanderbilt for the Ph.D. because his stories, Ransom wrote Lytle, "are not the money kind and he thinks he'll make teaching his profession and backlog."[25] He and his wife Shirley, and their children as they came along, liked to get to Gambier as often as possible. Helen and Duane Foreman and their two daughters, Robb Reavill and Elizabeth, lived in Baton Rouge, but Helen managed to bring the girls to Gambier, usually for a few days at Christmas and two or three weeks during the summer. Until the mid-1950s Ransom and Robb played golf regularly on the Mount Vernon Country Club course, Ransom continued to grow flowers and vegetables, and during the summers, when he was not away teaching, reading, or speaking, he loved to stay in Gambier, as he wrote Tate, "in my capacity of a gentleman of leisure, playing croquet and chatting with the distinguished guests."[26] But it was only on the croquet court, according to Denham Sutcliffe, also a member of the Kenyon English department, that Ransom was not the epitome of the gracious and considerate gentleman:

Ordinary mankind, having struck an opponent's ball, puts a foot on his own ball and knocks the opponent's ball a few yards off. Not John. He would knock the opponent in front of the next wicket; take his own ball through; hit the opponent again; proceed to the next wicket; repeat. He would carry the opponent all the way to the stake, never, of course, taking him through a wicket. And, then, having securely won the game, he would knock the opponent's ball into Licking County. I have seen the tea-and-toast variety of croquet players reduced nearly to tears.[27]

During the fifties Ransom regularly taught courses in modern poetry and on occasion, when someone was on leave or when for other reasons the department was shorthanded, he added a section of freshman composition. More than once he gave courses in the philosophy department. But these organized classes did not constitute the major portion of his teaching assignment. By this time he was attracting a third generation of students; and these were not only different from those he had taught at Vanderbilt, they had little in common with the first group he had taught at Kenyon. But he was rendering the same service he had always given his students. They brought him manuscripts, as had the two generations preceding them; he read them and usually found some grounds for encouraging the aspiring young poet or critic. Among this post-World War II group was Anthony Hecht, who had come to Kenyon at the suggestion of Robie Macauley. (Ransom's best students seem to have come to him because of the recommendation of a former student. Peter Taylor said he was "sent" to Ransom by Allen Tate.) Hecht recalls that he was a member of a "small but dedicated group who wanted to write poetry" and who "carefully read and discussed Mr. Ransom's poems, as well as his critical and theoretical prose." They wrote poems and passed those they liked among themselves in an attempt to imitate the procedure Ransom and his friends at Vanderbilt had followed twenty or twenty-five years before. Finally they would get enough courage to show their work to Ransom, and his "pronouncements" on it, Hecht has written, "were couched in a language" that could not be imitated, but the effect on all the young writers was the same:

We would all leave his office, confident that we were poets of manifest genius, and very nearly in the same league as Wordsworth or Keats. The next hour or so would be spent in a laureate daze, trying exactly to reconstruct the terms of his praise so as properly to relish them again and to report them to our friends. And this process of reconstruction was absolutely oracular, salutary, and magical. For it frequently appeared that what Mr. Ransom had said was not necessarily to be construed as simple praise. It took a little further meditation and thought to discover that like the Pythoness' advice to King Croesus, it was susceptible to more than one interpretation.[28]

The effect of this tact, Hecht believes, was most successful. Another member of the English department could recall no time at which Ransom's comment when he returned a student paper was sterner than "mighty fine, mighty fine." Ronald Sanders, who attended Kenyon during the mid-fifties, has written that to the end of his career Ransom's relationship with his students remained essentially unchanged.[29] He was interested in each of them individually, gave unstintingly of his time to them and their efforts at creativity, but though unfailingly affable and courteous, he was always a little withdrawn. He had no favorites and some of his students felt he devoted so much time and energy to those with little interest in and less talent for writing that he was not always available to those who could profit most from his insights and wisdom. But this group of students, most of whom were not from the South or the Midwest but from the large cities of the East, were surprised that the "short man with the white hair and the calm blue eyes," the reserved and dignified manner, and the unusual-sounding Anglicized southern speech, really understood them. These young men, Ransom seemed to believe, were willing to make almost any sacrifice to learn to write, and a similar ambition had dominated his life for more than fifty years. He knew, too, how few of them would actually succeed in this, the most hazardous of undertakings, and certainly he could have told even those who would break into the charmed circle of authorship of the many disappointments and the periods of agonizing self-doubt that lay ahead. He read their manuscripts, talked about them, and gave as much encouragement as he thought he could without fostering expectations completely unfounded. To all of these students, he was a "serene teacher and guide," a "good country gentleman" who received them and offered them in "quiet generosity the hope that we might become something like him." But in one sense Ransom must have spoiled them. No matter what they put on paper, he seemed to understand it, and it did not appear strange or unusual to these budding young writers that such an eminent figure in the literary world had the time, the patience, and the interest to read their manuscripts, talk about them, and formulate criticisms of them. Few of these students ever received again such treatment from the editor of an internationally known literary quarterly.

Ransom's teaching, as Allen Tate said on the occasion of his eightieth birthday, was never inspirational.[30] Surely his greatest achievements occurred outside the classroom, for his techniques before a class were far from those recommended in courses in teaching methods:

He was very nearly incapable of giving a formal lecture and he rightly avoided giving any. It is hard to say what his form of delivery was. The nearest thing to it is the style of the poet who gives a reading of his own verses, making comments along the way. This is what Ransom did with the poems of whatever period or author we happened to be studying. The effect was one of complete formlessness, but, in retrospect, it all seems to have been done with a great deal of precision.[31]

The manner in the classroom was similar to that in the poetry and analytical prose—"analytical, tentative, and understated." The role he represented was that of a character "to emulate not to imitate," for, as Tate says, "nothing could have disturbed John Ransom so much as to turn out diminutive copies of himself." That his students, some of the most distinguished writers of three generations, "did not have to commit regicide" in order to be themselves is perhaps his greatest achievement as a teacher.[32]

The last half a dozen or so years of Ransom's tenure at Kenyon were among the most active of his career. Although he gave as many as twenty or twenty-five public lectures and readings each year, he was never able to fill the demand. Even after declining invitations he was flattered to receive, he could not always meet commitments he had made to old friends and former students. He remained actively involved, too, in the administration of the School of Letters of Indiana University, serving as one of its senior fellows from 1951 to 1972. During these years he attended almost all of the meetings of the senior fellows, most of which were held in New York, and assisted in formulating the basic principles and procedures for operating the school. Between meetings he assumed an active role in planning the summer sessions—recommending courses, selecting teaching fellows, and arranging schedules—and taught in three of them: 1952, 1954, and 1958.[33]

In the first of these summers he gave a course entitled "Keats, with a Brief Consideration of Shelley." Because Robb was expecting Helen, Reavill, and their families for extended visits, she could not come with him to Bloomington. He and R. P. Blackmur set up bachelors' quarters at 708 Ballantine Street, the home of Miss Josephine Piercy, a member of the Indiana University faculty. Although the summer was very hot and the three two-hour class meetings each week were exhausting, he and Blackmur enjoyed their time together. Concerned apparently that she had left her home in the charge of two unattached males, whose living habits were unknown to her, Miss Piercy left detailed instructions for its care and maintenance, and Ransom was given the responsibility of reporting to her. "I have been reading the Blue Book devotedly," he wrote on June 29, "and we have been going by all your instructions and directions." The cleaning woman was coming at the times she was supposed to, the lawn man had cut the grass and dusted the roses, and the garbage was being "disposed of in the way you described." On August 1, 1952, he informed her that they were leaving and the only thing broken that he knew of was the "wire of a little picture over the books in the SE bedroom and that just fell of its own accord." It has been a good summer, he wrote Tate on August 17, after hurrying home to spend some time with Helen and her daughters before they had to return to Baton Rouge. Particularly was he pleased at the opportunity to form a closer acquaintance with Blackmur, with whom he had had some critical differences in the past and whom he had had to "rally a little about the necessity of his not being exclusive of his friends and inclusive of the aliens." After several prolonged discussions he was happy to report that he was "pretty sure everything is all right" and that he liked and admired "Richard much more than the contrary."[34]

He returned to Bloomington in the summer of 1954 to offer "Poetry of Our Own Century: Studies Particularly of T. S. Eliot, W. H. Auden, Wallace Stevens, and Thomas Hardy," the area in which most of his teaching had been concentrated for more than thirty years. He was extremely pleased, in spite of the extra work it imposed on him, that Professor Newton P. Stallknecht, the director of the School of Letters, could not keep enrollment below "twice the number ordinarily allowed in such courses." In 1958 he went back for what he wrote Arthur Mizener was likely to be his last teaching,[35] and this time he occupied, with Blackmur and Kenneth Burke, the MacClintock house; it was only a short walk from the building in which he would have his classes, a fact which pleased him very much since recurring attacks of vertigo had made him leery of driving a car. He looked forward to the summer and to the living arrangements, he wrote Stallknecht on February 8, 1958, because he was exited about a new course he wanted to offer and because he was delighted by the prospect of living with Burke and Blackmur, the company of both being "something rare." His new course would be, he wrote, a development of a lecture he had given in January in the Coolidge Auditorium of the Library of Congress. He was tentatively calling it "The Literary Anthropologist"—a title he later changed to "English Poetry: A Study for the Literary Anthropologist"—and since he did not know how it should be presented in the bulletin, he thought he ought to give in some detail his loosely drawn concept of the course:

I begin with the huge surplus of young poets, at all times hopeful and aggressive, even in a field where many offer and few are chosen. What sort of thing is it to be an accepted poet? I put together a lot of considerations, most of them commonplace, and see what we might get as an (idealized) anthropologist might see it. . . . Many poems will be discussed in an informal but persistent effort to generalize the quasi-religious and social purposes in the making of poetry.

He realized that he was dealing with some "Big Problems," but he meant "to touch on them as simply" as he could. He wanted to speak for the psychologist and the sociologist as well as the anthropologist, he wrote, but the "last term is the cleanest and most comprehensive of them." Although no special comments are available on the manner in which this course was accepted, enrollment, as always, was high and auditors took every remaining seat in the classroom. Ransom thought what he then considered to be his last teaching assignment extremely successful, and at the conclusion of the course he talked to a reporter from the Indianapolis *Star* who attempted to summarize, too simplistically to be sure, how Ransom thought literature served the layman: "Literature, which is life in form, explains life, says Ransom. It gives us life values, enriching our everyday living and giving us more experience than we, as individuals, could ever know."[36]

In the last decade of his editorship of the *Kenyon Review,* Ransom produced some of the most important of his critical writings, essays which show his continuing preoccupation with the unique nature of poetry and demonstrate the remarkable consistency of his basic critical position over a period of fifty years. In these last essays he covers much of the ground he has been over before as he attempts to clear up misunderstood statements or badly expressed concepts. His definition of the poem is unaltered, even in language: it remains a "logical structure having a local texture."[37] In "Old Age of an Eagle" he presents what he calls the three dimensions of a poem: "First the plot, or argument, a human representation struck off smartly, developed clearly and rounded off to a nicety. Then the meters. . . . And finally, the poetic language, the flowering habit of a thing that is alive, displaying its grace generally and coming into intermittent focus in special configuration of leaf or blossom."[38] A few years earlier he had suggested, that although the new meanings which the formal critics find in the poetic text are "profound and moving," they leave a distorted and incomplete view of poetry because they never discover its "perennial human values." The meaning of a "poetic text and its logical paraphrase" are not the same because the paraphrase always reduces the text. A poem has two kinds of meanings: the "ostensible argument" which can be rendered in prose and the "tissue of meaning" which cannot. Although a poem "is not included in its paraphrase," it must "include its own paraphrase." Contrary to the belief of some critics, the paraphrase is both "useful" and "reputable" because it "straightens out the text and prunes meaning down" and the critic can demonstrate that the poem is "decent enough to make formal sense."[39]

Many formal critics are at fault by not pointing out that a poem, like a Freudian dream, has both a "manifest and permissible content" and a "latent and suspected content," most of them concentrating their vigor on revealing the latter. This structure-texture dualism may be explained in terms of Freud's discussion of the ego and the id. The "thought work in the poem," its structure, belongs to the ego but the "interpolated material which does not relate to the argument" may be regarded as the work of the id. The critic should understand that a "powerful sensibility is recording in the poem, and the result might be a tropical wilderness of dense figurations, therefore humanly a waste, a nothing; but an equally powerful scheme of order is working there, too, to manage the riches of sense." A poem is conceived under both sensibility and intelligence acting in "opposed parts," like counterpoint in music.[40]

Two of Ransom's most significant essays—though the first of these is less an essay than a series of partially developed reflections on the subject—are those which he published in the mid-fifties on the concrete univeral.[41] The initial essay, Ransom says, was motivated by reading W. K. Wimsatt's *The Verbal Icon*, which contains the suggestion that the understanding of a poem can be fitted pretty well into a kind of Hegelian disposition: "a poem is a structure which may be viewed as a Concrete Universal." Hegel argues, Ransom says, that "the author of the poem is Spirit residing though partially and intermittently in the poet, and identical with that Spirit of the Universe which is God, or that Spirit of History which continually creates in order to objectify itself." [42] The amplitude of this Spirit is so great that it can be expressed only through the "plenitude of concreteness" and not through scientific concepts, which are hopelessly abstract. With these principles Ransom agrees, as he does with the assertion that the technical sciences use the natural world only to take what they want from it. But he cannot accept completely Hegel's argument that poetic language is the "perfect Synthesis of the Thesis (or Universal) and the Antithesis (or Concrete)," that the concrete is wholly assimilated in the universal and that the universal extends over the whole concretion. He will continue to insist that the "concrete detail is partly extraneous to the abstract universal," that it would be impossible ever to render in logical terms the complete meaning of a poem. Because the universal never quite grasps the concrete, the logical paraphrase is never equivalent to the poem.

These ruminations on the justification for a concrete universal as opposed to a scientific universal—an indication of the significance of poetry in a world almost completely dominated by science—leads him to attempt again to define the unique nature of that precious object, the poem,[43] by describing how language functions in its development:

About fifteen years ago I was thinking of the poem as having a logical structure or framework, and a texture whose character was partly irrelevant to the logical form and purpose. My "texture" in particular has given offense, and the fact is that I had no sooner uttered it than it struck me as a flat and inadequate figure for that vivid and easily felt part of the poem which we associate peculiarly with poetic language. I wish now to recast my definition entirely, though I shall only employ another figure whose disabilities I am aware of in advance.

.   .   .   .

Suppose we say that the poem is an organism. Then it has a physiology. We will figure its organs, and to me it seems satisfactory if we say they are three: the head, the heart, the feet. In this organism the organs work all at the same time, but the peculiarity of the joint production is that it still consists of the several products of the organs working individually.[44]

All of these organs work together to produce a poem. Each speaks, but in a different language: "the head in an intellectual language, the heart in an affective language, the feet in a rhythmical language."[45] On the intellectual level the poem is a logical whole; therefore it has a beginning, a middle, and an end as well as whatever connective and transitional devices as are needed to hold it together and suggest the relationships existing among its various parts. With their strong focus on the richness of the particulars, their minute scrutiny of the individual phrase and the specific figure, many modern critics have created a belief that a poem cannot be perceived as a completely unified whole, Ransom maintained.

In his second essay on the concrete universal Ransom sets out to demonstrate why he regards Kant, not Hegel, as his mentor. The concept of a concrete universal, though a "working phrase of Hegel's," is really a development of Kant's thought and may be defined as "any idea in the mind which proposes a little universe or organized working combination of parts" in order to attempt to produce a single effect. To create this single impression each part must do its work, its several duties, completely and effectively; a chemical formula, a recipe, a blueprint, or even Newman's idea of a university may be considered examples of universals. It is an idea, a design as it exists in the understanding, and it becomes a concrete universal when it is actually working. There are two kinds of concrete universals: those of applied science in which there is no "essential part missing, no unnecessary part showing," each part acting precisely and exactly as it should; and those of the arts, of poetry, which do not satisfy an organic need and are not located in the "animal perspective of human nature." Hegel argued that man does not need an awareness of the concrete particularities of nature to complete his realization of existence; he merely has to apply his own universal, his own self-imposed concept of order upon the world to make it orderly and understandable. Kant felt, however, that man should not be too aggressive in his attempt to know the world; he should try to establish a relationship with nature so that he could know the beauty that comes neither from nature nor from man's mind but in the process of man's becoming aware of nature.

From Kant's view of the concrete universal Ransom learned to differentiate between the scientific universal and the moral universal.

The scientific universal has a practical end in mind; it would alter the materials of nature until they fit a preconceived notion. The critic accepting this view would insist "that the universal or logical plan of the poem is borne out perfectly in the sensuous detail which puts it into action" and "that the concrete is used up so completely in the service of the universal that there is no remainder." The pure universal is a concept in the mind which will not stand confrontation with the actual world; it will appear fragmentary and distorted in the light of the world's unpredicated and phenomenal mystery. The complete realization of this pure universal in matter is the concrete universal, only a portion of which is included in the scientific universal. There is also the moral universal, which is more concerned with the realization of self and may be found in poetry of the right kind. Although it is not in didactic verse, which tries to tell us how to act, nor in the kind of poetry which would attempt to prescribe a specific mode of thought, it is in that kind of poetry which would assist the reader in knowing the world. In poetry of this type the imagination, through metaphor, makes the moral universal, which is abstract and conceptual, perceptual and concrete. The universal is referred to nature and particularized, given sensuous detail, through this reference; therefore nature is an essential element for poetry. To abandon nature is to abandon metaphor and without metaphor there can be no poetry. Ransom's interest in this subject did not diminish in these later years; his last published essay was on the concrete universal.

As Ransom passed his sixtieth birthday and moved nearer to the end of his career as a full-time editor and teacher, he received a large number of awards in recognition of his significant contributions to literature over the previous three decades. In late 1947, when he was informed of his selection to life membership in the National Institute of Arts and Letters, he had written Tate of his inclination to decline the invitation because he hated the "feel and reputation of honors of all sorts." But Tate had urged him to change his mind, pointing out that not only was it a distinct and well-deserved honor but that membership in the institute would give him opportunities to serve his fellow artists that he would not otherwise have. Consequently, when the formal invitation came he accepted and on December 30, 1947, he was installed, along with W. H. Auden, Padraic Colum, Bernard DeVoto, Matthew Josephson, F. O. Matthiessen, and John Hall Wheelock, as a lifetime member of the National Institute of Arts and Letters.[46] Shortly afterwards, on April 3, 1950, he declined a second opportunity to become consultant in poetry at the Library of Congress.[47] He had written Conrad Aiken earlier that he could not accept the position because the salary offered was considerably below what he was earning at Kenyon. Aiken consulted the Librarian of Congress, "who upped the salary to $7,500"; still he could not accept because the "new stipend would be $1,000 to $1,500 short." [48]

Early the next year he was honored twice. On January 22, 1951, it was announced that he had won the Bollingen Prize in Poetry, which in 1948 had gone to Ezra Pound and in 1949 to Wallace Stevens.[49] "Naturally I was 100% surprised," he wrote Tate on February 3, "and 99% pleased, of course; the small reservation being the faint suspicion that I may have owed it in some degree to the Committee's (unconscious) idea of using Ransom as a stick to beat Hillyer and the *Saturday Review of Literature* with." [50] But, he continued, "this reflects on me as a suspicious creature, as well as on the Committee, and it hasn't been more than a sneak of a suspicion, as I said above. So, flatly, I'm mighty pleased." As Conrad Aiken—chairman of a committee composed of Robert Penn Warren, W. H. Auden, Leonie Adams, and Karl Shapiro—explained, the prize could be given either for a book published in the preceding year or, as was the case with Ransom, "on the basis of a poet's entire work," for his overall "contribution to American poetry." Reacting to a reporter's question of how it felt to win the nation's leading poetry award, Ransom commented: "I am surprised. There is nothing recent of mine for the committee to have considered and my old work is small in volume when the inferior things are screened out. I know that when I was writing it, I had no sound education in poetry, and was in torture trying to escape from the stilted and sentimental verbal habits which conditioned me. My stuff came out of the academy. I am sure that is apparent." [51]

A few weeks later, on a visit to Nashville, he repeated a declaration he was often making in these years. He did intend to write more poetry, he told Ralph Morrisey of the Nashville *Tennessean,* but it would not be the "same kind of thing" he had done before. As he grew older, he said, composition was slower because "I find myself taking more time with my work, seeking that perfection which attracts all poets." He had to rewrite and revise carefully because he did not want to inflict on others the hurt "I always suffer when reading a poem that's not as good as it should be." Writing poetry, he concluded, is very complex, for "the fires must be built up, a creative tension evoked, which drives relentlessly this way and that. It's almost impossible for me to plan a poem."[52]

Most of the comment on Ransom's receiving the award was favorable. Writing in the *Saturday Review,* Oscar Williams pointed out that the fact that the prize had been given to Stevens and Ransom made it a high "honor indeed, for such prizes receive their worth from the recipients." The choice of Ransom, "whose every poem has the quality of enduring greatness," Williams wrote, "should undermine even the heaviest pessimism about the condition of poetry in America. . . . The existence of a healthy and high stratum of literary appreciation is proven by this latest award as by the one that preceded it last year."[53] A correspondent in *Time* applauded the committee's selection, pointing out that perhaps American readers would now read Ransom's verse. Heretofore, the "contribution to American poetry," for which Conrad Aiken said he had been given the prize, was known to few Americans, either "from lack of interest or pure defensive caution." If these readers get to Ransom, they will not find the kind of incomprehensible poetry they expect, the article continues, for "lucid, logical John Ransom is not that kind of poet." A skilled craftsman, he writes "movingly and hauntingly" about the death of children or "worldly-wisely" about the decay of youthful beauty, always in a manner almost as "transparent as a weather report." If this poetry by a poet "who has something to say, and who wants to talk to someone besides himself or the other poets" were more widely known, everyone would profit.[54]

Less than three weeks after this article appeared, and almost as if a direct result of it, Ransom received a letter which, he wrote Tate, "is worth a great deal to me, yet has its comic side. I am to be recipient of a prize from the National Institute of Arts and Letters in the amount of $1,000. In the letter it seems they like to 'recognize' work all the more if it has not been 'publicly appreciated.'" The "prize" Ransom had received was the Russell Loines Award for Poetry, given by the National Institute of Arts and Letters "from time to time to an American or English poet, not as a prize but as a recognition of value, preferably of value not widely recognized."[55] In his presentation remarks William Carlos Williams pointed out that Ransom had been the unacknowledged leader of the Fugitives, yet he had never restricted himself to a group. Although "you went to Kenyon and gathered about you young writers whose aims took in a wider tolerance than that envisioned by your earlier acceptances," Williams continued, "you remain still a Fugitive, as are all men who carry about with them that which you have been destined to preserve." In his response Ransom indicated his approval of the dignified manner in which the Institute "confers its award upon a public occasion," making the "impression of Academicians dedicated to the cause of arts and letters." But the honor of being "named publicly by the Institute" is enhanced by the "solid cash benefit that goes with it." It is a well-known fact that the arts "do not bring material rewards which are commensurate with those obtained in business or professional pursuits," and the artist himself understands that the more serious his art the "less is his ground for expecting the quick wide fame which brings occasionally the big money." Since the pursuit of the arts "brings in something less than a livelihood," he is not going to question the judgment of those who have conferred this honor upon him; instead he will only "register a gratitude which is uncomplicated and unstinted."

In the fall of 1955 the editors of *Hika,* Kenyon's undergraduate magazine, began serious preparations for a "special issue honoring John Crowe Ransom"; they wrote letters to "some of his interested friends and accomplished former students" asking for contributions. Instead of an "expression of personal praise," the editors requested independent work, unless someone had already prepared "something in particular on Mr. Ransom."[56] Considering the fact that contributors were not paid, the editors must have been surprised to receive poems by James Wright and Howard Nemerov, essays by R. P. Blackmur, Eric Bentley, George Hemphill, and Arthur Mizener; and the overall excellence of the issue was enhanced by the four drawings contributed by Phil Rice. Ransom secured permission for the reprinting of "Spectral Lovers" and "Painted Head," and the publication was, as the brief dedicatory statement expressed it, "a most impressive tribute" to a "poet, critic, teacher and gentleman of aristocratic and Southern manners," although it was not a "symposium of elaborate consideration and praise," only one contribution, that of George Hemphill, being specifically on Ransom.[57]

On August 16, 1957, upon the recommendation of Randall Jarrell, who was then serving as consultant in poetry, Ransom was appointed honorary consultant in American literature for the Library of Congress, his appointment as fellow in American literature having recently expired. Shortly thereafter he was selected to give one of the Gertrude Clark Whittall poetry lectures at the Library of Congress, an "annual series devoted to a common theme." On January 13 Ransom read his essay entitled "New Poets and Old Muses"; he was followed on January 20 by Delmore Schwartz ("The Present State of Poetry") and on January 27 by John Hall Wheelock ("The Two Knowledges: An Essay on a Certain Resistance"). All three of these essays were published under the title *American Poetry at Mid-Century*. After Jarrell's tenure was completed, Ransom was again urged to accept the position of consultant in poetry, which he wrote Tate on November 23, 1957, "is now a nice job, paying $8,000 and allowing for the incumbent's private trips round to make speeches, and his private writings, and holding him to only 9 months residence, and lasting for two years." But he had again declined, he wrote, because he was thinking of nothing but "retirement and private life (and work) after commencement next spring."

Later the same year Ransom was informed of another award he could expect in the near future. "Thank you for telling me about the medal which they have assigned to me at Brandeis," he wrote Tate on November 23; "I'll certainly want to accept it, coming from that committee you mention, and that institution, but I do hope they won't ask me to take the trip just for receiving it! I hope there will be some adjustments of the time possible so that I can be east already." On January 27, 1958, he wrote that he had just received formal notification of his selection and that the medal would be awarded on March 5. The official press release from Brandeis, on March 6, 1958, indicated that the Creative Arts Award Committee had been formed in May,

1956, for the purpose of extending "recognition and assistance for outstanding achievement in the fields of music, literature, fine arts, and the theater." Under its chairman, Louis Kronenberger, the commission was honoring, with a medal and a grant of $1,000, for aggregate achievement during their lives, four distinguished American artists: Roger Sessions (music), Jacques Lipchitz (sculpture), Stark Young (theater), and John Crowe Ransom (poetry).

Despite the genuine pleasure he received from this widespread recognition, and the cash awards which he and Robb were saving to apply on the cost of their first home, which they had begun to think seriously about, nothing pleased him more than to learn from Randall Stewart, chairman of the English department at Vanderbilt, that through the American Studies Association the Rockefeller Foundation had expressed its willingness to underwrite the expenses of bringing together at Vanderbilt for readings, papers, and conversations the members of the group that thirty years before had edited and published the *Fugitive*. "I'm for the Fugitive reunion," he wrote Stewart on October 29, 1955; "[it] seems to me a wonderful idea for the Fugitives themselves, and I'd hope some of the passion might spill over and be a credit on the public side."

By early January, 1956, Stewart had also received responses from Tate, Warren, and Merrill Moore, all endorsing the plan for a reunion and indicating their willingness to participate; at Vanderbilt, therefore, Stewart and Donald Davidson were trying to set a definite date and make specific plans for the conference. Stewart first suggested the dates of October 18–20, beginning with Thursday dinner and ending with luncheon Saturday, to coincide with "Homecoming Weekend so that we can provide something literary to these dates—the idea of combining this meeting with Vanderbilt's homecoming was particularly objectionable—and after two or three other possibilities were rejected, everyone finally agreed on May 3, 4, and 5, 1956, and Stewart was able to move on to other details. Since the general public, who certainly "will want to see something of the Fugitives while they are here," cannot attend the three "closed sessions" in which the Fugitives "will record for future historical use whatever they wish to say," there must be some sessions to which everyone will be invited. For these general meetings, Stewart proposed: (1) a "poetry reading at which Ransom, Tate, Davidson, Warren, and Moore will read" ("This will be a 'big event,'" Stewart wrote, "certain to fill the largest auditorium on campus. A local television station has requested permission to telecast a portion of it"); (2) a dinner at the Belle Meade Country Club for a hundred or more official guests of the board of trust; (3) a dinner on the Vanderbilt campus for members of the English department, their wives, and other "friends of the Fugitives."[58]

As soon as he could Ransom responded to Stewart's tentative program, indicating that most of his objections were provisional, since he "would not hold out against the wishes of the others if my views aren't accepted." To Stewart's suggestion that he assume his "natural position as leader" of the group, Ransom's objection was most firm. "I can't accept the role of a leader in any sense," he wrote on February 18, 1956; "we were too democratic or communal for that sort of thing and much too equal in any objective sense." He thought, too, that the proposed agenda placed the group too much in the public eye; he had hoped "that there would be some long sessions together with the old crowd, and the chance of making some decisions, and just a little bit of joint publicity and applause." Even from his "limited experience" he knew that nothing is "quite so painful as being 'honored,'" especially when the "socialites who don't know anything about one's work are enlisted to shed their own glory over the occasion." All of this was especially relevant to the cocktail party and the dinner at the Belle Meade Country Club at which Ransom was "slated to address Board and guests about matters on which one cannot speak intimately because of the disparity between the subjects and the audience. Horrors!" His hope was that the Fugitives could be in some peaceful place for at least two days; perhaps the place might be "that nice hotel (used to be nice, anyhow) down at Murfreesboro." These meetings should be supplemented by two reading sessions, one could be held in connection with "an open tea of the unexpensive sort, for the general public." These would be "memorable programs, with some definition to them."

Somewhat surprised, obviously, by the vehemence of Ransom's objections to some of the details that he and Davidson had worked out, Stewart responded immediately.[59] Although his convictions about affairs of this kind did not differ from Ransom's, he began, he was in a difficult spot because a lot of people, including the chancellor and members of the board of trust, had given him suggestions; nevertheless his one abiding principle was that the "active Fugitives should have the say." But even this is not a perfect solution, he continued, because there are disagreements among the Fugitives. Merrill Moore, for example, had insisted on inviting Henry W. Wells, of whom he was sure no one else would approve, and he also was strongly urging the inclusion of representatives of *Time, Life, Newsweek,* and the national television networks. On March 6, Stewart summarized the points on which there was general agreement. There would be four sessions attended only by the Fugitives and a few especially invited scholars and critics to assist in accomplishing the objectives which the Rockefeller Foundation had in mind in making the grant to support the conference. Those objectives, Stewart reported, were succinctly stated in a letter he had recently received from the foundation: "Mr. Marshall's understanding was that the Foundation's grant would be used only to make possible a small, working conference composed of representative members of the original group and a few interlocutor-critics who had studied its work, and so were in a position to ask leading questions, with the aim of producing a stenographic record which would constitute a kind of documentary source on how the group operated as a group." To give these sessions some kind of structure, though a very informal one, he had asked Cleanth Brooks, he reported, to serve as moderator and to select in advance a general set of topics to guide discussion in each of the sessions.[60] When Louis D. Rubin, Jr., who as secretary of the American Studies Association had persuaded the Rockefeller Foundation to support the conference, received this letter, he informed Stewart that the foundation "expects the closed conferences to cover certain definite topics and to answer, after a fashion, certain questions."[61] These topics, Rubin wrote Stewart on March 8, are: "One session would be devoted in general to what there was in the time and place and region that made the Fugitives possible," and another should be concerned with such questions as " 'What did you get out of being a member of the Fugitives?' 'What did it mean to you as a young poet?' . . . If these topics are dealt with . . . we'll be fulfilling our obligation."

Although Ransom was delighted at the prospect of seeing all of his old friends again, he deplored the public nature of some of the activities on the schedule. He was particularly displeased that the big cocktail party and dinner at the Belle Meade Country Club had not been dropped and that there before "two or three hundred people" he was expected to speak on some such topic as "Thoughts on the Present Occasion," "Poetry and the Modern World," or offer remarks on "What Vanderbilt could do to encourage a new literary movement."[62] "I guess I'm whipped," he wrote Stewart on April 2, "and therefore with every possible becoming show of reluctance I concur with your plan to seat me at the high table with the Chancellor and be prepared to make some remarks." So that they could be listed on the printed program, he sent a list of the poems he would read: "Janet Waking," "Antique Harvesters," "The Equilibrists," and "Prelude to an Evening." It did not take much persuading to get Robb, who was always willing to visit Nashville, to accompany him; they made reservations to join the other official guests at the Allen Hotel, just off the Vanderbilt campus.

At the first session, which began at 3 P.M. in Neely Auditorium and later adjourned to Alumni Hall for an exhibition of Fugitive books and manuscripts, Andrew Lytle, Allen Tate, and Robert Penn Warren made brief addresses. That evening a dinner was held in Rand Hall on the Vanderbilt campus; Alec Stevenson served as toastmaster, Jesse Wills and Alfred Starr gave brief reminiscences, and Donald Davidson presented an address which he later published in a much revised form as "Poetry as Tradition." Afterwards the Fugitives and the "interlocutor-critics" retired to Randall Stewart's apartment on Elliston Place for the first of the "closed sessions."[63] Here the discussion, although prompted by Davidson's paper, really took up an argument, as Louis Rubin explains, which had been suspended thirty years before:

Once the individual Fugitives were convened together behind closed doors, and the tape recorders began turning, something strange, even a little awesome, happened. They became a group again. The various individuals, despite some thirty years of separate and individual achievement, became the Nashville Fugitives once more. They began arguing, and the argument soon assumed, what was instantly and thrillingly recognizable to those who witnessed it, precisely the same lines of demarcation that had existed during the 1920's. Why, they began discussing, had none of the Fugitives succeeded in writing an epic? It was Tate, Ransom, Warren, Davidson, and Andrew Lytle on one side, Elliott and Alfred Starr on the other. The first five were those members of the Fugitives . . . who had gone on to become professional men of letters, who had committed themselves entirely and occupationally to literature.[64]

Professor Rubin's assignment of allegiances in this discussion is certainly correct; the division here is the same as that which was characteristic of the group thirty years before as it debated the relative virtues of the ancients and the moderns. In those discussions Davidson had supported the moderns, but in the late 1920s Ransom and Tate had adopted critical positions which he found objectionable, and the paper he read on this occasion, as well as some of his remarks in this first closed session, state this position. As Tate had written in the late twenties, there "are no important themes for modern poets" because "our culture is dissolving." Epic poetry can be produced only at a time when a society agrees on a common myth, and such a production is not possible in an age, such as this one, characterized by disunity, dissociation, and a lack of faith.[65] The discussion was not really about whether one or more of the Fugitives could or should have written an epic but whether poetry of the sort written and favored by Ransom, Tate, Warren, and other moderns—a poetry "composed *for* the printed page" and "received by the solitary, silent reader who ponders it in voiceless seclusion"—is not destructive and, therefore, indefensible.[66] When the poet made his work literary at the expense of his bardic role, neglected the oral character of his verse, Davidson had argued in his paper, and Elliott and Starr agreed in the ensuing discussion, he not only limited the value and influence of his own verse but contributed to the destruction of all poetry.

The second and third closed sessions were held at the home of Jesse Wills. Louis Rubin began the first of these by asking a question that focused the discussion for a time on one of the topics he had suggested that the group consider. He asked Ransom if he thought his poetry would have been the same if he "had not been at Vanderbilt with the Fugitives from 1920 to 1925." Decidedly not, Ransom responded; "the tremendous advance" between *Poems About God* and the later poetry he attributed almost entirely to his association with this group and, specifically, to Allen Tate's introducing him to modern poetry and criticism, particularly to the works of Eliot. The discussions in the group meetings, the private conversations, and the reading he was motivated to do were most helpful to him, he said, "because I was a homemade English scholar, and my preparation was not for teaching English at all" so there was a "crudeness and greenness about my work" that needed the "minute and very honest inspection" it received. "I know," he concluded, "it saved many painful years for me in such little progress as I was capable of making."[67] Then, after considering briefly the effects of this intimate and prolonged association on the poetry written by the Fugitives, the discussion turned to why the group had stayed together so long, to the influence of Vanderbilt, particularly of its faculty, upon them, to the beginning of the *Fugitive* and, finally, to the "dialectical leadership" of Sidney Hirsch.[68]

After lunch, which was served to the entire group by Ellen and Jesse Wills, the third closed session opened with Ransom as moderator. In a brief opening statement he turned the discussion back toward the topic of the first session, what he called "the characteristic Fugitive prejudice—dogma it might be—about what makes good poetry." Although Louise Cowan raised the question of why some of the Fugitives had become Agrarians—especially "those who experimented with technique and who didn't want to concern themselves with subject matter"—everyone was so deeply involved in the discussion of the nature and uses of poetry and of the reasons why some of the group had apparently abandoned poetry for criticism that this topic had to be delayed until the final closed session on Saturday morning.

At the dinner that evening Robb and Ransom, because he was listed for "Remarks," were seated at the head table with others on the program.[69] Although there is no record of what Ransom said on this occasion—other than his vague memory of expressing thanks for the university's "recognition of the group, even if somewhat tardily"—he spoke very briefly, returning "most of the time I was allotted." Apparently the others kept their remarks within the suggested limits, because all of the speakers and readers were back at Neely Auditorium, where they were greeted by a packed house, in time for that session to begin shortly after the scheduled time of 8:30. Randall Stewart presided and called first on William Yandell Elliott, who spoke on "The Fugitives in Perspective," after which Warren, Moore, Tate, Davidson, and Ransom read for about ten to fifteen minutes each.[70] The program was enthusiastically received, each poet getting prolonged applause after he had read the poems listed on the program. Although no one accepted the insistent invitations for encores, it was after eleven before the Ransoms, the Tates, Warren, Brooks, and some of the others gathered at the apartment of Cleone and Randall Stewart for "a few drinks, some conversation, and a chance to relax" after a long and, as they all agreed, productive day.

Surely the group of middle-aged and elderly men who met at Alumni Hall at 10 A.M. the next morning felt the effects of travel and two days of almost continuous activity. Their physical condition seemed to have little effect, however, on the discussion at this final closed session, which one person present described as "a probing analysis of the relations between the Fugitive and Agrarian movements."[71] Davidson insisted that *I'll Take My Stand* is just as much "a defense of Merrill Moore as a poet, and of Bill Elliott as a poet, and as a student of government—a free student of government, not bound under a totalitarian regime—it's as much that as it is an exposition of the case of the South under the Agrarian conception."[72] Tate agreed, pointing out that an "underlying assumption" of the book is that a "kind of religious humanism is the moral and spiritual condition which is favorable to poetry" and the value of the book is that it is a reaffirmation of religious humanism.[73] Finally the discussion led again to the question of why the Fugitives turned from poetry to fiction and criticism. Everywhere he went, Ransom said, he was asked why he left poetry for criticism: "I have never been happy with the thought that I have left poetry. I've continued to make threats of writing more poems; I even still do. . . . Mencken used to say that everybody has got a little volume of verse that he did at eighteen years old; but he goes to prose when he grows up and he's mature." Ransom challenged this point of view, because poetry is "a much more versatile and comprehensive instrument than we give it credit for being." So poetry can accommodate one's developing and changing thought, as it did for Yeats, but "we are faced with a new culture in this country, the strings that bound us to Europe are all gone," and "we are starting all over in this country with a kind of culture which is based on mass consumption." He ended by saying that as "persons we have to meet so many situations" he wondered whether one could always "meet them poetically."

Shortly after returning to Gambier, Ransom wrote Arthur Mizener his impressions of the "big meeting" in Nashville.[74] "It was a wonderful experience for me," he began, "seeing all the boys again, and having discourse with them, if not downright polemics such as we used to." His only regret, although he was "slightly down" from having to leave after such a brief period many of his oldest and dearest friends, was that "we were so rushed with our business" that there was little chance for private conversation. Particularly was he "disappointed with the poor allowance" he had for seeing Andrew Lytle, with whom he had hoped to stage "a big get-together after long years,"[75] and Frances and Brainard Cheney, and one or two other old friends. "I left with an empty feeling," he wrote Lytle, "as far as you and they are concerned."

Ransom was undergoing at this time one of the most trying periods of his life. Not only was he concerned about his approaching retirement, which he tried to convince himself he was looking forward to, but he chaffed under restrictions in his personal activities imposed by the periodic attacks of vertigo brought on by his inner-ear trouble. He had given up golf, he drove the car seldom and only for short distances, and he found any kind of travel increasingly uncomfortable. Then a series of unexpected deaths quickly deprived him of his closest friends and associates at Kenyon. In the early morning of January 3, 1956, Phil Rice's car left the highway and plunged twenty-five feet into a creek bank; after lingering near death for three weeks, he died on January 25. Then, on May 8, 1956, in the Cape Code Hospital in Hyannis, Massachusetts, Gordon Keith Chalmers succumbed to a cerebral hemorrhage. Finally, on July 20, 1956, in San Marino, California, where he was doing research in the Huntington Library, Charles Coffin died of a coronary occlusion. The extent to which Ransom was affected by the deaths of the three persons with whom he had had the closest associations at Kenyon is difficult to determine. He was a private man who concealed his personal feelings as carefully as he controlled the sentiment embodied in his best poems. His reserved and dignified manner, despite his unfailing courtesy, allowed him to keep everyone at a certain distance. Even his best friends—Donald Davidson, Robert Penn Warren, and Allen Tate—complained that his sense of absolute propriety, combined with a natural inclination toward honest (and sometimes severe) judgments, produced a shell around the inner man that no one could penetrate. Like the character in one of his poems, he "assuredly" must have known grief, but if he were "shaken," it was "not as a leaf." If he experienced a feeling of personal loss, as he must have, he expressed it guardedly, if at all. In some of the most significant areas of his life, however, drastic changes came immediately. For years Rice had been his closest associate on the *Review* and the person whom Ransom could engage in discussion of the most minute point of aesthetic theory. This kind of activity was personally satisfying to Ransom, and he also found it an effective stimulant to creativity. His best poetry had been written during the period of his association with the Fugitives, and almost all of his creative ideas evolved from discussions and exchanges of letters with Rice, Tate, Robert Graves, and others, with any one of whom he could test the validity of his aesthetic speculations. Coffin was his nearest neighbor, a fellow gardener and bridge partner, a good conversationalist, a scholar with interests in literature and theology which Ransom shared, a friend of the *Review*, and an ally in the English department. Although Ransom's relations with Chalmers were almost entirely formal, he had found him a loyal supporter of the *Review*, in spite of their lack of agreement on some of its basic policies. More than once Chalmers had secured the means of bailing the journal out of financial difficulty, and Ransom realized that his death made the future of the *Kenyon Review* much less certain.

Ransom made no attempt to find anyone to do Rice's work. He regarded Rice as irreplaceable, and, too, he had little encouragement to add to the staff because Frank E. Bailey, who was acting president until a successor to Chalmers could be selected, was naturally reluctant to commit Kenyon College to support the *Review* beyond his own temporary appointment. In order to keep the journal in operation, however, until a new president was selected and had assumed office,

Ransom was asked to continue teaching and to remain as editor through the academic year of 1957/58.

Soon after F. Edward Lund became president, he assured Ransom that "he was determined to keep the *Kenyon Review* going" and appointed a committee composed of Ransom, Denham Sutcliffe, and himself to select the next editor.[76] Since he had "rather it broke up than be inferior," Ransom immediately wrote Tate asking him to suggest names of possible candidates since the "name of a young man who has his own distinction, stands for something in the set of his ideas" did not occur to him. He first asked Tate's opinion of Murray Krieger, whom he liked very much but whom he feared "might still have too academic a mind." Tate apparently vetoed Krieger, for Ransom wrote on October 2, "you have confirmed my fears" about him. He thanked Tate for recommending Robie Macauley, who had, he wrote, the distinct advantage of "being one of our own crowd," and Ransom preferred to identify with a man who started on the right side of the fence than with one who had been converted. Originally he had favored Peter Taylor for editor and a "young poet here, Ted Bogardus," as managing editor, but "Peter never quite got his own 100% of himself behind the project." He had consulted him about Macauley, however, and found that he "agreed entirely" with Tate's recommendation. Taylor also thought Jack Thompson, who had been at Kenyon at the time he and Robert Lowell were there, would be an excellent choice. Ransom remembered Thompson as a "bit of a playboy but wholly intelligent." On the basis of some critical writing he had recently published, however, Ransom was convinced that Thompson had "acquired a solid intellectual integrity," and he arranged to meet him in New York, where he was doing graduate work at Columbia, after which he wrote Tate: "I had Jack Thompson and Dilly [his wife] to cocktails at the Plaza Wednesday afternoon, and a good talk with Jack before Dilly came. I like Jack very much personally but he wasn't as impressive on the intellectual side as I had hoped. He is not decisive in my way of thinking." [77]

With Thompson removed from serious contention, Ransom asked Tate for other suggestions, in addition to Howard Nemerov and William Jay Smith whom he had already mentioned.[78] At about the same time R. P. Blackmur recommended Joseph Frank. Ransom knew little about Smith, but he did not "feel complete satisfaction" with Macauley, and he thought Nemerov a "little foolish in finding his praise for *Lolita*, Nabokov's naughty little novel," which he had found "rather pointless." He wanted Tate's reaction to Joseph Frank, "whom all the Princeton men are enthusiastic about." Is there, he asked, a "little aridity in his thinking?" What Ransom was looking for was a critic with real force, but not "an analyst like Frye, or some young Burke of merely technical powers." Although he suspected there would be a "good place for a merely 'literary' review, especially centered upon the actual printing of much contemporary fiction"—and this was the sort of magazine Macauley would have—he did not believe this "the kind of journal the *Kenyon* should become." It would become "undistinguished as compared with its rivals" because it would "lack the tone of criticism built in the Reviews as they have come to be."

After much thoughtful consideration of the names suggested by dozens of people from whom he had requested recommendations, Ransom wrote Tate on November 5, 1957, that he had narrowed the list to two candidates: Joseph Frank and Randall Jarrell. In a recent conference Lund had said he wanted a man strong enough to "stand on his own feet and run the magazine without any presidential advice or supervision whatever"; and since Ransom was "retiring completely from the picture" and Rice and Coffin were both gone, it seemed important that the editor be the "sort to generate broad support from the academic community." [79] In this respect, he continued, Jarrell is probably the better man. Since Frank is not a "poet or fictionist himself" and because his "critical principles are very high," he would not appeal to the general reader, as Jarrell would. But Jarrell, "who is too polemical and stylistically too journalistic and personally too fond of his enemies (of having enemies), is really not acceptable because he would change the *Review* too much toward the spectacular." Even so, Ransom was inclined to feel that Jarrell might be the right man for their unusual situation. "His way of life in a small community would make a riffle," he concluded, but he was yet to find in Jarrell "a lack of courage or of principle." He "has a great journalistic or publicist flair, and in the main it is directed against the Philistines. . . . I suspect that his selection right now might please the President a great deal and that the Review would at any rate prosper under his hands and have readers, even if many of whom would be those whom he had provoked."

In spite of Tate's objections to Jarrell, and Ransom agreed with many of them, he and Howard Nemerov were invited to the campus for interviews.[80] Ransom wrote Tate on January 27, 1958, that Jarrell had received the unanimous vote of the committee:

I had great fears of my own about Randall, and we had a good many letters about him, pro and con. But he was so strong, and at the same time scrupulous and temperate in his expressions, and in personal talks so gentle in all he said to me, and with such practical views of the editorship, that I had to give him the nod, as Lund and Dennie had done completely. He has far more personal force than Nemerov, though we thought Nemerov would do. I am of the opinion that he has emotionally matured, and far more thoroughly than I would have thought possible. That feeling was reinforced when I went to Washington to make a Whittall lecture. Randall had nothing to do with that, and he was in the background modestly and not at all unhappily so far as I could see. At Washington he did not recur at all to the interview here, nor to the decision which we had still not made, nor ever assumed that I was more than an anonymous member of the committee which would decide. So I do believe he would have satisfied yourself too, in his mature phase.

Now Ransom wondered what effect his appointment would have on the *Review*. Although he was not "technically a critic," he was a sort of "trail-blazer" and his "affections for the literary object are immense." He will attract a wide following and the shift in emphasis will probably be good for the *Review*. After twenty years Ransom was convinced the *Review* should drop the "technical emphasis on criticism and put forward the poems, fiction, and bits of theatre that come up in our time."[81] But three months later, he wrote that Jarrell had declined the position for reasons that he respected. Jarrell was not sure that "he was sufficiently in touch with the critics" and he did not want to give up a "congenial job and a home, which he owns." The position went to Macauley, "obviously a good man," and he and Bogardus would make a good team.[82] Ransom was pleased, he said, with the choice because "Robie is a man of taste, and a very good and fast improving writer, and as to his literary convictions they are just the same as this Review has always held to, without ever defining them."

With the immediate future of the *Review* settled, Ransom went into his last few months of teaching. His imminent retirement was noted in *Time*, in an article which observed that in the classroom and through the *Kenyon Review*, "one of the nation's best and healthiest literary quarterlies," he had waged a largely successful literary campaign, thought by many "to verge on the revolutionary," to reshape the approach to literature, particularly poetry. To list the important writers who studied and taught with him at Kenyon reminds us, this correspondent pointed out, that his influence cannot be overestimated. Although founding a journal of the stature of the *Kenyon Review* would certainly earn him a place of distinction in American letters, neither the reputation of that quarterly, the influence of his critical writings, nor the impact of him personally—or of his theories generally—upon the teaching of literature should shift our attention from his greatest achievement: he is one of the best poets in the language. In 1956, during a visit to Kenyon, Robert Frost told a student audience, "you have right here on this campus the greatest living American poet." The undergraduate writer who reported Frost's statement took exception to it, pointing out that the person deserving that distinction was the speaker. On June 2, 1958, during the ceremony at which Ransom was awarded the degree of doctor of letters, Virgil C. Aldrich, chairman of the philosophy department, emphasized his claim to distinction as "poet, critic, editor, father, and friend of the new poets and professors who now, in your seventieth year, hold up the standard of poetic achievement recognized by the whole world of letters." But, Aldrich was pleased to add, "your Olympian preoccupation does not prevent you from loving a ball game, a horse race, a political campaign, a televised western, and tomatoes in your garden. We are happy that you plan to continue living here on the hill in a new house right beside the old one."

Although Ransom agreed to edit the *Review* for one more year, he was already looking forward to his retirement, to writing the "book or two" of criticism he had planned, and to "trying my hand at poetry again." Both he and Robb were as "excited as two children," he wrote Davidson on June 10, 1958, over the house which was being constructed on the Kenyon campus a few hundred yards from the one they had occupied for almost twenty years. At first they could not decide whether to stay in Gambier or to return to Nashville. "I told John," Robb was quoted as saying, "that I'll go back to Nashville or I'll stay here. I don't care which; we know people to play bridge with both places. But I won't go anywhere else."[83] But, according to George Lanning, she "didn't mention the Cleveland Indians, to whom they are both devoted and who aren't, one supposes, often to be seen in Tennessee." Finally, they decided to remain in Gambier. "We'll settle here," Ransom wrote Andrew Lytle on August 31, 1957; "it's the easiest thing in the world, and we're thoroughly at ease in the community and the landscape, which is much like that of middle Tennessee, only with better grass and less heat." The retirement was not planned, even to this extent, according to George Lanning, who assisted Ransom with the *Review* and later served as its editor. "At any rate, because of the Indians, or the quality of the local bridge players," Lanning said, "they stayed in Gambier: or perhaps the truth is that they absent mindedly bought land from the College and started a house before they'd really settled anything."[84]

This house, which one resident of Gambier described as "Victorian ranch," was the first house he and Robb had ever owned and both of them took great interest in its construction. With his duties on the *Review*, his reading and speaking engagements, and his writing, Ransom's time was fully occupied. He declined several opportunities to teach at other institutions, including a semester at Vanderbilt, and seemed perfectly content with his state of semiretirement. In response to a letter Donald Davidson sent, with a copy of *Southern Writers in the Modern World,* on his seventieth birthday, Ransom admitted that the book induced "a nice nostalgia" but that he did not "dwell on the matter of age." "I seem to be pretty able-bodied (haven't been to a doctor yet)," he wrote, "and am under the illusion of being of sound mind, lacking a little in quick automatic memory." At the end of the current academic year, when he would be able to give up the *Review,* he would assume no other duties because "I have some things to write." In the meantime he enjoyed checking closely on the construction of the new house, which "right at this minute is going up right under our noses, and we'll be in it by Christmas. That promises to be fun."[85]

His last year on the *Review* caused little difficulty. He was pleased to be able to publish much of the material he had accepted, leaving as little backlog as possible so that Robie Macauley would find it easier to steer the journal in the new direction Ransom knew it would take. In the winter number (1959) he published the last of his essays that would appear there under his editorship, "The Idea of a Literary Anthropologist and What He Might Say of the *Paradise Lost* of Milton," an essay based on an address he had given the previous year at the dedication of the new Phi Beta Kappa building at William and Mary. After Ted Bogardus' untimely death, Ransom assisted Macauley in having Irving Krentz appointed managing editor, and in the issue for Autumn, 1959, Ransom announced that henceforth the new editor, whom he recommended without reservation and whom he wished a "long and happy tenure of office" would be in "full charge." From his "private residence in Gambier," he insisted, he would have no official connection with the *Review*.

That Ransom fully understood that the journal would assume a pattern very much different from the one developed under his editorship is indicated in the "official letter" circulated by the Kenyon news bureau at the time of his retirement. "Mr. Macauley has been well assured," Ransom wrote, "that he is under no obligation to continue the periodical in the same literary pattern it has had for twenty years. It is our understanding rather that he will direct it along the lines that seem best to him at this new time so that possibly it will show some differences." Perhaps it was because he wanted to honor this understanding that he seldom visited the office of the *Review* after his retirement, and when he did, according to George Lanning, he adopted the role of an interested but uninvolved visitor, "no proprietorial eye" was cast around, and no "outsider would ever guess that except for him none of us would be here. I have wondered whether—as he has discarded much of his poetry, so many of his books and other critical writings—he has discarded his time on the *Review* as irrelevant to his present undertakings."[86] Whatever his attitudes toward the *Review,* he obviously accepted the fact that one phase of his career was over, and all he could do was to be prepared as well as possible to move into the next. Relieved of the responsibilities for the *Review,* he was sure that now he could complete some of the writing projects he had been mulling over for years. Maybe he could even get back to poetry.

XIV The Culmination of Grave Rites 1960-1974

RANSOM WAS pleased to turn the *Kenyon Review* over to Robie Macauley because, as he wrote his publisher, he was eager to get back "in the verse patch again."[1] Before he entertained that delightful prospect, however, there were other commitments he had to get out of the way. He had agreed to do an essay on Emily Dickinson for the University of Minnesota Pamphlets on American Writers and to edit, with a critical introduction, a "very unwieldly collection of Valéry's essays in the Bollingen Series."[2] He also had long wanted to write an essay on Blake, and an invitation from John Palmer to contribute something to the anniversary issue of the *Yale Review* gave him, he thought, the "kind of stimulus" he needed. There was no lack of things he wanted to do in addition to the projects he had promised to complete or had agreed to consider. He had definitely promised Alfred Knopf to make a new selection of the poems, "bringing them up to 50, adding a few others (revised vitally) of the old ones and—as I hope—two or three new ones."[3] A part of his problem, he saw immediately, was setting some priorities, trying to decide which of these commitments to honor first. His complicated schedule became even more involved when both Knopf and New Directions invited him to prepare a new collection of essays from those that had appeared regularly in the *Kenyon Review* and elsewhere over the past twenty years, and Allen Tate informed him that Alan Swallow wanted to bring out new editions of *The World's Body, God Without Thunder,* and *The New Criticism.* This last proposal was really not too tempting, despite Tate's insistence that these books should be kept in print, because, he wrote, "I can't read my old things with pleasure now. *The World's Body,* with considerable excision and perhaps supplementation I've felt nearest to doing."[4]

With all of these "things frying over the fire," he did not think it wise to accept any of the attractive offers he had received for a semester or more of teaching at some of the most prestigious universities in the country. He thought he could continue to speak or to read his poetry a few times a year without interfering with his work. In fact, he felt that these one- two- or three-day stands, properly spaced, would provide opportunities to visit many of his friends and keep him informed of new developments in the literary community. But any extended absence from his books and the comfortable study he had just occupied in the basement of his new home, he was convinced, would prevent his completing some of the projects he had underway. His work on the new *Selected Poems*—he began this undertaking first because he thought revising some of the older poems would turn him to writing poetry again—was hardly underway, however, when he received a letter from Richard Ellmann urging him to accept an offer to visit Northwestern for a year. After some hesitation, always mindful of how "helpful that extra salary would be," he decided to go to Evanston for one term.

Although he taught only one course, there were other duties, and he was always being surprised, he wrote Robie Macauley on Feburary 11, 1960, "by interruptions I have not allowed for." Ellmann had not been able to find any place for him to live except in a high-rise residential hotel, an environment so different from Gambier and so far removed from his books and notes that he found he could get very little work done. For his public lecture he read a paper on Thomas Hardy which depicted him as "a modern naturalist wanting to find his God" and argued that "Hardy will rank with Tennyson and Browning as the three major poets of the Victorian era." For some time, even before his retirement, he had been working on a selection of Hardy's poems for Macmillan, for which he was preparing a lengthy introduction.[5] When he left the *Review* he had promised Macauley he would continue to contribute to it, and he expected his public lecture at

Northwestern to be his first contribution. After delivering the paper, however, he felt it needed extensive revisions, work he just could not find time to do. Some of the interruptions, to be sure, were most pleasant; like the time he went downtown to hear Isabella Gardner and Robert Lowell read and stayed for a party in their honor, which was followed by a private dinner with the Tates and the Lowells and conversation that lasted almost all night. After Macauley had waited as long as he could—and three weeks beyond his announced deadline—he sent Ransom a telegram saying he was holding up copy for the spring issue of the magazine waiting for the essay. Ransom could send him only half of it and promise the rest by the end of the week. "I could never get manuscripts out of Blackmur and a few others," he wrote in a brief accompanying note, "except two weeks after the deadline; I scolded and wrote and wired and telephoned. But I never dreamed I would be as difficult as Blackmur and it mortifies me that I am being so."

As soon as his term was over at Northwestern he went down to Nashville, where on April 20 and 21 he participated in the annual Vanderbilt Literary Symposium with Lionel Trilling and Peter Taylor. After the meeting he stayed in town over the weekend to visit Annie and Ellene. Soon after he returned to Gambier he was asked to replace Peter Taylor for a term at Ohio State University. Once he had broken his pledge not to accept teaching assignments, it seemed almost impossible to turn down other offers, particularly when by accepting he could accommodate such a close friend as Peter Taylor. He agreed, therefore, to come to Columbus for the winter term of 1961 to offer a graduate seminar in the poetry of Wallace Stevens and T. S. Eliot, an assignment he found particularly pleasant because for several years he had wanted "to write-up both of these poets."[6] Since about 1941 he had promised himself that he would write an extensive essay on Eliot. He was the most important poet of his generation and deserved such comment, and Ransom had long been convinced that on two previous occasions he had been less than generous in his remarks about Eliot.[7] He had also changed his mind about Stevens, whom he had once classified as a poet just below the rank of greatness[8] but whom he now considered a "major poet whose magnitude has been dawning only gradually upon us." He was particularly anxious to do an essay on Stevens because he was convinced "you never have a poet until you write on him."[9]

Shortly after his return to Gambier he heard again from Randall Stewart, who reminded him of the invitation extended at the Fugitive reunion five years before, to return to Vanderbilt for a "semester or a year" whenever he could. After consulting Robb, who assured him she would like to see her old Nashville friends again, he wrote Stewart that he would come for a term the following year. On January 9 he accepted an offer from Vice-Chancellor Rob Roy Purdy to be a visiting professor of English at Vanderbilt for the fall semester of 1961/62. During that winter and spring he corresponded frequently with Stewart, settling final details of the appointment. On January 23, 1961, he wrote that he would offer a course which he called "Studies in Individual Poets Old and New" and indicated he would cover many poets, including Keats, Whitman, William Carlos Williams, Stevens, and Eliot, but would concentrate on the last two because "I've got considerations involving their understanding of the art and the essays of Eliot as they bear on the poems." For the undergraduates in the class—and Stewart had warned him to expect at least a hundred students, mostly undergraduates, many of whom would not be English majors—he promised to offer "generalities and dig into the poems in plain English without many philosophical terms." Stewart also asked if he would give a "public lecture or two" and be " 'available' at stated times in the Old Central parlor for conversations with interested students."[10] He responded immediately that he would be "glad to make an occasional speech such as is within my competence whenever requested and to hold informal hours for group and individual conferences as you may judge they are needed."[11] On January 27 he asked Stewart to assist him in finding an apartment "within walking distance of the University" and one with a kitchenette so that he could get his own breakfast and "occasionally pick-up lunch out of the refrigerator."

When he came to Nashville in April to speak and read at the annual Southern Literary Festival (held that year at Belmont College), he found that most of the details concerning his extended visit to Vanderbilt had been arranged. After investigating several apartments within walking distance of the campus, Stewart had finally located what he thought was the ideal place. West Side Row, where Ransom had lived during his senior year, had been converted into bachelor apartments for faculty and staff, and Stewart had been able to sublet one of the most comfortable of these from a faculty member on leave. After looking at it, Ransom decided it would be large enough for him and Robb and was extremely pleased that he would have to walk only a hundred yards or so to his classes. The most pleasant occasion on this visit was the dinner party the Davidsons gave for him on Saturday night following the meetings at Belmont, to which they invited Randall and Cleone Stewart, Jesse and Ellen Wills, and Alec and Elise Stevenson. After dinner Wills and Davidson read some of their new verse. Although Ransom had nothing new of his own to read, he was pleased that "some of the Fugitives" had returned to poetry after forsaking it for other activities for so many years.[12] It was almost like an "old-time Fugitive meeting," he wrote Tate, and he had returned home excited about the prospects of next year, hoping that this renewed acquaintance with his old friends would get him "poetizing again."

Early in September, 1961, he moved into his furnished apartment. He was pleased to be sharing an office with Davidson, who during many afternoons took him for long drives into some of the beautiful countryside he remembered so well. They were often joined by another faculty couple or two for dinner at Miss Martha's in the Allen Hotel, for many years Davidson's favorite restaurant in Nashville. "It's going to be mighty nice getting back into my old association with you," he had written Davidson before leaving Gambier; "that's one of the main interests I have in mind." Although Davidson complained to Tate that he had not "been able to see nearly enough of Ransom," the time they were able to spend together did much to heal the breach that had developed between them twenty-five years earlier when Ransom had "repudiated Agrarianism," Davidson thought, in his essay "Art and the Human Economy."[13] Ransom was "flattered" that one hundred and fifteen students registered to take the course for credit and almost half that number signed up as official auditors, but he was also grateful to have two graduate students to assist with the reading of papers.

He worked steadily through the fall on the manuscript for the *Selected Poems*, taught his class, visited friends, gave a public reading of his poetry, and made an occasional speech. His class was so large that he had to lecture at every meeting, and this was not the kind of teaching he did best, but, he wrote Tate on January 14, 1962, he did not dislike it and "such was the ignorance of my students that my vein didn't quite run out." On November 2 and 3 he spoke at the meeting of the East Texas Teachers Association and just before Thanksgiving gave an address to the students and faculty in the Divinity School entitled "The Religious Situation in the Poem." Among the poems he read on the latter occasion, to emphasize his central thesis that "all poetry when it is serious concerns a religious situation," was Tate's "Seasons of the Soul." After she had driven him down and gotten him settled, Robb had returned to Gambier because Jack's family, which was "to be increased by a fourth member," engaged "her attention and protection," especially since Jack was away at work most of the week. Because he had to read ninety-odd student essays before he could submit the reports that were due in the registrar's office the week after Thanksgiving, Ransom did not go home for the holidays. He stayed in Nashville and worked, barely taking off long enough to have Thanksgiving dinner with the Davidsons at Miss Martha's; then late Saturday afternoon, with all of his papers read and the reports completed, he went up to Monteagle to spend the weekend with Andrew Lytle.

He did go to Gambier for Christmas and had two pleasant weeks with Robb, the children, and their families, including five grandchildren, Jack's daughter Jane having been born on December 12. When he returned to Nashville shortly after the new year, he was anxious to finish his work there so that he could get back to his writing. He was embarrassed that he could not meet the deadlines he had set for himself, and he was particularly displeased that he was already almost a year beyond the date he had promised Knopf the manuscript of the *Selected Poems*. Except for a little random reading, nothing had been done on the Emily Dickinson essay and very little on the Valéry; and, as he told a reporter for the Nashville *Tennessean*, he wanted to get back to his garden and to his poetry. His favorites among his own verse were "Prelude to an Evening" and "Painted

Head." Because he thought his later poetry achieved "a certain mass and depth of theme and color that I didn't have before," he was convinced he could write more, and maybe better, verse if he could only get down to it.[14]

The most enjoyable single occasion of this five-month sojourn in Nashville was a Saturday evening shortly after Christmas in the home of the Alec Stevensons. Also present were Donald and Theresa Davidson, Jesse Wills (Ellen had another engagement), and Randall and Cleone Stewart. After dinner, he wrote Tate, "we had a bit of a Fugitive session": Davidson read from a novel he was working on "with Grand Old Opry characters in it and Jesse and Alec had new poems, especially Jesse."[15] Ransom displayed some of the revisions he was doing for the new edition of his poems by reading a recently completed version of "Conrad in Twilight," now called "Master's in the Garden Again." This poem, he informed Tate, "seems like a new one now. I couldn't stand the stuttering old introductory part, so I dramatized it a little with a 'dialogue by Laforgue.'" Although Davidson apparently liked this "first stab at a new 'Conrad,'" Ransom was dissatisfied with it. Even as he read it, he said, he realized it "didn't come up to any solid unit."[16] As soon as he was back in Gambier, therefore, he completely revised the poem and sent a copy to Tate, with this comment: "So I've tinkered and tinkered and tinkered at various moments. I don't know if it is a whole; if it is, it's a queer thing. But here's my latest (I'm pretty sure my last) version of the thing. I don't want to expand it, as it's meant to be tense; so I've sectioned it. The value of it for me has been to get back in the groove of poetic language, even though I emphasize the technique of the tetrameters, try out its capabilities."[17] He hoped "before long to explore some ideas which are on my mind for verse—some new ones—" but he still was not satisfied with this poem. He wrote another version for the *Selected Poems*.

Now that he was home, with his vow not to accept anymore teaching assignments more firmly fixed than ever, he was able to complete the manuscript of the *Selected Poems* and get it off to the publisher. At Alfred Knopf's Ransom's editor, Judith P. Jones, saw the book through the press as quickly as possible so that it would appear for his seventy-fifth birthday. Although he had no new verse for the volume, he did increase the number of poems he wished to keep in print from forty-four to fifty-three. In *Selected Poems* (1963) he added eight from his previous collections: four from *Chills and Fever*—"Agitato ma non troppo," "First Travels of Max," "Prometheus in Straits," and "Philomela"—and four from *Two Gentlemen in Bonds*—"Vision by Sweetwater," "Hilda," "Persistent Explorer," and "Morning." He also included "Old Man Pondered," which he had not reprinted since its first appearance in the June 15, 1929, *Saturday Review of Literature.* "Tom, Tom, the Piper's Son" was printed in a much revised form as "The Vanity of the Bright Young Men," and "Conrad in Twilight" was reprinted with only minor revisions. A completely recast version of this last poem appeared, however, under the title "Master's in the Garden Again." This version is not the same as the one he read in Nashville in January, 1962, or that which he sent to Tate on April 16.[18] "Prelude to an Evening" appeared without change, except for the addition of a comma after "deprived" in line 21, but the collection contained a much different version of this poem under the title "Prelude to an Evening: Revised and Explicated."

The volume was widely and, for the most part, favorably reviewed, although most of the reviewers took exception to some of the revisions. "It is almost as if John Ransom, Critic," Roger Hecht wrote in the *Sewanee Review,* "had set out to scold and correct the work of John Ransom, Poet, for a rashness or boldness of past poetic conduct." A few of Ransom's best poems are so firmly fixed in the minds of his readers, Hecht argued, that they are beyond change and should be left "as they are known and remembered and cherished."[19] Writing in the *New Statesman* Alan Brownjohn claimed Ransom's "a wholly unique talent which at times touches greatness"; a half-dozen or so of the poems establish "his place securely as one of the most commanding and assured voices in the American poetry of our time."[20] A writer in *Time* proclaimed him, with the possible exception of Marianne Moore, "the finest poet in the United States today." At seventy-five, this critic continued, Ransom "typifies a chivalry of the intellectual life that is almost gone from America. The ceremonies of commendation are beginning to enfold Ransom in their stony embrace, and he meets them with courteous, ironic sagacity."[21]

Among the "ceremonies of commendation" to which this writer

was referring was one held at Kenyon at which the principal administrative building was named Ransom Hall. "John Ransom as a poet, teacher, and editor," F. Edward Lund said on that occasion, "has contributed more to the reputation of Kenyon College than any living man." During the dedication ceremonies, one witness reported, Ransom stood "patiently in the chilly mist, like a polite bystander." Afterward he admitted that "it took awhile to get up the courage" to look at his name chiseled in stone above the entrance to the newly christened Ransom Hall. "I hardly dared to look at it," he said, "but I glanced over my spectacles and I read it way up at the top there. It looked very holy and scared me a little, but there it is. It looks as though I have become a part of the campus." [22]

To celebrate jointly Ransom's seventy-fifth birthday and the twenty-fifth anniversary of the founding of the *Kenyon Review,* the *Collegian,* the college newspaper, published a special supplement, *John Crowe Ransom: A Tribute from the Community of Letters,* which contained contributions from friends, admirers, and well-wishers throughout the United States and England. [23] A reporter for the Cleveland *Plain Dealer* called Gambier the "literary capital of the United States" because from this little village, which might be a "divot scooped out of southern Massachusetts and replanted in the Ohio valley," had come the *Kenyon Review,* which "has probably been more influential than any other magazine in changing the course of American letters." [24] In a special editorial the *Times Literary Supplement* called the *Kenyon Review* the most significant of the literary quarterlies in the period following World War II, pointing out that it "has led the way in American literary criticism." William Van O'Connor wrote that the New Criticism "would not have existed in the form it finally took" if Ransom "had not been writing editorials, reexamining his own tenets, and engaging in arguments with I. A. Richards, William Empson, Yvor Winters, Cleanth Brooks and others." Randall Jarrell's comment on Ransom the poet has often been quoted: he is "one of the most eloquent and individual war correspondents who ever existed in our world's old war between power and love." [25]

Another indication of the importance with which Ransom was regarded in the world of letters was "A Tribute to John Crowe Ransom on His Seventy-Fifth Birthday" published in *Shenandoah* (Spring,

1963). A special section of this issue of the magazine carried essays by Cleanth Brooks, Allen Tate, Francis Fergusson, John L. Stewart, and Robert Penn Warren. "I consider him now," Tate wrote, "since the death of Stevens and Frost, the dean of American poetry, whose poetry can scarcely be read by a young, coarse, and ignorant generation; whose poetry therefore can have little influence on the young and cannot found a school." Francis Fergusson suggested that the distinctive voice in Ransom's poetry may sound a little muffled to some of those "on Manhattan Island," but it is "there for those who will lend ear, and I do not see how it can become obsolete." The "great quality that shines through" Ransom's best verse, in Warren's view, is charity, a "charity without condescension or connivance or self-indulgence." [26]

The birthday celebration at Kenyon reached an appropriate climax in a symposium, sponsored by the *Kenyon Review*, on the subject: "Quo Vadimus? Or the Books Still Unwritten." For two days a distinguished panel composed of Robert Penn Warren, Robert Lowell, Allen Tate, and Stephen Spender responded to questions Robie Macauley had submitted to them in advance: "What direction should literary criticism take?" "What present tendencies in poetry seem to be the ones that point to the future?" "What areas in American fiction are still left unexplored?" "What will happen to the novel and drama over the next twenty years?" Ransom attended these sessions and made occasional comments, but the portions of the festivities he enjoyed most were those brief periods between the luncheons, cocktail parties, dinners, and formal meetings when he had a little time for private conversation with his old friends and former students. Surely, as one present pointed out, nothing so magnificent as this celebration had ever occurred in Gambier before, a village where "neighbors socialize on Tuesday and Thursday afternoons between two and four at the local garbage dump" and one so quiet that the "greatest excitement before the coming of Ransom might have been the day John Dillinger robbed the People's Bank."

When Robie Macauley insisted that Ransom contribute to the one hundredth number of the *Kenyon Review*, he was delighted, he wrote Tate, to be stimulated to do "at long last a piece on Wallace Stevens, a poet and man I have much admired. I am more than anxious to do this after my second reading, just now, of Pearce's *Continuity of American Poetry*." But, he concluded, "my commendation of Stevens as perhaps the best natural poet our country has had does not mean that Stevens hewed to the best poetic line or that poems in general must not suit their own honest occasions."[27] This assignment and the other commitments he had made convinced Ransom that he must devote the next few months to a "lot of work in prose," which he hoped to "make a reasonably quick job of" so that he could try his "hand at some new verse, not salvage work." When he actually got down to writing the essay on Stevens, however, it did not go as easily as he had expected. Although he had read Stevens carefully for years and felt he knew his poetry as well as that of any other modern poet, with the possible exception of Yeats and Eliot, the essay just would not take shape. "I find," he wrote Tate, "I don't stand very well too many hours of working closely at my writing." Except for the occasional attacks of vertigo, which almost completely disabled him when they did occur, he felt his health was good for one who was "approaching the physical state of a gerontion" but was "yet in the senescent rather than the senile stage." He tired easily, however, and sometimes after a period of only a few minutes he could not concentrate and would have to turn to something else. He worked at the essay as steadily as he could all fall, but as late as Thanksgiving he was afraid he would miss another deadline. Early in December, however, he got an unexpected burst of creative energy, completed the piece, and turned it in to Macauley before celebrating Christmas with the children and grandchildren.

The essay opens with an admission that Stevens is a "major poet whose magnitude has been dawning only gradually upon us." Ransom and his friends first read him in 1923 and knew him then as a "new poet who spoke as having authority"; at the same time they were mystified that an insurance executive could write such poetry.[28] As he became better acquainted with the poetry, he was even more perplexed by the versatility of the businessman-poet, particularly after publishing in the *Kenyon Review* "three important poems" (the only ones Stevens submitted to him): "Variations on a Summer's Day," "Esthetique du Mal," and "The Auroras of Autumn." In 1942, therefore, when Ransom was teaching for the summer at Bread Loaf, he wrote Stevens to ask if he could stop by Hartford on his way back to Gambier for some good conversation. He wanted to meet this "capacious man with a double personality, having an ego and an alter ego too," who was the "business man at Hartford" and the "poet when he went to Florida." Stevens responded immediately that he could not allow Ransom to meet him in Hartford for a "little conversation"; instead he proposed to board his train when it came through Hartford and go with Ransom to New York where they could have a "big conversation." Unfortunately, "before the appointed day could arrive" Ransom received a telegram requiring him to "hurry home by the speediest route, and make no stops by the way." The two poets never met, and although Ransom's interest in Stevens' poetry continued, he was not finally convinced that this sometime poet belonged with Eliot, Pound, and Frost in the first rank of American poets until after his death in 1955.[29]

Following his long-since stated principle that literary criticism should not be "pursued in any way except in the constant company of the actual poems," Ransom comments on several of Stevens' poems—particularly "The Ordinary Women," "Sea Surface Full of Clouds," "Le Monocle de Mon Oncle," "The Jack-Rabbit," "Sunday Morning," "Extracts from Addresses to the Academy of Fine Ideas," and "Notes Toward a Supreme Fiction"—in an attempt to demonstrate that his slightly older contemporary "was a very good Kantian, though there is no evidence that he had ever read Kant seriously, and some evidence that he had not." There are three "economies," Ransom points out, by which man conducts his life: the scientific and business economy under which we "calendar the working days of our life"; the moral economy, "commonly administered by the Synagogue and the Western churches under the simplest and boldest of supernatural sanctions"; and the third economy, "a spontaneous and individual yet compulsive kind of activity not directed by institutions" and intended to "perform, let us say, the works of grace." These economies are concerned with "bread, the moral commandments, and beauty," and Stevens' career falls most decidedly into the first and third. Although Stevens encouraged "good minor and occasional poets," his bond was with "professional poets, who were concerned, like himself, with the definition of their faith." As his poetic program did not take all his strength, Stevens was able to engage fully in two of the three economics, and he had so much ability that he may have been a poet who turned into a saint:

We may imagine several kinds of sainthood. One might have consisted in an invincible benevolence; a tranquillity toward the people and places and faiths he had once scorned, as if now he conceded them their equal right to be. Another might have been a pure beatitude, as when the mind achieves a childhood innocence again, and is visited by visions and angels. Or a third kind, a more official sainthood, into which a little of vanity might enter: the sense that he had been a mighty and effectual evangelist of his faith. There was something of each of these in him.[30]

As Ransom moved beyond his seventy-fifth birthday, he realized that he was not "up to par." "I have still a case of vertigo due to an ear trouble," he wrote Newton P. Stallknecht. "I don't dare drive a car. I can't walk in the dark and at times I simply stumble along instead of walking."[31] But he remained as active as he could and continued to accept ten to fifteen speaking and reading engagements a year. Along with Allen Tate, Robert Lowell, Randall Jarrell, Richard Wilbur, and Karl Shapiro, he read from his verse to honor the fiftieth anniversary of the founding of *Poetry*.[32] During a twelve-month period, embracing the winter of 1963 and the spring of 1964, he read and lectured at Yale; read at Louisiana State University, the University of Minnesota, and Purdue University; attended a three-day writers' conference in Louisville, Kentucky, at which he read his verse, gave two prepared and several unprepared speeches, and judged the poetry manuscripts; and lectured to the Oklahoma Library Association. During the same period he was in New York, where on December 19, 1963, he was honored by the Academy of American Poets.[33] He began this strenuous period with a three-week visit to California, where he made ten appearances at six different institutions before hurrying back to introduce Robert Lowell when he read at Kenyon on October 19, 1963. He was guest of honor at the Southern Literary Festival, which was meeting at the Mississippi State College for Women as a "special memorial" to Ellene, who had died the previous year. Ellene had been dean at Mississippi State College for Women for ten years when she discovered at her routine physical check up that she had cancer. She told no one of her illness, but proceeded to get her affairs in order. Although she learned of the illness in February, she completed the school year before coming to Nashville to receive treatment. When she checked into the hospital, Annie notified Ransom, but he had no notion of the seriousness of her condition until she died a few days later, on June 6, 1964.

Just after his return from California he had written Tate: "You'd be surprised to see what good physical shape I'm in nowadays. I've picked up weight and feel very strong, at least for the short haul."[34] Francis Fergusson saw him in New York in December and was amazed at his vigor and energy and the "speed with which he went up three long flights of stairs carrying two heavy bags."[35] When he got back to Gambier, after three strenuous days in Columbus, Mississippi, and a two-day visit with Annie and his friends in Nashville, however, he felt "used up" and could do little work, even on the "prose writing for which I have specific datelines."[36]

He remained an active member of the board of senior fellows of the School of Letters until its program was terminated in 1972. Although he did not teach there after the 1958 summer session, he made a specific effort to attend the board's annual meetings, and over a twenty-year period he was absent only twice.

Throughout the 1960s Ransom also responded to requests from Horst Frenz and Stallknecht for recommendations for courses and staff. When Frenz wrote Ransom on October 6, 1961, asking for recommendations for the summer staff, Ransom responded immediately, suggesting Leonard Ungar whose essay on T. S. Eliot in the Minnesota Pamphlet series, "though crowded as it had to be in about 50 pp., is the best thing we have on that poet" and Wayne Booth, whose *The Rhetoric of Fiction* he had read in manuscript for the University of Chicago Press. "Its the fullest (by far) and the wisest on the forms and points of view of fiction," he wrote; "he shows how the author *always* reveals his own point of view, and defends novels which have no interior reporter, only the author's own (or ironic) will. He writes easily and brightly and his book will push his rating very high." If neither of these two was available, Ransom reminded Frenz that he could always depend on Kenneth Burke, whose recently published

Rhetoric of Religion "may well be his best book" and R. P. Blackmur, who "gets constantly deeper."[37]

In response to a letter asking him to suggest names of additional senior fellows, Ransom recommended Wallace Fowlie, who is "a master of French language and literature and well versed in our own verse," and Eric Heller, "who dittoes Fowlie in German language and literature"; either of these would be an important addition, because "such an appointment is necessary to improve comparative literature offerings." In the same letter he indicated he would "exclude Cleanth Brooks, Robert Lowell, and Randall Jarrell" whose names had come from other senior fellows, because "they are too close to Tate and me and would give too much weight to a single group." He would "react favorably" to some of the others suggested, he added, particularly to Arthur Mizener, who is "good at fiction" and to Leslie Fiedler, who is a "critic of traditional poetry and criticism and saner and less exclusive than Shapiro."[38] Later, when asked to choose between R. W. B. Lewis and Mizener, he agreed with Stallknecht that Lewis appeared to be the "stronger man."[39]

Soon after the School of English was moved from Gambier to Bloomington to become the School of Letters, Ransom wrote Tate several letters indicating that he felt they should withdraw from the board of senior fellows because he thought the venture had accomplished all that could be expected of it. It was not until the mid-1960s, however, that he began to express feelings of this kind to Stallknecht. The senior fellows should not be so much involved in the management of the school, he wrote on January 22, 1964, because the circumstances surrounding that operation then were far different from those that existed in the 1940s:

When the Rockefeller people gave Kenyon College the money . . . [we wanted] to staff . . . the School of English with the brightest *outside* people rather than Gambier people, so that our standard would surpass the local college standard by aiming at an absolute excellence. We had no four or five or six people at Gambier qualified as our . . . designated Senior Fellows of the School had to be. Our idea was to conduct . . . a School for summer instruction in the critical approach such as must be far beyond the instruction we could have tapped in the College. . . . The Review and the School of English went after

professional writers of criticism who could teach writing profession-
ally; and in those days that would have been a little different from
going after regular competent academic writers. Nowadays I suppose
there is not so marked a difference, partly because we have succeeded
so well in our instructions.

So, although he hoped the senior fellows would survive in principle,
he thought it time "to get a new slate of them, a group just as various
and catholic as those now serving, but even more aware of what is
going on critically.... Our crowd has grown old in the service, and
less active than it might be." A few months later he concluded a letter:
"I'm feeling quite superannuated about education nowadays, and
rather like asking you to take my name off the list. But I will always
feel full of best wishes for the School."[40] But Stallknecht apparently
ignored the request and Ransom did not renew it.

His health was good, having "recently regained all the weight I lost
over the past two years," he wrote Tate, and he felt the need to write,
especially "to get some new poems done," but he just could not work
"as long or as fast" as he could "a few decades ago." The essay on
Emily Dickinson, which he had been thinking about for two or three
years and trying to write for six months, would not take shape so he
put it aside, as he did the one on Valéry, and began working on Blake,
hoping to write a long piece to serve as the leading essay for the
collection he had promised New Directions.[41] On Saturday, February
13, 1965, he returned from a week in Texas, where he had lectured at
Rice and the University of Texas on the "Theory of Poetic Form," to
find a letter from Allen Tate, containing a request that turned his
attention to another project. Tate was bringing together a collection
of essays on T. S. Eliot and urged Ransom to contribute. Ransom
replied that he would be happy to "write on Eliot" because he had "an
intense sympathy for that tortured soul who achieved serenity." Since
he had notes that he had used in several speeches on Eliot, he thought
he could complete his essay long before the summer deadline.[42] In
mid-summer, however, he wrote that he had not finished the essay,
although it was in an "advanced stage." Since he had seen the list of
prospective contributors and was confident there would be a "lot of
mss of general tribute," he had changed his mind and thought now of
doing something entirely different from what he had first planned:

I'm thinking of a general word or so of honor as a preface ... and then a detailed study of "Gerontion." It has always interested me very much especially as to how he practices the lapses from prosody by finding the odd scraps of information and the unexpected words that make the style fresh and vital as if it were straight verse. I think there's no poet who can staisfy the modern taste without the leap into not-quite relevant images.[43]

He was thinking, he concluded, of a piece of "ten pages which is assembling itself now in my mind."

Three months later, however, the essay apparently was still being assembled, because in response to a telegram from Tate requesting it, he admitted that he had written only an introduction "about Eliot and his faith and then talked a little of the more indefinite faith of most poets such as myself; but most sympathetic." If there is still time to meet the deadline, he wrote, he could complete the manuscript within three or four days of his return from Emory and Henry College, where he was lecturing on November 22. To demonstrate that the essay was "already assembled in his mind," though not yet committed to the page, he presented a brief summary of the opening section and a plan for the remainder:

"Gerontion" is a revolutionary and successful experiment in loosening the strict bonds of the old pentameter verse. ... The great point Eliot was after, and got hold of, was the prosody of the *phrases* of his text, where time after time there is a rhythm, i.e. a repetition of the phrases containing one, two, three, or four stresses, which the unstressed syllables don't disturb. The first stanza is the most important, almost 100% Old English and therefore rather the hardest to make melody of. ... I am under the conviction that the well-voiced, linguistically-trained readers do not have the slightest sense of the *expression*, which they either don't follow, or don't care to render. It's an important poem, and I'd like to hear a "linguist" try to read it. ... I think he has launched a new age for poets who attend to their prosodical advantages.[44]

When the essay was not in by November 29, as Ransom had promised it would be, Tate had to submit copy for the special issue of the *Sewanee Review* without it. On December 4, Ransom sent the opening paragraph of his introductory statement, which was to be a brief tribute to Eliot whom he considered the "most important poet of his generation," and the "insets in which I try the scansions of several of its sections." In between these scanned sections, he explained in an accompanying letter, he would attempt "a little general talk about the other sections, prosodically." His "remarks on the substance," would be "much briefer than my running comments on the prosody of the insets." He ended the letter with a rather lengthy statement of how he intended to develop the introductory part of the essay:

There is just one excursion from "Gerontion" which follows my introductory paragraph. I speak of the man as a deeply religious one, even in the early poems where he has apparently lost his faith somewhere, but he is still wrestling with the problem; and it seems imperative to spend a page or two on the Prufrock because, true to form, he makes the reader use all the head he can to read him rightly; and even the best critics—about all I have read—take that poem as an uproarious comedy at Prufrock's expense; who appears to be unable to sue for his lady's hand. The complementary fact, in my judgment, is that he finds her unworthy, because she is incapable of religious understanding, and I cite the phrases which show that he thinks there is no use putting the "overwhelming question" to her, for she would turn away. So the joke is on the common reader who is not interested in that feature; as Eliot even with all his piety must have expected. He had a great wit.[45]

He could not send the complete text the next day, as he had promised, because as soon as he returned from posting the letter to Tate, James Wright brought Robert Bly, whom Ransom had never met, over for a visit. They stayed through lunch, at a restaurant in Mount Vernon, and for most of the afternoon. Although he was surprised that he and Bly "got on famously," he was worried, he wrote Tate a few days later, about Wright's health. As soon as his visitors left, however, Ransom typed out and mailed his introductory statement and the insets in which he had carefully "marked the prosodies" of the first "three movements" of the poem. His comments on all "five of the poem's movements" he promised to send shortly. Everything was in by December 10 and Ransom wrote Tate that he was going "to rest up for a week." The essay appeared in the *Sewanee Review* for Spring, 1966, the issue following the special Eliot number.

The difficulty Ransom had in completing this essay is another indication of his diminished energy. His letters in the middle and late

1960s contain many references to the fact that he could no longer work at his earlier pace. When he pushed himself, as he did with the Eliot essay, he found he had neither the strength nor the interest to do any kind of creative work for days or sometimes weeks, except, as he expressed it, to "tinker" with his verse. Four months after completing the essay on "Gerontion," he still felt "utterly exhausted." He wrote Tate on April 18, 1966, "I never worked as hard in my life as I did trying to get the Eliot essay ready." Since he could not get the piece on Blake going, he decided to attempt something different "as the lead in for a big book of essays long promised to Jay Laughlin." At Emory and Henry College he had talked about "the improvisations of the critic who wants to see the whole mind of the poet he is reading," and he proposed to develop an essay from notes he had made for the occasion. But six months later the project was not finished—there is no indication that it ever advanced beyond the planning stage—and he was still trying to wind up "one or two last critical essays" before doing a "few more poems." [46]

Ransom continued to receive the kinds of awards due one of the nation's most distinguished men of letters. On December 4, 1962, it was announced that he had been given a $5,000 fellowship by the Academy of American Poets for "Distinguished Poetic Achievement." [47] This honor was followed less than two years later, on March 10, 1964, by the National Book Award for *Selected Poems* (1963). On that occasion Ransom, the winners in the other categories, and hundreds of distinguished guests assembled in the grand ballroom of the New York Hilton for the ceremonies at which each winner was introduced by a brief statement from the committee honoring his book, [48] presented a check for $1,000, and allowed five minutes for an acceptance speech.

Ransom's acceptance was characteristically modest, witty, and provocative. He began by saying that he was grateful that the judges had given the award to "such an old-timer," but "this pleasure is compounded with a pain" when he thinks of his "good friends, the other poets who were passed over." But such is the nature of the world we must live in that "perhaps every pleasure is the denial of some other pleasure." Since he may never "confront another audience so committed to the production of literature" as this one is, he continued, he must not lose his chance to comment on a "queer confusion that readers often feel about a poet's work." There is often no general agreement on whether the poet really tried to be decent and hopeful and in the line of the highest moral standard." This confusion is usually the reader's failure to understand the unique nature of the poem and precisely how it functions:

It is widely understood by poets that a lyric poem does not mean to promote utility, as the mechanical sciences do, nor morality, as the Scriptures do. It is much more like a rapturous piety; a homage to external nature despite the griefs it causes us, and to human nature despite its hateful and treacherous tendencies; or a testimony to the unknown Artificer, that a little of the awful secret of creation is being grasped here and published, to his everlasting glory.
A rational structure such as the argument of a poem is an abstract that never exists in nature by itself, but is merely one of perhaps countless structures operating in the same time and space and perhaps not interfering much with each other. And the rational mind cannot express such multiple combinations. The best the poet can do is to introduce words and phrases related to the argument, but partly going off tangentially and rather spectacularly as if heading for some other structures. Students are taught to regard the act of composing a poem under the image of the rational mind furiously worrying and whipping the imagination to perform superhuman or at least irrational feats of language which the understanding by itself cannot discover. So the poet has hit awkwardly but truly upon the mystery of multiple creation. Philosophers might say that he has obtained a fragmentary vision of that Absolute which embraces all these little relatives at once.[49]

Shall we allow "horrid disasters and ugly evil" in the poem, even though they are "according to created nature"? If some poet seems "given altogether to the show of horrors," we should realize that "it is an insipid period when nobody seems conscious of the necessity of evil." Although Ransom said he used to think he had "discovered the drama of opposites" all by himself, he now knew that Heraclitus "long ago spelled it out," two thousand years later Leibniz "expressed it, and tagged it with a remarkable consequence:" this is indeed "the best of all possible worlds" because though "evil is too well established in nature ever to fail us," the "party of evil" is always "in the minority." This doctrine is not in the Scriptures, because the theologians and moralists are "incorrigible partisans for their side," causing the Devil to work all the harder.

Ransom was almost able to express, in the five minutes allowed him, one of his most compelling and lasting convictions about the nature of the world and a recurring theme in much of his poetry. Because he had gone a little beyond the permitted "word count," however, he feared he had "betrayed" his audience. "My deepest apologies," he concluded; "that was evil, and I do not know if I have done enough good to overcome it." He was seldom able to say more in such brief space and at the same time to demonstrate more convincingly Tate's assertion that his critical essays "have the formal felicities of his poetry, and are themselves works of literature." [50]

In its next issue *Time* indicated its approval of the committee's choice by reminding its readers of the many areas in which Ransom had influenced twentieth-century literature:

Fortnight ago, a silver-haired southern gentleman named John Crowe Ransom stood up to receive the 1964 National Book Award for poetry. As founder and editor of the *Kenyon Review,* mentor to a platoon of celebrated poets and writers, and father of the New Criticism, Ransom is probably the most influential scholar-critic of the past 40 years. As the author of a few slender books of poetry, he has drawn the highest praise from the knottiest intellectuals of his time. [51]

A few weeks after receiving this award, while Ransom was in Louisville, Kentucky, for two speeches, he complained mildly to a reporter: the "spate of honors that have come my way recently I find painful. I had to cancel a speech to go to New York to get the National Book Award. They said come get it, so I thought I had better go." But this was in part at least a pose; he was naturally pleased to remain in the public eye even though his major work was far behind him; writing to Tate and others he commented on how "amazed and terribly pleased" he was that his friends continued to "champion an old has-been like me." Apparently his friends continued their support, always for honors he richly deserved, for on December 16, 1966, he was elected—along with Kenneth Burke, Henry Steele Commager, Katherine Anne Porter, and John Hall Wheelock—to membership in the American Academy of Arts and Letters. [52] He was inducted in May, 1967, and two months later learned that he was one of five "distinguished senior American writers" who would receive individual grants of $10,000 from the National Endowment for the Arts.[53] These awards, the first made by the endowment for this purpose, were intended, according to the official announcement, "to honor writers who have heretofore not received all the recognition due them." These particular writers were decided upon, the announcement said, because of "many, many inquiries, pleas, and demands on their behalf from poets, novelists, editors and publishers throughout the country." Almost before he had time to recover from the shock of receiving the "ten grand," which, as he wrote Tate, "came entirely unexpected and unapplied for," he was honored again by the same agency. In June, 1967, the endowment initiated the *American Literary Anthology,* an "annual collection of the best poetry, fiction, essays and criticism selected by a panel of judges from literary magazines of limited circulation." Andrew Lytle and Allen Tate recommended Ransom's essay on "Gerontion," which appeared, along with the work of forty-seven other poets, in the first collection.[54]

As Ransom's eightieth birthday approached friends in many sections of the country planned celebrations. The first of these occurred a little more than a year early, on April 28, 1967, at Martin College in Pulaski, Tennessee, where Ransom was born and had lived for the first eighteen months of his life. Since he had not been back for more than seventy-five years, he "could not imagine" he would "know a soul there," but he was grateful for the honor and pleased that he would have an opportunity to see some old friends again.[55] He flew to Nashville on April 27 and had an evening with Allen Tate and his new wife, Helen Heinz. The next day he drove down to Pulaski with the Tates and Andrew Lytle. Both Tate and Lytle appeared on the program, at which Ransom made a few comments and read some of his poems, including by request "Piazza Piece" and "Old Mansion." He drove back to Nashville that night and spent the weekend with Annie before flying back to Columbus late Sunday afternoon.

Meanwhile in New York, Dallas, Gambier, and elsewhere other occasions were being planned. Early in 1967 David McDowell, senior editor of Crown Publishers and a former student of Ransom's, had undertaken the responsibility of interesting the national news media in the celebration President Lund and his associates at Kenyon were planning. He wrote Saul Maloff, the book review editor, and Kermit Lansirir, the managing editor, of *Newsweek*, "both of whom," McDowell informed Lund, "are receptive to the idea. So is *Time*. David Sherman of *Life* is planning to send a researcher to Gambier somewhat before the event and, later, a photographer to record it." [56] At about the same time President and Mrs. Donald Cowan, Professors Thomas Landess and M. E. Bradford, and other members of the faculty and staff at the University of Dallas were completing plans to have as many members of the Nashville Agrarians as possible to participate in the Southern Literary Festival and to remain in Dallas for two days of Agrarian conversations. On March 22, 1968, Ransom asked to be excused from the senior fellows meeting scheduled for later that month in Bloomington, because he had had another of the attacks of vertigo, which of late were almost continuous, and because he felt he should conserve his "declining energies to participate in a three-day Southern Literary Festival at Dallas in late April. I have to do that because the Fugitives and the Agrarians will be the speakers and the panel." [57] Just before the Dallas meeting the Louisiana State University Press issued *John Crowe Ransom: Critical Essays and a Bibliography,* which contained an exhaustive checklist of works by and about Ransom and sixteen critical essays indicating the development of Ransom's literary reputation and evaluating his achievements as poet, critic, editor, and man of letters. [58]

Ransom, Tate, Lytle, and Warren came to Dallas for the meetings; Davidson was too ill to attend, but he sent a statement to be read into the official record of the Agrarian sessions. [59] Although Ransom was, as he expressed it, a "little unsteady on his pins," several of his friends commented on how well he seemed to withstand five exhausting days: from eight or eight-thirty in the morning, when he joined his old friends for breakfast in the motel dining room, through a morning discussion, which was recorded; an official luncheon, usually preceded by whiskey sours, bloody Marys, or sherry; then, after a brief rest, an afternoon session (also recorded), followed by cocktails, dinner, and a third session of recorded conversations. At the end of this very full day everyone gathered in someone's motel room for talk and drinks. Ransom appeared alert, interested, and actively engaged. Reading the transcripts of those Agrarian conversations, however, one is immediately aware that Ransom's hearing was much worse than he was willing to admit. Many of his comments demonstrate that often he did not understand the question to which he was responding.

Many of the participants in the Agrarian conversations went directly from Dallas to Gambier, where they were joined by others equally distinguished, for the celebration there.[60] The formal dinner given on the evening of April 29 was followed by a program at 11 A.M. the next day in the Wertheimer Field House, at which Allen Tate gave the principal address. Ransom's poems, Tate said, are minor only in that they are not long; they are "major in their inclusive irony." From his first poem to his last he has told us that "nothing will last, all will go and that our mastery of decay and death is ironically the culmination of 'grave rites and funerals.' The man whom we honor today at the end of his eightieth year is one of the great elegiac poets of the English language." Not even T. S. Eliot "surpassed him in the awareness of the shadowy backroom of the human condition, where 'invisible evil deprived and bold' makes its bid for domination." Like Wallace Stevens, Ransom is a master of formal versification; he has a quality of diction that has been "superficially described as elegant," and he has always maintained a "fastidious detachment from the existential muddle of our time."[61] Surely Ransom was pleased to hear this perceptive comparison of his poetry to that of Eliot and Stevens, whose work he regarded as the most representative of the age, as he must have been to read in the next issue of the *Kenyon Review* Robert Penn Warren's estimate of his achievements as a poet.[62] There is "something inconclusive about Ransom's poems," Warren wrote, because the tensions with which they are concerned cannot be resolved. The poetry is durable because of "the voice, the tone, the scrupulous shadings of attitude, the wit, the passion."

The reporter *Life* sent to Gambier made thirteen pages of notes, and the next issue of the magazine carried an account, with photographs, of the festivities.[63] "Robert Lowell brought along a poem written for the occasion," the story begins; "Allen Tate gave a proper tribute, Ransom took a bow but said nothing." Later that morning, however, he admitted that he felt a little awkward because he "knew of few other poets thus fêted before death." That afternoon over beer around the long table at Dorothy's, he confessed: "I'd rather rest on my poetry than on anything else. I've always liked to write poems of sentiment, not soft but personal. I cut my meanness out on friends." Ransom's influence on American letters, however, "springs only in part from his own distinguished verse," the reporter concluded, for "as teacher and critic, this scholar who never sought any degree beyond a B.A. revolutionized poetic criticism and served as a personal focus for a generation of poets."

All the activities surrounding his eightieth birthday were brought to an approximate climax by the reissue of *The World's Body*, Ransom's most significant and influential book of criticism, and by the appearance of a third edition of *Selected Poems*. [64] In a postscript to *The World's Body* Ransom again recanted, as he had in the essay on "Gerontion" two years before, some of his earlier statements on Eliot. In his review of *The Waste Land*, he had charged Eliot with the "academic trick" of using "recondite allusions" and not employing a "firm and consistent prosody." He was aware almost immediately that he was mistaken about the allusions because it became apparent that they "meant a great deal to a very important public." It took much longer, he admitted, for him to see that his "charges against Eliot's prosody were not completely justified." He hoped he had partly rectified that error of judgment, however, in a recent essay in which he had argued that by "precept and example" Eliot had brought into the "music of poetry the grace and freedom which had arrived in the art of pure music many years before." [65] His other "unfortunate estimate" of Eliot was his review of *Murder in the Cathedral*, which "was composed in a fury," a "matter of a few hours," at a time when he was deeply immersed in *Samson Agonistes* and thought Eliot's play was always "running wild and rejecting its form." At first he had "disliked the Interlude containing the Beckett sermon, the language of the poor old women employed in the Chorus, and especially the speeches of the silly young Royalists who tried to justify themselves for murdering the Archbishop." But during the past thirty years, he wrote, he had come to realize that drama was subject to change, as is any other art form, and now he was not offended by the intrusion of large blocks of prose into poetic drama. Of even more importance, he had concluded that it would be destructive to remove the passages of prose from *Murder in the Cathedral* because "the prose is suited precisely to its important speakers in the crucial action of the play."[66] The other "lapse of judgment" he acknowledged in this postscript was in the essay "Shake-speare at Sonnets," written as he later said, when he "was too much under the influence of Donne."[67] Now he admitted that he was able to see that more of Shakespeare's sonnets than he had thought were "innocent of my charge of anticlimax in their descending quatrains, and the final couplets are pithier and more adequate to their arguments."

The final collection of Ransom's verse selected by him appeared in early 1969. Anyone who has followed the publishing history of his poetry is aware of the fact that in each edition Ransom became less restrictive and admitted new poems into the group that he wished to keep in print. *Selected Poems* (1945) contains forty-two poems; *Poems and Essays* (1955), forty-four; *Selected Poems* (1963), fifty-three; and *Selected Poems* (1969), eighty—if the two different versions of the eight poems included in the section "Sixteen Poems in Eight Pairings" are considered as separate poems. Each appearance of a selection of his verse gave Ransom the opportunity to publish a revised version of some of the poems, some of which were so completely recast that they became different poems. All of the fifty-three poems in *Selected Poems* (1963) appear in the 1969 edition, but thirty of them were revised, some drastically; twenty-seven poems, including two from *Poems About God,* are added. There are now in print eight versions of "Necrological"; six of "Armageddon"; five each of "Eclogue," "Emily Hardcastle, Spinster," "Old Mansion," and "Vaunting Oak"; and ten of "Tom, Tom, the Piper's Son."

When this latest collection appeared, many reviewers were concerned about Ransom's revisions. Most critics have not accepted the latest as the best version of the poems.[68] Many of them apparently agree with Roger Hecht's assertion that a poet should not "impose on work long past present standards and present language."[69] Robert Buffington argues convincingly that in his old age Ransom was "kindly disposed toward the world," that some of the earlier poems were revised because Ransom had come to mistrust many of the ambiguities they contained. "Tom, Tom, the Piper's Son" and "Prelude to an Evening," for example, are given happy endings. Not one of the revised versions in the "Sixteen Poems in Eight Pairings," Buffington believes, is superior to the original.[70] What he takes from these poems is the "haunting dualism of man's experience," "something simultaneously offered and denied," man's ability to retain his sanity in a world that demands that he "hold two opposing ideas in the mind at the same time."[71] Above all else, this poetry of "the master's old age" reveals a strong urge to resolve some of the conflicts, to ease some of the tensions that accrue to man as he attempts to maintain in perilous balance some of the contrarieties of modern life: heaven and hell, fire and ice, reason and emotion, love and honor. The publication of this collection indicates conclusively the urgent need for a variorum edition of Ransom's poetry, from which could come a reader's edition of the best versions of the best poems.[72]

After his return from Dallas, Ransom's health required that he limit his traveling. He went to Boston on May 9, 1968, however, to receive the Emerson-Thoreau Medal and an honorarium of $1,000, given annually by the American Academy of Arts and Sciences for "distinguished achievement in the broad field of literature." At the 188th annual meeting of the academy, Henri Peyre, Sterling Professor of French at Yale University and chairman of the Emerson-Thoreau Medal Committee, read the citation to Ransom: "He coined the phrase 'The New Criticism' and in Gambier, Ohio, location of Kenyon College, he guided and inspired a review and a group of critics which changed for the better the face of American literature."[73]

Ransom's ear trouble did not improve, and his letters during this period are filled with references to his illness. In the fall of 1967, Reavill, his wife Shirley, and their three children came for a ten-day visit and Ransom was more active than usual. But just before they left, he wrote Tate, "an old ailment of mine broke out—the dizziness caused by the bad state of my right ear. I found I couldn't get out of bed in the night without holding on around the walls—I refused to crawl. I haven't ventured to work in the garden or drive the car, but I've recovered nearly, though my walking is not firm yet."[74] Although for a time he seemed to respond well to a new kind of medication his doctor gave him, the improvement was only temporary, for a few months later he wrote that he had come "into a bad condition, a vertigo due to a faulty functioning of the Labyrinth of my right ear, which ought to furnish me with a balancing power. I can't walk at all in the dark and just stump around in the light. But I'm taking treatment and in any case I'm getting used to my bad locomotion and beginning to improve it."[75]

He became even more concerned about his condition after having a temporary blackout in the air terminal in Indianapolis on his way home from Bloomington, where he had attended a meeting of the senior fellows of the School of Letters.[76] Although he was determined to refuse all invitations to speak or read, he was persuaded to go to Gainesville, Florida, to participate in the Florida Writers' Conference because Andrew Lytle was to be given an honorary degree by the University of Florida, where for many years he had taught creative writing. Also he was told that Cleanth Brooks and Peter Taylor were to be on the program and other old friends would likely be there. But this occasion was not an altogether happy one because he did not perform well. His reading went all right, although he was completely exhausted when it was over, and he was able to respond to the students' questions because some of those present made sure he understood what he was being asked. As the time neared for him to speak, however, he could not find his notes. Although John Tyree Fain, a former student who was to introduce him that evening, went back to the room where he was staying and searched it thoroughly, no notes turned up. So Ransom tried to re-create from memory what he had intended to say, and the most charitable statement his friends could make about his performance was that his "remarks were disjointed" and his "mind seemed to wander."[77] He did not accept an invitation to read or speak outside Gambier again.

During his last years Ransom lived so quietly that many of the students at Kenyon did not know they were sharing the village of Gambier with the man who a few years before was a model for every undergraduate student of literature. Seldom did he go beyond the boundaries of his own yard. Even the three- or four-hundred-yard walk down Kenyon's Middle Path to the post office was too much for him. He stayed in the modest white clapboard house, where he had lived since his retirement, and welcomed his old students and occasional visitors. If his guests had literary interests, as they invariably did, he would give them a firm handshake, present them to Robb or to any other family members who happened to be present, and take them downstairs to his booklined study. There, under his "southern clock," so named because its hands moved backwards across its face, he might show the new edition of his poems he was working on—to contain eighty-three poems, three more than *Selected Poems* (1969)— or he might read one of Blake's poems, whom he would say he was "writing up" at the moment to demonstrate his conviction that Blake was the greatest English poet of the nineteenth century.[78]

Thomas Lask, a journalist from the New York *Times,* who came by to see him about two years before he died, described him as "slight, courtly in every gesture, with eyes alert and a wide-mouthed smile" but found him unwilling to talk on subjects that did not interest him. Although it is likely that Ransom just did not understand the questions and was too gentlemanly to ask that they be repeated or that his interviewer speak louder, the reporter thought he was using the "privilege of art to pick and choose among the questions":

Asked for example, whether he still believed as he wrote in one volume that the aesthetic experience is "beyond good and evil," he answered a little quizzically, "Did I say that?" and let the matter drop.

He had not yet seen his book, *Beating the Bushes* [a selection of his unpublished essays from the *Kenyon Review* plus "Wanted: An Ontological Critic"], until his visitor showed him his own copy. But he displayed little of the excitement that a newly published book brings on. "I had forgotten the title," he admitted.[79]

Although he had done a great deal of criticism when he was young, now that his "powers were falling way," it was difficult to go on, so he would have "to let it stand where it will." But, this reporter concluded, "no matter what Mr. Ransom says or does not say, the emphasis today as in the past is on structure and texture."

Even though Ransom's daughter Helen had divorced Duane Forman, Ransom was saddened by Duane's death. Still greater grief came to Ransom when John, Jack's oldest child, accidentally hanged himself in an attempt to imitate a television stunt he had seen.[80] But, as always, Ransom kept his feeling under close control. What he felt, not even Robb knew for certain. As he had written in one of his best-known poems, "assuredly I have a grief / And I am shaken; but not as a leaf." In this always less than perfect world, all have some share of troubles and it ill befits anyone to bemoan his fate; instead he should "mount one tear" and walk "with holy calm beside the terrible bier." Ransom's deeply imbedded and rigidly enforced sense of decorum did not permit his personal griefs to intrude—even upon his family or closest friends. The routine he had followed since his retirement went along without noticeable interruption.

On Feburary 27, 1973, Robert Penn Warren came to read his poetry at Kenyon, and Ransom made one of his few public appearances when he came out to introduce him. He was also motivated by Warren's visit to write his last poem, "Four Threesomes or Three Foursomes," which appeared in the *Sewanee Review* for Summer, 1973. He was pleased and flattered, too, when he learned that Paul Schwartz, who had been in Kenyon's music department since 1947, had set "Survey of Literature" to music. When Schwartz was working on the poem, he had several conversations with Ransom, which he later described as "highly stimulating sessions . . . going over some of the finer points of prosody and related matters."[81]

In one of his last essays, Ransom wrote on faith:

I have never imposed my own faith on anybody particularly, but for this occasion I do not mind calling it Unitarian. I had backslid from my father's faith to that position even before I came upon Kant the Transcendentalist, who did not dare make images of the Unknown God. And that is exactly the position which nowadays even the clergy of most churches, including the Roman Catholic, have found themselves desperately studying and frequently accepting. Wherever Christ is mentioned, not as the great Saint or Prophet but as a junior member of the Godhead, it is because he promised to his followers that immortality which Kant had named as the third of the three aspirations of the Pure Reason—the soul itself—even though it is the least capable of logical demonstration. And I think that most of the communicants, and many of the clergy itself, have little interest in that article of faith; but do not go about advertising their dissidence because they know that every now and then they will have to attend a service for the dead, where there will be a bereaved family who may find a vicarious comfort in the Promise read by the officiating clergy.[82]

Obviously Ransom's thought on Christian grace and redemption had changed very little since *God Without Thunder*; therefore, he could find little comfort in the "Promise read by the officiating clergy." His

attitude toward death and immortality is best expressed, outside his
poetry, in a statement he gave a reporter on his seventy-fifth birthday:

We survive the seasons of a year and we survive even the passing
years, but not the span of life allotted to us. The poet knows that he
will die, but he is prepared for it, he accepts it in advance. If he lives
out his three score and ten (as this poet did) he will come into the
peace which accompanies the sense of having achieved all the wisdom
that was available for him, and he will be happy to subside, happy but
used up, into the annihilation of death.[83]

Shortly after his eighty-sixth birthday, which the family celebrated
quietly in Gambier, Robb began to notice that Ransom was failing very
rapidly. He had lost his appetite and was so weak he could hardly
walk. He was quiet, too quiet, and seemed completely self-absorbed.
Sitting in a chair in the living room, for hours at a time not making a
sound, he appeared to be lost somewhere in his own meditation. His
deafness, which had increased in recent years, suddenly appeared
much worse, and even when she was able to disrupt his brown study, it
was only for a moment. After giving her a word or two and a smile, he
slipped back within himself. When she suggested that they go to the
doctor, he went without protest and Robb heard what she already
knew. The end was near. As soon as she got home, she called Reavill,
who came immediately. After he arrived, Ransom seemed more alert
and attempted to engage in the general conversation. On the evening
of July 2 the house was a little stuffy and Reavill suggested they take
their chairs outside to see if they could catch a breeze. They sat in the
yard and talked until about ten-thirty, a little later than Ransom had
stayed up in recent months, then he went inside and retired. The next
morning when Robb, as was her custom, went in to wake him for
breakfast, he did not respond. He was all used up and had subsided
into the annihilation of death.

Epilogue

RANSOM WAS cremated and his ashes were buried between the graves of his two good friends, Charles Coffin and Philip Blair Rice, behind the library named for his friend and benefactor Gordon P. Chalmers. His death was given the kind of respectful treatment due an internationally known man of letters. The Associated Press immediately released an account which included the basic facts of his life and literary career, the positions he had held, and the literary awards he had received. Most major daily newspapers carried a brief notice obviously based on this information, but some of them later printed more detailed obituaries. The Richmond *News-Leader* pointed out his connection with the Fugitives, as did almost all the accounts that went beyond the information supplied by the press services, calling the work of that group "one of the most notable poetry revivals in the country." The Richmond *Times-Dispatch* carried a brief news story on the day following his death and ten days later, on July 14, the entire column of Maurice Duke, book editor, was devoted to comments on Ransom's literary career. "Except for brief obituary notices and comments in the academic community," Duke pointed out, "the passing of John Crowe Ransom went largely unnoticed"; whereas he should have been mourned as "one of the major figures in American literature of this century." In a front-page story the Nashville *Tennessean* called him "a major force in American literature." The Washington *Post* proclaimed him a "major American poet and critic." Both the New York *Times* and the London *Times* carried full-scale obituaries. In the former Alden Whitman indicated that Ransom had been "immensely influential as the founder of a band of Southern poets that included Allen Tate and Robert Penn Warren" and added that he "was also widely regarded as a literary critic of the first rank, capable of flaying the hide off of a wrongdoer with the greatest of courtesy." The *Times* called him "one of the most influential of modern critics" and credited him, along with Tate and Warren, with founding the New Criticism. "It would be tempting to say," this unsigned story concludes, "that, with Ransom's death, a valuable part of America had disappeared. But this is not so. Manners change; but the spirit lives on. Whatever news the paper may be full of—the latest outrages, the peril of the streets—there are still Americans (and they are not few) who stand for what Ransom stood for: faith, hope, and charity, no less than liberty, equality, and fraternity."

Indicative of the fact that in their opinion Ransom was no longer a member of the literary establishment, some of the national news magazines treated the event much more casually; both *Time* and *Newsweek* carried only brief notices in their "Milestones" and "Transitions" sections. But other journals were more generous in their attention. Writing in the *National Observer* Hugh Kenner credits Ransom with exerting "more influence on humane learning in America than possibly anyone else in this century." In a piece arguing for Ransom's importance as poet rather than critic, Judson Jerome in the *Writer's Digest* says that "with the passing of John Crowe Ransom . . . we have lost almost the last of the great American poets." Both the *Mississippi Quarterly* and the *South Carolina Review* carried obituary notices, the former calling him "one of the most influential men of his generation" and his poetry "some of the most original and impressive verse written in this century," and the latter reminding us that "a fellow poet once called him 'the best Southern poet since Poe.'" The *New Review* published tributes by Robert Lowell, Denis Donoghue, Richard Ellmann, and Roy Fuller; and the *Sewanee Review* had a special Ransom section with essays by Allen Tate, Thomas Daniel Young, Louis D. Rubin, Jr., and George Core.

A statement adopted by the faculty of Kenyon College pointed out that he was "always a completely committed and fully active member of the Faculty of Kenyon College and of the village of Gambier." In addition, he "was an eminent and versatile teacher, a careful scholar, the innovative founding editor of one of the most influential literary reviews of the century, an elegant, subtle, incisive critic, and a refined and memorable poet." On November 1, 1974, a memorial service was held in the Church of the Holy Spirit on the Kenyon campus. On that occasion Robert Daniel, professor and former chairman of English at Kenyon, said, "We have come together . . . to remember and honor a man who, among many other accomplishments, did much to establish the reputation of literary studies at Kenyon" and "it is especially for his achievement as a teacher that the Department of English holds him in affectionate remembrance." Robert Penn Warren spoke of Ransom as man, poet, and philosopher:

If I understand my old teacher and friend, he was a man who very early in life, repudiated the more public and secular ambitions that his power of mind must have persuasively proposed. This repudiation was in favor of a more private, rare, and difficult joy.

Of his own poetry, John more than once said that he wanted to be a "domestic poet," that was his phrase, and most of his subjects are, on the surface at least, small, common domestic. . . . But beyond his domestic poetry, there was, willy-nilly, another range of thought and feeling. There was the philosopher with a profound awareness of the tensions of his age, and an ironist to whom irony was the only antidote for the tragedy of life. And this fact is what gives the peculiar resonance and indefinable sweetness and pang and the individuality even to poems most obviously domestic. John Crowe Ransom is a writer about the small whose poems loom larger and larger—more inimitable, more indispensable, more powerful—as the years pass. A poet, in fact, in whom classic clarity of outline and modern intensities and tensions find their unique fusion.

Warren's tribute, delivered at the meeting of December 6, 1974, of the American Academy of Arts and Letters, ends as follows:

John Crowe Ransom died calmly in his sleep, on July 3 of this year, at the age of 86. He once said that, in writing a poem, what he always wanted to do was to make "a beautiful thing." He made many beautiful things. . . . And these things, speaking to the heart in their special accent, bear all the marks of being a permanent treasure—at least as long as the heart prizes the "common actuals" of life. And it should be added, as long as the mind values even painful veracity more than self-indulgence and philosophic vision more than delusion.

Notes

THE LETTERS from Ransom to Allen Tate are in the Firestone Library of Princeton University; those from Ransom to Donald Davidson, Andrew Lytle, Caroline Gordon, Brainard Cheney, and Robert Graves are in the Jesse E. Wills Collection of the Joint University Libraries, Nashville, Tennessee. The letters of the Ransom family (including those of R. P. Ransom, Ella Crowe Ransom, Robb Reavill Ransom, and those from John Crowe Ransom to members of his family) are in the Ellene Ransom Papers in the Tennessee State Library and Archives, Nashville. Ransom's letters to Cleanth Brooks and Robert Penn Warren are in the Yale University Library; those to Merrill Moore are in the Library of Congress. Letters from Ransom to Christopher Morley are in the Haverford College Library. Those from Ransom to George Marion O'Donnell and Robert Duncan, and from Duncan and O'Donnell to Ransom, are in the Special Collection of Modern Literature, Washington University Libraries. The letters from James H. Kirkland, Edwin Mims, and Henry Rand, the minutes of the meetings of the Board of Trust of Vanderbilt University, and the unpublished autobiography of Edwin Mims are in the Vanderbilt University Archives.

The correspondence files of the *Kenyon Review*, the Kenyon School of English (in the Chalmers Library of Kenyon College), and those of the Indiana School of Letters (in the Lily Library of Indiana University) contain many letters to and from Ransom.

NOTES TO CHAPTER I

1 R. P. Ransom to John James Ransom, March 6, 1884. R. P. Ransom was John Crowe Ransom's grandfather; John James Ransom, his father. The Ransom genealogy given here was compiled by Miss Ada Young of Murfreesboro, Tennessee:

James Ransom
|
James Ransom m. Amy Davis
|
Richard Payne Ransom m. Kesiah Christian Portice in 1784
|
John Ransom m. Elizabeth Bowman in 1817
|
Richard Portice Ransom (1825–1897) m. Frances Bass in 1851 (she died in 1865)
|
John James Ransom (1853–1934) m. Annie Newman in 1878 (she died in 1879); m. Sara Ella Crowe (1859–1947) in 1884

2 *Ibid.*

3 D. C. Kelley, "R. P. Ransom," *Christian Advocate*, October 7, 1897, p. 13.

4 *Ibid.*

5 *Ibid.*

6 *Ibid.*

7 John James Ransom to R. P. Ransom, October, 1871.

8 R. P. Ransom to John James Ransom, November, 1871.

9 John James Ransom to R. P. Ransom, December 14, 1872.

10 John James Ransom to R. P. Ransom, April 2, 1873.

11 Whom he expects to marry is never mentioned; in fact none of his letters home discusses any particular girl he was seeing. Perhaps the young lady was someone who lived near the family home in Rutherford County or in one of the towns or villages in which his father had preached.

12 John James Ransom to R. P. Ransom, April 2, 1873.

13 He listed his living and school expenses for the spring semester as follows: "Bread and Meat $5.00 per month; room and heat $15.00 per month; table linen $1.75; cup, saucer and spoon .20; soap .60; apples .10; 1 shuck mattress $7.00; curtains and shades $2.50; hand soap .20; paper .50; note book .40; envelopes and stamps .65; ink .50; text books $8.75; tuition $50.00." On June 3, he wrote his father that he owed a graduation fee of $5.00 and $6.50 for meals in the college dining room for the last two weeks; he asked for this $11.50, the last he would request for college expenses. If the cost of this term was about average ($124.65), John James Ransom's college expenses must have been $250 a year, a considerable sum for a Methodist minister whose earnings seldom reached $1,000 a year.

14 Information compiled by Curtis B. Haley, editor, "General Minutes and Yearbook of the Tennessee Conference of the Methodist Episcopal Church, South," March 14, 1941.

15 "Beginnings in Brazil: An Interview with Dr. J. J. Ransom," *Missionary Voice*, October, 1926, p. 10.

16 Ella Crowe Ransom to Dr. Guy Samuel Inmon, January 25, 1939.

17 When John James Ransom left Brazil in 1886, the congregation at Cattete gave him a "walking cane—made of very rare 'holy wood' with these words carved on the gold head: to Reverend J. J. Ransom, Founder of the M. E. Church, South in Brazil."

18 John James Ransom to Ella Crowe, November 29, 1882.

19 This poem was included in his letter of January 10, 1883, with a brief note saying he hoped she would accept this "expression of New Year's greeting with cousinly affection":

Like gorgeous temples rise the years
   In solemn beauty through the land:
Their flags are met with pilgrim tears;
   Their music who can understand?

Oh solemn notes that echo round
   Through spaces dim, and drear, and vast.
Seraphic waves of melting sound,
   From what far organ were ye cast?

What master touch on titan keys
   First loosed the rich harmonious flood,
Like lapsing murmurs of the seas
   At last by mortals understood?

Thou, fellow pilgrim, at the door
   Of this fair temple, list the tone,
A melody unheard before,
   The New Year singing on its own;

And swiftly go with bated breath
   Within the portal open wide;
And mayst thou hear, or life or death,
   That all is well whatever betide.

20 Ella Crowe Ransom to Stanley Horn, March 22, 1939.

21 This James Crowe moved to Memphis, where he was very active, John Crowe Ransom recalled in 1970, "in a group that was going to run the blacks out of the South." Once when "Uncle Jim" was visiting his niece's family in Nashville, he and John Crowe, his grand nephew, took a streetcar down town. While they were waiting at the stop for the car to come along, they were joined by a Negro woman with a huge bundle of dirty clothes she had collected to take home to wash. When the car stopped, Uncle Jim took the clothes and put them aboard for her. Although Ransom was aware that some of the passengers on the streetcar looked at his uncle rather strangely, he was "very proud of him." (Interview with John Crowe Ransom, September 10, 1970.)

His grandson, also named James but called Pat by his family, was graduated from Vanderbilt in 1914. After a brief career in New York as a journalist, he volunteered for service in the United States Army Air Corps. While Ransom was serving in France, Pat came to visit him just a few days before his plane crashed and he was killed. After his death his experiences in the service were published as *Pat Crowe, Aviator*, ed. W. B. Chase (New York, 1919).

22 Ella Crowe Ransom to Stanley Horn, March 22, 1939.

23 From an undated newspaper clipping in the Ellene Ransom Papers. The clipping seems to be from the Pulaski paper, but I have not been able to locate its source.

24 Ella Crowe Ransom to John James Ransom, April 2, 1885.

25 Ella Crowe Ransom to John James Ransom, November 16, 1885.

26 John James Ransom to J. E. Newman, August 15, 1886.

27 John James Ransom to Robert Bruce Crowe, August 30, 1886.

28 John James Ransom to Ella Crowe Ransom, October 18, 1886.

29 Irene Crowe contracted tuberculosis and went shortly afterwards to live in West Texas, where she thought the climate would be more healthful. She never

completely recovered, but returned to live with the Ransoms and Ella nursed her in her last illness.

30 John James Ransom to Ella Crowe Ransom, September 27, 1889.

31 "Richard P. Ransom," *Christian Advocate*, October 7, 1897, p. 13.

32 Interview with John Crowe Ransom, September 11, 1970.

33 Interview with John Crowe Ransom, September 10, 1970.

34 Until John James Ransom went to Murfreesboro in 1907 as presiding elder, he had never earned as much as $1,000 a year.

35 Interview with John Crowe Ransom, September 11, 1970.

36 Interview with John Crowe Ransom, September 10, 1970.

37 *Ibid.*

38 *Newsweek*, January 27, 1964, pp. 79–80.

39 Interview with John Crowe Ransom, September 11, 1970.

40 One reason John James Ransom selected the Bowen School was that Mr. Bowen always charged sons of ministers a reduced tuition rate. In fact Mr. Ransom never received a bill for John's tuition.

41 John Crowe Ransom, "Angus G. Bowen," in W. O. Batts (ed.), *Private Secondary Schools for Boys in Tennessee* (Nashville: n.p., 1957), 32–35.

42 After Bowen had closed his school in 1919, he went into the insurance business in Nashville. Ransom had all of his insurance with him; even after he went to Kenyon, he kept these policies so that he could exchange "brief personal notes" with his old friend when they corresponded about business. Each time he returned to Nashville he always went by Bowen's office to see him and often found him sitting with "one of the Dialogues of Plato in his hand or laid open beside him on the desk." *Ibid.*, 34.

43 At the end of his junior year he had taken the examinations in Greek and mathematics.

44 *Bulletin of the College of Arts and Science of Vanderbilt University*, 1903–1904.

45 From 1900 to 1903 John James Ransom was assigned to the New Providence Church at an annual salary of $600.

46 *Proceedings and Addresses at the Installation and Inauguration of James Hamilton Kirkland* (Nashville: n.p., 1893), 46.

47 Baskerville preceded Jones as professor of English at Vanderbilt.

48 "Literature and the Student," *Vanderbilt Observer* (October, 1903), 5.

49 John Crowe Ransom, "Foreword," *Fugitive*, I (April, 1922), 1.

50 John Crowe Ransom, *The World's Body* (New York: Charles Scribner's Sons, 1938), viii.

NOTES TO CHAPTER II

1 *Minutes of the Annual Conference of the Methodist Episcopal Church, South, 1874–1934.*

2 Ransom to author, July 22, 1968.

3 *Ibid.*

4 Students' Records, Registrar's Office, Vanderbilt University.

5 Ransom to author, July 22, 1968.

6 *Ibid.*

7 Much of the information about the village of Taylorsville was taken from three unpublished manuscripts prepared by Miss Dorrence Eaton, who for many years taught English in the Taylorsville High School, and from conversations with Miss Eaton and her sister Corinne Eaton Watts of Sumrall, Mississippi. Both of these ladies were in school in Taylorsville at the time Ransom taught there, and Mrs. Watts was one of his students.

8 Interview with Ransom, February 12 and 13, 1971.

9 Ransom to author, July 22, 1968.

10 Interview with Miss Dorrence Eaton, September 21, 1972, and from an unpublished manuscript of Miss Eaton's entitled "Taylorsville High School."
11 Interview with Mrs. Corinne Eaton Watts, September 22, 1972.
12 *Ibid.*
13 *Ibid.*
14 Interviews with Ransom, February 12 and 13, 1971.
15 *Ibid.*
16 Miss Eaton's father was also a member of this Sunday school class.
17 Interview with Mrs. Watts, September 22, 1972.
18 Some of this information came from the interview with Miss Eaton and some of it from Mrs. Watts.
19 Interviews with Ransom, February 12, and 13, 1971.
20 *Ibid.*
21 Vanderbilt University *Bulletin*, 1907–1908, lists these fees; Ransom's attitude was expressed in the interview of February 12 and 13, 1971.
22 Vanderbilt University *Bulletin*, 1907–1908.
23 Students' Records, Registrar's Office, Vanderbilt University.
24 Vanderbilt University *Bulletin*, 1908–1909.
25 Letter of recommendation written for Ransom by John H. Murray, April 12, 1913, in Ellene Ransom Papers.
26 *Vanderbilt Observer*, May, 1909.
27 Interviews with Ransom, August 15–17, 1970.
28 George Mayfield, "The Calumet Club," Vanderbilt *Alumnus*, November, 1919, pp. 44–45.
29 *Vanderbilt Observer*, November, 1908, pp. 38–39.
30 The information in this paragraph and those immediately preceding it came from Ransom's editorials in the *Observer* for 1908–1909, one of which appeared in every issue.
31 Letter of recommendation written for Ransom by M. M. Summar, April 15, 1913, in Ellene Ransom Papers.
32 Interviews with Ransom, August 15–17, 1970.
33 William A. Stuart to author, March 6, 1972.
34 Stuart to author, January 31, 1972.
35 *Student Handbook of Christ Church College*, 18th ed., 134.
36 Rob Roy Purdy (ed.), *Fugitives' Reunion: Conversations at Vanderbilt, May 3–5, 1956* (Nashville: Vanderbilt University Press, 1959), 106–107.
37 Ransom to the committee on graduate instruction of Vanderbilt University, October 16, 1920.
38 Letter of recommendation for Ransom written by Robert Dundas, March 13, 1913, in Ellene Ransom Papers.
39 Letter of recommendation for Ransom by Murray, April 12, 1913.
40 Ransom to Ella Crowe Ransom, November 4, 1910.
41 Ransom to J. J. Ransom, December 22, 1910.
42 Stuart to author, March 6, 1972.
43 Ransom to Ella Crowe Ransom, November 4, 1910.
44 Ransom to Ella Crowe Ransom, undated, apparently written in November, 1911.
45 Ransom to J. J. Ransom, June 19, 1911.
46 Ransom to J. J. Ransom, July 16, 1911.
47 Ransom to Annie Ransom, September 11, 1911.
48 *Ibid.*
49 Ransom to Ella Crowe Ransom, undated, apparently written in November, 1911.
50 Ransom to Ella Crowe Ransom, November 6, 1911.
51 Ransom to Ella Crowe Ransom, November 14, 1911.

52 Ransom to Annie Ransom, December 4, 1911.
53 Ransom to J. J. Ransom, November 21, 1911.
54 *Ibid.*
55 Ransom to Ellene Ransom, June 10, 1912.
56 Stuart to author, March 6, 1972.
57 Stuart to author, January 31, 1972.
58 Ransom to J. J. Ransom, November 20, 1911.
59 Ransom to J. J. Ransom, December 28, 1911.
60 Ransom to Ellene Ransom, December 17, 1911.
61 Ransom to Ella Crowe Ransom, December 26, 1911.
62 Ransom to J. J. Ransom, January 4, 1912.
63 Ransom to Ella Crowe Ransom, January 8, 1912.
64 Ransom to J. J. Ransom, January 29, 1912.
65 Ransom to Ella Crowe Ransom, February 4, 1912.
66 Ransom to J. J. Ransom, March 26, 1912.
67 Ransom to Annie Ransom, April 10, 1912.
68 Ransom to Ella Crowe Ransom, May 8, 1912.
69 *Ibid.*
70 *Ibid.*
71 Ransom to J. J. Ransom, May 19, 1912.
72 Ransom to Ellene Ransom, July 5, 1912.
73 Ransom to J. J. Ransom, March 26, 1912.
74 Virginia Cowles, *1913: An End and a Beginning* (New York: Harper and Row, 1967),
   54–55.
75 *Ibid.*, 39.
76 Ransom to Ellene Ransom, July 5, 1912.
77 Ransom to Annie Ransom, July 12, 1912.
78 Stuart to author, January 31, 1972.
79 Ransom to J. J. Ransom, August 5, 1912.
80 Ransom to Ella Crowe Ransom, August 12, 1912.
81 Ransom to J. J. Ransom, September 2, 1912.
82 *Ibid.*
83 Ransom to J. J. Ransom, October 17, 1912.
84 *Ibid.*
85 John Crowe Ransom, *The World's Body* (New York: Charles Scribner's Sons, 1938),
   42.
86 *Ibid.*

NOTES TO CHAPTER III

1 Ransom to Ella Crowe Ransom, April 4, 1912.
2 Ransom to J. J. Ransom, March 26, 1912.
3 Ransom to Ella Crowe Ransom, May 8, 1912.
4 Ransom to Ellene Ransom, June 10, 1912.
5 Ransom to J. J. Ransom, February 2, 1913.
6 Letter of recommendation written on April 12, 1913, when Ransom was applying
   for a teaching position in one of the New England preparatory schools; copies of all
   these letters of recommendation are on file in the Ellene Ransom Papers.
7 Ransom to J. J. Ransom, March 28, 1913.
8 Ransom to Ella Crowe Ransom, April 9, 1913.
9 Ransom to J. J. Ransom, May 10, 1913.
10 Ransom to J. J. Ransom, May 13, 1913.
11 Ransom to Ella Crowe Ransom, June 30, 1913.
12 Ransom to Mr. and Mrs. J. J. Ransom, July 31, 1913.

13 Ransom outlined his plans in a letter to Annie Ransom, July 31, 1913.
14 Stuart to author, January 31, 1972.
15 Ransom to J. J. Ransom, September 23, 1913.
16 *Ibid.*
17 Ransom to Ella Crowe Ransom, October 1, 1913.
18 Ransom to Ellene Ransom, December 8, 1913.
19 Ransom to J. J. Ransom, November 3, 1913.
20 Charter members of the club included, besides Ransom, William A. Stuart and Christopher Morley.
21 Ransom to J. J. Ransom, February 4, 1914.
22 Ransom to Ella Crowe Ransom, February 25, 1914.
23 Ransom to J. J. Ransom, December 8, 1913.
24 Ransom to J. J. Ransom, January 9, 1914.
25 *Ibid.*
26 Ransom to Ella Crowe Ransom, January 27, 1914.
27 Ransom to Ellene Ransom, March 5, 1914.
28 Ransom to Ella Crowe Ransom, February 25, 1914.
29 *Ibid.*
30 Ransom to J. J. Ransom, November 3, 1913.
31 Ransom to Ella Crowe Ransom, April 3, 1914.
32 Ransom to J. J. Ransom, April 9, 1914.
33 Ransom to Ella Crowe Ransom, May 27, 1914.

NOTES TO CHAPTER IV

1 John L. Stewart, *The Burden of Time: The Fugitives and Agrarians* (Princeton: Princeton University Press, 1965), 14.
2 *Ibid.*
3 Quoted from an incomplete and unpublished manuscript, Edwin Mims, "Autobiography," in the Jesse E. Wills Collection of the Joint University Libraries, Nashville, Tennessee.
4 Donald Davidson, *Southern Writers in the Modern World* (Athens: University of Georgia Press, 1958), 10.
5 Interview with Jordon Stokes, April 12, 1971.
6 Rob Roy Purdy (ed.), *Fugitives' Reunion: Conversations at Vanderbilt, May 3–5, 1956* (Nashville: Vanderbilt University Press, 1959), 93.
7 *Ibid.*, 98.
8 *Ibid.*, 90.
9 *Ibid.*, 94.
10 Interview with Jordan Stokes, April 12, 1971.
11 Interview with Donald Davidson, October 14, 1966.
12 Mims, "Autobiography."
13 Louise Cowan, *The Fugitive Group: A Literary History* (Baton Rouge: Louisiana State University Press, 1959), 15.
14 Davidson, *Southern Writers*, 11–12.
15 Edwin Mims, *History of Vanderbilt University* (Nashville: Vanderbilt University Press, 1946), 247.
16 John Crowe Ransom, "The Question of Justice," *Yale Review*, IV (July, 1915), 684–98.
17 Interview with Alec B. Stevenson, March 18, 1965.
18 William Yandell Elliott to Alec B. Stevenson, July 23, 1915.
19 Davidson, *Southern Writers*, 14.
20 *Ibid.*, 12.

21 Stewart, *The Burden of Time,* 14.
22 Vanderbilt *Alumnus,* October, 1917, pp. 3–4.
23 Ransom to Ella Crowe Ransom, May 13, 1917.
24 Davidson, *Southern Writers,* 33–34.
25 Ransom to Ella Crowe Ransom, July 24, 1917.
26 Descriptions written by Ransom—an undated letter to the Dean of the College of Arts and Science of Vanderbilt University.
27 Ransom to Ella Crowe Ransom, December 22, 1917.
28 Ransom to J. J. Ransom, January 14, 1918.
29 Ransom to Ella Crowe Ransom, May 12, 1918.
30 Ransom to J. J. Ransom, March 7, 1919.
31 Vanderbilt *Alumnus,* April, 1918, p. 178.
32 Ransom to Ella Crowe Ransom, March 12, 1919.
33 Cowan, *The Fugitive Group,* 25.
34 Purdy (ed.), *Fugitives' Reunion,* 101–102.
35 *Ibid.,* 100.
36 Allen Tate, "The Fugitive, 1922–1925: A Personal Recollection Twenty Years After," *Princeton University Library Chronicle,* III (April, 1942), 77.
37 Minutes, Board of Trust meeting, January 10, 1918.

NOTES TO CHAPTER V

1 Ransom to Christopher Morley, November 12, 1918.
2 Ransom to Morley, June 17, 1919.
3 Ransom to Morley, August 27, 1919.
4 *Ibid.*
5 Mims to Kirkland, August 13, 1919.
6 *Ibid.*
7 *Ibid.*
8 Ella Crowe Ransom to Mrs. James Crowe, October, 1919.
9 Ransom to Morley, May 19, 1918.
10 Allen Tate, "The Fugitive, 1922–1925: A Personal Recollection Twenty Years After," *Princeton University Library Chronicle,* III (April, 1942), 77.
11 Donald Davidson, *Southern Writers in the Modern World* (Athens: University of Georgia Press, 1958), 15.
12 *Ibid.,* 14.
13 John Crowe Ransom, *Poems About God* (New York: Henry Holt, 1919), vi–vii.
14 *Ibid.,* v.
15 *Poetry,* XVI (April, 1920), 51–52.
16 *Bookman,* L (October, 1919), 222–23.
17 *Yale Review,* IX (April, 1920), 660–67.
18 *Nation,* CIX (July 26, 1919), 116.
19 *Dial,* LXVI (May 31, 1919), 562–63.
20 Davidson, *Southern Writers,* 14–15.
21 Vanderbilt *Alumnus,* May, 1919, p. 172.
22 Ransom to Tate, undated letter written sometime in the spring of 1927.
23 Ella Crowe Ransom to Mrs. James Crowe, October, 1919.
24 Kirkland to Mims, May 28, 1920.
25 Interview with Ransom, April 15, 1972.
26 *Ibid.*
27 Interview with Robb Reavill Ransom, April 16, 1972.
28 Ransom to Ella Crowe Ransom, July 26, 1920.
29 *History of Wyoming* (Chicago: S. J. Clark Publishing Co., 1918), 22–25.

30 Interview with Tobey Reavill, April 16, 1972.
31 Interview with Ransom, April 15, 1972.
32 Davidson, *Southern Writers*, 21.
33 Tate, "*The Fugitive*, 1922–1925," 77–78.
34 Davidson, *Southern Writers*, 19.
35 Tate, "*The Fugitive*, 1922–1925," p. 77.
36 *Fugitive*, I (April, 1922), 1.
37 When the poem appeared in *Chills and Fever*, Ransom had changed the title to "Plea in Mitigation" and made several small changes in the text.
38 *Fugitive*, I (April, 1922), 1.
39 Davidson, *Southern Writers*, 8.
40 Ransom to Graves, June 12, 1925.
41 Davidson, *Southern Writers*, 28.
42 Ransom to Graves, July 11, 1923.
43 *Ibid.*
44 Ransom responded to Graves's suggestion in a letter dated July 4, 1923.
45 Ransom to Graves, November 19, 1923.
46 Published in *Grace After Meat* as "Ilex Priscus" and later as "Vaunting Oak."
47 Ransom mentioned this fact in a letter to Graves, November 20, 1923.
48 *Ibid.*
49 Ransom to Tate, May 6, 1924.
50 *New York Times Book Review*, September 7, 1924.
51 *Independent*, CXIII (November, 1924), 347.
52 *Measure*, XLIX (March, 1925), 15–17.
53 *Bookman* LX (November, 1924), 345–46.
54 Robert Graves, Introduction to John Crowe Ransom, *Grace After Meat* (London: Hogarth Press, 1924), 9, 11.
55 *Saturday Review of Literature*, I (December 27, 1924), 412.
56 Tate to Davidson, January 7, 1925.
57 Nashville *Tennessean*, August 31, 1924, and November 30, 1924.
58 John Crowe Ransom, "In the Classical Tradition," *Guardian*, I (November, 1924), 25–26.
59 *Yale Review* (July, 1925), 791–97.
60 New Orleans *Times-Picayune*, February 22, 1925.
61 *New Republic*, XLIII (May 27, 1925), 23–24.
62 It was spelled "Ransome" every time it appeared.
63 *Saturday Review of Literature*, II (June 6, 1925), 807.
64 Ransom to Graves, June 12, 1925.
65 Louise Cowan, *The Fugitive Group: A Literary History* (Baton Rouge: Louisiana State University Press, 1959), 141.
66 *Fugitive*, I (October, 1922), 66.
67 Cowan, *The Fugitive Group*, 119.
68 Ransom to Tate, July 14, 1923.
69 Ransom to Tate, July 30, 1923.
70 Ransom to Davidson, August 21, 1923.
71 Davidson, *Southern Writers*, 8.
72 Ransom to Graves, September 23, 1925.
73 Ransom to Kirkland, January 2, 1926; Ransom was promoted to associate professor of English in 1924 and to professor of English in 1927.
74 George Core (ed.), *Regionalism and Beyond: Essays of Randall Stewart* (Nashville: Vanderbilt University Press, 1968), 234.
75 Ransom reported the offer in a letter to Mims, July 6, 1924.

76 *Ibid.*
77 *Ibid.*
78 Ransom to Kirkland, April 10, 1925.

NOTES TO CHAPTER VI

1 John Crowe Ransom, *The World's Body* (New York: Charles Scribner's Sons, 1938), vii.
2 *Fugitive,* I (October, 1922), 67–68.
3 *Fugitive,* I (December, 1922), 99–100.
4 Ransom, *The World's Body,* vii.
5 *Ibid.,* xv.
6 Ransom to Tate, December 17, 1922.
7 *Ibid.*
8 *Literary Review* of New York *Evening Post,* July 14, 1923, pp. 825–26. In 1974 Tate wrote: Ransom "attacked T. S. Eliot for the obvious reasons, such as fragmentary prosody and expository discontinuity or, as he would have later described it, lack of structure. I saw the attack as the result of his irritation with my praise of Eliot, which was that of a distant disciple, to the neglect of him, my actual master from whom I learned more than I could even now describe and acknowledge ("On the Death of Ransom," *Sewanee Review,* LXXXII, Fall, 1974, p. 547).
9 Tate to *Literary Review* of New York *Evening Post,* August 3, 1923.
10 Davidson to Tate, August 14, 1923.
11 John Crowe Ransom "The Future of Poetry," *Fugitive,* III (February, 1924), 2–4.
12 Allen Tate, "One Escape from the Dilemma," *Fugitive,* III (April, 1924), 34–36.
13 Ransom to Tate, April 22, 1924.
14 Tate's remarks were made to George Core, who reported them to me in a letter, February 26, 1975.
15 John Crowe Ransom, "Mixed Modes," *Fugitive,* IV (March, 1925), 28–29.
16 John Crowe Ransom, "Thoughts on the Poetic Discontent," *Fugitive,* IV (June, 1925), 63–64.
17 John Crowe Ransom, "A Doctrine of Relativity," *Fugitive,* IV (September, 1925), 93–94.
18 Ransom to Andrew Lytle, December 11, 1925.
19 Ransom to Graves, June 12, 1925.
20 *Fugitive,* IV (December, 1925), 125.
21 Ransom to Graves, June 12, 1925.
22 *Ibid.*
23 Ransom to Graves, December 2, 1925.
24 Ransom to Tate, June 18, 1926.
25 Ransom to Davidson, July 1, 1926.
26 Ransom to Tate, June 18, 1926.
27 Ransom to Davidson, July 1, 1926.
28 Ransom to Tate, September 13, 1926.
29 Ransom to Tate, June 3, 1926.
30 Ransom to Tate, September 13, 1926.
31 *Ibid.*
32 Ransom to Mims, September 27, 1926.
33 *Ibid.*
34 Ransom, *The World's Body,* vii.
35 Ransom to Tate, September 5, 1926.
36 Ransom to Davidson, September 30, 1926.
37 Ransom to Davidson, October 13, 1926.

38 Nashville *Tennessean*, January 23, 1927.
39 *New Republic*, XLIX (February 21, 1927), 310.
40 *New York Times Book Review*, March 27, 1927, p. 2.
41 *Independent*, CXVIII (February 26, 1927), 246.
42 *Bookman*, LXV (April 1, 1927), 220.
43 *Poetry*, XXX (June, 1927), 163–65.
44 *Monthly Criterion*, VI (July, 1927), 168–72.
45 *Nation*, CXXIV (March 30, 1927), 346.
46 Ransom to Tate, February 20, 1927.
47 Ransom to Tate, undated letter written sometime in the spring of 1927.
48 A note in the margin of Davidson's copy of *Homage to John Dryden*, apparently written while he was preparing a review of this book for *Fugitive*, IV (June, 1925), 61–62.
49 This letter is not in the files of the correspondence made available by the chancellor's office of Vanderbilt University, but a part of it is included in Mims, "Autobiography," in Jesse E. Wills Collection of the Joint University Libraries, Nashville, Tennessee.
50 Ransom to Tate, June 25, 1927.

NOTES TO CHAPTER VII

1 Ransom to Davidson, August 18, 1926.
2 Ransom to Tate, April 3, 1928.
3 Ransom to Kirkland, October 1, 1928.
4 John Crowe Ransom, "Classical and Romantic," *Saturday Review of Literature*, VI (September 14, 1929), 125–27.
5 Ransom to Tate, September 5, 1926.
6 John Crowe Ransom, *God Without Thunder: An Unorthodox Defense of Orthodoxy* (New York: Harcourt, Brace, 1930), x.
7 Ransom to Tate, July 4, 1929.
8 *Ibid.*
9 *Ibid.*
10 Ransom, *God Without Thunder*, x.
11 *Ibid.*, 114–25.
12 *Christian Century*, XLVII (December 3, 1930), 1490–91.
13 *Commonweal*, XIII (February 4, 1931), 385–86.
14 *Saturday Review of Literature*, VII (February 28, 1931), 627.
15 *Criterion*, XI (October, 1931), 127–31.
16 *Sewanee Review*, XXXIX (Jan.–Mar., 1931), 103–11.
17 *Times Literary Supplement*, December 24, 1931, p. 1036.
18 *Bookman*, LXXIII (March, 1931), 100–101, and *Virginia Quarterly Review* (July, 1931), 451–57.
19 *Virginia Quarterly Review* (July, 1931), 452.
20 Robert Penn Warren, "John Crowe Ransom: A Study in Irony," *Virginia Quarterly Review*, XI (January, 1935), 98–99.
21 Donald Davidson, *Southern Writers in the Modern World* (Athens: University of Georgia Press, 1958), 29–30.
22 Allen Tate, "*The Fugitive*, 1922–25: A Personal Recollection Twenty Years After," *Princeton University Library Chronicle*, III (April, 1942), 84. Louise Cowan thinks the date of this letter is 1927, but Virginia Rock establishes it as 1926. See Virginia Rock, "The Making and Meaning of *I'll Take My Stand*" (Ph.D. dissertation, University of Minnesota, 1961), 224.
23 Ransom to Tate, April 3, 1926, as dated by Allen Tate.
24 John Crowe Ransom, "The South Defends Its Heritage," *Harper's Magazine*, CLIX

(June, 1929), 108–18; John Crowe Ransom, "The South—Old or New?" *Sewanee Review*, XXXVI (Spring, 1928), 139–47.

25 Ransom to Tate. The letter is undated but appears to have been written in the late summer of 1929.

26 Davidson to Tate, August 10, 1929.

27 Davidson to Tate, October 26, 1926.

28 Warren to Tate, fall, 1929.

29 Ransom to Tate, January 25, 1930.

30 *Ibid.*

31 Ransom to Tate; the letter is dated only "Saturday the 15th," but it seems, as Virginia Rock argues, that the date is February rather than March.

32 Ransom, Davidson, Owsley, Wade, Lytle, and Lanier.

33 "Articles of an Agrarian Reform," is in the Jesse E. Wills Collection of the Joint University Libraries, Nashville, Tennessee; Virginia Rock has a succinct comparison of the two documents, "The Making and Meaning of *I'll Take My Stand*," 270–71.

34 Harper's gave a $300 advance, 10 percent royalties on 2,500 copies, 12 ½ percent to 5,000, and 15 percent thereafter.

35 Davidson to Tate, February 18, 1930.

36 Davidson to Tate, July 21, 1930.

37 Davidson to Tate, July 26, 1930.

38 See Virginia Rock, "The Making and Meaning of *I'll Take My Stand*," 252.

39 Quoted *ibid.*

40 *Ibid.*, 255 ff.

41 Davidson to Tate, letter headed "Saturday, 1930."

42 Rock, "The Making and Meaning of *I'll Take My Stand*," 256.

43 Davidson and Ransom to the Agrarians, September 5, 1930.

44 Tate to Davidson, September 7, 1930.

45 Louis D. Rubin, Jr., "Introduction," *I'll Take My Stand* (Harper Torchbook edition; New York, 1962), vi.

46 Donald Davidson, "The 'Mystery' of the Agrarians: Facts and Illusions about Some Southern Writers," *Saturday Review of Literature*, XXVI (January 23, 1943), 6–7.

47 *Saturday Review of Literature*, VII (December 20, 1930), 467.

48 Birmingham *Age-Herald*, February 18, 1931.

49 Allen Cleaton, Richmond *Times-Dispatch*, December 7, 1930.

50 DesMoines *Register*, November 19, 1930.

51 Macon *Telegraph*, November 27, 1930.

52 Nashville *Tennessean*, September 22, 1930.

53 *Nation*, CXXXII (January 14, 1930), 48.

54 Rubin, "Introduction" to *I'll Take My Stand*, vi.

55 Ransom to Tate, January 25, 1930.

56 This account of the Richmond debate relies heavily on an unpublished essay by Professor M. Thomas Inge of the Virginia Commonwealth University: "The Great Debate in Richmond: Industrialism vs. Agrarianism."

57 Richmond *Times-Dispatch*, November 13, 1930.

58 Lambert Davis to Donald Davidson, October 30, 1930.

59 Donald Davidson, "3500 Pack Hall as Ransom-Barr Debate Southern Problems," Chattanooga *News*, November 15, 1930. Davidson reported that James Branch Cabell "had a front seat and listened intently, without blinking an eye lid or changing expression for two hours and a half. I'm afraid he looked bored, but I'm told he always looks bored."

60 Such was Davidson's impression years later; interviews, September and October, 1966.

61 Richmond *Times-Disptach*, November 16, 1930.

62 Virginius Dabney, in Baltimore *Evening Sun*, reprinted in Virginia *Pilot*, December 18, 1930.
63 New York *Times*, November 30, 1930.
64 Ransom to Tate, December 1, 1930.
65 Interview with Ransom, September, 1970.
66 Reported in Atlanta *Constitution*, February 12, 1931.
67 *Sherwood Anderson, Memoirs* (New York: Harcourt, Brace, 1942), 458–59.
68 Ms in Jesse E. Wills Collection of the Joint University Libraries, Nashville, Tennessee.

NOTES TO CHAPTER VIII

1 Ransom's essay "Reconstructed but Unregenerate" is really a composite of two earlier essays—"The South—Old or New," *Sewanee Review*, XXXVI (April, 1928), 139–47, and "The South Defends Its Heritage," *Harper's Magazine*, CLIX (June, 1929), 108–18.
2 J. J. Ransom to J. M. Huddlestone, April 7, 1926.
3 Ransom to Kirkland, January 13, 1931.
4 Kirkland to Ransom, January 15, 1931.
5 Ransom was on leave during the fall term of 1926.
6 Henry Allen Moe to James H. Kirkland, March 5, 1931.
7 Many of the details of the family's year in England were taken from this diary.
8 Ransom to Lytle, January 31, 1932.
9 Ransom to Tate, November 23, 1931.
10 Unless otherwise indicated, the quoted material in this part of the chapter comes from Helen Ransom Forman's diary, which is in her possession.
11 Ransom to Davidson, December 13, 1931.
12 Ransom to Tate, January 3, 1932.
13 Ransom to Davidson, December 13, 1931.
14 Ransom to Tate, March 16, 1932.
15 Ransom to Lytle, January 31, 1932.
16 Ransom to Tate, June 20, 1932.
17 Ransom to Tate, March 16, 1932.
18 Ransom to Tate, November 23, 1931.
19 Ransom to Davidson, December 13, 1931.
20 *Ibid.*
21 Ransom to Tate, January 31, 1932.
22 John Crowe Ransom, "The State and the Land," *New Republic*, LXX (February 17, 1932), 8–10; "Land! An Answer to the Unemployment Problem," *Harper's Magazine*, CLXV (July, 1932), 216–24.
23 Ransom to Tate, January 31, 1932.
24 Ransom to Tate, May 19, 1932.
25 Ransom to Lytle, June 20, 1932.
26 Ransom to Davidson, December 13, 1931.
27 Ransom to Tate, December 18, 1931.
28 Both essays were reprinted in *The World's Body* (New York: Charles Scribner's Sons, 1938), the second as "Forms and Citizens."
29 Ransom to Tate, undated; Tate has dated the letter "Fall, 1931."
30 John Crowe Ransom, "Poetry: A Note in Ontology," *American Review*, II (May, 1934), 172–200; John Crowe Ransom, "Happy Farmers," *American Review*, I (October, 1933), 513–35.
31 Ransom to Tate, January 3, 1932.
32 Ransom to Tate, November 23, 1931.
33 Ransom to Tate, January 3, 1932.

34 *Ibid.*
35 Ransom to Tate, May 19, 1932.
36 Ransom to Tate, October 25, 1932.
37 One reason for the shortage of funds was that he had expected a $500 advance from Harper's for *Land!*
38 Ransom to Lytle, June 20, 1932.
39 Wesley Hall, a large old building on the Vanderbilt campus, was the home of the Divinity School, and it also provided rooms for students and a few apartments for faculty members.
40 Ransom, "The State and the Land," 8–10. Ransom, "Land!" 216–24.
41 Ransom, "Land!" 221–22.
42 Ransom, "Happy Farmers," 531.
43 John Crowe Ransom, "A Capital for the New Deal," *American Review*, I (December, 1933), 1929–42.
44 Ransom to Lytle, July 15, 1933.
45 Ransom to Tate, July 24, 1933.
46 Seward Collins to Davidson, March 8, 1933.
47 Davidson was spending the year in Marshallville, Georgia, and did not attend the Nashville meeting, but he joined the group after they had adjourned to Lytle's Alabama farm.
48 John Crowe Ransom, "The Aesthetic of Regionalism," *American Review*, II (January, 1934), 309–10.
49 Davidson could not finish an essay that pleased him in time to meet the deadline, so Ransom's "Poetry: A Note in Ontology" was used instead.
50 Ransom to Tate, undated; Tate dates the letter "Late Winter, 1933."
51 Ransom to Tate, February 23, 1933.
52 Ransom to Tate, undated; Tate dates the letter "Late Winter, 1933."
53 John Crowe Ransom, "Regionalism in the South," *New Mexico Quarterly*, IV (May, 1934), 112.
54 *American Review*, I (December, 1933), 231–37.
55 Donald Davidson, "The 'Mystery' of the Agrarians: Facts and Illusions about Some Southern Writers," *Saturday Review of Literature*, XXVI (January 23, 1943), 7.
56 Some new contributors attracted to the Agrarian cause were James Waller, George Marion O'Donnell, Cleanth Brooks, and T. J. Cauley.
57 This same attitude had been expressed in a letter to Tate.
58 Herbert Agar and Allen Tate (eds.), *Who Owns America? A New Declaration of Independence* (Boston: Houghton Mifflin, 1936), 185.
59 *Ibid.*, 191–92.
60 George Marion O'Donnell to Richmond Croom Beatty, May 5, 1936.
61 John Crowe Ransom, "The Making of a Modern: The Poetry of George Marion O'Donnell," *Southern Review*, I (Spring, 1936), 864–74.
62 This list also includes Herbert Agar, Conrad Aiken, Donald Davidson, Caroline Gordon, Andrew Lytle, Frank Lawrence Owsley, Robert Penn Warren, James T. Adams, Van Wyck Brooks, Lewis Mumford, and Hervey Allen.
63 Ransom to Tate, November 4, 1937.
64 In spite of this invitation, which Davidson in later years did not remember having received, he published neither essays nor poems in the *Kenyon Review*.
65 John Crowe Ransom, "Art and the Human Economy," *Kenyon Review*, VII (Autumn, 1945), 685–86. Before this essay was published he sent a copy of it to Tate, who urged "him to suppress" it, "on the ground that when one finds a new interest, one need not repudiate an old one: one simply moves on." See Allen Tate, "On the Death of Ransom," *Sewanee Review*, LXXXII (Fall, 1974), 550.
     After Ransom's essay appeared Davidson wrote Tate: "It is all right for John to

change his mind, of course. Who could prevent him? And to change it in public if he chooses. Already by his silence on anything but purely aesthetic issues he had in effect severed his connection with his old friends, all but officially, and had implicitly chosen a new alignment. I deplore that, and have long since grieved over it much, but John is and has been his own master; and furthermore there have been other occasions when he swung an axe wildly, not much regarding his friends" (October 3, 1944, in J. T. Fain and T. D. Young (eds.), *The Literary Correspondence of Donald Davidson and Allen Tate* (Athens: University of Georgia Press, 1974), 344.

66 *Ibid.*, 686.
67 *Ibid.*
68 Before appearing in *The World's Body* five of these essays were published in the *American Review*, five in the *Southern Review*, three in the *Virginia Quarterly Review*, and two in the *Yale Review*.
69 Interview with Ransom, June, 1968.
70 O'Donnell to Beatty, June 24, 1937.

NOTES TO CHAPTER IX

1 Reavill Ransom to Ellene Ransom, May 10, 1936.
2 Interview with Helen Ransom Forman, August 25, 1970.
3 *John Crowe Ransom: A Tribute from the Community of Letters,* Supplement to the *Kenyon Collegian,* LXXXX (1964), 7.
4 Interview with Ransom, August 26, 1970.
5 Tate to Charles Cason, June 1, 1937.
6 Donald Davidson to Allen Tate, May 26, 1937, in J. T. Fain and T. D. Young (eds.), *The Literary Correspondence of Donald Davidson and Allen Tate* (Athens: University of Georgia Press, 1974), 303.
7 Kirkland to Tate, May 25, 1937.
8 Mims to Kirkland, May 22, 1937.
9 Conversations with Davidson, spring, 1965.
10 Davidson to Tate, May 26, 1937.
11 *Ibid.*
12 Interview with Frances Cheney, October 19, 1970.
13 Tate to Mims, May 28, 1937.
14 Tate to Davidson, May 28, 1937.
15 Nashville *Tennessean,* May 27, 1937.
16 Interview with Peter Taylor, August 11, 1970.
17 Nashville *Tennessean,* May 27, 1937.
18 O'Donnell to Kirkland, June 2, 1937.
19 Frank C. Rand to Lytle, June 2, 1937.
20 Tate to O. C. Carmichael, June 1, 1937.
21 Telegram, Bernard De Voto to Kirkland, May 30, 1937.
22 Tate to De Voto, June 1, 1937.
23 Tate to De Voto, June 5, 1937.
24 Kirkland to Ransom, June 7, 1936.
25 Mims to Kirkland, June 4, 1937.
26 This "anonymous donor" was Frank C. Rand.
27 Kirkland to Mims, June 5, 1937. The facts of this closely guarded secret are as follows: Kenyon College offered $4,500 plus free rent in a campus house. Vanderbilt was authorized by the Board of Trust to offer $4,700—and Ransom had a most satisfactory house for $45 a month.
28 Nashville *Tennessean,* June 8, 1937.
29 Interview with Frances Cheney, October 19, 1970.
30 Nashville *Tennessean,* June 11, 1937.

31 *Ibid.*
32 *Ibid.*
33 Ransom to Tate, June 17, 1937.
34 Davidson to Tate, June 20, 1937.
35 Ransom to Tate, August 12, 1937.
36 Boulder (Colo.) *Daily Camera*, August 13, 1937.

NOTES TO CHAPTER X

1 Ransom to Tate, October 10, 1937.
2 *Ibid.*
3 Ransom to Carmichael, October 5, 1937.
4 Ransom to Tate, October 16, 1937.
5 Ransom to Tate, October 18, 1937.
6 *Ibid.*
7 Ransom to Cleanth Brooks, October 18, 1937.
8 Ransom to Tate, November 4, 1937.
9 Ransom to Brooks, October 18, 1937.
10 Ransom to Ella Crowe Ransom, October 29, 1937.
11 Ransom to Tate, November 22, 1937.
12 Ransom to Ella Crowe Ransom, October 29, 1937.
13 Ransom to Tate, November 22, 1937.
14 About a year before Ransom went to Kenyon, Grace Lumpkin, a southern novelist and a contributor to the *New Masses,* published an interview with Seward Collins in which he admitted that he was a fascist and an admirer of both Hitler and Mussolini. At the end of the interview Lumpkin links Collins with the southern Agrarians: "I think it is not necessary to say that I do not believe that Fascism is already upon us. I do believe after reading a number of books like 'God without Thunder,' 'I Take My Stand,' [*sic*] and copies of the *Southern Review* and the *American Review,* that in those who write for them (some very sensitive and fine writers) there is the beginning of a group that is preparing the philosophical and moral shirt-front for Fascism." See Grace Lumpkin, "I Want a King," *Fight Against War and Fascism* (February, 1936), 14. Allen Tate answered the charge immediately, protesting that he was "so deeply opposed to Fascism" that he would "choose communism if it were an alternative to it." See Allen Tate, "Fascism and the Southern Agrarians," *New Republic* (May 27, 1936), 75. On June 19, 1936, the *New Republic* carried a letter from Collins asserting that he had not spoken for Tate or for any of the other Agrarians. In spite of the continued protests of Tate, Herbert Agar, and others, the charge of fascism continued to appear. An editorial in the *New Republic* a few weeks later (probably written by Malcolm Cowley) insisted that some theories of the Agrarians were much like those of Hitler and Mussolini, and V. F. Calverton declared the southern group "most dangerously reactionary." That some members of the faculty at Kenyon associated Ransom with fascism is not surprising. For a detailed discussion of the charge of fascism against the Agrarians, see Virginia Rock, "The Making and Meaning of *I'll Take My Stand*" (Ph.D. dissertation, University of Minnesota, 1961), 401–14.
15 Ransom to Ella Crowe Ransom, October 29, 1937.
16 Robb Reavill Ransom to Ellene Ransom, November 21 and 28, 1937.
17 Ransom to Ella Crowe Ransom, December 4, 1937.
18 Gordon Keith Chalmers (1904–1956), the son of a Baptist minister, grew up in Philadelphia and attended Brown University (A.B., 1925), Oxford (B.A., 1928), and Harvard (Ph.D., 1933). After teaching English at Mount Holyoke, he served as president of Rockford College (1934–1937) and of Kenyon College (1937–1956). His wife Roberta Teale Schwartz published verse in the *Fugitive, Poetry,* the

Bookman, and the *Saturday Review of Literature.* Her two volumes of poetry are *Lilliput* (1926) and *Lord Juggler and Other Poems* (1932). "It was really Roberta," Ransom recalled in 1963, "who . . . founded the Review. During her college days a strong minded old mistress had enrolled her in a nineteenth century course and made her read the British quarterlies of the period; not without remarking that no review of such quality had yet appeared in America. Roberta at once resolved to remedy this disaster, and it is now known . . . that she early came to an understanding with Gordon that he would bring it about if and when he could: and so he did." *American Oxonion,* (April, 1963), 63.

19 Frost came to Nashville to read before the Centennial Club, after which there was a party in his honor. About three A.M. Ransom drove Frost to his hotel and there in the street before the hotel—both still in tuxedos—and in the lobby, the two poets talked until daylight. "Milkmen were on the street by the time we got to the hotel," Ransom recalled twenty-five years later, "and there we stood in our dress clothes, in the morning sun, still talking. People passing by must have thought it funny." Quoted by Louise Davis in the Nashville *Tennessean Magazine* (June 7, 1964), 10. At eight o'clock that morning Robb was awakened by the noise Ransom made as he changed his clothes. When she asked him what he was doing, he said "I must go to class but Robert Frost can sleep." Years later, one summer while Ransom was living and teaching in Bread Loaf, Frost came for dinner. After dinner the two poets sat on the porch and talked until almost midnight. When Frost started home, Ransom offered to walk part of the way with him. At Frost's gate, Ransom started back and Frost came with him, and they spent the remainder of the night walking from one gate to the other; they were so involved in their conversation they did not know they had talked the night away until Robb called them in for breakfast. (Interview with Robb Reavill Ransom, February 12, 1971.)

20 Ransom to Tate, October 29, 1937.

21 *Ibid.*

22 *Ibid.*

23 Ransom to Tate, November 11, 1937.

24 Ransom to Tate, December 10, 1937.

25 Ransom to Tate, January 1, 1938.

26 Ransom to Tate, May 28, 1938.

27 Ransom to Tate, September 22, 1938.

28 The circular was dated September 28, 1938.

29 In his letters to Tate, Ransom explains his reasons for some of these choices: "Mark Van Doren is in universal favor at Kenyon; Roberta Teale Schwartz is a very fine, sweet, thoughtful person, not a meddler, and a sort of proxy we could deal with for the president; she's thoroughly good though not a high-powered literary person . . . a person of mighty fine taste"; Philip Timberlake "is our local faculty man, a good though unambitious man"; Eliseo Vivas "is a philosopher, young, at Wisconsin, an excellent man, friend of Rice's . . . considered brilliant among the philosophy group"; Paul Rosenfeld, "to represent music and art." Ransom to Tate, September 22 and October 1, 1938.

30 He received $150 for his lectures at the Murray (Kentucky) State Teachers College and $150 for those at the University of Chattanooga, all of which he sent home to his mother. The Reverend Dr. J. J. Ransom had died October 18, 1934, at the age of eighty-one.

31 Ransom to Tate, April 22, 1938.

32 This piece by Ransom was delayed for three years and appeared as "Yvor Winters: The Logical Critic," *Southern Review,* VI (Winter, 1941), 558–83, and in an expanded form in *The New Criticism.*

33 John Crowe Ransom, "Mr. Empson's Muddles," *Southern Review,* IV (1938/39),

322–39. In a slightly revised form this essay appears in *The New Criticism*.

34 Ransom to Tate, April 22, 1938.

35 *Ibid.*

36 Thomas Merton, "Standards for Critics," New York *Herald Tribune Books*, XIV (May 8, 1938), 10.

37 Henry S. Canby, "A Prospectus for Criticism," *Saturday Review of Literature*, XVIII (May 21, 1938), 8–9.

38 Frederick A. Pottle, "Theory of Poetry," *Yale Review*, XXVIII (Autumn, 1938), 183–85.

39 Louis Kronenberger, "Poetry in the Modern World," *Nation*, CXLVII (August 13, 1938), 160–62.

40 Michael Roberts, review in *Criterion*, XVIII (Winter, 1938–1939), 152–54.

41 *Times Literary Supplement*, August 13, 1938, p. 532.

42 Percy Hutchison, review in *New York Times Book Review*, December 18, 1938, p. 12.

43 R. P. Blackmur, "In Our Ends Are Our Beginnings," *Virginia Quarterly Review*, XIV (Summer, 1938), 446–50.

44 Kenneth Burke, "On Poetry and Poetics," *Poetry*, LV (October, 1939), 51–54.

45 Arthur Mizener, "Recent Criticism," *Southern Review*, V (Autumn, 1939), 376–400.

46 John Crowe Ransom, *The World's Body* (New York: Charles Scribner's Sons, 1938), 200. All textual references are to this edition.

47 Ransom to Tate, September 5, 1926.

48 Ransom, *The World's Body*, 137. In a letter to Arthur Mizener (April 26, 1940) Ransom writes that "metaphysical poetry is certainly limited . . . . For instance, *wit* is a dangerous quality; it is as bad for poetry as it is good; and if *wit* is the predominant character of metaphysical poets I have to cross them off my list, with every reluctance."

49 Pottle, "Theory of Poetry," 185.

50 The best critique of Ransom's argument, as well as the most persuasive attempt to refute it, is Arthur Mizener's "The Structure of Figurative Language in Shakespeare's Sonnets," *Southern Review*, V (Spring, 1940), 730–40. After Ransom had read Mizener's essay, he responded that he did not think their "controversy . . . quite becoming to either of us as a son of the morning. I evidently was intemperate and got myself way out on a limb; you in returning the compliment are pretty extreme yourself." The greatest variance in their views, Ransom believed, was in "the bare ruined choir passage." Ransom argued: "Here I would propose: that it's entirely possible Shakespeare had his eye on the bird-choir effect the minute he thought about denoting the time of life by the autumn leaves; that he knows (intuitively . . .) that his singing birds don't belong very expressly to his tenor but almost exclusively to his vehicle, and he is not deterred, as I think he should not be; therefore [he] has an intermediate and transitional version of the vehicle, namely the cold bare bows shaking in the winter wind, a perfect adaptation of vehicle to tenor; and then after this introduction of vehicle [he] lets vehicle really develop itself into the choirs aspect with the birds; knowing that Mizener or any decent reader will see at once that it is beautiful in itself (pure vehicular beauty) and then will see to it if he is a logician (and Mizener is that, a cannier one than Ransom) that some kind of no-singing-strain-now can be worked up in the tenor if necessary." Ransom to Mizener, April 26, 1940.

To which statement, Mizener replied: "What you have to say about the sonnet piece is, in the large at least, very flattering: it takes me seriously, and in doing so causes a lot of fine questions. . . . Your hypothetical account of the genesis of the bare ruin'd choirs passage sounds very plausible indeed. It's like any poet, isn't it, to let the necessities of vehicle, rhyme, or what-not determine some aspect of the tenor. But no genetic fallacy, as I hear my philosophical friends saying; that is,

Shakespeare is no less serious about the no-singing-strains-now business than he is about anything else in the tenor simply because it was first suggested by the necessity of putting something between the autumn leaves and the choir." Mizener to Ransom, May 1, 1940.

See also Wilfred Lynskey's "A Critic in Action: Mr. Ransom," *College English*, V (February, 1944), 239–49. Many of the reviews cited earlier in this chapter also give typical reactions to the essay.

51 Ransom to Tate, April 22, 1938. Ransom's letters during this period contain many references to his desire to write detailed, analytical, structural studies of individual poems, such as those included in Cleanth Brooks's *The Well-Wrought Urn*. But he could never pull himself away from his "theorizing" on the nature of poetry and its function in a civilized society, except in a few instances.

52 Ransom to Tate, September 22, 1938.

53 Ransom to Tate, October 1, 1938.

54 Ransom to Tate, October 18, 1938.

55 Ransom to Tate, December 10, 1938.

56 John Peale Bishop, "The Sorrows of Thomas Wolfe"; Ford Madox Ford, "A Paris Letter"; Philip Rahv, "Franz Kafka: The Hero as Lonely Man"; and Paul Rosenfeld, "The Advent of American Music."

57 *Kenyon Review*, I (Winter, 1939), 75–84.

58 *Ibid.*, 81–82.

59 Ransom to Tate, May 18, 1939.

60 *Kenyon Review*, I (Spring, 1939), 194–99.

61 *Ibid.*, 198.

62 "Prelude to an Evening" was begun in the winter of 1933 and completed early the next year.

63 Ransom to Tate, April 22, 1939.

64 Laurence N. Barrett, "John Crowe Ransom: Teacher," in *John Crowe Ransom: A Tribute from the Community of Letters*, Supplement to the *Kenyon Collegian*, LXXXX (1964), 23–24.

65 Louise Davis, in Nashville *Tennessean Magazine* (June 7, 1964), 14.

66 In Thomas Daniel Young (ed.), *John Crowe Ransom: Critical Essays and a Bibliography* (Baton Rouge: Louisiana State University Press, 1968), 210–11.

NOTES TO CHAPTER XI

1 Ransom to Ella Crowe Ransom, January 11, 1939.

2 Ransom to Tate, January 31, 1939.

3 Robb Ransom to Ellene Ransom, January 6, 1939.

4 Ransom to Tate, November 29, 1938, and April 29, 1939.

5 Ransom to Ella Crowe Ransom, January 11, 1939.

6 Ransom to Ella Crowe Ransom, January 25, 1939.

7 Ransom to Tate, February 22, 1939.

8 He was pleased and flattered, however, when Chalmers reported that in spite of their realization that Ransom's salary exceeded some of theirs by a considerable amount, the members of the faculty council had instructed their president to use every "reasonable means" to induce Ransom to stay.

9 Ransom to Tate, February 22, 1939.

10 His mother's letter is lost, but Ransom quotes these phrases in his reply of March 5, 1939.

11 Ransom to Tate, March 29, 1939.

12 Ransom to Tate, April 15, 1939.

13 Ransom to Tate, April 24, 1939; Ransom wrote Tate that he liked regular teaching

better than "supervision of genius." Tate did not like North Carolina because he was only "window dressing," not a part of the regular teaching faculty.

14 Ransom wrote his mother that the Carnegie Foundation had given "a lump sum to the college for the encouragement of creative writing and their specific object specified was the employment of Ransom as editor to carry on the *Review* and to do light teaching." March 13, 1939.

15 Ransom to Tate, undated (Summer, 1939).

16 Quoted in Louise Davis, Nashville *Tennessean Magazine* (June 7, 1964), 14.

17 *John Crowe Ransom: A Tribute from the Community of Letters*, Supplement to the *Kenyon Collegian*, LXXXX (1964), 8.

18 Ransom to Brooks, April 20, 1939.

19 Ransom to Tate, undated (Summer, 1939).

20 Kenyon College *Bulletin*, Spring, 1939, p. 4.

21 The statistical information about the *Kenyon Review* comes from the annual reports submitted by Ransom and his staff to the president and trustees of the college. The report for 1941 indicates that subscribers live in forty-four states and the District of Columbia as well as in Canada, England, France, Norway, Sweden, Belgium, Switzerland, Turkey, South Africa, India, Ceylon, Japan, British Malaya, and the Dutch East Indies. In the fall of 1940 as an effort intended to increase circulation, thirty thousand circulars were sent to a mailing list which included the following: all members of Modern Language Association, present and former Rhodes Scholars, subscribers to the *Southern Review* and *Poetry*, everyone listed in *Who's Who* and *Who's Who in America* indicating an interest in art or literature. *Kenyon Review* also exchanged advertisements with the *American Scholar, Commonsense, Furioso*, the *London Bulletin, Nation, New Directions, New Republic, Partisan Review, Poetry, Review of Politics, Southern Review, Southwest Review, Twice a Year*, and *Twentieth-Century Verse*.

22 Ransom to Tate, September 4, 1941.

23 This statement is dated March 12, 1941.

24 The *Southern Review* contains "critical matter of the highest excellence," Ransom wrote, but it also publishes "a large body of political content and a section of short stories" and gives no space to any but the literary arts.

25 Although the Carnegie Foundation was definitely committed against subsidizing periodicals, Ransom thought there was "the chance of an emergency gift" if the *Review* could establish that it was "something special." Ransom to Tate, January 16, 1941.

26 Ransom to F. P. Keppel, February 15, 1941. Church might not have been as generous as Ransom expected because of Wallace Stevens' reaction to the request. On August 30, 1940, Stevens wrote Henry Church: "For one thing (since you asked me to comment) I cannot imagine you as content to share the pages of the *Kenyon Review*. This seems to me to be very much as if Ransom was giving you his old clothes in order to keep himself going. . . . The only thing that is going to please you is that *Mesures* should be wholly yours and wholly yourself. This eliminates joining up with the *Southern Review*, the *Kenyon Review*, etc. After all, take the latter: Why does it exist, if not for the very purpose of enabling Ransom to find himself in its pages?"

27 Ransom to Tate, January 28, 1942.

28 In a letter to Tate, June 2, 1942, Ransom speculated that the board of trustees of Louisiana State University did not approve the merger because the proposal included the stipulation that either Brooks or Warren should spend one term each year at Kenyon while on salary from L.S.U. The trustees did not want to enter into an agreement that included this kind of financial commitment.

29 Ransom to Keppel, September 11, 1942.

30 Ransom to Tate, March 20, 1943.
31 David H. Stevens to Ransom, July 20, 1943.
32 He came to Gambier on November 11 and 12, 1943.
33 Total income, including Church's $750, the trustees' $1,000, and the Foundation's $3,750 was $8,627.85; expenditures were $6,958.
34 During 1945/46, however, without the Rockefeller grant, expenditures exceeded income by $2,338.29 and the surplus fell to $1,160.25. Because of a rise in printing costs, Ransom went into his eighth year as editor of the *Review* faced with the necessity of having to raise at least $3,000.
35 The rate of $5.00 a page which the *Review* paid when it began had been reduced to $2.50 at the beginning of the war.
36 Volume I (1939) had contained 480 pages, no fiction, and 25 pages of verse; Volume IV (1942) had 440 pages, 75 pages of fiction (including Andrew Lytle's "Alchemy" which ran to 55 pages), and 21 pages of verse; Volume VII (1945) contained 734 pages, 169 pages of fiction, and 48 of verse.
37 The foundation also provided funds for "editorial assistance" for the *Review*. During 1944 and 1945 Harold Whitehead, Eric Bentley, Charles Riker, and Robert Penn Warren each served a term as Rockefeller fellows.
38 During 1944, there were 1,140 entries submitted in the short story contest, which was judged by Robert Penn Warren, Harold Whitehall, and Ransom. First prize of $500 went to Jean Garrigue for "The Snow Fall" and second prize to Frances Gray Patton for "A Piece of Bread." The following year John Berryman's "The Imaginary Jew" won first prize and Mona Van Duyn's "The Bell," second.
39 Ransom to Tate, November 19, 1940.
40 Ransom was confused about the dates; he probably began the essay in November but he was still working on it at Christmas.
41 John Crowe Ransom, "The Concrete Universal: Observations on the Understanding of Poetry, I," *Kenyon Review*, XVI (Autumn, 1954), 554–64, and "The Concrete Universal: Observations on the Understanding of Poetry, II," *Kenyon Review*, XVII (Summer, 1955), 383–407. A third essay, "The Concrete Universal," written in 1970, was published in *Beating the Bushes* (1972).
42 Ransom quotes Tate in his letter of May 23, 1941.
43 Philip Blair Rice to I. A. Richards, June 14, 1941.
44 Richards to Rice, July 11, 1941.
45 Louise Bogan, review in *Nation*, CLIII (July 12, 1941), 37.
46 Babette Deutsch, review in *New York Herald Tribune Books*, XVII (June 15, 1941), 11.
47 Alexander Cowie, review in *Saturday Review of Literature*, XXIV (July 5, 1941), 13.
48 Richard Eberhart, review in *Accent*, II (Autumn, 1941), 51–55.
49 Fred B. Millet, review in *American Literature*, XV (March, 1943), 82–84.
50 Kenneth Burke, review in *Kenyon Review*, IV (Winter, 1942), 126–32.
51 John Crowe Ransom, *The New Criticism* (Norfolk, Conn.: New Directions, 1941), x–xi. All textual references are to this edition.
52 Ransom did not use here "intentional fallacy," but the term was developed from statements such as this.
53 Ransom to Tate, April 14, 1941.
54 John Crowe Ransom, *The World's Body* (New York: Charles Scribner's Sons, 1938), x.
55 Ransom, *The New Criticism*, 281–94.
56 See particularly: John Crowe Ransom, "An Address to Kenneth Burke," *Kenyon Review*, IV (Spring, 1942), 218–37; "The Inorganic Muses," *Kenyon Review*, V (Spring, 1943), 278–300; "Positive and Near Positive Aesthetics," *Kenyon Review*, V (Summer, 1943), 443–47; "Art Needs a Little Separating," *Kenyon Review*, VI (Winter, 1944), 114–22; "Art Worries the Naturalists," *Kenyon Review*, VII (Spring, 1945), 282–99; "Beating the Naturalists with the Stick of Drama," *Kenyon Review*,

VII (Summer, 1945), 515-20; "Art and the Human Economy," *Kenyon Review*, VII (Autumn, 1945), 683-88.
57 Ransom to Tate, January 5, 1942.
58 Ransom to Tate, September 4, 1941.
59 Ransom to David H. Stevens, August 27, 1943.
60 Ransom to Tate, September 4, 1941.
61 Robb Ransom to Ellene Ransom, April 6, 1939.
62 Ransom to Tate, January 4, 1944.
63 Nashville *Tennessean*, June 17, 1945.
64 *Sewanee Review*, LVI (Summer, 1948), 388.
65 John Crowe Ransom, "A Plan for an Educational Project in the Humanities," Summer, 1946, copy in Kenyon College Archives.
66 John L. Stewart, "A Little Higher in Spirit," in *John Crowe Ransom: A Tribute from the Community of Letters*, Supplement to the *Kenyon Collegian*, LXXXX (1964), 9.

NOTES TO CHAPTER XII

1 Howard Moss, "Integrity, Patience, Discipline," *New York Times Book Review*, July 8, 1945, p. 6.
2 Theodore Spencer, in *Saturday Review of Literature*, XXVIII (July 14, 1945), 30.
3 *New Yorker*, July 7, 1945, p. 68.
4 Richard Eberhart, "The Search for Perfection," *Poetry*, LXVII (January, 1946), 214.
5 Dan Norton, "Ten Poets," *Virginia Quarterly Review*, XXII (Summer, 1946), 439.
6 Spencer, in *Saturday Review of Literature*, 31.
7 Moss "Integrity, Patience, Discipline," 6.
8 *Ibid.*
9 Arthur Mizener, "The Riddling Friar," *Quarterly Review of Literature*, II (1945), 367.
10 Spencer, in *Saturday Review of Literature*, 31.
11 Richmond Croom Beatty, "John Crowe Ransom as Poet," *Sewanee Review*, LXII (Summer, 1944), 366.
12 Mizener, "The Riddling Friar," 368.
13 Allen Tate, review in *Nation*, CXXIV (March 30, 1927), 310.
14 Robert Penn Warren, "John Crowe Ransom: A Study in Irony," *Virginia Quarterly Review*, XI (January, 1935), 109.
15 *New Yorker*, July 7, 1945, p. 68.
16 Spencer, in *Saturday Review of Literature*, 31.
17 My winter's leave was much too cold for smarting.
What bitter winds, and numbing snows and sorrows,
And wheezy pines, like old men undeparting,
To funeralize against all green young morrows!
18 The following changes were made later: line 9, "Better to walk forth in the frozen air" becomes "Better to walk forth in the murderous air"; line 13, "And where I went, the hugest winter blast" becomes "And where I walked, the murderous winter blast."
19 The lines added in *Two Gentlemen in Bonds* were:

He was not a beautiful boy, nor good, nor clever,
A black cloud full of storms too hot for keeping,
A sword beneath his mother's heart,—yet never
Woman bewept her babe as this is weeping.

20 An examination of these changes demonstrates rather clearly some of Ransom's intentions in the revisions.

3. And the country kin sit glowering on the transaction (original)

3. And neither the county kin love the transaction (TGB)
3. And none of the county kin like the transaction (SP)

9. A pig with a pasty face, I had long said (original)
9. A pig with a pasty face, I had always said (TGB)
9. A pig with a pasty face, so I had said (SP)

10. Squealing for cakes, and fixing his base pretense (original)
10. Squealing for cookies, kinned by pure pretense (TGB)
10. Squealing for cookies, kinned by poor pretense (SP)

12. And these are the very forbears' lineaments (original)
12. I can see the forbears' antique lineaments (TGB)
12. I see the forebears' antique lineaments (SP)

20. Aggrieving the sapless limbs, all shorn and shaken (original)
20. Aggrieving the sapless limbs, the shorn and shaken (TGB)
20. Grieving the sapless limbs, the shorn and shaken (SP)

21 In *Grace After Meat* the poem appears under the title "Ilex Priscus."

22 The deleted lines, which appear as lines 10 through 15 of the version which appeared in the *Fugitive*, II (December, 1923), 174–75, are as follows:

But hé casts the feeble generations of leaf,
And naked to the spleen of the cold skies eruptive
That howl on his defiant head in chief,

Bears out their frenzy to its period,
And hears in the spring, a little more rheumy and deaf,
After the tragedy the lyric palinode. . . .

23 Why should two lovers go frozen asunder in fear (CF)
Why should two lovers go frozen apart in fear (SP)

Of many delicate postures she cast a snare (CF)
Yet of evasions even she made a snare (SP)

24 "Tom" has also appeared as "The Vanity of the Male" and "The Vanity of the Bright Young Men." In his *The Poetry of John Crowe Ransom* (New Brunswick: Rutgers University Press, 1972), Miller Williams includes nine different versions of this poem and omits two others: the one that appeared in the *Fugitive*, III (August, 1924), 100–101, and that used by William Pratt in *The Fugitive Poets* (New York: E. P. Dutton, 1965).

25 David Mann and Samuel H. Woods, Jr., "John Crowe Ransom's Poetic Revisions," *PMLA*, LXXXIII (March, 1968), 15–21.

26 Allen Tate, "For John Ransom at Seventy-five," *Shenandoah*, XIV (Spring, 1963), 8.

27 In T. S. Eliot, *Homage to John Dryden: Three Essays on Poetry of the Seventeenth Century* (London: Hogarth Press, 1927), 31.

28 *Ibid.*, 38.

29 J. T. Fain and T. D. Young (eds.), *The Literary Correspondence of Donald Davidson and Allen Tate* (Athens: University of Georgia Press, 1974), 166.

30 Allen Tate, "Whose Ox?" *Fugitive*, I (December, 1922), 99.

31 John Crowe Ransom, "Thoughts on the Poetic Discontent," *Fugitive*, IV (June, 1925), 63–64.

32 John Crowe Ransom, "Mixed Modes," *Fugitive*, IV (March, 1925), 28.

33 Ransom, "Thoughts on the Poetic Discontent," 64.

34 Warren, "John Crowe Ransom: A Study in Irony," 93–111.

35 *Ibid.*, 102.

36 *Ibid.*, 103.

37 Note written by Davidson in his copy of *Homage to John Dryden,* which he reviewed for the *Fugitive,* IV (June, 1925), 61–62.

38 "Five Poets," *Southern Review,* I (January, 1936), 674. Davidson indicated his approval of this point of view in an essay-review in the next issue of the same journal: "Six Poets: A Study in Magnitude," *Southern Review,* I (April, 1936), 876.

39 Davidson to John Hall Wheelock, February 4, 1949, in Jesse E. Wills Collection of the Joint University Libraries, Nashville, Tennessee.

40 John Crowe Ransom, *The World's Body* (New York: Charles Scribner's Sons, 1938), viii, 140, and 142.

41 Williams, *The Poetry of John Crowe Ransom,* 29.

42 G. R. Wasserman, "The Irony of John Crowe Ransom," *University of Kansas City Review,* XXIII (Winter, 1956), 151–60.

43 Graham Hough, "John Crowe Ransom: The Poet and the Critic," *Southern Review,* n.s., I (January, 1965), 14.

44 Randall Jarrell, "John Ransom's Poetry," *Sewanee Review,* LVI (Summer, 1948), 378.

45 Bentley to Stevens, February 27, 1945.

46 Ransom to Stevens, March 5, 1945.

47 Tate resigned October 15, 1945; he and Caroline Gordon were divorced in January, 1946. But after they agreed to remarry in March, 1946, Ransom thought the Tates might decide to remain in Sewanee. Instead, after their marriage in April, they sold Benfolly and moved to an apartment at 108 Perry Street, New York City.

48 Ransom to Tate, April 22, 1946.

49 Ransom to Tate, May 2, 1946.

50 Tate to Ransom, July 22, 1946.

51 Ransom to Tate, August 22, 1946.

52 "Nothing has been written about F[aulkner]," Ransom wrote Tate on August 22, 1946, "that's better than Caroline's piece."

53 Tate to Ransom, August 30, 1946; Tate, who in the spring of 1946 had become editor of belles lettres for Henry Holt and Company, was at this time trying to establish a connection between that firm and the *Kenyon Review.* Ransom had suggested, in his letter to Tate of August 22, 1946, that for $2,000 the *Review* "would carry all the advertising that could be devised for one publisher short of a multitude of similar ads about different books. We could doubtless steer many young authors, if few prospective best sellers, to our publisher. And turn over every little while something book-size from our publishing." Later this year and for $1,000 Ransom made such an arrangement with Random House.

54 Ransom to Tate, September 19, 1946.

55 Ransom to Tate, September 12, 1947.

56 Ransom to Tate, July 17, 1946.

57 Ransom to Mizener, July 6, 1957.

58 Ransom to John Marshall, January 27, 1947.

59 Between the summer of 1947 and the autumn of 1951 the contributors who received the largest compensation from the *Kenyon Review* were (with number of items given in parenthesis): Eric Bentley (8), $1,094.62; R. P. Blackmur (7), $988.37; William Empson (5), $704.48; Parker Tyler (9), $703.18; Isaac Rosenfeld (6), $685.25; Harry Levin (3), $584.53; and Leslie Fiedler (5), $502.64.

60 Memorandum to Ransom, February 4, 1947.

61 Ransom to Marshall, February 11, 1947. The *Kenyon Review* received $4,500 from the Rockefeller Foundation and was able to increase payments to contributors from $2,963.49 in 1946/47 to $6,407.81 in 1947/48.

62 Ransom to Tate, August 2, 1948.

63 *Bulletin,* Kenyon School of English (1948), 3.

64 Ransom to Tate, February 24, 1948.

65 Each student could register for two classes from the following schedule: Eric Bentley, "Studies in Drama, As Literature and As Theatre"; Cleanth Brooks, "Milton"; Richard Chase, "Hawthorne and Melville"; F. O. Matthiessen, "Twentieth-Century American Poetry"; William Empson, "The Key Word in the Long Poem"; John Crowe Ransom, "The Study of Poetry: Shakespeare's Dramatic Verse"; Austin Warren, "Donne and Other Metaphysical Poets"; Allen Tate, "The Novel Since 1895."

66 The program of the forum for 1948 was the following:

June 30   The Social Responsibilities of the Critic—F. O. Matthiessen
July 7   Some Critical Strategies—John Crowe Ransom and Austin Warren
July 14   Charlie Chaplin's *Monsieur Verdoux*—Eric Bentley
July 21   The Relevance of Verbal Analysis in Criticism—William Empson
July 28   Milton's Metaphors—Cleanth Brooks
August 4   Is It the Artist's Fate to Be Isolated from His Culture—Allen Tate and Richard Chase

67 George Lanning, "Memories of the School of English," in *John Crowe Ransom: A Tribute from the Community of Letters,* Supplement to the *Kenyon Collegian,* LXXXX (1964), 33–34.

68 For 1949 courses and instructors were as follows: Eric Bentley, "Studies in Drama"; Philip Rahv, "Dostoevsky and Tolstoy"; John Crowe Ransom, "Wordsworth: His Practice and Theory of Verse"; Herbert Read, "Studies in English Prose"; Mark Schorer, "Techniques of Fiction: Six Novels"; Allen Tate, "Pope and Johnson"; René Wellek, "Theory of Literature"; Yvor Winters, "The English Lyric."

69 Ransom to Caroline Gordon and Allen Tate, December 10, 1949.

70 Robert Hillyer, who won the Pulitzer Prize for poetry in 1934, was appointed to the faculty of Kenyon College in the fall of 1949 and served until 1951. A severe opponent of the New Criticism and of the difficult, intellectual verse of the twenties and thirties (Ransom said he belonged to the "Transparent School of Poetry"), Hillyer was openly hostile to the kind of poetry and criticism published in the *Kenyon Review.* "American poetry at present," he wrote in the *American Mercury,* for January, 1950, "is the almost undisputed playground of a loose confederation of critics whom we may term the school of Eliot. Up to four or five years ago, their writings were confined to the more esoteric literary reviews, but through logrolling, discreet acquaintanceship, academic positions, and brow-beating the public . . . they have gradually acquired power in the book-review sections of the metropolitan press." A little later in the essay, after naming Eliot and Tate, he makes an obvious reference to others of the group. "The music of words is a subject repugnant to them, since they are wholly concerned with irony, the meaning of meaning, paradoxes, ambiguities, ambivalences, dichotomies—and, indeed, any double-talk. . . . They will tell you that the sonnets of Donne are better than the sonnets of Shakespeare" (p. 65). A later statement is even more explicit: "Though the symbolism of T. S. Eliot's poetry and the incoherence of Ezra Pound's *Cantos* have served as damaging models for younger men, the more nearly complete sterilization and confusion of recent American poetry were accomplished by the New Criticism . . . a group of poets who first called themselves the Fugitives, and then, under the leadership of John Crowe Ransom, turned from poetry to criticism." Hillyer indicated his complete agreement with Douglas Bush's statement that one "cannot miss the tone of conscious intellectual superiority, a superiority which arouses envious despair in the less highly endowed." See Hillyer's *In Pursuit of Poetry* (New York: McGraw-Hill, 1960), 193. This attitude of "envious despair" may offer a partial explanation for the intensity of Hillyer's personal dislike of Ransom.

The issue of the *Kenyon Collegian* for September 30, 1949, reported that over the summer "Robert Hillyer set off a political-cultural powder keg that ultimately may serve to loosen the stranglehold on American letters held these many years by mad Ezra Pound, T. S. Eliot, and other high priests of incomprehensibility worshipped by the 'New Critics.'" After a discussion of the New Critics, whose "current preoccupation is a new vocabulary that has no purpose but its own creation," the article ended with a direct reference to Ransom: "Kenyon, cathedra of John Crowe Ransom, archdeacon in Poetry's New Priesthood, and . . . bailiwick for the avant-garde *Kenyon Review*, undoubtedly is in for a series of minor tremors as critical reputations hit the dust." The tone of the article was so critical that Denham Sutcliffe, a colleague in the English department, asked Ransom, who was on leave at Indiana University, if he, Charles Coffin, and Philip Blair Rice should answer it. Ransom responded that although it made him "feel mighty good" to know his friends wanted to defend him in his absence, he thought the matter should be dropped. "That boy from Kenyon was sure to crop up," he wrote on October 5, 1949; "I'd have laughed at him I think. But his cropping up does show the harm that the sailor-poet's tactics have done. He's raised up the middle brows, like the woman in Yeats who 'set the little houses against the great' . . . and I'm afraid he'll offer a cheap currency which will drive out the dear (in the sense that his exercises will be simpler than ours)."

Although no one in the English department responded, the next issue of the paper carried a letter from Gordon Chalmers: "If one of the purposes of Mr. Lobdell's article in Friday's *Collegian* was to discredit the work of a distinguished man of letters and an admired member of the Kenyon faculty, John Crowe Ransom, I hope that your readers will reflect that his work is internationally held in high esteem and is one of the occasions for admiration of the college itself"(*Kenyon Collegian*, October 7, 1949).

71 Ransom to Tate, June 7, 1950.
72 Ransom to Tate, March 28, 1950.
73 Ransom to Tate, June 27, 1950.
74 Ransom to Tate, September 17, 1950.
75 Chalmers to Ransom, August 22, 1950.
76 He had received $13,333.33 each year from the Rockefeller Foundation.
77 Ransom to Tate, October 27, 1950.
78 Ransom to Kenyon School of English fellows, November 4, 1950.
79 Ransom to Tate, November 28, 1950.
80 Ransom taught in the summer of 1952, offering a course entitled "Keats, with a Brief Consideration of Shelley," and in 1954 he gave "Poetry of Our Century: T. S. Eliot, W. H. Auden, Wallace Stevens, Thomas Hardy." The faculty list of the School of Letters during the first few summers reads very much like that of the School of English at Kenyon. Soon the following teaching fellows were added to those who taught during the first summer: R. P. Blackmur, Kenneth Burke, Leslie Fiedler, Irving Howe, Robert Fitzgerald, Randall Jarrell, Delmore Schwartz, William Empson, Harold Whitehall, and Richard Chase. In 1954 Newton P. Stallknecht replaced Richard Hudson as Director, and Philip Rahv and Allen Tate became senior fellows.
81 Ransom to Marshall, January 9, 1948. One does note the appearance of more foreign contributors after 1948. During the tenure of this Rockefeller grant, from 1948 to 1952, the *Review* carried contributions by Donat O'Donnell, Paul Radin, Rene Leibowitz, Sean O'Faolain, Hisaye Yamamoto, Jean Barrault, Northrop Frye, T. S. Eliot, Jacques Maritain, Renato Poggioli, Marius Bewley, and Pier Pasinetti.
82 *Kenyon Review*, X (Autumn, 1948), 682–88.
83 William Barrett, "A Present Tendency in American Criticism"; R. P. Blackmur, "For

a Second Look"; Richard Chase, "New vs. Ordealist"; and Allen Tate, "A Note on Autotelism," all in *Kenyon Review*, XI (Winter, 1949).

84 Edited by Allen Tate and Robert Penn Warren, this special issue of *Sewanee Review* (Summer, 1948), presented as "Homage to John Crowe Ransom," included essays by Wallace Stevens, Andrew Lytle, Robert Lowell, Randall Jarrell, F. O. Matthiessen, Howard Nemerov, Cleanth Brooks, Donald A. Stauffer, and William Van O'Connor, as well as a checklist in three sections—"Books and Essays," "Reviews," and "Criticism on Ransom"—by Robert W. Stallman. When Ransom received the first copy of the issue at a special dinner given in his honor on July 14 at Kenyon, he commented in what *Newsweek* called his "soft Pulaski, Tennessee, accent"; "They let me down easy. I am glad that everyone of them got in a negative or two somewhere in the course of his essay," *Newsweek*, August 2, 1948, p. 73. There were not many of these "negatives."

85 Donald A. Stauffer, "Portrait of the Critic-Poet as Equilibrist," *Sewanee Review*, LVI (Summer, 1948), 426.

86 *Ibid.*, 427.

87 *Ibid.*, 428.

88 Cleanth Brooks, "The Doric Delicacy," *Sewanee Review*, LVI (Summer, 1948), 414–15.

89 F. O. Matthiessen, "Primarily Language," *Sewanee Review*, LVI (Summer, 1948), 397.

90 Wallace Stevens, "John Crowe Ransom: Tennessean," *Sewanee Review* LVI (Summer, 1948), 367–69.

91 Randall Jarrell, "John Ransom's Poetry," *Sewanee Review*, LVI (Summer, 1948), 381.

NOTES TO CHAPTER XIII

1 John Crowe Ransom, "An Age of Criticism," *New Republic*, CXXVI (March 31, 1952), 18.

2 In an address read before the Ohio English Association on April 6, 1951, Ransom pointed out that not since the first half of the seventeenth century had there been as much poetry of high quality produced in a similar period as between 1900 and 1950. The *major* poets of the period, in his view, were Thomas Hardy, W. B. Yeats, E. A. Robinson, Robert Frost, and T. S. Eliot. Among the most important of the *minor* poets he listed Robert Bridges, Walter de la Mare, John Masefield, Vachel Lindsay, William Carlos Williams, Ezra Pound, Marianne Moore, E. E. Cummings, Hart Crane, and Allen Tate. Four others fall between these two groups, and future critics may classify them as either *major* or *minor*: A. E. Housman, Wallace Stevens, W. H. Auden, and Dylan Thomas. The only change in these listings that Ransom later made was to move Stevens into the group of major poets.

3 This series had included Ransom's study of Wordsworth, Warren's of "The Ancient Mariner," and Arthur Mizener's of Tennyson. In a letter to Mizener, April 25, 1945, commissioning the essay on Tennyson, Ransom indicated his plan for the entire series of essays: "They ought to leave the common thing and the academic thing unsaid, and fix and focus on the bright meaning which makes the visions. . . . What we need is a new statement of Tennyson and not a synthesis of statements."

4 John Crowe Ransom, "Poetry: The Formal Analysis," *Kenyon Review*, IX (Summer, 1947), 436.

5 George Lanning, "Ransom as Editor," in Thomas Daniel Young (ed.), *John Crowe Ransom: Critical Essays and a Bibliography* (Baton Rouge: Louisiana State University Press, 1968), 218.

6 Ransom to Mizener, September 7, 1950.

7 Ransom to Tate, September 6, 1950.

8 Fergusson, Tate, Jarrell, Trilling, and Rahv did not contribute to the series.

9   The *Times Literary Supplement* carried a follow-up article on this subject on June 12, 1953.
10 Ransom to Tate, April 9, 1952.
11 News release from Kenyon College, January 20, 1953.
12 For 1954 the fellows were: poetry, W. S. Merwin; fiction, George Lanning and Flannery O'Connor; criticism, R. W. B. Lewis; for 1955: poetry, Edgar Collins Bogardus and Douglas Nichols; fiction, Howard Nemerov; criticism, Richard Ellmann. In some years dual awards were possible because the grant was for $9,000 a year to permit the appointment of three married fellows, if such appointments were necessary in order to give the awards to the best qualified applicants. Each unmarried fellow appointed, therefore, left a surplus of $1,000.
13 The *Kenyon Review* fellows for 1956, 1957, and 1958 were: poetry: Ruth Stone, Delmore Schwartz, Theodore Holmes, and James Wright; fiction: Andrew Lytle, Theodore Hoffman, J. F. Powers, and Elizabeth Spencer; criticism: Leslie Fiedler, Francis Fergusson, and Thomas Henry Carter.
14 Between 1953 and 1959 the *Kenyon Review* drew heavily from its fellows, publishing from this group eighteen book reviews, nineteen essays, ten stories, and fourteen poems.
15 Ransom published the first half of Robert Penn Warren's *Brother to Dragons* in the issue for Winter, 1953, and many of the poems collected in *Promises* (1957) first appeared in the pages of the *Kenyon Review*.
16 Lanning, "Ransom as Editor," 214.
17 *Ibid.*, 215.
18 Ransom to Brainard Cheney, March 25, 1957.
19 Flannery O'Connor to Ransom, November 1, 1953.
20 Andrew Lytle, "What Quarter of the Night," *Sewanee Review*, LXIV (Summer, 1956), 349–97; corresponds to "The Water Witch" section of *The Velvet Horn*.
21 Ransom to Lytle, August 31, 1957.
22 Warren to Ransom, March 30, 1955.
23 Ransom to Tate, June 3, 1950.
24 Ransom to Tate, January 11, 1952.
25 Ransom to Lytle, March 25, 1954.
26 Ransom to Tate, March 3, 1950.
27 Denham Sutcliffe, "On the Croquet Court," in *John Crowe Ransom: A Tribute from the Community of Letters*, Supplement to the *Kenyon Collegian*, LXXXX (1964), 12.
28 Anthony Hecht, "A Note of Gratitude," *ibid.*, 8–9.
29 Ronald Sanders, in Flushing (N.Y.) *Phoenix*, April 3, 1962. See also his *Reflections on a Teapot: The Personal History of a Time* (New York: Harper and Row, 1972), 281–300.
30 Allen Tate, "Gentleman in a Dustcoat," an address delivered at Kenyon College, April 30, 1968; published in *Sewanee Review*, LXXVI (Summer, 1968), 375–81.
31 Sanders, in Flushing (N.Y.) *Phoenix*, April 3, 1962.
32 Tate, "Gentleman in a Dustcoat," 381.
33 A letter written by Ransom on December 5, 1952, to the other senior fellows— Philip Rahv, Allen Tate, Lionel Trilling, and Austin Warren—and he wrote dozens more like it, demonstrates the kinds of things he concerned himself with in the operation of the School of Letters during the 1950s. After an exchange of several letters, Ransom wrote that Alfred Kazin had decided he was not qualified to offer Blake, as the senior fellows had suggested, and wanted to give a course with the very general title of "Studies in Fiction"; Kazin said he would discuss those "fictions which involve ideas about God." Although he would use some of the same books Irving Howe had on his reading list for his course in "The Political Novel," Ransom saw no serious duplication and would allow Kazin to change his course unless one of the

senior fellows raised an objection. He suggested that these two courses be put at the same hour, "which would be a good hour, so that nobody could take them both, and there might be a healthy sort of comparison in everybody's mind about the contents and ideas of the two courses." A second problem had arisen: "Cleanth Brooks has asked that a substitute be found to offer the first half of his course because he needs the extra time to devote to a writing problem in which he is engaged." Ransom had just learned that Robert Lowell was returning to America from Italy to offer a course spring semester at Iowa, and he asked permission to engage him to fill in for Brooks, for "he is well prepared for this particular course, and he is a good man to have on hand." All other teaching fellows proposed by the senior fellows "agreed to the courses as we defined them, except Stephen Spender." Ransom asked Tate if he had Spender's acceptance, and if he did to notify him or Newton P. Stallknecht, director of the School of English, immediately, so that the bulletin could be printed.

It is obvious that planning for an operation of the scale of the School of Letters at the detailed level suggested by this letter consumed a great deal of time, which had to be taken from a very busy schedule of editing, teaching, writing, and lecturing. Apparently Ransom was not involved in the operation of the School of English to this extent after the mid-1950s.

34 Ransom to Tate, August 17, 1952.
35 Ransom to Mizener, June 14, 1958; he had just retired from Kenyon.
36 Indianapolis *Star Magazine*, August 10, 1958.
37 John Crowe Ransom, "Criticism as Pure Speculation," in Donald A. Stauffer (ed.), *The Intent of the Critic* (Princeton: Princeton University Press, 1941), 110.
38 John Crowe Ransom, "Old Age of an Eagle," in his *Poems and Essays* (New York: Random House, 1955), 79; a briefer version of this essay first appeared in *New Republic*, May 12, 1952.
39 John Crowe Ransom, "Poetry, I: The Formal Analysis," *Kenyon Review*, IX (Summer, 1947), 436–56.
40 John Crowe Ransom, "More than Gesture," *Partisan Review*, XX (January–February, 1953), 108–11; a review of R. P. Blackmur's *Language as Gesture*.
41 John Crowe Ransom, "The Concrete Universal: Observations on the Understanding of Poetry, I," *Kenyon Review*, XVI (Autumn, 1954), 554–64, and "The Concrete Universal: Observations on the Understanding of Poetry, II," *Kenyon Review*, XVII (Summer, 1955), 383–407. At the end of the second essay Ransom indicated he had more to say on this subject, but the discussion was not resumed until the appearance of *Beating the Bushes* (1972), which included "The Concrete Universal," Ransom's last essay, written in 1970. The second of these essays received fairly wide distribution and became one of the best known of Ransom's critical pieces because it was written for *Poems and Essays*, a paperback collection of Ransom's work which included forty-four poems (all of those in *Selected Poems*, 1945, plus "Vision by Sweetwater" and "Persistent Explorer") and eight essays.
42 Ransom, "Concrete Universal, I," 555.
43 In "Poetry: The Final Cause," *Kenyon Review*, IX (Autumn 1947), 640–58, Ransom defines "Precious Objects" as those which are "beyond price, or valued at more than the market value of such objects"; they are "loved" not merely "used." An object which has been "abstracted from the substance" for the technical reason of "employment" in a desire process" cannot qualify. Like all other Precious Objects— "father, mother, husband, wife, child, friend, home, sun, moon, sky, sea, mountain"—a poem is likely to present "fresh aspects of a substance which is contingent and unpredictable."
44 Ransom, "Concrete Universal, I," 559–60.
45 In 1970, Ransom returns to this figure, defining a poem as an "organism in action":

The three organs are related to each other at least as nearly as are the parts of formal music. The head has to be the intellectual organ, and especially attentive to keeping the logical clarity of the text, and the finality of the conclusion. It has as much conscience in this respect as prose has, and is slow to waive its simple purity; for instance if the heart tries its patience by wanting to use words and phrases which are fateful and strange but too rich and rare for the common barbarian reader. But just often enough it is possible to persuade the honest head that a quotidian language will not do for good verse; till the head finally concurs, and is rewarded by receiving some rare intimations of immortality, for which it will be unexpectedly but eternally grateful.

But the give-and-take in the exchanges from organ to organ is often imperfect insofar as the feet—that is, the meters or rhythms, and the rhymes too if they are engaged—do not aspire faithfully to the obligations of reciprocity. *Beating the Bushes* (New York, 1972), 176.

46 Lifetime membership is limted to 250.

47 The first offer he had came at the end of a year's leave of absence, which he was spending at Indiana University, and he said he could not be away two years in a row.

48 Ransom to Tate, September 6, 1950.

49 Originally this prize was given by the Library of Congress, but after the furor that followed awarding of the prize to Ezra Pound in 1948, it has been awarded by Yale University. From funds granted by the Bollingen Foundation, a cash award is given each year to the American poet whose work in the opinion of the committee represents the highest achievement in the field of American poetry during the previous two-year period. Until 1960 the award was $1,000; from 1960 to 1963, it was $2,500; and since then it has been $5,000.

50 Through the pages of the *Saturday Review* Hillyer had objected to Pound's receiving the award.

51 New York *Times,* January 22, 1951.

52 Nashville *Tennessean,* March 4, 1951.

53 *Saturday Review,* XXXIV (February 3, 1951), 18. A writer in the St. Louis *Post-Dispatch* began his two-column account of the ceremonies with an obvious reference to Pound's having received the award: "Mr. Ransom is as sane and American as they come. Nor should his poems distress people who want to understand what they read, as do the poems of Wallace Stevens, another winner. The poetry of John Crowe Ransom is not to be read while running, but it all makes sense and very hard sense at that."

54 *Time,* February 12, 1951, p. 94.

55 The prize was given sixteen times between 1931 and 1970. Other winners include Robert Frost, William Carlos Williams, Kenneth Muir, Robert Graves, and John Berryman.

56 Melvyn Baron, member of the staff of *Hika,* to Allen Tate, November 16, 1955.

57 The issue also published two excellent pictures of Ransom, including one of the few available of him in academic dress, a letter from William Empson, and several poems by Kenyon undergraduates.

58 Randall Stewart to Ransom, February 14, 1956.

59 Stewart to Ransom, February 20, 1956.

60 Brooks remarked in accepting this responsibility that he doubted that these sessions would require a moderator. He was correct, as it turned out, for the informal conversation carried itself, much as it had in the original meetings. Brooks served as moderator of the first and fourth sessions, Willard Thorp of the second, and Ransom of the third.

61 Memorandum from Stewart, March 11, 1956, and addressed to Ransom, Davidson, Tate, Warren, Moore, Elliott, Brooks, and Lytle.

62 Ransom to Stewart, March 13, 1956.

63 The Fugitives at this session were Donald Davidson, William Yandell Elliott, Merrill Moore, John Crowe Ransom, Alfred Starr, Alec B. Stevenson, Allen Tate, Robert Penn Warren, and Jesse Wills. Sidney Mttron Hirsch joined the group for the third session on Friday afternoon. Other invited guests were Richmond Croom Beatty, Dorothy Bethurum, Cleanth Brooks, William Cobb, Louise Cowan, Robert Jacobs, Andrew Lytle, Frank Owsley, Louis D. Rubin, Jr., and Willard Thorp.

64 Louis D. Rubin, Jr., "Introduction" to Rob Roy Purdy (ed.) *Fugitives' Reunion: Conversations at Vanderbilt, May 3–5, 1956* (Nashville: Vanderbilt University Press, 1959), 16.

65 Tate to Davidson, May 14, 1926, in J. T. Fain and T. D. Young (eds.), *The Literary Correspondence of Donald Davidson and Allen Tate* (Athens: University of Georgia Press, 1974), 166.

66 Donald Davidson, *Still Rebels, Still Yankees and Other Essays* (Baton Rouge: Louisiana State University Press, 1972), 10.

67 Purdy (ed.), *Fugitives' Reunion*, 86–87.

68 Several of those present also discussed the influence of Ransom's teaching.

69 There were eighty-eight guests at the dinner, not the two or three hundred Ransom had expected.

70 Warren read "Pursuit," and "Meriwether Lewis"; Moore, "Outer Mongolia," "It Was As If the World," "The Book of How," "Ego," and "The Noise That Time Makes"; Tate, "Ode to the Confederate Dead" and "The Swimmers"; Davidson, "On a Replica of the Parthenon," "Randall, My Son," and "Lee in the Mountains"; Ransom, "Janet Waking," "Antique Harvesters," "The Equilibrists," and "Prelude to an Evening."

71 Purdy (ed.), *Fugitives' Reunion*, 6.

72 *Ibid.*, 181.

73 *Ibid.*, 182.

74 Ransom to Mizener, June 22, 1956.

75 Ransom to Lytle, August 31, 1957.

76 Ransom to Tate, September 24, 1957.

77 Ransom to Tate, October 25, 1957.

78 Ransom to Tate, October 18, 1957.

79 Ransom to Tate, November 5, 1957.

80 Joseph Frank was not invited because he was out of the country.

81 Ransom to Tate, April 21, 1958.

82 Edgar "Ted" Bogardus did not serve as Macauley's managing editor because he died from asphyxiation from a defective flue in the family home in Mount Vernon, Ohio, on May 11, 1958.

83 Lanning, "Ransom as Editor," in Young (ed.), *John Crowe Ransom*, 211.

84 Kenyon College gave Ransom the land on which the house was built.

85 Ransom to Davidson, June 10, 1958.

86 Lanning, "Ransom as Editor," in Young (ed.), *John Crowe Ransom*, 219–20.

NOTES TO CHAPTER XIV

1 Quoted on dust jacket of *Selected Poems* (New York: Alfred A. Knopf, 1969).

2 Ransom to Tate, October 21, 1961. Neither book was published.

3 *Ibid.*

4 *Ibid.*

5 *Selected Poems of Thomas Hardy*, edited with an introduction by John Crowe Ransom (New York: Macmillan, 1961).

6 Interview with Ransom, February 12, 1972.

7 John Crowe Ransom, "Waste Lands," *Literary Review*, III (July 14, 1923), 825–26, and his "A Cathedralist Looks at Murder," *Southern Review*, I (Winter, 1936), 609–23; the latter was reprinted in *The World's Body*. In the Postscript to the reprinting of *The World's Body* (Baton Rouge: Louisiana State University Press, 1968), Ransom wrote: "Perhaps about 1941, after the *Kenyon Review* had started publication, I wrote Eliot to send us a poem, or an essay. He responded promptly and politely that he had nothing at the moment, but added a wry postscript to remark that evidently he liked my verse better than I liked his. That was a blow that hurt. I knew that he meant no great compliment to my verse, for he knew as well as I that I was not of his stature. I had to make apology, but I could not simply write a little note to say that I thought he was a grand poet. I must write a very best essay, commending some notable verse of his without stinting" (p. 352).

8 John Crowe Ransom, "The Poetry of 1900–1950," *Kenyon Review*, XIII (Summer, 1951), 445–54.

9 Interview with Ransom, February 12, 1971.

10 Stewart to Ransom, January 11, 1961.

11 Ransom to Stewart, January 23, 1961.

12 Davidson had published the first edition of *American Composition and Rhetoric* in 1939, *The Tennessee: The Old River, Frontier to Secession* in 1946, and *The Tennessee: The New River, Civil War to TVA* in 1948; since his graduation from Vanderbilt, Wills had been an executive with the National Life and Accident Insurance Company.

13 Tate agreed with Davidson's conclusion. Many years later he wrote: "He sent me the typescript before he published it in the *Kenyon Review*. He dismissed Agrarianism as sentimental and nostalgic." See Allen Tate, "On the Death of Ransom," *Sewanee Review*, LXXXII (Fall, 1974), 550.

14 Much of the information about Ransom's semester at Vanderbilt comes from personal observations and from many conversations with him during that time. I sat in on his class and assisted him with some of the reports required by the dean and the registrar.

15 Ransom to Tate, January 14, 1962.

16 The original version of the poem:

Master's in the Garden Again
(with dialogue by Laforgue)

Twilight comes early now. It discovers
Exchange between these eldering lovers.

"Conrad, dear man, surprise! You are old
To be sitting so late in your sodden garden."

"Woman! intrusion! is this done well?
I'm nursing my knees, they are not very cold.
Have you known the fall of the year when it fell,
Or the wind's rant when the season was fell?
The health of the garden is Reason's burden."

"Conrad, your feet are dipping in muck,
The neuralgia will settle in your own back,
And whose health is it that gets the asthma?
O, come to your loving pipe, and your paper!"

"No," says the thinker. "Concede: I am here.
For your information, you're being improper.
I can do with a little cold and miasma,
But off with yourself!—for a while—my dear."

And the master's back does not uncurve
Nor the autumn's blow for an instant swerve.

Autumn days in our section
Are the most used-up thing on earth
(Or in the waters under the earth)
Having no more color nor predilection
Than cornstalks too wet for the fire,
A ribbon rotting on the byre,
A man's face as weathered as straw—
And the watery eye is part of the show.

17 Ransom to Tate, April 16, 1962, with the revised poem:

Master's in the Garden Again
(to the memory of Thomas Hardy)

I
Evening comes early, and soon discovers
Exchange between these conjugate lovers.

"Conrad, dear man, surprise! aren't you bold
To be sitting so late in your sodden garden?"

"Woman! intrusion! does this promise well?
I'm nursing my knees, they are not very cold.
Have you known the fall of a year when it fell?
Indeed it's a garden, but if you will pardon,
The health of a garden is reason's burden."

"Conrad, your feet are dripping in muck,
The neuralgia will settle in your own neck,
And whose health is it that catches an asthma?
Come in from foul weather for pity's sake!"

"No," says the thinker. "Concede. I am here,
Keeping guard in my garden and minding miasma.
You're lonely, my loony? Your house is up there.
Go and wait. If you won't I'll go jump in the lake."

II
And the master's back has not uncurved
Nor the autumn's blow for an instant swerved.

Autumn days in our section
Are the most used-up thing on earth
(Or in the waters under the earth)
Having no more color nor predilection
Than cornstalks too wet for the fire
And the leaves rotten on the byre.

The show is of death. There is no defection.

III
But the temple and brow, they frown like the law.
If the arm lies low, yet the rage looks high.
The accusing eye? It's a fierce round O.
The offense was raw, says the fix in the jaw.
We'll raise a rare now! we'll heave a brave blow!

A pantomine blow, if it damns him to do.

A yell mumming, too. And it's a gay garden now.
Play sweeter than pray, that the darkened be gay.

18 Line 11, "And chips on Conrad's hearth are blazing," becomes "And the log on Conrad's hearth is blazing"; and line 13 is changed *from* "Butter and toast, Conrad, are pleasing!" *to* "Butter and toast, Conrad, are meant for pleasing!"
   "I am pleased," he wrote Tate on February 27, 1963, "that you agree with my revisions of 'Conrad.' I'd advise against any such thing from a poet, but still I felt compelled to rewrite this one: and not honestly and completely to recant from the old version and commit it to the flames, but to leave it in the book too."

19 Roger Hecht, in *Sewanee Review*, LXXI (Autumn, 1963), 643-44.

20 Alan Brownjohn, in *New Statesman*, February 13,1970.

21 *Time*, January 27, 1967.

22 Louise Davis, Nashville *Tennessean*, June 7, 1964.

23 This issue, which ran to fifty-six pages, carried poems by Don Cameron Allen, Richard Eberhart, Dudley Fitts, Kenneth Burke, Robert Lowell, Roberta Teale Schwartz (Mrs. Gordon Chalmers), and W. H. Auden. Among dozens of congratulatory statements from scholars, poets, journalists, and men of letters were those from John L. Stewart, C. P. Snow, Granville Hicks, Leslie Fiedler, Jackson Mathews, Charles R. Anderson, Arthur Mizener, Northrop Frye, Karl Shapiro, René Wellek, Malcolm Cowley, R. P. Blackmur, Norman Podhoretz, William Van O'Connor, Allen Tate, Lawrence Ferlinghetti, Robert Penn Warren, Reed Whittemore, Howard Nemerov, R. S. Crane, Willard Thorp, Randall Jarrell, W. J. Bate, Mark Schorer, Eric Bentley, Cleanth Brooks, Jacques Barzun, William Empson, Donald Davidson, Delmore Schwartz, Bernard Weinberg, Robie Macauley, Austin Warren, Stephen Spender, and Marianne Moore. There were also an explication of Ransom's "Master's in the Garden Again" by W. D. Snodgrass and a brief review of Ransom's achievements as poet by Stanley Edgar Hyman.

24 Wes Lawrence, in Cleveland *Plain Dealer*, April 19, 1964. Lawrence points out that in twenty-five years the *Kenyon Review* had published work by winners of three Nobel Prizes, fourteen National Book Awards, and thirteen Pulitzer Prizes.

25 *John Crowe Ransom: A Tribute from the Community of Letters*, Supplement to the *Kenyon Collegian*, LXXXX (1964), 16, 30.

26 "A Tribute to John Crowe Ransom on His Seventy-Fifth Birthday," *Shenandoah*, XIV (Spring, 1963), 8, 14, 21.

27 Ransom to Tate, September 21, 1963.

28 John Crowe Ransom, "The Planetary Poet," *Kenyon Review*, XXVI (Winter, 1964), 233-64.

29 Ransom's feelings toward Frost were mixed. "I felt sad about Frost," he wrote Tate on February 27, 1963, "though I didn't go to the funeral. I generally had the curious feeling about him of being indebted to his achievement, in this sense: he was at his best a fine poet, but he chose not to be at his best generally, and therefore discharged the debt to the less literate society which we can't find in us to take seriously. That's a sort of missionary feeling, with relief that someone else is doing the job."

30 Ransom, "The Planetary Poet," 263-64.

31 Ransom to Newton P. Stallknecht, March 28, 1968.

32 November 5, 1962.

33 On that occasion Robert Penn Warren, the principal speaker, declared: "We are here to honor as best we can a man and a poet of rare quality and distinction. In a special sense, the man and the poet are scarcely to be separated. The two exist for us in almost unique, mutually fulfilling harmony—in a special blend of strength and gentleness, of wit and sympathy, of tough integrity and invincible gaiety of spirit.

His special tone of being is the most significant thing he has given his friends. In his poems it is what he has given the world"; see *A Tribute from the Community of Letters,* 20.

34 Ransom to Tate, May 18, 1963.

35 Conversation with Francis Fergusson, November 20, 1974.

36 Ransom to Stallknecht, November 21, 1963.

37 Ransom to Horst Frenz, October 30, 1961.

38 Ransom to Stallknecht, April 21, 1964.

39 Ransom to Stallknecht, November 21, 1964.

40 *Ibid.*

41 Five years later he was still working on this essay but had decided to go ahead and publish the collection without it. He had been reading Blake seriously for "five or six years," he told me on February 12, 1971, and considered him the "best poet of the nineteenth century," although "Wordsworth's 'Intimations Ode' is the greatest poem."

42 Ransom to Tate, February 16, 1965.

43 Ransom to Tate, August 24, 1965.

44 Ransom to Tate, November 20, 1965.

45 Ransom to Tate, December 4, 1965.

46 Ransom to Tate, January 12, 1967.

47 The board of chancellors who made this selection was composed of J. Donald Adams, W. H. Auden, Louise Bogan, Witter Bynner, Randall Jarrell, Robert Lowell, Marianne Moore, Robert Nathan, John G. Gerhardt, Frederick H. Pottle, John Hall Wheelock, and Richard Wilbur.

48 The poetry committee was composed of Jean Garrigue, Anthony Hecht, and John Hall Wheelock.

49 Carbon copies of Ransom's comments and Wheelock's introductory remarks are on file in the archives section of Chalmers Library at Kenyon.

50 Allen Tate, "For John Ransom at Seventy-Five," *Shenandoah,* XIV (Spring, 1963), 7.

51 *Time,* April 3, 1964.

52 The full complement of the American Academy of Arts and Letters is fifty, and all are selected from the 250 members of the National Institute of Arts and Letters. Ransom's chair, number forty-six, was formerly occupied by Hamilton Wright Mabie, Brand Whitlock, Mark Anthony DeWolfe Howe, and William Ernest Hocking. Ransom did not respond when he received notice of his selection—a few years before he had declined an offer of membership in the Institute until Tate reminded him of his duty to the community of letters—and Allen Tate and Malcolm Cowley both wrote, asking him to accept. On February 16, 1965, he replied to Tate: "And yes about the AAAL matter, where your urging supplements Malcolm Cowley's . . . I'm very grateful to you both, and I would be just plain obtuse to hold out."

53 The other four were Yvor Winters, Kenneth Patchen, Louise Bogan, and Malcolm Cowley.

54 Ransom received a check for $1,000 and the same amount went to the *Sewanee Review,* where the essay first appeared. Ransom to Tate, June 26, 1967.

55 Ransom to Tate, April 18, 1967.

56 David McDowell to F. Edmund Lund, March 14, 1967.

57 Ransom to Stallknecht, March 22, 1968.

58 Edited by Thomas Daniel Young, this collection contains essays by Robert Penn Warren, Edwin Berry Burgum, Delmore Schwartz, Cleanth Brooks, Randall Jarrell, F. O. Matthiessen, Donald A. Stauffer, Morgan Blum, Vivienne Koch, G. R. Wasserman, Louis D. Rubin, Jr., Kelsie B. Harder, Karl F. Knight, Graham Hough, F. P. Jarvis, and George Lanning. The bibliography is by Mildred Brooks Peters.

59 Frank Lawrence Owsley was represented at the session by his widow Harriet, and
   Lyle Lanier sent a telegram expressing his disappointment that he could not attend.
60 Out of town guests included—in addition to Warren, Tate, and Lytle—Robert
   Lowell, Elizabeth Hardwick, Peter Taylor, Eleanor Ross Taylor, David McDowell,
   Judith Jones (Ransom's editor at Knopf), and Robie Macauley.
61 Allen Tate, "Gentleman in a Dustcoat," *Sewanee Review,* LXXVI (Summer, 1968),
   375–81.
62 Robert Penn Warren, "Notes on the Poetry of John Crowe Ransom on His Eightieth
   Birthday," *Kenyon Review,* XXX (Autumn, 1968), 319–49.
63 "To Do a Poet Honor," *Life,* May 10, 1968.
64 *The World's Body* (Baton Rouge: Louisiana State University Press, 1968), and *Selected
   Poems* (New York: Knopf, 1969).
65 John Crowe Ransom, "Gerontion," *Sewanee Review,* LXXIV (Spring, 1966), 390.
66 Ransom, Postscript to *The World's Body* (1968), 366.
67 Interview with John Crowe Ransom, February 11, 1971.
68 In *John Crowe Ransom* (New York: Twayne, 1969), Thornton H. Parsons uses the
   text of *Poems and Essays.* Allen Tate says Ransom "ruined 'Prelude to an Evening'"
   by rewriting it and refers to "John's mania," the constant revision of some of his
   poetry, as the "last infirmity of a truly noble mind," in Tate's "Reflections on the
   Death of Ransom," *Sewanee Review,* LXXXII (Fall, 1974), 549. See also Thomas
   Daniel Young's essay in *Georgia Review,* XXVII (Summer, 1973), 275–83.
69 Roger Hecht, in *Sewanee Review,* LXXI (Autumn, 1963), 643.
70 In this collection Ransom goes back to the division that he had used in *Two
   Gentlemen in Bonds*: 1) "The Innocent Doves," 2) "The Manliness of Man," adding
   3) "Two Gentlemen in Bonds, *(in twelve sonnets)*," and 4) "Sixteen Poems in Eight
   Pairings *(with the original and final versions studied comparatively).*" The justification for
   this kind of division is discussed by Robert Penn Warren in his "Notes on the Poetry
   of John Crowe Ransom on His Eightieth Birthday," 335–36. The first section, "The
   Innocent Doves," is "clearly composed of poems about the gentle ones who are
   caught in the cleft stick of the world" and the second section, "The Manliness of
   Man," demonstrates the kind of "world man must live in and make his peace with,"
   the way man, "to fulfill his 'manliness,' must deal with this world." See also Robert
   Buffington, *The Equilibrist: A Study of John Crowe Ransom's Poems* (Nashville:
   Vanderbilt University Press, 1967).
71 Buffington, *The Equilibrist,* 14.
72 In recent years there have been a number of books and monographs devoted to
   Ransom's poetry and criticism: Robert Buffington, *The Equilibrist*; Karl F. Knight,
   The Poetry of John Crowe Ransom: A Study of Diction, Metaphor and Symbol (The Hague:
   Mouton, 1965); James E. Magner, *John Crowe Ransom: Critical Principles and
   Preoccupations* (The Hague: Mouton, 1971); Thornton H. Parsons, *John Crowe
   Ransom* (New York: Twayne, 1969); John L. Stewart, *John Crowe Ransom,* University
   of Minnesota pamphlets on American Writers (Minneapolis: University of
   Minnesota Press, 1962); Miller Williams, *The Poetry of John Crowe Ransom* (New
   Brunswick: Rutgers University Press, 1972); and Thomas Daniel Young, *John Crowe
   Ransom,* Southern Writers Series (Austin, Texas: Steck-Vaughn, 1971). The
   number and quality of some of these studies—and many others in which Ransom is
   included as a member of the Fugitives, the Agrarians, or the New Critics—indicate
   that at the time of his death he was regarded as an influential editor and teacher, a
   significant literary theorist, and one of the "greatest elegiac poets of the English
   language" (the phrase is Allen Tate's, "Gentleman in a Dustcoat," 375), a poet whose
   poetry, "hung high, with a long view, is swept and garlanded, and shines" (Robert
   Penn Warren, "Notes on the Poetry of John Crowe Ransom at His Eightieth
   Birthday," p. 349). Whatever future generations may think of his theoretical

criticism—and few critics in this century have offered more insight into the nature and function of poetry—most of the commentators are convinced that his poetry will endure. Miller Williams calls Ransom one of the few good love poets of the century and "Winter Remembered"—which "along with perhaps eight or ten or a dozen" other poems of Ransom's will be "read as long as poetry is read in English"—one of the "best love poems ever written by an American" (p. 121). Thornton Parsons maintains that "only a few poets of this century will add eleven works to the permanent tradition of English and American poetry" (p. 165). And Victor Howes says Ransom has a few poems "lodged where time cannot dislodge them" (*Christian Science Monitor,* December 18, 1969).

73 A copy of this statement is in the archives section of the Chalmers Library of Kenyon College. Other winners of this award include Robert Frost, T. S. Eliot, Katherine Anne Porter, Mark Van Doren, Edmund Wilson, Joseph Wood Krutch, and I. A. Richards.

74 Ransom to Tate, September 14, 1967.

75 Ransom to Tate, undated (1967).

76 Interview with John Crowe Ransom, August 3, 1973.

77 John Tyree Fain to author, September 27, 1974, and a conversation, November 2, 1974. Interview with Andrew Lytle, October 30, 1974.

78 On December 18, 1970, he wrote me: "I must tell you that just now I have made a big jump in the language of my book. For months I have been getting ready a fourth and final Edition. . . . I speak of a 'big jump'—I have brought in a few poems from *Poems About God,* and have taken up for a new try a number of the poems in the early editions."

79 Thomas Lask, New York *Times,* May 17, 1972. Ransom's collection of essays *Beating the Bushes* was published by New Directions in 1972.

80 The Mount Vernon *News* reported that young John Ransom hanged himself while "trying a stunt seen on television." A few evenings before he had seen a person "pretend to hang himself by placing a pad or some other apparatus under the neck. John tied a sweatshirt around his neck and hanged himself from a steel beam."

81 Paul Schwartz to author, September 24, 1974.

82 Ransom, Postscript to *The World's Body* (1968), 376–77.

83 *Time,* January 27, 1964.

Index

Serpent in Eden: H. L. Mencken and the South Edited by
Fred C. Hobson, Jr.

I'll Take My Stand: The South and the Agrarian Tradition
Twelve Southerners

The Fathers and Other Fiction Allen Tate

Gentleman in a Dustcoat: A Biography of John Crowe Ransom
Thomas Daniel Young

Helping Muriel Make It Through the Night Stories by Lee Zacharias

Bricks Without Straw Albion Tourgée. Edited by Otto H. Olsen

The Federalist Literary Mind: Selections from the *Monthly Anthology
and Boston Review*, 1803–1811, Including Documents Relating to the
Boston Athenaeum Edited by Lewis P. Simpson

Cabin Road John Faulkner

William Faulkner of Oxford Edited by James W. Webb and
A. Wigfall Green

The Mind and Art of Henry Miller William A. Gordon

A Bibliographical Guide to the Study of Southern Literature Edited by
Louis D. Rubin, Jr.

The Fugitive Group: A Literary History Louise Cowan

The World's Body John Crowe Ransom

My Mark Twain: Reminiscences and Criticisms William Dean Howells

The Clairvoyant Eye: The Poetry and Poetics of Wallace Stevens
Joseph N. Riddel

Rhetoric and Criticism Marie Hochmuth Nichols

Freudianism and the Literary Mind Frederick J. Hoffman

Who's Who in Faulkner Margaret P. Ford and Suzanne Kincaid

George W. Cable: A Biography Arlin Turner

POETRY

A Cage for Loulou Rudolph von Abele

Vacating: Hymn for Drum Rosanne Coggeshall

Why God Permits Evil Miller Williams